GW00601601

CONCISE COLLEGE TEXTS

"A" LEVEL LAW:
CASES AND MATERIALS

AUSTRALIA AND NEW ZEALAND
The Law Book Company Ltd.
Sydney : Melbourne : Perth

CANADA AND U.S.A.
The Carswell Company Ltd.
Agincourt, Ontario

INDIA
N. M. Tripathi Private Ltd.
Bombay
and
Eastern Law House Private Ltd.
Calcutta and Delhi
M.P.P. House
Bangalore

ISRAEL
Steimatzky's Agency Ltd.
Jerusalem : Tel Aviv : Haifa

MALAYSIA : SINGAPORE : BRUNEI
Malayan Law Journal (Pte.) Ltd.
Singapore and Kuala Lumpur

PAKISTAN
Pakistan Law House
Karachi

CONCISE COLLEGE TEXTS

"A" LEVEL LAW: CASES AND MATERIALS

BRIAN HOGAN, LL.B.
of Gray's Inn, Barrister,
Professor of Common Law, University of Leeds

PETER SEAGO, J.P., LL.M.
Senior Lecturer in Law,
Dean of the Faculty of Law, University of Leeds

GEOFFREY BENNETT, M.A.
of the Inner Temple, Barrister,
Lecturer in Law, University of Leeds

LONDON
SWEET & MAXWELL
1986

Published in 1986 by
Sweet & Maxwell Limited of
11 New Fetter Lane, London.
Printed in Great Britain by
Richard Clay (The Chaucer Press) Limited,
Bungay, Suffolk.

British Library Cataloguing in Publication Data

Hogan, Brian
    'A' level law: cases and materials.—
    (Concise college texts)
    1. Law—England
    I. Title   II. Seago, Peter   III. Bennett,
    Geoffrey, *1952*–   IV. Series
    344.2   KD661

    ISBN 0–421–35290–6

PREFACE

In our textbook *"A" Level Law* we included an Appendix I which indicated the basic texts we thought should be available to students reading for "A" Level Law. Although we still consider those materials to be the core of a basic library, it soon became apparent to us that very few students had access to such a range of sources. Accordingly we have produced this casebook in an attempt to reduce the gap between the ideal we believe should exist and the actual resources available to most students. We hope it will also serve as a structure which can be of assistance even to those students who do have wider access to materials and so enable them to pursue their studies more effectively.

Within the constraints necessarily imposed by the economics of publishing we have elected to reproduce substantial extracts from a relatively small number of cases and to avoid paraphrase and mere summaries. This, we think, is the best way in which a student can get a "feel" for the way lawyers think and express themselves, as well as giving a sense of what lies behind sometimes rather austere expressions of general principles.

A user of this book is also likely to be relying on a textbook. With this in mind we have frequently cross-referenced the casebook to our textbook *"A" Level Law* (referred to as H.S.B. in this casebook). We have also included an Appendix on the Police and Criminal Evidence Act 1984 and the Prosecution of Offences Act 1985 which updates the relevant section of our textbook. We hope in this way that the two books can be used together to complement each other. Even so, it should be stressed that the textbook and the casebook do not depend upon each other for their comprehensibility. Either can be used independently of the other. Indeed we hope that even students who do not use our textbook will still find the casebook helpful in studying syllabuses which involve an element of Crime or Contract in particular.

We have greatly benefited from the comments of teachers and students of "A" Level Law in producing this book. We would always be glad to hear comments on how we can best serve the needs of its users.

Leeds University
July, 1986

Brian Hogan
Peter Seago
Geoffrey Bennett

ADDENDUM

The following case appeared too late to be included in the text: it should be read along with *R. v. Moloney* (p. 180) and *R. v. Hancock* (p. 186).

R. v. Nedrick
The Times, July 11, 1986 (C.A.)

[Nedrick was convicted of murder. The prosecution's case had been that he had poured paraffin through the letter box and on to the front door of a woman against whom he had a grudge, and had set it alight. In the resulting fire one of the woman's children had been killed by asphyxiation and burns. In the appeal against conviction, the Court of Appeal had endeavoured to crystallise the effect of the speeches in *Moloney* and *Hancock*. In the majority of murder cases it would be sufficient for the judge to direct the jury that the prosecution had to prove that the accused either intended to kill or intended to do serious bodily harm.]

Lord Lane C.J. . . . In some cases, however, of which the present case was one, the defendant did an act which was manifestly dangerous and as a result someone died.

The primary desire or motive of the defendant might not have been to harm that person, or indeed anyone.

. . . . . .

It might be advisable first of all to explain to the jury that a man might intend to achieve a certain result while at the same time not desiring it to come about.

In *Moloney*, Lord Bridge of Harwich had given an illustration of the distinction, when he said:

> "A man who, at London Airport, boards a plane which he knows to be bound for Manchester, clearly intends to travel to Manchester, even though Manchester is the last place he wants to be and his motive for boarding the plane is simply to escape pursuit."

The man who knowingly boarded the Manchester aircraft wanted to go there in the sense that boarding was a voluntary act. His desire to leave London predominated over his desire not to go to Manchester. When he decided to board the aircraft, if not before, he formed the intention to travel to Manchester.

In *Hancock* the House decided that the *Moloney* guidelines required a reference to probability. Lord Scarman said:

> "They also require an explanation that the greater the probability of a consequence the more likely it is that the

consequence was foreseen and that if that consequence was foreseen the greater the probability is that that consequence was also intended."

When determining whether the defendant had the necessary intent it might, therefore, be helpful for a jury to ask themselves:

1   How probable was the consequence which resulted from the defendant's voluntary act?

2   Did he foresee that consequence?

If he did not appreciate that death or really serious harm was likely to result from his act, he could not have intended to bring it about.

If he did, but thought that the risk to which he was exposing the person killed was only slight, then it might be easy for the jury to conclude that he did not intend to bring about that result.

On the other hand, if the jury were satisfied that at the material time the defendant recognized that death or serious harm would be virtually certain — barring some unforeseen intervention — to result from his voluntary act, then that was a fact from which they might find it easy to infer that he intended to kill or do serious bodily harm, even though he might not have had any desire to achieve that result.

As Lord Bridge had said in *Moloney*:

> ". . . the probability of the consequence taken to have been foreseen must be little short of overwhelming before it will suffice to establish the necessary intent."

He used the expression "moral certainty" and said, "will lead to a certain consequence unless something unexpected supervenes to prevent it".

Where the charge was murder and in the rare cases where the simple direction was not enough, the jury should be directed that they were not entitled to infer the necessary intention unless they felt sure that death or serious bodily harm was a virtual certainty — barring some unforeseen intervention — as a result of the defendant's actions and that the defendant appreciated that such was the case.

Where a man realized that it was for all practical purposes inevitable that his actions would result in death or serious harm, the inference might be irresistible that he intended that result, however little he might have desired or wished it to happen.

The decision was one for the jury to be reached on a consideration of all the evidence.

Appeal allowed.
Verdict of manslaughter substituted.

ACKNOWLEDGMENTS

Crown copyright material is reprinted by kind permission of the Controller of Her Majesty's Stationery Office.

Extracts from various law reports reproduced by kind permission of: The Incorporated Council for Law Reporting and Butterworth & Co. (Publishers) Ltd.

The extract from Cross, *Precedent in English Law* (3rd ed.), 1977, reproduced by kind permission of Oxford University Press.

TABLE OF CONTENTS

TABLE OF CASES

Page references in **bold** type denote cases which are digested or quoted from in the text of the work.

TABLE OF STATUTES

Page references in **bold** type indicate where statutory material is set out either in part or in full in the text.

PART ONE

ENGLISH LEGAL SYSTEM

Chapter 1

SOURCES OF LAW AND THE DOCTRINE
OF PRECEDENT

1. THE INTERPRETATION OF STATUTES

Heydon's Case
(1584) 3 Co. Rep. 7a

[I]t was resolved by [the Court] that for the sure and true interpretation of all statutes in general (be they penal or beneficial, restrictive or enlarging of the common law,) four things are to be discerned and considered: -

1st. What was the common law before the making of the Act.

2nd. What was the mischief and defect for which the common law did not provide.

3rd. What remedy the Parliament hath resolved and appointed to cure the disease of the commonwealth.

And, 4th. The true reason of the remedy; and then the office of all the Judges is always to make such construction as shall suppress the mischief, and advance the remedy, and to suppress subtle inventions and evasions for continuance of the mischief, and *pro privato commodo*, and to add force and life to the cure and remedy, according to the true intent of the makers of the Act, *pro bono publico*.

Magor and St. Mellons v. Newport Corporation
[1952] A.C. 189 (H.L.)

Lord Simonds. My Lords, I have had the advantage of reading the opinion which my noble and learned friend, Lord Morton of Henryton, is about to deliver, and I fully concur in his reasons and conclusion, as I do in those of Parker, J., and the majority of the Court of Appeal. Nor should I have thought it necessary to add any observations of my own were it not that the dissenting opinion of Denning, L.J., appears to invite some comment.

My Lords, the criticism which I venture to make of the judgment of the learned Lord Justice is not directed at the conclusion that he reached. It is after all a trite saying that on questions of construction different minds may come to different conclusions and I am content to say that I agree with my noble and learned friend. But it is on the approach of the Lord Justice to what is a question of construction and nothing else that I think it desirable to make some comment, for at a time when so large a proportion of the cases that are brought before the courts depend on the construction of modern statutes it would not be right for this House to pass unnoticed the propositions which the learned Lord Justice lays down for the guidance of himself and, presumably, of others. "We sit here," he says, "to find out the intention of Parliament and of Ministers and carry it out, and we do this better by filling in the gaps and making sense of the enactment than by opening it up to destructive analysis." The first part of this passage appears to be an echo of what was said in *Heydon's Case* 300 years ago and, so regarded, is not objectionable. But the way in which the learned Lord Justice summarizes the broad rules laid down by Sir Edward Coke in that case may well induce grave misconception of the function of the court. The part which is played in the judicial interpretation of a statute by reference to the circumstances of its passing is too well known to need re-statement. It is sufficient to say that the general proposition that it is the duty of the court to find out the intention of Parliament – and not only of Parliament but of Ministers also – cannot by any means be supported. The duty of the court is to interpret the words that the legislature has used. Those words may be ambiguous, but, even if they are, the power and duty of the court to travel outside them on a voyage of discovery are strictly limited . . . .

The second part of the passage that I have cited from the judgment of the learned Lord Justice is, no doubt, the logical sequel of the first. The court, having discovered the intention of Parliament and of Ministers too, must proceed to fill in the gaps. What the legislature has not written, the court must write. This proposition which re-states in a new form the view expressed by the lord justice in the earlier case of *Seaford Court Estates Ld.* v. *Asher* (1950) (to which the lord justice himself refers), cannot be supported. It appears to me to be a naked usurpation of the legislative function under the thin disguise of interpretation, and it is the less justifiable when it is guesswork with what material the legislature would, if it had discovered the gap, have filled it in. If a gap is disclosed, the remedy lies in an amending Act.

Note

While the so-called Mischief Rule derived from *Heydon's Case* is by no means a dead letter, it is doubtful whether any judge would accept it in detail or subscribe to its underlying philosophy. The duty of the court, as Lord Simonds says, is to interpret the words which the legislature has used. This - the so-called Literal Rule - no doubt most accurately expresses the prevailing judicial attitude to the interpretation of statutes. But as a principal of interpretation the Literal Rule may be stated in different terms as the following judicial views show:

"If the words of an Act are clear, you must follow them, even though they lead to a manifest absurdity. The court has nothing to do with the question whether the legislature has committed an absurdity." *R . v. The Judge of the City of London Court* (1892) *per* Lord Esher M.R.

"If the language of a statute be plain, admitting of only one meaning, the Legislature must be taken to have meant and intended what it has plainly expressed, and whatever it has in clear terms enacted must be enforced though it should lead to absurd or mischievous results." *Vacher v. London Society of Compositors* (1913) *per* Lord Atkinson.

"A judge must not alter the material of which [a statute] is woven, but he can and should iron out the creases." *Eddis v. Chichester -Constable* (1969) *per* Fenton Atkinson L.J.

"The duty of the courts is to ascertain and give effect to the will of Parliament as expressed in its enactments. In the performance of this duty the judges do not act as computers into which are fed the statute and the rules for the construction of statutes and from whom issues forth the mathematically correct answer. The interpretation of statutes is a craft as much as a science and the judges, as craftsmen, select and apply the appropriate rules as the tools of their trade. They are not legislators, but finishers, refiners and polishers of legislation which comes to them in a state requiring varying degrees of further processing." *Corocraft* v. *Pan American Airways* (1969) *per* Donaldson J.

But however the Literal Rule is expressed, and whether in broader or narrower terms, the governing principle is that the words of a statute must be given their ordinary meaning in the context in which they occur. "In determining the meaning of any word or phrase in a statute," said Lord Reid in *Pinner v. Everett* (1969), "the first question to ask always is what is the natural or ordinary meaning of that word or phrase in its context in the statute."

This, then, is the agreed starting point, but the question Lord Reid requires the interpreter to first ask himself does not provide its own answer. In determining, for example, whether a telephone kiosk or a bandstand is a "building" for the purposes of section 9 of the Theft Act, or who is an "occupier" for the purposes of the Occupiers' Liability Act 1957, how helpful is it to say that "building" and "occupier" should be given their ordinary meanings?

And who is to determine the ordinary meaning of words and phrases? Until 1972 it appears clearly to have been assumed that the interpretation of statutes was a matter of law for the judge, but in that year the House of Lords decided in *Brutus* v. *Cozens* (1973) that the meaning of "ordinary" words was a matter of fact for the trier of fact to determine. The issue was whether the appellant who, as part of a protest against apartheid in South Africa, had run onto the centre court at Wimbledon during the tennis championship blowing a whistle and distributing pamphlets, was guilty of "insulting" behaviour likely to occasion a breach of the peace contrary to section 5 of the Public Order Act 1936. In his speech Lord Reid said:

"The meaning of an ordinary word of the English language is not a question of law. The proper construction of a statute is a question of law. If the context shows that a word is used in an unusual sense the court will determine in other words what that unusual sense is. But here there is in my opinion no question of the word 'insulting' being used in any unusual sense. It appears to me, for reasons which I shall give later, to be intended to have Ats ordinary meaning. It is for the tribunal which decides the case to consider, not as law but as fact, whether in the whole circumstances the words of the statute do or do not as a matter of ordinary usage of the English language cover or apply to the facts which have been proved. If it is alleged that the tribunal has reached a wrong decision then there can be a question of law but only of a limited character. The question would normally be whether their decision was unreasonable in the sense that no tribunal acquainted with the ordinary use of language could reasonably reach that decision.

Were it otherwise we should reach an impossible position. When considering the meaning of a word one often goes to a dictionary. There one finds other words set out. And if one wants to pursue the matter and find the meaning of those other words the dictionary will give the meaning of those other words in still further words which often include the word for whose meaning one is searching. No doubt the court could act as a dictionary. It could direct the tribunal to take some word or phrase other than the word in the statute and consider whether that word or phrase applied to or covered the facts proved. But we have been warned time and again not to substitute other words for the words of a statute. And there is very good reason for that. Few words have exact synonyms. The overtones are almost always different. Or the court could frame a definition. But then again the tribunal would be left with words to consider. No doubt a statute may contain a definition - which incidentally often creates more problems than it solves - but the purpose of a definition is to limit or modify the ordinary meaning of a word and the court is not entitled to do that.

So the question of law in this case must be whether it was unreasonable to hold that the appellant's behaviour was not insulting. To that question there could in my view by only one answer - No. . . .

We were referred to a number of dictionary meanings of 'insult' such as treating with insolence or contempt or indignity or derision or dishonour or offensive disrespect. Many things otherwise unobjectionable may be said or done in an insulting way. There can be no definition. But an ordinary sensible man knows an insult when he sees or hears it.

Taking the passage which I have quoted, 'affront' is much too vague a word to be helpful; there can often be disrespect without insult, and I do not think that contempt for a person's rights as distinct from contempt for the person himself would generally be held to be insulting. Moreover there are many grounds other than insult for feeling resentment or protesting. I do not agree that there can be conduct which is not insulting in the ordinary sense of the word but which is 'insulting for the purpose of this section'. If the view of the Divisional Court was that in this section the word 'insulting' has some special or unusually wide meaning, then I do not agree. Parliament has given no indication that the word is to be given any unusual meaning. Insulting means insulting and nothing else.

If I had to decide, which I do not, whether the appellant's conduct insulted the spectators in this case, I would agree with the justices. The spectators may have been very angry and justly so. The appellant's conduct was deplorable. Probably it ought to be punishable. But I cannot see how it insulted the spectators."

Perhaps the most striking development following *Brutus* v. *Cozens* has concerned the interpretation of "dishonesty" for the purposes of the Theft Acts. (See below, p. 237.) It is for the jury to determine whether the defendant's conduct is dishonest by reference to the standards of reasonable and honest people. The underlying idea seems to be that the ordinary man (*ie* the ordinary magistrate or juryman) can recognise dishonesty when he sees it.

Questions

1. Is it true to say that the ordinary man can recognise dishonesty when he sees it? Is the ordinary judge any better qualified to say what dishonesty means? What arguments can be advanced for saying that dishonesty should be defined by the judge as a matter of law or should be left to the magistrates or jury to determine as a matter of fact?

2. Suppose that in *Brutus* v. *Cozens* the magistrates had concluded that the appellant's behaviour had been insulting and had convicted him. Would Lord Reid have supported the conviction?

While the first thing to be considered is the ordinary meaning of the word or phrase in its context, it may be that the ordinary meaning leads to an absurd result. Lord Atkinson in the passage quoted above was prepared to say then so be it; it was for Parliament and not the courts to put the matter right. It is unlikely that any judge would now take so very literal a stance. There would probably be general agreement with the view expressed by Lord Reid in *Pinner* v. *Everett* that when the ordinary meaning leads to a result which cannot reasonably be supposed to have been the intention of Parliament, it becomes permissible to look for some other meaning of the word or phrase. This is the so-called Golden Rule: that statutes should be construed so as to avoid absurdity. But notice that Lord Reid said this approach was permissible *only* where the ordinary interpretation led to an absurd result and in *Jones* v. *DPP* (1962) he added:

"It is a cardinal principle applicable to all kinds of statutes that you may not for any reason attach to a statutory provision a meaning which the words of that provision cannot reasonably bear. If they are capable of more than one meaning, then you can choose between those meanings, but beyond that you must not go."

Hence in *IRC* v. *Hinchy* (1960) where income tax legislation provided that a person who failed to submit a correct return was liable to forfeit £20 plus "treble the tax which he ought to be charged" the defendant was held liable to pay some £438 (calculated on the basis of his total tax liability for the year multiplied by three) though his return failed to declare only some £14 of taxable income. The trial judge, the Court of Appeal and the House of Lords were all agreed that Parliament could not reasonably be supposed to have intended so extravagant and extreme a penalty but the House, unlike the trial judge and the Court of Appeal, held that it was not possible to attach any other construction to the statute. Simply because the ordinary construction leads to an absurd result does not of itself justify the court coming to some other conclusion.

The principles and practice of statutory interpretation was considered by the Law Commission's: *The Interpretation of Statutes*, Law Com. No. 21 (1969). Their general conclusion was that in the hands of the courts interpretation had become too restrictive. They said in paras. 29-33 of their Report:

"The three so-called rules which have been described above do not call for criticism if they are to be regarded simply as convenient headings by reference to which the different approaches of the courts to problems of interpretation may be described. They are less satisfactory, when they, or equivalent propositions in other language, are used to justify the meaning given to a provision. In our view, the ultimate function of a court in the interpretative process is not simply to decide whether it is bound to follow a literal interpretation on the one hand or to adopt on the other an interpretation reached in the light of the golden or mischief rules. It is rather to decide the meaning of the provision, taking into account, among other matters, the light which the actual language used, and the broader aspects of legislative policy arrived at by the golden and mischief rules, throw on that meaning.

To place undue emphasis on the literal meaning of the words of a provision is to assume an unattainable perfection in draftsmanship; it presupposes that the draftsmen can always choose words to describe the situations intended to be covered by the provision which will leave no room for a difference of opinion as to their meaning. Such an approach ignores the limitations of language, which is not infrequently demonstrated even at the level of the House of Lords when Law Lords differ as to the so-called "plain meaning" of words. . . . .

When we turn from the literal rule to the golden rule, we find that this rule sets a purely negative standard by reference to absurdity, inconsistency or inconvenience, but provides no clear means to test the existence of these characteristics or to measure their quality or extent. When a court decides that a particular construction is absurd, it implies, although often tacitly, that the construction is absurd because it is irreconcilable with the general policy of the legislature. Thus in *R*. v. *Oakes*(1959) (where the Court read "aids and abets *and* does any act preparatory to the commission of an offence" in s.7 of the Official Secrets Act 1920 as "aids and abets *or* does any act preparatory to the commission of an offence") the underlying assumption was that the Act was framed to fit in with the general pattern of the criminal law. Similarly, in *Riddell* v. *Reid* (1942) (where the majority of the House of Lords held that the words "outside the area of the building under construction" in the preamble to the Building Regulations 1926 made under s.79 of the Factory and Workshop Act 1901 could be read in effect as "outside the area used in the building operations") the finding that a strict construction would be "narrow and unprofitable" (Lord Thankerton), "illogical and inexplicable" (Lord Russell of Killowen) and "paradoxical" and "generally inconvenient and unworkable" (Lord Wright) can only be explained by reference to the purpose of the Building Regulations and their parent Act. In fact the golden rule on closer examination turns out to be a less explicit form of the mischief rule.

The mischief rule as expressed in *Heydon's Case* (1584) describes in our view a somewhat more satisfactory approach to the interpretation of statutes. But, apart from the archaism of its language, it reflects a very different constitutional balance between the Executive, Parliament and the public than would now be acceptable. Hence, particularly under its fourth head, in its emphasis on the suppression of the mischief and, in effect, adaptation of the remedy for that purpose, it does not make it clear to what extent the judge should consider the actual language in which the specific remedies contained in the statute are communicated to the public. *Heydon's Case* is also somewhat outdated in its approach, because it assumes that statute is subsidiary or supplemental to the common law, whereas in modern conditions many statutes mark a fresh point of departure rather than a mere addition to, and qualification of, common law principles. Furthermore, the mischief rule was enunciated before the rules excluding certain material, which might bear on the mischief and "true reason of the remedy", had been developed. If a court has inadequate means of discovering the policy behind a statute, a mere exhortation to consider that policy may not be very effective. . . . ."

Smith v. Hughes
[1960] 1 W.L.R. 830 (D.C.)

Lord Parker C.J. These are six appeals by way of case stated by one of the stipendiary magistrates sitting at Bow Street, before whom informations were preferred by police officers against the defendants, in each case that she "being a common prostitute, did solicit in a street for the purpose of prostitution, contrary to section 1(1) of the Street Offences Act, 1959." The magistrate in each case found that the defendant was a common prostitute, that she had solicited and that the solicitation was in a street, and in each case fined the defendant.

The facts, to all intents and purposes, raise the same point in each case; there are minute differences. The defendants in each case were not themselves physically in the street but were in a house adjoining the street. In one case the defendant was on a balcony and she attracted the attention of men in the street by tapping and calling down to them. In other cases the defendants were in ground-floor windows, either closed or half open, and in another case in a first-floor window.

The sole question here is whether in those circumstances each defendant was soliciting in a street or public place. The words of section 1(1) of the Act of 1959 are in this form: "It shall be an offence for a common prostitute to loiter or solicit in a street or public place for the purpose of prostitution." Observe that it does not say there specifically that the person who is doing the soliciting must be in the street. Equally, it does not say that it is enough if the person who receives the solicitation or to whom it is addressed is in the street. For my part, I approach the matter by considering what is the mischief aimed at by this Act. Everybody knows that this was an Act intended to clean up the streets, to enable people to walk along the streets without being molested or solicited by common prostitutes. Viewed in that way, it can matter little whether the prostitute is soliciting while in the street or is standing in a doorway or on a balcony, or at a window, or whether the window is shut or open or half open; in each case her solicitation is projected to and addressed to somebody walking in the street. For my part, I am content to base my decision on that ground and that ground alone. I think the magistrate came to a correct conclusion in each case, and that these appeals should be dismissed.

Fisher v. Bell
[1960] 3 W.L.R. 919 (D.C.)

[By section 1(1) of the Restriction of Offensive Weapons Act 1959 "Any person who manufactures, sells or hires or offers for sale or hire or lends or gives to any other person - (a) any knife which has a blade which opens automatically by hand pressure applied to a button, spring or other device in or attached to the handle of the knife, sometimes known as a 'flick knife' . . . shall be guilty of an offence . . . .

The defendant displayed in his shop window a knife bearing a ticket which stated, "Ejector knife - 4s." When a constable entered the shop and told him he would be reported for offering the knife for sale the defendant replied, "Fair enough."]

Lord Parker C.J. read s. 1(1), Restriction of Offensive Weapons Act, 1959, stated the facts and continued: The sole question is whether the exhibition of that knife in the window with the ticket constituted an offer for sale within the statute. I confess that I think most lay people and, indeed, I myself when I first read the papers, would be inclined to the view that to say that if a knife was displayed in a window like that with a price attached to it was not offering it for sale was just nonsense. In ordinary language it is there inviting people to buy it, and it is for sale; but any statute must of course be looked at in the light of the general law of the country. Parliament in its wisdom in passing an Act must be taken to know the general law. It is perfectly clear that according to the ordinary law of contract the display of an article with a price on it in a shop window is merely an invitation to treat. It is in no sense an offer for sale the acceptance of which constitutes a contract. That is clearly the general law of the country. Not only is that so, but it is to be observed that in many statutes and orders which prohibit selling and offering for sale of goods it is very common when it is so desired to insert the words "offering or exposing for sale," "exposing for sale" being clearly words which would cover the display of goods in a shop window. Not only that, but it appears that under several statutes - we have been referred in particular to the Prices of Goods Act, 1939, and the Goods and Services (Price Control) Act, 1941 - Parliament, when it desires to enlarge the ordinary meaning of those words, includes a definition section enlarging the ordinary meaning of "offer for sale" to cover other matters including, be it observed, exposure of goods for sale with the price attached.

In those circumstances I am driven to the conclusion, though I confess reluctantly, that no offence was here committed. At first sight it sounds absurd that knives of this sort cannot be manufactured, sold, hired, lent, or given, but apparently they can be displayed in shop windows; but even if this - and I am by no means saying it is - is a casus omissus it is not for this court to supply the omission. I am mindful of the strong words of Lord Simonds in *Magor and St. Mellons Rural District Council v. Newport Corporation* (1952). In that case one of the Lords Justices in the Court of Appeal had, in effect, said that the court having discovered the supposed intention of Parliament must proceed to fill in the gaps - what the legislature has not written the court must write - and in answer to that contention Lord Simonds in his speech said: "It appears to me to be a naked usurpation of the legislative function under the thin disguise of interpretation."

Approaching this matter apart from authority, I find it quite impossible to say that an exhibition of goods in a shop window is itself an offer for sale. We were, however, referred to several cases, one of which is *Keating* v. *Horwood* (1926) a decision of this court. There, a baker's van was being driven on its rounds. There was bread in it that had been ordered and bread in it that was for sale, and it was found that that bread was underweight contrary to the Sale of Food Order, 1921. That order was an order of the sort to which I have referred already which prohibited the offering or exposing for sale. In giving his judgment, Lord Hewart C.J. said this: "The question is whether on the facts there were, (1) an offering, and (2) an exposure, for sale. In my opinion, there were both." Avory J. said: "I agree and have nothing to add." Shearman J., however, said: "I am of the same opinion. I am quite clear that this bread was exposed for sale, but have some doubt whether it can be said to have been offered for sale until a particular loaf was tendered to a particular customer." There are three matters to observe on that case. The first is that the order plainly contained the words "expose for sale," and on any view there was an exposing for sale. Therefore the question whether there was an offer for sale was unnecessary for decision. Secondly, the principles of general contract law were never referred to, and thirdly, albeit all part of the second ground, the respondent was not represented and there was in fact no argument. I cannot take that as an authority for the proposition that the display here in a shop window was an offer for sale.

. . . Accordingly, I have come to the conclusion in this case that the justices were right, and this appeal must be dismissed.

Questions

1. Was not what was done by the defendant in *Fisher* v. *Bell* within the mischief aimed at by the Act? If so, why did not Lord Parker C.J. apply the Mischief Rule as he had done in *Smith* v. *Hughes* (1960)?

2. Would *Smith* v. *Hughes* (1960) have been decided the same way by applying the Literal Rule? Note that Hilberry J., while agreeing with Lord Parker, said that the men were solicited "in a street" since that was where the soliciting took place. But on this view what would the position be if the prostitute was in the street and solicited a man who was on private premises?

3. Lord Parker admits in *Fisher* v. *Bell* that most lay people (note that most members of Parliament are lay people) would think it was "nonsense" to say that the defendant was not offering the flick knife for sale. In that case should not the ordinary meaning of the phrase (*ie* the meaning as understood by ordinary people) have been given to it? Would this have been a case where Lord Reid (*cf*. his views as expressed in *Brutus* v. *Cozens* above) would have said that "offers

for sale" was used in an unusual sense?

4. If the court in *Fisher* v. *Bell* had given to "offers for sale" its "usual" as opposed to its "unusual" meaning (*i.e.* the technical meaning the phrase has for the lawyer) would Lord Simonds really have regarded this as "a naked usurpation of the the legislative function"?

Adler v. George
[*1964*] 2 *Q.B.* 7 (*D.C.*)

Lord Parker C.J. This is an appeal by way of case stated from a decision of justices for the county of Norfolk sitting at Downham Market who convicted the defendant of an offence contrary to section 3 of the Official Secrets Act, 1920, in that, in the vicinity of a prohibited place, namely, Marham Royal Air Force station, he obstructed a member of Her Majesty's Forces engaged in security duty in relation to the said prohibted place.

Section 3 provides that: "No person in the vicinity of any prohibited place shall obstruct, knowingly mislead or otherwise interfere with or impede, the chief officer or a superintendent or other officer of police, or any member of His Majesty's forces engaged on guard, sentry, patrol, or other similar duty in relation to the prohibited place, and, if any person acts in contravention of, or fails to comply with, this provision, he shall be guilty of a misdemeanour." In the present case the defendant had obtained access to - it matters not how - and was on the Air Force station on May 11, 1963, and there and then, it was found, he obstructed a member of Her Majesty's Royal Air Force.

The sole point here, and a point ably argued by the defendant, is that if he was on the station he could not be in the vicinity of the station, and it is only an offence under this section to obstruct a member of Her Majesty's Forces while he is in the vicinity of the station. The defendant has referred to the natural meaning of "vicinity," which I take to be, quite generally, the state of being near in space, and he says that it is inapt to and does not cover being in fact on the station as in the present case.

I am quite satisfied that this is a case where no violence is done to the language by reading the words "in the vicinity of" as meaning "in or in the vicinity of." Here is a section in an Act of Parliament designed to prevent interference with members of Her Majesty's forces, among others, who are engaged on guard, sentry, patrol or other similar duty in relation to a prohibited place such as this station. It would be extraordinary, I venture to think it would be absurd, if an indictable offence was thereby created when the obstruction took place outside the precincts of the station, albeit in the vicinity, and no offence at all was created if the obstruction occurred on the station itself. It is to be observed that if the defendant is right, the only offence committed by him in obstructing such a member of the Air Force would be an offence contrary to section 193 of the Air Force Act, 1955, which creates a summary offence, the maximum sentence for which is three months, whereas section 3 of the Official Secrets Act, 1920, is, as one would expect, dealing with an offence which can be tried on indictment and for which, under section 8, the maximum sentence of imprisonment is one of two years. There may be, of course, many contexts in which "vicinity" must be confined to its literal meaning of "being near in space" but under this section, I am quite clear that the context demands that the words should be construed in the way I have said. I would dismiss this appeal.

Questions

1. In this case Lord Parker adds two words, "in or," to the statute which were not there before. Is this not a naked usurpation of the legislative function?

2. Since it was clear in *Fisher* v. *Bell* that Parliament meant to penalise the shopkeeper who placed flick knives in his window, could not Lord Parker, on the reasoning of *Adler* v. *George*, have just as easily added two words so that the section would have read "offers *or exposes* for sale"?

2. CASE LAW

Cross, Precedent in English Law (3rd ed.), pp. 38-40

According to the preliminary statement of the English rules of precedent contained in the last chapter, every court is bound to follow any case decided by a court above it in the hierarchy, and appellate courts (other than the House of Lords) are bound by their previous decisions. This statement is too concise because it does not indicate that the only part of a previous case which is binding is the *ratio decidendi* (reason for deciding). The principal object of the present chapter is to consider what is meant by the *ratio decidendi* of a case when the phrase is used by judges and other lawyers and by what methods it may be determined. This will show what is entailed by "following" or "applying" a case and by being "bound" by a previous decision, although these matters are not discussed until the beginning of the next chapter.

The *ratio decidendi* is best approached by a consideration of the structure of a typical judgment. The contemporary English judge almost invariably gives reasons for his decision in a civil case. Assuming that the trial is by a judge alone without a jury, he generally summarizes the evidence, announces his findings of fact, and reviews the arguments that have been addressed to him by counsel for each of the parties. If a point of law has been raised, he often discusses a number of previous decisions. Nowadays it is comparatively seldom that a civil case is tried by a judge and jury. When there is a jury, the judge sums the evidence up to them and bases his judgment on their findings of fact. In criminal cases tried on indictment, the all-important feature from the point of view of a lawyer is the summing up to the jury. The form of the judgments in appllellate courts is similar to that of a judge who tries a civil case without a jury. It consists of a review of the facts and arguments and a discussion of relevant questions of law. Several opinions are frequently delivered in appellate courts because appeals are always heard by more than one judge.

It is not everything said by a judge when giving judgment that constitutes a precedent. In the first place, this status is reserved for his pronouncements on the law, and no disputed point of law is involved in the vast majority of cases that are tried in any year. The dispute is solely concerned with the facts. For example, the issue may be whether a particular motorist was driving carelessly by failing to keep a proper lookout or travelling at an excessive speed. No one doubts that a motorist owes a legal duty to drive carefully and, very frequently, the only question is whether he was in breach of that duty when he caused damage to a pedestrian or another motorist. Cases in which the only issues are questions of fact are usually not reported in any series of law reports, but it is not always easy to distinguish law from fact and the reasons which led a judge of first instance or an appellate court to come to a factual conclusion are sometimes reported at length. For example, an employer is under a legal duty to provide his employees with a reasonably safe system of working. The question whether that duty has been broken is essentially one of fact, but the law reports contain a number of cases in which judges have expressed their views concerning the precautions which an employer should have taken in particular instances. When an injury would not have occurred if a workman had been wearing protective clothing it has been said that his employer ought to have insisted that such clothing should have been worn instead of merely rendering it available for those who desired to wear it, but the House of Lords has insisted that observations of this nature are not general propositions of law necessarily applicable to future cases and the decisions based upon them do not constitute a precedent. There is no point in endeavouring to ascertain the *ratio decidendi* of such cases.

The second reason why it is not everything said by a judge in the course of his judgment that constitutes a precedent is that, among the propositions of law enunciated by him, only those which he appears to consider necessary for his decision are said to form part of the *ratio decidendi* and thus to amount to more than an *obiter dictum*. If the judge in a later case is bound by the precedent according to the English doctrine of *stare decisis*, he must apply the earlier *ratio decidendi* however much he disapproves of it, unless, to use the words of Lord Reid, he considers that the two cases are "reasonably distinguishable". Dicta in earlier cases are, of course, frequently followed or applied, but dicta are never of more than persuasive authority. There is no question of any judge being bound to follow them. Even when the *ratio decidendi* of a previous case is merely a persuasive authority, it must be followed in later cases unless the judge has good reason to disapprove of it. It constitutes a precedent, and the difference between a persuasive precedent and an *obiter dictum* is only slightly less significant than that between binding and persuasive precedents. If, for example, a High Court judge of first instance comes to the conclusion that a proposition of law contained in a previous opinion of another High Court judge of first instance is *ratio*, he will be a great deal more reluctant to differ from it than would be the case if he was satisfied that it was merely a *dictum*, although a judge of first instance is not bound to follow the decision of another judge of first instance.

The law student soon learns to appreciate the importance of the distinction between *ratio* and *obiter dicta* but to realise that the distinction is important itself provides no test for determining which is which. And there is of course no test, in the sense of a formula, capable of being applied to a case which will automatically provide the answer.

Take *Felthouse* v. *Bindley* (below, p. 291) for example. The case might be said to be authority for the proposition that silence cannot be construed as assent. But what it really decides is that on the facts of that case John Bindley's failure to reply to his nephew's offer did not bind John; it is not an authority for a general proposition that in no circumstances may silence be taken as assent.

Professor Goodhart ("The Ratio Decidendi of a Case," *Essays in Jurisprudence and Common Law*) thought that in determining the *ratio* of a case certain things had to be kept in mind. Of prime importance, he thought, was to discover which facts the judge found and which of these he considered material. Note, it is the facts which the judge considers to be material, *not* the facts which we think he ought to have regarded as material (why?). The judge, however, will only rarely say which facts he regards as material and leaves this for others to determine; but if he does indicate which facts he regards as material and which he regards as immaterial then those facts must be accordingly so regarded. Goodhart then says:

"Having established the material and the immaterial facts of the case as seen by the court, we can then proceed to state the principle of the case. It is found in the conclusion reached by the judges on the basis of the material facts and on the exclusion of the immaterial ones. In a certain case the court finds that facts *A*, *B* and *C* exist. It then excludes fact *A* as immaterial, and on facts *B* and *C* it reaches conclusion *X*. What is the *ratio decidendi* of this case? There are two principles: (*a*) in any future case in which the facts are *A*, *B* and *C*, the court must reach conclusion *X*, and (*b*) in any future case in which the facts are *B* and *C*, the court must reach conclusion *X*. In the second case the absence of fact *A* does not affect the result, for fact *A* has been held to be immaterial. The court, therefore, creates a principle when it determines which are the material and which are the immaterial facts on which it bases its decision.

It follows that a conclusion based on a fact, the existence of which has not been determined by the court, cannot establish a principle. We then have what is called a *dictum*. If, therefore, a judge in the course of his opinion suggests a hypothetical fact, and then states what conclusion he would reach if that fact existed, he is not creating a principle."

Consider *Carlill* v. *Carbolic Smoke Ball Co.* (below, p. 279). Write down what you consider to be the material facts of the case and its *ratio.* Obviously the sex of the plaintiff was not considered material; only Lindley L.J. tells us that the plaintiff was female but it is clear that he attaches no importance to this fact. Was it material that it was a Carbolic Smoke Ball that was sold to the plaintiff? Lindley L.J. helps here by saying, "What that is I do not know," and since he did not trouble to find out he cannot have regarded it as material. So what was material? That it was a patent medicine? Or is the case authority for the more general proposition that whenever the defendant claims certain properties for his wares, the goods must have those properties? Was it material that the defendants had lodged £1,000 with the Alliance Bank? All the judges mention this fact and lay at least some stress on it. Would the case have been decided otherwise if the £1,000 had not been deposited with the bank?

All cases are subject to this form of analysis. The lawyer is always concerned to determine (i) precisely for what does a case constitute a precedent; and (ii) does that precedent govern the case he has at hand. He will of course attempt to show that precedents he sees as favourable to his case are not properly distinguishable while he will seek to distinguish precedents he sees as unfavourable. To distinguish a case he must show that the facts are distinguishable in a material respect, so material that a different legal consequence must follow.

Chapter 2

THE OPERATION OF THE DOCTRINE
OF PRECEDENT

1. THE HOUSE OF LORDS

London Street Tramways v. London County Council
[1898] A.C. 375 (H.L.)

Earl of Halsbury L.C. My Lords, for my own part I am
prepared to say that I adhere in terms to what has been said by
Lord Campbell and assented to by Lord Wensleydale, Lord
Cranworth, Lord Chelmsford and others, that a decision of this
House once given upon a point of law is conclusive upon this
House afterwards, and that it is impossible to raise that
question again as if it was res integra and could be reargued,
and so the House be asked to reverse its own decision. That is a
principle which has been, I believe, without any real decision
to the contrary, established now for some centuries, and I am
therefore of opinion that in this case it is not competent for us
to rehear and for counsel to reargue a question which has been
recently decided.

. . . . . .

My Lords, it is totally impossible, as it appears to me, to
disregard the whole current of authority upon this subject, and
to suppose that what some people call an "extraordinary case,"
an "unusual case," a case somewhat different from the
common, in the opinion of each litigant in turn, is sufficient to
justify the rehearing and rearguing before the final Court of
Appeal of a question which has been already decided. Of
course I do not deny that cases of individual hardship may
arise, and there may be a current of opinion in the profession
that such and such a judgment was erroneous; but what is that
occasional interference with what is perhaps abstract justice
as compared with the inconvenience - the disastrous
inconvenience - of having each question subject to being
reargued and the dealings of mankind rendered doubtful by
reason of different decisions, so that in truth and in fact there
would be no real final Court of Appeal? My Lords, "interest rei

publicae" there should be "finis litium" at some time, and that there could be no "finis litium" if it were possible to suggest in each case that it might be reargued, because it is "not an ordinary case," whatever that may mean. Under these circumstances I am of opinion that we ought not to allow this question to be reargued.

Practice Statement (Judicial Precedent)
[1966] 1 W.L.R. 1234

Lord Gardiner L.C. Their Lordships regard the use of precedent as an indispensable foundation upon which to decide what is the law and its application to individual cases. It provides at least some degree of certainty upon which individuals can rely in the conduct of their affairs, as well as a basis for orderly development of legal rules.

Their Lordships nevertheless recognise that too rigid adherence to precedent may lead to injustice in a particular case and also unduly restrict the proper development of the law. They propose, therefore, to modify their present practice and, while treating former decisions of this House as normally binding, to depart from a previous decision when it appears right to do so.

In this connection they will bear in mind the danger of disturbing retrospectively the basis on which contracts, settlements of property and fiscal arrangements have been entered into and also the especial need for certainty as to the criminal law.

This announcement is not intended to affect the use of precedent elsewhere than in this House.

Since this Practice Direction previous decisions of the House of Lords have only exceptionally been seriously questioned and none appears to have been directly and explicitly overruled. In *Moloney* (1985), below, p. 180) the House defined the *mens rea* of murder in terms markedly different from those set by its previous decision in *Hyam* (1975) but did not take the formal step of overruling *Hyam*. In *British Railways Board* v. *Herrington* (1972) the House stated an occupier's duty to trespassers in terms much more generous to the trespasser than had been stated in its decision in *Addie* v. *Dumbreck* (1929) but the law reporter cautiously noted that *Addie* had merely been "reconsidered."

Questions

1. Was the House of Lords ever bound by its own decisions? May the House in some future case properly decide that it is bound by its own decisions?

2. Why the "especial" need for certainty in the criminal law? Is it not more important to avoid injustice in criminal cases than in civil cases? Compare the attitude of the Court of Appeal (Criminal Division) in this respect, below, p. 27.

2. COURT OF APPEAL (CIVIL DIVISION)

Young v. Bristol Aeroplane Company
[1944] K.B. 718 (C.A.)

Lord Greene M.R. The question thus raised as to the jurisdiction of this court to refuse to follow decisions of its own was obviously one of great general importance and directions were given for the appeal to be argued before the full court. It is surprising that so fundamental a matter should at this date still remain in doubt. To anyone unacquainted with the rare cases in which it has been suggested or asserted that this court is not bound to follow its own decisions or those of a court of co-ordinate jurisdiction the question would, we think, appear to be beyond controversy. Cases in which this court has expressed its regret at finding itself bound by previous decisions of its own and has stated in the clearest terms that the only remedy of the unsuccessful party is to appeal to the House of Lords are within the recollection of all of us and numerous examples are to be found in the reports. When in such cases the matter has been carried to the House of Lords it has never, so far as we know, been suggested by the House that this view was wrong and that this court could itself have done justice by declining to follow a previous decision of its own which it considered to be erroneous. On the contrary, the House has, so far as we are aware, invariably assumed and in many cases expressly stated that this court was bound by its own previous decision to act as it did. . . .

In considering the question whether or not this court is bound by its previous decisions and those of courts of co-ordinate jurisdiction, it is necessary to distinguish four classes of case. The first is . . . where this court finds itself confronted with one or more decisions of its own or of a court of co-ordinate jurisdiction which cover the question before it and there is no conflicting decision of this court or of a court of co-ordinate jurisdiction. The second is where there is such a conflicting decision. The third is where this court comes to the conclusion that a previous decision, although not expressly overruled, cannot stand with a subsequent decision of the House of Lords. The fourth (a special case) is where this court comes to the conclusion that a previous decision was given per incuriam. In the second and third classes of case it is beyond question that the previous decision is open to examination. In the second class, the court is unquestionably entitled to choose between the two conflicting decisions. In the third class of case the court is merely giving effect to what it considers to have been a decision of the House of Lords by which it is bound. The fourth class requires more detailed examination and we will refer to it again later in this judgment.

[His lordship reviewed previous decisions where conflicting views had been expressed on whether the Court of Appeal was bound by its previous decisions and continued:]

It remains to consider the quite recent case of *Lancaster Motor Co. (London)* v. *Bremith. Ld.* (1941) in which a court consisting of the present Master of the Rolls, Clauson L.J. and Goddard L.J., declined to follow an earlier decision of a court consisting of Slesser L.J. and Romer L.J. This was clearly a case where the earlier decision was given per incuriam. It depended on the true meaning (which in the later decision was regarded as clear beyond argument) of a rule of the Supreme Court to which the court was apparently not referred and which it obviously had not in mind. The Rules of the Supreme Court have statutory force and the court is bound to give effect to them as a statute. Where the court has construed a statute or a rule having the force of a statute its decision stands on the same footing as any other decision on a question of law, but where the court is satisfied that an earlier decision was given in ignorance of the terms of a statute or a rule having the force of a statute the position is very different. It cannot, in our opinion, be right to say that in such a case the court is entitled to disregard the statutory provision and is bound to follow a decision of its own given when that provision was not present to its mind. Cases of this description are examples of decisions given per incuriam. We do not think that it would be right to say that there may not be other cases of decisions given per incuriam in which this court might properly consider itself entitled not to follow an earlier decision of its own. Such cases would obviously be of the rarest occurrence and must be dealt with in accordance with their special facts. . . .

On careful examination of the whole matter we have come to the clear conclusion that this court is bound to follow previous decisions of its own as well as those of courts of co-ordinate jurisdiction. The only exceptions to this rule (two of them apparent only) are those already mentioned which for convenience we here summarize: (1.) The court is entitled and bound to decide which of two conflicting decisions of its own it will follow. (2.) The court is bound to refuse to follow a decision of its own which, though not expressly overruled, cannot, in its opinion, stand with a decision of the House of Lords. (3.) The court is not bound to follow a decision of its own if it is satisfied that the decision was given per incuriam.

[*Young* was regarded as settling the question of precedent in the Court of Appeal until Lord Denning became Master of the Rolls in 1962. In a number of cases he expressed his dislike for the principle in *Young* and the high point came in *Davis* v. *Johnson* (1978) (C.A.) where three (Lord Denning M.R., Baker P. and Shaw L.J.) of the five judges in the Court of Appeal stated that the Court of Appeal was not always bound by its previous decisions. Lord Denning did so on the broad ground that the Court of Appeal could depart from a previous decision where it was convinced it was wrong. Baker P. and Shaw L.J. expressed the power in more limited terms which appear in the next extract.

In the House of Lords (1978), where the decision of the Court of Appeal as to the merits was upheld, their Lordships were unanimous that the Court of Appeal should follow *Young*.]

Davis v. Johnson
[*1978*] 2 W.L.R. 553 (H.L.)

Lord Diplock. So far as civil matters are concerned the law upon this question is now clear and unassailable. It has been so for more than 30 years. I do not find it necessary to trace the origin and development of the doctrine of stare decisis before the present structure of the courts was created in 1875. In that structure the Court of Appeal in civil actions has always played, save in a few exceptional matters, an intermediate and not a final appellate role. The application of the doctrine of stare decisis to decisions of the Court of Appeal was the subject of close examination by a Court of Appeal composed of six of its eight regular members in *Young* v. *Bristol Aeroplane Co. Ltd.* (1944). . . .

The rule as expounded in the *Bristol Aeroplane* case was not new in 1944. It had been acted upon on numerous occasions and had, as recently as the previous year, received the express confirmation of this House of Viscount Simon L.C. with whose speech Lord Atkin agreed: see *Perrin* v. *Morgan* (1943). Although prior to 1944 there had been an occasional deviation from the rule, which was why a court of six was brought together to consider it, there has been none since. It has been uniformly acted upon by the Court of Appeal and re-affirmed, notably in a judgment of a Court of Appeal of five, of which Lord Denning as Denning L.J. was a member, in *Morelle Ltd.* v. *Wakeling* (1955). This judgment emphasised the limited scope of the per incuriam exception to the general rule that the

Court of Appeal is bound by its own previous decisions. The rule has also been uniformly accepted by this House as being correct. . . .

Furthermore, the provisions of the Administration of Justice Act 1969 which authorise "leap-frog" appeals in civil cases direct from the High Court to this House are based on the tacit assumption that the rule as stated in the *Bristol Aeroplane* case is correct. One of the two grounds on which a High Court judge may authorise a "leap frog" appeal is if he is satisfied that a point of law of general importance involved in his decision:

> "is one in respect of which the judge is bound by a decision of the Court of Appeal or of the House of Lords in previous proceedings, and was fully considered in the judgments given by the Court of Appeal or the House of Lords (as the case may be) in those previous proceedings": s. 12(3)(*b*).

The justification for by-passing the Court of Appeal when the decision by which the judge is bound is one given by the Court of Appeal itself in previous proceedings is because that court also is bound by the decision, if the point of law was fully considered and not passed over per incuriam.

So the rule as it had been laid down in the *Bristol Aeroplane* case (1944) had never been questioned thereafter until, following upon the announcement by Lord Gardiner L.C. in 1966 [*Practice Statement (Judicial Precedent) (1966)*] that the House of Lords would feel free in exceptional cases to depart from a previous decision of its own, Lord Denning M.R. conducted what may be described, I hope without offence, as a one-man crusade with the object of freeing the Court of Appeal from the shackles which the doctrine of stare decisis imposed upon its liberty of decision by the application of the rule laid down in the *Bristol Aeroplane* case to its own previous decisions; or, for that matter, by any decisions of this House itself of which the Court of Appeal disapproved: see *Broome* v. *Cassell & Co. Ltd.* (1972) and *Schorsch Meier G.m.b.H.* v. *Hennin* (1975). In his judgment in the instant appeal, Lord Denning M.R. refers to a number of cases after 1966 in which he suggests that the Court of Appeal has either refused to apply the rule as laid down in the *Bristol Aeroplane* case or has added so many other exceptions to the three that were stated by Lord Greene M.R. that it no longer operates as a curb on the power of the Court of Appeal to disregard any previous decision of its own which the majority of those members who happen to be selected to sit on a particular appeal think is wrong. Such, however, has not been the view of the other two members of the Court of Appeal who were sitting with the Master of the Rolls in any of those cases to which he refers. Where they felt able to disregard a previous decision of the Court of Appeal this was only because, in their opinion, it fell within the first or second exception stated in the *Bristol Aeroplane* case.

. . . . . .

The reasons why his colleagues had not agreed to follow him are plain enough. In an appellate court of last resort a balance must be struck between the need on the one side for the legal certainty resulting from the binding effort of previous decisions, and, on the other side the avoidance of undue restriction on the proper development of the law. In the case of an intermediate appellate court, however, the second desideratum can be taken care of by appeal to a superior appellate court, if reasonable means of access to it are available; while the risk to the first desideratum, legal certainty, if the court is not bound by its own previous decisions grows ever greater with increasing membership and the number of three-judge divisions in which it sits - as the arithmetic which I have earlier mentioned shows. So the balance does not lie in the same place as in the case of a court of last resort. That is why the Lord Chancellor's announcement about the future attitude towards precedent of the House of Lords in its judicial capacity concluded with the words: "This announcement is not intended to affect the use of precedent elsewhere than in this House." . . . . . .

In the instant case Lord Denning M.R. in effect reiterated his opinion that the Court of Appeal in relation to its own previous decisions should adopt the same rule as that which the House of Lords since the announcement in 1966 has applied in relation to its previous decisions. Sir George Baker P., on the other hand, preferred to deal with the problem of stare decisis by adding a new exception to the rule in the *Bristol Aeroplane* case (1944), which he formulated as follows (1978):

"The court is not bound to follow a previous decision of its own if satisfied that that decision was clearly wrong and cannot stand in the face of the will and intention of Parliament expressed in simple language in a recent statute passed to remedy a serious mischief or abuse, and further adherence to the previous decision must lead to injustice in the particular case and unduly restrict proper development of the law with injustice to others."

Shaw L.J. phrased the exception rather differently. He said:

"It would be in some such terms as that the principle of stare decisis should be relaxed where its application would have the effect of depriving actual and potential victims of violence of a vital protection which an Act of Parliament was plainly designed to afford to them, especially where, as in the context of domestic violence, that deprivation must inevitably give rise to an irremediable detriment to such victims and create in regard to them an injustice irreversible by a later decision of the House of Lords."

My Lords, the exception as stated by Sir George Baker P. would seem wide enough to cover any previous decision on the construction of a statute which the majority of the court thought was wrong and would have consequences that were regrettable, at any rate if they felt sufficiently strongly about it. As stated by Shaw L.J. the exception would appear to be what might be termed a "one-off" exception. It is difficult to think of any other statute to which it would apply.

In my opinion, this House should take this occasion to reaffirm expressly, unequivocably and unanimously that the rule laid down in the *Bristol Aeroplane* case (1944) as to stare decisis is still binding on the Court of Appeal.

Question

Is the Court of Appeal bound by what the House of Lords said in *Davis* v. *Johnson* insofar as it relates to the operation of the doctrine of precedent in the Court of Appeal?

Williams v. Fawcett
[*1985*] *1 All E.R. 787 (C.A.)*

[The respondent was allegedly in breach of a court order not to molest the applicant and the applicant sought an order committing him for contempt. The respondent appealed on the grounds that the order did not specify the alleged breaches and was not signed by a "proper officer" of the court. The appeal was allowed on the first ground but the Court of Appeal held that notwithstanding decisions of its own to the contrary there was no requirement that the order be signed by a proper officer of the court.]

Sir John Donaldson M.R. If we are bound by these decisions, and we are unless they can be treated as having been reached per incuriam, they represent a very considerable change in the law for which, so far as I can see, there is absolutely no warrant. The change to which I refer is, of course, a requirement that these notices shall be signed by the proper officer. The rule of stare decisis is of the very greatest importance, particularly in an appellate court, such as this, which sits in six or seven divisions simultaneously. But for this rule, the law would not only bifurcate; it would branch off in six or seven different directions.

That of course has been stressed over and over again. It was emphasised in the classic case of *Young v Bristol Aeroplane Co Ltd* (1944) and in *Morelle Ltd v Wakeling* (1955) which considered *Young's* case. But in each of those cases, as I will demonstrate briefly, the court retained the power in an exceptional case to depart from its previous decisions. Thus in *Young's* case (1944) Lord Greene MR said:

> "Where the court has construed a statute or a rule having the force of a statute, its decision stands on the same footing as any other decision on a question of law. But where the court is satisfied that an earlier decision was given in ignorance of the terms of a statute or a rule having the force of a statute the position is very different. It cannot, in our opinion, be right to say that in such a case the court is entitled to disregard the statutory provision and is bound to follow a decision of its own given when that provision was not present to its mind. Cases of this description are examples of decisions given *per incuriam*. We do not think that it would be right to say that there may not be other cases of decisions given *per incuriam* in which this court might properly consider itself entitled not to follow an earlier decision of its own. Such cases would obviously be of the rarest occurrence and must be dealt with in accordance with their special facts."

Morelle's case was a five-judge Court of Appeal, although I hasten to add that it is now well-established that a five-judge Court of Appeal has no more authority than a three-judge Court of Appeal. It consisted of Evershed MR, Denning, Jenkins, Morris and Romer LJJ. I read from the judgment:

"As a general rule the only cases in which decisions should be held to have been given per incuriam are those of decisions given in ignorance or forgetfulness of some inconsistent statutory provision or of some authority binding on the court concerned: so that in such cases some part of the decision or some step in the reasoning on which it is based is found, on that account, to be demonstrably wrong. This definition is not necessarily exhaustive, but cases not strictly within it which can properly be held to have been decided per incuriam must, in our judgment, consistently with the stare decisis rule which is an essential feature of our law, be, in the language of Lord Greene, M.R., of the rarest occurrence. In the present case, it is not shown that any statutory provision or binding authority was overlooked . . . As we have already said, it is, in our judgment, impossible to fasten on any part of the decision under consideration, or on any step in the reasoning on which the judgments were based, and to say of it: 'Here was a manifest slip or error'."

In my judgment, one *can* say that in so far as the authorities which I have cited decide that a notice to show cause must be signed by the "proper officer" there was a manifest slip or error. There is no warrant for that proposition whatsoever either in the rules or in the statute. So I ask myself: is this case exceptional? I remind myself of the dangers of treating a decision as given per incuriam simply on the ground that it can be demonstrated to be wrong, even if the error is fairly clear on an examination of the authorities. However, for my part I think there are very exceptional features about the four decisions of this court to which I have referred and they are these.

There is, first of all, the clearness with which the growth of the error can be detected if the decisions are read consecutively. Second, these cases are all concerned with the liberty of the subject. It is true that if we were to leave the law as it has been declared to be, namely that these notices have to be signed by the proper officer, there are a number of subjects who would have to be released forthwith, because it is almost unknown for any notice to show cause to be signed by the proper officer. The change would, therefore, be beneficial to some subjects. But the other side of the coin is that these cases are also concerned with the maintenance of the authority of the courts to insist on obedience to their orders. They are therefore in a very special category. They are also, as I have said, cases which appear to be by no means unusual. Unfortunately there are a number of committals for contempt, particularly in the field of domestic violence. They are cases which are most unlikely to reach the House of Lords, which, if we do not act, is alone able to correct the error which has crept into the law.

I say that such a case is unlikely to reach the House of Lords because if the law is to be left as it has evolved, then this court would quash the committal order and it would be for the respondent to take the case to the House of Lords. I doubt whether any respondents would take that course, bearing in mind that there would be a substantial delay before the appeal to the House of Lords was heard and that he or she would, probably rightly, consider it unlikely that the House of Lords would require the contemnor to return to prison to complete his sentence.

3. COURT OF APPEAL (CRIMINAL DIVISION)

R. v. Gould
[1968] 2 Q.B. 65 (C.A.)

Diplock L.J. The question of law in this appeal is whether, on a charge of bigamy under section 57 of the Offences against the Person Act, 1861, a defendant's honest belief upon reasonable grounds that at the time of his second marriage his former marriage had been dissolved is a good defence to the charge. In *R.* v. *Wheat* (1921) the Court of Criminal Appeal decided that it was not. The deputy chairman rightly regarded himself as bound by that decision. But we are not.

In its criminal jurisdiction, which it has inherited from the Court of Criminal Appeal, the Court of Appeal does not apply the doctrine of stare decisis with the same rigidity as in its civil jurisdiction. If upon due consideration we were to be of opinion that the law had been either misapplied or misunderstood in an earlier decision of this court or its predecessor, the Court of Criminal Appeal, we should be entitled to depart from the view as to the law expressed in the earlier decision notwithstanding that the case could not be brought within any of the exceptions laid down in *Young* v. *Bristol Aeroplane Co. Ltd.* (1944) as justifying the Court of Appeal in refusing to follow one of its own decisions in a civil case (*Rex* v. *Taylor*) (1950). A fortiori, we are bound to give effect to the law as we think it is if the previous decision to the contrary effect is one of which the ratio decidendi conflicts with that of other decisions of this court or its predecessors of co-ordinate jurisdiction.

Questions

1. Why should the rules relating to the precedent differ according to whether the Court of Appeal is exercising civil or criminal jurisdiction?

2. Why should the house of Lords recognise (see *Practice Statement* above, p. 18) the especial need for certainty in the criminal law which the Court of Appeal does not apparently recognise?

4. DIVISIONAL COURTS

Police Authority for Huddersfield v. Watson
[1947] K.B. 842 (D.C.)

Lord Goddard C.J. Mr. Streatfeild has argued that it is open to us to depart from *Garvin's* case (1944) if we think it was wrongly decided. As we have not heard his full argument, I prefer only to say this: Nothing that I have heard in this case, as far as the argument has gone, satisfies me that *Garvin's* case was wrongly decided; but whether it was rightly decided or not I am clearly of opinion that we ought to follow it. This court is made a final court of appeal in these matters, and I can imagine nothing more disastrous than that where the court has given a decision upon the construction or application of this Act another court should give a decision contrary to the decision already given, because there then would be two conflicting cases. You might get a court consisting perhaps of different judges choosing one of those decisions, and another court choosing the other decision, and there would be no finality in the matter at all. For myself, I think we ought to hold that we are bound by this decision, and I say so for this reason: The Court of Appeal in *Young* v. *Bristol Aeroplane Co., Ld.* (1944), held, after argument before the full court of six judges, that the Court of Appeal was bound by its own decisions, with certain well-defined exceptions. [His Lordship referred to the *Young* exceptions and continued:]

If that is the rule which is applicable in the Court of Appeal - it is to be remembered that Court of Appeal judgments are reviewable in the House of Lords, at any rate by leave - and the Master of the Rolls pointed out in the course of his judgment that in some cases Court of Appeal judgments are final, as in bankruptcy, and in others are reviewable by the House of Lords, and yet he draws no distinction - and if, therefore, in a court most of whose decisions are reviewable, although it may be only by leave, in the House of Lords, those decisions are binding on the court, how much more important is it that this court, which is a final court, should follow its own decisions and consider that it ought to give full force and effect to them. Otherwise, as I have said, a great deal of uncertainty would be introduced into the law.

I know that in the writings of various eminent people the doctrine of stare decisis has been canvassed from time to time. In my opinion, if one thing is certain it is that stare decisis is part of the law of England, and in a system of law such as ours, where the common law, and equity largely, are based on decisions, it seems to me it would be very unfortunate if a court of final appeal has given a decision and has laid down a definite principle and it cannot be said the court has been misled in any way by not being referred to authorities, statutory or judicial, which bear on the question, that it should then be said that that decision was not to be a binding authority.

Watson's case concerned a matter of civil law but in *Younghusband* v. *Luftig* (1949) it was confirmed that the position was the same in relation to criminal cases.

5. OTHER COURTS

Judges of the High Court are not bound by the decisions of their fellow judges in the High Court. It has been assumed, though not authoritatively established, that circuit judges and magistrates are bound by decisions of the High Court.

PART TWO

CRIMINAL LAW

Chapter 1

ACTUS REUS AND MENS REA: THE INGREDIENTS OF A CRIME

1. ACTUS REUS

A. All Elements of the Actus Reus Must be Proved

R. v. Dyson
[1908] 2 K.B. 454 (C.C.A.)

[D. was charged with the manslaughter of his child. There was evidence that he had inflicted injuries upon the child in November 1906 and again in December 1907. The child died on March 5, 1908. At the trial the judge told the jury that they were entitled to convict D. even if they thought that the death was wholly caused by the injuries inflicted in November 1906. On appeal against conviction:]

Lord Alverstone C.J. The jury convicted the prisoner, who appeals against that conviction upon the ground that the judge misdirected the jury in that he left it to them to find the prisoner guilty if they considered the death to have been caused by the injuries inflicted in 1906. That was clearly not a proper direction, for, whatever one may think of the merits of such a rule of law, it is still undoubtedly the law of the land that no person can be convicted of manslaughter where the death does not occur within a year and a day after the injury was inflicted, for in that event it must be attributed to some other cause. Under these circumstances, there having been a misdirection, the question arises whether the Court can nevertheless dismiss the appeal under s. 4, sub-s. 1, of the Criminal Appeal Act, 1907, upon the ground that no substantial miscarriage of justice has actually occurred by reason of the conviction. The proper question to have been submitted to the jury was whether the prisoner accelerated the child's death by the injuries which he inflicted in December, 1907. For if he did, the fact that the child was already suffering from meningitis, from which it would in any event have died before long, would afford no answer to the charge of causing its death: *Rex* v. *Martin* (1832). And if that question had been left to the jury, they would in all probability have found the prisoner guilty on that ground; indeed it was the only ground upon which counsel for the prosecution invited them to convict. But it is one thing to say that the jury on a proper direction would probably have so convicted; it is another to say positively that there has been no substantial miscarriage of justice. We feel that we cannot act upon the proviso in sub-s. 1 of s. 4, for it is in our judgment plain that we cannot substitute ourselves for the jury and find the facts which are necessary to support the conviction. The proviso is intended to apply to a case in which the evidence is such that the jury must have found the prisoner guilty if they had been properly directed. It does not apply where the evidence leaves it in doubt whether they would have so found; and here the medical evidence established that there were no external marks of recent injury, a fact which might have induced the jury to find that the assault committed in December, 1907, did not accelerate the death. . . . It is to be regretted that the Legislature when passing the Criminal Appeal Act did not empower the Court to order a new trial, for the present is a case in which it is eminently desirable that such a power should exist. But they did not think fit to do so, and we have no choice but to allow the appeal.

Conviction quashed.

Questions

1. The "year and a day rule" is still a part of the *actus reus* of murder and manslaughter today. What purpose does it serve? Is it still needed today? (See 14th Report of the Criminal Law Revision Committee, *Offences Against the Person*, para. 39 (Cmnd. 7844, 1980).

2. Section 4(1) of the Criminal Appeal Act 1907 became section 2(1) of the Criminal Appeal Act 1968. There is now a limited power to order a new trial - but only where the appeal has been allowed solely on the basis of fresh evidence: section 7(1) of the Criminal Appeal Act 1968. Would this have been of assistance to Lord Alverstone in *Dyson*?

Note

Further illustrations of the need to establish the *actus reus* can be found in *Deller* (1952). But *cf. Dadson* (1850) (See H.S.B., p. 132.)

B. The Need for Voluntary Conduct

Bratty v. Att.-Gen. for Northern Ireland
[1963] A.C. 386 (H.L.)

[B. was charged with the murder by strangulation of an 18 year old girl. He told the police that "I had some terrible feeling and then a sort of blackness." The jury were asked, by the defence, to reach one of three conclusions: (1) that B. had been acting in a state of automatism; (2) that B. had been incapable of forming the necessary intent for murder and was guilty, therefore, only of manslaughter;

(3) that B. was not guilty on the basis of insanity. In the event the trial judge left only the defence of insanity to the jury founded on the defence suggestion that B. had suffered an attack of psychomotor epilepsy. The jury convicted B. of murder. His appeal that the trial judge wrongfully refused to leave defences (1) and (2) to the jury was considered eventually by the House of Lords.]

Lord Denning. My Lords, in the case of *Woolmington* v. *Director of Public Prosecutions* [see below, p. 128] Viscount Sankey L.C. said that "when dealing with a murder case the Crown must prove (a) death 'as the result of a voluntary act of the accused and (b) malice of the accused." The requirement that it should be a voluntary act is essential, not only in a murder case, but also in every criminal case. No act is punishable if it is done involuntarily: and an involuntary act in this context - some people nowadays prefer to speak of it as "automatism" - means an act which is done by the muscles without any control by the mind, such as a spasm, a reflex action or a convulsion; or an act done by a person who is not conscious of what he is doing, such as an act done whilst suffering from concussion or whilst sleep-walking. The point was well put by Stephen J. in 1889: "Can anyone doubt that a man who, though he might be perfectly sane, committed what would otherwise be a crime in a state of somnambulism, would be entitled to be acquitted? And why is this? Simply because he would not know what he was doing," see *Reg.* v. *Tolson* (1889). The term "involuntary act" is, however, capable of wider connotations: and to prevent confusion it is to be observed that in the criminal law an act is not to be regarded as an involuntary act simply because the doer does not remember it. When a man is charged with dangerous driving, it is no defence to him to say "I don't know what happened. I cannot remember a thing," see *Hill* v. *Baxter* (1958). Loss of memory afterwards is never a defence in itself, so long as he was conscious at the time. ... Nor is an act to be regarded as an involuntary act simply because the doer could not control his impulse to do it. When a man is charged with murder, and it appears that he knew what he was doing, but he could not resist it, then his assertion "I couldn't help myself" is no defence in itself . . . : though it may go towards a defence of diminished responsibility, in places where that defence is available (see *R.* v. *Byrne*, below, p. 135): but it does not render his act involuntary so as to entitle him to an unqualified acquittal. Nor is an act to be regarded as an involuntary act simply because it is unintentional or its consequences are unforeseen. When a man is charged with dangerous driving, it is no defence for him to say, however truly, "I did not mean to drive dangerously." There is said to be an absolute prohibition against that offence, whether he had a guilty mind or not, see *Hill* v. *Baxter per* Lord Goddard C.J. But even though it is absolutely prohibited, nevertheless he has a defence if he can show that it was an involuntary act in the sense that he was unconscious at the time and did not know what he was doing . . . .

Another thing to be observed is that it is not every involuntary act which leads to a complete acquittal. Take first an involuntary act which proceeds from a state of drunkenness. If the drunken man is so drunk that he does not know what he is doing, he has a defence to any charge, such as murder or wounding with intent, in which a specific intent is essential, but he is still liable to be convicted of manslaughter or unlawful wounding for which no specific intent is necessary. . .

[See below, p. 139.]

Again, if the involuntary act proceeds from a disease of the mind, it gives rise to a defence of insanity, but not to a defence of automatism. Suppose a crime is committed by a man in a state of automatism or clouded consciousness due to a recurrent disease of the mind. Such an act is no doubt involuntary, but it does not give rise to an unqualified acquittal, for that would mean that he would be let at large to do it again. The only proper verdict is one which ensures that the person who suffers from the disease is kept secure in a hospital so as not to be a danger to himself or others. That is, a verdict of guilty but insane.

Once you exclude all the cases I have mentioned, it is apparent that the category of involuntary acts is very limited. So limited, indeed, that until recently there was hardly any reference in the English books to this so-called defence of automatism.

My Lords, I think that the difficulty is to be resolved by remembering that, whilst the *ultimate* burden rests on the Crown of proving every element essential in the crime, nevertheless in order to prove that the act was a voluntary act, the Crown is entitled to rely on the *presumption* that every man has sufficient mental capacity to be responsible for his crimes: and that if the defence wish to displace that presumption they must give some evidence from which the contrary may reasonably be inferred. Thus a drunken man is presumed to have the capacity to form the specific intent necessary to constitute the crime, unless evidence is given from which it can reasonably be inferred that he was incapable of forming it .... So also it seems to me that a man's act is presumed to be a voluntary act unless there is evidence from which it can reasonably be inferred that it was involuntary. To use the words of Devlin J., the defence of automatism "ought not to be considered at all until the defence has produced at least *prima facie* evidence," see *Hill* v. *Baxter*; and the words of North J. in New Zealand "unless a proper foundation is laid," .... The necessity of laying the proper foundation is on the defence: and if it is not so laid, the defence of automatism need not be left to the jury, any more than the defence of drunkenness . . . , provocation . . . or self-defence . . . need be.

What, then, is a proper foundation? The presumption of mental capacity of which I have spoken is a provisional presumption only. It does not put the legal burden on the defence in the same way as the presumption of sanity does. It leaves the legal burden on the prosecution, but nevertheless, until it is displaced, it enables the prosecution to discharge the ultimate burden of proving that the act was voluntary. Not because the presumption is evidence itself, but because it takes the place of evidence. In order to displace the presumption of mental capacity, the defence must give sufficient evidence from which it may reasonably be inferred that the act was involuntary. The evidence of the man himself will rarely be sufficient unless it is supported by medical evidence which points to the cause of the mental incapacity. It is not sufficient for a man to say "I had a black-out": for "black-out" as Stable J. said . . . "is one of the first refuges of a guilty conscience and a popular excuse." The words of Devlin J. in *Hill* v. *Baxter* should be remembered: "I do not doubt that there are genuine cases of automatism and the like, but I do not see how the layman can safely attempt without the help of some medical or scientific evidence to distinguish the genuine from the fraudulent." When the only cause that is assigned for an involuntary act is drunkenness, then it is only necessary to leave drunkenness to the jury, with the consequential directions, and not to leave automatism at all. When the only cause that is assigned for it is a disease of the mind, then it is only necessary to leave insanity to the jury, and not automatism. When the cause assigned is concussion or sleep-walking, there should be some evidence from which it can reasonably be inferred before it should be left to the jury. If it is said to be due to concussion, there should be evidence of a severe blow shortly beforehand. If it is said to be sleep-walking, there should be some credible support for it. His mere assertion that he was asleep will not suffice.

Once a proper foundation is thus laid for automatism, the matter becomes at large and must be left to the jury. As the case proceeds, the evidence may weigh first to one side and then to the other: and so the burden may appear to shift to and fro. But at the end of the day the legal burden comes into play and requires that the jury should be satisfied beyond reasonable doubt that the act was a voluntary act.

[Lord Denning concluded that since the only evidence tendered in support of the defence of automatism was that of psychomotor epilepsy the trial judge was right not to leave the issue to the jury. Psychomotor epilepsy was evidence of insanity and since this had been rejected, there was no other evidence to go to the jury.]

Note

Questions of automatism are often bound up with the defence of insanity (see below, p. 134). What are the practical differences between the defences of non-insane automatism on the one hand and insanity or insane automatism on the other? Similarly issues of automatism and drunkenness may arise together (see below, p. 143).

C. Liability for a State of Affairs

Winzar v. Chief Constable of Kent
The Times, March 28, 1983, (D.C.)

Robert Goff L.J. The appellant had been charged with an offence under Section 12 of the Licensing Act 1872, *viz.* that he had been found drunk in a highway called Westcliff Road, contrary to that Section. The Ramsgate Justices heard the charge on the 6th October 1981 and they convicted him and imposed a fine of £15. The appeal came before the Crown Court, and Judge Edie and the two magistrates dismissed the appeal against conviction and sentence.

The facts found by the Crown Court are as follows: "(1) At 11.50 p.m. on the 24th August 1981 the Appellant was brought in on a stretcher to Ramsgate General Hospital. Dr. Sparkes examined him, and though the Appellant was able to give an account of himself, and mentioned that he suffered from a low sugar condition, Dr. Sparkes formed the opinion that he was drunk, that he was fit to leave the hospital, and thereupon asked him to do so. Dr. Sparkes later saw him slumped on a seat in the corridor and the police were called. (2) W.P.C. Washer arrived at the hospital at 1.15 a.m., saw the Appellant being carried into Westcliff Road, she then spoke to him, he was not able to answer, and she formed the opinion he was drunk. (3) The Appellant was placed in a police car stationed on the hospital forecourt in Westcliff Road, and taken to Ramsgate Police Station where he was charged with being found drunk in the highway called Westcliff Road, Ramsgate, cautioned, and made no reply."

It appears that the Appellant advanced the following argument before the Crown Court. First, his condition was not brought on by drink; secondly, he was not found on a highway as he had been carried to a police car which was stationed in the hospital forecourt; thirdly, his presence on the highway was momentary; and, fourthly, he was not there of his own volition but only for the purpose of being transported from the hospital to the police car.

The conclusion of the Crown Court was that the Appellant had been drunk and that he had been found on the highway known as Westcliff Road, Ramsgate, even though his presence on the highway was momentary and not of his own volition.

The question posed for the decision of the court is as follows: "Would a drunken person, lawfully ejected from premises after a request to leave, and consequently ascertained to be on the highway, even though momentarily and not of his volition, nevertheless be found on a highway within the meaning of Section 12 of the Licensing Act 1872?" . . .

We turn then to the question which was raised by the Crown Court, which was in effect: Does the fact that the Appellant was only momentarily on the highway and not there of his own volition, prevent his conviction of the offence of being found drunk in a highway?

We were referred to an Australian case, which was the only case found by counsel of direct relevance to the point we have to consider. That is the case of *Sheehan* v. *Piddington* (1955). In that case Mr. Piddington was found drunk in a public place, Marshall Street, Goondiwindi. The evidence showed that the Appellant entered a house in Goondiwindi and woke up a lodger, who was a friend of his. He began to converse with his friend in a manner which led the latter to form the opinion that the Appellant was drunk. A police constable called at the house, and the Appellant was asked to leave several times. He refused, and was finally removed by the police constable on to the footpath of Marshall Street. The police officer advised the Appellant to go home. However, he would not do so. He staggered three or four paces away and then turned round and lurched back towards the gate of the house from which he had already been removed. The police constable decided that he had had enough, and that the man had become a drunken nuisance. Accordingly, he arrested him.

On those facts, it was the conclusion of the full court, - the judgment being given by Macrossan C.J., that the offence of being found drunk in a public place had been proved. It was held that the mere fact that the man had been removed into the public place by force, and had not gone there of his own volition, did not prevent him from being found guilty of the crime for which he had been charged.

It is right to point out that on page 583 of the report, the Chief Justice said: "It is unnecessary to consider in this case what would have been the position had the Appellant been merely ejected by Constable Sheehan from his residence and without any interval of time arrested in Marshall Street." Plainly, that point was reserved by the Chief Justice because it did not arise on the facts of the case before him. On the evidence in that case, the Appellant had been given a chance to go home. He had then tried to get back into the house again and after that, not surprisingly, the police officer arrested him.

That case is persuasive authority for the view that it makes no difference in a case of this kind whether the person charged with the offence has gone into the highway or public place of his own volition or not.

In my judgment, looking at the purpose of this particular offence, it is designed, as Mr. Goymer has submitted, to deal with the nuisance which can be caused by persons who are drunk in a public place. This kind of offence is caused quite simply when a person is found drunk in a public place or in a highway.

Mr. Goymer gave an example which illustrates how sensible that conclusion is. Suppose a person was found as being drunk in a restaurant or a place of that kind and was asked to leave. If he was asked to leave, he would walk out of the door of the restaurant and would be in a public place or in a highway of his own volition. He would be there of his own volition because he had responded to a request. However, if a man in a restaurant made a thorough nuisance of himself, was asked to leave, objected and was ejected, in those circumstances, he would not be in a public place of his own volition because he would have been put there either by a gentleman on the door of the restaurant, or by a police officer, who might have been called to deal with the man in question. It would be nonsense if one were to say that the man who responded to the plea to leave could be said to be found drunk in a public place or in a highway, whereas the man who had been compelled to leave could not.

This leads me to the conclusion that a person is "found to be drunk in a public place or in a highway," within the meaning of those words as used in the section, when he is perceived to be drunk in a public place. It is enough for the commission of the offence if (1) a person is in a public place or a highway, (2) he is drunk, and (3) in those circumstances he is perceived to be there and to be drunk. Once those criteria have been fulfilled, he is liable to be convicted of the offence of being found drunk in a highway.

Appeal dismissed.

Note

See also *R . v. Larsonneur* (1933).

Questions

1. Would it be nonsense to say that "the man who responded to the plea to leave the restaurant could be said to be found drunk in a public place or in a highway, whereas the man who had been compelled to leave could not."?

2. What does this case say about the meaning of the phrase "be found."?

3. Would it have made any difference had the eviction from the hospital been unlawful?

D. Liability for Failure to Act

R. v. Gibbins and Proctor
(1918) 82 J.P. 287 (C.C.A.)

[G. and his mistress P. were charged with the murder by starvation of Nelly, G.'s seven year old daughter. The prosecution alleged that G. gave P. enough money to maintain all the family in good health, but that she so hated Nelly that she starved her to death, and did so with the full knowledge of G.]

Darling, J. It has been said that there ought not to have been a finding of guilty of murder against Gibbins. The court agrees that the evidence was less against Gibbins than Proctor; Gibbins gave her money, and, as far as we can see, it was sufficient to provide for the wants of themselves and all the children. But he lived in the house, and the child was his own, a little girl of seven, and he grossly neglected the child. He must have known what her condition was if he saw her, for she was little more than a skeleton. He is in this dilemma: if he did not see her the jury might well infer that he did not care if she died; if he did he must have known what was going on. The question is whether there was evidence that he so conducted himself as to show that he desired that grievous bodily injury should be done to the child. He cannot pretend that he showed any solicitude for her. He knew that Proctor hated her, knew that she was ill, and that no doctor had been called in, and the jury may have come to the conclusion that he was so infatuated with Proctor, and so afraid of offending her, that he preferred that the child should starve to death rather than that he should be exposed to any injury or unpleasantness from Proctor. It is unnecessary to say more than that there was evidence that Gibbins did desire that grievous bodily harm should be done to the child; he did not interfere in what was being done, and he comes within the definition which I have read, and is therefore guilty of murder.

The case of Proctor is plainer. She had charge of the child. She was under no obligation to do so or to live with Gibbins, but she did so, and receiving money, as it is admitted she did, for the purpose of supplying food, her duty was to see that the child was properly fed and looked after, and to see that she had medical attention if necessary. We agree with what Lord Coleridge, C.J., said in *R*. v. *Instan* (1893). "There is no case directly in point, but it would be a slur upon, and a discredit to the administration of, justice in this country if there were any doubt as to the legal principle, or as to the present case being within it. The prisoner was under a moral obligation to the deceased from which arose a legal duty towards her; that legal duty the prisoner has wilfully and deliberately left unperformed, with the consequence that there has been an acceleration of the death of the deceased owing to the non-performance of that legal duty." Here Proctor took upon herself the moral obligation of looking after the children; she was *de facto*, though not *de jure*, the wife of Gibbins, and had excluded the child's own mother. She neglected the child undoubtedly, and the evidence shows that as a result the child died. So a verdict of manslaughter was inevitable.

But it is necessary to go further and see whether it was murder. The evidence is that she had plenty of money; that she kept the child upstairs insufficiently supplied with food; that she hated the child and hit her. There is also evidence that when the child died of starvation both appellants took part in hiding the body and preventing the death from being known. They concocted a story that she had been sent away and was still alive. There is evidence that Proctor told Gibbins to bury the child out of sight, and that he did so in the brickyard where he worked. The jury came to the conclusion that she had done more than wickedly neglect the child; she had deliberately withheld food from it, and therefore we come to the conclusion that there was evidence which justified the jury in returning a verdict against her, not merely of manslaughter, but of murder. The appeals are therefore dismissed.

Appeals dismissed.

Note

A person will be held criminally liable for failure to act only where the law imposes a duty to act. A duty may be imposed:
  (1) expressly by statute;
  (2) because of status (*ie* Gibbins was under a legal obligation to maintain his child);
  (3) by contractual undertaking (*Pittwood* (1902));
  (4) by voluntary assumption of the duty (Proctor has assumed the moral responsibility for the child);
  (5) by conduct, *eg Miller*, below.

R. v. Miller
[1983] A.C. 161 (H.L.)

[M. had returned from the pub at closing time to the house where he was squatting. He lay on his mattress and lit a cigarette. He fell asleep and awoke to find his mattress on fire. Not having anything with which to extinguish the fire he simply moved to another room and went back to sleep. The house was badly damaged by the fire he had started. He was charged with arson contrary to section 1(1) and (3) of the Criminal Damage Act 1971. (See below, p. 269 for the provisions of the Act.)]

Lord Diplock. The first question to be answered where a completed crime of arson is charged is: "Did a physical act of the accused start the fire which spread and damaged property belonging to another (or did his act cause an existing fire, which he had not started but which would otherwise have burnt itself out harmlessly, to spread and damage property belonging to another)?" I have added the words in brackets for completeness. They do not arise in the instant case; in cases where they do, the accused, for the purposes of the analysis which follows, may be regarded as having started a fresh fire.

The first question is a pure question of causation; it is one of fact to be decided by the jury in a trial upon indictment. It should be answered "No" if, in relation to the fire during the period starting immediately before its ignition and ending with its extinction, the role of the accused was at no time more than that of a passive bystander. In such a case the subsequent questions to which I shall be turning would not arise. The conduct of the parabolical priest and Levite on the road to Jericho may have been indeed deplorable, but English law has not so far developed to the stage of treating it as criminal; and if it ever were to do so there would be difficulties in defining what should be the limits of the offence.

If on the other hand the question, which I now confine to: "Did a physical act of the accused start the fire which spread and damaged property belonging to another?" is answered "Yes," as it was by the jury in the instant case, then for the purpose of the further questions the answers to which are determinative of his guilt of the offence of arson, the conduct of the accused, throughout the period from immediately before the moment of ignition to the completion of the damage to the property by the fire, is relevant; so is his state of mind throughout that period.

Since arson is a result-crime the period may be considerable, and during it the conduct of the accused that is causative of the result may consist not only of his doing physical acts which cause the fire to start or spread but also of his failing to take measures that lie within his power to counteract the danger that he has himself created. And if his conduct, active or passive, varies in the course of the period, so may his state of mind at the time of each piece of conduct. If at the time of any particular piece of conduct by the accused that is causative of the result, the state of mind that actuates his conduct falls within the description of one or other of the states of mind that are made a necessary ingredient of the offence of arson by section 1(1) of the Criminal Damage Act 1971 (*i.e.* intending to damage property belonging to another or being reckless as to whether such property would be damaged) I know of no principle of English criminal law that would prevent his being guilty of the offence created by that subsection. Likewise I see no rational ground for excluding from conduct capable of giving rise to criminal liability, conduct which consists of failing to take measures that lie within one's power to counteract a danger that one has oneself created, if at the time of such conduct one's state of mind is such as constitutes a necessary ingredient of the offence. I venture to think that the habit of lawyers to talk of "*actus reus*," suggestive as it is of action rather than inaction, is responsible for any erroneous notion that failure to act cannot give rise to criminal liability in English law.

No one has been bold enough to suggest that if, in the instant case, the accused had been aware at the time that he dropped the cigarette that it would probably set fire to his mattress and yet had taken no steps to extinguish it he would not have been guilty of the offence of arson, since he would have damaged property of another being reckless as to whether any such property would be damaged.

I cannot see any good reason why, so far as liability under criminal law is concerned, it should matter at what point of time before the resultant damage is complete a person becomes aware that he has done a physical act which, whether or not he appreciated that it would at the time when he did it, does in fact create a risk that property of another will be damaged; provided that, at the moment of awareness, it lies within his power to take steps, either himself or by calling for the assistance of the fire brigade if this be necessary, to prevent or minimise the damage to the property at risk.

. . . . . .

The recorder, in his lucid summing up to the jury (they took 22 minutes only to reach their verdict) told them that the accused having by his own act started a fire in the mattress which, when he became aware of its existence, presented an obvious risk of damaging the house, became under a duty to take some action to put it out. The Court of Appeal upheld the conviction, but their ratio decidendi appears to be somewhat different from that of the recorder. As I understand the judgment, in effect it treats the whole course of conduct of the accused, from the moment at which he fell asleep and dropped the cigarette on to the mattress until the time the damage to the house by fire was complete, as a continuous act of the accused, and holds that it is sufficient to constitute the statutory offence of arson if at any stage in that course of conduct the state of mind of the accused, when he fails to try to prevent or minimise the damage which will result from his initial act, although it lies within his power to do so, is that of being reckless as to whether property belonging to another would be damaged.

My Lords, these alternative ways of analysing the legal theory that justifies a decision which has received nothing but commendation for its accord with commonsense and justice, have, since the publication of the judgment of the Court of Appeal in the instant case, provoked academic controversy. Each theory has distinguished support. Professor J.C. Smith espouses the "duty theory"; Professor Glanville Williams who, after the decision of the Divisional Court in *Fagan* v. *Metropolitan Police Commissioner* (1969) appears to have been attracted by the duty theory, now prefers that of the continuous act. When applied to cases where a person has unknowingly done an act which sets in train events that, when he becomes aware of them, present an obvious risk that property belonging to another will be damaged, both theories lead to an identical result; and since what your Lordships are concerned with is to give guidance to trial judges in their task of summing up to juries, I would for this purpose adopt the duty theory as being the easier to explain to a jury; though I would commend the use of the word "responsibility," rather than "duty" which is more appropriate to civil than to criminal law, since it suggests an obligation owed to another person, *i.e.*, the person to whom the endangered property belongs, whereas a criminal statute defines combinations of conduct and state of mind which render a person liable to punishment by the state itself.

Note

See below, p. 66 for an appropriate direction on the *mens rea* requirement in such a case.

E. Causation

(1) *The accused's conduct must amount to a factual cause of the prohibited conduct*

The principles of causation apply to any crime in which the prosecution must prove that the accused caused a prohibited result, *eg* damage to property, but they are nearly always seen in the context of causing death.

Note

See *Dalloway* (1847); H.S.B., p. 141.

(2) *The accused's conduct must be capable of amounting to a legal cause of the prohibited result*

R. v. Malchereck and Steele
(1981) 73 Cr.App.R. 173 (C.A.)

[In a combined appeal the Court of Appeal was asked to consider the legal principles involved in cases where the victim's death could be arguably attributed to a doctor turning off a life support system. In the first case M. had stabbed his wife several times causing, *inter alia*, a deep abdominal wound. She received perfectly normal hospital treatment, but later her heart stopped. After treatment for this emergency it was found that she had suffered brain damage as a result of lack of oxygen. Eventually using five of the six Royal Medical Colleges' tests, irreversible brain damage was diagnosed and the life support system was switched off. The question for the Court of Appeal was 'who had caused her death?' M., by stabbing her, or the doctors, by turning off the machine? The facts of *Steele* are omitted].

Lord Lane C.J. The question posed for answer to this Court is simply whether the judge in each case was right in withdrawing from the jury the question of causation. Was he right to rule that there was no evidence on which the jury could come to the conclusion that the assailant did not cause the death of the victim?

The way in which the submissions are put by Mr. Field-Fisher on the one hand and by Mr. Wilfred Steer on the other is as follows; the doctors, by switching off the ventilator and the life support machine were the cause of death or, to put it more accurately, there was evidence which the jury should have been allowed to consider that the doctors, and not the assailant, in each case may have been the cause of death.

In each case it is clear that the initial assault was the cause of the grave head injuries in the one case and of the massive abdominal haemorrhage in the other. In each case the initial assault was the reason for the medical treatment being necessary. In each case the medical treatment given was normal and conventional. At some stage the doctors must decide if and when treatment has become otiose. This decision was reached, in each of the two cases here, in circumstances which have already been set out in some detail. It is no part of the task of this Court to inquire whether the criteria, the Royal Medical College confirmatory tests, are a satisfactory code of practice. It is no part of the task of this Court to decide whether the doctors were, in either of these two cases, justified in omitting one or more of the so called "confirmatory tests." The doctors are not on trial: the applicant and the appellant respectively were.

There are two comparatively recent cases which are relevant to the consideration of this problem. The first is the case of *Jordan* (1956). That was a decision of the Court of Criminal Appeal, presided over by Hallett J. There the appellant stabbed his victim on May 4, 1956. The victim died in hospital on May 12. At the trial the pathologist who carried out the autopsy gave evidence that the cause of death was bronchopneumonia following a penetrating abdominal injury. The main burden of the appeal was whether fresh medical evidence, which was not called at the trial, should be admitted and considered by the

Court of Criminal Appeal.

In due course, in what was described as the exceptional or the exceedingly unusual circumstances of the case, that evidence was admitted. Evidence was given, accordingly, by two pathologists who said that in their opinion death had not been caused by the initial stab wound, which had almost healed at the time of the death, but by the introduction of terramycin after the deceased man had shown himself to be intolerant to that drug, and also by the intravenous introduction of huge quantities of liquid, which was an abnormal medical treatment and which, in these circumstances, was quite wrong. The conviction was quashed because the Court came to the conclusion, in effect, that the further evidence demonstrated that the death of the victim might not have resulted from normal treatment employed to cope with a felonious injury but that the treatment administered, the terramycin and the intravenous fluid, was an abnormal treatment which was palpably wrong which, in its turn, caused the death at a time when the original wound was in the process of healing and indeed had practically healed.

The other decision is that of *Smith* (1959). In that case the appellant had stabbed a fellow soldier with a bayonet. One of the wounds had pierced the victim's lung and had caused bleeding. Whilst being carried to the medical hut or reception centre for treatment, the victim was dropped twice and then, when he reached the treatment centre, he was given treatment which was subsequently shown to have been incorrect. [*Note. In fact, evidence was tendered in Smith to show that had the correct procedure been followed the chances of recovery would have been as high as 75 per cent.*] Lord Parker C.J., who gave the judgment of the Court, stressed the fact - if it needed stressing - that the case of *Jordan* (*supra*) was a very particular case depending upon its own exact facts, as indeed Hallett J. himself in that case had said.

In *Smith* (*supra*) counsel for the appellant argued that if there was any other cause, whether resulting from negligence or not, operating; if something happened which impeded the chance of the deceased recovering, then the death did not result from that wound.

A very similar submission to that has been made to this Court by counsel in the instant case. The Court in *Smith* (*supra*) was quite unable to accept that contention . . . . Lord Parker C.J. said . . . : "It seems to the Court that if at the time of death the original wound is still an operating cause and a substantial cause, then the death can properly be said to be the result of the wound, albeit that some other cause of death is also operating. Only if it can be said that the original wounding is merely the setting in which another cause operates can it be said that the death does not result from the wound. Putting it in another way, only if the second cause is so overwhelming as to make the original wound merely part of the history can it be said that the death does not flow from the wound."

In the view of this Court, if a choice has to be made between the decision in *Jordan* (*supra*) and that in *Smith* (*supra*) which we do not believe it does (*Jordan* (*supra*) being a very exceptional case), then the decision in *Smith* (*supra*) is to be preferred.

. . . . . .

There is no evidence in the present case here that at the time of conventional death, after the life support machinery was disconnected, the original wound or injury was other than a continuing, operating and indeed substantial cause of the death of the victim, although it need hardly be added that it need not be substantial to render the assailant guilty. There may be occasions, although they will be rare, when the original injury has ceased to operate as a cause at all, but in the ordinary case if the treatment is given bona fide by competent and careful medical practitioners, then evidence will not be admissible to show that the treatment would not have been administered in the same way by other medical practitioners. In other words, the fact that the victim has died, despite or because of medical treatment for the initial injury given by careful and skilled medical practitioners, will not exonerate the original assailant from responsibility for the death. It follows that so far as the ground of appeal in each of these cases relates to the direction given on causation, that ground fails. It also follows that the evidence which it is sought to adduce now, although we are prepared to assume that it is both credible and was not available properly at the trial - and a reasonable explanation for not calling it at the trial has been given - if received could, under no circumstances, afford any ground for allowing the appeal.

The reason is this. Nothing which any of the two or three medical men whose statements are before us could say would alter the fact that in each case the assailant's actions continued to be an operating cause of the death. Nothing the doctors could say would provide any ground for a jury coming to the conclusion that the assailant in either case might not have caused the death. The furthest to which their proposed evidence goes, as already stated, is to suggest, first, that the criteria or the confirmatory tests are not sufficiently stringent and, secondly, that in the present case they were in certain respects inadequately fulfilled or carried out. It is no part of this Court's function in the present circumstances to pronounce upon this matter, nor was it a function of either of the juries at these trials. Where a medical practitioner adopting methods which are generally accepted comes bona fide and conscientiously to the conclusion that the patient is for practical purposes dead, and that such vital functions as exist - for example, circulation - are being maintained solely by mechanical means, and therefore discontinues treatment, that does not prevent the person who inflicted the initial injury from being responsible for the victim's death. Putting it in another way, the discontinuance of treatment in those circumstances does not break the chain of causation between the initial injury and the death.

Although it is unnecessary to go further than that for the purpose of deciding the present point, we wish to add this thought. Whatever the strict logic of the matter may be, it is perhaps somewhat bizarre to suggest, as counsel have impliedly done, that where a doctor tries his conscientious best to save the life of a patient brought to hospital *in extremis,* skilfully using sophisticated methods, drugs and machinery to do so, but fails in his attempt and therefore discontinues treatment, he can be said to have caused the death of the patient.

(3) *Does unreasonable conduct by the victim break the chain of causation?*

R. v. Blaue
(1975) 61 Cr.App.R. 271 (C.A.)

[B. had stabbed and seriously wounded a girl of 18. She refused a blood transfusion on the ground she was a Jehovah's Witness, and later died. It seems fairly clear that the blood transfusion would have given her the chance to undergo surgery which would have had a high chance of success.]

Lawton L.J. In *R.* v. *Holland* (1841) the defendant, in the course of a violent assault, had injured one of his victim's fingers. A surgeon had advised amputation because of danger to life through complications developing. The advice was rejected. A fortnight later the victim died of lockjaw: " ... the real question is", said Maule J, "whether in the end the wound inflicted by the prisoner was the cause of death?" That distinguished judge left the jury to decide that question as did the judge in this case. They had to decide it as juries always do, by pooling their experience of life and using their common sense. They would not have been handicapped by a lack of training in dialectics or moral theology.

Maule J's direction to the jury reflected the common law's answer to the problem. He who inflicted an injury which resulted in death could not excuse himself by pleading that his victim could have avoided death by taking greater care of himself. . . . The common law in Sir Matthew Hale's time probably was in line with contemporary concepts of ethics. A man who did a wrongful act was deemed *morally* responsible for the natural and probable consequences of that act. Counsel for the appellant asked us to remember that since Sir Matthew Hale's day the rigour of the law relating to homicide has been eased in favour of the accused. It has been - but this has come about through the development of the concept of intent, not by reason of a different view of causation. . . .

The physical cause of death in this case was the bleeding into the pleural cavity arising from the penetration of the lung. This had not been brought about by any decision made by the deceased girl but by the stab wound.

Counsel for the appellant tried to overcome this line of reasoning by submitting that the jury should have been directed that if they thought the girl's decision not to have a blood transfusion was an unreasonable one, then the chain of causation would have been broken. At once the question arises - reasonable by whose standards? Those of Jehovah's Witnesses? Humanists? Roman Catholics? Protestants of Anglo-Saxon descent? The man on the Clapham omnibus? But he might well be an admirer of Eleazar who suffered death rather than eat the flesh of swine; or of Sir Thomas Moore who, unlike nearly all his contemporaries, was unwilling to accept Henry VIII as Head of the Church of England. Those brought up in the Hebraic and Christian traditions would probably be reluctant to accept that these martyrs caused their own deaths.

As was pointed out to counsel for the appellant in the course of argument, two cases, each raising the same issue of reasonableness because of religious beliefs, could produce different verdicts depending on where the cases were tried. A jury drawn from Preston, sometimes said to be the most Catholic town in England, might have different views about martyrdom to one drawn from the inner suburbs of London.

Counsel for the appellant accepted that this might be so; it was, he said, inherent in trial by jury. It is not inherent in the common law as expounded by Sir Matthew Hale and Maule J. It has long been the policy of the law that those who use violence on other people must take their victims as they find them. This in our judgment means the whole man, not just the physical man. It does not lie in the mouth of the assailant to say that his victim's religious beliefs which inhibited him from accepting certain kinds of treatment were unreasonable. The question for decision is what caused her death. The answer is the stab wound. The fact that the victim refused to stop this end coming about did not break the causal connection between the act and death.

Questions

Is this case authority for the proposition that failure by a victim to take proper care of himself can never excuse the initial assailant from responsibility? Does it make any difference whether the initial wound was trivial or serious? Would it support a conclusion that a rapist should be held responsible for the subsequent suicide of his distraught victim?

R. v. Pagett
(1983) 76 Cr.App.R. 279 (C.A.)

[P. had forcibly abducted a young girl. Armed police had surrounded the house where he was holding the girl and he threatened to shoot her. He later tried to leave the house holding the girl in front of him as a shield. He fired shots at the police who instinctively fired back. Police bullets struck and killed the girl.]

Goff L.J. In our judgment, the question whether an accused person can be held guilty of homicide, either murder or manslaughter, of a victim the immediate cause of whose death is the act of another person must be determined on the ordinary principles of causation, uninhibited by any such rule of policy as that for which Lord Gifford has contended. We therefore reject the second ground of appeal.

We turn to the first ground of appeal, which is that the learned judge erred in directing the jury that it was for him to decide *as a matter of law* whether by his unlawful and deliberate acts the appellant caused or was a cause of Gail Kinchen's death. It is right to observe that this direction of the learned judge followed upon a discussion with counsel, in the absence of the jury; though the appellant, having dismissed his own counsel, was for this purpose without legal representation. In the course of this discussion, counsel for the prosecution referred the learned judge to a passage in Professor Smith and

Professor Hogan's *Criminal Law* (4th ed. (1978), p. 272), which reads as follows: "Causation is a question of both fact and law. D's act cannot be held to be the cause of an event if the event would have occurred without it. The act, that is, must be a *sine qua non* of the event and whether it is so is a question of fact. But there are many acts which are *sine qua non* of a homicide and yet are not either in law, or in ordinary parlance, the cause of it. If I invite P to dinner and he is run over and killed on the way, my invitation may be a *sine qua non* of his death, but no one would say I killed him and I have not caused his death in law. Whether a particular act which is a *sine qua non* of an alleged *actus reus* is also a cause of it is a question of law. Where the facts are admitted the judge may direct the jury that a particular act did, or did not, cause a particular result." There follows a reference to *Jordan* (1956).

For the appellant, Lord Gifford criticised the statement of the learned authors that "Whether a particular act which is a *sine qua non* of an alleged *actus reus* is also a cause of it is a question of law." He submitted that that question had to be answered by the jury as a question of fact. In our view, with all respect, both the passage in Smith and Hogan's *Criminal Law,* and Lord Gifford's criticism of it, are over-simplifications of a complex matter.

We have no intention of embarking in this judgment on a dissertation of the nature of causation, or indeed of considering any matters other than those which are germane to the decision of the issues now before us. Problems of causation have troubled philosophers and lawyers throughout the ages; and it would be rash in the extreme for us to trespass beyond the boundaries of our immediate problem. Our comments should therefore be understood to be confined not merely to the criminal law, but to cases of homicide (and possibly also other crimes of violence to the person); and it must be emphasised that the problem of causation in the present case is specifically concerned with the intervention of another person (here one of the police officers) whose act was the immediate cause of the death of the victim, Gail Kinchen.

In cases of homicide, it is rarely necessary to give the jury any direction on causation as such. Of course, a necessary ingredient of the crimes of murder and manslaughter is that the accused has by his act caused the victim's death. But how the victim came by his death is usually not in dispute. What is in dispute is more likely to be some other matter: for example, the identity of the person who committed the act which indisputably caused the victim's death; or whether the accused had the necessary intent; or whether the accused acted in self-defence, or was provoked. Even where it is necessary to direct the jury's minds to the question of causation, it is usually enough to direct them simply that in law the accused's act need not be the sole cause, or even the main cause, of the victim's death, it being enough that his act contributed significantly to that result. It is right to observe in passing, however, that even this simple direction is a direction of law relating to causation, on the basis of which the jury are bound to act in concluding whether the prosecution has established, as a matter of fact, that the accused's act did in this sense cause the victim's death. Occasionally, however, a specific issue of causation may arise. One such case is where, although an act of the accused constitutes a *causa sine qua non* of (or necessary condition for) the death of the victim, nevertheless the intervention of a third person may be regarded as the sole cause of the victim's death, thereby relieving the accused of criminal responsibility. Such intervention, if it has such an effect, has often been described by lawyers as a *novus actus interveniens*. We are aware that this time-honoured Latin term has been the subject of criticism. We are also aware that attempts have been made to translate it into English; though no simple translation has proved satisfactory, really because the Latin term has become a term of art which conveys to lawyers the crucial feature that there has not merely been an intervening act of another person, but that that act was so independent of the act of the accused that it should be regarded in law as the cause of the victim's death, to the exclusion of the act of the accused. At the risk of scholarly criticism, we shall for the purposes of this judgment continue to use the Latin term.

Now the whole subject of causation in the law has been the subject of a well-known and most distinguished treatise by Professors Hart and Honoré, *Causation in the Law*. Passages from this book were cited to the learned judge, and were plainly relied upon by him; we, too, wish to express our indebtedness to it. It would be quite wrong for us to consider in this judgment the wider issues discussed in that work. But, for present purposes, the passage which is of most immediate relevance is to be found in Chapter XII, in which the learned authors consider the circumstances in which the intervention of a third person, not acting in concert with the accused, may have the effect of relieving the accused of criminal responsibility. The criterion which they suggest should be applied in such circumstances is whether the intervention is voluntary, *i.e.* whether it is "free, deliberate and informed." We resist the temptation of expressing the judicial opinion whether we find ourselves in complete agreement with that definition; though we certainly consider it to be broadly correct and supported by authority. Among the examples which the authors give of non-voluntary conduct, which is not effective to relieve the accused of responsibility, are two which are germane to the present case, *viz.* a reasonable act performed for the purpose of self-preservation, and an act done in performance of a legal duty.

There can, we consider, be no doubt that a reasonable act performed for the purpose of self-preservation, being of course itself an act caused by the accused's own act, does not operate as a *novus actus interveniens*. If authority is needed for this almost self-evident proposition, it is to be found in such cases as *Pitts* (1842) and *Curley* (1909). In both these cases, the act performed for the purpose of self-preservation consisted of an act by the victim in attempting to escape from the violence of the accused, which in fact resulted in the victim's death. In each case it was held as a matter of law that, if the victim acted in a reasonable attempt to escape the violence of the accused, the death of the victim was caused by the act of the accused. Now one form of self-preservation is self-defence; for present purposes, we can see no distinction in principle between an attempt to escape the consequences of the accused's act, and a response which takes the form of self-defence. Furthermore, in our judgment, if a reasonable act of self-defence against the act of the accused causes the death of a third party, we can see no reason in principle why the act of self-defence, being an involuntary act caused by the act of the accused, should relieve the accused from criminal responsibility for the death of the third party. Of course, it does not necessarily follow that the accused will be guilty of the murder, or even of the manslaughter, of the third party; though in the majority of cases he is likely to be guilty at least of manslaughter. Whether he is guilty of murder or manslaughter will depend upon the question whether all the ingredients of the relevant offence have been proved; in particular, on a charge of murder, it will be necessary that the accused had the necessary intent.

. . . . . .

There is however one further aspect of the present case to which we must advert. On the evidence, Gail Kinchen was not just an innocent bystander killed by a shot fired from the gun of a police officer who, acting in reasonable self-defence, fired his gun in response to a lethal attack by the appellant: though on those facts alone it would, in our opinion, have been open to the jury to convict the appellant of murder or manslaughter. But if, as the jury must have found to have occurred in the present case, the appellant used Gail Kinchen by force and against her will as a shield to protect him from any shots fired by the police, the effect is that he committed not one but two unlawful acts, both of which were dangerous - the act of firing at the police, and the act of holding Gail Kinchen as a shield in front of him when the police might well fire shots in his direction in self-defence. Either act could in our judgment, if on the principles we have stated it was held to cause the death of Gail Kinchen, constitute the *actus reus* of the manslaughter or, if the necessary intent were established, murder of Gail Kinchen by the appellant, even though the shot which killed her was fired not by the appellant but by a police officer.

2. MENS REA

A. Degrees of Culpability: Definitions

Law Commission: Codification of the Criminal Law, Clause 22

(*Law Com. No. 143; 1985*)

Fault

22. For the purposes of this Act and of any Code Fault terms: offence—

    (*a*) a person acts in respect of an element of an offence—

        "purposely" when he wants it to exist or *Purpose.* occur;

        "intentionally" when he wants it to exist *Intention.* or occur, is aware that it exists or is almost certain that it exists or will exist or occur;

        "knowingly" when he is aware that it exists or is almost certain that it exists or will exist or occur;

        "recklessly" when— *Recklessness*

            (i) he is aware of a risk that it exists

or will exist or occur; and

(ii) it is, in the circumstances known to him, unreasonable to take the risk;

"heedlessly" when— *Heedlessnes*

(i) he gives no thought to whether there is a risk that it exists or will exist or occur although the risk would be obvious to any reasonable person; and

(ii) it is in the circumstances unreasonable to take the risk:

(*b*) a person acts—

"negligently" when his act is a very *Criminal* serious deviation from the standard of care *negligence.* to be expected of a reasonable person;

"carelessly" when his act is a deviation *Carelessness.* from the standard of care to be expected of a reasonable person;

and these and like words shall be construed accordingly unless the context otherwise requires.

Model Penal Code

Section 2.02. General Requirements of Culpability

(1) *Minimum Requirements of Culpability*

Except as provided in Section 2.05, a person is not guilty of an offense unless he acted purposely, knowingly, recklessly or negligently, as the law may require, with respect to each material element of the offence.

(2) *Kinds of Culpability Defined*

(a) Purposely.

A person acts purposely with respect to a material element of an offense when:

(i) if the element involves the nature of his conduct or a result thereof, it is his conscious object to engage in conduct of that nature or to cause such a result; and

(ii) if the element involves the attendant circumstances, he is aware of the existence of such circumstances or he believes or hopes that they exist.

(b) Knowingly.

A person acts knowingly with respect to a material element of an offense when:

   (i)   if the element involves the nature of his conduct or the attendant circumstances, he is aware that his conduct is of that nature or that such circumstances exist; and

  (ii)   if the element involves a result of his conduct, he is aware that it is practically certain that his conduct will cause such a result.

(c) Recklessly.

A person acts recklessly with respect to a material element of an offense when he consciously disregards a substantial and unjustifiable risk that the material element exists or will result from his conduct. The risk must be of such a nature and degree that, considering the nature and purpose of the actor's conduct and the circumstances known to him, its disregard involves a gross deviation from the standard of conduct that a law-abiding person would observe in the actor's situation.

(d) Negligently.

A person acts negligently with respect to a material element of an offense when he should be aware of a substantial and unjustifiable risk that the material element exists or will result from his conduct. The risk must be of such a nature and degree that the actor's failure to perceive it, considering the nature and purpose of his conduct and the circumstances known to him, involves a gross deviation from the standard of care that a reasonable person would observe in the actor's situation.

B. Intention and Knowledge

In most crimes liability can be established by proof of intention or recklessness; and so a precise definition of intention does not have to be attempted. In some crimes, intention only will suffice (in respect of at least one element of the *actus reus*); in these crimes it is necessary to know what constitutes intention.

Cunliffe v. Goodman
[*1950*] *2 K.B. 237 (C.A.)*

Asquith L.J. An "intention" to my mind connotes a state of affairs which the party intending; I will call him X - does more than merely contemplate: it connotes a state of affairs which, on the contrary, he decides, so far as in him lies, to bring about, and which in point of possibility, he has a reasonable prospect of being able to bring about by his own act of volition.

Note

See further *R. v. Moloney* (below, p. 180); *R. v. Hancock and Shankland* (below, p. 186).

Question

X plants a bomb in a local public house which he desires to destroy. He gives the landlord 60 seconds warning knowing that this is almost certainly not enough time to evacuate the premises. Five people are seriously wounded. Can he be convicted of unlawfully and maliciously wounding these people with intent to cause them grievous bodily harm?

C. Recklessness

As a result of recent decisions it can be said that recklessness involves the taking of an unjustified risk either deliberately or without adverting to the existence of the risk.

(1) *Deliberate risk taking*

R. v. Cunningham
[*1957*] *2 Q.B. 396 (C.C.A.)*

[C. had wrenched a gas meter off the wall in a cellar in order to steal its contents. As a result escaping gas seeped through a wall of loose stone rubble which divided the cellar of the house from the cellar of the adjoining house. The escaping gas partially asphyxiated a woman occupant in the adjoining house. He was charged with unlawfully and maliciously causing a certain noxious thing to be taken by the victim so as thereby to endanger her life (Offences Against the Person Act 1861, s. 23). The trial judge directed the jury that "'Malicious' for this purpose means wicked - some thing which he has no business to do and perfectly well knows it.' On appeal against conviction:]

Byrne J. With the utmost respect to the learned judge, we think it is incorrect to say that the word "malicious" in a statutory offence merely means wicked. We think the judge was, in effect, telling the jury that if they were satisfied that the appellant acted wickedly – and he had clearly acted wickedly in stealing the gas meter and its contents – they ought to find that he had acted maliciously in causing the gas to be taken by Mrs. Wade so as thereby to endanger her life.

In our view it should have been left to the jury to decide whether, even if the appellant did not intend the injury to Mrs. Wade, he foresaw that the removal of the gas meter might cause injury to someone but nevertheless removed it. We are unable to say that a reasonable jury, properly directed as to the meaning of the word "maliciously" in the context of section 23, would without doubt have convicted.

In these circumstances this court has no alternative but to allow the appeal and quash the conviction.

Appeal allowed.

(2) *Inadvertent risk taking*

R. v. Caldwell
[1982] A.C. 341 (H.L.)

[C. set fire to a hotel where 10 guests were in residence, believing he had a grievance against the proprietor. No great damage was caused. He was charged under section 1 of the Criminal Damage Act 1971 which is set out in Chapter 10. In the indictment count 2 contained a charge under section 1(1) of the Act which is the basic offence of criminal damage; to this he pleaded guilty. In another count he was charged with an offence under section 1(2) which involves intentionally or recklessly endangering life to which he pleaded not guilty. The House was mainly concerned with the question of whether self-induced intoxication could provide a defence to this second charge, but in the course of the speeches attention was given to the meaning of the word "reckless."]

Lord Diplock. My Lords, the Criminal Damage Act 1971 replaced almost in their entirety the many and detailed provisions of the Malicious Damage Act 1861. Its purpose, as stated in its long title, was to *revise* the law of England and Wales as to offences of damage to property. As the brevity of the Act suggests, it must have been hoped that it would also simplify the law.

In the Act of 1861, the word consistently used to describe the mens rea that was a necessary element in the multifarious offences that the Act created was "maliciously" – a technical expression, not readily intelligible to juries, which became the subject of considerable judicial exegesis. This culminated in a judgment of the Court of Criminal Appeal in *Reg.* v. *Cunningham* (1957) (above) which approved, as an accurate statement of the law, what had been said by Professor Kenny in the first edition of his *Outlines of Criminal Law* published in 1902:

"In any statutory definition of a crime, malice must be taken . . . as requiring either (1) an actual intention to do the particular kind of harm that in fact was done; or (2) recklessness as to whether such harm should occur or not (*i.e.,* the accused has foreseen that the particular kind of harm might be done and yet has gone on to take the risk of it)."

My Lords, in this passage Professor Kenny was engaged in defining for the benefit of students the meaning of "malice" as a term of art in criminal law. To do so he used ordinary English words in their popular meaning. Among the words he used was "recklessness," the noun derived from the adjective "reckless," of which the popular or dictionary meaning is: careless, regardless, or heedless, of the possible harmful consequences of one's acts. It presupposes that if thought were given to the matter by the doer before the act was done, it would have been apparent to him that there was a real risk of its having the relevant harmful consequences; but, granted this, recklessness covers a whole range of states of mind from failing to give any thought at all to whether or not there is any risk of those harmful consequences, to recognising the existence of the risk and nevertheless deciding to ignore it. Conscious of this imprecision in the popular meaning of recklessness as descriptive of a state of mind, Professor Kenny, in the passage quoted, was, as it seems to me, at pains to indicate by the words in brackets the particular species within the genus reckless states of mind that constituted "malice" in criminal law. This parenthetical restriction on the natural meaning of recklessness was necessary to an explanation of the meaning of the adverb "maliciously" when used as a term of art in the description of an offence under the Malicious Damage Act 1861 (which was the matter in point in *Reg.* v. *Cunningham* (1957); but it was not directed to and consequently has no bearing on the meaning of the adjective "reckless" in section 1 of the Criminal Damage Act 1971. To use it for that purpose can, in my view, only be misleading.

My Lords, the restricted meaning that the Court of Appeal in *Reg.* v. *Cunningham* had placed upon the adverb "maliciously" in the Malicious Damage Act 1861 in cases where the prosecution did not rely upon an actual intention of the accused to cause the damage that was in fact done, called for a meticulous analysis by the jury of the thoughts that passed through the mind of the accused at or before the time he did the act that caused the damage, in order to see on which side of a narrow dividing line they fell. If it had crossed his mind that there was a risk that someone's property might be damaged but, because his mind was affected by rage or excitement or confused by drink, he did not appreciate the seriousness of the risk or trusted that good luck would prevent its happening, this state of mind would amount to malice in the restricted meaning placed upon that term by the Court of Appeal; whereas if, for any of these reasons, he did not even trouble to give his mind to the question whether there was any risk of damaging the property, this state of mind would not suffice to make him guilty of an offence under the Malicious Damage Act 1861.

Neither state of mind seems to me to be less blameworthy than the other; but if the difference between the two constituted the distinction between what does and what does not in legal theory amount to a guilty state of mind for the purposes of a statutory offence of damage to property, it would not be a practicable distinction for use in a trial by jury. The only person who knows what the accused's mental processes were is the accused himself - and probably not even he can recall them accurately when the rage or excitement under which he acted has passed, or he has sobered up if he were under the influence of drink at the relevant time. If the accused gives evidence that because of his rage, excitement or drunkenness the risk of particular harmful consequences of his acts simply did not occur to him, a jury would find it hard to be satisfied beyond reasonable doubt that his true mental process was not that, but was the slightly different mental process required if one applies the restricted meaning of "being reckless as to whether" something would happen, adopted by the Court of Appeal in *Reg.* v. *Cunningham.*

My Lords, I can see no reason why Parliament when it decided to revise the law as to offences of damage to property should go out of its way to perpetuate fine and impracticable distinctions such as these, between one mental state and another. One would think that the sooner they were got rid of, the better.

When cases under section 1(1) of the New Act, in which the prosecution's case was based upon the accused having been "reckless as to whether . . . property would be destroyed or damaged," first came before the Court of Appeal, the question as to the meaning of the expression "reckless" in the context of that subsection appears to have been treated as soluble simply by posing and answering what had by then, unfortunately, become an obsessive question among English lawyers: Is the test of recklessness "subjective" or "objective"? The first two reported cases, in both of which judgments were given off the cuff, are first *Reg.* v. *Briggs (Note)* (1977) which is reported in a footnote to the second, *Reg.* v. *Daryl Parker* (1977). Both classified the test of recklessness as "subjective." This led the court in *Reg.* v. *Briggs (Note)* (1977) to say: "A man is reckless in the sense required when he carries out a deliberate act knowing that there is some risk of damage resulting from that act but nevertheless continues in the performance of that act." This leaves over the question whether the risk of damage may not be so slight that even the most prudent of men would feel justified in taking it, but it excludes that kind of recklessness that consists of acting without giving any thought at all to whether or not there is any risk of harmful consequences of one's act; even though the risk is great and would be obvious if any thought were given to the matter by the doer of the act. *Reg.* v. *Daryl Parker* (1977), however, opened the door a chink by adding as an alternative to the actual knowledge of the accused that there is some risk of damage resulting from his act and his going on to take it, a mental state described as "closing his mind to the obvious fact" that there is such a risk.

Reg. v. *Stephenson* (1979), the first case in which there was full argument, though only on one side, and a reserved judgment, slammed the door again upon any less restricted interpretation of "reckless" as to whether particular consequences will occur than that originally approved in *Reg.* v. *Briggs (Note)* (1977). The appellant, a tramp, intending to pass the night in a hollow in the side of a haystack, had lit a fire to keep himself warm; as a result of this the stack itself caught fire. At his trial he was not himself called as a witness but a psychiatrist gave evidence on his behalf that he was schizophrenic and might not have had the same ability to foresee or appreciate risk as a mentally normal person. The judge had given to the jury the direction on the meaning of reckless that had been approved in *Reg.* v. *Daryl Parker* (1977). The argument for the appellant on the appeal was that this let in an "objective" test whereas the test should be entirely "subjective." It was buttressed by copious citation from previous judgments in civil and criminal cases where the expressions "reckless" or "recklessness" had been used by judges in various contexts. Counsel for the Crown expressed his agreement with the submissions for the appellant. The judgment of the court contains an analysis of a number of the cited cases, mainly in the field of civil law. These cases do not disclose a uniform judicial use of the terms; and as respects judicial statements made before the current vogue for classifying all tests of legal liability as either "objective" or "subjective" they are not easily assignable to one of those categories rather than the other. The court, however, reached its final conclusion by a different route. It made the assumption that although Parliament in replacing the Act of 1861 by the Act of 1971 had discarded the word "maliciously" as descriptive of the mens rea of the offences of which the actus reus is damaging property, in favour of the more explicit phrase "intending to destroy or damage any such property or being reckless as to whether any such property would be destroyed," it nevertheless intended the words to be interpreted in precisely the same sense as that in which the single adverb "maliciously" had been construed by Professor Kenny in the passage that received the subsequent approval of the Court of Appeal in *Reg.* v. *Cunningham* (1957).

My Lords, I see no warrant for making any such assumption in an Act whose declared purpose is to revise the then existing law as to offences of damage to property, not to perpetuate it. "Reckless" as used in the new statutory definition of the mens rea of these offences is an ordinary English word. It had not by 1971 become a term of legal art with some more limited esoteric meaning than that which it bore in ordinary speech - a meaning which surely includes not only deciding to ignore a risk of harmful consequences resulting from one's acts that one has recognised as existing, but also failing to give any thought to whether or not there is any such risk in circumstances where, if any thought were given to the matter, it would be obvious that there was.

If one is attaching labels, the latter state of mind is neither more nor less "subjective" than the first. But the label solves nothing. It is a statement of the obvious; mens rea is, by definition, a state of mind of the accused himself at the time he did the physical act that constitutes the actus reus of the offence; it cannot be the mental state of some non-existent, hypothetical person.

Nevertheless, to decide whether someone has been "reckless" as to whether harmful consequences of a particular kind will result from his act, as distinguished from his actually intending such harmful consequences to follow, does call for some consideration of how the mind of the ordinary prudent individual would have reacted to a similar situation. If there were nothing in the circumstances that ought to have drawn the attention of an ordinary prudent individual to the possibility of that kind of harmful consequence, the accused would not be described as "reckless" in the natural meaning of that word for failing to address his mind to the possibility; nor, if the risk of the harmful consequences was so slight that the ordinary prudent individual upon due consideration of the risk would not be deterred from treating it as negligible, could the accused be described as "reckless" in its ordinary sense if, having considered the risk, he decided to ignore it. (In this connection the gravity of the possible harmful consequences would be an important factor. To endanger life must be one of the most grave.) So to this extent, even if one ascribes to "reckless" only the restricted meaning, adopted by the Court of Appeal in *Reg.* v. *Stephenson* (1979) and *Reg.* v. *Briggs* (*Note*) (1977) of foreseeing that a particular kind of harm might happen and yet going on to take the risk of it, it involves a test that would be described in part as "objective" in current legal jargon. Questions of criminal liability are seldom solved by simply asking whether the test is subjective or objective.

In my opinion, a person charged with an offence under section 1(1) of the Criminal Damage Act 1971 is "reckless as to whether any such property would be destroyed or damaged" if (1) he does an act which in fact creates an obvious risk that property will be destroyed or damaged and (2) when he does the act he either has not given any thought to the possibility of there being any such risk or has recognised that there was some risk involved and has nonetheless gone on to do it. That would be a proper direction to the jury; cases in the Court of Appeal which held otherwise should be regarded as overruled.

Where the charge is under section 1 (2) the question of the state of mind of the accused must be approached in stages, corresponding to paragraphs (*a*) and (*b*). The jury must be satisfied that what the accused did amounted to an offence under section 1 (1), either because he actually intended to destroy or damage the property or because he was reckless (in the sense that I have described) as to whether it might be destroyed or damaged. Only if they are so satisfied must the jury go on to consider whether the accused also either actually intended that the destruction or damage of the property should endanger someone's life or was reckless (in a similar sense) as to whether a human life might be endangered.

Appeal dismissed.

Notes

1. The question of self-induced intoxication is considered below, p. 138.]
2. Where the prosecution are relying on recklessness in a case where liability is based upon a failure to act (see above, p. 43) Lord Diplock said that a modified direction to the jury would be necessary.

R. v. Miller
[1983] A.C. 161 (H.L.)

Lord Diplock. While in the general run of cases of destruction or damage to property belonging to another by fire (or other means) where the prosecution relies upon the recklessness of the accused, the direction recommended by this House in *Reg.* v. *Caldwell* (1982) is appropriate, in the exceptional case, (which is most likely to be one of arson and of which the instant appeal affords a striking example) where the accused is initially unaware that he has done an act that in fact sets in train events which, by the time the accused becomes aware of them, would make it obvious to anyone who troubled to give his mind to them that they present a risk that property belonging to another would be damaged, a suitable direction to the jury would be: that the accused is guilty of the offence under section 1 (1) of the Criminal Damage Act 1971 if, when he does become aware that the events in question have happened as a result of his own act, he does not try to prevent or reduce the risk of damage by his own efforts or if necessary by sending for help from the fire brigade, and the reason why he does not is either because he has not given any thought to the possibility of there being any such risk or because, having recognised that there was some risk involved, he has decided not to try to prevent or reduce it.

Question

Lord Diplock talks of recklessness as involving, *inter alia*, the creation of an "obvious risk." What does he mean by this? To whom must the risk be obvious
   (i)   to the accused;
   (ii) to a reasonable person;
   (iii) to a reasonable person of the accused's age with such of his characteristics as would affect his appreciation of the risk?

R. v. Rogers
(1984) 149 J.P. 89 (C.A.)

[R. was convicted, at the age of 15, of several offences, one of which was arson
with intent to endanger life (or being reckless as to whether the life of another
would be endangered), contrary to section 1(2) and (3) of the Criminal Damage
Act 1971.]

Ackner L.J. That question - "had he acted recklessly?" - was
the real issue. Mr Timms at the beginning of the trial sought a
ruling from the trial Judge as to the direction which the learned
Judge would give on the subject of recklessness. He submitted
that when considering recklessness, the jury could only convict
the appellant if he did an act which created a risk to life
obvious to someone of his age and with such of his
characteristics as would affect his appreciation of the risk. He
should not in law be capable of being convicted if the act
created a risk which was obvious to an ordinary prudent person
of mature years and understanding, but was not obvious to him
at his age and with his characteristics. The learned Judge ruled
against that submission and accordingly Mr Timms, with
characteristic good sense, advised his client to alter his plea.
The appellant then pleaded guilty and was sentenced as we
have indicated.

The point of law which is raised before us is the point which
Mr Timms took before HH Judge Abdela. It is said that the
learned Judge erred in law in deciding that the test of
recklessness as to whether life was endangered was as follows:
A person is guilty of an offence if (i) he does an act which in
fact creates a risk to the ordinary prudent man, *i.e.* one of
mature years and understanding, that life will be endangered;
(ii) he did the act not having given thought to the possibility of
such a risk; or (iii) recognizing that there was some risk, he
nonetheless continued to act. The learned Judge, it is urged,
was wrong in law because he failed to apply the law in relation
to what constitutes the "ordinary prudent man" and failed
adequately to consider *DPP* v. *Camplin* (1978). (See below, p.
195.) He should have found that the ordinary prudent man is
synonymous with the reasonable man and therefore the jury
should have had regard to the particular situation of the
appellant, namely his age, and any other characteristics which
would affect his appreciation of the risk.

This arson, it is accepted by Mr Timms (who has argued this
case with great skill and competence) was serious. For the

ordinary prudent adult there was plainly an obvious risk of endangering the life of another. Thus the sole question which this appeal raises is whether the learned Judge was wrong in the ruling which he gave. As we have indicated, Mr Timms' main complaint is that the case of *Camplin*, a decision of the House of Lords, makes it clear that when considering the question of provocation the jury are to be directed to take into account, amongst other things, the age of the defendant, and this approach was not applied here. Mr Timms submits that the same approach as in *Camplin* applies where recklessness is the issue before the jury.

Camplin's case was concerned with the defence of provocation provided by s. 2 of the Homicide Act 1957. What the jury have to decide, pursuant to that section, is whether the provocation which resulted in the accused killing someone was enough to make a reasonable man do as he did. In order to answer that question the House of Lords decided in *Camplin* that the jury must take into account the age, sex and such of the accused's characteristics as would affect the gravity of the provocation to him (per Lord Diplock). They have to consider whether the defendant reacted as a reasonable man in his situation (per Lord Morris). The jury have to take into account the entire factual situation, including the characteristics of the accused (per Lord Simon). However, under the section of the Criminal Damage Act 1971 with which we are concerned, the jury have to consider whether the defendant intended by the damage which he committed to endanger the life of another or was reckless as to whether the life of another would thereby be endangered. Thus the issue is, have the prosecution proved that the defendant had the requisite intention or, alternatively, has he taken what the law considers to be an unjustifiable risk? This seems to us to be quite a different question from that raised under the Homicide Act 1957 and accounts for the fact that *Camplin's* case was not mentioned in *Caldwell's* case or in the cases of *Lawrence* or *Miller*, the recent cases on recklessness.

[Ackner L.J. said the issue relating to the unjustifiable risk had been considered by the House of Lords in *Caldwell*, *Lawrence* and *Miller* (see above).]

The Divisional Court considered these principles recently in the case of *Elliott* v. *C* (1983). That was an appeal by the prosecution by way of case stated from the justices of the petty sessional division of Canterbury, who on September 28, 1982 found that the respondent C, who was a minor, was not guilty of a charge and dismissed an information which alleged that she on June 16, 1982 without lawful excuse had destroyed by fire a shed and its contents intending to destroy such property or being reckless whether such property would be destroyed contrary to the same section in the Criminal Damage Act 1971 as that with which we are concerned. She was a schoolgirl who had reached the age of 14 years in May 1982. She lived with her foster mother and was in a remedial class at school. On the evening of June 15, 1982 she went out with an older schoolfriend. She hoped to stay the night at the friend's home, but was unable to do so. She did not return to her own home, but stayed out all night, not sleeping for the whole of the night. At about 5 am on June 16, 1982 she entered Mr. Davies' garden shed. She found white spirit in a plastic container. She poured this onto the carpet on the floor of the shed, threw two lighted matches onto the spirit, the second of which ignited. The fire immediately flared up out of control and the girl left the shed. In due course proceedings were taken against her.

The magistrates found that while she had realized that the contents of the bottle which contained the white spirit were possibly inflammable, she had not handled it before and had not appreciated how explosively it would burn and immediately become out of her control, thus destroying the shed and its contents, placing her own life at risk. She had not given thought at the time that she started the fire to the possibility of there being a risk that the shed and its contents would be destroyed by her actions. In the circumstances the risk would not have been obvious to her or been appreciated by her if she had given thought to it. In reaching their findings the magistrates said that they had paid due regard to the girl's age and understanding, her lack of experience in dealing with inflammable spirit and the fact that she must have been tired and exhausted at the time. They had had the case of *Caldwell* drawn to their attention and they said that they found it implicit in the decision that a defendant should only be held to have acted recklessly by virtue of his failure to give any thought to an obvious risk that property would be destroyed or damaged where such risk would be obvious to him if he had given any thought to the matter. They therefore dismissed the information.

[Ackner L.J. said that in the Divisional Court, Glidewell J. had felt that the correct interpretation of the three House of Lords authorities compelled him to hold that the prosecuting counsel was right in his submission that the risk had to be obvious to a reasonable prudent man, not necessarily to the particular defendant if he or she had given thought to it.]

Robert Goff L.J., in his judgment – and we should perhaps emphasize that both judgments were reserved – expressed his unhappiness at having to reach the same conclusion, but held compelled by the authorities, to which we have referred, to do so. He referred to certain articles written by jurists which were critical of Lord Diplock's statement of principle, unless that principle was to be taken as qualified to the extent that the defendant should be regarded as having acted recklessly by virtue of his failure to give any thoughts to an obvious risk that property would be destroyed or damaged (or for that matter the life of another would be endangered) only where such risk would have been obvious to him if he had given any thought to the matter. However, for the reasons given by Robert Goff, L.J., in his characteristically careful analysis of the matter, such a qualification, in his judgment, had been clearly rejected by Lord Diplock and by the majority of the court in *Caldwell's* case. . . . . .

In the face of that difficult situation, Mr Timms sought to induce us to adopt a via media. He said he accepted it would be wrong to ask the question whether the defendant himself was aware of the risk, but it would be right to inquire whether a person of the age of the defendant and with his characteristics which might be relevant to his ability to foresee the risk, would have appreciated it. He drew our attention in particular to the submission made by the prosecution before the magistrates in *Elliott's* case . . . "that in relation to the defendant aged 14 years, the proper approach was whether such risk would have been obvious to a normal 14 year old child". Therefore he said he was not seeking to relate the test to the particular defendant, but merely, so to speak, to a class of which he is a member. This, he says, provides him with the same logical basis of approach to the reasonable man or the reasonably prudent person as *Camplin* had suggested. We do not think that that via media was for one moment in the mind of Lord Diplock. The opportunity so to ingraft this important modification on the principle which he had enunciated had arisen in the subsequent cases and would have been just the sort of point (if it was a valid one) which we would have expected the House of Lords to have desired to have dealt with, thus clearing up the position, when they had the opportunity to do so when considering whether or not to give leave in *Elliott's* case. If they had desired to say, for instance, that the age of the defendant was a factor to which particular regard must be had in applying the test, then *Elliott* was just the sort of case to do that, excising, if appropriate, any reference to any other ephemeral characteristics such as exhaustion from which the girl was said to be suffering. But they did not take that opportunity. We do not think that we should seek by this subtlety to avoid applying principles which we also have difficulty in accepting. We respectfully share the regrets voiced by Robert Goff LJ that in essence "recklessness" has now been construed synonymously with "carelessness". Like the editor of the current edition of Archbold we find difficulty in reconciling the following excerpts from the speech of Lord Hailsham, LC, with Lord Diplock's conclusion in *R. v. Lawrence*, with which he agreed. Lord Hailsham said . . . . "It only surprises me that there should have been any question regarding the existence of mens rea in relation to the words 'reckless', 'recklessly' or 'recklessness'. Unlike most English words it has been in the English language as a word in general use at least since the eighth century A.D. almost always with the same meaning, applied to a person or conduct evincing a state of mind stopping short of deliberate intention, and going beyond mere inadvertence, or in its modern, though not its etymological and original sense, mere carelessness". The excerpt from the speech of Lord Diplock . . . where he refers to *Caldwell's* case (is): "The conclusion reached by the majority was that the adjective 'reckless' when used in a criminal statute, *i.e.* the Criminal Damage Act 1971, had not acquired a special meaning as a term of legal art, but bore its popular or dictionary meaning of careless, regardless, or heedless of the possible harmful consequences of one's acts. The same must be true of the adverbial derivative 'recklessly'".

We therefore dismiss the appeal against conviction. Although we would have preferred that the Judge should have at least been entitled in law to have left the jury the question, would a boy of the defendant's age have appreciated that to have thrown petrol bombs very close to the windows of this dwelling house was a danger to the life of the occupants of that house, we have little doubt that on the facts of this case the answer would have been clearly in the affirmative. As we have already stressed, this was a ground floor flat and the petrol bombs were thrown so close to the window where the girl whom it was sought, so it was said, to frighten her, had her bedroom, that one landed within 18 inches of that window.

. . . . . .

Questions

1. To what crimes will the *Caldwell* definition apply? (See Lord Diplock in *Lawrence* (1982).)

Lord Roskill in *Seymour* (1983) speaking of the statutory offence of causing death by reckless driving and the common law offence of "motor" manslaughter said:

> My Lords, I would accept the submission of counsel for the Crown that once it is shown that the two offences co-exist it would be quite wrong to give the adjective "reckless" or the adverb "recklessly" a different meaning according to whether the statutory or the common law offence is charged. "Reckless" should today be given the same meaning in relation to all offences which involve "recklessness" as one of the elements unless Parliament has otherwise ordained.

2. Does the *Caldwell* test apply to "recklessness" in the definition of rape? (See the Sexual Offences Amendment Act 1976, s. 1, below, p. 270.)

R. v. Satnam and Kewal
(*1984*) 78 Cr.App.R. 149 (C.A.)

Bristow J. We think that in enacting [section 1 of the Sexual Offences Amendment Act 1976] Parliament must have accepted the recommendations of the Heilbron Committee, so that the provisions are declaratory of the existing law as stated in *D.P.P.* v. *Morgan* [below, p. 80].

Any direction as to the definition of rape should therefore be based upon section 1 of the 1976 Act and upon *D.P.P.* v. *Morgan*, without regard to *R.* v. *Caldwell* or *R.* v. *Lawrence*, which were concerned with recklessness in a different context and under a different statute.

The word "reckless" in relation to rape involves a different concept to its use in relation to malicious damage or, indeed, in relation to offences against the person. In the latter cases the foreseeability, or possible foreseeability, is as to the consequences of the criminal act. In the case of rape the foreseeability is as to the state of mind of the victim.

. . . . . .

In summing-up a case of rape which involves the issue of consent, the judge should, in dealing with the state of mind of the defendant, first of all direct the jury that before they could convict of rape the Crown has to prove either that the defendant knew the woman did not want to have sexual intercourse, or was reckless as to whether she wanted to or not.

If they were sure he knew she did not want to they should find him guilty of rape knowing there to be no consent. If they were not sure about that, then they would find him not guilty of such rape and should go on to consider reckless rape. If they thought he might genuinely have believed that she did want to, even though he was mistaken in his belief, they would find him not guilty. In considering whether his belief was genuine, they should take into account all the relevant circumstances (which could at that point be summarised) and ask themselves whether, in the light of those circumstances, he had reasonable grounds for such a belief. If, after considering those circumstances, they were sure he had no genuine belief that she wanted to, they would find him guilty. If they came to the conclusion that he could not care less whether she wanted to or not, but pressed on regardless, then he would have been reckless and could not have believed that she wanted to, and they would find him guilty of reckless rape.

Notes

1. What meaning should be given to the word "reckless" in section 15(4) of the Theft Act 1968 (below, p. 267)?

2. Does the *Caldwell* definition of "recklessness" apply to assaults? (See Smith and Hogan, *Criminal Law* (5th ed.), p. 354.)

D. Negligence

Blyth v. Birmingham Waterworks Co.
(1856) 11 Exch. 781

Alderson B. Negligence is the omission to do something which a reasonable man, guided upon those considerations which ordinarily regulate the conduct of human affairs, would do, or doing something which a prudent and reasonable man would not do.

This is a definition of negligence in a civil law case.

Questions

1. In which crimes does negligence form the basis for liability? (See section 3 Road Traffic Act 1972; *Morgan* (below, p. 80); manslaughter (below, p. 201).) Although negligence is rarely the direct basis for criminal liability it may arise indirectly (for example as a defence to strict liability offences). (See H.S.B., p. 168 and p. 151.)

2. How does negligence, as defined by Alderson B. differ from recklessness as defined by Lord Diplock in *Caldwell* (above, p. 60)?

E. Blameless Inadvertence

In the states of mind so far considered there can be detected at least some element of culpability. Where the accused cannot be said to be at fault in his failure to perceive some element of the *actus reus*, it is sometimes said that he is, in respect of that element, blamelessly inadvertent. Does it therefore follow that he cannot be convicted of the offence in question?

R. v. Prince
(1875) L.R. 2 C.C.R 154 (Court for Crown Cases Reserved)

[P. was charged under the then equivalent of section 20 of the Sexual Offences Act 1956 which provides:

"It is an offence for a person acting without lawful authority or excuse to take an unmarried girl under the age of 16 out of the possession of her parent or guardian against his will."

He knew full well that her father would not consent and that he had no right to take her out of her father's possession. However he honestly and, in the eyes of the jury, reasonably believed that she was 18 years old. So as far as that aspect of the *actus reus* was concerned he might be said to lack *mens rea.*]

Bramwell B. read a judgment to which *Kelly C.B., Cleasby B., Grove J., Pollock B.*, and *Amphlett B.* assented.

. . . It is impossible to suppose that a person taking a girl out of her father's possession against his will is guilty of no offence within the statute unless he, the taker, knows she is under 16 - that he would not be guilty if the jury were of opinion he knew neither one way nor the other. Let it be then that the question is whether he is guilty where he knows, as he thinks, that she is over 16. This introduces the necessity for reading the statute with some strange words introduced; as thus: "Whosoever shall take any unmarried girl being under the age of sixteen, and not believing her to be over the age of sixteen, out of the possession", etc. Those words are not there, and the question is whether we are bound to construe the statute as though they were, on account of the rule that mens rea is necessary to make an act a crime.

I am of opinion that we are not, nor as though the word "knowingly" was there, and for the following reasons. The act forbidden is wrong in itself, if without lawful cause. I do not say illegal, but wrong. I have not lost sight of this, that though the statute probably principally aims at seduction for carnal purposes, the taking may be by a female, with a good motive. Nevertheless, though there may be cases which are not immoral in one sense, I say that the act forbidden is wrong. Let us remember what is the case supposed by the statute. It supposes that there is a girl - it does not say a woman, but a girl something between a child and a woman - it supposes she is in the possession of her father or mother, or other person having lawful care and charge of her, and it supposes there is a taking, and that that taking is against the will of the person in whose possession she is. It is, then, a taking of a girl in the possession of someone, against his will. I say that done without lawful cause is wrong, and that the legislature meant it should be at the risk of the taker, whether or not the girl was under 16. I do not say that taking a woman of 50 from her brother's or even father's house is wrong. She is at an age when she has a right to choose for herself; she is not a girl, nor of such tender age that she can be said to be in possession of or under the care or in the charge of anyone. If I am asked where I draw the line, I answer at when the female is no longer a girl in anyone's possession. But what the statute contemplates, and what I say is wrong, is the taking of a female of such tender years that she is properly called a girl, and can be said to be in another's possession, and in that other's care or charge. No argument is necessary to prove this; it is enough to state the case. The legislature has enacted that if anyone does this wrong act he does it at the risk of the girl turning out to be under 16. This opinion gives full scope to the doctrine of mens rea. If the taker believed he had the father's consent, though wrongly, he would have no mens rea. So if he did not know she was in anyone's possession, nor in the care or charge of anyone. In those cases he would not know he was doing the act forbidden by the statute, an act which, if he knew she was in the possession and care or charge of anyone, he would know was a crime or not according as she was under 16 or not. He would know he was doing an act wrong itself, whatever was his intention, if done without lawful cause. In addition to these considerations one may add that the statute does use the word "unlawfully", and does not use the words "knowingly or not believing to the contrary". If the question was whether his act was unlawful there would be no difficulty as it clearly was not lawful. . . .

Blackburn J. read the following judgment to which *Cockburn C.J., Mellor, Quain, Lush, Archibald, Field* and *Lindley JJ.* assented. . . . The question, therefore is reduced to whether the words in s. 55 of the Offences against the Person Act 1861, that whosoever shall unlawfully take "any unmarried girl being under the age of sixteen, out of the possession of her father" are to be read as if they were "being under the age of sixteen, and he knowing she was under that age". No such words are contained in the statute, nor is there the word "maliciously", "knowingly", or any other word used that can be said to involve a similar meaning. The argument in favour of the prisoner must, therefore, entirely proceed on the ground that in general a guilty mind is an essential ingredient in a crime, and that where a statute creates a crime the intention of the legislature should be presumed to be to include "knowingly" in the definition of the crime, and the statute should read as if that word were inserted, unless the contrary intention appears. We need not inquire at present whether the canon of construction goes quite so far as above stated, for we are of opinion that the intention of the legislature sufficiently appears to have been to punish the abductor unless the girl, in fact, was of such an age as to make her consent an excuse irrespective of whether he knew her to be too young to give an effectual consent, and to fix that age at 16.

The section in question is one of a series of enactments beginning with s. 50 forming a code for the protection of women and the guardians of young women. These enactments are taken with scarcely any alteration from the repealed statute, the Offences against the Person Act 1828, which had collected them into a code from a variety of old statutes all repealed by it. Section 50 enacts that:

> "Whosoever shall unlawfully and carnally know and abuse any girl under the age of ten years, shall be guilty of felony."

By s. 51:

> "Whosoever shall unlawfully and carnally know and abuse any girl being above the age of ten years and under the age of twelve years, shall be guilty of a misdemeanour."

It seems impossible to suppose that the intention of the legislature in those two sections could have been to make the crime depend upon the knowledge of the prisoner of the girl's actual age. It would produce the monstrous result that a man who had carnal connection with a girl in reality not quite ten years old, but whom he, on reasonable grounds, believed to be a little more than ten, was to escape altogether. He could not, in that view of the statute, be convicted of the felony, for he did not know her to be under ten. He could not be convicted of the misdemeanour because she was, in fact, not above the age of ten. It seems to us that the intention of the legislature was to punish those who had connection with young girls, though with their consent, unless the girl was, in fact, old enough to give a valid consent. The man who has connection with a child relying on her consent does it at his peril if she is below the statutable age.

Section 55, on which the present case arises, uses precisely the same words as those in ss. 50 and 51, and must be construed in the same way, and if we refer to the repealed statute 4 & 5 Phil. & Mary, c. 8 (Abduction Act 1557), from s. 3 of which the words in s. 55 are taken with very little alteration, it strengthens the inference that such was the intention of the legislature. The preamble states as the mischief aimed at, that female children, heiresses, and others having expectations, were, unawares of their friends, brought to contract marriages of disparagement "to the great heaviness of their friends", and then to remedy this enacts by the first section that it shall not be lawful for anyone to take an unmarried girl being under 16 out of the custody of her father or the person to whom he either, by will or by act in his lifetime, gives the custody, unless it be bona fide done by or for the master or mistress of such child, or the guardian in chivalry or in socage of such child. This recognises a legal right to the possession of the child depending on the real age of the child, and not on what appears. The object of the legislature, being as it appears by the preamble to protect this legal right to the possession, would be baffled if it was an excuse that the person guilty of the taking thought the child above sixteen. The words "unlawfully take" as used in s. 3 of 4 & 5 Phil. & Mary, c. 8 (Abduction Act 1557), mean without the authority of the master, or mistress, or guardian mentioned in the immediately preceding section. . . .

Note

This case is one of the leading authorities in what is known as strict (or absolute) liability. See further *Hibbert* (1869) for an interesting comparison (see H.S.B., p. 162). Strict liability will be considered further in Chapter 2; see below, p. 89.

Question

The imposition of liability without fault certainly makes the task of the prosecutor more straightforward. Should all crimes be dealt with in this way, leaving the issue of culpability as a matter of relevance only to the sentence? What sentence would you deem appropriate for *Prince*? He received six months imprisonment.

F. Coincidence of Actus Reus and Mens Rea

R. v. Church
[1966] 1 Q.B. 59 (C.C.A.)

[C. had taken a woman in his van for sexual purposes. He had been unable to satisfy her and she reproached him and slapped his face. In an ensuing fight he knocked her out and was unable to revive her. He then panicked, dragged her out of the van and threw her into the river.]

Edmund Davies J. The outline of the case for the prosecution, was this: The gravity of the injuries inflicted during life clearly pointed to an intention by the appellant to cause grievous bodily harm to or the death of Mrs. Nott. Her death was in fact brought about by the action of the appellant in shortly thereafter throwing her still-living body into the river. Did it make any difference, as far as the murder charge was concerned, whether or not the appellant believed she was then already dead? On this question the trial judge gave this direction: "His case is that he genuinely and honestly believed that she was dead. I direct you that, if that was his genuine and honest belief, then when he threw what he thought to be a dead body into the river he obviously was not actuated by any intention to cause death or grievous bodily harm: you cannot cause death or serious bodily harm to a corpse. Therefore the question for you is: have the prosecution satisfied you that his story told before you today . . . that he believed she was dead, is untrue; and that the truth is that he threw her into the river not caring whether she was alive or dead but simply to get her body out of his van, so that he would not be caught and punished for what he had already done to her?"

The jury were thus told in plain terms that they could not convict of murder unless it had been proved that the appellant knew that Mrs. Nott was still alive when he threw her into the river or (at least) that he did not then believe she was dead. We venture to express the view that such a direction was unduly benevolent to the appellant and that the jury should have been told that it was still open to them to convict of murder, notwithstanding that the appellant may have thought his blows and attempt at strangulation had actually produced death when he threw the body into the river, if they regarded the appellant's behaviour from the moment he first struck her to the moment when he threw her into the river as a series of acts designed to cause death or grievous bodily harm. See *Meli* v. *The Queen* (1954). In the present case, the jury, directed as they were, acquitted of murder. They had, however, been told that the trial judge could see no ground upon which the appellant could be acquitted of all crime and they convicted him of manslaughter.

Note

See also *Att.-Gen.'s Reference (No. 4 of 1980) (1981)* (H.S.B., p. 153).

G. Transferred Malice

R. v. Latimer
(1886) 17 Q.B.D. 359

[L. who had argued with X in a public house aimed a blow at him with a belt. The belt lightly struck X, but glanced off severely cutting Y's face. He was charged, *inter alia*, with unlawfully and maliciously wounding Y.]

Lord Coleridge C.J. We are of opinion that this conviction must be sustained. It is common knowledge that a man who has an unlawful and malicious intent against another, and, in attempting to carry it out, injures a third person, is guilty of what the law deems malice against the person injured; because the offender is doing an unlawful act, and has that which the judges call general malice, and that is enough. Such would be the case if the matter were *res integra*, and it is not so, for *R. v. Hunt* is an express authority on the point. There a man intended to injure *A*, and said so, and, in the course of doing it, stabbed the wrong man, and had clearly malice in fact, but no intention of injuring the man who was stabbed. . . . The indictment in *R. v. Pembliton* (1874) was on the Act making unlawful and malicious injury to property a statutory offence; and the jury expressly negatived, and the facts expressly negatived, any intention to do injury to property; and the court held that under the Act making it an offence to injure any property there must be an intent to injure property. *R. v. Pembliton,* therefore, does not govern the present case; and on no other ground is there anything to be said for the prisoner.

Questions

1. In *Pembliton* (1874) the accused was involved in a fight outside a public house. He picked up a large stone and threw it at the people he had been fighting. It flew over the heads of the intended victims and smashed a large plate glass window behind them. P. was charged with the then equivalent of criminal

damage (see below, p. 269). Could he have been convicted of such an offence? What other offences may he have committed? Why was his conviction quashed?

2. In *Latimer* it would seem that L. would be guilty whether or not he foresaw the harm to Y - or was not even negligent in respect of such harm. Is there a case for saying that liability in these cases should depend on at least the existence of negligence?

H. Mistake

Question

X has been charged with abducting Y, a 15 year old girl. Would he have any defence if he believed:

(1) abducting 15 year old girls was no criminal offence? (See *Esop* (1836) H.S.B., p. 155);
(2) that Y was in fact 16 years old (see *Prince* above, p. 74);
(3) that Y was a common prostitute? (see *Hibbert* (1869) H.S.B., p. 162).

D.P.P. v. Morgan
[*1976*] *A.C. 182 (H.L.)*

[M. invited some friends to his house to have intercourse with his wife. He told them to ignore any signs of resistance as this would just be his wife's way of increasing her enjoyment. M. and his friends were charged with rape. The friends pleaded not guilty on the ground that they believed that the wife had consented to intercourse. The trial judge directed the jury that such a belief would afford a defence only if it had been based on reasonable grounds. It would not suffice that the accused honestly believed she had consented. Their appeals against conviction were dismissed by the Court of Appeal, but leave was granted to appeal to the House of Lords.]

Lord Cross. . . . Secondly, I would say something as to how far - if at all - the decision in *Reg.* v. *Tolson*, (1889), which was, of course, a case of bigamy, has a bearing on this case. The statute there provided that "Whosoever, being married, shall marry any other person during the life of the former husband or wife, . . . shall be guilty of felony," with a proviso that

"nothing in this section contained shall extend . . . to any person marrying a second time whose husband or wife shall have been continually absent from such person for the space of seven years then last past, and shall not have been known by such person to be living within that time. . . ."

The defendant who was found by the jury to have had reasonable grounds for believing that her husband was then dead - though in fact he was not - went through a ceremony of marriage with another man within seven years of the time when she last knew of his being alive. She therefore fell within the very words of the statute. Nevertheless, the majority of the Court of Crown Cases Reserved held that she was entitled to be acquitted because on general principles of criminal liability, having no particular relation to the crime of bigamy, a mistaken belief based on reasonable grounds in the existence of facts, which, if true, would have made the act charged against her innocent, afforded her a defence since it was not to be supposed that Parliament intended bigamy to be an "absolute" offence to the commission of which the state of mind of the defendant was wholly irrelevant. The minority of the judges, on the other hand, thought that the existence of the proviso which gave an express exemption from liability in certain circumstances made it impossible to imply an exemption from liability in other circumstances not covered by it. If the Sexual Offences Act 1956 had provided that it was an offence for a man to have sexual intercourse with a woman who did not consent to it then the case of *Reg.* v.*Tolson* would undoubtedly have been in point; but what the Act says is that it is an offence for a man to "rape" a woman and, as I see it, one cannot say that *Reg.* v. *Tolson* applies to rape unless one reads the words "rape a woman" as equivalent to "have intercourse with a woman who is not consenting to it." Counsel for the Director says, of course, that they are equivalent but the question remains whether he is right.

Finally, I must refer to an alternative submission, made by counsel for the appellant - namely, that in *Reg.* v. *Tolson* the court was wrong in saying that to afford a defence to a charge of bigamy the mistaken belief of the defendant had to be based on reasonable grounds. It is, of course, true that the question whether a mistaken belief honestly held but based on no reasonable grounds would have afforded a defence was not argued in that case. There had been several conflicting decisions by judges on assize - one saying that an honest belief would be a defence, others that a belief on reasonable grounds would be a defence, and yet others that not even a belief on reasonable grounds would be a defence. In *Reg.* v. *Tolson* Stephen J. asked the jury whether they thought that the defendant in good faith and on reasonable grounds believed her husband to be dead at the date of her second marriage. Having obtained an affirmative answer he then, in order to get the point settled by the Court of Crown Cases Reserved, directed the jury - contrary to his own opinion - that such a

belief would not be a defence and, after they had duly
convicted Mrs. Tolson, sentenced her to one day's
imprisonment. On her appeal against her conviction, her
counsel was not, of course, concerned to dispute the view that a
mistaken belief had to be based on reasonable grounds, since
the jury had held that his client had had reasonable grounds for
her belief, and the question whether an honest belief would
have been enough was never argued. If it had been argued, it is
possible that some of the judges who were in the majority -
though having regard to the way in which he framed his
question, I do not think that Stephen J. would have been one of
them - might have held that a mistaken belief honestly but
unreasonably held was enough. But *Reg.* v. *Tolson* was decided
over 80 years ago. It is accepted as a leading authority in the law
of bigamy not only in this country . . . but also in Australia . . . .
Moreover, the phrase "an honest and reasonable belief
entertained by the accused of the existence of facts, which, if
true, would make the act charged against him innocent" has
been adopted on several occasions as a definition of mens rea
generally applicable to cases where the offence is not an
absolute one but the words defining it do not expressly or
impliedly indicate that some particular mens rea is required to
establish it. . . . Counsel did not refer us to any case in which the
propriety of the inclusion of the element of "reasonableness"
has been doubted; and its inclusion was, in fact, approved in
Reg. v. *King* (1964) and by Lord Diplock in *Sweet* v. *Parsley*
[below, p. 89]. So, even if I had been myself inclined to think
that the inclusion of the element of reasonableness was wrong,
I would not have thought it right for us to call it in question in
this case. In fact, however, I can see no objection to the
inclusion of the element of reasonableness in what I may call a
"*Tolson*" case. If the words defining an offence provide either
expressly or impliedly that a man is not to be guilty of it if he
believes something to be true, then he cannot be found guilty if
the jury think that he may have believed it to be true, however
inadequate were his reasons for doing so. But, if the definition
of the offence is on the face of it "absolute" and the defendant
is seeking to escape his prima facie liability by a defence of
mistaken belief, I can see no hardship to him in requiring the
mistake - if it is to afford him a defence - to be based on
reasonable grounds. As Lord Diplock said in *Sweet* v. *Parsley*
(1970), there is nothing unreasonable in the law requiring a
citizen to take reasonable care to ascertain the facts relevant to
his avoiding doing a prohibited act. To have intercourse with a

woman who is not your wife is, even today, not generally considered to be a course of conduct which the law ought positively to encourage and it can be argued with force that it is only fair to the woman and not in the least unfair to the man that he should be under a duty to take reasonable care to ascertain that she is consenting to the intercourse and be at the risk of a prosecution if he fails to take such care. So if the Sexual Offences Act 1956 had made it an offence to have intercourse with a woman who was not consenting to it, so that the defendant could only escape liability by the application of the *"Tolson"* principle, I would not have thought the law unjust.

But, as I have said, section 1 of the Act of 1956 does not say that a man who has sexual intercourse with a woman who does not consent to it commits an offence; it says that a man who rapes a woman commits an offence. Rape is not a word in the use of which lawyers have a monopoly and the first question to be answered in this case, as I see it, is whether according to the ordinary use of the English language a man can be said to have committed rape if he believed that the woman was consenting to the intercourse and would not have attempted to have it but for this belief, whatever his grounds for so believing. I do not think that he can. Rape, to my mind, imports at least indifference as to the woman's consent. I think, moreover, that in this connection the ordinary man would distinguish between rape and bigamy. To the question whether a man who goes through a ceremony of marriage with a woman believing his wife to be dead, though she is not, commits bigamy, I think that he would reply "Yes, - but I suppose that the law contains an escape clause for bigamists who are not really to blame." On the other hand, to the question whether a man, who has intercourse with a woman believing that she is consenting to it, though she is not, commits rape, I think that he would reply "No. If he was grossly careless then he may deserve to be punished but not for rape." That being my view as to the meaning of the word "rape" in ordinary parlance, I next ask myself whether the law gives it a different meaning. There is very little English authority on the point but what there is - namely, the reported directions of several common law judges in the early and the middle years of the last century - accords with what I take to be the ordinary meaning of the word. The question has been canvassed in a number of recent cases in New South Wales and Victoria but there is only one of them - *Reg.* v. *Daly* (1968) - that I find of much assistance. In none of the others do the judges advert to the fact that to include an intention to have intercourse whether or not the woman consents in the definition of rape and to say that a reasonable mistake with regard to consent is an available defence to a charge of rape are two incompatible alternatives which cannot be combined in a single direction to a jury – as, incidentally, the judge combined them in one passage in his summing up in this case. In *Reg.* v. *Daly* the court, as well as drawing that distinction which I regard as fundamental, indicated pretty clearly that it thought – as I do – that the former approach to the problem was the right one. For these reasons, I think that the summing up contained a misdirection.

Proviso applied.

Questions

1. Why does a belief that one is free to marry have to be reasonable on a charge of bigamy, yet a belief that an alleged rape victim was consenting need only to be genuine?

The speeches in *Morgan* led to the establishment of a Committee under Heilbron J. (Cmnd. 6352 (1975)) and subsequently to the Sexual Offences (Amendment) Act 1976 (below, p. 270).

2. In the crime of assault the accused may have a defence if the prosecution fails to prove he acted unlawfully. The touching of another may be lawful if: (a) the person consents to be touched; (b) the accused was acting reasonably in self defence or to prevent the commission of a crime. Where the accused mistakenly believes the other consented or that his action is necessary, *e g .* to prevent a crime, is it sufficient that he genuinely holds that belief or must it be based upon reasonable grounds?

R. v. Gladstone Williams
(1984) 78 Cr.App.R. 176 (C.A.)

[W. saw M. knock a black youth to the ground. M. told W. that the black youth had mugged a woman and that he was arresting him. M. claimed, falsely, to be a police officer. W. asked to see his identity and when this could not be produced a struggle followed in which W. punched M. in the face. W. was charged with assault occasioning actual bodily harm contrary to section 47 of the Offences Against the Person Act 1861. W. claimed he was acting lawfully to prevent the commission of a crime. The judge directed the jury that, if M. were acting lawfully, W. would still have a defence if he had an honest belief based upon reasonable grounds that reasonable force was necessary to prevent a crime. W. appealed against his conviction.]

Lord Lane C.J. One starts off with the meaning of the word "assault." "Assault" in the context of this case, that is to say using the word as a convenient abbreviation for assault and battery, is an act by which the defendant, intentionally or recklessly, applies unlawful force to the complainant. There are circumstances in which force may be applied to another lawfully. Taking a few examples: first, where the victim consents, as in lawful sports, the application of force to another will, generally speaking, not be unlawful. Secondly, where the defendant is acting in self-defence: the exercise of any necessary and reasonable force to protect himself from unlawful violence is not unlawful. Thirdly, by virtue of section 3 of the Criminal Law Act 1967, a person may use such force as is reasonable in the circumstances in the prevention of crime or in effecting or assisting in the lawful arrest of an offender or suspected offender or persons unlawfully at large. In each of those cases the defendant will be guilty if the jury are sure that first of all he applied force to the person of another, and secondly that he had the necessary mental element to constitute guilt.

The mental element necessary to constitute guilt is the intent to apply unlawful force to the victim. We do not believe that the mental element can be substantiated by simply showing an intent to apply force and no more.

What then is the situation if the defendant is labouring under a mistake of fact as to the circumstances? What if he believes, but believes mistakenly, that the victim is consenting, or that it is necessary to defend himself, or that a crime is being committed which he intends to prevent? He must then be judged against the mistaken facts as he believes them to be. If judged against those facts or circumstances the prosecution fail to establish his guilt, then he is entitled to be acquitted.

The next question is, does it make any difference if the mistake of the defendant was one which, viewed objectively by a reasonable onlooker, was an unreasonable mistake? In other words should the jury be directed as follows: "Even if the defendant may have genuinely believed that what he was doing to the victim was either with the victim's consent or in reasonable self-defence or to prevent the commission of crime, as the case may be, nevertheless if you, the jury, come to the conclusion that the mistaken belief was unreasonable, that is to say that the defendant as a reasonable man should have realised his mistake, then you should convict him."

It is upon this point that the large volume of historical precedent with which Mr. Howard threatened us at an earlier stage is concerned. But in our judgment the answer is provided by the judgment of this Court in *Kimber* (1983), by which, as already stated, we are bound. There is no need for me to rehearse the facts, save to say that that was a case of an alleged

indecent assault upon a woman. Lawton L.J. deals first of all
with the case of *Albert* v. *Lavin* (1981): "The application of the
Morgan principle (above, p. 80) to offences other than indecent
assault on a woman will have to be considered when such
offences come before the courts. We do, however, think it
necessary to consider two of them because of what was said in
the judgment. The first is a decision of the Divisional Court in
Albert v. *Lavin* (1981). The offence charged was assaulting a
police officer in the execution of his duty, contrary to section
51 of the Police Act 1964. The defendant in his defence
contended, *inter alia*, that he had not believed the police
officer to be such and in consequence had resisted arrest. His
counsel analysed the offence in the same way as we have done
and referred to the reasoning in *Director of Public Prosecutions*
v. *Morgan*. Hodgson J. delivering the leading judgment,
rejected this argument and in doing so said: 'In my judgment
Mr Walker's ingenious argument fails at an earlier stage. It does
not seem to me that the element of unlawfulness can properly
be regarded as part of the definitional elements of the offence.
In defining a criminal offence the word "unlawful" is surely
tautologous and can add nothing to its essential ingredients . . .
And no matter how strange it may seem that a defendant
charged with assault can escape conviction if he shows that he
mistakenly but unreasonably thought his victim was
consenting but not if he was in the same state of mind as to
whether his victim had a right to detain him, that in my
judgment is the law.' We have found difficulty in agreeing
with this reasoning" - and I interpolate, so have we - "even
though the judge seems to be accepting that belief in consent
does entitle a defendant to an acquittal on a charge of assault.
We cannot accept that the word 'unlawful' when used in a
definition of an offence is to be regarded as 'tautologous.' In
our judgment the word 'unlawful' does import an essential
element into the offence. If it were not there social life would
be unbearable, because every touching would amount to a
battery unless there was an evidential basis for a defence. This
case was considered by the House of Lords. The appeal was
dismissed, but their Lordships declined to deal with the issue
of belief."

That is the end of the citation from *Kimber* (*supra*) in so far as
it is necessary for the second point. I read a further passage . . .
which sets out the proper direction to the jury, and is relevant
to the first leg of the appellant's argument in this case. It reads
as follows: "In our judgment the learned recorder should have

directed the jury that the prosecution had to make them sure that the appellant never had believed that Betty was consenting. As he did not do so, the jury never considered an important aspect of his defence."

We respectfully agree with what Lawton L.J. said there with regard both to the way in which the defence should have been put and also with regard to his remarks as to the nature of the defence. The reasonableness or unreasonableness of the defendant's belief is material to the question of whether the belief was held by the defendant at all. If the belief was in fact held, its unreasonableness, so far as guilt or innocence is concerned, is neither here nor there. It is irrelevant. Were it otherwise, the defendant would be convicted because he was negligent in failing to recognise that the victim was not consenting or that a crime was not being committed and so on. In other words the jury should be directed first of all that the prosecution have the burden or duty of proving the unlawfulness of the defendant's actions; secondly, if the defendant may have been labouring under a mistake as to the facts, he must be judged according to his mistaken view of the facts; thirdly, that is so whether the mistake was, on an objective view, a reasonable mistake or not.

In a case of self-defence, where self-defence or the prevention of crime is concerned, if the jury came to the conclusion that the defendant believed, or may have believed, that he was being attacked or that a crime was being committed, and that force was necessary to protect himself or to prevent the crime, then the prosecution have not proved their case. If however the defendant's alleged belief was mistaken and if the mistake was an unreasonable one, that may be a powerful reason for coming to the conclusion that the belief was not honestly held and should be rejected.

Even if the jury come to the conclusion that the mistake was an unreasonable one, if the defendant may genuinely have been labouring under it, he is entitled to rely upon it.

We have read the recommendations of the Criminal Law Revision Committee, Part IX, paragraph 72(a), in which the following passage appears: "The common law defence of self-defence should be replaced by a statutory defence providing that a person may use such force as is reasonable in the circumstances as he believes them to be in the defence of himself or any other person." In the view of this Court that represents the law as expressed in *D.P.P.* v. *Morgan* (*supra*) and in *Kimber* (*supra*) and we do not think that the decision of the

Divisional Court in *Albert* v. *Lavin* (*supra*) from which we have cited can be supported.

For those reasons this appeal must be allowed and the conviction quashed.

Appeal allowed.
Conviction quashed.

Chapter 2

STRICT LIABILITY

1. DEFINITION

Where blameless inadvertence suffices as to an element of the *actus reus*, the crime is said to be an offence of strict liability (see above, p. 74)?

2. HOW CAN YOU RECOGNISE CRIMES OF STRICT LIABILITY?

Sweet v. Parsley
[1970] A.C. 132 (H.L.)

[The appellant who had leased a farm to tenants was charged with being concerned in the management of premises which were used for the purpose of smoking cannabis contrary to section 5(*b*) of the Dangerous Drugs Act 1965. The magistrates convicted her even though they found she had no knowledge that her tenants were smoking drugs. Her appeal was dismissed by the divisional court and she appealed to the House of Lords.]

Lord Reid. My Lords, a Divisional Court dismissed her appeal, holding that she had been concerned in the management of those premises. The reasons given for holding that she was managing the property were that she was in a position to choose her tenants: that she could put them under as long or as short a tenancy as she desired: and that she could make it a term of any letting that smoking of cannabis was not to take place. All these reasons would apply to every occupier who lets out parts of his house or takes in lodgers or paying guests. But this was held to be an absolute offence, following the earlier decision in *Yeandel* v. *Fisher* (1966).

How has it come about that the Divisional Court has felt bound to reach such an obviously unjust result? It has in effect held that it was carrying out the will of Parliament because Parliament has chosen to make this an absolute offence. And, of course, if Parliament has so chosen the courts must carry out its will, and they cannot be blamed for any unjust consequences. But has Parliament so chosen?

I dealt with this matter at some length in *Warner's* case (1969). On reconsideration I see no reason to alter anything which I there said. But I think that some amplification is necessary. Our first duty is to consider the words of the Act: if they show a clear intention to create an absolute offence that is an end of the matter. But such cases are very rare. Sometimes the words of the section which creates a particular offence make it clear that mens rea is required in one form or another. Such cases are quite frequent. But in a very large number of cases there is no clear indication either way. In such cases there has for centuries been a presumption that Parliament did not intend to make criminals of persons who were in no way blameworthy in what they did. That means that whenever a section is silent as to mens rea there is a presumption that, in order to give effect to the will of Parliament, we must read in words appropriate to require mens rea.

Where it is contended that an absolute offence has been created, the words of Alderson B. in *Attorney-General* v. *Lockwood* (1842) have often been quoted:

> "The rule of law, I take it, upon the construction of all statutes, and therefore applicable to the construction of this is, whether they be penal or remedial, to construe them according to the plain, literal, and grammatical meaning of the words in which they are expressed, unless that construction leads to a plain and clear contradiction of the apparent purpose of the Act, or to some palpable and evident absurdity."

That is perfectly right as a general rule and where there is no legal presumption. But what about the multitude of criminal enactments where the words of the Act simply make it an offence to do certain things but where everyone agrees that there cannot be a conviction without proof of mens rea in some form? This passage, if applied to the present problem, would mean that there is no need to prove mens rea unless it would be "a plain and clear contradiction of the apparent purpose of the Act" to convict without proof of mens rea. But that would be putting the presumption the wrong way round: for it is firmly established by a host of authorities that mens rea is an essential ingredient of every offence unless some reason can be found for holding that that is not necessary.

It is also firmly established that the fact that other sections of the Act expressly require mens rea, for example because they contain the word "knowingly," is not in itself sufficient to justify a decision that a section which is silent as to mens rea creates an absolute offence. In the absence of a clear indication in the Act that an offence is intended to be an absolute offence, it is necessary to go outside the Act and examine all relevant circumstances in order to establish that this must have been the intention of Parliament. I say "must have been" because it is a universal principle that if a penal provision is reasonably capable of two interpretations, that interpretation which is most favourable to the accused must be adopted.

What, then, are the circumstances which it is proper to take into account? In the well known case of *Sherras* v. *De Rutzen* (1895) Wright J. only mentioned the subject matter with which the Act deals. But he was there dealing with something which was one of a class of acts which "are not criminal in any real sense, but are acts which in the public interest are prohibited under a penalty". It does not in the least follow that when one is dealing with a truly criminal act it is sufficient merely to have regard to the subject matter of the enactment. One must put oneself in the position of a legislator. It has long been the practice to recognise absolute offences in this class of quasi-criminal acts, and one can safely assume that, when Parliament is passing new legislation dealing with this class of offences, its silence as to mens rea means that the old practice is to apply. But when one comes to acts of a truly criminal character, it appears to me that there are at least two other factors which any reasonable legislator would have in mind. In the first place a stigma still attaches to any person convicted of a truly criminal offence, and the more serious or more disgraceful the offence the greater the stigma. So he would have to consider whether, in a case of this gravity, the public interest really requires than an innocent person should be prevented from proving his innocence in order that fewer guilty men may escape. And equally important is the fact that fortunately the Press in this country are vigilant to expose injustice and every manifestly unjust conviction made known to the public tends to injure the body politic by undermining public confidence in the justice of the law and of its administration. But I regret to observe that, in some recent cases where serious offences have been held to be absolute offences, the court has taken into account no more than the wording of the Act and the character and seriousness of the mischief which constitutes the offence.

The choice would be much more difficult if there were no other way open than either mens rea in the full sense or an absolute offence; for there are many kinds of case where putting on the prosecutor the full burden of proving mens rea creates great difficulties and may lead to many unjust acquittals. But there are at least two other possibilities.

Parliament has not infrequently transferred the onus as regards mens rea to the accused, so that, once the necessary facts are proved, he must convince the jury that on balance of probabilities he is innocent of any criminal intention. I find it a little surprising that more use has not been made of this method: but one of the bad effects of the decision of this House in *Woolmington* v. *Director of Public Prosecutions* (1935) (below, p. 128) may have been to discourage its use. The other method would be in effect to substitute in appropriate classes of cases gross negligence for mens rea in the full sense as the mental element necessary to constitute the crime. It would often be much easier to infer that Parliament must have meant that gross negligence should be the necessary mental element than to infer that Parliament intended to create an absolute offence. A variant of this would be to accept the view of Cave J. in *Reg.* v. *Tolson* (1889). This appears to have been done in Australia where authority appears to support what Dixon J. said in *Proudman* v. *Dayman* (1941):

> "As a general rule an honest and reasonable belief in a state of facts which, if they existed, would make the defendant's act innocent affords an excuse for doing what would otherwise be an offence."

It may be that none of these methods is wholly satisfactory but at least the public scandal of convicting on a serious charge persons who are in no way blameworthy would be avoided.

If this section means what the Divisional Court have held that it means, then hundreds of thousands of people who sublet part of their premises or take in lodgers or are concerned in the management of residential premises or institutions are daily incurring a risk of being convicted of a serious offence in circumstances where they are in no way to blame. For the greatest vigilance cannot prevent tenants, lodgers or inmates or guests whom they bring in from smoking cannabis cigarettes in their own rooms. It was suggested in argument that this appellant brought this conviction on herself because it is found as a fact that when the police searched the premises there were people there of the "beatnik fraternity." But surely it would be going a very long way to say that persons managing premises of any kind ought to safeguard themselves by refusing accommodation to all who are of slovenly or exotic appearance, or who bring in guests of that kind. And unfortunately drug taking is by no means confined to those of unusual appearance.

Speaking from a rather long experience of membership of both Houses, I assert with confidence that no Parliament within my recollection would have agreed to make an offence of this kind an absolute offence if the matter had been fully explained to it. So, if the court ought only to hold an offence to be an absolute offence where it appears that that must have been the intention of Parliament, offences of this kind are very far removed from those which it is proper to hold to be absolute offences.

I must now turn to the question what is the true meaning of section 5 of the 1965 Act. It provides:

> "If a person - (*a*) being the occupier of any premises, permits those premises to be used for the purpose of smoking cannabis or cannabis resin or of dealing in cannabis or cannabis resin (whether by sale or otherwise); or (*b*) is concerned in the management of any premises used for any such purpose as aforesaid; he shall be guilty of an offence against this Act."

We are particularly concerned with paragraph (*b*), and the first question is what is meant by "used for any such purpose." Is the "purpose" the purpose of the smoker or the purpose of the management? When in *Warner's* case (1969) I dealt briefly with *Yeandel's* case (1966), I thought it was the purpose of the smoker, but fuller argument in the present case brought out that an identical provision occurs in section 8(*d*) which deals with opium. This latter provision has been carried on from the Dangerous Drugs Act, 1920, and has obviously been copied into the later legislation relating to cannabis. It would require strong reasons - and there are none - to justify giving this provision a new meaning in section 5 different from that which it had in the 1920 Act and now has in section 8 of the 1965 Act. I think that in section 8 it is clear that the purpose is the purpose of the management. The first purpose mentioned is the purpose of the preparation of opium for smoking which can only be a purpose of the management. I believe that opium cannot be smoked casually anywhere at any time as can a cannabis cigarette. The section is dealing with "opium dens" and the like when the use of opium is the main purpose for which the premises are used. But it is a somewhat strained use of language to say that an ordinary room in a house is "used for the purpose" of smoking cannabis when all that happens is that some visitor lights a cannabis cigarette there. Looking to the origin and context of this provision, I have come to the conclusion that it cannot be given this wide meaning. No doubt this greatly reduces the scope of this provision when applied to the use of cannabis. But that is apt to happen when a draftsman simply copies an existing provision without regard to the different circumstances in which it is to operate. So, if the purpose is the purpose of the management, the question whether the offence with regard to opium in 1920, and now with regard to cannabis, is absolute can hardly arise. It could only arise if, although the manager not only knew about cannabis smoking and conducted the premises for that purpose, some person concerned in the management had no knowledge of that. One would first have to decide whether a person who is not actually assisting in the management can be regarded as being "concerned in the management," although ignorant of the purpose for which the manager was using the premises. Even if such a person could be regarded as "concerned in the management," I am of opinion that, for the reasons which I have given, he could not be convicted without proof of mens rea.

I would allow the appeal and quash the appellant's conviction.

Lord Diplock. Where the crime consists of doing an act which is prohibited by statute the proposition as to the state of mind of the doer which is contained in the full definition of the crime must be ascertained from the words and subject-matter of the statute. The proposition, as Stephen J. pointed out, may be stated explicitly by the use of such qualifying adverbs as "maliciously," "fraudulently," "negligently" or "knowingly" - expressions which in relation to different kinds of conduct may call for judicial exegesis. And even without such adverbs the words descriptive of the prohibited act may themselves connote the presence of a particular mental element. Thus where the prohibited conduct consists in permitting a particular thing to be done the word "permit" connotes at least knowledge or reasonable grounds for suspicion on the part of the permittor that the thing will be done and an unwillingness to use means available to him to prevent it and, to take a recent example, to have in one's "possession" a prohibited substance connotes some degree of awareness of that which was within the possessor's physical control: *Reg.* v. *Warner* (1969).

But only too frequently the actual words used by Parliament to define the prohibited conduct are in themselves descriptive only of a physical act and bear no connotation as to any particular state of mind on the part of the person who does the act. Nevertheless, the mere fact that Parliament has made the conduct a criminal offence gives rise to *some* implication about the mental element of the conduct proscribed. . . .

This implication stems from the principle that it is contrary to a rational and civilised criminal code, such as Parliament must be presumed to have intended, to penalise one who has performed his duty as a citizen to ascertain what acts are prohibited by law (ignorantia juris non excusat) and has taken all proper care to inform himself of any facts which would make his conduct lawful.

Where penal provisions are of general application to the conduct of ordinary citizens in the course of their every day life the presumption is that the standard of care required of them in informing themselves of facts which would make their conduct unlawful, is that of the familiar common law duty of care. But where the subject-matter of a statute is the regulation of a particular activity involving potential danger to public health, safety or morals in which citizens have a choice as to whether they participate or not, the court may feel driven to infer an intention of Parliament to impose by penal sanctions a higher duty of care on those who choose to participate and to place upon them an obligation to take whatever measures may be necessary to prevent the prohibited act, without regard to those considerations of cost or business practicability which play a part in the determination of what would be required of them in order to fulfil the ordinary common law duty of care. But such an inference is not lightly to be drawn, nor is there any room for it unless there is something that the person on whom the obligation is imposed can do directly or indirectly, by supervision or inspection, by improvement of his business methods or by exhorting those whom he may be expected to influence or control, which will promote the observance of the obligation (see *Lim Chin Aik* v. *The Queen* (1963)).

Gammon (Hong Kong) Ltd. v. Att.-Gen.
[1984] 3 W.L.R. 347 (P.C.)

Lord Scarman. In their Lordships' opinion, the law relevant to this appeal may be stated in the following propositions (the formulation of which follows closely the written submission of the appellants' counsel, which their Lordships gratefully acknowledge): (1) there is a presumption of law that mens rea is required before a person can be held guilty of a criminal offence; (2) the presumption is particularly strong where the offence is "truly criminal" in character; (3) the presumption applies to statutory offences, and can be displaced only if this is clearly or by necessary implication the effect of the statute; (4) the only situation in which the presumption can be displaced is where the statute is concerned with an issue of social concern; public safety is such an issue; (5) even where a statute is concerned with such an issue, the presumption of mens rea stands unless it can also be shown that the creation of strict liability will be effective to promote the objects of the statute by encouraging greater vigilance to prevent the commission of the prohibited act.

Notes

Since strict liability occurs almost exclusively in statutory offences, identification is largely a matter of statutory interpretation. The starting point is the presumption that *actus non facit reum nisi mens sit rea*. This presumption is, however, rebuttable. The following factors have been held to be matters to be taken into consideration.

(i) The presumption is more readily rebuttable in crimes which are regarded as not truly criminal in nature "but are acts which in the public interest are prohibited under a penalty." See, *eg Alphacell* v. *Woodward* (1972). (See H.S.B., p. 166.)

(ii) Certain words may indicate the requirement or otherwise of *mens rea*.

   permit and *allow* generally indicate the need to prove *mens rea*;
   cause and *use* generally indicate strict liability;
   possess indicates a partial requirement of mens rea;
   knowingly normally indicates the need for mens rea, but occasionally may be used indirectly to impose strict liability. This may occur when section (A) of an Act contains the word "knowingly" but section (B) does not. The courts may conclude that the absence of the word in section (B) means Parliament intended that section to impose strict liability.
   (See further H.S.B., p. 163.)

(iii) Strict liability can be said to be more frequently found in certain factual situations, *eg* legislation regulating sale of food and drink, control of pollution, and road traffic offences. (See H.S.B., p. 166).

(iv) It was said that strict liability is normally restricted to offences bearing only a small penalty. This, however, should not be regarded as a reliable guideline in view of Lord Scarman's remarks in *Gammon (Hong Kong) Ltd*. v. *Att.-Gen*. (1984).

   "The severity of the maximum penalties is a more formidable point. But it has to be considered in the light of the ordinance read as a whole. For reasons which their Lordships have already developed, there is nothing inconsistent with the purpose of the ordinance in imposing severe penalties for offences of strict liability. The legislature could reasonably have intended severity to be a significant deterrent, bearing in mind the risks to public safety arising from some contraventions of the ordinance. Their Lordships agree with the view on this point of the Court of Appeal. It must be crucially important that those who participate in or bear responsibility for the carrying out of works in a manner which complies with the requirements of the ordinance should know that severe penalties await them in the event of any contravention or non-compliance with the ordinance by themselves or by anyone over whom they are required to exercise supervision or control.''

3. DEFENCES

Statutes are now providing defences to offences of strict liability. Such defences may take the form of providing the accused with a defence if he can prove that he was not negligent, and they may require that he proves that a third party was, in reality, responsible for the prohibited act. The following are two examples of such legislation.

Section 28 of the Misuse of Drugs Act 1971 provides a defence, *inter alia*, for persons charged with possession of controlled drugs.

"(2) Subject to subsection (3) below, in any proceedings for an offence to which this section applies it shall be a defence for the accused to prove that he neither knew nor suspected nor had reason to suspect the existence of some fact alleged by the prosecution which it is necessary for the prosecution to prove if he is to be convicted of the offence charged.''

Section 113 of the Food and Drugs Act 1955 provides a good illustration of what is known of as the third party defence.

"A person against whom proceedings are brought under this Act shall, upon information duly laid by him and on giving to the prosecution not less than three clear days' notice of his intention, be entitled to have any person to whose act or default he alleges that the contravention of the provisions in question was due brought before the court in the proceedings; and if, after the contravention has been proved, the original defendant proves that the contravention was due to the act or default of that other person, that other person may be convicted of the offence, and, if the original defendant further proves that he has used all due diligence to secure that the provisions in question were complied with, he shall be acquitted of the offence.''

See further H.S.B., p. 168.

Chapter 3

PARTIES TO CRIMINAL CONDUCT

1. PRINCIPAL OR PERPETRATOR

The principal or perpetrator is one who, with the relevant mens rea, by his own act or omission immediately brings about the actus reus. For example, in murder the one who fires the gun, in criminal damage the one who breaks the window, in burglary the one who enters the building. His identification is normally straightforward but not always, see *Abbott* v. *R*.(below, p. 150 and *Graham* (H.S.B. p. 202).

2. SECONDARY PARTIES

Callow v. Tillstone
(*1900*) 83 L.T. 411 (*D.C.*)

[G., a butcher, was convicted of the offence of exposing for sale meat which was unsound and unfit for human consumption. The meat in question was from a heifer which had been destroyed after becoming ill from eating yew leaves. C., a veterinary surgeon, had negligently carried out an examination of the dead beast and had pronounced it sound and healthy. C. was now charged with aiding and abetting G, the principal offender, who had been convicted despite being blameless - see above, p. 74.]

Lawrance. J. In this case we have no doubt that the justices came to a wrong conclusion in finding that the appellant Callow was guilty of the offence charged against him. What they had found him guilty of was only negligence, and the question now arises upon that finding whether Callow, who was the veterinary surgeon called in in the case, can be found guilty of aiding and abetting the exposing for sale of this unsound meat, when all that the justices find against him is negligence. The justices found that Callow had been guilty of negligence and thereby abetted Grey, and upon that they convicted him. We think that is not sufficient, and the case of *Benfield* v. *Simms* (1898) is very strong to show that it is not sufficient. In that case, where there was a conviction, the defendant, a veterinary surgeon, had - according to the finding of the justices - knowingly counselled the owner of a horse to cause the act of cruelty in question and Channell J. says at the end of his judgment, that the decision of the court in that case "afforded no ground whatever for supposing that a veterinary surgeon who gives a wrong opinion and commits an error in judgment is liable to be convicted of cruelty if the effect of his opinion being followed is that the act of cruelty does in fact result." I think, therefore, the appeal must be allowed.

Kennedy J. I am entirely of the same opinion. It seems to me that all that is found by the justices against the appellant is negligence, and to my mind a person cannot be convicted of aiding and abetting the commission of this offence upon such a finding. In this case the appellant gave his certificate, one is bound to assume, quite honestly, and therefore it seems to me he ought not to be convicted under s. 5 of aiding and abetting the exposing of the meat for sale.

Appeal allowed. Convicted quashed

Att.-Gen.'s Reference (No.1 of 1975)
[*1975*] *Q.B. 773 (C.A.)*

Lord Widgery C.J. gave the following opinion of the court. This case comes before the court on a reference from the Attorney-General, under section 36 of the Criminal Justice Act 1972, and by his reference he asks the following question:

"Whether an accused, who surreptitiously laced a friend's drinks with double measures of spirits when he knew that his friend would shortly be driving his car home, and in consequence his friend drove with an excess quantity of alcohol in his body and was convicted of the offence under section 6 (1) of the Road Traffic Act 1972, is entitled to a ruling of no case to answer on being later charged as an aider and abettor counsellor and procurer, on the ground that there was no shared intention between the two, that the accused did not by accompanying him or otherwise positively encourage the friend to drive, or on any other ground."

. . . . . .

The language in the section which determines whether a "secondary party," as he is sometimes called, is guilty of a criminal offence committed by another embraces the four words "aid, abet, counsel or procure." The origin of those words is to be found in section 8 of the Accessories and Abettors Act 1861, which provides;

"Whosoever shall aid, abet, counsel or procure the commission of any misdemeanor, whether the same be a

misdemeanor at common law or by virtue of any Act passed
or to be passed, shall be liable to be tried, indicted and
punished as a principal offender."

Thus, in the past, when the distinction was still drawn
between felony and misdemeanor, it was sufficient to make a
person guilty of a misdemeanor if he aided, abetted, counselled
or procured the offence of another. When the difference
between felonies and misdemeanors was abolished in 1967,
section 1 of the Criminal Law Act 1967 in effect provided that
the same test should apply to make a secondary party guilty
either of treason or felony.

Of course it is the fact that in the great majority of instances
where a secondary party is sought to be convicted of an offence
there has been a contact between the principal offender and the
secondary party. Aiding and abetting almost inevitably
involves a situation in which the secondary party and the main
offender are together at some stage discussing the plans which
they may be making in respect of the alleged offence, and are
in contact so that each knows what is passing through the mind
of the other.

In the same way it seems to us that a person, who counsels the
commission of a crime by another, almost inevitably comes to a
moment when he is in contact with that other, when he is
discussing the offence with that other and when, to use the
words of the statute, he counsels the other to commit the
offence.

The fact that so often the relationship between the secondary
party and the principal will be such that there is a meeting of
minds between them caused the trial judge in the case from
which this reference is derived to think that this was really an
essential feature of proving or establishing the guilt of the
secondary party and, as we understand his judgment, he took
the view that in the absence of some sort of meeting of minds,
some sort of mental link between the secondary party and the
principal, there could be no aiding, abetting or counselling of
the offence within the meaning of the section.

So far as aiding, abetting and counselling is concerned we
would go a long way with that conclusion. It may very well be
as I said a moment ago, difficult to think of a case of aiding,
abetting or counselling when the parties have not met and have
not discussed in some respects the terms of the offence which
they have in mind. But we do not see why a similar principle
should apply to procuring. We approach section 8 of the Act of

1861 on the basis that the words should be given their ordinary meaning, if possible. We approach the section on the basis also that if four words are employed here, "aid, abet, counsel or procure," the probability is that there is a difference between each of those four words and the other three, because, if there were no such difference, then Parliament would be wasting time in using four words where two or three would do. Thus, in deciding whether that which is assumed to be done under our reference was a criminal offence we approach the section on the footing that each word must be given its ordinary meaning.

To procure means to produce by endeavour. You procure a thing by setting out to see that it happens and taking the appropriate steps to produce that happening. We think that there are plenty of instances in which a person may be said to procure the commission of a crime by another even though there is no sort of conspiracy between the two, even though there is no attempt at agreement or discussion as to the form which the offence should take. In our judgment the offence described in this reference is such a case.

If one looks back at the facts of the reference: the accused surreptitiously laced his friend's drink. This is an important element and, although we are not going to decide today anything other than the problem posed to us, it may well be that, in similar cases where the lacing of the drink or the introduction of the extra alcohol is known to the driver, quite different considerations may apply. We say that because, where the driver has no knowledge of what is happening, in most instances he would have no means of preventing the offence from being committed. If the driver is unaware of what has happened, he will not be taking precautions. He will get into his car seat, switch on the ignition and drive home and, consequently, the conception of another procuring the commission of the offence by the driver is very much stronger where the driver is innocent of all knowledge of what is happening, as in the present case where the lacing of the drink was surreptitious.

The second thing which is important in the facts set out in our reference is that, following and in consequence of the introduction of the extra alcohol, the friend drove with an excess quantity of alcohol in his blood. Causation here is important. You cannot procure an offence unless there is a causal link between what you do and the commission of the offence, and here we are told that in consequence of the addition of this alcohol the driver, when he drove home, drove with an excess quantity of alcohol in his body.

Giving the words their ordinary meaning in English, and asking oneself whether in those circumstances the offence has been procured, we are in no doubt that the answer is that it has. It has been procured because, unknown to the driver and without his collaboration, he has been put in a position in which in fact he has committed an offence which he never would have committed otherwise. We think that there was a case to answer and that the trial judge should have directed the jury that an offence is committed if it is shown beyond reasonable doubt that the defendant knew that his friend was going to drive, and also knew that the ordinary and natural result of the additional alcohol added to the friend's drink would be to bring him above the recognised limit of 80 milligrammes per 100 millilitres of blood.

It was suggested to us that, if we held that there may be a procuring on the facts of the present case, it would be but a short step to a similar finding for the generous host, with somewhat bibulous friends, when at the end of the day his friends leave him to go to their own homes in circumstances in which they are not fit to drive and in circumstances in which an offence under the Road Traffic Act 1972 is committed. The suggestion has been made that the host may in those circumstances be guilty with his guests on the basis that he has either aided, abetted, counselled or procured the offence.

The first point to notice in regard to the generous host is that that is not a case in which the alcohol is being put surreptitiously into the glass of the driver. That is a case in which the driver knows perfectly well how much he has to drink and where to a large extent it is perfectly right and proper to leave him to make his own decision.

Furthermore, we would say that, if such a case arises, the basis on which the case will be put against the host is, we think, bound to be on the footing that he has supplied the tool with which the offence is committed. This, of course, is a reference back to such cases as those where oxy-acetylene equipment was bought by a man knowing it was to be used by another for a criminal offence: see *Reg.* v. *Bainbridge* (1960). There is ample and clear authority as to the extent to which supplying the tools for the commission of an offence may amount to aiding and abetting for present purposes.

Accordingly, so far as the generous host type of case is concerned, we are not concerned at the possibility that difficulties will be created, as long as it is borne in mind that in those circumstances the matter must be approached in accordance with well known authority governing the provision of the tools for the commission of an offence, and never forgetting that the introduction of the alcohol is not there surreptitious, and that consequently the case for saying that the offence was procured by the supplier of the alcohol is very much more difficult.

Our decision on the reference is that the question posed by the Attorney-General should be answered in the negative.

A. The Actus Reus of Secondary Participation

R. v. Clarkson
[1971] 3 All E.R. 344 (C.M.A.C.)

[A girl was subjected to a brutal multiple rape in military barracks in Germany. The accused in question had been drinking and had entered the room where the rapes occurred and stood watching.]

Megaw L.J. As has been said, there was no evidence on which the prosecution sought to rely that either the appellant Clarkson or the appellant Carroll had done any physical act or uttered any word which involved direct physical participation or verbal encouragement. There was no evidence that they had touched the girl, helped to hold her down, done anything to her, done anything to prevent others from assisting her or to prevent her from escaping, or from trying to ward off her attackers, or that they had said anything which gave encouragement to the others to commit crime or to participate in committing crime. Therefore, if there was here aiding and abetting by the appellants Clarkson or Carroll it could only have been on the basis of inferences to be drawn that by their very presence they, each of them separately as concerns himself, encouraged those who were committing rape. Let it be accepted, and there was evidence to justify this assumption, that the presence of those two appellants in the room where the offence was taking place was not accidental in any sense and that it was not by chance, unconnected with the crime, that they were there. Let it be accepted that they entered the room when the crime was committed because of what they had heard, which indicated that a woman was being raped, and they remained there.

R. v. Coney (1882) decided that non-accidental presence at the scene of the crime is not conclusive of aiding and abetting.

The jury has to be told by the judge, or as in this case the court-martial has to be told by the judge-advocate, in clear terms what it is that has to be proved before they can convict of aiding and abetting; what it is of which the jury or the court-martial, as the case may be, must be sure as matters of inference before they can convict of aiding and abetting in such a case where the evidence adduced by the prosecution is limited to non-accidental presence. What has to proved is stated by Hawkins J. in a well-known passage in his judgment in *R. v. Coney* where he said:

> "In my opinion, to constitute an aider and abettor some active steps must be taken by word, or action, with the intent to instigate the principal or principals. Encouragement does not of necessity amount to aiding and abetting, it may be intentional or unintentional, a man may unwittingly encourage another in fact by his presence, by misinterpreted words, or gestures, or by his silence, or non-interference, or he may encourage intentionally by expressions, gestures, or actions intended to signify approval. In the latter case he aids and abets, in the former he does not. It is no criminal offence to stand by, a mere passive spectator of a crime, even of a murder. Non-interference to prevent a crime is not itself a crime. But the fact that a person was voluntarily and purposely present witnessing the commission of a crime, and offered no opposition to it, though he might reasonably be expected to prevent and had the power to do so, or at least to express his dissent, might under some circumstances, afford cogent evidence upon which a jury would be justified in finding that he wilfully encouraged and so aided and abetted. But it would be purely a question for the jury whether he did so or not."

It is not enough, then, that the presence of the accused has, in fact, given encouragement. It must be proved that the accused intended to give encouragement; that he *wilfully* encouraged. In a case such as the present, more than in many other cases where aiding and abetting is alleged, it was essential that the element should be stressed; for there was here at least the possibility that a drunken man with his self discipline loosened by drink, being aware that a woman was being raped, might be attracted to the scene and might stay on the scene in the capacity of what is known as a voyeur; and, while his presence should offer encouragement to rapers and would-be rapers or discouragement to the victim, he might not realise that he was giving encouragement; so that, while encouragement there might be it would not be a case in which, to use the words of Hawkins J., the accused person "wilfully encouraged".

A further point is emphasised in passages in the judgment of the Court of Criminal Appeal in *R. v. Allan* (1965). That was a case concerned with participation in an affray. Edmund Davies J., giving the judgment of the court, said:

> "In effect, it amounts to this: that the learned judge thereby directed the jury that they were in duty bound to convict an accused who was proved to have been present and witnessing an affray if it was also proved that he nursed an intention to join in if help was needed by the side which he favoured, and this notwithstanding that he did nothing by words or deeds to evince his intention and outwardly played the rôle of a purely passive spectator. It was said that, if that direction is right, where A and B behave themselves to all outward appearances in an exactly similar manner, but it be proved that A had the intention to participate if needs be, whereas B had no such intention, then A must be convicted of being a principal in the second degree to the affray, whereas B should be acquitted. To do that, it is objected, would be to convict A on his thoughts, even though they found no reflection in his actions."

The other passage in the judgment is this:

> "In our judgment, before a jury can properly convict an accused person of being a principal in the second degree to an affray, they must be convinced by the evidence that, at the very least, he by some means or other encouraged the participants. To hold otherwise would be, in effect, as counsel for the appellants rightly expressed it, to convict a man on his thoughts, unaccompanied by any physical act other than the fact of his mere presence."

From that it follows that mere intention is not in itself enough. There must be an intention to encourage; and there must also be encouragement in fact, in cases such as the present case.

So we come to what was said by the judge-advocate. First there was the guidance which he gave to the court after the submissions had been made at the close of the prosecution's case. The relevance of that to the matters which the court now has to decide has already been mentioned. There is a passage in that guidance in which the judge-advocate said this:

> "You have been told, correctly, the position as regards an aider and abettor, and that is all that the [appellant] is charged with in these three charges. To be an aider and abettor, a person need not take any active steps in the commission of a crime, but he must be in a position to render assistance or encouragement by actual or constructive presence, and he must share a common intention with them that the crime should be committed. An illustration is that of a jeweller's shop. One man will throw a brick through the window and somebody else will snatch the valuables inside. It might be said that they were the people who actually committed the offence itself, but on such an occasion there will be somebody standing by with a motor car to enable the others to make their getaway. Probably someone is on the corner to make sure there is no policeman about to arrive on the scene. One or two others may be present to thrust out a leg and trip up anybody who may interfere or get in the way, if necessary, of those who will go in pursuit. They are sharing a common intention that the offence should be committed and they are aiders and abettors. Other people may be standing by, but the mere fact that a person watches and just stands by without sharing the common purpose of the others, is not guilty of aiding and abetting."

The judge-advocate draws the analogy which is commonly drawn where direction is given of two persons jointly indicted, for example, of committing burglary. One actually enters the house and the other stands outside to keep watch. That analogy, in the view of this court, is misleading in relation to what was involved in the present case, for it presupposes a prior meeting of minds between the persons concerned as to the crime to be committed. The man who stands outside and does not go in is guilty of burglary; but it cannot in such a case properly be said that he has taken no active step in the commission of the offence. He has gone to the place where he is, and he has conducted himself as he does, as part of the joint plan which, in its totality, it intended to procure commission of the crime.

In the view of this court the echo of that false analogy

unfortunately continued throughout when the judge-advocate came to sum up the matter to the court-martial. . . .

There are other passages in the summing-up relating to the same matter, which are susceptible of the same criticism. We do not propose to refer to them individually. It is right to say that towards the very end of the summing-up, the judge-advocate comes nearer, if we may put it that way, to expressing the principal correctly. Indeed, if that passage stood alone the court might well have had to consider with very great care whether it should not take the view that that passage, by itself and in itself, while subject to verbal criticism, might be regarded as having put the matter with sufficient clarity to the court. But when that passage is read, as it must be read, with the other passages in the summing-up and with the passages in the original direction on the submission, this court has come to the conclusion that the court might have misunderstood the relevant principles that ought to be applied. It might have been left under the impression that it could find the two appellants guilty on the basis of their continuing, non-accidental, presence, even though it was not sure that the necessary inferences to be drawn from the evidence included (i) an intention to encourage and (ii) actual encouragement. While we have no doubt that those inferences could properly have been drawn in respect of each appellant on each count, so that verdicts of guilty could properly have been returned, we cannot say that the court-martial, properly directed, would necessarily have drawn those inferences. Accordingly the convictions of the appellants Clarkson and Carroll must be quashed.

Question

Can a defendant be liable as a secondary party by failing to act?

Du Cros v. Lambourne
[1907] 1 K.B. 40 (D.C.)

[The accused had been charged with driving a car at a speed dangerous to the public. It appeared that though the car was his, it had been driven by another. (It is generally accepted that an indictment need not specify whether the accused was the principal or secondary party - so long as the crime was perpetrated by someone and the accused was a party to it.)]

Lord Alverstone. C.J. It has been contended on his behalf that there was no evidence, and reliance was placed on certain of the judgments in *Reg.* v. *Coney* in support of this contention.

Reg. v. *Coney* was a case of spectators at a prize-fight, and I do not think that the general language used in the judgments was intended to be, or can be, treated as applying to every kind of case. We have to consider the facts found in this case. The case states that the appellant must have known that the speed of the car was dangerous; that if Miss Godwin was driving, she was doing so with the consent and approval of the appellant, who was in control of the car, and that he could, and ought to, have prevented her from driving at this excessive and dangerous speed, but that he allowed her to do so and did not interfere in any way. I will not attempt to lay down any general rule or principle, but having regard to these findings of fact, it is, in my opinion, impossible to say that there was in this case no evidence of aiding and abetting on the part of the appellant. The case further states that, having regard to the above facts, the Court of quarter sessions dismissed the appeal, holding that it was not necessary to decide whether the appellant was himself driving or not. This can only mean that the mind of the Court had been addressed to the question of aiding and abetting, and it being in my opinion impossible to say that there was no evidence on which the appellant could be convicted of aiding and abetting, this appeal must be dismissed.

B. *Mens Rea of Secondary Participation*

R. v. Bainbridge
[*1959*] *3 All E.R. 200 (C.C.A.)*

[B. purchased some oxygen cutting equipment for some men who six weeks later used it for breaking into the Midland Bank at Stoke Newington: B. said that he thought the equipment was probably going to be used for an illegal purpose - possibly breaking up stolen goods, but he had no idea that it was to be used for breaking into a bank. On appeal against conviction of B. as a secondary party to the break-in;]

Lord Parker C.J. Counsel for the appellant, who argued this case very well, contended that that direction was wrong. As he put it, in order that a person should be convicted of being accessory before the fact, it must be shown that, at the time when he bought the equipment in a case such as this, he knew that a particular crime was going to be committed; and by "a particular crime" counsel meant that the premises in this case which were going to be broken into were known to the appellant and contemplated by him, and not only the premises in question but the date when the crime was going to occur; in other words, that he must have known that on a particular date the Stoke Newington branch of the Midland Bank was intended to be broken into.

The court fully appreciates that it is not enough that it should be shown that a person knew that some illegal venture was intended. To take this case, it would not be enough if the appellant knew - he says that he only suspected - that the equipment was going to be used to dispose of stolen property. That would not be enough. Equally, this court is quite satisfied that it is unnecessary that knowledge of the intention to commit the particular crime which was in fact committed should be shown, and by "particular crime" I am using the words in the same way as that in which counsel for the appellant used them, namely, on a particular date and particular premises.

It is not altogether easy to lay down a precise form of words which will cover every case that can be contemplated, but, having considered the cases and the law, this court is quite clear that the direction of Judge Aarvold in this case cannot be criticised. Indeed, it might well have been made with the passage in *Foster's Crown Cases* (3rd Edn.) (1792) at p. 369 in mind, because there the learned author says:

"If the principal totally and substantially varieth, if being solicited to commit a felony of one kind he *wilfully and knowingly* committeth a felony of another, *he* will stand single in that offence, and the person soliciting will not be involved in his guilt. For on *his* part it was no more than a fruitless ineffectual temptation."

The converse of course is that, if the principal does not totally and substantially vary the advice or the help and does not wilfully and knowingly commit a different form of felony altogether, the man who has advised or helped, aided or abetted, will be guilty as an accessory before the fact.

Judge Aarvold in this case, in the passages to which I have referred, makes it clear that there must be not merely suspicion but knowledge that a crime of the type in question was intended, and that the equipment was bought with that in view. In his reference to the felony of the type intended it was, as he states, the felony of breaking and entering premises and the stealing of property from those premises. The court can see nothing wrong in that direction.

Appeal dismissed.

D.P.P. for Northern Ireland v. Maxwell
[*1978*] *1 W.L.R. 1350*

[M. was a member of the Ulster Volunteer Force a unit proscribed in Northern Ireland. On the night in question he guided some terrorists to a public house where they planted a bomb. It was found at first instance that he knew that what was planned would be violent, involving danger to persons or premises. He did not, however, know exactly what offence would be committed. He appealed against his conviction for secondary participation. The judgment of the Court of Criminal Appeal in Northern Ireland was delivered by Lord Lowry C.J. A further appeal by Maxwell was dismissed by the House of Lords. Their Lordships strongly approved the judgment of Lord Lowry C.J.]

Lord Lowry C.J. Once the "particular crime" theory of guilty knowledge is rejected in favour of the *Bainbridge* principle, the question arises how far that principle goes. In a practical sense the question is whether the principle applies to the facts proved in this case.

Suppose the intending principal offender (whom I shall call "the principal") tells the intended accomplice (whom I shall call "the accomplice") that he means to shoot A or else leave a bomb at A's house and the accomplice agrees to drive the principal to A's house and keep watch while there, it seems clear that the accomplice would be guilty of aiding and abetting whichever crime the principal committed, because he would know that one of two crimes was to be committed, he would have assisted the principal and he would have intended to assist him. Again, let us suppose that the principal tells the accomplice that the intention is to murder A at one house but, if he cannot be found or the house is guarded, the alternative plan is to go to B's house and leave a bomb there or thirdly to rob a particular bank (or indeed murder somebody, or bomb somebody's house or rob any bank, as to which see *R. v. Bainbridge*) and requests the accomplice to make a reconnaissance of a number of places and report on the best way of gaining access to the target. The accomplice agrees and makes all the reconnaissances and reports, and the principal then without a further communication, selects a target and commits the crime. It seems clear that, whichever crime the principal commits, all the ingredients of the accomplice's guilt are present. In each of these examples the accomplice knows exactly what is contemplated and the only thing he does not know is to which particular crime he will became an accessory when it is committed. His guilt springs from the fact that he contemplates the commission of one (or more) of a number of crimes by the principal and he intentionally lends his assistance in order that such a crime will be committed. In other words, he knows that the principal is committing or about to commit one of a number of specified illegal acts and with that knowledge he helps him to do so.

The situation has something in common with that of two persons who agree to rob a bank on the understanding, either express or implied from conduct (such as the carrying of a loaded gun by one person with the knowledge of the other), that violence *may* be resorted to. The accomplice knows, not that the principal *will* shoot the cashier, but that he may do so; and, if the principal does shoot him, the accomplice will be guilty of murder. A different case is where the accomplice has only offence A in contemplation and the principal commits offence B. Here the accomplice, although morally culpable (and perhaps guilty of conspiring to commit offence A), is not guilty of aiding and abetting offence B. The principle with which we are dealing does not seem to us to provide a warrant, on the basis of combatting lawlessness generally, for convicting an alleged accomplice of *any* offence which, helped by his preliminary acts, a principal may commit. The relevant crime must be within the contemplation of the accomplice and only exceptionally would evidence be found to support the allegation that the accomplice had given the principal a completely blank cheque.

Interesting hypothetical problems can be posed, if, for example, one person supplies to another house-breaking implements or weapons which are used, and perhaps used repeatedly, by the person supplied or by a third person, either immediately or months or years later. Such questions must, we think, be solved by asking whether the crime actually committed is fairly described as the crime or one of a number of crimes within the contemplation of the accomplice. They are typical of the kind of problem which may be encountered in the application of any principle of the common law which, while requiring to be soundly based, can only proceed from one instance to another. But those questions do not arise in the present case.

The facts found here show that the appellant, as a member of an organisation which habitually perpetrates sectarian acts of violence with firearms and explosives, must, as soon as he was briefed for his role, have contemplated the bombing of the Crosskeys Inn as not the only possibility but one of the most obvious possibilities among the jobs which the principals were likely to be undertaking and in the commission of which he was intentionally assisting. He was therefore in just the same situation, so far as guilty knowledge is concerned, as a man who had been given a list of jobs and told that one of them would be carried out. And so he is guilty of the offence alleged against him in count 1.

[Lord Dilhorne and Lord Edmund Davies said though the indictment could not technically be challenged, where the accused was not being charged as a principal offender, it would be better if the particulars of the offence could indicate the exact nature of the allegations against the accused.]

National Coal Board v. Gamble
[*1959*] *1 Q.B. 11 (D.C.*)

[The N.C.B. supplied X with coal. One of X's drivers would load his lorry with coal and would then proceed to have his lorry weighed. If the weight was correct an employee of the N.C.B. would issue the driver with a ticket and the driver would then drive out onto the public roads. On the occasion in question the weighbridge operator noticed that the lorry was overloaded. It is a criminal offence to drive a lorry on a public road where the load exceeds a certain weight. The driver said he would take the risk and the weighbridge operator issued a ticket. The driver committed the offence as a principal offender as soon as he drove onto the road. The question for the court was whether the weighbridge operator was a secondary party and further whether the N.C.B was liable for the acts of its employee.]

Devlin J. A person who supplies the instrument for a crime or anything essential to its commission aids in the commission of it; and if he does so knowingly and with intent to aid, he abets it as well and is therefore guilty of aiding and abetting. I use the word "supplies" to comprehend giving, lending, selling or any other transfer of the right of property. In a sense a man who gives up to a criminal a weapon which the latter has a right to demand from him aids in the commission of the crime as much as if he sold or lent the article. But this has never been held to be aiding in law.... The reason, I think, is that in the former case there is in law a positive act and in the latter only a negative one. In the transfer of property there must be either a physical delivery or a positive act of assent to a taking. But a man who hands over to another his own property on demand, although he may physically be performing a positive act, in law is only refraining from detinue. Thus in law the former act is one of assistance voluntarily given and the latter is only a failure to prevent the commission of the crime by means of a forcible detention, which would not even be justified except in the case of felony. Another way of putting the point is to say that aiding and abetting is a crime that requires proof of mens rea, that is to say of intention to aid as well as of knowledge of the circumstances, and that proof of the intent involves proof of a positive act of assistance voluntarily done.

These considerations make it necessary to determine at what point the property in the coal passed from the board and what the board's state of knowledge was at that time. If the property had passed before the board knew of the proposed crime, there was nothing they could legally do to prevent the driver of the lorry from taking the overloaded lorry out onto the road. If it had not, then they sold the coal with knowledge that an offence was going to be committed.

[It was found, by the justices at the trial, that the weighbridge operator could have refused to transfer the property after he had discovered the excess weight].

This is the conclusion to which the justices came. Mr. Thompson submits on behalf of the board that it does not justify a verdict of guilty of aiding and abetting. He submits, first, that even if knowledge of the illegal purpose had been acquired before delivery began, it would not be sufficient for the verdict; and secondly, that if he is wrong about that, the knowledge was acquired too late, and the board was not guilty of aiding and abetting simply because Haslam failed to stop the process of delivery after it had been initiated.

On his first point Mr.Thompson submits that the furnishing of an article essential to the crime with knowledge of the use to which it is to be put does not of itself constitute aiding and abetting; there must be proved in addition a purpose or motive of the defendant to further the crime or encourage the criminal. Otherwise, he submits, there is no mens rea.

I have already said that in my judgment there must be proof of intent to aid. . . . I would agree that proof that the article was knowingly supplied is not conclusive evidence of intent to aid. *Rex* v. *Steane*, (1947) in which the defendant was charged with having acted during the war with intent to assist the enemy contrary to the Defence Regulations then in force, makes the same point. But prima facie - and *Rex* v. *Steane* makes this clear also - a man is presumed to intend the natural and probable consequences of his acts, and the consequence of supplying essential material is that assistance is given to the criminal. It is always open to the defendant, as in *Rex* v. *Steane*, to give evidence of his real intention. But in this case the defence called no evidence. The prima facie presumption is therefore enough to justify the verdict, unless it is the law that some other mental element besides intent is necessary to the offence.

This is what Mr.Thompson argues, and he describes the additional element as the purpose or motive of encouraging the crime. No doubt evidence of an interest in the crime or of an express purpose to assist it will greatly strengthen the case for the prosecution. But an indifference to the result of the crime does not of itself negative abetting. If one man deliberately sells to another a gun to be used for murdering a third, he may be indifferent about whether the third man lives or dies and interested only in the cash profit to be made out of the sale, but he can still be an aider and abettor. To hold otherwise would be to negative the rule that mens rea is a matter of intent only and does not depend on desire or motive.

The authorities, I think, support this conclusion, though none has been cited to us in which the point has been specifically argued and decided. . . . The same principle has been applied in civil cases where the seller has sued upon a contract for the supply of goods which he knew were to be used for an illegal purpose. . . .

The case chiefly relied on by Mr.Thompson was *Reg.* v. *Coney* (1882). In that case the defendants were charged with aiding and abetting an illegal prize fight at which they had been present. The judgments all refer to "encouragement," but it would be wrong to conclude from that that proof of encouragement is necessary to every form of aiding and abetting. Presence on the scene of the crime without encouragement or assistance is no aid to the criminal; the supply of essential material is. Moreover, the decision makes it clear that encouragement can be inferred from mere presence. Cave J., who gave the leading judgment, said of the summing-up: "It may mean either that mere presence unexplained is evidence of encouragement, and so of guilt, or that mere presence unexplained is conclusive proof of encouragement, and so of guilt. If the former is the correct meaning I concur in the law so laid down; if the latter, I am unable to do so." This dictum seems to me to support the view I have expressed. If voluntary presence is prima facie evidence of encouragement and therefore of aiding and abetting, it appears to me to be a fortiori that the intentional supply of an essential article must be prima facie evidence of aiding and abetting.

As to Mr Thompson's alternative point, I have already expressed the view that the facts show an act of assent made by Haslam after knowledge of the proposed illegality and without which the property would not have passed. If some positive act to complete delivery is committed after knowledge of the illegality, the position in law must, I think, be just the same as if the knowledge had been obtained before the delivery had been begun. Of course, it is quite likely that Haslam was confused about the legal position and thought that he was not entitled to withhold the weighbridge ticket. There is no mens rea if the defendant is shown to have a genuine belief in the existence of circumstances which, if true, would negative an intention to aid; see *Wilson* v. *Inyang* (1951). But this argument, which might have been the most cogent available to the defence, cannot now be relied upon, because Haslam was not called to give evidence about what he thought or believed.

The fact that no evidence was called for the defence makes this case a peculiar one. We were told that the board desired to obtain a decision on principle which would enable them to regulate their practice in the future. They therefore accepted responsibility for Haslam's act without going into any questions of vicarious liability; and they called no evidence in order, we were told, that the decision might be given on facts put against them as strongly as might be. What they wished to establish was that responsibility for overloaded lorries rested solely with the carrier and that the sale and delivery of the coal could not, if that was all that could be proved, involve them in a breach of the criminal law. For the reasons I have given I think that the law cannot be so stated and that the appeal should be dismissed.

Note

For requirements of vicarious liability see H.S.B., p. 184.

Question

Would it make any difference that the accused hoped that the criminal offence would not be committed, and had even tried to persuade the would-be principal offender against it?

Lynch v. D.P.P. for Northern Ireland
[1975] A.C. 653 (H.L.)

[The defendant had driven two men to the place where they killed another. The majority of the speeches are concerned with the defence of duress. The above question was however considered.]

Lord Morris of Borth-y-Gest. If in the present case the jury were satisfied that the car was driven towards the garage in pursuance of a murderous plan and that the appellant knew that that was the plan and intentionally drove the car in execution of that plan, he could be held to have aided and abetted even though he regretted the plan or indeed was horrified by it. However great his reluctance, he would have intended to aid and abet.

C. Liability for Unforeseen Consequences

Questions

1. A provides B with a gun to kill C. B aims at C but misses and accidentally hits D, killing him. Is A a secondary party to the killing?

2. A and B plan a burglary. A will drive the getaway car while B will enter the house to steal money. It is agreed B should carry a cosh to protect himself against the occupiers should they be aroused. C, the occupier, is awakened and comes down to investigate. B coshes him, causing him serious injury. Is A a secondary party to the attack on C? Would it make any difference if B had, unknown to A, taken a gun which he used to kill C?

Davies v. D.P.P.
[*1954*] *A.C. 378 (H.L.)*

[A fight between two rival gangs had broken out on Clapham Common during the course of which it was alleged that D. had knifed and killed a member of the rival gang. The prosecution called Lawson, a member of D.'s gang, to give evidence against D. Under the rules of evidence if the jury found L. to be an accomplice in the killing, his evidence could only be relied upon if the trial judge had warned the jury of the dangers of acting upon the uncorroborated evidence of an accomplice. No such warning was given and the House of Lords had to determine whether there was any evidence upon which the jury could have held L. to be an accomplice in the killing.]

Lord Simonds L.C.   In particular, I can see no reason why, if half a dozen boys fight another crowd, and one of them produces a knife and stabs one of the opponents to death, all the rest of his group should be treated as accomplices in the use of a knife and the infliction of mortal injury by that means, unless there is evidence that the rest intended or concerted or at least contemplated an attack with a knife by one of their number, as opposed to a common assault. If all that was designed or envisaged was in fact a common assault, and there was no evidence that Lawson, a party to that common assault, knew that any of his companions had a knife, then Lawson was not an accomplice in the crime consisting in its felonious use.

R. v. Anderson and Morris
[1966] 2 All E.R. 644 (C.C.A.)

[After W. had attacked A.'s wife, A. armed himself with a knife and, accompanied by M., went to look for W. When A. found W. a fight ensued in the course of which A. stabbed and killed W. In the light of new evidence submitted in the Court of Criminal Appeal a new trial was ordered in the case of A. who had been convicted of murder. M. argued that his conviction for manslaughter should be quashed.]

Lord Parker C.J. What is complained of is a passage in the summing-up. It is unnecessary to read the direction on law in full. The material direction is where the judge said:

"If you think there was a common design to attack [the applicant Welch] but it is not proved, in the case of [the applicant Morris], that he had any intention to kill or cause grievous bodily harm but that [the applicant Anderson], without the knowledge of [the applicant Morris], had a knife, took it from the flat and at some time formed the intention to kill or cause grievous bodily harm to Welch and did kill him - an act outside the common design to which [the applicant Morris] is proved to have been a party - then you would or could on the evidence find it proved that [the applicant Anderson] committed murder and [the applicant Morris] would be liable to be convicted of manslaughter provided you are satisfied that he took part in the attack or fight with Welch."

In passing, I should say that this court has very grave doubts whether the judge really intended to say what he did, and for this reason, that as I have already said, he attached very great importance to the evidence of Mr. Christopher, and indeed had in a later passage gone so far as to say that unless the jury felt sure that they could accept Mr. Christopher's evidence they were to acquit the applicant Morris altogether. Bearing that in mind, one would expect the judge to be giving a direction on the basis that Mr. Christopher's evidence was accepted, and that the jury were satisfied that the applicant Morris knew that the applicant Anderson had this knife and had in a moment of anger armed himself with it. However, whatever we think, the judge on the transcript had told the jury that they could convict or indeed should convict the applicant Morris even though he had no idea that the applicant Anderson had armed himself with a knife. In other words, this court must approach the case on the basis that the jury fully understood that that was being put before them as a direction in law.

Counsel for the applicant Morris submits that that was a clear misdirection. He would put the principle of law to be invoked in this form: that where two persons embark on a joint enterprise, each is liable for the acts done in pursuance of that joint enterprise, that that includes liability for unusual consequences if they arise from the execution of the agreed joint enterprise but (and this is the crux of the matter) that if one of the adventurers goes beyond what has been tacitly agreed as part of the common enterprise, his co-adventurer is not liable for the consequences of that unauthorised act. Finally, he says it is for the jury in every case to decide whether what was done was part of the joint enterprise, or went beyond it and was in fact an act unauthorised by that joint enterprise. In support of that, he refers to a number of authorities to which this court finds it unnecessary to refer in detail, but which in the opinion of this court shows that at any rate for the last 130 or 140 years that has been the true position. This matter was in fact considered in some detail in *R*. v. *Smith* (1961), which was heard by a court of five judges presided over by Hilbery, J., on Nov. 6, 1961, a case in which Slade, J., gave the judgment of the court. That case was referred to at some length in the later decision in this court of *R*. v. *Betty* (1963). It is unnecessary to go into that case in any detail. It followed the judgment of Slade, J., in *R*. v. *Smith* (1963), and it did show the limits of the general principle which counsel for the applicant Morris invokes in the present case. In *R*. v. *Smith* (1963), the co-adventurer who in fact killed was known by the accused to have knife, and it was clear on the facts of that case that the common design involved an attack on a man, in that case a barman, in which the use of a knife would not be outside the scope of the concerted action. Reference was there made to the fact that the case might have been different if in fact the man using the knife had used a revolver, a weapon which he had, unknown to Smith. The court in *R*. v. *Betty* (1963) approved entirely of what had been said in *R*. v. *Smith* (1963), and in fact added to it. In passing, it is to be observed that, as counsel for the applicant Morris has pointed out, the headnote to *R*. v. *Betty* (1963) may go somewhat further and may have led the judge in the present case to think that there were no such limits to the principle. Counsel for the Crown, on the other hand, while recognising that he cannot go beyond this long string of decided cases, has said that they are really all part and parcel of a much wider principle which he would put in this form, that if two or more persons engage in an unlawful act and one suddenly develops an intention to kill whereby death results, not only is he guilty of murder, but all those who have engaged in the unlawful act are guilty of manslaughter. He recognises that the present trend of authority is against that proposition, but he goes back to *R. v. Salisbury* (1553). In that case a master had lain in wait to attack a man and his servants who had no idea of what his, the master's idea was, joined in the attack, whereby the man was killed. It was held there that those servants were themselves guilty of manslaughter. The court is by no means clear on the facts as reported that that case is really on all fours, but it is in the opinion of the court quite clear that that principle is wholly out of touch with the position today. It seems to this court that to say that adventurers are guilty of manslaughter when one of them has departed completely from the concerted action of the common design and has suddenly formed an intent to kill and has used a weapon and acted in a way which no party to that common design could suspect is something which would revolt the conscience of people today. Counsel for the Crown in his attractive argument points to the fact that it would seem to be illogical that, whereas if two people had formed a common design to do an unlawful act and death resulted by an unforeseen consequence, they should be held, as they would undoubtedly be held, guilty of manslaughter; yet if one of them in those circumstances had in a moment of passion decided to kill, the other would be acquitted altogether. The law, of course, is not completely logical, but there is nothing really illogical in such a result, in that it could well be said as a matter of common-sense that in the latter circumstances the death resulted or was caused by the sudden action of the adventurer who decided to kill and killed. Considered as a matter of causation, there may well be an overwhelming supervening event which is of such a character that it will relegate into history matters which would otherwise be looked on as causative factors. Looked at in that way, there is really nothing illogical in the result to which counsel for the Crown points. Be that as it may, this court is quite satisfied that they should follow the long line of cases to which I have referred, and it follows accordingly that, whether intended or not, the jury were misdirected in the present case, and misdirected in a manner which really compels this court to quash the conviction of the applicant Morris. In the result leave to appeal will be granted to both the applicants; this will be treated as the hearing of the appeal and in the case of the applicant Anderson, instead of quashing the conviction, the court will direct a new trial under s.1 of the Criminal Appeal Act 1964. In the case of he applicant Morris, they will allow the appeal and quash the conviction.

D. No Conviction of Principal Offender

Question

Is it possible to convict the defendant as an accomplice to an offence in the absence of a conviction of the principal offender?

(i) There is no objection to convicting A as a secondary party where the principal is not convicted
 (a) because he has not been apprehended;
 (b) because he has a defence not available to A;
 (c) because evidence admissible against A is not available against the principal.
(ii) Where the evidence against A, the accomplice and B, the principal, is substantially the same then it will normally be wrong to acquit B yet convict A.
(iii) There must, however, be a crime to which A can be a secondary party:

Thornton v. Mitchell
[1940] 1 All E.R. 339 (D.C.)

[A bus conductor was helping his driver to reverse their bus by ringing the bell to indicate that there were no persons behind the bus. He negligently rang the bell when two pedestrians were behind the bus. The driver reversed injuring both, one fatally. The charge against the driver of driving without due care and attention was dismissed, but the magistrates convicted the conductor of aiding and abetting that offence.]

Lord Hewart C.J. [The magistrates say:]

"We, being of opinion that the conductor [had been very negligent], held that he was guilty of aiding and abetting, counselling and procuring the said Hollinrake to drive without due care and attention, and accordingly we inflicted a fine."

In my opinion, this case is *a fortiori* upon *Morris* v. *Tolman* (1923), to which our attention has been directed. I will read one sentence from the judgment of Avory. J.:

" . . . in order to convict, it would be necessary to show that the respondent was aiding the principal, but a person cannot aid another in doing something which that other has not done."

That, I think, is the very thing which these justices have decided that this bus conductor did. In one breath they say that the principal did nothing which he should not have done, and in the next breath they hold that the bus conductor aided and abetted the driver in doing something which had not been done or in not doing something which he ought to have done. I really think that, with all respect to the ingenuity of counsel for the respondent, the case is too plain for argument, and this appeal must be allowed and the conviction quashed.

Question

W as there a charge which might successfully have been brought against the conductor?

R. v. Cogan and Leak
[1976] Q.B. 217 (C.A.)

[L. had invited C. to have sexual intercourse with his (L.'s) wife. It is clear that she did not consent to the intercourse but did so because she was afraid of her husband. The jury found that C. honestly believed she was consenting, but that he had no reasonable grounds for such a belief. In the light of the decision of the House of Lords in *Morgan* (above, p. 80) C.'s conviction for rape was quashed. L., however, had no such belief that his wife was consenting, but in this country a man cannnot (subject to certain exceptions which were not applicable here) rape his own wife as a principal offender. The question for the Court of Appeal was whether, following C.'s acquittal, L.'s conviction for aiding and abetting the rape of his wife could still be upheld.]

Lawton L.J. The only case which Mr. Herrod submitted had a direct bearing upon the problem of Leak's guilt was *Walters* v. *Lunt* (1951). In that case the respondents had been charged, under section 33(1) of the Larceny Act 1916, with receiving from a child aged seven years, certain articles knowing them to have been stolen. In 1951, a child under eight years was deemed in law to be incapable of committing a crime: it followed that at the time of receipt by the respondents the articles had not been stolen and that the charge had not been proved. That case is very different from this because here one fact is clear - the wife had been raped. Cogan had had sexual intercourse with her without her consent. The fact that Cogan was innocent of rape because he believed that she was consenting does not affect the position that she was raped.

Her ravishment had come about because Leak had wanted it to happen and had taken action to see that it did by persuading Cogan to use his body as the instrument for the necessary physical act. In the language of the law the act of sexual intercourse without the wife's consent was the actus reus: it had been procured by Leak who had the appropriate mens rea, namely, his intention that Cogan should have sexual intercourse with her without her consent. In our judgment it is irrelevant that the man whom Leak had procured to do the physical act himself did not intend to have sexual intercourse with the wife without her consent. Leak was using him as a means to procure a criminal purpose.

Before 1861 a case such as this, pleaded as it was in the indictment, might have presented a court with problems arising from the old distinctions between principals and accessories in felony. Most of the old law was swept away by section 8 of the Accessories and Abettors Act 1861 and what remained by section 1 of the Criminal Law Act 1967. The modern law allowed Leak to be tried and punished as a principal offender. In our judgment he could have been indicted as a principal offender. It would have been no defence for him to submit that if Cogan was an "innocent" agent, he was necessarily in the old terminology of the law a principal in the first degree, which was a legal impossibility as a man cannot rape his own wife during cohabitation. The law no longer concerns itself with the niceties of degrees in participation in crime; but even if it did Leak would still be guilty. The reason a man cannot by his own physical act rape his wife during cohabitation is because the law presumes Bonsent from the marriage ceremony: see *Hale, Pleas of the Crown* (1778), vol. 1, p. 629. There is no such presumption when a man procures a drunken friend to do the physical act for him. Hale C.J. put this case in one sentence, at p. 629:

" . . . tho in marriage she hath given up her body to her husband, she is not to be by him prostituted to another".

Had Leak been indicted as a principal offender, the case against him would have been clear beyond argument. Should he be allowed to go free because he was charged with "being aider and abettor to the same offence"? If we are right in our opinion that the wife had been raped (and no one outside a court of law would say that she had not been), then the particulars of offence accurately stated what Leak had done, namely, he had procured Cogan to commit the offence. This would suffice to uphold he conviction. We would prefer, however, to uphold it on a wider basis. In our judgment convictions should not be upset because of mere technicalities of pleading in an indictment. Leak knew what the case against him was and the facts in support of that case were proved. But for the fact that the jury thought that Cogan in his intoxicated condition might have mistaken the wife's sobs and distress for expressions of her consent, no question of any kind would have arisen about the form of pleading. By his written statement Leak virtually admitted what he had done. As Judge Chapman said in *Reg.* v. *Humphreys* (1965).

> "It would be anomalous if a person who admitted to a substantial part in the perpetration of a misdemeanour as aider and abettor could not be convicted on his own admission merely because the person alleged to have been aided and abetted was not or could not be convicted."

In the circumstances of this case it would be more than anomalous: it would be an affront to justice and to the common sense of ordinary folk. It was for these reasons that we dismissed the appeal against conviction.

Notes

1. See also *Bourne* (1952).
2. In *Richards* (1974) the Court of Appeal refused to convict a secondary party of a greater offence than that for which the principal offenders were convicted. This may have been because the secondary party was not present at the scene of the crime, but it is more likely that the court was applying a general principle that secondary party liability should not exceed that of the principal. But see now *R*.v. *Howe*, below, p. 145.

E. Repentance by Secondary Party

R. v. Becerra
[1976] 62 Cr.App.R. 212 (C.A.)

[B. together with C. and G. went to burgle a flat. During the burglary they were disturbed by L., the tenant. B. called out, "let's go" and climbed out of a window, followed by G. C., who had been handed a knife by B., stabbed and killed L. B. and C. were charged with murder. On appeal against conviction B. argued that even if there were a joint plan between himself and C. to meet resistance with serious violence or even death, he had effectively withdrawn from the common venture before it was put into effect.]

Roskill L.J. Mr. Owen says that . . . the learned judge in effect, though perhaps not in so many words, withdrew the defence of "withdrawal" from the jury, because the learned judge was saying to the jury that the only evidence of Becerra's suggested "withdrawal" was the remark, if it were made, "Come on let's go," coupled with the fact of course that Becerra then went out through the window and ran away and that that could not in those circumstances amount to "withdrawal" and therefore was not available as a defence, even if they decided the issue of common design against Becerra. It is upon that passage in the summing-up that Mr. Owen has principally focused his criticism.

It is necessary, before dealing with that argument in more detail, to say a word or two about the relevant law. It is a curious fact, considering the number of times in which this point arises where two or more people are charged with criminal offences, particularly murder or manslaughter, how relatively little authority there is in this country upon the point. But the principle is undoubtedly of long standing.

Perhaps it is best first stated in *Saunders and Archer* (1577) (in the eighteenth year of the first Queen Elizabeth) at p. 476 in a note by *Plowden*, thus: " ... for if I command one to kill J. S. and before the Fact done I go to him and tell him that I have repented, and expressly charge him not to kill J. S. and he afterwards kills him, there I shall not be Accessory to this Murder, because I have countermanded my first Command, which in all Reason shall discharge me, for the malicious Mind of the Accessory ought to continue to do ill until the Time of the Act done, or else he shall not be charged; but if he had killed J. S. before the Time of my Discharge or Countermand given, I should have been Accessory to the Death, notwithstanding my private Repentance."

The next case to which I may usefully refer is some 250 years later, but over 150 years ago: *Edmeads and Others* (1828), where there is a ruling of Vaughan B. at a trial at Berkshire Assizes, upon an indictment charging Edmeads and others with unlawfully shooting at game keepers. At the end of his ruling the learned Baron said on the question of common intent, "that is rather a question for the jury; but still, on this evidence, it is quite clear what the common purpose was. They all draw up in lines, and point their guns at the game-keepers, and they are all giving their countenance and assistance to the one of them who actually fires the gun. If it could be shown that either of them separated himself from the rest, and showed distinctly that he would have no hand in what they were doing, the objection would have much weight in it"

I can go forward over 100 years. Mr Owen (to whose juniors

we are indebted for their research into the relevant Canadian and United States cases) referred us to several Canadian cases, to only one of which is it necessary to refer in detail, a decision of the Court of Appeal of British Columbia in *Whitehouse (alias Savage)* (1941). I need not read the headnote. The Court of Appeal held that the trial judge concerned in that case, which was one of murder, had been guilty of misdirection in his direction to the jury on this question of "withdrawal." The matter is, if I may most respectfully say so, so well put in the leading judgment of Sloan J.A., that I read the whole of the passage: "Can it be said on the facts of this case that a mere change of mental intention and a quitting of the scene of the crime just immediately prior to the striking of the fatal blow will absolve those who participate in the commission of the crime by overt acts up to that moment from all the consequences of its accomplishment by the one who strikes in ignorance of his companions' change of heart? I think not. After a crime has been committed and before a prior abandonment of the common enterprise may be found by a jury there must be, in my view, in the absence of exceptional circumstances, something more than a mere mental change of intention and physical change of place by those associates who wish to dissociate themselves from the consequences attendant upon their willing assistance up to the moment of the actual commission of that crime. I would not attempt to define too closely what must be done in criminal matters involving participation in a common unlawful purpose to break the chain of causation and responsibility. That must depend upon the circumstances of each case but it seems to me that one essential element ought to be established in a case of this kind: Where practicable and reasonable there must be timely communication of the intention to abandon the common purpose from those who wish to dissociate themselves from the contemplated crime to those who desire to continue in it. What is 'timely communication' must be determined by the facts of each case but where practicable and reasonable it ought to be such communication, verbal or otherwise, that will serve unequivocal notice upon the other party to the common unlawful cause that if he proceeds upon it he does so without the further aid and assistance of those who withdraw. The unlawful purpose of him who continues alone is then his own and not one in common with those who are no longer parties to it nor liable to its full and final consequences." The learned judge then went on to cite a passage from 1 Hale's *Pleas of the*

Crown 618 and the passage from *Saunders and Archer* (*supra*) to which I have already referred.

In the view of each member of this Court, that passage, if we may respectfully say so, could not be improved upon and we venture to adopt it in its entirety as a correct statement of the law which is to be applied in this case.

The last case, an English one, is *Croft* (1944), a well known case of a suicide pact where, under the old law, the survivor of a suicide pact was charged with and convicted of murder. It was sought to argue that he had withdrawn from the pact in time to avoid liability (as the law then was) for conviction for murder.

The Court of Criminal Appeal, comprising Lawrence J. (as he then was), Lewis and Wrottesley JJ. dismissed the appeal and upheld the direction given by Humphreys J. to the jury at the trial. Towards the end of the judgment Lawrence J. said: " . . . counsel for the appellant complains - although I do not understand that the point had ever been taken in the court below - that the summing-up does not contain any reference to the possibility of the agreement to commit suicide having been determined or countermanded. It is true that the learned judge does not deal expressly with that matter except in a passage where he says: 'Even if you accept his statement in the witness-box that the vital and second shot was fired when he had gone through that window, he would still be guilty of murder if she was then committing suicide as the result of an agreement which they had mutually arrived at that that should be the fate of both of them, and it is no answer for him that he altered his mind after she was dead and did not commit suicide himself' . . . the authorities, such as they are, show in our opinion, that where a person has acted as an accessory before the fact, in order that he should not be held guilty as an accessory before the fact, he must give express and actual countermand or revocation of the advising, counselling, procuring, or abetting which he had given before."

It seems to us that those authorities make plain what the law is which has to be applied in the present case.

We therefore turn back to consider the direction which the learned judge gave in the present case to the jury and what was the suggested evidence that Becerra had withdrawn from the common agreement. The suggested evidence is the use by Becerra of the words "Come on let's go," coupled, as I said a few moments ago, with his act in going out through the window. The evidence, as the judge pointed out, was that

Cooper never heard that nor did the third man. But let it be supposed that that was said and the jury took the view that it was said.

On the facts of this case, in the circumstances then prevailing, the knife having already been used and being contemplated for further use when it was handed over by Becerra to Cooper for the purpose of avoiding (if necessary) by violent means the hazards of identification, if Becerra wanted to withdraw at that stage, he would have to "countermand," to use the word that is used in some of the cases or "repent" to use another word so used in some manner vastly different and vastly more effective than merely to say "Come on, let's go" and go out through the window.

It is not necessary, on this application, to decide whether the point of time had arrived at which the only way in which he could effectively withdraw, so as to free himself from joint responsibility for any act Cooper thereafter did in furtherance of the common design, would be physically to intervene so as to stop Cooper attacking Lewis, as the judge suggested, by interposing his own body between them or somehow getting in between them or whether some other action might suffice. That does not arise for decision here. Nor is it necessary to decide whether or not the learned judge was right or wrong, on the facts of this case, in that passage . . . which Mr. Owen criticised: "and at least take all reasonable steps to prevent the commission of the crime which he had agreed the others should commit." It is enough for the purposes of deciding this application to say that under the law of this country as it stands, and on the facts (taking them at their highest in favour of Becerra), that which was urged as amounting to withdrawal from the common design was not capable of amounting to such withdrawal. Accordingly Becerra remains responsible, in the eyes of the law, for everything that Cooper did and continued to do after Becerra's disappearance through the window as much as if he had done them himself.

Appeal dismissed.

Chapter 4

DEFENCES

1. INTRODUCTION

In a criminal case it is the duty of the prosecution to establish the accused's guilt. What exactly does that mean?

Woolmington v. D.P.P.
[1935] A.C. 462 (H.L.)

[W.'s wife had left him and had returned to live with her mother. W. went to try to persuade her to return. While at his mother-in-law's house his wife was killed by a shot from a gun he was carrying. His story was that he had taken the gun to frighten her by saying he would kill himself if she did not return, and that it had gone off accidentally.

In directing the jury Swift J. said:]

"If you come to the conclusion that she died in consequence of injuries from the gun which he was carrying, you are put by the law of this country into this position: The killing of a human being is homicide, however he may be killed, and all homicide is presumed to be malicious and murder, unless the contrary appears from circumstances of alleviation, excuse, or justification. 'In every charge of murder, the fact of killing being first proved, all the circumstances of accident, necessity, or infirmity are to be satisfactorily proved by the prisoner, unless they arise out of the evidence produced against him: for the law will presume the fact to have been founded in malice until the contrary appeareth.' That has been the law of this country for all time since we had law. Once it is shown to a jury that somebody has died through the act of another, that is presumed to be murder, unless the person who has been guilty of the act which causes the death can satisfy a jury that what happened was something less, something which might be alleviated, something which might be reduced to a charge of manslaughter, or was something which was accidental, or was something which could be justified."

[W. was convicted of murder. His appeal against conviction finally reached the House of Lords. Viscount Sankey L.C., having reviewed the various authorities concluded:]

Viscount Sankey L.C. If at any period of a trial it was permissible for the judge to rule that the prosecution had established its case and that the onus was shifted onto the prisoner to prove that he was not guilty and that unless he discharged that onus the prosecution was entitled to succeed, would be enabling the judge in such a case to say that the jury must in law find the prisoner guilty and so make the judge decide the case and not the jury, which is not the common law. It would be an entirely different case from those exceptional instances of special verdicts where a judge asks the jury to find certain facts and directs them that on such facts the prosecution is entitled to succeed. Indeed, a consideration of such special verdicts shows that it is not till the end of the evidence that a verdict can properly be found and that at the end of the evidence it is not for the prisoner to establish his innocence, but for the prosecution to establish his guilt. Just as there is evidence on behalf of the prosecution so there may be evidence on behalf of the prisoner which may cause a doubt as to his guilt. In either case, he is entitled to the benefit of the doubt. But while the prosecution must prove the guilt of the prisoner, there is no such burden laid on the prisoner to prove his innocence and it is sufficient for him to raise a doubt as to his guilt; he is not bound to satisfy the jury of his innocence.....

This is the real result of the perplexing case of *Rex* v. *Abramovitch* (1914), which lays down the same proposition, although perhaps in somewhat involved language. Juries are always told that, if conviction there is to be, the prosecution must prove the case beyond reasonable doubt. This statement cannot mean that in order to be acquitted the prisoner must "satisfy" the jury. This is the law as laid down in the Court of Criminal Appeal in *Rex* v. *Davies* (1913), the headnote of which correctly states that where intent is an ingredient of a crime there is no onus on the defendant to prove that the act alleged was accidental. Throughout the web of the English Criminal Law one golden thread is always to be seen, that it is the duty of the prosecution to prove the prisoner's guilt subject to what I have already said as to the defence of insanity and subject also to any statutory exception. If, at the end of and on the whole of the case, there is a reasonable doubt, created by the evidence given by either the prosecution or the prisoner, as to whether the prisoner killed the deceased with a malicious intention, the prosecution has not made out the case and the prisoner is entitled to an acquittal. No matter what the charge or where the trial, the principle that the prosecution must prove the guilt of the prisoner is part of the common law of England and no attempt to whittle it down can be entertained.

Note

The standard of proof required is proof beyond reasonable doubt.

Question

If X is charged with murder what is the position if:
(i)   he claims it was an accident;
(ii) he claims he was acting in self defence;
(iii) he claims he was acting in a state of automatism;
(iv) he claims he was insane at the time he committed the offence;
(v)   he claims he was suffering from diminished responsibility?

2. MENTAL ABNORMALITY

A. Insanity

R. v. M'Naghten
(1843) 10 C. & Fin. 200

[M. had killed the secretary to Sir Robert Peel by shooting him in the back. His acquittal on the ground of insanity attracted a good deal of controversy. The House of Lords debated the matter and summoned the judges to answer certain questions which were put.]

Tindal L.C.J. The first question proposed by your Lordships is this: "What is the law respecting alleged crimes committed by persons afflicted with insane delusion in respect of one or more particular subjects or persons; as, for instance, where, at the time of the commission of the alleged crime, the accused knew he was acting contrary to law, but did the act complained of with a view, under the influence of insane delusion, of redressing or revenging some supposed grievance or injury, or of producing some supposed public benefit?"

In answer to which question, assuming that your Lordships' inquiries are confirmed [*sic*] to those persons who labour under such partial delusions only, and are not in other respects insane, we are of opinion that (notwithstanding the party accused did the act complained of with a view, under the influence of insane delusion, of redressing or revenging some supposed grievance or injury, or of producing some public benefit) he is nevertheless punishable, according to the nature of the crime committed, if he knew, at the time of committing such crime, that he was acting contrary to law; by which expression we understand your Lordships to mean the law of the land.

Your Lordships are pleased to inquire of us, secondly: "What are the proper questions to be submitted to the jury, where a person alleged to be afflicted with insane delusion respecting one or more particular subjects or persons is charged with the commission of a crime (murder, for example), and insanity is set up as a defence?" And, thirdly: "In what terms ought the question to be left to the jury as to the prisoner's state of mind at the time when the act was committed?" And as these two questions appear to us to be more conveniently answered together, we have to submit our opinion to be that *the jury ought to be told in all cases that every man is to be presumed to be sane, and to possess a sufficient degree of reason to be responsible for his crimes, until the contrary be proved to their satisfaction; and that, to establish a defence on the ground of insanity, it must be clearly proved that, at the time of the committing of the act, the party accused was labouring under such a defect of reason, from disease of the mind, as not to know the nature and quality of the act he was doing; or, if he did know it, that he did not know he was doing what was wrong.* [Author's italics.] The mode of putting the latter part of the question to the jury on these occasions has generally been whether the accused at the time of doing the act knew the difference between right and wrong; which mode, though rarely, if ever, leading to any mistake with the jury, is not, as we conceive, so accurate when put generally, and in the abstract, as when put with reference to the party's knowledge of right and wrong in respect to the very act with which he is charged. If the question were to be put as to the knowledge of the accused, solely and exclusively with reference to the law of the land, it might tend to confound the jury, by inducing them to believe that an actual knowledge of the law of the land was essential in order to lead to a conviction; whereas the law is administered upon the principle that every one must be taken conclusively to know it, without proof that he does know it. If the accused was conscious that the act was one which he ought not to do, and if that act was at the same time contrary to the law of the land, he is punishable. The usual course, therefore, has been to leave the question to the jury, whether the party accused had a sufficient degree of reason to know that he was doing an act that was wrong; and this course we think is correct, accompanied with such observations and explanations as the circumstances of each particular case may require.

The fourth question which your Lordships have proposed to us is this: "If a person under an insane delusion as to existing facts commits an offence in consequence thereof, is he thereby excused?" To which question the answer must of course depend on the nature of the delusion; but, making the same assumption as we did before, namely, that he labours under such partial delusion only, and is not in other respects insane, we think he must be considered in the same situation as to responsibility as if the facts with respect to which the delusion exists were real. For example, if, under the influence of his delusion, he supposes another man to be in the act of attempting to take away his life, and he kills that man, as he supposes, in self-defence, he would be exempt from punishment. If his delusion was that the deceased had inflicted a serious injury to his character and fortune, and he killed him in revenge for such supposed injury, he would be liable to punishment.

The question lastly proposed by your Lordships is: "Can a medical man, conversant with the disease of insanity, who never saw the prisoner previously to the trial, but who was present during the whole trial and the examination of all the witnesses, be asked his opinion as to the state of the prisoner's mind at the time of the commission of the alleged crime, or his opinion whether the prisoner was conscious at the time of doing the act that he was acting contrary to law, or whether he was labouring under any and what delusion at the time?" In answer thereto, we state to your Lordships that we think the medical man, under the circumstances supposed, cannot in strictness be asked his opinion in the terms above stated, because each of those questions involves the determination of the truth of the facts deposed to, which it is for the jury to decide, and the questions are not mere questions upon a matter of science, in which case such evidence is admissable. But, where the facts are admitted, or not disputed, and the question becomes substantially one of science only, it may be convenient to allow the question to be put in the general form, though the same cannot be insisted on as a matter of right.

Questions

1. In the italicised passage what is meant by "not to know the nature and quality of the act he was doing?"

2. In the passage "that he did not know he was doing what was wrong" what is meant by "wrong"?

3. Is there a recognised medical concept known as insanity?

4. What is a disease of the mind?

R. v. Sullivan
[1984] A.C. 156 (H.L.)

[S. during an epileptic fit, had attacked P. He was charged with causing grievous bodily harm with intent (Offences Against the Person Act 1861, s. 18) and inflicting grievous bodily harm (Offences Against the Person Act 1861, s. 20). He pleaded not guilty to both, but on a ruling that if the jury accepted his story they would be bound to bring in a verdict of not guilty by reason of insanity, he changed his plea to guilty of an assault occasioning actual bodily harm. On appeal against his conviction, in the House of Lords, Lord Diplock considered whether psychomotor epilepsy was rightly held to be a "disease of the mind."]

Lord Diplock. The nomenclature adopted by the medical profession may change from time to time. . . . But the meaning of the expression "disease of the mind" as the cause of "a defect of reason" remains unchanged for the purposes of the application of the M'Naghten Rules. I agree with what was said by Devlin J. in *Reg.* v. *Kemp* (1957), that "mind" in the M'Naghten Rules is used in the ordinary sense of the mental faculties of reason, memory and understanding. If the effect of a disease is to impair these faculties so severely as to have either of the consequences referred to in the latter part of the rules, it matters not whether the aetiology of the impairment is organic, as in epilepsy, or functional, or whether the impairment itself is permanent or is transient and intermittent, provided that it subsisted at the time of commission of the act. The purpose of the legislation relating to the defence of insanity, ever since its origin in 1800, has been to protect society against recurrence of the dangerous conduct. The duration of a temporary suspension of the mental faculties of reason, memory and understanding, particularly if, as in Mr. Sullivan's case, it is recurrent, cannot on any rational ground be relevant to the application by the courts of the M'Naghten Rules, though it may be relevant to the course adopted by the Secretary of State, to whom the responsibility for how the defendant is to be dealt with passes after the return of the special verdict of "not guilty by reason of insanity."

To avoid misunderstanding I ought perhaps to add that in expressing my agreement with what was said by Devlin J. in *Kemp*, where the disease that caused the temporary and intermittent impairment of the mental faculties was arteriosclerosis, I do not regard that learned judge as excluding the possibility of non-insane automatism (for which the proper verdict would be a verdict of "not guilty") in cases where temporary impairment (not being self-induced by consuming drink or drugs) results from some external physical factor such as a blow on the head causing concussion or the administration of an anaesthetic for therapeutic purposes. . . . . . .

My Lords, it is natural to feel reluctant to attach the label of insanity to a sufferer from psychomotor epilepsy of the kind to which Mr. Sullivan was subject, even though the expression in the context of a special verdict of "not guilty by reason of insanity" is a technical one which includes a purely temporary and intermittent suspension of the mental faculties of reason, memory and understanding resulting from the occurrence of an epileptic fit. But the label is contained in the current statute, it has appeared in this statute's predecessors ever since 1800. It does not lie within the power of the courts to alter it. Only Parliament can do that. It has done so twice; it could do so once again.

Sympathise though I do with Mr. Sullivan, I see no other course open to your Lordships than to dismiss this appeal.

R. v. Quick
[1973] Q.B. 910 (C.A.)

[Q., a psychiatric nurse, had assaulted a patient whilst suffering from hypoglycaemia. He was a diabetic and on this occasion the evidence suggested that the episode was brought on by an insulin injection rather than by the diabetes itself. The trial judge ruled that this amounted to insanity and not non-insane automatism. Quick changed his plea to one of guilty. On appeal against conviction:]

Lawton L.J. Our task has been to decide what the law means now by the words "disease of the mind." In our judgment the fundamental concept is of a malfunctioning of the mind caused by disease. A malfunctioning of the mind of transitory effect caused by the application to the body of some external factor such as violence, drugs, including anaesthetics, alcohol and hypnotic influences cannot fairly be said to be due to disease. Such malfunctioning, unlike that caused by a defect of reason from disease of the mind, will not always relieve an accused from criminal responsibility. A self-induced incapacity will not excuse (see *Reg.* v. *Lipman* (1970)), nor will one which could have been reasonably foreseen as a result of either doing, or omitting to do something, as, for example, taking alcohol against medical advice after using certain prescribed drugs, or failing to have regular meals while taking insulin. From time to time difficult border line cases are likely to arise. When they do, the test suggested by the New Zealand Court of Appeal in *Reg.* v. *Cottle* (1958) is likely to give the correct result, viz., can this mental condition be fairly regarded as amounting to or producing a defect of reason from disease of the mind?

In this case Quick's alleged mental condition, if it ever existed, was not caused by his diabetes but by his use of the insulin prescribed by his doctor. Such malfunctioning of his mind as there was, was caused by an external factor and not by a bodily disorder in the nature of a disease which disturbed the working of his mind. It follows in our judgment that Quick was entitled to have his defence of automatism left to the jury and that Bridge J.'s ruling as to the effect of the medical evidence called by him was wrong.

Question

What would be the position if the court had found that although the hypoglycaemic episode had been caused by the injection of insulin, the attack would not have occurred but for the failure of the accused to heed the advice of his doctor to eat sufficient food after each injection? (See *Bailey* (1983) below, p. 143.)

B. Diminished Responsibility

See Homicide Act 1957, s. 2 (below, p. 261).

R. v. Byrne
[1960] 2 Q.B. 396 (C.A.)

[B. killed a girl and then perpetrated horrifying mutilations on her body. The only defence was that the accused was suffering from diminished responsibility. It was accepted that he was a sexual psychopath and that as such he suffered from violent perverted sexual desires which he found difficult or impossible to control. The trial judge gave the jury a direction which, in effect, told the jury that B.'s condition did not constitute diminished responsibility. On appeal against conviction:]

Lord Parker C.J. [His Lordship reviewed the defence of insanity and continued:] The ability of the accused to control his physical acts by exercise of his will was relevant before the passing of the Homicide Act, 1957, in one case only: that of provocation. Loss of self-control on the part of the accused so as to make him for the moment not master of his mind had the effect of reducing murder to manslaughter if: (i) it was induced by an act or series of acts done by the deceased to the accused, and (ii) such act or series of acts would have induced a reasonable man to lose his self-control and act in the same manner as the accused acted. . . .

Whether loss of self-control induced by provocation negatived the ordinary presumption that a man intends the natural ordinary consequences of his physical acts so that, in such a case, the prosecution had failed to prove the essential mental element in murder (namely, that the accused intended to kill or to inflict grievous bodily harm) is academic for the purposes of our consideration. What is relevant is that loss of self-control has always been recognised as capable of reducing murder to manslaughter, but that the criterion has always been the degree of self-control which would be exercised by a reasonable man, that is to say, a man with a normal mind.

It is against that background of the existing law that section 2(1) of the Homicide Act, 1957, falls to be construed. To satisfy the requirements of the subsection the accused must show: (a) that he was suffering from an abnormality of mind, and (b) that such abnormality of mind (i) arose from a condition of arrested or retarded development of mind or any inherent causes, or was induced by disease or injury and (ii) was such as substantially impaired his mental responsibility for his acts in doing or being a party to the killing.

"Abnormality of mind," which has to be contrasted with the time-honoured expression in the M'Naughten Rules "defect of reason," means a state of mind so different from that of ordinary human beings that the reasonable man would term it abnormal. It appears to us to be wide enough to cover the mind's activities in all its aspects, not only the perception of physical acts and matters, and the ability to form a rational judgment as to whether an act is right or wrong, but also the ability to exercise will power to control physical acts in accordance with that rational judgment. The expression "mental responsibility for his acts" points to a consideration of the extent to which the accused's mind is answerable for his physical acts which must include a consideration of the extent of his ability to exercise will power to control his physical acts.

Whether the accused was at the time of the killing suffering from any "abnormality of mind" in the broad sense which we have indicated above is a question for the jury. On this question medical evidence is no doubt of importance, but the jury are entitled to take into consideration all the evidence, including the acts or statements of the accused and his demeanour. They are not bound to accept the medical evidence if there is other material before them which, in their good judgment, conflicts with it and outweighs it.

The aetiology of the abnormality of mind (namely, whether it arose from a condition of arrested or retarded development of mind or any inherent causes, or was induced by disease of injury) does, however, seem to be a mater to be determined on expert evidence.

Assuming that the jury are satisfied on the balance of probabilities that the accused was suffering from "abnormality of mind" from one of the causes specified in the parenthesis of the subsection, the crucial question nevertheless arises: was the abnormality such as substantially impaired his mental responsibility for his acts in doing or being a party to the killing? This is a question of degree and essentially one for the jury. Medical evidence is, of course, relevant, but the question involves a decision not merely as to whether there was some impairment of the mental responsibility of the accused for his acts but whether such impairment can properly be called "substantial," a matter upon which juries may quite legitimately differ from doctors.

Furthermore, in a case where the abnormality of mind is one which affects the accused's self-control the step between "he did not resist his impulse" and "he could not resist his impulse" is, as the evidence in this case shows, one which is incapable of scientific proof. A fortiori there is no scientific measurement of the degree of difficulty which an abnormal person finds in controlling his impulses. These problems which in the present state of medical knowledge are scientifically insoluble, the jury can only approach in a broad, common-sense way. This court has repeatedly approved directions to the jury which have followed directions given in Scots cases where the doctrine of diminished responsibility forms part of the common law. We need not repeat them. They are quoted in *Reg.* v. *Spriggs* (1958). They indicate that such abnormality as "substantially impairs his mental responsibility" involves a mental state which in popular language (not that of the M'Naghten Rules) a jury would regard as amounting to partial insanity or being on the border-line of insanity.

It appears to us that the judge's direction to the jury . . . amounted to a direction that difficulty or even inability of an accused person to exercise will power to control his physical acts could not amount to such abnormality of mind as substantially impairs his mental responsibility. For the reasons which we have already expressed we think that this construction of the Act is wrong. Inability to exercise will power to control physical acts, provided that it is due to abnormality of mind from one of the causes specified in the parenthesis in the subsection is, in our view, sufficient to entitle the accused to the benefit of the section; difficulty in controlling his physical acts depending on the degree of difficulty, may be. It is for the jury to decide on the whole of the evidence whether such inability or difficulty has, not as a matter of scientific certainty but on the balance of probabilities, been established, and in the case of difficulty whether the difficulty is so great as to amount in their view to a substantial impairment of the accused's mental responsibility for his acts. The direction in the present case thus withdrew from the jury the essential determination of fact which it was their province to decide.

As already indicated, the medical evidence as to the appellant's ability to control his physical acts at the time of the killing was all one way. The evidence of the revolting circumstances of the killing and the subsequent mutilations as of the previous sexual history of the appellant pointed, we think plainly, to the conclusion that the accused was what would be described in ordinary language as on the border-line of insanity or partially insane. Properly directed, we do not think that the jury could have come to any other conclusion than that the defence under section 2 of the Homicide Act was made out.

The appeal will be allowed and a verdict of manslaughter substituted for the verdict of murder. The only possible sentence having regard to the tendencies of the accused is imprisonment for life. The sentence will, accordingly, not be disturbed.

Appeal allowed.

3. INTOXICATION

R. v. Majewski
[1977] A.C. 433 (H.L.)

[M. was charged with various assaults occasioning actual bodily harm and assaults on a police constable in the execution of his duty. His defence was that voluntary consumption of alcohol and drugs had so affected him that he could recall nothing of the alleged incidents. The trial judge told the jury that they could ignore the subject of drink and drugs as being in any way a defence to any of the charges against the accused. This was because these offences were offences of basic intent; self induced intoxication could only be a defence to a crime requiring specific intent. His appeal against conviction was dismissed by the Court of Appeal but that Court certified that the following point of law of general public importance was involved:

"Whether a defendant may properly be convicted of assault notwithstanding that, by reason of his self-induced intoxication, he did not intend to do the act alleged to constitute the assault."]

Lord Elwyn-Jones L.C. The appeal raises issues of considerable public importance. In giving the judgment of the Court of Appeal, Lawton L.J. rightly observed that

"The facts are commonplace - indeed so commonplace that

their very nature reveals how serious from a social and public standpoint the consequences would be if men could behave as the [appellant] did and then claim that they were not guilty of any offence."

... [T]he crux of the case for the Crown was that, illogical as the outcome may be said to be, the judges have evolved for the purpose of protecting the community a substantive rule of law that, in crimes of basic intent as distinct from crimes of specific intent, self-induced intoxication provides no defence and is irrelevant to offences of basic intent, such as assault.

What then is the mental element required in our law to be established in assault? This question has been most helpfully answered in the speech of Lord Simon of Glaisdale in *Reg.* v. *Morgan* (1976):

"By 'crimes of basic intent' I mean those crimes whose definition expresses (or, more often, implies) a mens rea which does not go beyond the actus reus. The actus reus generally consists of an act and some consequence. The consequence may be very closely connected with the act or more remotely connected with it: but with a crime of basic intent the mens rea does not extend beyond the act and its consequence, however remote, as defined in the actus reus. I take assault as an example of a crime of basic intent where the consequence is very closely connected with the act. The actus reus of assault is an act which causes another person to apprehend immediate and unlawful violence. The mens rea corresponds exactly. The prosecution must prove that the accused foresaw that his act would probably cause another person to have apprehension of immediate and unlawful violence, or would possibly have that consequence, such being the purpose of the act, or that he was reckless as to whether or not his act caused Buch apprehension. This foresight (the term of art is 'intention') or recklessness is the mens rea in assault. For an example of a crime of basic intent where the consequence of the act involved in the actus reus as Befined in the crime is less immediate, I take the crime of unlawful wounding. The act is, say, the squeezing of a trigger. A number of consequences (mechanical, chemical, ballistic and physiological) intervene before the final consequence involved in the defined actus reus - namely, the wounding of another person in circumstances unjustified by law. But

again here the mens rea corresponds closely to the actus
reus. The prosecution must prove that the accused foresaw
that some physical harm would ensue to another person in
circumstances unjustified by law as a probable (or possible
and desired) consequence of his act, or that he was reckless
as to whether or not such consequence ensued."

How does the fact of self-induced intoxication fit into that
analysis? If a man consciously and deliberately takes alcohol
and drugs not on medical prescription, but in order to escape
from reality, to go "on a trip," to become hallucinated,
whatever the description may be and thereby disables himself
from taking the care he might otherwise take and as a result by
his subsequent actions causes injury to another - does our
criminal law enable him to say that because he did not know
what he was doing he lacked both intention and recklessness
and accordingly is entitled to an acquittal?

[Lord Elwyn-Jones reviewed the authorities, especially *DPP* v. *Beard*
(1920) in which Lord Birkenhead L.C. concluded that (except in cases where
insanity is pleaded) the decisions "establish that where a specific intent is an
essential element in the offence, evidence of a state of drunkenness rendering the
accused incapable of forming such an intent should be taken into consideration
in order to determine whether he had in fact formed the intent necessary to
constitute the particular crime. If he was so drunk that he was incapable of
forming the intent required he could not be convicted of a crime which was
committed only if the intent was proved. ... In a charge of murder based upon
intention to kill or to do grievous bodily harm, if the jury are satisfied that the
accused was, by reason of his drunken condition, incapable of forming the intent
to kill or to do grievous bodily harm ... he cannot be convicted of murder. But
nevertheless unlawful homicide has been committed by the accused, and
consequently he is guilty of unlawful homicide without malice aforethought, and
that is manslaughter: *per* Stephen J. in *Reg.* v. *Doherty* (1887)."
The passage concludes: "the law is plain beyond all question that in cases
falling short of insanity a condition of drunkenness at the time of committing an
offence causing death can only, when it is available at all, have the effect of
reducing the crime from murder to manslaughter." Lord Elwyn-Jones
continued:]

From this it seemed clear - and this is the interpretation which
the judges have placed upon the decision during the ensuing
half century - that it is only in the limited class of cases
requiring proof of specific intent that drunkenness can
exculpate. Otherwise in no case can it exempt completely from
criminal liability.

[Lord Elwyn-Jones concluded his review of the authorities by noting that this
principle had never been overruled by the House of Lords and it remained to
determine whether it should be. He continued:]

I do not for my part regard that general principle as either
unethical or contrary to the principles of natural justice. If a

man of his own volition takes a substance which causes him to cast off the restraints of reason and conscience, no wrong is done to him by holding him answerable criminally for any injury he may do while in that condition. His course of conduct in reducing himself by drugs and drink to that condition in my view supplies the evidence of mens rea, of guilty mind certainly sufficient for crimes of basic intent. It is a reckless course of conduct and recklessness is enough to constitute the necessary mens rea in assault cases: see *Reg.* v. *Venna* (1976). The drunkenness is itself an intrinsic, an integral part of the crime, the other part being the evidence of the unlawful use of force against the victim. Together they add up to criminal recklessness. On this I adopt the conclusion of Stroud in (1920) 36 L.Q.R. 273 that:

". . . it would be contrary to all principle and authority to suppose that drunkenness" (and what is true of drunkenness is equally true of intoxication by drugs) "can be a defence for crime in general on the ground that 'a person cannot be convicted of a crime unless the mens was rea.' By allowing himself to get drunk, and thereby putting himself in such a condition as to be no longer amenable to the law's commands, a man shows such regardlessness as amounts to mens rea for the purpose of all ordinary crimes."

This approach is in line with the American Model Penal Code (s. 2.08(2)):

"When recklessness establishes an element of the offence, if the actor, due to self-induced intoxication, is unaware of a risk of which he would have been aware had he been sober, such unawareness is immaterial."

The final question that arises is whether section 8 of the Act of 1967 [see below, p. 262] has had the result of abrogating or qualifying the common law rule. That section emanated from the consideration the Law Commission gave to the decision of the house in *Director of Public Prosecutions* v. *Smith* (1961). Its purpose and effect was to alter the law of evidence about the presumption of intention to produce the reasonable and probable consequences of one's acts. It was not intended to change the common law rule. In referring to "all the evidence" it meant all the *relevant* evidence. But if there is a substantive rule of law that in crimes of basic intent, the factor of intoxication is irrelevant (and such I hold to be the substantive law), evidence with regard to it is quite irrelevant. Section 8 does not abrogate the substantive rule and it cannot properly be said that the continued application of that rule contravenes the section. For these reasons, my conclusion is that the certified question should be answered "Yes," that there was no misdirection in this case and that the appeal should be dismissed.

My noble and learned friends and I think it may be helpful if we give the following indication of the general lines on which in our view the jury should be directed as to the effect upon the criminal responsibility of the accused of drink or drugs or both, whenever death or physical injury to another person results from something done by the accused for which there is no legal justification and the offence with which the accused is charged is manslaughter or assault at common law or the statutory offence of unlawful wounding under section 20, or of assault occasioning actual bodily harm under section 47 of the Offences against the Person Act 1861.

In the case of these offences it is no excuse in law that, because of drink or drugs which the accused himself had taken knowingly and willingly, he had deprived himself of the ability to exercise self-control to realise the possible consequences of what he was doing, or even to be conscious that he was doing it. As in the instance case, the jury may be properly instructed that they "can ignore the subject of drink or drugs as being in any way a defence" to charges of this character.

Note

In *Caldwell* (above, p. 60) Lord Diplock held that where the charge of an offence under section 1(2) of the Criminal Damage Act 1971 is framed so as to charge the defendant only with "*intending* by the destruction or damage [of the property] to endanger the life of another," evidence of self-induced intoxication can be relevant to his defence. If, however, the charge is, or includes, a reference to his being "reckless as to whether the life of another would thereby be endangered," this is a basic intent offence to which evidence of self-induced intoxication cannot be relevant.

Question

What approach should be taken by the court in a case where the accused has "committed" an offence in a state of automatism induced by a medically prescribed drug? (see *Sullivan*, above, p. 132). Should the answer be different if the symptoms were caused by the accused's failure to observe his doctor's instructions as to diet or consumption of alcohol? Is this another area in which the courts should distinguish between crimes of basic and specific intent?

R. v. Bailey
(*1983*) *77 Cr.App.R. 76 (C.A.*)

[B. was a diabetic who took insulin to control his condition. On the occasion in question he claimed that he assaulted his victim during a period of unconsciousness caused by hypoglycaemia because of his failure to take sufficient food following his last dose of insulin. He was convicted of wouding with intent (Offences Against the Person Act 1861, s. 18); the jury were not required to give a verdict on an alternative count of unlawful wounding (Offences Against the Person Act 1861, s. 20). He appealed to the Court of Appeal against conviction. Clearly the defence would be available to the charge of wounding with intent; was it, however, available to the basic intent offence of unlawful wounding under s. 20 Offences Against the Person Act 1861?]

Griffiths L.J. Automatism resulting from intoxication as a result of a voluntary ingestion of alcohol or dangerous drugs does not negative the *mens rea* necessary for crimes of basic intent, because the conduct of the accused is reckless and recklessness is enough to constitute the necessary *mens rea* in assault cases where no specific intent forms part of the charge. See *D.P.P.* v. *Majewski* (*supra*) in the speech of Lord Edmund-Davies where he said: "The law therefore establishes a conclusive presumption against the admission of proof of intoxication for the purpose of disproving *mens rea* in ordinary crimes. Where this presumption applies, it does not make 'drunkenness' itself a crime but the drunkenness is itself an integral part of the crime, as forming, together with the other unlawful conduct charged against the defendant, a complex act of criminal recklessness."

The same considerations apply where the state of automatism is induced by the voluntary taking of dangerous drugs. See *Lipman* (1969) where a conviction for manslaughter was upheld, the appellant having taken L.S.D. and killed his mistress in the course of an hallucinatory trip. It was submitted on behalf of the Crown that a similar rule should be applied as a matter of public policy to all cases of self-induced automatism. But it seems to us that there may be material distinctions between a man who consumes alcohol or takes dangerous drugs and one who fails to take sufficient food after insulin to avert hypoglycaemia.

It is common knowledge that those who take alcohol to excess or certain sorts of drugs may become aggressive or do dangerous or unpredictable things; they may be able to foresee the risks of causing harm to others, but nevertheless persist in their conduct. But the same cannot be said without more of a man who fails to take food after an insulin injection. If he does appreciate the risk that such a failure may lead to aggressive, unpredictable and uncontrollable conduct and he nevertheless deliberately runs the risk or otherwise disregards it, this will amount to recklessness. But we certainly do not think that it is common knowledge, even among diabetics, that such is a consequence of a failure to take food; and there is no evidence that it was known to this appellant. Doubtless he knew that if he failed to take his insulin or proper food after it, he might lose consciousness, but as such he would only be a danger to himself unless he put himself in charge of some machine such as a motor car, which required his continued conscious control.

In our judgment, self-induced automatism, other than that due to intoxication from alcohol or drugs, may provide a defence to crimes of basic intent. The question in each case will be whether the prosecution have proved the necessary element of recklessness. In cases of assault, if the accused knows that his actions or inaction are likely to make him aggressive, unpredictable or uncontrolled with the result that he may cause some injury to others and he persists in the action or takes no remedial action when he knows it is required, it will be open to the jury to find that he was reckless.

. . . . . .

In the present case the recorder never invited the jury to consider what the appellant's knowledge or appreciation was of what would happen if he failed to take food after his insulin or whether he realised that he might become aggressive. Nor were they asked to consider why the appellant had omitted to take food in time. They were given no direction on the elements of recklessness. Accordingly, in our judgment, there was also a misdirection in relation to the second count in the indictment of unlawful wounding.

But we have to consider whether, notwithstanding these misdirections, there has been any miscarriage of justice and whether the jury properly directed could have failed to come to the same conclusion. As Lawton L.J. said in *Quick's* case (1973), referring to the defence of automatism, it is a "quagmire of law, seldom entered nowadays save by those in desperate need of some kind of defence." This case is no exception. We think it very doubtful whether the appellant laid a sufficient basis for the defence to be considered by the jury at all. But even if he did, we are in no doubt that the jury properly directed must have rejected it. Although an episode of sudden transient loss of consciousness or awareness was theoretically possible, it was quite inconsistent with the graphic description that the appellant gave to the police both orally and in his written statement. There was abundant evidence Bhat he had armed himself with the iron bar and gone to Harrison's house for the purpose of attacking him, because he wanted to teach him a lesson and because he was in the way.

Moreover, the doctor's evidence to which we have referred showed it was extremely unlikely that such an episode could follow some five minutes after taking sugar and water. For these reasons we are satisfied that no miscarriage of justice occurred and the appeal will be dismissed.

Appeal dismissed.
Proviso applied.

4. DURESS AND NECESSITY

A. Duress

R. v. Howe
[1986] 2 W.L.R. 294 (C.A.)

Lord Lane C.J. read the following judgment of the court. These appeals arise out of two separate cases. The issues in each are largely similar. We therefore decided, with the consent of the parties, to hear them together.

Regina v. *Howe; Regina* v. *Bannister*

Howe and Bannister were convicted . . . on two counts of murder (counts 1 and 2) and one count of conspiracy to murder (count 3). Howe received concurrent sentences of custody for life; Bannister of life imprisonment.

There were two other men, Murray and Bailey, charged jointly with them. These two changed their pleas to guilty during the trial. Bailey was sentenced to concurrent terms of custody for life; Murray to concurrent terms of life imprisonment with a recommendation that he should serve a minimum of 25 years.

At the time of the offences Howe and Bailey were 19, Bannister 20 and Murray 35. . . . Murray was the dominant figure. He was evidently a dishonest, powerful, violent and sadistic man.

Count 1: murder of Elgar

The first victim was a 17-year old youth called Elgar. He was offered a job as a driver by Murray. On the evening of 10 October 1983 all five men were driven by Murray up into the hills between Stockport and Buxton, eventually stopping at some public lavatories at a remote spot called Goytsclough. Murray at some stage told both appellants in effect that Elgar was a "grass," and that they were going to kill him. Bannister was threatened with violence if he did not give Elgar "a bit of a battering." From thenceforwards Elgar, who was naked, sobbing and begging for mercy, was tortured, compelled to undergo appalling sexual perversions and indignities, he was kicked and punched. Bannister and Howe were doing the kicking and punching. The coup de grace was executed by Bailey, who strangled Elgar with a headlock. It is unnecessary to go into further details of the attack on Elgar which are positively nauseating.

In brief the two appellants asserted that they had only acted as they did through fear of Murray, believing that they would be treated in the same way as Elgar had been treated if they did not comply with Murray's directions.

The prosecution were content to assent to the proposition that death had been caused by Bailey strangling the victim, although the kicks and punches would have resulted in death moments later even in the absence of the strangulation. The body was hidden by the appellants and the other two men.

On this basis the appellants were in the position of what would have earlier been principals in the second degree and duress was left to the jury as an issue on this count.

Count 2: murder of Pollitt

Very much the same course of conduct took place as with Elgar. On 11 October 1983 the men picked up Pollitt, a 19-year old labourer, and took him to the same place where all four men kicked and punched the youth. Murray told Howe and Bannister to kill Pollitt, which they did by strangling him with Bannister's shoe lace. As the appellants were in the position of principals in the first degree, the judge did not leave duress to the jury on this count.

Count 3: conspiracy to murder Redfern

The third intended victim was a 21-year old man. The same procedure was followed, but Redfern suspected tht something was afoot and managed with some skill to escape on his motorcycle from what would otherwise have inevitably been another horrible murder. The judge left the defence of duress to the jury on this charge of conspiracy to murder.

The grounds of appeal, which are the same in respect of each of these appellants, are as follows. That the judge erred in directing the jury (1) in respect of count 2, that the defence of duress was not available to a principal in the first degree to the actual killing; (2) in respect of counts 1 and 3, that the test as to whether the appellants were acting under duress contains an "objective" element; that is to say, if the prosecution prove that a reasonable man in the position of the defendant would not have felt himself forced to comply with the threats, the defence fails.

Regina v. *Burke; Regina* v. *Clarkson*

I now turn to the case of Burke and Clarkson. These two appellants . . . were convicted of murder. Burke was sentenced to custody for life (misdescribed in the sentencing remarks); Clarkson was sentenced to life imprisonment with a recommendation that he serve a minimum of 25 years.

The facts were as follows . . . Burke, then aged 18, shot a 63-year old criminal called Henry Botton at point blank range with a sawn-off shotgun on the doorstep of Botton's house. The prosecution's case was that Burke had done this at the request of Clarkson, who was anxious to prevent Botton from giving evidence against him.

Clarkson's defence was that he had nothing to do with the shooting at all. Burke's defence was that he had agreed to shoot Botton because of his fear that Clarkson would kill him if he did not, but when it came to the event, the gun went off accidentally and the killing therefore was unintentional and amounted to no more than manslaughter. Burke's defence of duress was only left to the jury in respect of manslaughter.

Burke's grounds of appeal are that (1) the judge was wrong in not leaving the defence of duress to the jury so far as murder was concerned, i.e., a similar submission to that contained in the first ground of appeal in the Howe and Bannister case; and (2) that the judge was wrong in directing the jury that the culpability of a secondary party can be no higher than that of the principal party, and that accordingly if they found Burke guilty of manslaughter only, then Clarkson could only be guilty at the most of manslaughter, and if they acquitted Burke on the grounds of duress, Clarkson too must be acquitted altogether.

Counsel for Burke submits that that alleged misdirection may have induced the jury to return a perverse verdict of guilty of murder against Burke when they did not believe him to be guilty, simply to ensure that they could convict Clarkson whom they no doubt believed to be the real villain. . . .

What then was the law relating to duress in murder cases which these two judges were obliged to expound?

Until 1975 there was, we think, no difficulty. *Kenny's Outlines of Criminal Law* . . . expresses the matter with his usual felicity

> "It is . . . clear that threats of the immediate infliction of death, or even of grievous bodily harm, will excuse *some* crimes that have been committed under the influence of such threats. It is impossible to say with precision for what crimes the defence will be allowed to avail. It certainly will not excuse murder.

Russell on Crime, citing *Hale's Pleas of the Crown* and *East's Pleas of the Crown*, comes to a similar conclusion.

In the light of that weight of authority it is not surprising that no one in this country seems to have advanced duress as a defence to murder over the best part of two centuries. There is one possible exception. Killing under duress per minas seems to us to differ little, if at all, in principle from killing by reason of a necessity imposed by circumstances. In each case the necessary mens rea exists in the intention to kill. In each case the wish to kill is absent. In each case the wish not to kill is overborne by the knowledge that the defendant's own death will be the inevitable or almost inevitable result of not killing.

Thus the judgment of Lord Coleridge C.J. in the famous case of *Reg.* v. *Dudley and Stephens* (1884) where the necessity was imposed by circumstances, and where the defence of necessity was indeed advanced, seems to be relevant. We cite from that judgment two passages, the first:

> "There remains to be considered the real question in the case - whether killing under the circumstances set forth in the verdict be or be not murder. The contention that it could be anything else was, to the minds of us all, both new and strange, and we stopped the Attorney-General in his negative argument in order that we might hear what could be said in support of a proposition which appeared to us to be at once dangerous, immoral, and opposed to all legal

principle and analogy."

Again, he said:

> "There are many conceivable states of things in which it might possibly be true, but if Lord Bacon meant to lay down the broad proposition that a man may save his life by killing, if necessary, an innocent and unoffending neighbour, it certainly is not law at the present day."

There is no need for us to cite further authorities. They are set out in the dissenting opinions of Lord Simon of Glaisdale in *Director of Public Prosecutions for Northern Ireland* v. *Lynch* (1975).

It is to *Lynch's* case that we now turn. In *Lynch's* case by a majority of three to two the House of Lords decided that duress was open as a defence to a person charged with murder, other than as a principal in the first degree. Of the majority Lord Morris of Borth-y-Gest and Lord Wilberforce were careful to confine their opinions to the facts of the case before them.

Lynch had been ordered by one, M., to drive M. and two others to a point where those three alighted from the car and shot a policeman. They then got back into the car and Lynch drove them to their starting point. The case against Lynch was that he had aided and abetted the killing. The defence was duress: that Lynch had believed in effect that M. would shoot him if he did not do as he was told. The judge ruled that that defence was not open to him.

The majority reached their decision on the basis that the principal in the second degree or accessory before the fact - the terms seem to be used almost interchangeably - can logically be distinguished from the principal in the first degree and that the former is entitled to rely on duress as a possible defence. The majority declined to give a ruling on the position of the principal in the first degree.

Lord Morris of Borth-y-Gest said:

> "The issue in the present case is therefore whether there is any reason why the defence of duress, which in respect of a variety of offences has been recognised as a possible defence, may not also be a possible defence on a charge of being a principal in the second degree to murder. I would confine my decision to that issue. It may be that the law must deny such a defence to an actual killer, and that the

law will not be irrational if it does so." . . . .

Lynch's appeal was accordingly allowed, but a retrial was ordered (which, although permissible by the law of Northern Ireland, is not in these circumstances permissible here) and Lynch at the second trial was again convicted.

The result of the decision of the House of Lords in that case, which is of course binding on this court as it was upon the trial judges, is that duress is open as a defence to a person who is charged with aiding and abetting a murder whether (it seems) he is present at the killing or not, provided that he did not himself do the killing. The position in law of the actual killer remains the same as it was before this decision of the House of Lords. That is to say, for the reasons already adumbrated, he does not have the defence of duress available to him.

We are reinforced in this view by the majority decision of the Judicial Committee of the Privy Council in *Abbott* v. *The Queen* (1977). This decision, although not strictly binding upon us, is of great persuasive authority. In that case the appellant had assisted in the burying alive of a mortally wounded girl at the behest of one Malik. Malik was an extremely dangerous man and the appellant contended that he was convinced that if he did not obey Malik's instructions he and/or members of his family would be killed. It was clear on the facts that the appellant was a principal in the first degree to the murder of the girl in that he took an active and indeed a leading part in the killing. The trial judge declined to leave the defence of duress to the jury. The principal ground of appeal to the Judicial Committee of the Privy Council was that the judge was wrong in that decision.

Lord Salmon, delivering the majority opinion of the Board considered the question whether *Lynch's* case (1975) could properly be regarded as any authority for the proposition advanced on behalf of the appellant that duress affords a complete defence, although the appellant was a principal in the first degree. His Lordship examined the speeches of Lords Morris of Borth-y-Gest and Wilberforce together with the speeches of the two dissenting members of the House and came to the following conclusion, at p. 764:

> "It seems to their Lordships that . . . the majority of the House was of the opinion that duress is not a defence to a charge of murder against anyone proved to have done the actual killing. However this may be, their Lordships are

clearly of the opinion that in such a case, duress, as the law now stands, affords no defence. For reasons which will presently be explained, their Lordships, whilst loyally accepting the decision in *Lynch's* case, are certainly not prepared to extend it."

In our judgment the two judges in the present cases were correct in their view as to what the law is at present and their directions to the jury accurately reflected the true position.

It is true that to allow the defence to the aider and abettor but not to the killer may lead to illogicality, as was pointed out by this court in *Reg.* v. *Graham (Paul)* (1982), where the question in issue in the instant case was not argued, but that is not to say that any illogicality should be cured by making duress available to the actual killer rather by removing it from the aider and abettor.

Assuming that a change in the law is desirable or necessary, we may perhaps be permitted to express a view. The whole matter was dealt with in extenso by Lord Salmon in his speech in *Abbott* v. *The Queen* (1977) to which reference has already been made. He dealt there with the authorities. It is unnecessary for us in the circumstances to repeat the citations which he there makes. It would moreover be impertinent for us to try to restate in different terms the contents of that speech with which we respectfully agree. Either the law should be left as it is or the defence of duress should be denied to anyone charged with murder, whether as a principal in the first degree or otherwise. It seems to us that it would be a highly dangerous relaxation in the law to allow a person who has deliberately killed, maybe a number of innocent people, to escape conviction and punishment altogether because of a fear that his own life or those of his family might be in danger if he did not; particularly so when the defence of duress is so easy to raise and may be so difficult for the prosecution to disprove beyond reasonable doubt, the facts of necessity being as a rule known only to the defendant himself. That is not to say that duress may not be taken into account in other ways, for example by the parole board.

Even if, contrary to our views, it were otherwise desirable to extend the defence of duress to the actual killer, this is surely not the moment to make any such change, when acts of terrorism are commonplace and opportunities for mass murder have never been more readily to hand.

In any event, if it is to be permitted as a defence to murder at all, duress should in our view, by analogy with provocation, only reduce the offence to manslaughter and not result in an outright acquittal. That would mean that the effect and gravity of the duress in a particular case could fairly be reflected in the sentence imposed.

We turn now to consider the second ground of appeal advanced on behalf of Burke, namely, that the judge was wrong in directing the jury that if Burke was guilty of manslaughter and not of murder, then Clarkson could be found guilty at the worst only of manslaughter.

The judge based himself on a decision of this court in *Reg.* v. *Richards* (1974) Q.B. 776. The facts in that case were that Mrs. Richards paid two men to inflict injuries on her husband which she intended should "put him in hospital for a month." The two men wounded the husband but not seriously. They were acquitted of wounding with intent but convicted of unlawful wounding. Mrs. Richards herself was convicted of wounding with intent, the jury plainly, and not surprisingly, believing that she had the necessary intent, though the two men had not.

She appealed against her conviction on the ground that she could not properly be convicted as accessory before the fact to a crime more serious than that committed by the principals in the first degree. The appeal was allowed and the conviction for unlawful wounding was substituted. The court followed a passage from *Hawkins' Pleas of the Crown*, vol. 2. c. 29, para. 15:

> "I take it to be an uncontroverted rule that [the offence of the accessory can never rise higher than that of the principal]; it seeming incongruous and absurd that he who is punished only as a partaker of the guilt of another, should be adjudged guilty of a higher crime than the other."

James L.J., delivering the judgment in *Reg.* v. *Richards*, said:

> "If there is only one offence committed, and that is the offence of unlawful wounding, then the person who has requested that offence to be committed, or advised that that offence be committed, cannot be guilty of a graver offence than that in fact which was committed."

The decision in *Reg.* v. *Richards* has been the subject of some criticism - see for example Smith and Hogan, *Criminal Law*, 5th ed. (1983).

Counsel before us posed the situation where A hands a gun to D informing him that it is loaded with blank ammunition only and telling him to go and scare X by discharging it. The ammunition is in fact live, as A knows, and X is killed. D is convicted only of manslaughter, as he might be on those facts. It would seem absurd that A should thereby escape conviction for murder.

We take the view that *Reg. v. Richards* (1974) was incorrectly decided, but it seems to us that it cannot properly be distinguished from the instant case. In those circumstances we are obliged to follow the decision until such time as it is overruled. Our liberty to depart from a precedent which we think to be erroneous is restricted, generally speaking, to cases where the departure is in favour of the appellant. . . .

In cases such as the present where an accessory before the fact has prevailed upon another to commit a criminal act, a more satisfactory rule would be to allow each to be convicted of the offence appropriate to his intention, whether or not that would involve the accessory in being convicted of a more serious offence than the principal. In our view the judge was in the circumstances right to direct the jury as he did.

We wish to add this. If we had come to the opposite conclusion, namely, that the judge should have directed the jury that it was open to them to convict Clarkson of murder and Burke of manslaughter, we should nevertheless have dismissed Burke's appeal. The suggestion that the jury may have convicted Burke of murder not because they believed him to be guilty but because they wished to ensure Clarkson's conviction, seems to us to be fanciful, to say the least.

Finally we turn to the second ground of appeal in the case of Howe and Bannister, namely, that the judge was wrong in directing the jury that there is an "objective" element in the defence of duress. The judge directed the jury on this point as follows: "The test is whether the threat was of such gravity that it might well have caused a reasonable man placed in the same situation as the defendant to act as the defendant did." And a little later on the judge put it in this way: "Would a sober person of reasonable firmness sharing the defendant's characteristics have responded to the threats by taking part in the killing . . . ?"

It seems to us that this direction was in accordance with the judgment of this court in *Reg. v. Graham (Paul)* (1982). Consequently this ground of appeal likewise fails.

In the result all these appeals are dismissed.

Appeals dismissed.

The court certified that the decision involved the following points of law of general public importance. "(1) Is duress available as a defence to a person charged with murder as a principal in the first degree (actual killer)? (2) Can one who incites or procures by duress another to kill or to be a party to a killing be convicted of murder if that other is acquitted by reason of duress? (3) Does the defence of duress fail if the prosecution prove that a person of reasonable firmness sharing the characteristics of the defendant would not have given way to the threats as did the defendant?"

B. Necessity

R. v. Dudley and Stephens
(1884) 14 Q.B.D. 273 (Q.B.D.)

[The two accused had been charged with the murder of a cabin boy. D. and S. together with the cabin boy and another had been forced to take to a lifeboat following a storm at sea. After 20 days in the boat, the last eight of which had been without food or water, desperte for survival, they killed the cabin boy and fed off his flesh and blood. Four days later they were picked up. (The jury returned a special verdict.)]

Lord Coleridge C.J. The verdict finds in terms that "if the men had not fed upon the body of the boy they would *probably* not have survived," and that "the boy being in a much weaker condition was *likely* to have died before them." They might possibly have been picked up next day by a passing ship; they might possibly not have been picked up at all; in either case it is obvious that the killing of the boy would have been an unnecessary and profitless act. It is found by the verdict that the boy was incapable of resistance, and, in fact, made none; and it is not even suggested that his death was due to any violence on his part attempted against, or even so much as feared by, those who killed him. Under these circumstances the jury say that they are ignorant whether those who killed him were guilty of murder, and have referred it to this Court to determine what is the legal consequence which follows from the facts which they have found.

. . . . . .

Now it is admitted that the deliberate killing of this unoffending and unresisting boy was clearly murder, unless the killing can be justified by some well-recognised excuse admitted by the law. It is further admitted that there was in this case no such excuse, unless the killing was justified by what has been called "necessity." But the temptation to the act which existed here was not what the law has ever called necessity. Nor is this to be regretted. Though law and morality are not the same, and many things may be immoral which are not necessarily illegal, yet the absolute divorce of law from morality would be of fatal consequence; and such divorce would follow if the temptation to murder in this case were to be held by law an absolute defence of it. It is not so. To preserve one's life is generally speaking a duty, but it may be the plainest and the highest duty to sacrifice it. War is full of instances in which it is a man's duty not to live, but to die. The duty, in case of shipwreck, of a captain to his crew, of the crew to the passengers, of soldiers to women and children, as in the noble case of the *Birkenhead*; these duties impose on men the moral necessity, not of the preservation, but of the sacrifice of their lives for others, from which in no country, least of all, it is to be hoped, in England, will men ever shrink, as indeed, they have not shrunk. It is not correct, therefore, to say that there is any absolute or unqualified necessity to preserve one's life. "Necesse est ut eam, non ut vivam," is a saying of a Roman officer quoted by Lord Bacon himself with high eulogy in the very chapter on necessity to which so much reference has been made. It would be a very easy and cheap display of commonplace learning to quote from Greek and Latin authors, from Horace, from Juvenal, from Cicero, from Euripides, passage after passage, in which the duty of dying for others has been laid down in glowing and emphatic language as resulting from the principles of heathen ethics; it is enough in a Christian country to remind ourselves of the Great Example whom we profess to follow. It is not needful to point out the awful danger of admitting the principle which has been contended for. Who is to be the judge of this sort of necessity? By what measure is the comparative value of lives to be measured? Is it to be strength, or intellect, or what? It is plain that the principle leaves to him who is to profit by it to determine the necessity which will justify him in deliberately taking another's life to save his own. In this case the weakest, the youngest, the most unresisting, was chosen. Was it more necessary to kill him than one of the grown men? The answer must be "No" –

> "So spake the Fiend, and with necessity,
> The tyrant's plea, excused his devilish deeds."

It is not suggested that in this particular case the deeds were "devilish," but it is quite plain that such a principle once admitted might be made the legal cloak for unbridled passion and atrocious crime. There is no safe path for judges to tread but to ascertain the law to the best of their ability and to declare it according to their judgment; and if in any case the law appears to be too severe on individuals, to leave it to the Sovereign to exercise that prerogative of mercy which the Constitution has intrusted to the hands fittest to dispense it.

It must not be supposed that in refusing to admit temptation to be an excuse for crime it is forgotten how terrible the temptation was; how awful the suffering; how hard in such trials to keep the judgment straight and the conduct pure. We are often compelled to set up standards we cannot reach ourselves, and to lay down rules which we could not ourselves satisfy. But a man has no right to declare temptation to be an excuse, though he might himself have yielded to it, nor allow compassion for the criminal to change or weaken in any manner the legal definition of the crime. It is therefore our duty to declare that the prisoners' act in this case was wilful murder, that the facts as stated in the verdict are no legal justification of the homicide; and to say that in our unanimous opinion the prisoners are upon this special verdict guilty of murder.

[The sentence of death was later commuted to six months' imprisonment without hard labour.]

Question

Would or should the court have taken a different line had the cabin boy consented to die or had the crew drawn lots to select the victim?

Note

In a civil action concerning the power of the chief officer of the London Fire Brigade to instruct his drivers that, with care, they might disobey a red traffic sign, Lord Denning M.R. said - in *Buckoke* v. *Greater London Council* (1971):

"During the argument I raised the question: Might not the driver of a fire engine be able to raise the defence of necessity? I put this illustration: A driver of a fire escape with ladders approaches the traffic lights. He sees 200 yards down the road a blazing house with a man at an upstairs window in extreme peril. The road is clear in all directions. At that moment the lights turn red. Is the driver to wait for 60 seconds, or more, for the lights to turn green? If the driver waits for that time, the man's life will be lost. I suggested to both counsel that the driver might be excused in crossing the lights to save the man. He might have the defence of necessity. Both counsel denied it. They would not allow him any defence in law. The circumstances went to mitigation, they said, and did not take away his guilt. If counsel are correct - and I accept that they are - nevertheless such a man should not be prosecuted.

He should be congratulated."

(But the actual controversy in the case has now been removed by a regulation which permits drivers of fire engines to treat the red light as a warning rather than a mandatory stop sign).

5. SELF DEFENCE, PREVENTION OF CRIME, DEFENCE OF PROPERTY

Criminal Law Act 1967, s.3

3. - (1) A person may use such force as is reasonable in the circumstances in the prevention of crime, or in effecting or assisting in the lawful arrest of offenders or suspected offenders or of persons unlawfully at large.

(2) Subsection (1) above shall replace the rules of the common law on the question when force used for a purpose mentioned in the subsection is justified by that purpose.

Att.-Gen. for Northern Ireland's Reference (No. 1 of 1975) *[1977] A.C. 105 (H.L.)*

[The accused had been charged with murder. He had shot the victim in the mistaken belief that the victim was a member of an illegal organisation - the I.R.A.]

Lord Diplock. [interpreting the Criminal Law Act (Northern Ireland) 1967, s. 3 which is in the same terms as the Criminal Law Act 1967, s. 3.] What amount of force is "reasonable in the circumstances" for the purpose of preventing crime is, in my view, always a question for the jury in a jury trial, never a "point of law" for the judge.

The form in which the jury would have to ask themselves the question in a trial for an offence against the person in which this defence was raised by the accused, would be: Are we satisfied that no reasonable man (a) with knowledge of such facts as were known to the accused or *reasonably* believed by him to exist (b) in the circumstances and time available to him for reflection (c) could be of opinion that the prevention of the risk of harm to which others might be exposed if the suspect were allowed to escape justified exposing the suspect to the risk of harm to him that might result from the kind of force that the accused contemplated using?

To answer this the jury would have first to decide what were the facts that did exist and were known to the accused to do so and what were mistakenly believed by the accused to be facts.

In respect of the latter the jury would have had to decide whether any *reasonable man on the material available to the accused* could have shared that belief. To select, as is done in paragraph 2(xiii) of the reference, two specific inferences of fact as to which it is said that the accused had no belief is merely to exclude them from the jury's consideration as being facts mistakenly believed by the accused to exist; but this does not preclude the jury from considering what inferences of fact a *reasonable* man would draw from the primary facts known to the accused.

The jury would have also to consider how the circumstances in which the accused had to make his decision whether or not to use force and the shortness of the time available to him for reflection, might affect the judgment of a reasonable man. In the facts that are to be assumed for the purposes of the reference there is material upon which a jury might take the view that the accused had reasonable grounds for apprehension of imminent danger to himself and other members of the patrol if the deceased were allowed to get away and join armed fellow-members of the Provisional I.R.A. who might be lurking in the neighbourhood, and that the time available to the accused to make up his mind what to do was so short that even a reasonable man could only act intuitively. This being so, the jury in approaching the final part of the question should remind themselves that the postulated balancing of risk against risk, harm against harm, by the reasonable man is not undertaken in the calm analytical atmosphere of the courtroom after counsel with the benefit of hindsight have expounded at length the reasons for and against the kind and degree of force that was used by the accused; but in the brief second or two which the accused had to decide whether to shoot or not and under all the stresses to which he was exposed.

In many cases where force is used in the prevention of crime or in effecting an arrest there is a choice as to the degree of force to use. On the facts that are to be assumed for the purposes of the reference the only options open to the accused were either to let the deceased escape or to shoot at him with a service rifle. A reasonable man would know that a bullet from a self-loading rifle if it hit a human being, at any rate at the range at which the accused fired, would be likely to kill him or to injure him seriously. So in one scale of the balance the harm to which the deceased would be exposed if the accused aimed to hit him was predictable and grave and the risk of its occurrence high. In the other scale of the balance it would be open to the jury to take the view that it would not be unreasonable to assess the kind of harm to be averted by preventing the accused's escape as even graver - the killing or wounding of members of the patrol by terrorists in ambush, and the effect of this success by members of the Provisional I.R.A. in encouraging the continuance of the armed insurrection and all the misery and destruction of life and property that terrorist activity in Northern Ireland has entailed. The jury would have to consider too what was the highest degree at which a reasonable man could have assessed the likelihood that such consequences might follow the escape of the deceased if the facts had been as the accused knew or believed them reasonably to be.

Note

The words italicised should now be read in the light of *Gladstone Williams* (see above, p. 84. It is submitted that it suffices that the accused honestly held his mistaken view. It remains, of course, the position that the amount of force he uses in the circumstances which actually exist or which he mistakenly believes to exist, must be reasonable. What if the jury reach the conclusion he was right to use some force, but not as much as he, in fact, used?

R. v. McInnes
[1971] 1 W.L.R. 1600 (C.A.)

[During the course of a fight between "skinheads" and "greasers" the accused stabbed and killed a member of the rival gang. At his trial he pleaded that it was an accident. He was convicted and in his appeal to the Court of Appeal he argued, *inter alia*, that the trial judge had not properly directed the jury on the issue of excessive force used in self defence.]

Edmund-Davies L.J. The final criticism levelled against the summing up is that the judge wrongly failed to direct the jury that, if death resulted from the use of excessive force by the accused in defending himself against the aggressiveness of the deceased, the proper verdict was one of not guilty of murder but guilty of manslaughter. Certainly no such direction was given, and the question that arises is whether its omission constitutes a defect in the summing up.

The Privy Council decision in *Palmer* v. *The Queen* (1971) provides high persuasive authority which we, for our part, unhesitatingly accept, that there is certainly *no* rule that, in every case where self-defence is left to the jury, such a direction is called for.

But where self-defence fails on the ground that the force used went clearly beyond that which was reasonable in the light of the circumstances as they reasonably appeared to the accused, is it the law accused, is it the law that the inevitable result must be that he can be convicted of manslaughter only, and not of murder? It seems that in Australia that question is answered in the affirmative . . . but not, we think, in this country. On the contrary, if a plea of self-defence fails for the reason stated, it affords the accused no protection at all. But it is important to stress that the facts upon which the plea of self-defence is unsuccessfully sought to be based may nevertheless serve the defendant in good stead. They may, for example, go to show that he may have acted under provocation or that, although acting unlawfully, he may have lacked the intent to kill or cause serious bodily harm, and in that way render the proper verdict one of manslaughter.

The court elicited from defence counsel . . . that his researches had revealed no authority for the proposition he advanced, and which was described by the Court of Criminal Appeal in *Reg.* v. *Hassin* (1963) as "a novelty in present times." For our part, we think that at least persuasive authority to the contrary is not lacking. Thus, in *Palmer* v. *The Queen* (1971) Lord Morris of Borth-y-Gest said:

"There are no prescribed words which must be employed in or adopted in a summing up. All that is needed is a clear exposition, in relation to the particular facts of the case, of the conception of necessary self-defence. If there has been no attack, then clearly there will have been no need for defence. If there has been attack so that defence is reasonably necessary it will be recognised that a person defending himself cannot weigh to a nicety the exact measure of his necessary defensive action. If a jury thought that in a moment of unexpected anguish a person attacked had only done what he honestly and instinctively thought was necessary that would be most potent evidence that only reasonable defensive action had been taken. A jury will be told that the defence of self-defence, where the evidence makes its raising possible, will only fail if the prosecution show beyond doubt that what the accused did was not by way of self-defence. But their Lordships consider, in agreement with the approach in the *De Freitas* case (1960), that if the prosecution have shown that what was done was not done in self-defence then that issue is eliminated from the case. If the jury consider that an accused acted in self-defence or if the jury are in doubt as to this then they will acquit. The defence of self-defence either succeeds so as to result in an acquittal or it is disproved, in which case as a defence it is rejected. In a homicide case the circumstances may be such that it will become an issue as to whether there was provocation so that the verdict might be one of manslaughter. Any other possible issues will remain. If in any case the view is possible that the intent necessary to constitute the crime of murder was lacking then that matter would be left to the jury."

. . . . . .

Section 3(1) of the Criminal Law Act 1967 provides that: "A person may use such force as is reasonable in the circumstances in the prevention of crime . . . ," and in our judgment the degree of force permissible in self-defence is similarly limited. Deliberate stabbing was so totally unreasonable in the circumstances of this case, even on the defendant's version, that self-defence justifying a complete acquittal was not relied upon before us, and rightly so. Despite the high esteem in which we hold our Australian brethren, we respectfully reject as far as this country is concerned the refinement sought to be introduced that, if the accused, in defending himself during a fisticuff's encounter, drew out against his opponent (who he had no reason to think was armed) the deadly weapon which he had earlier unsheathed and then, "let him have it," the jury should have been directed that, even on those facts, it was open to them to convict of manslaughter. They are, in our view, the facts of this case. It follows that in our judgment no such direction was called for.

In the result, we hold that, upon abundant evidence and following a summing up which is not open to substantial criticism, the jury arrived at a verdict which ought not to be disturbed. We accordingly dismiss this appeal.

Appeal dismissed.

Note

In *Shannon* (1980) the Court of Appeal reaffirmed the view that although self defence either succeeded or failed, juries must be directed to take account of the circumstances in which the accused had to make his decision.

Self-defence and defence of property

In the large majority of cases where the accused acts to defend himself or his property, the would be assailant will be attempting to commit a crime. Thus the situation will fall within the ambit of section 3 of the Criminal Law Act 1967. It is clear, however, that the law still recognises the existence of the common law

Defences

defences of self-defence and defence of property and from time to time (as in *Bird*, below) the court will be asked to decide whether any of the special rules relating to those defences still apply. On the whole, however, the courts are likely to try to unify all these varying defences under the principles governing section 3.

R. v. Bird
[1985] 2 All E.R. 513 (C.A.)

[B. was charged with unlawful wounding contrary to section 20 of the Offences Against the Person Act 1861. On appeal against conviction she argued that the judge was in error in directing the jury that self-defence could only be relied upon if the accused had demonstrated by her action that she did not want to fight. In the defence of self-defence at common law it was generally agreed that there was a duty to retreat first. This was stated in its modern form by Widgery L.J. in *Julien* (1969):

"The third point taken by counsel for the appellant is that the learned deputy chairman was wrong in directing the jury that before the appellant could use force in self-defence he was required to retreat. The submission here is that the obligation to retreat before using force in self-defence is an obligation which only arises in homicide cases. As the court understands it, it is submitted that if the injury results in death then the accused cannot set up self-defence except on the basis that he had retreated before he resorted to violence. On the other hand, it is said that where the injury does not result in death (as in the present case) the obligation to retreat does not arise. The sturdy submission is made that an Englishman is not bound to run away when threatened, but can stand his ground and defend himself where he is. In support of this submission no authority is quoted, save that counsel for the appellant has been at considerable length and diligence to look at the textbooks on the subject, and has demonstrated to us that the textbooks in the main do not say that a preliminary retreat is a necessary prerequisite to the use of force in self-defence. Equally, it must be said that the textbooks do not state the contrary either; and it is, of course, well known to us all that for very many years it has been common form for judges directing juries where the issue of self-defence is raised in any case (be it a homicide case or not) that the duty to retreat arises. It is not, as we understand it, the law that a person threatened must take to his heels and run in the dramatic way suggested by counsel for the appellant; but what is necessary is that he should demonstrate by his actions that he does not want to fight. He must demonstrate that he is prepared to temporise and disengage and perhaps to make some physical withdrawal; and to the extent that that is necessary as a feature of the justification of self-defence, it is true, in our opinion, whether the charge is a homicide charge or something less serious. Accordingly, we reject counsel for the appellant's third submission."]

Lord Lane C.J. The matter is dealt with accurately and helpfully in Smith and Hogan *Criminal Law* (5th edn, 1983) p. 327 as follows:

"There were formerly technical rules about the duty to retreat before using force, or at least fatal force. This is now simply a factor to be taken into account in deciding whether it was necessary to use force, and whether the force was reasonable. If the only reasonable course is to retreat, then it would appear that to stand and fight must be to use unreasonable force. There is, however, no rule of law that a person attacked is bound to run away if he can; but it has been said that - ' . . . what is necessary is that he should demonstrate by his actions that he does not want to fight. He must demonstrate that he is prepared to temporise and disengage and perhaps to make some physical withdrawal.' It is submitted that it goes too far to say that action of this kind is *necessary*. It is scarcely consistent with the rule that it is permissible to use force, not merely to counter an actual attack, but to ward off an attack honestly and reasonably believed to be imminent. A demonstration by D. [the defendant] at the time that he did not want to fight is, no doubt, the best evidence that he was acting reasonably and in good faith in self-defence; but it is no more than that. A person may in some circumstances so act without temporising, disengaging or withdrawing; and he should have a good defence."

We respectfully agree with that passage. If the defendant is proved to have been attacking or retaliating or revenging himself, then he was not truly acting in self-defence. Evidence that the defendant tried to retreat or tried to call off the fight may be a cast-iron method of casting doubt on the suggestion that he was the attacker or retaliator or the person trying to revenge himself. But it is not by any means the only method of doing that.

It seems to us therefore that in this case the trial judge (we hasten to add through no fault of his own), by using the word "necessary" as he did in the passages in the summing up to which we have referred, put too high an obligation on the appellant.

Appeal allowed.

Chapter 5

ATTEMPTS

1. THE ACTUS REUS OF ATTEMPTS

O'Brien v. Anderton
March 14, 1984 Lexis (D.C.)

Kerr L.J. This is a case stated by the Justices for the County of Greater Manchester, acting in and for the City of Manchester sitting in the Magistrates' Court at Crown Square. It concerns the conviction of the Appellant for attempted burglary on the 1st December, 1982. The charge was that he, together with another man, was guilty of an attempt to commit burglary by attempting to enter warehouse premises belonging to William O'Hanlon and Co., at 8 Tariff Street, Manchester, with intent to steal therein, contrary to Section 1(1) of the Criminal Attempts Act 1981. The Appellant consented to be tried summarily and pleaded not guilty.

I read the facts as found by the justices.

"(a) at 1.35 a.m. on 17th November, 1982 the Appellant was one of four men seen by police officers on Tariff Street, outside the premises of William O'Hanlon and Company.

"(b) No unauthorised person had any right or authority to enter or damage property in the building at 8 Tariff Street belonging to William O'Hanlon and Company.

"(c) The Appellant was standing on a plastic bread crate which was leaning against a wall underneath a broken window outside 8 Tariff Street, the ledge of the window being approximately 5 feet from the pavement.

"(d) The Appellant was looking into the premises through the broken window.

"(e) There was no evidence to suggest that the Appellant was responsible for breaking the window.

"(f) When the police officers approached the men, the Appellant jumped from the crate on to the pavement and ran in the opposite direction from the police officers.

"(g) After a brief struggle, the Appellant was apprehended by the police.

"(h) The Appellant, although being constantly abusive, made no admissions during his interviews with the police officers.

"3. It was contended by the Respondent that the Appellant was attempting to enter the premises with the intention to steal therein. 4. It was contended on behalf of the Appellant that the Respondent had adduced insufficient evidence for a finding of guilt with regard to the 'attempt' element of the charge 5. No cases were cited in argument before us, nor did we deem it necessary to seek the advice of our clerk.

"6. We were of the opinion that the Appellant's actions and the surrounding circumstances were a step towards the commission of the offence of burglary and such actions were immediately connected with that offence and if the Appellant had not been interrupted it would have resulted in the commission of the offence of burglary. Accordingly, we found the Appellant guilty."

The question for the opinion of this court is as follows: "Was there evidence sufficient to prove the offence charged, in particular was there an act or acts which showed that he was trying to commit the crime charged?"

The charge, as I have already mentioned, was under Section 1(1) of the Criminal Attempts Act 1981, to which the justices were referred. That reads as follows: "If, with intent to commit an offence to which this section applies, a person does an act which is more than merely preparatory to the commission of the offence, he is guilty of attempting to commit the offence."

Mr. Aston has submitted that the act of the Appellant was not capable, in law, of constituting an attempt of burglary because, as I understand his submission, it was not an act more than merely preparatory to the commission of the offence. The words "more than merely preparatory" have replaced the various ways of seeking to define the concept of an attempt which one finds in many earlier authorities. In my view, whether an act is more than merely preparatory to the commission of an offence must be a question of degree in the nature of a jury question. Obviously, acts which are merely preparatory, such as reconnaissance of the scene of the intended crime, cannot amount to attempts. They must be more than merely preparatory. If they go close to the actual commission of the offence, they may still form part of the acts necessary to carry out the complete offence, and may, in that sense, still be preparatory. But if they are properly to be regarded as more than merely preparatory, then they constitute an attempt.

I have already read the reasoning of the justices. The Appellant's actions and the surrounding circumstances were a step towards the commission of the offence of burglary and such actions were immediately connected with that offence. The justices went on to say that they concluded that if the Appellant had not been interrupted, it would have resulted in the commission of the offence of burglary.

The facts are wholly consistent with these conclusions. The Appellant was standing underneath a broken window of warehouse premises which was only about 5 feet above the pavement. He was standing on a plastic crate which was leaning against the wall. He was found in that position at 1.35 a.m. outside those premises. In my judgment, although the Appellant had not yet done any act connected with actual entry, what he had done, and being in the position in which he was, was something which it was perfectly open to the justices to regard as more than a merely preparatory act to the offence of burglary.

In those circumstances, I conclude that there was ample evidence to entitle the justices to regard the offence as proved and to convict the Appellant of attempted burglary. I would dismiss this appeal.

2. MENS REA

Section 1 makes it clear that this is an offence requiring proof of intention. The Act says "with intent to commit an offence." Thus if X is to be convicted of attempted rape it must be proved he intended to have intercourse with the victim knowing she did not consent. If *Prince* (above, p. 74) had been stopped before he could get away with Annie Phillips would it have been a defence that he did not know she was under 16?

3. ATTEMPTING THE IMPOSSIBLE

R. v. Shivpuri
[1986] 2 W.L.R. 988 (H.L.)

Lord Bridge of Harwich. My Lords, On 23 February 1984 the appellant was convicted at the Crown Court at Reading of two attempts to commit offences. The offences attempted were being knowingly concerned in dealing with (count 1) and in harbouring (count 2) a Class A controlled drug namely diamorphine, with intent to evade the prohibition of importation imposed by section 3(1) of the Misuse of Drugs Act 1971, contrary to section 170(1)(*b*) of the Customs and Excise Management Act 1979. On 5 November 1984 the Court of Appeal (Criminal Division) dismissed his appeals against conviction but certified that a point of law of general public importance was involved in their decision and granted leave to appeal to your Lordships' House. The certified question granted on 13 November 1984 reads:

> "Does a person commit an offence under section 1 of the Criminal Attempts Act 1981 where, if the facts were as that person believed them to be, the full offence would have been committed by him, but where on the true facts the offence which that person set out to commit was in law impossible, e.g., because the substance imported and believed to be heroin was not heroin but a harmless substance?"

The facts plainly to be inferred from the evidence, interpreted in the light of the jury's guilty verdicts, may be shortly summarised. The appellant, on a visit to India, was approached by a man named Desai, who offered to pay him £1,000 if, on his return to England, he would receive a suitcase which a courier would deliver to him containing packages of drugs which the appellant was then to distribute according to instructions he would receive. The suitcase was duly delivered to him in Cambridge. On 30 November 1982, acting on instructions, the appellant went to Southall station to deliver a package of drugs to a third party. Outside the station he and the man he had met by appointment were arrested. A package containing a powdered substance was found in the appellant's shoulder bag. At the appellant's flat in Cambridge, he produced to customs officers the suitcase from which the lining had been ripped out and the remaining packages of the same powdered substance. In answer to questions by customs officers and in a long written statement the appellant made what amounted to a full confession of having played his part, as described, as recipient and distributor of illegally imported drugs. The appellant believed the drugs to be either heroin or cannabis. In due course the powdered substance in the several packages was scientifically analysed and found not to be a controlled drug but snuff or some similar harmless vegetable matter.

[Lord Bridge then considered an entirely separate ground of appeal, which was not raised in the Court of Appeal, before turning to the certified question. This concerned the interpretation of provisions of the drugs legislation and is not relevant here.]

. . . . .

The certified question depends on the true construction of the Criminal Attempts Act 1981. That Act marked an important new departure since, by section 6, it abolished the offence of attempt at common law and substituted a new statutory code governing attempts to commit criminal offences. It was considered by your Lordships' House last year in *Anderton v. Ryan* (1985) after the decision in the Court of Appeal which is the subject of the present appeal. That might seem an appropriate starting point from which to examine the issues arising in this appeal. But your Lordships have been invited to exercise the power under the *Practice Statement* (*Judicial Precedent*) (1966) to depart from the reasoning in that decision if it proves necessary to do so in order to affirm the convictions appealed against in the instant case. I was not only a party to the decision in *Anderton v. Ryan*, I was also the author of one of the two opinions approved by the majority which must be taken to express the House's ratio. That seems to me to afford a sound reason why, on being invited to re-examine the language of the statute in its application to the facts of this appeal, I should initially seek to put out of mind what I said in *Anderton v. Ryan*. Accordingly I propose to approach the issue in the first place as an exercise in statutory construction, applying the language of the Act to the facts of the case, as if the matter were res integra. If this leads me to the conclusion that the appellant was not guilty of any attempt to commit a relevant offence, that will be the end of the matter. But if this initial exercise inclines me to reach a contrary conclusion, it will then be necessary to consider whether the precedent set by *Anderton v. Ryan* bars that conclusion or whether it can be surmounted either on the ground that the earlier decision is distinguishable or that it would be appropriate to depart from it under the Practice Statement.

[Section 1 of the Criminal Attempts Act 1981 was set out in full; see below, p. 273].

Applying this language to the facts of the case, the first question to be asked is whether the appellant intended to commit the offences of being knowingly concerned in dealing with and harbouring drugs of Class A or Class B with intent to evade the prohibition on their importation. Translated into more homely language the question may be rephrased, without in any way altering its legal significance, in the following terms: did the appellant intend to receive and store (harbour) and in due course pass on to third parties (deal with) packages of heroin or cannabis which he knew had been smuggled into England from India? The answer is plainly yes, he did. Next, did he in relation to each offence, do an act which was more than merely preparatory to the commission of the offence? The act relied on in relation to harbouring was the receipt and retention of the packages found in the lining of the suitcase. The act relied on in relation to dealing was the meeting at Southall station with the intended recipient of one of the packages. In each case the act was clearly more than preparatory to the commission of the *intended* offence; it was not and could not be more than merely preparatory to the commission of the *actual* offence, because the facts were such that the commission of the actual offence was impossible. Here then is the nub of the matter. Does the "act which is more than merely preparatory to the commission of the offence" in section 1(1) of the Act of 1981 (the actus reus of the statutory offence of attempt) require any more than an act which is more than merely preparatory to the commission of the offence which the defendant intended to commit? Section 1(2) must surely indicate a negative answer; if it were otherwise, whenever the facts were such that the commission of the actual offence was impossible, it would be impossible to prove an act more than merely preparatory to the commission of that offence and subsections (1) and (2) would contradict each other.

This very simple, perhaps over simple, analysis leads me to the provisional conclusion that the appellant was rightly convicted of the two offences of attempt with which he was charged. But can this conclusion stand with *Anderton v. Ryan*? The appellant in that case was charged with an attempt to handle stolen goods. She bought a video recorder believing it to be stolen. On the facts as they were to be assumed it was not stolen. By a majority the House decided that she was entitled to be acquitted. I have re-examined the case with care. If I could extract from the speech of Lord Roskill or from my own speech a clear and coherent principle distinguishing those cases of attempting the impossible which amount to offences under the statute from those which do not, I should have to consider carefully on which side of the line the instant case fell. But I have to confess that I can find no such principle.

Running through Lord Roskill's speech and my own in *Anderton v. Ryan* is the concept of "objectively innocent" acts which, in my speech certainly, are contrasted with "guilty acts." A few citations will make this clear. Lord Roskill said:

"My Lords, it has been strenuously and ably argued for the respondent that these provisions involve that a defendant is liable to conviction for an attempt even where his actions are innocent but he erroneously believes facts which, if true, would make those actions criminal, and further, that he is liable to such conviction whether or not in the event his intended course of action is completed."

He proceeded to reject the argument. . . . I referred to the appellant's purchase of the video recorder and said:

"Objectively considered, therefore, her purchase of the recorder was a perfectly proper commercial transaction."

A further passage from my speech proceeded, as:

"The question may be stated in abstract terms as follows. Does section 1 of the Act of 1981 create a new offence of attempt where a person embarks on and completes a course of conduct which is objectively innocent, solely on the ground that the person mistakenly believes facts which, if true, would make that course of conduct a complete crime? If the question must be answered affirmatively it requires convictions in a number of surprising cases: the classic case, put by Bramwell B. in *Reg.* v. *Collins* (1864), of the man who takes away his own umbrella from a stand, believing it not to be his own and with intent to steal it; the case of the man who has consensual intercourse with a girl over 16 believing here to be under that age; the case of the art dealer who sells a picture which he represents to be and which is in fact a genuine Picasso, but which the dealer mistakenly believes to be a fake.

The common feature of all these cases, including that under appeal, is that the mind alone is guilty, the act is innocent."

I then contrasted the case of the man who attempts to pick the empty pocket, saying:

"Putting the hand in the pocket is the guilty act, the intent to steal is the guilty mind, the offence is appropriately dealt with as an attempt, and the impossibility of committing the full offence for want of anything in the pocket to steal is declared by [subsection (2)] to be no obstacle to conviction."

If we fell into error, it is clear that our concern was to avoid convictions in situations which most people, as a matter of common sense, would not regard as involving criminality. In this connection it is to be regretted that we did not take due note of paragraph 2.97 of the Law Commission's report (Criminal Law: Attempt, and Impossibility in Relation to Attempt, Conspiracy and Incitement (1980) (Law Commission No. 102)) which preceded the enactment of the Act of 1981, which reads:

"If it is right in principle that an attempt should be chargeable even though the crime which it is sought to commit could not possibly be committed, we do not think that we should be deterred by the consideration that such a change in our law would also cover some extreme and exceptional cases in which a prosecution would be theoretically possible. An example would be where a person is offered goods at such a low price that he believes that they are stolen, when in fact they are not; if he actually purchases them, upon the principles which we have discussed he would be liable for an attempt to handle stolen goods. Another case which has been much debated is that raised in argument by Bramwell B. in *Reg.* v. *Collins* (1864). If A takes his own umbrella, mistaking it for one belonging to B and intending to steal B's umbrella, is he guilty of attempted theft? Again, on the principles which we have discussed he would in theory be guilty, but in neither case would it be realistic to suppose that a complaint would be made or that a prosecution would ensue."

The prosecution in *Anderton* v. *Ryan* itself falsified the Commission's prognosis in one of the "extreme and exceptional cases." It nevertheless probably holds good for other such cases, particularly that of the young man having sexual intercourse with a girl over 16, mistakenly believing her to be under that age, by which both Lord Roskill and I were much troubled.

However that may be, the distinction between acts which are "objectively innocent" and those which are not is an essential element in the reasoning in *Anderton* v. *Ryan* and the decision, unless it can be supported on some other ground, must stand or fall by the validity of this distinction. I am satisfied on further consideration that the concept of "objective innocence" is incapable of sensible application in relation to the law of criminal attempts. The reason for this is that any attempt to commit an offence which involves "an act which is more than merely preparatory to the commission of the offence" but for any reason fails, so that in the event no offence is committed, must *ex hypothesi*, from the point view of the criminal law, be "objectively innocent." What turns what would otherwise, from the point of view of the criminal law, be an innocent act into a crime is the intent of the actor to commit an offence. I say "from the point of view of the criminal law" because the law of tort must surely here be quite irrelevant. A puts his hand into B's pocket. Whether or not there is anything in the pocket capable of being stolen, if A intends to steal, his act is a criminal attempt; if he does not so intend, his act is innocent. A plunges a knife into a bolster in a bed. To avoid the complication of an offence of criminal damage, assume it to be A's bolster. If A believes the bolster to be his enemy B and intends to kill him, his act is an attempt to murder B; if he knows the bolster is only a bolster, his act is innocent. These considerations lead me to the conclusion that the distinction sought to be drawn in *Anderton* v. *Ryan* between innocent and guilty acts considered "objectively" and independently of the state of mind of the actor cannot be sensibly maintained.

Another conceivable ground of distinction which was to some extent canvassed in argument, both in *Anderton* v. *Ryan* and in the instant case, though no trace of it appears in the speeches in *Anderton* v. *Ryan*, is a distinction which would make guilt or innocence of the crime of attempt in a case of mistaken belief dependent on what, for want of a better phrase, I will call the defendant's dominant intention. According to the theory necessary to sustain this distinction, the appellant's dominant intention in *Anderton* v. *Ryan* was to buy a cheap video recorder; her belief that it was stolen was merely incidental. Likewise in the hypothetical case of attempted unlawful sexual intercourse, the young man's dominant intention was to have intercourse with the particular girl; his mistaken belief that she was under 16 was merely incidental. By contrast, in the instant case the appellant's dominant intention was to receive and distribute illegally imported heroin or cannabis.

Whilst I see the superficial attraction of this suggested ground of distinction, I also see formidable practical difficulties in its application. By what test is a jury to be told that a defendant's dominant intention is to be recognised and distinguished from his incidental but mistaken belief? But there is perhaps a more formidable theoretical difficulty. If this ground of distinction is relied on to support the acquittal of the appellant in *Anderton* v. *Ryan*, it can only do so on the basis that her mistaken belief that the video recorder was stolen played no significant part in her decision to buy it and therefore she may be acquitted of the intent to handle stolen goods. But this line of reasoning runs into head-on collision with section 1(3) of the Act of 1981. The theory produces a situation where, apart from the subsection, her intention would not be regarded as having amounted to any intent to commit an offence. Section 1(3)(*b*) then requires one to ask whether, if the video recorder had in fact been stolen, her intention would have been regarded as an intent to handle stolen goods. The answer must clearly be yes, it would. If she had bought the video recorder knowing it to be stolen, when in fact it was, it would have availed her nothing to say that her dominant intention was to buy a video recorder because it was cheap and that her knowledge that it was stolen was merely incidental. This seems to me fatal to the dominant intention theory.

I am thus led to the conclusion that there is no valid ground on which *Anderton* v. *Ryan* can be distinguished. I have made clear my own conviction, which as a party to the decision (and craving the indulgence of my noble and learned friends who agreed in it) I am the readier to express, that the decision was wrong. What then is to be done? If the case is indistinguishable, the application of the strict doctrine of precedent would require that the present appeal be allowed. Is it permissible to depart from precedent under the *Practice Statement (Judicial Precedent)* (1966) notwithstanding the especial need for certainty in the criminal law? The following considerations lead me to answer that question affirmatively. First, I am undeterred by the consideration that the decision in *Anderton* v. *Ryan* was so recent. The Practice Statement is an effective abandonment of our pretention to infallibility. If a serious error embodied in a decision of this House has distorted the law, the sooner it is corrected the better. Secondly, I cannot see how, in the very nature of the case, anyone could have acted in reliance on the law as propounded in *Anderton* v. *Ryan* in the belief that he was acting innocently and now find that, after all, he is to be held to have committed a criminal offence. Thirdly, to hold the House bound to follow *Anderton* v. *Ryan* because it cannot be distinguished and to allow the appeal in this case would, it seems to me, be tantamount to a declaration that the Act of 1981 left the law of criminal attempts unchanged following the decision in *Reg.* v. *Smith (Roger)* (1975). Finally, if, contrary to my present view, there is a valid ground on which it would be proper to distinguish cases similar to that considered in *Anderton* v. *Ryan*, my present opinion on that point would not foreclose the option of making such a distinction in some future case.

I cannot conclude this opinion without disclosing that I have had the advantage, since the conclusion of the argument in this appeal, of reading an article by Professor Glanville Williams entitled "*The Lords and Impossible Attempts, or Quis Custodiet Ipsos Custodes?*" [1986] C.L.J. 33. The language in which he criticises the decision in *Anderton* v. *Ryan* is not conspicuous for its moderation, but it would be foolish, on that account, not to recognise the force of the criticism and churlish not to acknowledge the assistance I have derived from it.

I would answer the certified question in the affirmative and dismiss the appeal.

[Lord Scarman delivered a speech in agreement with Lord Bridge.

The Lord Chancellor agreed with the speech of Lord Bridge, but added that had he been unable to depart from *Anderton* v. *Ryan*, he would be able to distinguish the cases.

Lord Elwyn-Jones and Lord Mackay of Clashfern agreed with the Lord Chancellor.]

Question

Albert comes from a country where sexual intercourse with a girl under the age of 21 is a criminal offence. He assumes that this is also the law in England, but nevertheless has intercourse with his 19 year old girl friend. Does he commit any criminal offence?

Chapter 6

HOMICIDE

1. STATISTICS

Criminal Statistics : England and Wales 1983
(*HMSO; Cmnd. 9349*)

4.1 Introduction. The term "homicide" covers the offences of murder, manslaughter and infanticide, for which the maximum penalty is imprisonment for life. Offences of causing death by reckless driving and certain other offences where a death has occurred are not covered here, unless they were at some stage classified by the police as homicide (in 1983 there were 189 offences of causing death by reckless driving recorded by the police which were not included in the homicide figures). In this chapter, offences are shown according to the year in which the offence was initially recorded by the police as homicide; this is not necessarily the year in which the incident which led to the death took place, nor the year in which any court decision was made (which is the year the conviction is recorded in the statistics of court proceedings).

4.2 Offences initially recorded as homicide. 553 offences were initially recorded as homicide in 1983, much lower than the numbers recorded in the peak years of 1979 (629), 1980 (621) and 1982 (618) but similar to the number in 1981. The number recorded in 1980 included nearly 100 associated with fires started deliberately which in other years has been less than 30. The number of homicides is relatively small so considerable year-to-year variation is to be expected. The total number of offences initially recorded as homicide in the ten-year period 1974 to 1983 was about 40 per cent higher than the total in the period 1964 to 1973. Over the same period the number of other "more serious offences" of violence against the person (Table 2.8) increased by the same proportion.

4.3 Outcome of offences initially recorded as homicide; offences currently recorded as homicide. Where an offence is initially recorded by the police as homicide, it remains so classified unless the police or the courts decide that no offence of homicide took place. In the period 1973-83, an average of about 12 per cent of offences initially recorded as homicide in each year were decided by the courts or the police to be a lesser offence or no offence. All other offences remain recorded as homicide even where no court decision has been or can be made. In cases where there is more than one suspect, the most serious of the possible classifications is allocated to the offence, e.g. if one suspect is found guilty of a lesser offence than homicide or of no offence and another suspect has committed suicide or died or has been found insane, the offence remains currently recorded as homicide. The number of offences initially recorded as homicide in 1983 which were currently recorded as homicide as at 1 June 1984 was 506. For 128 offences court decisions were still pending and it is estimated that a further 3 per cent of the 1983 offences currently recorded as homicide as at 1 June 1984 will subsequently be decided by the courts not to be homicide; on this assumption, the number of offences currently recorded as homicide for 1983 will become about 490, fewer than in each of the years 1979-82 but more than in earlier years (except for 1974).

4.4 Method of killing. In 1983, the proportionate use of different methods of killing was similar to the pattern in most of the previous ten years; the pattern in 1980 was different because of the exceptionally large number of homicides recorded in that year which occured in fires. In 1983, as in earlier years, the most common method of killing was a sharp instrument (about 1 in 3). In 1983, as in 1982, strangulation or asphyxiation was the method of killing in about 1 in 5 homicides; hitting, kicking etc. and a blunt instrument was the method each in about 1 in 7 homicides. The number of homicides in 1983 by shooting was 39 (1 in 13) close to the average for 1973-82.

4.5 Relationship between victim and suspect. In 1983, the pattern of relationship between victim and suspect was similar to that in most earlier years. Offences in which the victim was acquainted with the suspect accounted for about three-quarters of all offences currently recorded as homicide; in about two fifths of the offences of homicide in 1983 the victim was a member of the suspect's family or was the suspect's cohabitant or lover, similar to the proportion in 1982 but a slightly lower proportion than in earlier years. The number and proportion of victims who were sons or daughters of the suspects in 1983 were similar to the figures in 1981 and 1982 but lower than in some earlier years. The proportion of victims who were not known to the suspect in 1983 (1 in 5) was similar to the proportion in most earlier years. Three police officers were killed while on duty in 1983; all three were victims of the terrorist bomb incident in London in December. This brought the total number of police officers on duty killed over the period 1973-83 to 21.

4.6 Circumstances. As might be expected from the preponderance of victims known to or related to suspects, in 1983, as in most years, about half of the offences currently recorded as homicide were committed during quarrels or bouts of temper. In 1983, 49 homicides were associated with robbery or other incidents in furtherance of theft or gain, similar to the numbers in earlier years; the proportion (about 1 in 10) was also similar to most previous years; the victim and suspect were not known to each other in about 60 per cent of this type of homicide, as compared with about 20 per cent for all homicides. There were 14 homicides as the result of arson in 1983, fewer than in 1982 (18) and the exceptionally large number in 1980 (84), but more than in other years. Six homicides attributed to acts of terrorism were recorded following the bomb incident outside Harrods in London in December 1983, for which the Provisional IRA claimed responsibility; the victims were the three police officers referred to in paragraph 4.5 and three members of the public. This brought the total number of homicides attributed to acts of terrorism over the period 1973-83 to 90. In 1983 there were no victims of homicide while the suspects were resisting or avoiding arrest.

4.7 Age and sex of victims. In 1983, there were 10 victims of homicide per million population, a lower rate than in 1978-82, and similar to the average rate in 1973-77. Throughout the period 1973-83 it was the "under 1 year" age group which was most at risk; the rate in 1983 - 45 per million population aged under 1 year - was about the same as in 1979-82, but lower than the average of about 55 per million in 1973-78. The age group "5 and under 16" was least at risk throughout the period 1973-83 - about 2 per million population in 1983, lower than in any year in the period 1973-82. In 1983 the number of victims per million population in the age group "1 and under 5" (13 per million population) was higher than in 1973-82 (except 1979), and in the age group "70 years and over" (10 per million population) was also higher than in 1973-82 (except 1980).

4.8 Suspects of offences of homicide. A suspect is defined as (i) a person who has been arrested in respect of an offence initially classified as homicide and has been charged, though not necessarily charged at court, with homicide or (ii) a person who is suspected by the police of having committed the offence but is known to have died or committed suicide prior to arrest. More than one suspect may be tried for one offence and one suspect may be tried for more than one offence; for some offences no suspect is ever brought to trial. The number of suspects shown in this section of the chapter is therefore different from the number of offences initially recorded (i.e. victims). There were 586 suspects of the 553 offences initially recorded as homicide in 1983; about 5 per cent of the 586 suspects committed suicide or died before committal proceedings were completed, about 6 per cent. were not proceeded against, discharged as a result of the committal proceedings, convicted summarily of a lesser offence or committed for trial for a lesser offence; and about 5 per cent had not yet been the subject of committal proceedings. Of the 494 persons (84 per cent) committed for trial for homicide, 365 were tried by 1 June 1984 and 129 were still awaiting trial. The following paragraphs cover those who were tried at the Crown Court for homicide in 1983 - 296 for murder, 63 for manslaughter and 6 for infanticide.

4.9 Suspects indicted for homicide; suspects convicted of homicide. Of the 365 persons indicted before 1 June 1984 for homicides initially recorded in 1983, about 80 per cent were convicted of homicide, a lower proportion than in 1981 and 1982 (about 85 per cent), similar to the proportion in 1977-80 and slightly higher than the proportion in 1973-76 when the average was under 80 per cent. Before 1 June 1984, 296 suspects of homicides recorded in 1983 were indicted for murder and 100 of these were in the event convicted of murder and given life imprisonment. When results are known relating to the 129 suspects whose trials are pending the number is likely to increase to about 145, lower than the peak numbers in 1979, 1981 and 1982 but higher than in any other year. For 1983, 34 per cent of persons indicted for murder were convicted of murder - about the same as the average for 1979-82, and a slightly higher proportion than the average for the period 1973-78 (28 per cent); a further 23 per cent were convicted of manslaughter under section 2 of the Homicide Act 1957, where the only or principal defence was that of diminished responsibility - the same proportion as in 1982 and a slightly higher proportion than the average for 1973-81. For persons indicted for all offences of homicide and acquitted on all charges relating to the incident, the proportion for 1983 (at 1 June 1984) at 11 per cent was similar to that in 1981 and 1982, and lower than the average of about 14 per cent for the period 1973-80.

4.10 Of the 69 suspects convicted before 1 June 1984 of section 2 manslaughter for homicide offences initially recorded in 1983, 5 were sentenced to life imprisonment - the final number and proportion given life imprisonment are likely to be much lower than in the previous decade. A further 25 were sentenced to other terms of imprisonment - the final proportion for 1983 is likely to be higher than in the previous decade. For 1983, there were 26 hospital orders with restrictions on discharge under sections 37/41 of the Mental Health Act 1983 given to persons convicted of section 2 manslaughter, the proportionate use was 38 per cent for 1983, higher than the average for the period 1974-82 (about 27 per cent). In total, including hospital orders with restrictions, about 80 per cent of those convicted of section 2 manslaughter for 1983 offences were given an immediate custodial sentence, higher than the average proportion in the period 1973-82 (about 75 per cent). For 1983, 8 persons convicted of section 2 manslaughter were given a probation order, lower than the number in most years in the period 1973-82.

4.11 For 1983, of the 123 persons convicted before 1 June 1984 of manslaughter other than section 2 manslaughter, 111 were given sentences of immediate custody; the proportion given these types of sentence for 1983 (about 90 per cent) was higher than the average proportion in the period 1973-82 (about 80 per cent). For 1983, the proportionate use of other types of sentence (mainly fully suspended sentence and probation order) was correspondingly lower than in most previous years.

2. MURDER AND MANSLAUGHTER

The *actus reus* for both murder and manslaughter is the unlawful killing of a human being; death occurring within a year and a day of the injury inflicted by the accused on the victim (see *Dyson*, above, p. 33). The distinction between the two lies in the mens rea.

R. v. Moloney
[1985] 1 All E.R. 1025 (H.L.)
[See also *R. v. Nedrick*, Preface.]

[M. was charged with the murder of his stepfather, P. It was accepted by both sides that M. had shot and killed P. with a shotgun at about 4 a.m. following a party to celebrate P.'s wedding anniversary. M. and P. had both consumed much alcohol and had got into a heated discussion about M.'s future in the army. The other guests had all gone to bed by about 1 a.m. At 4 a.m. they were aroused by the sound of a gunshot. They discovered M. telephoning the police to say he had just "murdered" his stepfather. M. claimed that as the argument progressed P. challenged M. to see who could load and fire a shotgun the faster. M. had easily won and had pulled the trigger of the empty chamber, whereupon P. had taunted him by saying that he knew M. would not have the nerve to fire the gun. M. said that in his drunken state he responded by pulling the other trigger. His defence was that he in no way intended to harm, let alone kill, P.]

Lord Bridge. The judge correctly directed the jury that, in order to prove the appellant guilty of murder, "the prosecution have to prove that he intended either to kill his stepfather or to cause him some really serious bodily injury." But he had earlier given the following direction on intent:

"When the law requires that something must be proved to have been done with a particular intent, it means this: a man intends the consequences of his voluntary act (a) when he desires it to happen, whether or not he foresees that it probably will happen, and (b) when he foresees that it will probably happen, whether he desires it or not."

[The jury convicted M. of murder. His appeal was dismissed by the Court of Appeal who certified that a point of law of general public importance was involved, namely:

"Is malice aforethought in the crime of murder established by proof that when doing the act which causes the death of another the accused either: (a) intends to kill or do serious harm; or (b) foresees that death or serious harm will probably occur, whether or not he desires either of those consequences?"]

Lord Bridge. The true and only basis of the appellant's defence that he was guilty not of murder but of manslaughter was encapsulated in the two sentences in his statement: "I didn't aim the gun. I just pulled the trigger and he was dead." The appellant amplified this defence in two crucial passages in his evidence. He said: "I never deliberately aimed at him and fired at him intending to hurt him or to aim close to him intending to frighten him." A little later he said he had no idea in discharging the gun that it would injure his father: "In my state of mind I never considered that the probable consequence of what I might do might result in injury to my father. I never conceived that what I was doing might cause injury to anybody. It was just a lark."

This being the evidence, the issue for the jury was a short and simple one. If they were sure that, at the moment of pulling the trigger which discharged the live cartridge, the appellant realised that the gun was pointing straight at his stepfather's head, they were bound to convict him of murder. If, on the other hand, they thought it might be true that, in the appellant's drunken condition and in the context of this ridiculous challenge, it never entered the appellant's head when he pulled the trigger that the gun was pointing at his father, he should have been acquitted of murder and convicted of manslaughter. . . .

The fact that, when the appellant fired the gun, the gun was pointing directly at his stepfather's head at a range of about six feet was not, and could not be, disputed. The sole issue was whether, when he pressed the trigger, this fact and its inevitable consequence were present to the appellant's mind. If they were, the inference was inescapable, using words in their ordinary, everyday meaning, that he intended to kill his stepfather. The undisputed facts that the appellant loved his stepfather and that there was no premeditation or rational motivation could not, as any reasonable juror would understand, rebut this inference. If, on the other hand, as the appellant was in substance asserting, it never crossed his mind, in his more or less intoxicated condition and when suddenly confronted by his stepfather's absurd challenge, that by pulling the trigger he might injure, let alone kill, his stepfather, no question of foresight of consequences arose for consideration. Whatever his state of mind, the appellant was undoubtedly guilty of a high degree of recklessness. But, so far as I know, no one has yet suggested that recklessness can furnish the necessary element in the crime of murder.

If the jury had not demonstrated, by the question they asked after four hours of deliberation, that the issue of intent was one they did not understand, there might be room for further argument as to the outcome of this appeal. As it is, the jury's question, the terms of the judge's further direction and the jury's decision, just over an hour later, to return a unanimous verdict of guilty of murder leave me in no doubt, with every respect to the trial judge, and the Court of Appeal, that this was an unsafe and unsatisfactory verdict.

That conclusion would be sufficient to dispose of this appeal. But, since I regard it as of paramount importance to the due administration of criminal justice that the law should indicate the appropriate direction to be given as to the mental element in the crime of murder, or indeed in any crime of specific intent, in terms which will be both clear to judges and intelligible to juries, I must first examine the present state of the law on that subject, and, if I find that it leads to some confusion, I must next consider whether it is properly within the judicial function of your Lordships' House to attempt some clarification and simplification. I emphasise at the outset that this is in no sense an academic, but is essentially a practical, exercise . . . .

The golden rule should be that, when directing a jury on the mental element necessary in a crime of specific intent, the judge should avoid any elaboration or paraphrase of what is meant by intent, and leave it to the jury's good sense to decide whether the accused acted with the necessary intent, unless the judge is convinced that, on the facts and having regard to the way the case has been presented to the jury in evidence and argument, some further explanation or elaboration is strictly necessary to avoid misunderstanding. In trials for murder or wounding with intent, I find it very difficult to visualise a case where any such explanation or elaboration could be required, if the offence consisted of a direct attack on the victim with a weapon, except possibly the case where the accused shot at A and killed B, which any first year law student could explain to a jury in the simplest of terms.

I do not, of course, by what I have said in the foregoing paragraph, mean to question the necessity, which frequently arises, to explain to a jury that intention is something quite distinct from motive or desire. But this can normally be quite simply explained by reference to the case before the court or, if necessary, by some homely example. A man who, at London airport, boards a plane which he knows to be bound for Manchester, clearly intends to travel to Manchester, even though Manchester is the last place he wants to be and his motive for boarding the plane is simply to escape pursuit. The possibility that the plane may have engine trouble and be diverted to Luton does not affect the matter. By boarding the Manchester plane, the man conclusively demonstrates his intention to go there, because it is a moral certainty that that is where he will arrive.

I return to the two uncertainties noted by the Criminal Law Revision Committee in the report referred to above as arising from *Hyam* v. *DPP* which still remain unresolved. I should preface these observations by expressing my view that the differences of opinion to be found in the five speeches in *Hyam* v. *DPP* have, as I believe, caused some confusion in the law in an area where, as I have already indicated, clarity and simplicity are, in my view, of paramount importance. I believe it also follows that it is within the judicial function of your Lordships' House to lay down new guidelines which will achieve those desiderata, if we can reach broad agreement what they should be. . . .

Starting from the proposition established by *R* v. *Vickers* (1957), as modified by *DPP* v. *Smith* (1961), that the mental element in murder requires proof of an intention to kill or cause really serious injury, the first fundamental question to be answered is whether there is any rule of substantive law that foresight by the accused of one of those eventualities as a probable consequence of his voluntary act, where the probability can be defined as exceeding a certain degree, is equivalent or alternative to the necessary intention. I would answer this question in the negative. Here I derive powerful support from the speech of Lord Hailsham in *Hyam* v. *DPP* (1974), where he said:

> "I do not, therefore, consider, as was suggested in argument, that the fact that a state of affairs is correctly foreseen as a highly probable consequence of what is done is the same thing as the fact that the state of affairs is intended."

And again:

> " . . . I do not think that foresight as such of a high degree of probability is at all the same thing as intention, and, in my view, it is not foresight but intention which constitutes the mental element in murder."

The irrationality of any such rule of substantive law stems from the fact that it is impossible to define degrees of probability, in any of the infinite variety of situations arising in human affairs, in precise or scientific terms. As Lord Reid said in *Southern Portland Cement Ltd* v. *Cooper* (1974):

> "Chance probability or likelihood is always a matter of degree. It is rarely capable of precise assessment. Many different expressions are in common use. It can be said that the occurrence of a future event is very likely, rather likely, more probable than not, not unlikely, quite likely, not improbable, more than a mere possibility, etc. It is neither practicable nor reasonable to draw a line at extreme probability."

I am firmly of opinion that foresight of consequences, as an element bearing on the issue of intention in murder, or indeed any other crime of specific intent, belongs not to the substantive law but to the law of evidence. Here again I am happy to find myself aligned with Lord Hailsham in *Hyam* v. *DPP* (1974), where he said: "Knowledge or foresight is at the best material which entitles or compels a jury to draw the necessary inference as to intention." A rule of evidence which judges for more than a century found of the utmost utility in directing juries was expressed in the maxim, "A man is presumed to intend the natural and probable consequences of his acts". In *DPP* v. *Smith* (1960) your Lordships' House, by treating this rule of evidence as creating an irrebuttable presumption and thus elevating it, in effect, to the status of a rule of substantive law, predictably provoked the intervention of Parliament by s. 8 of the Criminal Justice Act 1967 to put the issue of intention back where it belonged, viz in the hands of the jury, "drawing such inferences from the evidence as appear proper in the circumstances". I do not by any means take the conjunction of the verbs "intended or foresaw" and "intend or foresee" in that section as an indication that Parliament treated them as synonymous; on the contrary, two verbs were needed to connote two different states of mind.

I think we should now no longer speak of presumptions in this context but rather of inferences. In the old presumption that a man intends the natural and probable consequences of his acts the important word is "natural". This word conveys the idea that in the ordinary course of events a certain act will lead to a certain consequence unless something unexpected supervenes to prevent it. One might almost say that, if a consequence is natural, it is really otiose to speak of it as also being probable.

Section 8 of the Criminal Justice Act 1967 leaves us at liberty to go back to the decisions before that of this House in *DPP* v. *Smith* and it is here, I believe, that we can find a sure, clear, intelligible and simple guide to the kind of direction that should be given to a jury in the exceptional case where it is necessary to give guidance how, on the evidence, they should approach the issue of intent.

I know of no clearer exposition of the law than that in the judgment of the Court of Criminal Appeal (Lord Goddard CJ, Atkinson and Cassels JJ) delivered by Lord Goddard CJ in *R. v. Steane* (1947) where he said:

> "No doubt, if the prosecution prove an act the natural consequences of which would be a certain result and no evidence or explanation is given, then a jury may, on a proper direction, find that the prisoner is guilty of doing the act with the intent alleged, but if, on the totality of the evidence, there is room for more than one view as to the intent of the prisoner, the jury should be directed that it is for the prosecution to prove the intent to a jury's satisfaction, and if, on a review of the whole evidence, they either think that the intent did not exist or they are left in doubt as to the intent, the prisoner is entitled to be acquitted."

In the rare cases in which it is necessary to direct a jury by reference to foresight of consequences, I do not believe it is necessary for the judge to do more than invite the jury to consider two questions. First, was death or really serious injury in a murder case (or whatever relevant consequence must be proved to have been intended in any other case) a natural consequence of the defendant's voluntary act? Second, did the defendant foresee that consequence as being a natural consequence of his act? The jury should then be told that if they answer Yes to both questions it is a proper inference for them to draw that he intended that consequence.

My Lords, I would answer the certified question in the negative. I would allow the appeal, set aside the verdict of murder, substitute a verdict of manslaughter and remit the case to the Court of Appeal, Criminal Division to determine the appropriate sentence. Having regard to the time the appellant has already spent in custody, the case should be listed for hearing at the earliest possible date.

Appeal allowed. Verdict of murder set aside and verdict of manslaughter substituted; case remitted to Court of Appeal, Criminal Division to determine appropriate sentence.

R. v. Hancock and Shankland
[1986] 2 W.L.R. 357 (H.L.)
[See also *R . v. Nedrick*, Preface.]

Lord Scarman. My Lords, in this case the Director of Public Prosecutions appeals against the decision of the Court of Appeal (Criminal Division) quashing the respondents' convictions of murder and substituting verdicts of manslaughter. The appeal is brought to secure a ruling from the House upon the refusal of the Court of Appeal to accept as sound the guidelines formulated by this House in a recent case in which the House gave guidance as to the direction appropriate to be given by the judge to the jury in a murder trial in which the judge considers it necessary to direct the jury upon the issue of intent by reference to foresight of consequences. The case is *Reg.* v. *Moloney* (above p. 180) and the guidance was in these terms:

> "In the rare cases in which it is necessary to direct a jury by reference to foresight of consequences, I do not believe it is necessary for the judge to do more than invite the jury to consider two questions. First, was death or really serious injury in a murder case (or whatever relevant consequence must be proved to have been intended in any other case) a natural consequence of the defendant's voluntary act? Secondly, did the defendant foresee that consequence as being a natural consequence of his act? The jury should then be told that if they answer yes to both questions it is a proper inference for them to draw that he intended that consequence."

In the present case, the trial judge having based his direction to the jury on the guidance which I have quoted, the two accused (respondents to this appeal) were convicted of murder. The Court of Appeal quashed the convictions on the ground that the judge's guidance may well have misled the jury. The court refused leave to appeal but certified the following point of general public importance:

> "Do the questions to be considered by a jury set out in the speech of Lord Bridge of Harwich in *Reg* v. *Moloney* as a model direction require amplification?"

It will be observed that the questions which it was suggested in *Moloney* that the jury should ask themselves refer to a "natural" consequence, not a "natural and probable" consequence. The Director now appeals with the leave of the House.

The appeal is of importance for two reasons. First, of course, there is the need to settle a point of difference between this House and the Court of Appeal. The *Moloney* guidance was intended to be authoritative in the sense that it was given to be followed by judges in appropriate cases, *i.e.* those "exceptional" cases, as the House thought, where the foreseeability of death or serious bodily harm may be relevant to a decision as to the intent underlying the act of violence. The House realised and declared, however, that the guidance was no part of the ratio decidendi in the case. ... The guidance was offered as an attempt in a practical way to clarify and simplify the task of the jury. It was not intended to prevent judges from expressing in other language, if they should deem it wise in a particular case, guidance designed to assist the jury to reach a conclusion on the facts in evidence. ...

The dangers inherent in general guidance for the assistance of juries in determining a question of fact lead me to the second reason for the importance of the appeal, namely that the cases to which the guidance was expressly limited by the House in *Moloney*, *i.e.* the "rare cases" in which it is necessary to direct a jury by reference to foresight of consequences, are unlikely to be so rare or so exceptional as the House believed. As the House then recognised, the guidelines as formulated are applicable to cases of any crime of specific intent, and not merely murder. But further and disturbingly, crimes of violence where the purpose is by open violence to protest, demonstrate, obstruct, or frighten are on the increase. Violence is used by some as a means of public communication. Inevitably there will be casualties: and inevitably death will on occasions result. If death results, is the perpetrator of the violent act guilty of murder? It will depend on his intent. How is the specific intent to kill or to inflict serious harm proved? Did he foresee the result of his action? Did he foresee it as probable? Did he foresee it as highly probable? If he did, is he guilty of murder? How is a jury to weigh up the evidence and reach a proper conclusion amidst these perplexities? The best guidance that can be given to a trial judge is to stick to his traditional function, *i.e.* to limit his direction to the applicable rule (or rules) of law, to emphasise the incidence and burden of proof, to remind the jury that they are the judges of fact, and against that background of law to discuss the particular questions of fact which the jury have to decide, indicating the inferences which they may draw if they think it proper from the facts which they find established. Should not appellate guidance emphasise the importance of particular facts and avoid generalisation? This is a question to be considered. The facts of this case would appear to indicate an affirmative answer.

. . . Reginald Dean Hancock and Russell Shankland were convicted of the murder of Mr. Wilkie. In the dark hours of the early morning of November 30, 1984 Mr. David Wilkie was driving his taxi along the Heads of the Valley Road. As he approached the bridge over the road at Rhymney he was killed when two lumps of concrete hit the car. The two lumps, a block and a post, had been dropped from the bridge as he approached it.

Mr. Wilkie's passenger was a miner going to work. Mr. Hancock and Mr. Shankland were miners on strike, and strongly objected to Mr. Wilkie's passenger going to work. That morning they had collected the block and the post from nearby, had brought them to the bridge under which the Heads of the Valley Road runs through a cutting, and had placed them on the parapet on the side facing towards the Rhymney roundabout. They then awaited the arrival of a convoy escorting the miner on his way to work. The convoy approached the bridge at about 5.15 a.m.: it consisted of a police motor-cycle, a police Land Rover, the taxi driven by Mr. Wilkie, and a police Sherpa van. The convoy was travelling from the Rhymney roundabout towards the bridge in the nearside lane of the carriageway. Estimates of its speed varied: it was put somewhere between 30 and 40 m.p.h. As the convoy neared the bridge, the concrete block struck the taxi's windscreen. The post struck the carriageway some 4ft. 8 ins. from the nearside verge. Before, however, the post subsided on the ground, it was hit by the taxi. The taxi skidded out of control, coming to rest on the embankment. Mr. Wilkie died from the injuries he received in the wrecking of the taxi by the two lumps of concrete.

The case for the prosecution was that the two concrete objects were either thrown from the bridge or pushed over its parapet in the path of the taxi at a time when the taxi could not avoid being struck by one or both of them. And, as the trial judge told the jury, the prosecution case could be compressed into one question and answer, the question being "what else could a person who pushed or threw such objects have intended but to cause really serious bodily harm to the occupants of the car?" The answer in the prosecution's submission was that a person acting in that way could in the circumstances have intended nothing less.

The defence was simple enough: that the two men intended to block the road, to stop the miner going to work, but not to kill or to do serious bodily harm to anyone. Hancock told Detective Chief Superintendent Caisley that he did not throw the two pieces of "masonry" over the bridge but merely "dropped" them. He told him that he dropped them on the side of the bridge "nearest to the roundabout where I could see them coming." At a later interview Hancock admitted "shoving" the block of concrete over the parapet of the bridge, but declared that he believed when he did so that he was standing "over the *middle* lane," *i.e.* not over the nearside lane, along which the convoy was moving. He said that he did not mean to do anyone damage - "just to frighten him [*i.e.* the miner going to work] more than anything." Shankland admitted that he was party to the plan to obstruct the road but denied that they intended to hurt anyone. Like Hancock, he emphasised that their plan was to drop the objects in the middle lane of the carriageway, *i.e.* clear of the lane alongside which the convoy was travelling, and that they believed that this was what they did.

Hancock and Shankland were prepared to plead guilty to manslaughter but the Crown decided to pursue the charge of murder. The issue was ultimately one of intention. Did they (or either of them) intend to kill or to cause anyone serious bodily harm?

The case called for a careful direction by judge to jury as to the state of mind required by law to be proved to their satisfaction before they could return a verdict of murder. The jury would also want his help in weighing up the evidence. The judge's direction as to the intention required by law was impeccable. He said:

> "If the prosecution has made you satisfied so as to be sure that Dean Hancock and Russell Shankland agreed that they would, in concert, push or throw missiles from the bridge, each having the intention either to kill or to cause really serious injury, then you will find each of them guilty of murder as the block was thrown or pushed by Dean Hancock in pursuance of the agreement."

When he came to help them on the facts, he offered guidance

along the *Moloney* lines:

> "You may think that critical to the resolution of this case
> is the question of intent. In determining whether a person
> intended to kill or to cause really serious injury, you must
> have regard to all of the evidence which has been put before
> you, and draw from it such inferences as to you seem
> proper and appropriate. You may or may not, for the
> purpose of considering what inferences to draw, find it
> helpful to ask: Was death or serious injury a natural
> consequence of what was done? Did a defendant foresee
> that consequence as a natural consequence? That is a
> possible question which you may care to ask yourselves. If
> you find yourselves not satisfied so as to be sure that there
> was an intent to kill or to cause really serious injury, then it
> is open to you to return a verdict of not guilty of murder,
> but guilty of manslaughter."

The jury was out for five hours. When they returned they told
the judge that they had failed to reach agreement. The judge
now gave them the option of a majority verdict. A few minutes
later he received a note from the jury in these terms:

> "Your Lordship,
> "With respect, the jury has discussed at great length the
> factual aspects of this case and feel, under the
> circumstances, confident in dealing with this matter.
> However, the precise legal definitions regarding the
> committing of murder and manslaughter are causing
> dissent because of lack of knowledge, particularly with
> regard to intent and foreseeable consequences."

The jury were plainly perplexed. The judge gave them a
further direction but did not go beyond what he had already
said in summing up. If they were puzzled by the way in which
the judge had then dealt with the issue of intent, the second
direction would not have helped them. Their problem was how
to relate foresight to intention – a problem which they did not
find solved by asking themselves the two questions relating to
natural consequences and foresight which the judge had put to
them.

In the Court of Appeal Lord Lane C.J. delivered the
judgment of the court. The court found itself driven to the
conclusion that the use by the judge of the *Moloney* guidelines

may have misled the jury. The guidelines offered the jury no assistance as to the relevance or weight of the probability factor in determining whether they should, or could properly, infer from foresight of a consequence (in this case, of course, death or serious bodily harm) the intent to bring about that consequence. This was, in the court's view, a particularly serious omission because the case law, as Lord Bridge of Harwich in *Moloney* had recognised, indicated "that the probability of the consequence taken to have been foreseen must be little short of overwhelming before it will suffice to establish the necessary intent." In the court's view the judge's failure to explain the factor of probability was because he faithfully followed *Moloney*: "[he] was unwittingly led into misdirecting the jury by reason of the way in which the guidelines in *Moloney* were expressed:"

The question for the House is, therefore, whether the *Moloney* guidelines are sound. In *Moloney's* case the ratio decidendi was that the judge never properly put to the jury the defence, namely that the accused was unaware that the gun was pointing at his stepfather. The House, however, held it necessary in view of the history of confusion in this branch of the law to attempt to clarify the law relating to the establishment of the mental element necessary to constitute the crime of murder and to lay down guidelines for assisting juries to determine in what circumstances it is proper to infer intent from foresight. The House certainly clarified the law. First, the House cleared away the confusions which had obscured the law during the last 25 years laying down authoritatively that the mental element in murder is a specific intent, the intent to kill or to inflict serious bodily harm. Nothing less suffices: and the jury must be sure that the intent existed when the act was done which resulted in death before they can return a verdict of murder.

Secondly, the House made it absolutely clear that foresight of consequences is no more than evidence of the existence of the intent; it must be considered, and its weight assessed, together with all the evidence in the case. Foresight does not necessarily imply the existence of intention, though it may be a fact from which when considered with all the other evidence a jury may think it right to infer the necessary intent. Lord Hailsham of St. Marylebone L.C. put the point succinctly and powerfully in his speech in *Reg.* v. *Moloney*:

"I conclude with the pious hope that your Lordships will

not again have to decide that foresight and foreseeability are not the same thing as intention although either may give rise to an irresistible inference of such, and that matters which are essentially to be treated as matters of inference for a jury as to a subjective state of mind will not once again be erected into a legal presumption. They should remain, what they always should have been, part of the law of evidence and inference to be left to the jury after a proper direction as to their weight, and not part of the substantive law."

Thirdly, the House emphasised that the probability of the result of an act is an important matter for the jury to consider and can be critical in their determining whether the result was intended.

These three propositions were made abundantly clear by Lord Bridge of Harwich. His was the leading speech and received the assent of their other Lordships, Lord Hailsham of St. Marylebone L.C., Lord Fraser of Tullybelton. Lord Edmund-Davies, and Lord Keith of Kinkel. His speech has laid to rest ghosts which had haunted the case law ever since the unhappy decision of your Lordships' House in *Reg.* v. *Smith* (1961) and which were given fresh vigour by the interpretation put by some upon the speeches of members of this House in *Reg.* v. *Hyam* (1975).

It is only when Lord Bridge of Harwich turned to the task of formulating guidelines that difficulty arises. It is said by the Court of Appeal that the guidelines by omitting any express reference to probability are ambiguous and may well lead a jury to a wrong conclusion. The omission was deliberate. Lord Bridge omitted the adjective "probable" from the time-honoured formula "foresight of the natural and probable consequences of his acts" because he thought that "if a consequence is natural, it is really otiose to speak of it as also being probable." But is it?

Lord Bridge of Harwich did not deny the importance of probability. He put it thus;

"But looking on their facts at the decided cases where a crime of specific intent was under consideration, including *Reg.* v. *Hyam* (1975) A.C. 55 itself, they suggest to me that the probability of the consequence taken to have been foreseen must be little short of overwhelming before it will suffice to establish the necessary intent."

In his discussion of the relationship between foresight and intention, Lord Bridge of Harwich reviewed the case law since the passing of the Homicide Act 1957 and concluded, at p. 928:

> "foresight of consequences, as an element bearing on the issue of intention in murder, or indeed any other crime of specific intent, belongs, not to the substantive law, but to the law of evidence."

He referred to the rule of evidence that a man is presumed to intend the natural and probable consequences of his acts, and went on to observe that the House of Lords in *Smith's* case (1961) had treated the presumption as irrebuttable, but that Parliament intervened by section 8 of the Criminal Justice Act 1967 to return the law to the path from which it had been diverted, leaving the presumption as no more than an inference open to the jury to draw if in all the circumstances it appears to them proper to draw it.

Yet he omitted any reference in his guidelines to probability. He did so because he included probability in the meaning which he attributed to "natural." My Lords, I very much doubt whether a jury without further explanation would think that "probable" added nothing to "natural." I agree with the Court of Appeal that the probability of a consequence is a factor of sufficient importance to be drawn specifically to the attention of the jury and to be explained. In a murder case where it is necessary to direct a jury on the issue of intent by reference to foresight of consequences the probability of death or serious injury resulting from the act done may be critically important. Its importance will depend on the degree of probability: if the likelihood that death or serious injury will result is high, the probability of that result may, as Lord Bridge of Harwich noted and the Lord Chief Justice emphasised, be seen as overwhelming evidence of the existence of the intent to kill or injure. Failure to explain the relevance of probability may, therefore, mislead a jury into thinking that it is of little or no importance and into concentrating exclusively on the causal link between the act and its consequence. In framing his guidelines Lord Bridge of Harwich emphasised that he did not believe it necessary to do more than to invite the jury to consider his two questions. Neither question makes any reference (beyond the use of the word "natural") to probability. I am not surprised that when in this case the judge faithfully followed this guidance the jury found themselves perplexed and unsure. In my judgment, therefore, the *Moloney* guidelines as they stand are unsafe and misleading. They require a reference to probability. They also require an explanation that the greater the probability of a consequence the more likely it is that the consequence was foreseen and that if that consequence was foreseen the greater the probability is that that consequence was also intended. But juries also require to be reminded that the decision is theirs to be reached upon a consideration of all the evidence.

Accordingly, I accept the view of the Court of Appeal that the *Moloney* guidelines are defective. I am, however, not persuaded that guidelines of general application, albeit within a limited class of case, are wise or desirable. Lord Lane C.J. formulated in this case guidelines for the assistance of juries but for the reason which follows, I would not advise their use by trial judges when summing up to a jury.

I fear that their elaborate structure may well create difficulty. Juries are not chosen for their understanding of a logical and phased process leading by question and answer to a conclusion but are expected to exercise practical common sense. They want help on the practical problems encountered in evaluating the evidence of a particular case and reaching a conclusion. It is better, I suggest, notwithstanding my respect for the comprehensive formulation of the Court of Appeal's guidelines, that the trial judge should follow the traditional course of a summing up. He must explain the nature of the offence charged, give directions as to the law applicable to the particular facts of the case, explain the incidence and burden of proof, put both sides' cases making especially sure that the defence is put; he should offer help in understanding and weighing up all the evidence and should make certain that the jury understand that whereas the law is for him the facts are for them to decide. Guidelines, if given, are not to be treated as rules of law but as a guide indicating the sort of approach the jury may properly adopt to the evidence when coming to their decision on the facts.

In a case where foresight of a consequence is part of the evidence supporting a prosecution submission that the accused intended the consequence, the judge, if he thinks some general observations would help the jury, could well, having in mind section 8 of the Criminal Justice Act 1967, emphasise that the probability, however high, of a consequence is only a factor, though it may in some cases be a very significant factor, to be considered with all the other evidence in determining whether the accused intended to bring it about. The distinction between the offence and the evidence relied on to prove it is vital. Lord Bridge's speech in *Moloney* made the distinction crystal clear: it would be a disservice to the law to allow his guidelines to mislead a jury into overlooking it.

For these reasons I would hold that the *Moloney* guidelines are defective and should not be used as they stand without further explanation. The laying down of guidelines for use in directing juries in cases of complexity is a function which can be usefully exercised by the Court of Appeal. But it should be done sparingly, and limited to cases of real difficulty. If it is done, the guidelines should avoid generalisation so far as is possible and encourage the jury to exercise their common sense in reaching what is their decision on the facts. Guidelines are not rules of law: judges should not think that they must use them. A judge's duty is to direct the jury in law and to help them upon the particular facts of the case.

Accordingly, I would answer the certified question in the affirmative and would dismiss the appeal. I would propose that the costs of all parties be paid out of central funds.

Appeal dismissed.

3. VOLUNTARY MANSLAUGHTER AND PROVOCATION

D.P.P. v. Camplin
[1978] A.C. 705 (H.L.)

[C., a 15 year old boy, was charged with the murder of K. At his trial C. alleged that K. had forcibly buggered him and had then laughed at him, whereupon C. hit him over the head with a heavy chapati pan. The prosecution appealed to the House of Lords against the decision of the Court of Appeal to substitute a verdict of manslaughter for that of murder on the basis that C. had been provoked.]

Lord Diplock. The point of law of general public importance involved in the case has been certified as being:

"Whether, on the prosecution for murder of a boy of 15, where the issue of provocation arises, the jury should be directed to consider the question, under s. 3 of the Homicide Act 1957, whether the provocation was enough to make a reasonable man do as he did by reference to a 'reasonable adult' or by reference to a 'reasonable boy of 15'."

My Lords, the doctrine of provocation in crimes of homicide

has always represented an anomaly in English law. In crimes of violence which result in injury short of death, the fact that the act of violence was committed under provocation, which has caused the accused to lose his self-control, does not affect the nature of the offence of which he is guilty: it is merely a matter to be taken into consideration in determining the penalty which it is appropriate to impose: whereas in homicide provocation effects a change in the offence itself from murder, for which the penalty is fixed by law (formerly death and now imprisonment for life), to the lessor offence of manslaughter, for which the penalty is in the discretion of the judge.

[Lord Diplock then reviewed the history of provocation showing how until 1957 the conduct of the deceased had to be of such a kind as was capable in law of constituting provocation and that this was a question of law for the judge. This meant that a trial judge could withdraw the issue of provocation from the jury on the basis that a reasonable man would not have reacted as the accused did. For example reasonable men were not provoked by words alone; they did not possess short tempers nor unusual characteristics; when provoked they tempered their reaction in proportion to the degree of provocation offered. He continued:]

My Lords, this was the state of law when *Bedder* (1954) fell to be considered by this House. The accused had killed a prostitute. He was sexually impotent. According to his evidence he had tried to have sexual intercourse with her and failed. She taunted him with his failure and tried to get away from his grasp. In the course of her attempts to do so she slapped him in the face, punched him in the stomach and kicked him in the groin, whereupon he took a knife out of his pocket and stabbed her twice and caused her death. The struggle that led to her death thus started because the deceased taunted the accused with his physical infirmity; but in the state of the law as it then was, taunts unaccompanied by any physical violence did not constitute provocation. The taunts were followed by violence on the part of the deceased in the course of her attempt to get away from the accused, and it may be that this subsequent violence would have a greater effect on the self-control of an impotent man already enraged by the taunts than it would have had on a person conscious of possessing normal physical attributes. So there might be some justification for the judge to instruct the jury to ignore the fact that the accused was impotent when they were considering whether the deceased's conduct amounted to such provocation as would cause a reasonable or ordinary person to lose his self-control. This indeed appears to have been the ground on which the Court of Criminal Appeal had approved the summing-up when they said:

" . . . no distinction is to be made in the case of a person who, though it may not be a matter of temperament is physically impotent, is conscious of that impotence, *and therefore mentally liable to be more excited unduly* if he is 'twitted' or attacked on the subject of that particular infirmity."

This statement, for which I have myself supplied the emphasis, was approved by Lord Simonds L.C. speaking on behalf of all the members of this House who sat on the appeal; but he also went on to lay down the broader proposition that:

"It would be plainly illogical not to recognise an unusually excitable or pugnacious temperament in the accused as a matter to be taken into account but yet to recognise for that purpose some unusual physical characteristic, be it impotence or another."

Section 3 of the 1957 Act is in the following terms:

"Where on a charge of murder there is evidence on which the jury can find that the person charged was provoked (whether by things done or by things said or by both together) to lose his self-control, the question whether the provocation was enough to make a reasonable man do as he did shall be left to be determined by the jury; and in determining that question the jury shall take into account everything both done and said according to the effect which, in their opinion, it would have on a reasonable man."

My Lords, this section was intended to mitigate in some degree the harshness of the common law of provocation as it had been developed by recent decisions in this House. It recognises and retains the dual test: the provocation must not only have caused the accused to lose his self-control but also be such as might cause a reasonable man to react to it as the accused did. Nevertheless it brings about two important changes in the law. The first is it abolishes all previous rules of law as to what can or cannot amount to provocation and in particular the rule of law that words unaccompanied by violence could not do so. Secondly it makes it clear that if there was any evidence that the accused himself at the time of the act which caused the death in fact lost his self-control in consequence of some provocation however slight it might appear to the judge, he was bound to leave to the jury the question, which is one of opinion not of law, whether a reasonable man might have reacted to that provocation as the accused did.

I agree with my noble and learned friend, Lord Simon of Glaisdale, that since this question is one for the opinion of the jury the evidence of witnesses as to how they think a reasonable man would react to the provocation is not admissible.

The public policy that underlay the adoption of the "reasonable man" test in the common law doctrine of provocation was to reduce the incidence of fatal violence by preventing a person relying on his own exceptional pugnacity or excitability as an excuse for loss of self-control. The rationale of the test may not be easy to reconcile in logic with more universal propositions as to the mental element in crime. Nevertheless it has been preserved by the 1957 Act but falls to be applied now in the context of a law of provocation that is significantly different from what it was before the Act was passed.

Although it is now for the jury to apply the "reasonable man" test, it still remains for the judge to direct them what, in the new context of the section, is the meaning of this apparently inapt expression, since powers of ratiocination bear no obvious relationships to powers of self-control. Apart from this the judge is entitled, if he thinks it helpful, to suggest considerations which may influence the jury in forming their own opinions as to whether the test is satisfied; but he should make it clear that these are not instructions which they are required to follow; it is for them and no one else to decide what weight, if any, ought to be given to them.

As I have already pointed out, for the purposes of the law of provocation the "reasonable man" has never been confined to the adult male. It means an ordinary person of either sex, not exceptionally excitable or pugnacious, but possessed of such powers of self-control as everyone is entitled to expect that his fellow citizens will exercise in society as it is today. A crucial factor in the defence of provocation from earliest times has been the relationship between the gravity of provocation and the way in which the accused retaliated, both being judged by the social standards of the day. When Hale was writing in the 17th century pulling a man's nose was thought to justify retaliation with a sword; when *Mancini* was decided by this

House, a blow with a fist would not justify retaliation with a deadly weapon. But so long as words unaccompanied by violence could not in common law amount to provocation the relevant proportionality between provocation and retaliation was primarily one of degrees of violence. Words spoken to the accused before the violence started were not normally to be included in the proportion sum. But now that the law has been changed so as to permit of words being treated as provocation, even though unaccompanied by any other acts, the gravity of verbal provocation may well depend on the particular characteristics or circumstances of the person to whom a taunt or insult is addressed. To taunt a person because of his race, his physical infirmities or some shameful incident in his past may well be considered by the jury to be more offensive to the person addressed, however equable his temperament, if the facts on which the taunt is founded are true than it would be if they were not. It would stultify much of the mitigation of the previous harshness of the common law in ruling out verbal provocation as capable of reducing murder to manslaughter if the jury could not take into consideration all those factors which in their opinion would affect the gravity of taunts and insults when applied to the person to whom they are addressed. So to this extent at any rate the unqualified proposition accepted by this House in *Bedder* that for the purposes of the "reasonable man" test any unusual physical characteristics of the accused must be ignored requires revision as a result of the passing of the 1957 Act.

That he was only 15 years of age at the time of the killing is the relevant characteristic of the accused in the instant case. It is a characteristic which may have its effects on temperament as well as physique. If the jury think that the same power of self-control is not to be expected in an ordinary, average or normal boy of 15 as in an older person, are they to treat the lesser powers of self-control possessed by an ordinary, average or normal boy of 15 as the standard of self-control with which the conduct of the accused is to be compared?

It may be conceded that in strict logic there is a transition between treating age as a characteristic that may be taken into account in assessing the gravity of the provocation addressed to the accused and treating it as a characteristic to be taken into account in determining what is the degree of self-control to be expected of the ordinary person with whom the accused's conduct is to be compared. But to require old heads on young shoulders is inconsistent with the law's compassion of human infirmity to which Sir Michael Foster ascribed the doctrine of provocation more than two centuries ago. The distinction as to the purpose for which it is legitimate to take the age of the accused into account involves considerations of too great nicety to warrant a place in deciding a matter of opinion, which is no longer one to be decided by a judge trained in logical reasoning but by a jury drawing on their experience of how ordinary human beings behave in real life.

There is no direct authority prior to the Act that states expressly that the age of the accused could not be taken into account in determining the standard of self-control for the purposes of the reasonable man test, unless this is implicit in the reasoning of Lord Simonds LC in *Bedder*. The Court of Appeal distinguished the instant case from that of *Bedder* on the ground that what it was there said must be ignored was an unusual characteristic that distinguished the accused from ordinary normal persons, whereas nothing could be more ordinary or normal than to be aged 15. The reasoning in *Bedder* would, I think, permit of this distinction between normal and abnormal characteristics, which may affect the powers of self-control of the accused; but for reasons that I have already mentioned the proposition stated in *Bedder* requires qualification as a consequence of changes in the law affected by the 1957 Act. To try to salve what can remain of it without conflict with the Act could in my view only lead to unnecessary and unsatisfactory complexity in a question which has now become a question for the jury alone. In my view *Bedder*, like *Mancini* and *Holmes*, ought no longer to be treated as an authority on the law of provocation.

In my opinion a proper direction to a jury on the question left to their exclusive determination by s. 3 of the 1957 Act would be on the following lines. The judge should state what the question is, using the very terms of the section. He should then explain to them that the reasonable man referred to in the question is a person having the power of self-control to be expected of an ordinary person of the sex and age of the accused, but in other respects sharing such of the accused's characteristics as they think would affect the gravity of the provocation to him, and that the question is not merely whether such a person would in like circumstances be provoked to lose his self-control but also would react to the provocation as the accused did.

I accordingly agree with the Court of Appeal that the judge ought not to have instructed the jury to pay no account to the age of the accused even though they themselves might be of opinion that the degree of self-control to be expected in a boy of that age was less than in an adult. So to direct them was to impose a fetter on the right and duty of the jury which the 1957 Act accords to them to act on their own opinion on the matter.

I would dismiss this appeal.

Note

In *Newell* (1980) the Court of Appeal held that the court may only use a "characteristic" to distinguish the accused from ordinary men if that characteristic possesses a sufficient degree of permanency and if the provocative action was directed against that characteristic. This was certainly the case in *Bedder* but does it explain the approach adopted in *Camplin*? The Court may not take account of the fact that the accused was unduly short tempered or drunk.

4. INVOLUNTARY MANSLAUGHTER

A. Gross Negligence Manslaughter

R. v. Bateman
(1925) 19 Cr.App.R. 8. (C.C.A.)

[B. had been charged with manslaughter following his treatment of a woman patient during and after childbirth.]

Lord Hewart C.J. In expounding the law to juries on the trial of indictments for manslaughter by negligence, judges have often referred to the distinction between civil and criminal liability for death by negligence. If A has caused the death of B by alleged negligence, then, in order to establish civil liability, the plaintiff must prove (in addition to pecuniary loss caused by death) that A owed a duty to B to take care, that that duty was not discharged, and that the default caused the death of B. To convict A of manslaughter, the prosecution must prove the three things above mentioned and must satisfy the jury, in addition, that A's negligence amounted to a crime. In the civil action, if it is proved that A fell short of the standard of reasonable care required by law, it matters not how far he fell short of that standard. The extent of his liability depends not on the degree of negligence, but on the amount of the damage done. In a criminal court, on the contrary, the amount and degree of negligence are the determining question. There must be a mens rea.

... In explaining to juries the test which they should apply to determine whether the negligence, in the particular case, amounted or did not amount to a crime, judges have used many epithets, such as "culpable," "criminal," "gross," "wicked," "clear," "complete." But whatever epithet be used, and whether an epithet be used or not, in order to establish criminal liability the facts must be such that, in the opinion of the jury, the negligence of the accused went beyond a mere matter of compensation between subjects and showed such disregard for the life and safety of others as to amount to a crime against the state and conduct deserving punishment. . . .

Andrews v. D.P.P.
[*1937*] *A.C. 576 (H.L.*)

[The following is a passage from the speeches in the House of Lords following the conviction for manslaughter of a motorist whose dangerous driving had resulted in the death of a pedestrian. After considering the above passage from *Bateman*, Lord Atkin continued:

Lord Atkin. Here again I think with respect that the expressions used are not, indeed they probably were not intended to be, a precise definition of the crime. I do not myself find the connotations of *mens rea* helpful in distinguishing between degrees of negligence, nor do the ideas of crime and punishment in themselves carry a jury much further in deciding whether in a particular case the degree of negligence shown is a crime and deserves punishment. But the substance of the judgment is most valuable, and in my opinion is correct. In practice it has generally been adopted by judges in charging juries in all cases of manslaughter by negligence, whether in driving vehicles or otherwise. The principle to be observed is that cases of manslaughter in driving motor cars are but instances of a general rule applicable to all charges of homicide by negligence. Simple lack of care such as will constitute civil liability is not enough: for purposes of the criminal law there are degrees of negligence; and a very high degree of negligence is required to be proved before the felony is established. Probably of all the epithets than can be applied, "reckless" most nearly covers the case. It is difficult to visualize a case of death caused by reckless driving in the connotation of that term in ordinary speech which would not justify a conviction for manslaughter; but it is probably not all-embracing, for "reckless" suggests an indifference to risk whereas the accused may have appreciated the risk and intended to avoid it and yet shown such a high degree of negligence in the means adopted to avoid the risk as would justify a conviction. If the principle of *Bateman's Case* is observed it will appear that the law of manslaughter has not changed by the introduction of motor vehicles on the road. Death caused by their negligent driving, though unhappily much more frequent, is to be treated in law as death caused by any other form of negligence; and juries should be directed accordingly.

B. *Constructive Manslaughter*

D.P.P. v. Newbury
[*1977*] *A.C. 500* (*H.L.*)

[Two boys (aged 15) pushed a piece of paving stone off a railway bridge into the path of an oncoming train. The guard in the train was killed and the boys were tried for and convicted of manslaughter. The House of Lords was asked whether an accused could be properly convicted of manslaughter, when his mind is not affected by drink or drugs, if he did not forsee that his act might cause harm to another.]

Lord Salmon. ... The learned trial judge did not direct the jury that they should acquit the appellants unless they were satisfied beyond a reasonable doubt that the appellants had foreseen that they might cause harm to someone by pushing the piece of paving stone off the parapet into the path of the approaching train. In my view the learned trial judge was quite right not to give such a direction to the jury. The direction which he gave is completely in accordance with established law, which, possibly with one exception to which I shall presently refer, has never been challenged. In *R.* v. *Larkin* (1942), Humphreys J. said:

"Where the act which a person is engaged in performing is unlawful, then if at the same time it is a dangerous act, that is, an act which is likely to injure another person, and quite inadvertently the doer of the act causes death of that other person by that act then he is guilty of manslaughter."

I agree entirely with Lawton LJ. that that is an admirably clear statement of the law which has been applied many times. It makes it plain (a) that an accused is guilty of manslaughter if it is proved that he intentionally did an act which was unlawful and dangerous and that that act inadvertently caused death and (b) that it is unnecessary to prove that the accused knew that the act was unlawful or dangerous. This is one of the reasons why cases of manslaughter vary so infinitely in their gravity.

They may amount to little more than pure inadvertence and sometimes to little less than murder.

I am sure that in *R.* v. *Church* (1966) Edmund-Davies J. in giving the judgment of the court, did not intend to differ from or qualifying anything which had been said in *R.* v. *Larkin*, (1942). Indeed he was restating the principle laid down in that case by illustrating the sense in which the word "dangerous" should be understood. Edmund-Davies J. said, at p. 70:

> "For such a verdict '(guilty of manslaughter)' inexorably to follow, the unlawful act must be such as all sober and reasonable people would inevitably recognise must subject the other person to, at least, the risk of some harm resulting therefrom, albeit not serious harm."

The test is still the objective test. In judging whether the act was dangerous the test is not did the accused recognise that it was dangerous but would all sober and reasonable people recognise its danger.

Notes

1. In many cases the jury will be asked to return a verdict of manslaughter based either on gross negligence or on the unlawful act doctrine; see *eg Lamb* (1967).

2. In order to form the basis of constructive manslaughter the unlawful act referred to in the above passage:

   (a) cannot be a failure to act; *Lowe* (1973);
   (b) must be an act which is unlawful in itself (such as an assault) and not a lawful act which has become unlawful because of the negligent way in which it was performed; *Andrews* v. *DPP* (1937);
   (c) must be an act which is likely to cause some physical harm and not just emotional disturbance; *Dawson* (1985).

C. Causing Death by Reckless Driving and Manslaughter

(1) Causing death by reckless driving (Road Traffic Act 1972, s.1)

The prosecution must establish (i) that the accused was driving recklessly and (ii) that the reckless nature of the driving caused the death of another. What is meant by reckless driving?

R. v. Lawrence
[1982] A.C. 510 (H.L.)

Lord Diplock. In my view, an appropriate instruction to the jury on what is meant by driving recklessly would be that they must be satisfied of two things: first, that the defendant was in fact driving the vehicle in such a manner as to create an obvious and serious risk of causing physical injury to some other person who might happen to be using the road or of doing substantial damage to property; and, second, that in driving in that manner the defendant did so without having given any thought to the possibility of there being any such risk or, having recognised that there was some risk involved, had none the less gone on to take it. It is for the jury to decide whether the risk created by the manner in which the vehicle was being driven was both obvious and serious and, in deciding this, they may apply the standard of the ordinary prudent motorist as represented by themselves. If satisfied that an obvious and serious risk was created by the manner of the defendant's driving, the jury are entitled to infer that he was in one or other of the states of mind required to constitute the offence and will probably do so; but regard must be given to any explanation he gives as to his state of mind which may displace the inference.

(2) Causing death by reckless driving or manslaughter?

R. v. Seymour
(1983) 77 Cr.App. R. 215 (H.L.)

[S. was charged with (motor) manslaughter following an incident in which he had crushed a woman between two vehicles. He had been prepared to plead guilty to causing death by reckless driving, but the prosecution were unwilling to accept this plea due to the seriousness of the allegations. Lord Roskill in the House of Lords expressly approved the following direction by the trial judge to the jury.]

Lord Roskill. The second question you have to decide: was the driving that caused those injuries reckless? If so, then it is manslaughter. If you are not satisfied that it was reckless, then the verdict is not guilty. To amount to reckless driving mere negligence is not enough. His conduct must go beyond the question of compensation between citizens and amount to, in your view, criminal conduct requiring punishment. You have to be satisfied on the question of recklessness that he drove in such a manner as to create an obvious and serious risk of causing physical harm to some other person who might happen to be using the road at the time. . . . Once you are satisfied that the manner of his driving was such as to create an obvious and serious risk of causing physical harm to a person using the road at the time, you also have to be satisfied that driving in that manner he did so without having given any thought to the possibility of there being any such risk, or alternatively, having recognised that there was some risk involved, none the less went on to take it; in other words, he was reckless. He reckoned not of the consequences. In determining the quality of his driving, you apply the standards of the ordinary reasonable motorist. You, of course, take into account all the evidence including his explanation.

Notes

Before *Seymour* the law appeared to recognise the following categories of manslaughter:

(i) Gross negligence. Here the prosecution had to prove that the accused had behaved in a highly negligent fashion which was likely (in the eyes of reasonable people) to cause death (or possibly really serious bodily harm).

(ii) Constructive manslaughter. This required that the prosecution prove that the accused had committed an unlawful act which was likely to subject another to the risk of some harm (albeit slight harm).

(iii) Reckless manslaughter. It was generally accepted that the prosecution would obtain a conviction for manslaughter if it could prove that the *accused foresaw* that his conduct was likely to cause another some bodily harm, or some injury to their health or welfare (if this meant something different from bodily injury).

These three categories of manslaughter are recognisable in the pre *Seymour* cases and each had its own set of requirements. *Seymour* and a later decision of the Privy Council in *Kong Cheuk Kwan* v. *R*. (1985) appear to have had the following effects.

1. In *Seymour* the House of Lords was concerned with the choice between gross negligence manslaughter and causing death by reckless driving. Lord Roskill said that both crimes depended upon the reckless taking of an unjustified risk. In reckless driving this was the unjustifiable risk of causing an obvious and serious risk of physically harming other road users or of causing substantial damage to property. In "motor" manslaughter (a term used by Lord Roskill in this case in place of gross negligence manslaughter) it was the unjustifiable risk of causing an obvious and serious risk of physical harm to another.

2. Recklessness in both manslaughter and causing death by reckless driving meant what Lord Diplock had said it meant in *Caldwell* (1982). In itself this is not particularly earth shattering since there seems to be little difference between gross negligence as defined in *Bateman* (1925) and *Caldwell* recklessness. Further, in *Kong Cheuk Kwan* v. *R*. Lord Roskill said that directions couched in terms of gross negligence and compensation are probably of little assistance to jurors. So Lord Roskill seems to be substituting the term "recklessness" for "gross negligence" in category (i). However there is a more significant change. It was generally accepted that when a prosecutor sought to establish gross negligence manslaughter he would have to prove that the accused's conduct was likely to cause death (or possibly really serious bodily harm). A risk of some physical harm would only suffice as the basis for manslaughter under category (iii) - reckless manslaughter - but there reckless had its subjective (*Cunningham*) meaning. In other words under category (iii) the prosecutor would have to prove that the accused had deliberately taken the risk of physically injuring another. Lord Roskill would seem to have merged categories (i) and (iii) in a way highly favourable to the prosecution. Under the direction given in *Seymour* the prosecution need only prove that the accused was reckless (in the *Caldwell* sense) as to causing *some* physical harm. On the other hand, at the end of his speech in *Seymour*, Lord Roskill added that in a case of motor manslaughter it would be appropriate for the trial judge to tell the

jury that to constitute motor manslaughter the risk of death being caused by the defendant's method of driving must be very high. Was this a modification of his earlier direction that the jury should be told that the accused could be convicted of manslaughter if he was reckless as to causing *some* physical injury? Apparently not, since in *Kong Cheuk Kwan* v. *R*. he said that the remarks about the high risk of death in *Seymour* were merely intended to point to those cases in which a charge of motor manslaughter would be more appropriate than one of causing death by dangerous driving. The remarks were not intended to alter the pre-existing law as to manslaughter by recklessness. The remarks about the high risk of death are merely a recognition that in reality juries will only convict motorists of manslaughter where their driving created a high risk of death. This is not part of the formula to be left to the jury on motor manslaughter and indeed in *Kong Cheuk Kwan* v. *R*. there is no reference to a high risk of death in the formula which is approved.

3. *Seymour* was a case involving, in Lord Roskill's words, "motor" manslaughter. It might be argued that the direction on manslaughter approved in that case was to be restricted to such cases - though there appears to be no very good reason why motorists should have a category of manslaughter all to themselves. However, in *Kong Cheuk Kwan* v. *R*. Lord Roskill approved the *Seymour* direction in a case involving a collision between two hydrofoil ferries. Again, in this case, there are passages which suggest that he did so because the case had distinct factual similarities to *Seymour*- both cases involving death from bad driving. It is more likely that this new approach is to replace gross negligence manslaughter entirely in which case the categories of manslaughter would now read as follows:

(i) Reckless manslaughter (replacing old categories (i) and (iii)). The prosecution would have to prove that the accused recklessly (in the *Caldwell* sense) caused an obvious and serious risk of some physical injury (and this might also include injury to health or welfare if this means something different from physical injury).

(ii) Constructive manslaughter. This category clearly survives the decisions in *Seymour* and *Kong Cheuk Kwan* v. *R*. though its scope for application seems to have been greatly reduced. It could be argued that there will be very few cases which would previously have been brought under this head which could not now more easily be brought under category (i).

4. Conclusion. It seems that the cases of *Seymour* and *Kong Cheuk Kwan* v. *R*. may have effected a great simplification in the law relating to involuntary manslaughter while at the same time widening its scope.

One final point should be made. Throughout this note it has been assumed that there is really no difference between gross negligence and *Caldwell* recklessness. Others have argued that there is one significant difference. This is best explained by an illustration. X is driving his car behind Y. He pulls out to overtake Y and sees Z coming in the opposite direction. If a reasonable man would realise that X has virtually no chance of passing Y before he hits Z but X does not see this risk then he is clearly grossly negligent and reckless in the *Caldwell* sense. The same is true if X sees that he is unlikely to get past but deliberately takes the risk. If, however, X adverts to the risk but genuinely concludes that there is no risk some would argue that he may be grossly negligent but he does not fall within the strict wording of Diplock's test for recklessness in *Caldwell* since he has not failed to see the risk. However there appears little to choose between a person who does not see an obvious risk and one who having seen the risk stupidly concludes that it does not exist. It seems likely that a court would conclude that the driver was reckless in this third situation, in which case there would be no difference between gross negligence and *Caldwell* recklessness.

Chapter 7

NON FATAL OFFENCES AGAINST THE PERSON

1. ASSAULT AND BATTERY

A. General Requirements of Assault and Battery

Fagan v. Metropolitan Police Commissioner
[1969] 1 Q.B. 439 (D.C.)

[A police constable had asked the defendant to park his car so that he could inspect the defendant's driving documents. The constable stood in the road to indicate exactly where the car should be parked. The defendant drove forward and came to a halt with the front offside wheel on the constable's foot. The constable said "Get off you are on my foot!" to which the defendant replied "F . . . you, you can wait." The car's engine stopped running. The constable several times asked the defendant to move - and eventually the defendant reluctantly and slowly did so. The magistrates convicted Fagan of assaulting a police constable in the execution of his duty (Police Act 1964, s.51). His appeal was dismissed by Quarter Sessions which court stated a case for the Divisional Court. The problem was that in the absence of a finding that the defendant deliberately drove on to the constable's foot, it was difficult to say that after he had realised that his car was on the constable's foot that he did anything which would amount to an assault.]

James J. Mr. Abbas for the appellant . . . contends that on the finding of the justices the initial mounting of the wheel could not be an assault and that the act of the wheel mounting the foot came to an end without there being any mens rea. It is argued that thereafter there was no act on the part of the appellant which could constitute an actus reus but only the omission or failure to remove the wheel as soon as he was asked. That failure, it is said, could not in law be an assault, nor could it in law provide the necessary mens rea to convert the original act of mounting the foot into an assault.

Mr. Rant for the respondent argues that the first mounting of the foot was an actus reus which act continued until the moment of time at which the wheel was removed. During that continuing act, it is said, the appellant formed the necessary intention to constitute the element of mens rea and once that element was added to the continuing act, an assault took place. In the alternative, Mr. Rant argues that there can be situations in which there is a duty to act and that in such situtations an omission to act in breach of duty would in law amount to an assault. It is unnecessary to formulate any concluded views on this alternative.

In our judgment the question arising, which has been argued on general principles, falls to be decided on the facts of the particular case. An assault is any act which intentionally - or possibly recklessly - causes another person to apprehend immediate and unlawful personal violence. Although "assault" is an independent crime and is to be treated as such, for practical purposes today "assault" is generally synonymous with the term "battery" and is a term used to mean the actual intended use of unlawful force to another person without his consent. On the facts of the present case the "assault" alleged involved a "battery." Where an assault involves a battery, it matters not, in our judgment, whether the battery is inflicted directly by the body of the offender or through the medium of some weapon or instrument controlled by the action of the offender. An assault may be committed by the laying of a hand upon another, and the action does not cease to be an assault if it is a stick held in the hand and not the hand itself which is laid on the person of the victim. So for our part we see no difference in principle between the action of stepping on to a person's toe and maintaining that position and the action of driving a car on to a person's foot and sitting in the car whilst its position on the foot is maintained.

To constitute the offence of assault some intentional act must have been performed: a mere omission to act cannot amount to an assault. Without going into the question whether words alone can constitute an assault, it is clear that the words spoken by the appellant could not alone amount to an assault: they can only shed a light on the appellant's action. For our part we think the crucial question is whether in this case the act of the appellant can be said to be complete and spent at the moment of time when the car wheel came to rest on the foot or whether his act is to be regarded as a continuing act operating until the wheel was removed. In our judgment a distinction is to be drawn between acts which are complete - though results may continue to flow - and those acts which are continuing. Once the act is complete it cannot thereafter be said to be a threat to inflict unlawful force upon the victim. If the act, as distinct from the results thereof, is a continuing act there is a continuing threat to inflict unlawful force. If the assault involves a battery and that battery continues there is a continuing act of assault.

For an assault to be committed both the elements of actus reus and mens rea must be present at the same time. The "actus reus" is the action causing the effect on the victim's mind. . . . The "mens rea" is the intention to cause that effect. It is not necessary that mens rea should be present at the inception of the actus reus; it can be superimposed upon an existing act. On the other hand the subsequent inception of mens rea cannot convert an act which has been completed without mens rea into an assault.

In our judgment the Willesden magistrates and quarter sessions were right in law. On the facts found the action of the appellant may have been initially unintentional, but the time came when knowing that the wheel was on the officer's foot the appellant (1) remained seated in the car so that his body through the medium of the car was in contact with the officer, (2) switched off the ignition of the car, (3) maintained the wheel of the car on the foot and (4) used words indicating the intention of keeping the wheel in that position. For our part we cannot regard such conduct as mere omission or inactivity.

There was an act constituting a battery which at its inception was not criminal because there was no element of intention but which became criminal from the moment the intention was formed to produce the apprehension which was flowing from the continuing act. The fallacy of the appellant's argument is that it seeks to equate the facts of this case with such a case as where a motorist has accidentally run over a person and, that action having been completed, fails to assist the victim with the intent that the victim should suffer.

We would dismiss this appeal.

Notes

1. See also *Miller* (above, p. 43).

2. It is generally accepted that the *mens rea* of assault and battery is intention or recklessness. In *Venna* (1976) it was held that recklessness should receive the subjective interpretation derived from *Cunningham* (see above, p. 59). However, certain doubt has been cast on this by statements of Lord Roskill in *Seymour* (above, p. 72) where he said that the word recklessness should always receive the same definition, namely that found in *Caldwell* (above, p. 60). It is submitted that the definition of recklessness in *Caldwell* should be confined to these cases where the word is used in a statute. In assaults, recklessness suffices by reason of the common law and thus until any express statement emerges from the courts *Venna* should be treated as authoritative.

Smith v. Chief Superintendent, Woking Police Station
(1983) 76 Cr.App.R. 234 (C.A.)

[The defendant entered a private garden at night and looked through the windows of the complainants' bed sitting room. She was in her night clothes and became extremely terrified when she saw his face close against the windows. The defendant was charged under section 4 Vagrancy Act 1824 which required, *inter alia*, proof that the defendant's purpose was to assault the complainant.]

Kerr L.J. It is also common ground that the definition of an assault as stated, for instance, in *Archbold* (41st ed.), para. 20-114, is correct in law: "An assault is any act which intentionally - or recklessly - causes another to apprehend immediate and unlawful violence." It is stated later on in the passage that there must be, on the part of the defendant, a hostile intent calculated to cause apprehension in the mind of the victim.

In the present case, on the findings which I have summarised, there was quite clearly an intention to cause fear, an intention to frighten, and that intention produced the intended effect as the result of what the defendant did, in that it did frighten and indeed terrify Miss Mooney to the extent that she screamed. It is not a case where she was merely startled or surprised or ashamed to be seen in her night-clothes; she was terrified as the result of what the defendant deliberately did, knowing and either intending or being reckless as to whether it would cause that fear in her.

Ultimately, as it seems to me, the only point taken by Mr. Denny which requires some consideration is whether there was a sufficient apprehension, within the definition which I have read, of immediate and unlawful violence. He takes the point that there is no finding here that what Miss Mooney was terrified of was some violence, and indeed some violence which can be described as immediate. However, as it seems to me, Mr. Greenbourne is right when he submits, really in the form of a question: "What else, other than some form of immediate violence, could Miss Mooney have been terrified about?"

When one is in a state of terror one is very often unable to analyse precisely what one is frightened of as likely to happen next. When I say that, I am speaking of a situation such as the present, where the person who causes one to be terrified is immediately adjacent, albeit on the other side of a window. Mr. Denny relied on a sentence in Smith and Hogan's *Criminal Law* (4th ed.), p. 351, where an illustration is given as follows:

"There can be no assault if it is obvious to P" - the complainant - "that D" - the defendant - "is unable to carry out his threat, as where D shakes his fist at P who is safely locked inside his car." That may be so, but those are not the facts of the present case.

In the present case the defendant intended to frighten Miss Mooney and Miss Mooney was frightened. As it seems to me, there is no need for a finding that what she was frightened of, which she probably could not analyse at that moment, was some innominate terror of some potential violence. It was clearly a situation where the basis of the fear which was instilled in her was that she did not know what the defendant was going to do next, but that, whatever he might be going to do next, and sufficiently immediately for the purposes of the offence, was something of a violent nature. In effect, as it seems to me, it was wholly open to the justices to infer that her state of mind was not only that of terror, which they did find, but terror of some immediate violence. In those circumstances, it seems to me that they were perfectly entitled to convict the defendant who had gone there, as they found, with the intention of frightening her and causing her to fear some act of immediate violence, and therefore with the intention of committing an assault upon her. Accordingly, I would dismiss this appeal.

Glidewell J. I agree, and there is nothing I can usefully add.

Appeal dismissed.

Note

In some cases this requirement that the victim be placed in fear of immediate personal violence appears to receive a rather generous interpretation. This is often because a technical assault is required as the basis of a more serious offence; this used to be the position under section 20 of the Offences Against the Person Act 1861, see below, p. 217.

B. Unlawfulness

The prosecution must prove that the conduct of the defendant was unlawful in that (1) no justification existed for his conduct and (2) that the victim did not consent to the conduct. (See *Williams* see above, p. 84.) An assault may arise as a charge of common assault where the injuries may be trivial or non-existent or it may form the basis of a more serious offence such as an assault occasioning actual bodily harm (Offences Against the Person Act 1861, s. 47 which carries up to five years imprisonment) where the injuries may be serious. Does consent still operate as a defence in these more serious cases?

Att.-Gen.'s Reference (No. 6 of 1980)
[1981] 3 W.L.R. 125 (C.A.)

Lord Lane C.J. The point of law upon which the court is asked to give its opinion is as follows:

> "Where two persons fight (otherwise than in the course of sport) in a public place can it be a defence for one of those persons to a charge of assault arising out of the fight that the other consented to fight?"

. . . . . .

For convenience we use the word "assault" as including "battery," and adopt the definition of James J. in *Fagan* v. *Commissioner of Metropolitan Police* (1969), 444, namely: "the actual intended use of unlawful force to another person without his consent," to which we would respectfully add "or any other lawful excuse."

We think that it can be taken as a starting point that it is an essential element of an assault that the act is done contrary to the will and without the consent of the victim and it is doubtless for this reason that the burden lies on the prosecution to negative consent. Ordinarily, then, if the victim consents, the assailant is not guilty.

But the cases show that the courts will make an exception to this principle where the public interest requires: *Reg.* v. *Coney* (1882) ("the prize fight case"). The 11 judges were of opinion that a prize fight is illegal, that all persons aiding and abetting were guilty of assault, and that the consent of the actual fighters was irrelevant. Their reasons varied as follows: Cave J., that the blow was struck in anger and likely to do corporal hurt, as opposed to one struck in sport, not intended to cause bodily harm; Mathew J., the dangerous nature of the proceedings; Stephen J., what was done was injurious to the public, depending on the degree of force and the place used; Hawkins J., the likelihood of a breach of the peace, and the degree of force and injury; Lord Coleridge C.J., breach of the peace and protection of the public.

The judgment in *Rex* v. *Donovan* (1934) (beating for the purposes of sexual gratification), the reasoning in which seems to be tautologous, proceeds upon a different basis, starting with the proposition that consent is irrelevant if the act complained of is "unlawful . . . in itself," which it will be if it involves the infliction of bodily harm.

Bearing in mind the various cases and the views of the text book writers cited to us, and starting with the proposition that ordinarily an act consented to will not constitute an assault, the question is: at what point does the public interest require the court to hold otherwise?

In answering this question the diversity of view expressed in the previous decisions, such as the two cases cited, make some selection and a partly new approach necessary. Accordingly we have not followed the dicta which would make an act, even if consensual, an assault if it occurred in public, on the ground that it constituted a breach of the peace, and was therefore itself unlawful. These dicta reflect the conditions of the times when they were uttered, when there was little by way of an established police force and prize fights were a source of civil disturbance. Today, with regular policing, conditions are different. Statutory offences, and indeed by-laws, provide a sufficient sanction against true cases of public disorder, as do the common law offences of affray, etc. Nor have we followed the Scottish case of *Smart* v. *H.M. Advocate* (1975), holding the consent of the victim to be irrelevant on a charge of assault, guilt depending upon the "evil intent" of the accused, irrespective of the harm done.

The answer to this question, in our judgment, is that it is not in the public interest that people should try to cause, or should cause, each other actual bodily harm for no good reason. Minor struggles are another matter. So, in our judgment, it is immaterial whether the act occurs in private or in public; it is an assault if actual bodily harm is intended and/or caused. This means that most fights will be unlawful regardless of consent.

Nothing which we have said is intended to cast doubt upon the accepted legality of properly conducted games and sports, lawful chastisement or correction, reasonable surgical interference, dangerous exhibitions, etc. These apparent exceptions can be justified as involving the exercise of a legal right, in the case of chastisement or correction, or as needed in the public interest, in the other cases.

Our answer to the point of law is No, but not, as the reference implies, because the fight occurred in a public place, but because, wherever it occurred, the participants would have been guilty of assault, subject to self-defence, if, as we understand was the case, they intended to and/or did cause actual bodily harm.

The point of law referred to us by the Attorney-General has revealed itself as having been the subject of much interesting legal and philosophical debate, but it does not seem that the particular uncertainty enshrined in the reference has caused practical inconvenience in the administration of justice during the last few hundred years. We would not wish our opinion on the point to be the signal for unnecessary prosecutions.

Opinion accordingly.

Bolduc and Bird v. R.
(1967) 63 D.L.R. (2d.) 82 (Sup. Ct. of Canada.)

[Bolduc was a qualified medical practitioner and Bird was a musician who claimed to be interested in entering the medical profession. Bolduc was due to perform a vaginal examination of the complainant. He introduced Bird to her as a medical student and asked if she minded if he remained during the examination. As she believed him to be a bona fide student she consented. When the true facts emerged Bolduc and Bird were convicted of an indecent assault. (In order to establish indecent assault, the prosecution must establish an assault.) On appeal to the Supreme Court of Canada from a decision of the Court of Appeal which had dismissed their first appeal:]

Hall J. The question for decision is whether on those facts and in the circumstances so described the appellants Bolduc and Bird were guilty of an indecent assault upon the person of the complainant contrary to s.141 of the *Criminal Code* which reads:

141 (1) Every one who indecently assaults a female person is guilty of an indictable offence and is liable to imprisonment for five years and to be whipped.

(2) An accused who is charged with an offence under subsection (1) may be convicted if the evidence establishes that the accused did anything to the female person with her consent that, but for her consent, would have been an indecent assault, if her consent was obtained by false and fraudulent representation as to the nature and quality of the act.

With respect, I do not agree that an indecent assault was committed within the meaning of this section. What Bolduc did was unethical and reprehensible in the extreme and was something no reputable medical practitioner would have countenanced. However, Bolduc's unethical conduct and the fraud practised upon the complainant do not of themselves necessarily imply an infraction of s.141. It is common ground that the examination and treatment, including the insertion of the speculum were consented to by the complainant. The question is: "Was her consent obtained by false and fraudulent representations as to the nature and quality of the act?" Bolduc did exactly what the complainant understood he would do and intended that he should do, namely, to examine the vaginal tract and to cauterize the affected parts. Inserting the speculum was necessary for these purposes. The was no fraud on his part as to what he was supposed to do and in what he actually did. The complainant knew that Bird was present and consented to his presence. The fraud that was practised on her was not as to the nature and quality of what was to be done but was as to Bird's identity as a medical intern. His presence as distinct from some overt act by him was not an assault. However, any overt act either alone or in common with Bolduc would have transposed the situation into an unlawful assault, but Bird did not touch the complainant; he merely looked on and listened to Bolduc's comments on what was being done because of the condition then apparent in the vaginal tract. Bird was in a sense a "peeping tom". . . .

The question of fraud vitiating a woman's consent in the case of rape or indecent assault was fully canvassed by Stephen, J., in *R. v. Clarence* (1888), and by the High Court of Australia in *Papadimitropoulos v. The Queen* (1957), where the Court, in concluding a full review of the relevant law and cases decided up to that . . . time said [p. 261]:

> To return to the central point; rape is carnal knowledge of a woman without her consent: carnal knowledge is the physical fact of penetration; it is the consent to that which is in question; such a consent demands a perception as to what is about to take place, as to the identity of the man and the character of what he is doing. But once the consent is comprehending and actual the inducing causes cannot destroy its reality . . .

The complainant here knew what Bolduc was proposing to do to her, for this was one in a series of such treatments. Her consent to the examination and treatment was real and comprehending and it cannot, therefore, be said that her consent was obtained by false or fraudulent representations as to the nature and quality of the act to be done, for that was not the fraud practised on her. The fraud was as to Bird being a medical intern and it was not represented that he would do anything but observe. It was intended that the examination and treatment would be done by Bolduc and this he did without assistance or participation by Bird.

I would, accordingly, allow the appeals, quash the convictions and direct that a verdict of acquittal be entered for both appellants.

Question
In what situations would fraud vitiate consent?

2. SECTIONS 18 AND 20 OF THE OFFENCES AGAINST THE PERSON ACT 1861

(See below, p. 258 for details of these provisions.)

A. Section 20. "Inflicting" Grievous Bodily Harm

It will be noted that in section 18 of the Act the prosecution must prove that the accused *caused* grievous bodily harm whereas under section 20 it must prove that the accused *inflicted* grievous bodily harm. Until recently this use of different terminology was taken to mean that under section 20 grievous bodily harm was only *inflicted* if the prosecution could establish that it had resulted from an assault. The courts were often, therefore, faced with the need to find an assault in order to sustain a conviction under section 20 and this led to ever increasing liberal interpretations of what constituted an assault. (See H.S.B., p. 241, 2.) Recently, however, the matter has been considered by the House of Lords.

Commissioner of Police of the Metropolis v. Wilson
[*1984*] *A.C.* 242 (*H.L.*)

[The case was directed towards a technical question of alternative verdicts. In the course of answering the certified question Lord Roskill said of the word "inflict":]

Lord Roskill. What, then, are the allegations expressly or impliedly included in a charge of "inflicting grievous bodily harm." Plainly that allegation must, so far as physical injuries are concerned, at least impliedly if not indeed expressly, include the infliction of "actual bodily harm" because infliction of the more serious injuries must include the infliction of the less serious injuries. But does the allegation of "inflicting" include an allegation of "assault"? The problem arises by reason of the fact that the relevant English case law has proceeded along two different paths. In one group it has, as has already been pointed out, been held that a verdict of assault was a possible alternative verdict on a charge of inflicting grievous bodily harm contrary to section 20. In the other group grievous bodily harm was said to have been inflicted without any assault having taken place, unless of course the offence of assault were to be given a much wider significance than is usually attached to it. This problem has been the subject of recent detailed analysis in the Supreme Court of Victoria in *Reg. v. Salisbury* (1976). In a most valuable judgment - I most gratefully acknowledge the assistance I have derived from that judgment in preparing this speech - the full court drew attention, in relation to comparable legislation in Victoria, to the problems which arose from this divergence in the main stream of English authority. The problem with which your Lordships' House is now faced arose in *Salisbury* in a different way from the present appeals. There, the appellant was convicted of an offence against the Victorian equivalent of section 20. He appealed on the ground that the trial judge had refused to leave to the jury the possibility of convicting him on that single charge of assault occasioning actual bodily harm or of common assault. The full court dismissed the appeal on the ground that at common law these latter offences were not "necessarily included" in the offence of "inflicting grievous bodily harm." The reasoning leading to this conclusion is plain:

> "It may be that the somewhat different wording of section 20 of the English Act has played a part in bringing about the existence of the two lines of authority in England, but, be that as it may, we have come to the conclusion that, although the word 'inflicts' . . . does not have as wide a meaning as the word 'causes' . . . the word 'inflicts' does have a wider meaning than it would have if it were construed so that inflicting grievous bodily harm always involved assaulting the victim. In our opinion, grievous bodily harm may be inflicted . . . either where the accused has directly and violently 'inflicted' it by assaulting the victim, or where the accused has 'inflicted' it by doing something, intentionally, which, though it is not itself a direct application of force to the body of the victim, does directly result in force being applied violently to the body of the victim, so that he suffers grievous bodily harm. Hence, the lesser misdemeanours of assault occasioning actual bodily harm and common assault . . . are not necessarily included in the misdemeanour of inflicting grievous bodily harm . . . " (See p. 461.)

This conclusion was reached after careful consideration of English authorities such as *Reg. v. Taylor*, (1869) *Reg. v. Martin* (1881) *Reg. v. Clarence* (1888) and *Reg. v. Halliday*

(1889). My Lords, it would be idle to pretend that these cases are wholly consistent with each other, or even that, as in *Clarence*, though there was a majority in favour of quashing the conviction then in question, the judgments of those judges among the 13 present who formed the majority are consistent with each other. Some of these cases were not argued on both sides. Others are very inadequately reported and different reports vary. Thus, Stephen J., who was in the majority in *Clarence*, described the infliction of grievous bodily harm in these words, at p. 41:

"The words appears [*sic*] to me to mean the direct causing of some grievous injury to the body itself with a weapon, as by a cut with a knife, or without a weapon, as by a blow with the fist, or by pushing a person down. Indeed, though the word 'assault' is not used in the section, I think the words imply an assault and battery of which a wound or grievous bodily harm is the manifest immediate and obvious result. This is supported by *Taylor* . . . "

But Wills J., also in the majority, was clearly of the view that grievous bodily harm could be inflicted without an assault, as for example, by creating panic. On the other hand, in *Taylor* (1869), where the accused was charged on two counts, one under each limb of section 20, the jury convicted him of common assault. Kelly C.B. said that each count was for an offence which necessarily included an assault, and a verdict of guilty of common assault was upheld. *Taylor* is not easy to reconcile with the later cases unless it is to be supported on the basis of the wounding count in the indictment. In *Martin* (1881), on the other hand, there was no reference to the issue whether the accused's conduct in creating panic among a theatre audience constituted assault. He did an unlawful act calculated to cause injury and injury was thereby caused. He was thus guilty of an offence against section 20.

My Lords, I doubt whether any useful purpose would be served by further detailed analysis of these and other cases, since to do so would only be to repeat less felicitously what has already been done by the full court of Victoria in *Salisbury* (1976). I am content to accept, as did the full court, that there can be an infliction of grievous bodily harm contrary to section 20 without an assault being committed.

Note

It is thus clear that the word *"inflict"* does not necessarily mean that section 20 involves proof of an assault whereby the grievous bodily harm resulted. The problem remains, however, that the word *"inflict"* is used in section 20 whereas the word *"cause"* is used in section 18. It is thus possible for the courts to find a distinction between these two words. (See H.S.B., p. 241.)

B. Mens Rea in Sections 18 and 20 of the Offences Against the Person Act 1861

R. v. Mowatt
[1968] 1 Q.B. 421 (C.A.)

[The facts appear in the judgment of Diplock L.J.]

Diplock L.J. [In referring to the case of *Cunningham* (above p. 59) and its treatment of the word "malice":] But the court in that case also expressed approval obiter of a more general statement by Professor Kenny, [Kenny's Outlines of Criminal Law, 18th ed. (1962), p. 202] which runs as follows:

> "in any statutory definition of a crime, 'malice' must be taken not in the old vague sense of wickedness in general, but as requiring either (1) an actual intention to do the particular kind of harm that in fact was done, or (2) recklessness as to whether such harm should occur or not (*i.e.* the accused has foreseen that the particular kind of harm might be done, and yet has gone on to take the risk of it). It is neither limited to, nor does it indeed require, any ill will towards the person injured."

This generalisation is not, in our view, appropriate to the specific alternative statutory offences described in sections 18 and 20 of the Offences against the Person Act, 1861, and section 5 of the Prevention of Offences Act, 1851, and if used in that form in the summing-up is liable to bemuse the jury. In section 18 the word "maliciously" adds nothing. The intent expressly required by that section is more specific than such element of foresight of consequences as is implicit in the word "maliciously" and in directing a jury about an offence under this section the word "maliciously" is best ignored.

In the offence under section 20, and in the alternative verdict which may be given on a charge under section 18, for neither of which is any specific intent required, the word "maliciously" does import upon the part of the person who unlawfully inflicts the wound or other grievous bodily harm an awareness that his act may have the consequence of causing some physical harm to some other person. That is what is meant by "the particular kind of harm" in the citation from Professor Kenny. It is quite unnecessary that the accused should have foreseen that his unlawful act might cause physical harm of the gravity described in the section, *i.e.,* a wound or serious physical injury. It is enough that he should have foreseen that some physical harm to some person, albeit of a minor character, might result.

In many cases in instructing a jury upon a charge under section 20, or upon the alternative verdict which may be given under that section when the accused is charged under section 18, it may be unnecessary to refer specifically to the word "maliciously." The function of a summing-up is not to give the jury a general dissertation upon some aspect of the criminal law, but to tell them what are the issues of fact on which they must make up their minds in order to determine whether the accused is guilty of a particular offence. There may, of course, be cases where the accused's awareness of the possible consequences of his act is genuinely in issue. *Reg.* v. *Cunningham* [above, p. 59] is a good example. But where the evidence for the prosecution, if accepted, shows that the physical act of the accused which caused the injury to another person was a direct assault which any ordinary person would be bound to realise was likely to cause some physical harm to the other person (as, for instance, an assault with a weapon or the boot or violence with the hands) and the defence put forward on behalf of the accused is not that the assault was accidental or that he did not realise that it might cause some physical harm to the victim, but is some other defence such as that he did not do the alleged act or that he did it in self-defence, it is unnecessary to deal specifically in the summing-up with what is meant by the word "maliciously" in the section. It can only confuse the jury to invite them in the summing-up to consider an improbability not previously put forward and to which no evidence has been directed, to wit - that the accused did not realise what any ordinary person would have realised was a likely consequence of his act, and to tell the jury that the onus lies, not upon the accused to establish, but upon the prosecution to negative that improbability and to go on to talk about presumptions. To a jury who are not jurisprudents that sounds like jargon. In the absence of any evidence that the accused did not realise that it was a possible consequence of his act that some physical harm might be caused to the victim, the prosecution satisfy the relevant onus by proving the commission by the accused of an act which any ordinary person would realise was likely to have that consequence. There is no issue here to which the jury need direct their minds and there is no need to give to them any specific directions about it.

In such a case, and these are the commonest of cases under section 18, the real issues of fact on which the jury have to make up their minds are: (1) are they satisfied that the accused did the act? (2) if so, are they satisfied that the act caused a wound or other serious physical injury? (3) If the defence of self-defence is raised or there is any evidence to support it, do they think that the accused may have done the act in self-defence? (4) If the answer to (1) and (2) is "yes" and to (3), if raised, is "no," are they satisfied that when he did the act he intended to cause a wound or other really serious physical injury? If (3), if raised, is answered "no" and (1) and (2) are answered "yes," the lesser offence under section 20 is made out; and if (4) is also answered "yes" the graver offence under section 18 is made out.

In any case under section 18 where the physical act of the accused was a direct assault which any ordinary person would have realised was likely to cause some physical harm to the victim and there is no evidence that the accused himself did not realise that it might do so, if those issues, which we have stated, are put fairly and squarely to the jury it is the view of this court that the summing-up is not open to criticism. There is no need for any general dissertation about the meaning of the word "maliciously." The less said about it in such a case the better.

The only remaining issue is whether the present case is one of this kind. The relevant evidence for the prosecution was that of the complainant and the two police officers. The complainant, in the early hours of the morning of September 30, was returning home, according to his evidence, and was stopped in a street by two men, one of whom was the defendant. They asked him if there was a club anywhere about, and then one of them, not the defendant, snatched a £5 note from the complainant's breast pocket and ran off. The complainant said he chased him without success, returned to the defendant, grasped him by his lapels and demanded to know the whereabouts of his mate. The defendant then (and this was common ground) hit out at the complainant and knocked him down. That was the first assault. Two off-duty police officers then saw the defendant, according to their evidence, sitting astride the complainant, and they saw the defendant strike him several violent blows in the face with his fist and pull him to his feet, strike him again in the face, knocking him down and making him virtually unconscious. The defendant was, according to the police, trying to pull up the complainant again when the police arrested him. When the defendant was taken to the station, he was found to be concealing a £5 note in his hand.

The judge directed the jury to acquit of robbery with violence, because the evidence showed no violence but a snatching. That left larceny from the person, of which the jury convicted him. As regards the count of wounding, in effect, the judge directed the jury to acquit the appellant of any offence if they accepted that only the first blow, which he admitted, had been struck. He directed them that on the evidence there would be justification in self-defence for that. As regards the blows seen to be struck by the police, the defendant sitting astride the complainant and raining a series of blows upon his face, lifting him up, casting him down again, the only issues before the jury was whether that happened at all and, if so, whether they were inflicted with intent to do grievous bodily harm. If the jury accepted that it did happen, then clearly any ordinary man would realise that some physical harm would be sustained by the victim, even though he might not have any specific intent to break the skin or amount to serious physical injury.

In the view of this court, this was clearly a case where in relation to the lesser offence of which the defendant was convicted it was quite unnecessary for the judge to give the jury any instructions upon the meaning of the word "maliciously."

Another point was raised by Mr. Briggs on behalf of the defendant, namely, that the directions as given by the judge to the jury upon the issue of self-defence were inadequate. In the view of this court, there is nothing in that contention; and this appeal is accordingly dismissed.

Appeal dismissed.

Questions

1. What is the *mens rea* of an offence

(1) under section 47 of the Offences Against the Person Act 1861;
(2) under section 20 of the Offences Against the Person Act 1861;
(3) under section 18 of the Offences Against the Person Act 1861?

2. What effect, if any, does section 8 of the Criminal Justice Act 1967 have on *Mowatt?* (See Smith and Hogan *Criminal Law* (5th ed.), p. 377.)

3. INDECENT ASSAULT

Faulkner v. Talbot
[1981] 3 All E.R. 468 (D.C.)

Lord Lane C.J. The way in which the case arises is this. The appellant was convicted by the justices on 5th February 1980 of indecent assault on a boy, who was then aged 14 years, contrary to s15(1) of the Sexual Offences Act 1956. The events happened at the appellant's home, and there is no dispute as to the material facts. The 14-year-old boy was living in the appellant's home, having left his parents. The appellant and the boy watched a horror film on the television; the boy was scared, or said he was scared, by the film. As a result of that the appellant told the boy that he could sleep with her if he wished. That he chose to do.

Once they were in bed together, the appellant invited the boy to have sexual intercourse with her. The boy's account, in so far as it was material, was this: the appellant tried to put her hand on his penis, but he would not let her. She then pulled the boy on top of her; she took hold of his penis and put it inside her vagina. On those facts the charge was laid.

It is a well-known fact that there is no statutory provision specifically forbidding a woman to have sexual intercourse with a boy of 14. But what s15 of the Sexual Offences Act 1956, under which this case was brought, says is as follows:

"(1) It is an offence for a person to make an indecent assault on a man.

(2) A boy under the age of sixteen cannot in law give any consent which would prevent an act being an assault for the purposes of this section . . . "

The way in which counsel for the appellant, in his attractive argument to this court, has put the matter is as follows. He submits that, since the act of sexual intercourse in these circumstances is not an offence on the part of the woman, therefore that touching of the boy as a prelude to, or as part of, or as postlude to, the act of sexual intercourse cannot in logic itself be an offence.

He submits, secondly, if, for example, in an act of sexual intercourse, in the way described by Wien J in *R v Upward* (7th October 1976, unreported), to which reference will be made later, a woman lies passively and does nothing at all except let the boy have sexual intercourse, that, suggests counsel, would be no offence; whereas if she took any part in the act, by touching the boy for instance on the buttock during the act of sexual intercourse, it would be an offence. That, counsel submits, is contrary to common sense and contrary to logic and therefore, he goes on to argue, it cannot be right that the act of sexual intercourse under any circumstances can amount to indecent assault by the woman on the boy.

We have been referred to a number of authorities and it is right, both for the purpose of clarity and in deference to the arguments addressed to us, that I should refer to them. The first case we were referred to was *Hare* (1934). The appellant was a woman who had been convicted under s 62 of the Offences against the Person Act 1861 (which was a precursor of the 1956 Act) of indecent assault on a boy of 12. In so far as it was material, that section of the 1861 Act read: "Whosoever . . . shall be guilty . . . of any indecent Assault upon any Male Person shall be guilty of a misdemeanour . . . "

The judgment of the court was delivered by Avory J. Having stated the facts, he went on as follows:

> "We are asked in this case to hold that it was not competent to the Recorder to leave the case to the jury or for the jury to convict the appellant. The argument put forward on behalf of the appellant is that the charge being laid under s. 62 of the Offences against the Person Act, 1861, no woman can be convicted of the offences charged. The boy, being under the age of sixteen, was by law incompetent to consent to any such conduct as took place between him and the appellant. There is no question that the nature of that which took place between them was indecent. The whole question is, as has been concisely put by counsel for the appellant, whether the offence under s. 62 is to be limited to an indecent assault of a sodomitical character . . . there is no reason for saying that the phrase: 'Whosoever . . . shall be guilty . . . of any indecent assault' does not include a woman."

That case provides a formidable hurdle for counsel for the appellant to clear.

The next case to which we were referred was *Director of Public Prosecutions* v. *Rogers* (1953). That was a case where the facts were somewhat special, as will be observed. The headnote reads:

> "On two occasions, the respondent, when alone in the

house with his daughter aged 11, put his arm round her and led her upstairs, and when they were upstairs exposed his person and invited her to masturbate him, which she did. No compulsion or force was used by the defendant, and the child neither objected nor resisted, but submitted to the defendant's request. Justices dismissed informations charging the defendant with indecent assault on the child."

The Divisional Court held, on those facts, "that as the defendant had not used compulsion or force, or acted in a hostile manner towards the child, there had been no assault, and consequently no indecent assault on her, and that the decision of the justices was, therefore, right." The facts were that the father, being alone in the house with the little daughter, put his arms round her and said "come upstairs." She made no objection or resistance and no force was used on either of the two occasions. That was the basis for the decision of the court, namely that the justices were right and the appeal was dismissed.

It seems to me that the circumstances there were exceptional. There was no reason why the father should not put his arm round the shoulder of his daughter; there was a lawful excuse for doing that, because he was the father. There was no touching of the child in an indecent way.

The next case was *R* v. *Mason* (1968). The headnote reads as follows:

"The defendant, a married woman, was arraigned on a number of counts, each alleging indecent assault against one of six different boys, all between the ages of fourteen and sixteen years. Over a substantial period of time she had been visited by the boys, sometimes singly, sometimes more than one at a time, and had had sexual intercourse with them. There was no suggestion that she had used force or committed any hostile act against any of the boys. Intercourse had taken place sometimes at her suggestion, sometimes at the suggestion of the boys themselves. *Held*, that as there was no evidence of the use of any force or of any hostile act by the defendant, there had been no assault, and consequently no indecent assault, so that the counts must be quashed."

I read one passage from the judgment of Veale J, which was really the high spot of counsel's argument (at 18):

"I am further prepared to hold that acts of touching readily submitted to and enjoyed during or preliminary to intercourse in such circumstances should be regarded as part of the intercourse and are equally not an assault by the woman on the boy."

These words were echoed in a different form in a case to which we have been referred, *R* v. *Upward* (7th October 1976, unreported) which was heard at Caernarvon before Wien J and a jury. Wien J was there, in the passage to which we have been referred, informing the jury of the reason why he was directing them to acquit the woman in similar circumstances to those which I have described in *Mason*. Wien J, as I say, echoed and expanded the words used by Veale J in *Mason*.

One turns now to consider whether those two passages correctly reflect the law as it stands at the moment and in order to reach that decision it is necessary to look at two more recent decisions. The first is *R.* v. *McCormack* (1969). That was a decision of the Court of Appeal, Criminal Division, before Fenton Atkinson LJ, Melford Stevenson and James JJ. The headnote reads as follows:

"A charge of unlawful sexual intercourse with a girl under sixteen necessarily includes an allegation of indecent assault on the same girl and, where there is clear evidence of indecent assault, the judge should leave this lesser offence also to the jury, even though the prosecution have not relied on it. When a man inserts his finger into the vagina of a girl under sixteen, this is an indecent assault, however willing and co-operative the girl may be."

I read a passage from the judgment of the court delivered by Fenton Atkinson LJ.

"Then there followed an argument by counsel for the appellant, which he has repeated to this court and put very attractively before us, whether in view of the girl's consent, there could be a conviction of indecent assault, there being here a willing girl and no evidence of any compulsion or hostility; and he referred to a line of authorities such as *Fairclough* v. *Whipp* (1951) and *Director of Public Prosecutions* v. *Rogers* (1953), cases which have shown that where the accused adult invites a child, for example, to touch his private parts, but exercises no sort of compulsion and there is no hostile act, the charge of indecent assault is not appropriate. But, in our view, that line of authorities has no application here, and, in the view of the members of this court, it is plain beyond argument that if a man inserts a finger into the vagina of a girl under sixteen that is an indecent assault, in view of her age, and it is an indecent assault however willing and co-operative she may in fact be."

Finally, so far as authorities are concerned, I turn to *R* v *Sutton* (1977). In that case the facts were that the appellant took three boys, all under the age of 14, to his home and photographed them partially clothed and in the nude. He remained fully clothed. He neither touched or fondled the boys, except touch them on the hands and legs and bodies in order to arrange their poses for the purpose of photography. The boys consented to these acts.

The appellant was charged with indecently assaulting the boys contrary to s 15(1) of the 1956 Act. The jury were directed that any touching without consent was an assault and the law did not permit persons under 16 to consent to the touching, if it was accompanied by circumstances of indecency. The jury convicted. On appeal it was held by the Court of Appeal, Criminal Division, that they had been misdirected.

The holding was:

"that whereas section 15(2) of the Sexual Offences Act 1956 bars consent from preventing an act with a boy under 16 from being an indecent assault - i.e. if the act alleged to constitute the assault is itself an indecent act - and thus the defence of consent will not avail a defendant; in the present case the touching of the boys by the appellant, which was merely to indicate a pose, was not of itself indecent, was consented to and was not hostile or threatening, the consent of the boys to the acts complained of prevented such acts being an assault, and, therefore, an indecent assault; thus the question of indecency did not arise; accordingly, the jury had been misdirected and the appeal would be allowed and the conviction quashed."

One turns, in the light of those authorities, to present the case. First of all what is an assault? An assault is any intentional touching of another person without the consent of that person and without lawful excuse. It need not necessarily be hostile or rude or aggressive, as some of the cases seem to indicate. If the touching is an indecent touching, as in this case it plainly was because the appellant took hold of the boy's penis, then the provisions of s 15(2) of the Sexual Offences Act 1956 come into play: "A boy under the age of sixteen cannot in law give any consent which would prevent an act being an assault for the purposes of this section." Consequently, the touching undoubtedly being indecent, the boy in this case, being aged 14, could not consent to it. It was intentional touching; it was touching without lawful excuse, and in view of s 15(2) it was a touching to which the boy could not in law consent and therefore did not consent. Accordingly, as I see it, one has all the necessary ingredients of the offence of indecent assault, and the consequence is that the recorder was correct in the conclusion to which he came.

The question which is asked by the case is as follows:

" . . . whether the acts of the appellant to which the complainant consented in pulling him on top of her and touching his penis immediately before sexual intercourse by him with her were an indecent assault by the appellant on the complainant contrary to s.15(1) of the Sexual Offences Act, 1956?"

The answer I would give to that is Yes, it was an indecent assault. In my judgment the decision of Veale J in *Mason* was wrong, and in so far as it is necessary to refer to the matter, where Wien J was making explanation to the jury, he was likewise in error.

For these reasons I would dismiss this appeal.

Chapter 8

OFFENCES UNDER THE THEFT ACT 1968

1. THEFT

A. Meaning of Appropriation

R. v. Morris; R. v. Burnside
[1984] A.C. 320 (H.L.)

[Both cases involved defendants substituting lower priced labels to goods in a
supermarket intending to induce the shop to sell the goods at the lower price. In
Morris the accused was charged and paid the lower price; in *Burnside* the
defendant was arrested before he paid for the goods. Both defendants were
convicted at their trials. Their appeals were dismissed by the Court of Appeal
and divisional court respectively. The House of Lords considered their further
appeals as a consolidated appeal.]

Lord Roskill. My Lords, in his submissions for the
appellants . . . Mr. Denison urged that on these simple facts
neither appellant was guilty of theft. He accepted that Morris
would have had no defence to a charge under section 15(1) of
obtaining property by deception for he dishonestly paid the
lesser prices and passed through the checkpoint having done so
before he was arrested. But Morris, he said, was not guilty of
theft because there was no appropriation by him before
payment at the checkpoint sufficient to support a charge of
theft, however dishonest his actions may have been in
previously switching the labels.

Mr. Denison pointed out that if, as he accepted, an offence
was committed against section 15(1) and if the prosecution case
were right, Morris would be liable to be convicted of obtaining
property by deception which he had already stolen - a situation
which learned counsel suggested was somewhat anomalous.

As regards Burnside, Mr. Denison submitted that for the
same reason there was no appropriation before his arrest
sufficient to support a charge of theft. He also submitted that
Burnside's actions however dishonest would not support a
charge of attempting to obtain property by deception contrary
to section 15(1) since his dishonest act was no more than an act

preparatory to obtaining property by deception and was not sufficiently proximate to an attempt to obtain property by deception.

My Lords, if these submissions be well founded it is clear that, however dishonest their actions, each respondent was wrongly convicted of theft. The question is whether they are well founded. The answer must depend upon the true construction of the relevant sections of the Act of 1968 and it is to these that I now turn. . . .

. . . . . .

It is to be observed that the definition of "appropriation" in section 3(1) is not exhaustive. But section 1(1) and section 3(1) show clearly that there can be no conviction for theft contrary to section 1(1) even if all the other ingredients of the offence are proved unless "appropriation" is also proved.

The starting point of any consideration of Mr. Denison's submissions must, I think, be the decision of this House in *Reg. v. Lawrence (Alan)* (1972). In the leading speech, Viscount Dilhorne expressly accepted the view of the Court of Appeal (Criminal Division) in that case that the offence of theft involved four elements, (1) a dishonest (2) appropriation (3) of property belonging to another, (4) with the intention of permanently depriving the owner of it. Viscount Dilhorne also rejected the argument that even if these four elements were all present there could not be theft within the section if the owner of the property in question had consented to the acts which were done by the defendant. That there was in that case a dishonest appropriation was beyond question and the House did not have to consider the precise meaning of that word in section 3(1).

Mr. Denison submitted that the phrase in section 3(1) "any assumption by a person of *the rights*" (my emphasis) "of an owner amounts to an appropriation" must mean any assumption of "*all* the rights of an owner." Since neither respondent had at the time of the removal of the goods from the shelves and of the label switching assumed *all* the rights of the owner, there was no appropriation and therefore no theft. Mr. Jeffreys for the prosecution, on the other hand, contended that *the* rights in this context only meant *any* of the rights. An owner of goods has many rights - they have been described as "a bundle or package of rights." Mr. Jeffreys contended that on a fair reading of the subsection it cannot have been the intention that every one of an owner's rights had to be assumed by the alleged thief before an appropriation was proved and that essential ingredient of the offence of theft established.

My Lords, if one reads the words "the rights" at the opening of section 3(1) literally and in isolation from the rest of the section, Mr. Denison's submission undoubtedly has force. But the later words "any later assumption of a right" in subsection (1) and the words in subsection (2) "no later assumption by him of rights" seem to me to militate strongly against the correctness of the submission. Moreover the provisions of section 2(1)(*a*) also seem to point in the same direction. It follows therefore that it is enough for the prosecution if they have proved in these cases the assumption by the respondents of *any* of the rights of the owner of the goods in question, that is to say, the supermarket concerned, it being common ground in these cases that the other three of the four elements mentioned in Viscount Dilhorne's speech in *Reg. v. Lawrence (Alan)* had been fully established.

My Lords, Mr. Jeffreys sought to argue that any removal from the shelves of the supermarket, even if unaccompanied by label switching, was without more an appropriation. In one passage in his judgment in Morris's case, the learned Lord Chief Justice appears to have accepted the submission, for he said:

"it seems to us that in taking the article from the shelf the customer is indeed assuming one of the rights of the owner - the right to move the article from its position on the shelf to carry it to the check-out."

With the utmost respect, I cannot accept this statement as correct. If one postulates an honest customer taking goods from a shelf to put in his or her trolley to take to the checkpoint there to pay the proper price, I am unable to see that any of these actions involves any assumption by the shopper of the rights of the supermarket. In the context of section 3(1), the concept of appropriation in my view involves not an act expressly or impliedly authorised by the owner but an act by way of adverse interference with or usurpation of those rights. When the honest shopper acts as I have just described, he or she is acting with the implied authority of the owner of the supermarket to take the goods from the shelf, put them in the trolley, take them to the checkpoint and there pay the correct price, at which moment the property in the goods will pass to the shopper for the first time. It is with the consent of the owners of the supermarket, be that consent express or implied, that the shopper does these acts and thus obtains at least control if not actual possession of the goods preparatory, at a later stage, to obtaining the property in them upon payment of the proper amount at the checkpoint. I do not think that section 3(1) envisages any such act as an "appropriation," whatever may be the meaning of that word in other fields such as contract or sale of goods law.

If, as I understand all your Lordships to agree, the concept of appropriation in section 3(1) involves an element of adverse interference with or usurpation of some right of the owner, it is necessary next to consider whether that requirement is satisfied in either of these cases. As I have already said, in my view mere removal from the shelves without more is not an appropriation. Further, if a shopper with some perverted sense of humour, intending only to create confusion and nothing more both for the supermarket and for other shoppers, switches labels, I do not think that that act of label switching alone is without more an appropriation, though it is not difficult to envisage some cases of dishonest label-switching which could be. In cases such as the present, it is in truth a combination of these actions, the removal from the shelf and the switching of the labels, which evidences adverse interference with or usurpation of the right of the owner. Those acts, therefore, amount to an appropriation and if they are accompanied by proof of the other three elements to which I have referred, the offence of theft is established. Further, if they are accompanied by other acts such as putting the goods so removed and relabelled into a receptacle, whether a trolley or the shopper's own bag or basket, proof of appropriation within section 3(1) becomes overwhelming. It is the doing of one or more acts which individually or collectively amount to such adverse interference with or usurpation of the owner's rights which constitute appropriation under section 3(1) and I do not think it matters where there is more than one such act in which order the successive acts take place, or whether there is any interval of time between them. To suggest that it matters whether the mislabelling precedes or succeeds removal from the shelves is to reduce this branch of the law to an absurdity.

My Lords, it will have been observed that I have endeavoured so far to resolve the question for determination in these appeals without reference to any decided cases except *Reg. v. Lawrence (Alan)* (1972) which alone of the many cases cited in argument is a decision of this House. If your Lordships accept as correct the analysis which I have endeavoured to express by

reference to the construction of the relevant sections of the
Theft Act, a trail through a forest of decisions, many briefly
and indeed inadequately reported, will tend to confuse rather
than to enlighten. There are however some to which brief
reference should perhaps be made.

First, *Reg. v. McPherson* (1973). Your Lordships have had the
benefit of a transcript of the judgment of Lord Widgery C.J. I
quote from page 3 of the transcript:

> "Reducing this case to its bare essentials we have this: Mrs.
> McPherson in common design with the others takes two
> bottles of whisky from the stand, puts them in her shopping
> bag; at the time she intends to take them out without paying
> for them, in other words she intends to steal them from the
> very beginning. She acts dishonestly as the jury found, and
> the sole question is whether that is an appropriation of the
> bottles within the meaning of section 1. We have no
> hesitation whatever in saying that it is such an
> appropriation and indeed we content ourselves with a
> judgment of this brevity because we have been unable to
> accept or to find any argument to the contrary, to suggest
> that an appropriation is not effective in those simple
> circumstances."

That was not, of course, a label switching case, but it is a plain
case of appropriation effected by the combination of the acts
of removing the goods from the shelf and K of concealing them
in the shopping bag. *Reg. v. McPherson* is to my mind clearly
correctly decided as are all the cases which have followed it. It
is wholly consistent with the principles which I have
endeavoured to state in this speech.

It has been suggested that *Reg. v. Meech* (1974), *Reg. v. Skipp*
(1975) – your Lordships also have a transcript of the judgment
in this case – and certain other cases are inconsistent with *Reg.
v. McPherson*. I do not propose to examine these or other cases
in detail. Suffice it to say that I am far from convinced that
there is any inconsistency between them and other cases, as has
been suggested, once it is appreciated that facts will vary
infinitely. The precise moment when dishonest acts, not of
themselves amounting to an appropriation, subsequently,
because of some other and later acts combined with those
earlier acts, do bring about an appropriation within section
3(1), will necessarily vary according to the particular case in
which the question arises.

Of the other cases referred to, I understand all your Lordships to agree that *Anderton v. Wish* (*Note*) (1980) was rightly decided for the reasons given. I need not therefore refer to it further. *Eddy v. Niman* (1981) was in my view also correctly decided on its somewhat unusual facts. I think that Webster J., giving the first judgment, asked the right question at p. 241, though, with respect, I think that the phrase "some overt act . . . inconsistent with the true owner's rights" is too narrow. I think that the act need not necessarily be "overt."

Kaur (Dip) v. Chief Constable for Hampshire (1981) is a difficult case. I am disposed to agree with the learned Lord Chief Justice that it was wrongly decided but without going into further detail I respectfully suggest that it is on any view wrong to introduce into this branch of the criminal law questions whether particular contracts are void or voidable on the ground of mistake or fraud or whether any mistake is sufficiently fundamental to vitiate a contract. These difficult questions should so far as possible be confined to those fields of law to which they are immediately relevant and I do not regard them as relevant questions under the Theft Act 1968.

My Lords, it remains briefly to consider any relationship between section 1 and section 15. If the conclusion I have reached that theft takes place at the moment of appropriation and before any payment is made at the checkpoint be correct it is wrong to assert, as has been asserted, that the same act of appropriation creates two offences, one against section 1(1) and the other against section 15(1), because the two offences occur at different points of time; the section 15(1) offence is not committed until payment of the wrong amount is made at the checkpoint while the theft has been committed earlier. It follows that in cases such as Morris's two offences were committed. I do not doubt that it was perfectly proper to add the third count under section 15(1) in this case. I think the assistant recorder was right to leave all three counts to the jury. While one may sympathise with his preventing them from returning a verdict on the third count once they convicted on the theft counts if only in the interests of simplification, the counts were not alternative as he appears to have treated them. They were cumulative and once they were left to the jury verdicts should have been taken on all of them.

My Lords, these shoplifting cases by switching labels are essentially simple in their facts and their factual simplicity should not be allowed to be obscured by ingenious legal arguments upon the Theft Act which for some time have bedevilled this branch of the criminal law without noticeably contributing to the efficient administration of justice - rather the reverse. The law to be applied to simple cases, whether in magistrates' courts or the Crown Court, should if possible be equally simple. I see no reason in principle why, when there is clear evidence of both offences being committed, both offences should not be charged. But where a shoplifter has passed the checkpoint and quite clearly has, by deception, obtained goods either without paying or by paying only a lesser price than he should, those concerned with prosecutions may in future think it preferable in the interests of simplicity to charge only an offence against section 15(1). In many cases of that kind it is difficult to see what possible defence there can be and that course may well avoid any opportunity for further ingenious legal arguments upon the first few sections of the Theft Act. Of course when the dishonesty is detected before the defendant has reached the checkpoint and he or she is arrested before that point so that no property has been obtained by deception, then theft is properly charged and if "appropriation," within the meaning that I have attributed to that word in this speech, is proved as well as the other three ingredients of the offence of theft, the defendant is plainly guilty of that offence.

My Lords, as already explained I have not gone through all the cases cited though I have mentioned some. Of the rest those inconsistent with this speech must henceforth be treated as overruled.

I would answer the certified questions in this way:

"There is a dishonest appropriation for the purposes of the Theft Act 1968 where by the substitution of a price label showing a lesser price on goods for one showing a greater price, a defendant either by that act alone or by that act in conjunction with another act or other acts (whether done before or after the substitution of the labels) adversely interferes with or usurps the right of the owner to ensure that the goods concerned are sold and paid for at that greater price."

I would dismiss these appeals.

Note

Morris gives approval to the decisions on the facts in *McPherson*, *Skipp* and *Eddy* v. *Niman*, the facts of which can be found in H.S.B., pp. 256 *et seq*.

Lord Roskill, however, appears to disapprove the decision in *Kaur* v. *Chief Constable for Hampshire*. In that case the defendant while looking at shoes on a rack in a department store discovered a pair of shoes, one of which had been incorrectly priced lower. She took the pair of shoes to the till and handed them to the cashier without comment. The cashier entered the incorrect lower price and the defendant took the shoes. She was arrested as she left the shop, and admitted that she had been dishonest. She was charged with theft. Now clearly the appropriation in this case must have occurred after the cashier had rung up the lower price since there was no allegation that she had interfered with the labels. Whose shoes was she therefore appropriating? The magistrates held that the cashier had no authority to sell at the lower price, and the contract was therefore void. Since ownership of property is not transferred under a void contract, the shoes remained the store's property. The defendant thus appropriated property belonging to another, and in doing so committed theft. The divisional court, however, held that the contract was not void, but voidable. This means there was a contract for the sale of the shoes which could be set aside by the store once it had discovered its mistake. In the meantime the shoes belonged to the defendant who had thus appropriated *her own property* and this was not theft. Lord Roskill disapproved the introduction of complex civil law issues, but with respect this seems unavoidable in this type of case. It is also equally difficult to believe that such conduct should constitute theft.

B. Dishonestly

A jury (or bench of magistrates) may not convict a defendant of theft unless the prosecution have proved that the defendant had acted dishonestly. "Dishonestly" receives a partial definition in section 2(1) of the Theft Act 1968, but the courts have accepted that there still remains a general jury issue of whether the defendant's conduct was "dishonest." In effect, this allows the tribunal of fact to decide whether the conduct in question merits a criminal sanction. In many cases the answer will be obvious, but certain situations might be viewed quite differently by different jurors. Consider the following situations. Do you consider the conduct of X, Y and Z to be (a) dishonest and/or (b) deserving of punishment?

(a) X works at a local shop. His employer has told him never to borrow money from the cash till. One rainy evening he is forced to work late and misses his last train home. He has insufficient money for a taxi fare and so he takes £5 from the till and leaves an IOU note. He has £50 at home from which he intends to repay the money on the following morning.

(b) Y works in a factory which makes paper. All employees are forbidden to remove paper for personal use. Y takes home some scrap paper for his children to draw on.

(c) Z has been instructed by his employer that he should always travel first class when on firm's business. Z believes this to be a waste of money and so always travels second class. However in order to appear to be following instructions he always claims the first class fare and donates the difference to charity.

For the purposes of the Theft Acts 1968 and 1978 should the jury be instructed that the defendant has acted dishonestly if they find:

(1) that the defendant believed that he was acting dishonestly;
(2) that ordinary decent people would think that the defendant was acting dishonestly;
(3) that the defendant knew that ordinary decent people would regard his conduct as dishonest?

R. v. Ghosh
[1982] 3 W.L.R. 110 (C.A.)

[The Court of Appeal reviewed its previous decision in *R.v. McIvor* (1982) where two lines of approach to the issue of dishonesty were identified.]

Lord Lane C.J. When *Reg.* v. *McIvor* (1982) came before the Court of Appeal, there were two conflicting lines of authority. On the one hand there were cases which decided that the test of dishonesty for the purposes of the Theft Act 1968 is, what we venture to call, subjective - that is to say the jury should be directed to look into the mind of the defendant and determine whether he knew he was acting dishonestly: see *Reg.* v. *Landy* (1981), where Lawton L.J. giving the reserved judgment of the Court of Appeal said:

"An assertion by a defendant that throughout a transaction he acted honestly does not have to be accepted but has to be weighed like any other piece of evidence. If that was the defendant's state of mind, or may have been, he is entitled to be acquitted. But if the jury, applying their own notions of what is honest and what is not, conclude that he could not have believed that he was acting honestly, then the element of dishonesty will have been established. What a jury must not do is to say to themselves: 'If we had been in his place we would have known we were acting dishonestly so he must have known he was.'"

On the other hand there were cases which decided that the test of dishonesty is objective. Thus in *Reg.* v. *Greenstein* (1975), the judge had directed the jury:

" . . . there is nothing illegal in stagging. The question you have to decide and what this case is all about is whether these defendants, or either of them, carried out their stagging operations in a dishonest way. To that question you apply your own standards of dishonesty. It is no good, you see, applying the standards of anyone accused of dishonesty otherwise everybody accused of dishonesty, if he were to be tested by his own standards, would be acquitted automatically, you may think. The question is essentially the one for a jury to decide and it is essentially one which the jury must decide by applying its own standards."

The Court of Appeal, in a reserved judgment, approved that direction.

[Lord Lane said that in *McIvor* the Court of Appeal had attempted to reconcile these two approaches by holding that the objective approach was correct when the defendant was charged with theft under s. 1 Theft Act 1968. The subjective approach was to be used in cases such as conspiracy to defraud, and obtaining property by deception contrary to section 15 Theft Act 1968. His Lordship continued:]

We feel, with the greatest respect, that in seeking to reconcile the two lines of authority in the way we have mentioned, the Court of Appeal in *Reg.* v. *McIvor* was seeking to reconcile the irreconcilable. It therefore falls to us now either to choose between the two lines of authority or to propose some other solution.

In the current supplement to *Archbold Criminal Pleading Evidence & Practice*, 40th ed. (1979), paragraph 1460, the editors suggest that the observations on dishonesty by the Court of Appeal in *Reg.* v. *Landy* can be disregarded "in view of the wealth of authority to the contrary." The matter, we feel, is not as simple as that.

In *Reg.* v. *Waterfall* (1970), the defendant was charged under section 16 of the Theft Act 1968 with dishonestly obtaining a pecuniary advantage from a taxi driver. Lord Parker C.J., giving the judgment of the Court of Appeal, said:

"The sole question as it seems to me in this case revolves round the third ingredient, namely, whether what was done was done dishonestly. In regard to that the deputy recorder directed the jury in this way: 'If on reflection and deliberation you came to the conclusion that this defendant never did have any genuine belief that Mr. Tropp [the accountant] would pay the taxi fare, then you would be entitled to convict him. . . . ' In other words, in that passage the deputy recorder is telling the jury they had to consider what was in this particular defendant's mind: had he a genuine belief that the accountant would provide the money? That, as it seems to this court, is a perfectly proper direction subject to this, that it would be right to tell the jury that they can use as a test, though not a conclusive test, whether there were any reasonable grounds for that belief. Unfortunately, however, just before the jury retired, in two passages the deputy recorder, as it seems to this court, was saying: you cannot hold that this man had a genuine belief unless he had reasonable grounds for that belief."

Lord Parker then sets out the passages in question and continues:

"the court is quite satisfied that those directions cannot be justified. The test here is a subjective test, whether the particular man had an honest belief, and of course whereas the absence of reasonable ground may point strongly to the fact that that belief is not genuine, it is at the end of the day for the jury to say whether or not in the case of this particular man he did have that genuine belief."

That decision was criticised by academic writers. But it was followed shortly afterwards in *Reg.* v. *Royle* (1971), another case under section 16 of the Theft Act 1968. Edmund Davies L.J. giving the judgment of the court said:

"The charges being that debts had been dishonestly 'evaded' by deception, contrary to section 16(2)(*a*), it was incumbent on the commissioner to direct the jury on the fundamental ingredient of dishonesty. In accordance with *Reg.* v. *Waterfall* (1970) they should have been told that the test is whether the accused had an honest belief and that, whereas the absence of reasonable ground might point strongly to the conclusion that he entertained no genuine belief in the truth of his representation, it was for them to say whether or not it had been established that the appellant had no such genuine belief."

It is to be noted that the court in that case treated the "fundamental ingredient of dishonesty" as being the same as whether the defendant had a genuine belief in the truth of the representation.

In *Reg* v. *Gilks* (1972), which was decided by the Court of Appeal the following year, the appellant had been convicted of theft contrary to section 1 of the Theft Act 1968. The facts were that he had been overpaid by a bookmaker. He knew that the bookmaker had made a mistake, and that he was not entitled to the money. But he kept it. The case for the defence was that "bookmakers are a race apart." It would be dishonest if your grocer gave you too much change and you kept it, knowing that he had made a mistake. But it was not dishonest in the case of a bookmaker. The judge directed the jury:

> "Well, it is a matter for you to consider, members of the jury, but try and place yourselves in that man's position at that time and answer the question whether in your view he thought he was acting honestly or dishonestly."

Cairns L.J. giving the judgment of the Court of Appeal held that that was, in the circumstances of the case, a proper and sufficient direction on the matter of dishonesty. He continued:

> "On the face of it the defendant's conduct was dishonest: the only possible basis on which the jury could find that the prosecution had not established dishonesty would be if they thought it possible that the defendant did have the belief which he claimed to have."

A little later *Reg.* v. *Feely* (1973) came before a court of five judges. The case is often treated as having laid down an objective test of dishonesty for the purpose of section 1 of the Theft Act 1968. But what it actually decided was (i) that it is for the jury to determine whether the defendant acted dishonestly and not for the judge, (ii) that the word "dishonestly" can only relate to the defendant's own state of mind, and (iii) that it is unnecessary and undesirable for judges to define what is meant by "dishonestly."

It is true that the court said:

> "Jurors, when deciding whether an appropriation was dishonest can be reasonably expected to, and should, apply the current standards of ordinary decent people."

It is that sentence which is usually taken as laying down the objective test. But the passage goes on:

> "In their own lives they have to decide what is and what is not dishonest. We can see no reason why, when in a jury box, they should require the help of a judge to tell them what amounts to dishonesty."

The sentence requiring the jury to apply current standards leads up to the prohibition on judges from applying *their* standards. That is the context in which the sentence appears. It seems to be reading too much into that sentence to treat it as authority for the view that "dishonesty can be established independently of the knowledge or belief of the defendant." If it could, then any reference to the state of mind of the defendant would be beside the point.

This brings us to the heart of the problem. Is "dishonestly" in section 1 of the Theft Act 1968 intended to characterise a course of conduct? Or is it intended to describe a state of mind? If the former, then we can well understand that it could be established independently of the knowledge or belief of the accused. But if, as we think, it is the latter, then the knowledge and belief of the accused are at the root of the problem.

Take for example a man who comes from a country where public transport is free. On his first day here he travels on a bus. He gets off without paying. He never had any intention of paying. His mind is clearly honest; but his conduct, judged objectively by what he has done, is dishonest. It seems to us that in using the word "dishonestly" in the Theft Act 1968, Parliament cannot have intended to catch dishonest conduct in that sense, that is to say conduct to which no moral obloquy could possibly attach. This is sufficiently established by the partial definition in section 2 of the Theft Act itself. All the matters covered by section 2(1) relate to the belief of the accused. Section 2(2) relates to his willingness to pay. A man's belief and his willingness to pay are things which can only be established subjectively. It is difficult to see how a partially subjective definition can be made to work in harness with the test which in all other respects is wholly objective.

If we are right that dishonesty is something in the mind of the accused (what Professor Glanville Williams calls "a special mental state"), then if the mind of the accused is honest, it cannot be deemed dishonest merely because members of the jury would have regarded it as dishonest to embark on that course of conduct.

So we would reject the simple uncomplicated approach that the test is purely objective, however attractive from the practical point of view that solution may be.

There remains the objection that to adopt a subjective test is to abandon all standards but that of the accused himself, and to bring about a state of affairs in which "Robin Hood would be no robber": *Reg.* v. *Greenstein*. This objection misunderstands the nature of the subjective test. It is no defence for a man to say "I knew that what I was doing is generally regarded as dishonest; but I do not regard it as dishonest myself. Therefore

I am not guilty." What he is however entitled to say is "I did not know that anybody would regard what I was doing as dishonest." He may not be believed; just as he may not be believed if he sets up "a claim of right" under section 2(1) of the Theft Act 1968, or asserts that he believed in the truth of a misrepresentation under section 15 of the Act of 1968. But if he *is* believed, or raises a real doubt about the matter, the jury cannot be sure that he was dishonest.

In determining whether the prosecution has proved that the defendant was acting dishonestly, a jury must first of all decide whether according to the ordinary standards of reasonable and honest people what was done was dishonest. If it was not dishonest by those standards, that is the end of the matter and the prosecution fails.

If it was dishonest by those standards, then the jury must consider whether the defendant himself must have realised that what he was doing was by those standards dishonest. In most cases, where the actions are obviously dishonest by ordinary standards, there will be no doubt about it. It will be obvious that the defendant himself knew that he was acting dishonestly. It is dishonest for a defendant to act in a way which he knows ordinary people consider to be dishonest, even if he asserts or genuinely believes that he is morally justified in acting as he did. For example, Robin Hood or those ardent anti-vivisectionists who remove animals from vivisection laboratories are acting dishonestly, even though they may consider themselves to be morally justified in doing what they do, because they know that ordinary people would consider these actions to be dishonest.

Cases which might be described as borderline, such as *Boggeln* v. *Williams* (1978), will depend upon the view taken by the jury as to whether the defendant may have believed what he was doing was in accordance with the ordinary man's idea of honesty. A jury might have come to the conclusion that the defendant in that case was disobedient or impudent, but not dishonest in what he did.

2. BURGLARY

R. v. Collins
[*1973*] *Q.B. 100 (C.A.)*

Edmund Davies L.J. gave the judgment of the court. This is about as extraordinary a case as my brethren and I have ever heard either on the bench or while at the bar. Stephen William George Collins was convicted on October 29, 1971, at the Essex Assizes of burglary with intent to commit rape and he was sentenced to 21 months' imprisonment. He is a 19-year old youth, and he appeals against that conviction by the certificate of the judge. The terms in which that certificate is expressed reveal that the judge was clearly troubled about the case and the conviction.

Let me relate the facts. Were they put into a novel or portrayed on the stage, they would be regarded as being so improbable as to be unworthy of serious consideration and as verging at times on farce. At about 2 o'clock in the early morning of Saturday, July 24, 1971, a young lady of 18 went to bed at her mother's home in Colchester. She had spent the evening with her boyfriend. She had taken a certain amount of drink, and it may be that this fact affords some explanation of her inability to answer satisfactorily certain crucial questions put to her at the trial.

She has the habit of sleeping without wearing night apparel in a bed which is very near the lattice-type window of her room. At one stage in her evidence she seemed to be saying that the bed was close up against the window which, in accordance with her practice, was wide open. In the photographs which we have before us, however, there appears to be a gap of some sort between the two, but the bed was clearly quite near the window.

At about 3.30 or 4 o'clock she awoke and she then saw in the moonlight a vague form crouched in the open window. She was unable to remember, and this is important, whether the form was on the outside of the window sill or on that part of the sill which was inside the room, and for reasons which will later become clear, that seemingly narrow point is of crucial importance.

The young lady then realised several things: first of all that the form in the window was that of a male; secondly that he was a naked male; and thirdly that he was a naked male with an erect penis. She also saw in the moonlight that his hair was blond. She thereupon leapt to the conclusion that her boyfriend, with whom for some time she had been on terms of regular and frequent sexual intimacy, was paying her an ardent nocturnal visit. She promptly sat up in bed, and the man descended from the sill and joined her in bed and they had full sexual intercourse. But there was something about him which made her think that things were not as they usually were between her and her boyfriend. The length of his hair, his voice as they had exchanged what was described as "love talk," and other features led her to the conclusion that somehow there was something different. So she turned on the bed-side light, saw that her companion was not her boyfriend and slapped the face of the intruder, who was none other than the defendant. He said to her, "Give me a good time tonight," and got hold of her arm, but she bit him and told him to go. She then went into the bathroom and he promptly vanished.

The complainant said that she would not have agreed to intercourse if she had known that the person entering her room was not her boyfriend. But there was no suggestion of any force having been used upon her, and the intercourse which took place was undoubtedly effected with no resistance on her part.

The defendant was seen by the police at about 10.30 later that same morning. According to the police, the conversation which took place then elicited these points. He was very lustful the previous night. He had taken a lot of drink, and we may here note that drink (which to him is a very real problem) had brought this young man into trouble several times before, but never for an offence of this kind. He went on to say that he knew the complainant because he had worked around her house. On this occasion, desiring sexual intercourse - and according to the police evidence he added that he was determined to have a girl, by force if necessary, although that part of the police evidence he challenged - he went on to say that he walked around the house, saw a light in an upstairs bedroom, and he knew that this was the girl's bedroom. He found a step ladder, leaned it against the wall and climbed up and looked into the bedroom. He could see through the wide-open window a girl who was naked and asleep. So he descended the ladder and stripped off all his clothes, with the exception of his socks, because apparently he took the view that if the girl's mother entered the bedroom it would be easier to effect a rapid escape if he had his socks on than if he was in his bare feet. That is a matter about which we are not called upon to express any view, and would in any event find ourselves unable to express one.

Having undressed, he then climbed the ladder and pulled himself up on to the window sill. His version of the matter is that he was pulling himself in when she awoke. She then got up and knelt on the bed, she put her arms around his neck and body, and she seemed to pull him into the bed. He went on:

"I was rather dazed because I didn't think she would want to know me. We kissed and cuddled for about 10 or 15 minutes and then I had it away with her but found it hard because I had had so much to drink."

The police officer said to the defendant:

"It appears that it was your intention to have intercourse with this girl by force if necessary, and it was only pure coincidence that this girl was under the impression that you were her boyfriend and apparently that is why she consented to allowing you to have sexual intercourse with her." It was alleged that he then said, "Yes, I feel awful about this. It is the worst day of my life, but I know it could have been worse."

Thereupon the officer said to him - and he challenges this: "What do you mean, you know it could have been worse?", to which he is alleged to have replied:

"Well, my trouble is drink and I got very frustrated. As I've told you, I only wanted to have it away with a girl and I'm only glad I haven't really hurt her."

Then he made a statement under caution, in the course of which he said:

"When I stripped off and got up the ladder I made my mind up that I was going to try and have it away with this girl. I feel terrible about this now, but I had too much to drink. I am sorry for what I have done."

In the course of his testimony, the defendant said that he would not have gone into the room if the girl had not knelt on the bed and beckoned him into the room. He said that if she had objected immediately to his being there or to his having intercourse he would not have persisted. While he was keen on having sexual intercourse that night, it was only if he could find someone who was willing. He strongly denied having told the police that he would, if necessary, have pushed over some girl for the purpose of having intercourse.

There was a submission of no case to answer on the ground that the evidence did not support the charge, particularly that ingredient of it which had reference to entry into the house "as a trespasser." But the submission was overruled, and, as we have already related, he gave evidence.

Now, one feature of the case which remained at the conclusion of the evidence in great obscurity is where exactly Collins was at the moment when, according to him, the girl manifested that she was welcoming him. Was he kneeling on the sill outside the window or was he already inside the room, having climbed through the window frame, and kneeling upon the inner sill? It was a crucial matter, for there were certainly three ingredients that it was incumbent upon the Crown to establish. Under section 9 of the Theft Act 1968, which renders a person guilty of burglary if he enters any building or part of a building as a trespasser and with the intention of committing rape, the entry of the accused into the building must first be proved. Well, there is no doubt about that, for it is common ground that he did enter this girl's bedroom. Secondly, it must be proved that he entered as a trespasser. We will develop that point a little later. Thirdly, it must be proved that he entered as a trespasser with intent at the time of entry to commit rape therein.

The second ingredient of the offence - the entry must be as a trespasser - is one which has not, to the best of our knowledge, been previously canvassed in the courts. Views as to its ambit have naturally been canvassed by the textbook writers, and it is perhaps not wholly irrelevant to recall that those who were advising the Home Secretary before the Theft Bill was presented to Parliament had it in mind to get rid of some of the frequently absurd technical rules which had been built up in relation to the old requirement in burglary of a "breaking and entering." The cases are legion as to what this did or did not amount to, and happily it is not now necessary for us to consider them. But it was in order to get rid of those technical rules that a new test was introduced, namely, that the entry must be "as a trespasser."

What does that involve? According to the editors of *Archbold Criminal Pleading Evidence & Practice*, 37th ed. (1969), para. 1505:

> "Any intentional, reckless or negligent entry into a building will, it would appear, constitute a trespass if the building is in the possession of another person who does not consent to the entry. Nor will it make any difference that the entry was the result of a reasonable mistake on the part of the defendant, so far as trespass is concerned."

If that be right, then it would be no defence for this man to say (and even were he believed in saying), "Well, I honestly thought that this girl was welcoming me into the room and I therefore entered, fully believing that I had her consent to go in." If *Archbold* is right, he would nevertheless be a trespasser, since the apparent consent of the girl was unreal, she being mistaken as to who was at her window. We disagree. We hold that, for the purposes of section 9 of the Theft Act, a person entering a building is not guilty of trespass if he enters without knowledge that he is trespassing or at least without acting recklessly as to whether or not he is unlawfully entering.

A view contrary to that of the editors of *Archbold* was expressed in Professor Smith's book on *The Law of Theft*, 1st ed. (1968), where, having given an illustration of an entry into premises, the author comments, at paragraph 462:

> "It is submitted that . . . D should be acquitted on the ground of lack of mens rea. Though, under the civil law, he entered as a trespasser, it is submitted that he cannot be convicted of the criminal offence unless he knew of the facts which caused him to be a trespasser or, at least, was reckless."

The matter has also been dealt with by Professor Griew, who in paragraph 4-05 of his work *The Theft Act 1968* has this passage:

> "What if D wrongly believes that he is not trespassing? His belief may rest on facts which, if true, would mean that he was not trespassing: for instance, he may enter a building by mistake, thinking that it is the one he has been invited to enter. Or his belief may be based on a false view of the legal effect of the known facts: for instance, he may misunderstand the effect of a contract granting him a right of passage through a building. Neither kind of mistake will protect him from tort liability for trespass. In either case, then, D satisfies the literal terms of section 9(1): he 'enters. . . as a trespasser.' But for the purposes of criminal liability a man should be judged on the basis of the facts as he believed them to be, and this should include making allowances for a mistake as to rights under the civil law. This is another way of saying that a serious offence like burglary should be held to require mens rea in the fullest

sense of the phrase: D should be liable for burglary only if he knowingly trespasses or is reckless as to whether he trespasses or not. Unhappily it is common for Parliament to omit to make clear whether mens rea is intended to be an element in a statutory offence. It is also, though not equally, common for the courts to supply the mental element by construction of the statute."

We prefer the view expressed by Professor Smith and Professor Griew to that of the editors of *Archbold*. In the judgment of this court there cannot be a conviction for entering premises "as a trespasser" within the meaning of section 9 of the Theft Act unless the person entering does so knowing that he is a trespasser and nevertheless deliberately enters, or, at the very least, is reckless as to whether or not he is entering the premises of another without the other party's consent.

Having so held, the pivotal point of this appeal is whether the Crown established that this defendant at the moment that he entered the bedroom knew perfectly well that he was not welcome there or, being reckless as to whether he was welcome or not, was nevertheless determined to enter. That in turn involves consideration as to where he was at the time that the complainant indicated that she was welcoming him into her bedroom. If, to take an example that was put in the course of argument, her bed had not been near the window but was on the other side of the bedroom, and he (being determined to have her sexually even against her will) climbed through the window and crossed the bedroom to reach her bed, then the offence charged would have been established. But in this case, as we have related, the layout of the room was different, and it became a point of nicety which had to be conclusively established by the Crown as to where he was when the girl made welcoming signs, as she unquestionably at some stage did.

How did the judge deal with this matter? We have to say regretfully that there was a flaw in his treatment of it. Referring to section 9, he said:

"There are three ingredients. First is the question of entry. Did he enter into that house? Did he enter as a trespasser? This is to say, was the entry, if you are satisfied there was an entry, intentional or reckless? And, finally, and you may think this is the crux of the case as opened to you by Mr.

Irwin, if you are satisfied that he entered as a trespasser, did he have the intention the rape this girl?"

The judge then went on to deal in turn with each of these three ingredients. He first explained what was involved in "entry" into a building. He then dealt with the second ingredient. But here he unfortunately repeated his earlier observation that the question of entry as a trespasser depended on "was the entry intentional or reckless?" We have to say that this was putting the matter inaccurately. This mistake may have been derived from a passage in the speech of counsel for the Crown when replying to the submission of "no case." Mr. Irwin at one stage said: "Therefore, the first thing that the Crown have got to prove, my Lords, is that there has been a trespass which may be an intentional trespass, or it may be a reckless trespass." Unfortunately the judge regarded the matter as though the second ingredient in the burglary charged was whether there had been an intentional or reckless entry, and when he came to develop this topic in his summing up that error was unfortunately perpetuated. The judge told the jury:

"He had no right to be in that house, as you know, certainly from the point of view of the girl's parent. But if you are satisfied about entry, did he enter intentionally or recklessly? What the prosecution say about that is, you do not really have to consider recklessness because when you consider his own evidence he intended to enter that house, and if you accept the evidence I have just pointed out to you, he in fact did so. So, at least, you may think, it was intentional. At the least, you may think it was reckless because as he told you he did not know whether the girl would accept him."

We are compelled to say that we do not think the judge by these observations made sufficiently clear to the jury the nature of the second test about which they had to be satisfied before this young man could be convicted of the offence charged. There was no doubt that his entry into the bedroom was "intentional." But what the accused had said was, "She knelt on the bed, she put her arms around me and then I went in." If the jury thought he might be truthful in that assertion, they would need to consider whether or not, although entirely surprised by such a reception being accorded to him, this young man might not have been entitled reasonably to regard her action as amounting to an invitation to him to enter. If she in fact appeared to be welcoming him, the Crown do not suggest that he should have realised or even suspected that she was so behaving because, despite the moonlight, she thought he was someone else. Unless the jury were entirely satisfied that the defendant made an effective and substantial entry into the bedroom without the complainant doing or saying anything to cause him to believe that she was consenting to his entering it, he ought not to be convicted of the offence charged. The point is a narrow one, as narrow maybe as the window sill which is crucial to this case. But this is a criminal charge of gravity and, even though one may suspect that his intention was to commit the offence charged, unless the facts show with clarity that he in fact committed it he ought not to remain convicted.

Some question arose as to whether or not the defendant can be regarded as a trespasser *ab initio*. But we are entirely in agreement with the view expressed in *Archbold*, again in paragraph 1505, that the common law doctrine of trespass *ab initio* has no application to burglary under the Theft Act 1968. One further matter that was canvassed ought perhaps to be mentioned. The point was raised that, the complainant not being the tenant or occupier of the dwelling house and her mother being apparently in occupation, this girl herself could not in any event have extended an effective invitation to enter, so that even if she had expressly and with full knowledge of all material facts invited the defendant in, he would nevertheless be a trespasser. Whatever be the position in the law of tort, to regard such a proposition as acceptable in the criminal law would be unthinkable.

We have to say that this appeal must be allowed on the basis that the jury were never invited to consider the vital question whether his young man did enter the premises as a trespasser, that is to say knowing perfectly well that he had no invitation to enter or reckless of whether or not his entry was with permission. The certificate of the judge, as we have already said, demonstrated that he felt there were points involved calling for further consideration. That consideration we have given to the best of our ability. For the reasons we have stated, the outcome of the appeal is that this young man must be acquitted of the charge preferred against him. The appeal is accordingly allowed and his conviction quashed.

Appeal allowed.

Questions

1. What error(s), in the opinion of the Court of Appeal, did the trial judge make in his direction to the jury?

2. What other offences, if any, might have been committed by the defendant?

Chapter 9

CRIMINAL STATISTICS

Each year the Home Office publishes its annual review of Criminal Statistics. These statistics provide much useful information and all those concerned in the administration of the criminal justice system should take time to examine them. Below are extracted just a small selection of tables which outline the number of offences recorded by the Police [Criminal Statistics; 1983 H.M.S.O. Cmnd. 9349].

Fig. 2.5 Notifiable offences recorded by the police England and Wales 1983

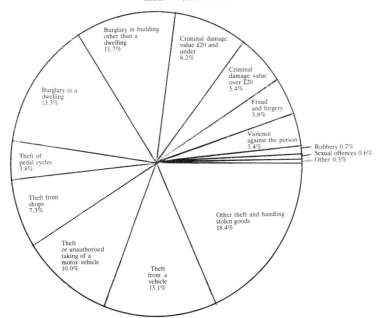

Table 2.8 Notifiable[1] offences of violence against the person recorded by the police by offence
England and Wales

Number of offences

Offence		Offences recorded											Offences cleared up 1983	
		1973	1974	1975	1976	1977	1978	1979	1980	1981	1982	1983	Number	Percentage
4A Murder, Manslaughter, Infanticide } Homicide		456	600	515	565	482	532	629	620	559	618	550	520	95
2 Attempted murder		429	371	499	239	222	185	158	155	182	173	128	113	88
3 Threat or conspiracy to murder[2]		134	131	94	131	165	254	425	528	620	707	688	455	66
4B Child destruction		1	2	—	—	1	2	2	2	1	—	—	—	—
4C Causing death by dangerous or reckless driving[3]		769	654	690	595	602	313	225	235	234	269	189	185	98
5 Wounding or other act endangering life		3,891	4,240	4,399	4,144	4,354	4,504	4,475	4,390	4,685	4,713	5,086	3,857	76
6 Endangering railway passenger		52	40	41	45	26	31	29	38	28	28	34	30	(88)
More serious offences		5,741	6,038	6,238	5,719	5,852	5,821	5,943	5,968	6,309	6,508	6,675	5,160	77
7 Endangering life at sea		5	1	—	—	—	—	—	—	—	—	—	—	—
8 Other wounding etc.		54,545	56,500	63,520	71,188	75,472	80,524	88,327	90,654	93,336	101,566	103,894	77,926	75
9 Assault		879	1,138	1,141	785	783	655	619	557	497	560	693	570	82
12 Abandoning a child under two years		7	9	7	4	7	12	12	8	11	15	22	13	(59)
13 Child stealing		61	53	63	31	51	39	48	48	28	28	44	33	(75)
14 Procuring illegal abortion		36	21	14	9	11	7	3	2	3	3	5	6	(120)[4]
15 Concealment of birth		25	21	19	12	14	15	8	9	23	15	9	8	(89)
Less serious offences		55,558	57,743	64,764	72,029	76,338	81,252	89,017	91,278	93,898	102,187	104,667	78,556	75
Total violence against the person		61,299	63,781	71,002	77,748	82,190	87,073	94,960	97,246	100,207	108,695	111,342	83,716	75

1 In 1978 and earlier years were 'indictable'.
2 Under the Criminal Law Act 1977 this offence was broadened from 8 September 1977 to include verbal threats to kill.
3 Under the Criminal Law Act 1977 this offence was limited as from 1 December 1977 to reckless driving.
4 Offences cleared up in current year may have been initially recorded in an earlier year.
( ) Percentages in brackets are based on totals of less than 100.

Table 2.10 Offences of burglary and robbery recorded by the police by offence

England and Wales

Number of offences

	Offence	Offences recorded											Offences cleared up 1983	
		1973	1974	1975	1976	1977	1978	1979	1980	1981	1982	1983	Number	Percentage
28	Burglary in a dwelling	178,174	213,819	237,353	230,236	262,131	256,759	252,288	294,375	349,011	406,398	431,031	118,305	27
29	Aggravated burglary in a dwelling	241	337	419	404	475	528	484	558	681	690	1,008	309	31
30	Burglary in a building other than a dwelling	205,508	259,138	277,551	279,312	335,725	302,732	291,178	323,373	368,579	398,209	376,196	122,437	33
31	Aggravated burglary in a building other than a dwelling	112	113	106	96	90	90	87	84	110	92	106	67	63
33	Going equipped for stealing etc.	9,130	10,425	6,438	5,400	5,629	5,601	5,101	4,257	4,837	5,197	5,045	4,974	99
	Total burglary	393,165	483,832	521,867	515,448	604,050	565,710	549,138	622,647	723,218	810,586	813,386	246,092	30
34	Robbery	7,338	8,666	11,311	11,611	13,730	13,150	12,482	15,006	20,282	22,837	22,119	5,258	24

Table 2.12 Offences of theft and handling stolen goods recorded by the police by offence

England and Wales

Number of offences

	Offences	Offences recorded											Offences cleared up 1983[1]	
		1973	1974	1975	1976	1977	1978	1979	1980[1]	1981[1]	1982[1]	1983[1]	Number	Percentage
39	Theft from the person of another	10,807	16,092	20,851	24,015	27,545	27,064	26,797	28,775	29,636	28,907	27,913	3,711	13
40	Theft in a dwelling other than from automatic machine or meter	42,609	46,816	49,665	49,828	50,277	45,965	44,418	45,335	46,415	47,980	47,797	18,943	40
41	Theft by an employee	26,464	30,980	31,280	29,513	31,656	32,175	32,587	27,642	23,577	21,918	21,138	19,252	91
42	Theft or unauthorised taking from mail	1,319	1,718	1,584	1,597	1,650	1,571	1,391	1,298	1,285	1,868	1,892	896	47
43	Abstracting electricity	...	...	...	...	...	6,076	6,140	6,906	6,761	6,275	5,688	5,138	90
44	Theft of pedal cycle	53,842	66,097	78,602	86,317	95,663	87,497	96,993	99,910	109,843	124,992	124,648	19,108	15
45	Theft from vehicle	186,714	219,453	239,432	241,397	295,411	293,667	278,349	294,948	379,640	449,037	424,238	105,422	25
46	Theft from shops	130,161	164,063	175,552	180,993	217,276	203,643	203,122	206,175	225,342	242,304	235,512	205,253	87
47	Theft from automatic machine or meter	30,666	29,186	27,164	23,613	23,297	22,056	20,749	24,648	29,441	31,962	34,320	18,603	54
48	Theft or unauthorised taking of motor vehicle	195,518	251,382	264,896	264,537	310,294	316,948	309,245	324,354	332,590	351,230	325,699	85,715	26
49	Other theft or unauthorised taking	281,611	318,622	333,070	339,524	386,576	357,055	351,062	364,663	377,828	405,791	412,208	105,207	26
54	Handling stolen goods	39,099	45,454	45,578	44,338	47,904	47,536	45,290	38,815	40,793	43,589	44,871	44,475	99
	Total theft and handling stolen goods	998,810	1,189,863	1,267,674	1,285,672	1,487,549	1,441,253	1,416,143	1,463,469	1,603,151	1,755,853	1,705,924	631,723	37

1 Figures for 1980 onwards are not comparable with those for previous years because of changes to improve the consistency of recording multiple, continuous and repeated offences.

... Not separately available. Included under classification 99 "other notifiable offence."

Table 2.13 Offences of theft recorded by the police by offence and value of property stolen

England and Wales 1983

Number of offences

	Offence	Total	Value stolen										Average value of property stolen[2] £	Total value of property stolen £ thousand	Total value of property recovered £ thousand
			Nil[1]	Under £5	£5 and under £25	£25 and under £100	£100 and under £500	£500 and under £1,000	£1,000 and under £5,000	£5,000 and under £10,000	£10,000 and under £50,000	£50,000 and over			
39	Theft from the person of another	27,913	1,724	2,105	8,034	10,738	4,267	563	421	41	20	—	123	3,214	177
40	Theft in a dwelling other than from automatic machine or meter	47,797	1,201	8,032	10,274	14,145	10,729	2,005	1,276	95	36	4	175	8,170	776
41	Theft by an employee	21,138	504	3,073	5,623	4,690	4,189	1,252	1,371	231	169	36	625	12,891	2,284
42	Theft or unauthorised taking from mail	1,892	200	845	258	428	124	12	19	3	2	1	142	239	49
43	Abstracting electricity	5,688	1,638[3]	169	555	1,042	1,353	927	113	58	2	—	114	463	16
44	Theft of pedal cycle	124,648	921	169	10,606	68,800	43,848	244	56	4	—	—	85	10,487	812
45	Theft from vehicle	424,238	20,687	54,331	86,182	141,309	104,248	11,388	5,470	408	199	16	143	57,647	4,518
46	Theft from shops	235,512	5,792	102,098	82,039	31,104	11,943	1,785	672	58	20	—	36	8,328	2,697
47	Theft from automatic machine or meter	34,320	4,118	4,866	10,953	10,656	3,583	123	21	—	—	—	47	1,417	56
48	Theft or unauthorised taking of motor vehicle	325,699	10,149	248	948	9,103	149,064	70,632	76,521	7,122	1,814	98	1,014	319,979	224,915
49	Other theft or unauthorised taking	412,208	11,402	56,621	102,839	134,863	81,870	13,584	9,563	984	430	52	180	72,061	7,043
	Total of these theft offences	1,661,053	58,337	232,943	318,798	427,189	414,792	101,701	95,448	8,948	2,690	207	309	494,894	243,343

1 Most of these offences will be attempts, but some offences of unknown value may be included
2 Excluding offences where the value was recorded as nil
3 Including 655 offences for which the value was unknown

Chapter 10

STATUTES ON CRIMINAL LAW

Accessories and Abettors Act 1861

As to abettors in misdemeanours

8. Whosoever shall aid, abet, counsel, or procure the commission of any misdemeanour whether the same be a misdemeanour at common law or by virtue of any Act passed or to be passed, shall be liable to be tried, indicted, and punished as a principal offender.

Offences Against the Person Act 1861

Shooting or attempting to shoot, or wounding, with intent to do grievous bodily harm, or to resist apprehension

18. Whosoever shall unlawfully and maliciously by any means whatsoever wound or cause any grievous bodily harm to any person, with intent to do some grievous bodily harm to any person, or with intent to resist or prevent the lawful apprehension or detainer of any person, shall be guilty of felony, and being convicted thereof shall be liable to be kept in penal servitude for life.

Inflicting bodily injury, with or without weapon

20. Whosoever shall unlawfully and maliciously wound or inflict any grievous bodily harm upon any other person, either with or without any weapon or instrument, shall be guilty of a misdemeanour, and being convicted thereof shall be liable to be kept in penal servitude.

Assault occasioning bodily harm, common assault

47. Whosoever shall be convicted on indictment of any assault occasioning actual bodily harm shall be liable to be kept in penal servitude and whosoever shall be convicted upon an

Indictment for a common Assault shall be liable, at the Discretion of the Court, to be imprisoned for any Term not exceeding One Year, with or without Hard Labour.

Sexual Offences Act 1956

Rape

1. - (1) It is felony for a man to rape a woman.

(2) A man who induces a married woman to have sexual intercourse with him by impersonating her husband commits rape.

Indecent assault on a woman

14. - (1) It is an offence, subject to the exception mentioned in subsection (3) of this section, for a person to make an indecent assault on a woman.

(2) A girl under the age of sixteen cannot in law give any consent which would prevent an act being an assault for the purposes of this section.

(3) Where a marriage is invalid under section two of the Marriage Act, 1949, or section one of the Age of Marriage Act, 1929 (the wife being a girl under the age of sixteen), the invalidity does not make the husband guilty of any offence under this section by reason of her incapacity to consent while under that age, if he believes her to be his wife and has reasonable cause for the belief.

(4) A woman who is a defective cannot in law give any consent which would prevent an act being an assault for the purposes of this section, but a person is only to be treated guilty of an indecent assault on a defective by reason of that incapacity to consent, if that person knew or had reason to suspect her to be a defective.

Indecent assault on a man

15. - (1) It is an offence for a person to make an indecent assault on a man.

(2) A boy under the age of sixteen cannot in law give any consent which would prevent an act being an assault for the purposes of this section.

(3) A man who is a defective cannot in law give any consent which would prevent an act being an assault for the purposes of

this section, but a person is only to be treated as guilty of an indecent assault on a defective by reason of that incapacity to consent, if that person knew or had reason to suspect him to be a defective.

(4) . . . .

(5) For the purposes of the last foregoing subsection a person shall be presumed, unless the contrary is proved, to have been under the age of seventeen, at the time of the offence charged if he is stated in the charge or indictment, and appears to the court, to have been so.

Abduction of unmarried girl under eighteen from parent or guardian

19. - (1) It is an offence, subject to the exception mentioned in this section, for a person to take an unmarried girl under the age of eighteen out of the possession of her parent or guardian against his will, if she is so taken with the intention that she shall have unlawful sexual intercourse with men or with a particular man.

(2) A person is not guilty of an offence under this section because he takes such a girl out of the possession of her parent or guardian as mentioned above, if he believes her to be of the age of eighteen or over and has reasonable cause for the belief.

(3) In this section "guardian" means any person having the lawful care or charge of the girl.

Abduction of unmarried girl under sixteen from parent or guardian

20. - (1) It is an offence for a person acting without lawful authority or excuse to take an unmarried girl under the age of sixteen out of the possession of her parent or guardian against his will.

(2) In the foregoing subsection "guardian" means any person having the lawful care or charge of the girl.

Homicide Act 1957

Abolition of "constructive malice"

1. - (1) Where a person kills another in the course or furtherance of some other offence, the killing shall not amount to murder unless done with the same malice aforethought (express or implied) as is required for a killing to amount to murder when not done in the course or furtherance of another offence.

(2) For the purposes of the foregoing subsection, a killing done in the course or for the purpose of resisting an officer of justice, or of resisting or avoiding or preventing a lawful arrest, or of effecting or assisting an escape or rescue from legal custody, shall be treated as a killing in the course or furtherance of an offence.

Persons suffering from diminished responsibility

2. - (1) Where a person kills or is a party to the killing of another, he shall not be convicted of murder if he was suffering from such abnormality of mind (whether arising from a condition of arrested or retarded development of mind or any inherent causes or induced by disease or injury) as substantially impaired his mental responsibility for his acts and omissions in doing or being a party to the killing.

(2) On a charge of murder, it shall be for the defence to prove that the person charged is by virtue of this section not liable to be convicted of murder.

(3) A person who but for this section would be liable, whether as principal or as accessory, to be convicted of murder shall be liable instead to be convicted of manslaughter.

(4) The fact that one party to a killing is by virtue of this section not liable to be convicted of murder shall not affect the question whether the killing amounted to murder in the case of any other party to it.

Provocation

3. Where on a charge of murder there is evidence on which the jury can find that the person charged was provoked (whether by things done or by things said or by both together) to lose his self-control, the question whether the provocation was enough to make a reasonable man do as he did shall be left to be determined by the jury; and in determining that question the jury shall take into account everything both done and said according to the effect which, in their opinion, it would have on a reasonable man.

Indecency with Children Act 1960

Indecent conduct towards young child

1. - (1) Any person who commits an act of gross indecency with or towards a child under the age of fourteen, or who incites a child under that age to such an act with him or another, shall be liable on conviction on indictment to imprisonment for a term not exceeding two years, or on summary conviction to imprisonment for a term not exceeding six months, to a fine not exceeding [four hundred pounds] or to both.

Criminal Justice Act 1967

Proof of criminal intent

8. A court or jury, in determining whether a person has committed an offence -

(a)   shall not be bound in law to infer that he intended or foresaw a result of his actions by reason only of its being a natural and probable consequence of those actions; but

(b)   shall decide whether he did intend or foresee that result by reference to all the evidence, drawing such inferences from the evidence as appear proper in the circumstances.

Theft Act 1968

Definition of "theft"

Basic definition of theft

1. - (1) A person is guilty of theft if he dishonestly appropriates property belonging to another with the intention of permanently depriving the other of it; and "thief" and "steal" shall be construed accordingly.

(2) It is immaterial whether the appropriation is made with a view to gain, or is made for the thief's own benefit.

(3) The five following sections of this Act shall have effect as regards the interpretation and operation of this section (and, except as otherwise provided by this Act, shall apply only for

purposes of this section).

"Dishonestly"

2. - (1) A person's appropriation of property belonging to another is not to be regarded as dishonest –

(a) if he appropriates the property in the belief that he has in law the right to deprive the other of it, on behalf of himself or of a third person; or

(b) if he appropriates the property in the belief that he would have the other's consent if the other knew of the appropriation and the circumstances of it; or

(c) (except where the property came to him as trustee or personal representative) if he appropriates the property in the belief that the person to whom the property belongs cannot be discovered by taking reasonable steps.

(2) A person's appropriation of property belonging to another may be dishonest notwithstanding that he is willing to pay for the property.

"Appropriates"

3. - (1) Any assumption by a person of the rights of an owner amounts to an appropriation, and this includes, where he has come by the property (innocently or not) without stealing it, any later assumption of a right to it by keeping or dealing with it as owner.

(2) Where property or a right or interest in property is or purports to be transferred for value to a person acting in good faith, no later assumption by him of rights which he believed himself to be acquiring shall, by reason of any defect in the transferor's title, amount to theft of the property.

"Property"

4. - (1) "Property" includes money and all other property, real or personal, including things in action and other intangible property.

(2) A person cannot steal land, or things forming part of land and severed from it by him or by his directions, except in the following cases, that is to say –

(a)   when he is a trustee or personal representative, or is authorised by power of attorney, or as liquidator of a company, or otherwise, to sell or dispose of land belonging to another, and he appropriates the land or anything forming part of it by dealing with it in breach of the confidence reposed in him; or

(b)   when he is not in possession of the land and appropriates anything forming part of the land by severing it or causing it to be severed, or after it has been severed; or

(c)   when, being in possession of the land under a tenancy, he appropriates the whole or part of any fixture or structure let to be used with the land.

For purposes of this subsection "land" does not include incorporeal hereditaments; "tenancy" means a tenancy for years or any less period and includes an agreement for such a tenancy, but a person who after the end of a tenancy remains in possession as statutory tenant or otherwise is to be treated as having possession under the tenancy, and "let" shall be construed accordingly.

(3) A person who picks mushrooms growing wild on any land, or who picks flowers, fruit or foliage from a plant growing wild on any land, does not (although not in possession of the land) steal what he picks, unless he does it for reward or for sale or other commercial purpose.

For purposes of this subsection "mushroom" includes any fungus, and "plant" includes any shrub or tree.

(4) Wild creatures, tamed or untamed, shall be regarded as property; but a person cannot steal a wild creature not tamed nor ordinarily kept in captivity, or the carcase of any such creature unless either it has been reduced into possession by or on behalf of another person and possession of it has not since been lost or abandoned, or another person is in course of reducing it into possession.

"Belonging to another"

5. - (1) Property shall be regarded as belonging to any person having possession or control of it, or having in it any proprietary right or interest (not being an equitable interest arising only from an agreement to transfer or grant an interest).

(2) Where property is subject to a trust, the persons to whom it belongs shall be regarded as including any person having a right to enforce the trust, and an intention to defeat the trust

shall be regarded accordingly as an intention to deprive of the property any person having that right.

(3) Where a person receives property from or on account of another, and is under an obligation to the other to retain and deal with that property or its proceeds in a particular way, the property or proceeds shall be regarded (as against him) as belonging to the other.

(4) Where a person gets property by another's mistake, and is under an obligation to make restoration (in whole or in part) of the property or its proceeds or of the value thereof, then to the extent of that obligation the property or proceeds shall be regarded (as against him) as belonging to the person entitled to restoration, and an intention not to make restoration shall be regarded accordingly as an intention to deprive that person of the property or proceeds.

(5) Property of a corporation sole shall be regarded as belonging to the corporation notwithstanding a vacancy in the corporation.

"With the intention of permanently depriving the other of it"

6. - (1) A person appropriating property belonging to another without meaning the other permanently to lose the thing itself is nevertheless to be regarded as having the intention of permanently depriving the other of it if his intention is to treat the thing as his own to dispose of regardless of the other's rights: and a borrowing or lending of it may amount to so treating it if, but only if, the borrowing or lending is for a period and in circumstances making it equivalent to an outright taking or disposal.

(2) Without prejudice to the generality of subsection (1) above, where a person, having possession or control (lawfully or not) of property belonging to another, parts with the property under a condition as to its return which he may not be able to perform, this (if done for purposes of his own and without the other's authority) amounts to treating the property as his own to dispose of regardless of the other's rights.

Theft, robbery, burglary, etc.

Theft

7. A person guilty of theft shall on conviction on indictment be liable to imprisonment for a term not exceeding ten years.

Robbery

8. - (1) A person is guilty of robbery if he steals, and immediately before or at the time of doing so, and in order to do so, he uses force on any person or puts or seeks to put any person in fear of being then and there subjected to force.

(2) A person guilty of robbery, or of an assault with intent to rob, shall on conviction on indictment be liable to imprisonment for life.

Burglary

9. - (1) A person is guilty of burglary if -

(a) he enters any building or part of a building as a trespasser and with intent to commit any such offence as is mentioned in subsection (2) below; or

(b) having entered any building or part of a building as a trespasser he steals or attempts to steal anything in the building or that part of it or inflicts or attempts to inflict on any person therein any grievous bodily harm.

(2) The offences referred to in subsection (1)(*a*) above are offences of stealing anything in the building or part of a building in question, of inflicting on any person therein any grievous bodily harm or raping any woman therein, and of doing unlawful damage to the building or anything therein.

(3) References in subsections (1) and (2) above to a building shall apply also to an inhabited vehicle or vessel, and shall apply to any such vehicle or vessel at times when the person having a habitation in it is not there as well as at times when he is.

(4) A person guilty of burglary shall on conviction on indictment be liable to imprisonment for a term not exceeding fourteen years.

. . . .

Abstracting of electricity

13. A person who dishonestly uses without due authority, or dishonestly causes to be wasted or diverted, any electricity shall on conviction on indictment be liable to imprisonment for a term not exceeding five years.

. . . .

Obtaining property by deception

15. - (1) A person who by any deception dishonestly obtains property belonging to another, with the intention of permanently depriving the other of it, shall on conviction on indictment be liable to imprisonment for a term not exceeding ten years.

(2) For purposes of this section a person is to be treated as obtaining property if he obtains ownership, possession or control of it, and "obtain" includes obtaining for another or enabling another to obtain or to retain.

(3) Section 6 above shall apply for purposes of this section, with the necessary adaptation of the reference to appropriating, as it applies for purposes of section 1.

(4) For purposes of this section "deception" means any deception (whether deliberate or reckless) by words or conduct as to fact or as to law, including a deception as to the present intentions of the person using the deception or any other person.

Obtaining pecuniary advantage by deception

16. - (1) A person who by any deception dishonestly obtains for himself or another any pecuniary advantage shall on conviction on indictment be liable to imprisonment for a term not exceeding five years.

(2) The cases in which a pecuniary advantage within the meaning of this section is to be regarded as obtained for a person are cases where -

(a)   [*Repealed by Theft Act 1978, s. 5(5)*.]
(b)   he is allowed to borrow by way of overdraft, or to take out any policy of insurance or annuity contract, or obtains an improvement of the terms on which he is allowed to do so; or
(c)   he is given the opportunity to earn remuneration or greater remuneration in an office or employment, or to win money by betting.

(3) For purposes of this section "deception" has the same meaning as in section 15 of this Act.

False accounting

17. - (1) Where a person dishonestly, with a view to gain for himself or another or with intent to cause loss to another, -

(a) destroys, defaces, conceals or falsifies any account or any record or document made or required for any accounting purpose; or

(b) in furnishing information for any purpose produces or makes use of any account, or any such record or document as aforesaid, which to his knowledge is or may be misleading, false or deceptive in a material particular;

he shall, on conviction on indictment, be liable to imprisonment for a term not exceeding seven years.

(2) For purposes of this section a person who makes or concurs in making in an account or other document an entry which is or may be misleading, false or deceptive in a material particular, or who omits or concurs in omitting a material particular from an account or other document, is to be treated as falsifying the account or document.

. . . .

Blackmail

21. - (1) A person is guilty of blackmail if, with a view to gain for himself or another or with intent to cause loss to another, he makes any unwarranted demand with menaces; and for this purpose a demand with menaces is unwarranted unless the person making it does so in the belief -

(a) that he has reasonable grounds for making the demand; and

(b) that the use of the menaces is a proper means of reinforcing the demand.

(2) The nature of the act or omission demanded is immaterial, and it is also immaterial whether the menaces relate to action to be taken by the person making the demand.

(3) A person guilty of blackmail shall on conviction on indictment be liable to imprisonment for a term not exceeding fourteen years.

Handling stolen goods

22. - (1) A person handles stolen goods if (otherwise than in the course of the stealing) knowing or believing them to be stolen goods he dishonestly receives the goods, or dishonestly undertakes or assists in their retention, removal, disposal or realisation by or for the benefit of another person, or if he arranges to do so.

(2) A person guilty of handling stolen goods shall on conviction on indictment be liable to imprisonment for a term not exceeding fourteen years.

. . . .

Going equipped for stealing, etc.

25. - (1) A person shall be guilty of an offence if, when not at his place of abode, he has with him any article for use in the course of or in connection with any burglary, theft or cheat.

(2) A person guilty of an offence under this section shall on conviction on indictment be liable to imprisonment for a term not exceeding three years.

(3) Where a person is charged with an offence under this section, proof that he had with him any article made or adapted for use in committing a burglary, theft or cheat shall be evidence that he had it with him for such use.

(4) Any person may arrest without warrant anyone who is, or whom he, with reasonable cause, suspects to be, committing an offence under this section.

(5) For the purposes of this section an offence under section 12(1) of this Act of taking a conveyance shall be treated as theft, and "cheat" means an offence under section 15 of this Act.

Criminal Damage Act 1971

Destroying or damaging property

1. - (1) A person who without lawful excuse destroys or damages any property belonging to another intending to destroy or damage any such property or being reckless as to whether any such property would be destroyed or damaged shall be guilty of an offence.

(2) A person who without lawful excuse destroys or damages any property, whether belonging to himself or another -

(a) intending to destroy or damage any property or being reckless as to whether any property would be destroyed or damaged; and

(b) intending by the destruction or damage to endanger the

life of another or being reckless as to whether the life of another would be thereby endangered;

shall be guilty of an offence.

(3) An offence committed under this section by destroying or damaging property by fire shall be charged as arson.

Sexual Offences (Amendment) Act 1976

Meaning of "rape" etc.

1. - (1) For the purposes of section 1 of the Sexual Offences Act 1956 (which relates to rape) a man commits rape if -

(a)   he has unlawful sexual intercourse with a woman who at the time of the intercourse does not consent to it; and

(b)   at that time he knows that she does not consent to the intercourse or he is reckless as to whether she consents to it;

references to rape in other enactments (including the following provisions of this Act) shall be construed accordingly.

(2) It is hereby declared that if at a trial for a rape offence the jury has to consider whether a man believed that a woman was consenting to sexual intercourse, the presence or absence of reasonable grounds for such a belief is a matter to which the jury is to have regard, in conjunction with any other relevant matters, in considering whether he so believed.

Theft Act 1978

Obtaining services by deception

1. - (1) A person who by any deception dishonestly obtains services from another shall be guilty of an offence.

(2) It is an obtaining of services where the other is induced to confer a benefit by doing some act, or causing or permitting some act to be done, on the understanding that the benefit has been or will be paid for.

Evasion of liability by deception

2. - (1) Subject to subsection (2) below, where a person by any deception -

(a) dishonestly secures the remission of the whole or part of any existing liability to make a payment, whether his own liability or another's; or

(b) with intent to make permanent default in whole or in part on any existing liability to make a payment, or with intent to let another do so, dishonestly induces the creditor or any person claiming payment on behalf of the creditor to wait for payment (whether or not the due date for payment is deferred) or to forgo payment; or

(c) dishonestly obtains any exemption from or abatement of liability to make a payment;

he shall be guilty of an offence.

(2) For the purposes of this section "liability" means legally enforceable liability; and subsection (1) shall not apply in relation to liability that has not been accepted or established to pay compensation for a wrongful act or omission.

(3) For purposes of subsection (1)(*b*) a person induced to take in payment a cheque or other security for money by way of conditional satisfaction of a pre-existing liability is to be treated not as being paid but as being induced to wait for payment.

(4) For purposes of subsection (1)(*c*) "obtains" includes obtaining for another or enabling another to obtain.

Making off without payment

3. - (1) Subject to subsection (3) below, a person who, knowing that payment on the spot for any goods supplied or service done is required or expected from him, dishonestly makes off without having paid as required or expected and with intent to avoid payment of the amount due shall be guilty of an offence.

(2) For purposes of this section "payment on the spot" includes payment at the time of collecting goods on which work has been done or in respect of which service has been provided.

(3) Subsection (1) above shall not apply where the supply of the goods or the doing of the service is contrary to law, or where the service done is such that payment is not legally enforceable.

(4) Any person may arrest without warrant anyone who is, or whom he, with reasonable cause, suspects to be, committing or attempting to commit an offence under this section.

Punishments

4. - (1) Offences under this Act shall be punishable either on conviction on indictment or on summary conviction.

(2) A person convicted on indictment shall be liable -

(a)   for an offence under section 1 or section 2 of this Act, to imprisonment for a term not exceeding five years; and

(b)   for an offence under section 3 of this Act, to imprisonment for a term not exceeding two years.

(3) A person convicted summarily of any offence under this Act shall be liable -

(a)   to imprisonment for a term not exceeding six months; or

(b)   to a fine not exceeding the prescribed sum for the purposes of [section 32 of the Magistrates' Courts Act 1980]; (punishment on summary conviction of offences triable either way: £1,000 or other sum substituted by order under that Act),

or to both.

Supplementary

5. - (1) For the purposes of sections 1 and 2 above "deception" has the same meaning as in section 15 of the Theft Act 1968, that is to say, it means any deception (whether deliberate or reckless) by words or conduct as to fact or as to law, including a deception as to the present intentions of the persons using the deception or any other person; and section 18 of that Act (liability of company officers for offences by the company) shall apply in relation to sections 1 and 2 above as it applies in relation to section 15 of that Act.

(2) Sections 30(1) (husband and wife), 31(1) (effect on civil proceedings) and 34 (interpretation) of the Theft Act 1968, so far as they are applicable in relation to this Act, shall apply as they apply in relation to that Act.

(3) In the Schedule to the Extradition Act 1873 (additional list of extradition crimes), after "Theft Act 1968" there shall be inserted "or the Theft Act 1978"; and there shall be deemed to be included among the descriptions of offences set out in Schedule 1 to the Fugitive Offenders Act 1967 any offences under this Act.

(4) In the Visiting Forces Act 1952, in paragraph 3 of the Schedule (which defines for England and Wales "offences against property" for purposes of the exclusion in certain cases of the jurisdiction of United Kingdom courts) there shall be added at the end -
"(*j*) the Theft Act 1978".

Criminal Attempts Act 1981

Attempting to commit an offence

1. - (1) If, with intent to commit an offence to which this section applies, a person does an act which is more than merely preparatory to the commission of the offence, he is guilty of attempting to commit the offence.

(2) A person may be guilty of attempting to commit an offence to which this section applies even though the facts are such that the commission of the offence is impossible.

(3) In any case where -

(a) apart from this subsection a person's intention would not be regarded as having amounted to an intent to commit an offence; but
(b) if the facts of the case had been as he believed them to be, his intention would be so regarded,

then, for the purposes of subsection (1) above, he shall be regarded as having had an intent to commit that offence.

(4) This section applies to any offence which, if it were completed, would be triable in England and Wales as an indictable offence, other than -

(a) conspiracy (at common law or under section 1 of the Criminal Law Act 1977 or any other enactment);
(b) aiding, abetting, counselling, procuring or suborning the commission of an offence;
(c) offences under section 4(1) (assisting offenders) or 5(1) (accepting or agreeing to accept consideration for not disclosing information about an arrestable offence) of the Criminal Law Act 1967.

Trial and penalties

4. - (1) A person guilty by virtue of section 1 above of attempting to commit an offence shall -

(a) if the offence is murder or any other offence the sentence for which is fixed by law, be liable on conviction on indictment to imprisonment for life; and

(b) if the offence attempted is indictable but does not fall within paragraph (*a*) above, be liable on conviction on indictment to any penalty to which he would have been liable on conviction on indictment of that offence; and

(c) if the offence attempted is triable either way, be liable on summary conviction to any penalty to which he would have been liable on summary conviction of that offence.

(2) In any case in which a court may proceed to summary trial of an information charging a person with an offence and an information charging him with an offence under section 1 above of attempting to commit it or an attempt under a special statutory provision, the court may, without his consent, try the informations together.

(3) Where, in proceedings against a person for an offence under section 1 above, there is evidence sufficient in law to support a finding that he did an act falling within subsection (1) of that section, the question whether or not his act fell within that subsection is a question of fact.

(4) Where, in proceedings against a person for an attempt under a special statutory provision, there is evidence sufficient in law to support a finding that he did an act falling within subsection (3) of section 3 above, the question whether or not his act fell within that subsection is a question of fact.

(5) Subsection (1) above shall have effect –

(a) subject to section 37 of and Schedule 2 to the Sexual Offences Act 1956 (mode of trial of and penalties for attempts to commit certain offences under that Act); and

(b) notwithstanding anything –
  (i) in section 32(1) (no limit to fine on conviction on indictment) of the Criminal Law Act 1977; or
  (ii) in section 31(1) and (2) (maximum of six months' imprisonment on summary conviction unless express provision made to the contrary) of the Magistrates' Courts Act 1980.

Conspiracy

Extension of definition of the offence of conspiracy

5. - (1) For subsection (1) of section 1 of the Criminal Law Act 1977 (definition of the offence of conspiracy) there shall be substituted the following subsection) -

"(1) Subject to the following provisions of this Part of this Act, if a person agrees with any other person or persons that a course of conduct shall be pursued which, if the agreement is carried out in accordance with their intentions, either -
(*a*) will necessarily amount to or involve the commission of any offence or offences by one or more of the parties to the agreement, or
(*b*) would do so but for the existence of facts which render the commission of the offence or any of the offences impossible,
he is guilty of conspiracy to commit the offence or offences in question."

(2) This section shall not apply where an agreement was entered into before the commencement of this Act unless the conspiracy continued to exist after that date.

Supplementary

Effect of Part I on common law

6. - (1) The offence of attempt at common law and any offence at common law of procuring materials for crime are hereby abolished for all purposes not relating to acts done before the commencement of this Act.

(2) Except as regards offences committed before the commencement of this Act, references in any enactment passed before this Act which fall to be construed as references to the offence of attempt at common law shall be construed as references to the offence under section 1 above.

PART THREE

CONTRACT

Chapter 1

OFFER AND ACCEPTANCE

1. THE INGREDIENTS OF A CONTRACT

Carlill v. Carbolic Smoke Ball Company
[1893] 1 Q.B. 256 (C.A.)

[The defendants were the sellers of a medical preparation picturesquely
described as the "Carbolic Smoke Ball." They placed an advertisement in the
Pall Mall Gazette stating that they would pay £100 to anyone who bought and
used the ball according to their directions and who still contracted influenza.
They mentioned that £1,000 had been deposited with their bankers to show their
sincerity in the matter. Despite using the ball as prescribed, the plaintiff
contracted 'flu. She thereupon sued the defendants for her £100.]

Bowen L.J. We were asked to say that this document was a
contract too vague to be enforced.

The first observation which arises is that the document itself
is not a contract at all, it is only an offer made to the public. The
defendants contend next, that it is an offer the terms of which
are too vague to be treated as a definite offer, inasmuch as
there is no limit of time fixed for the catching of the influenza,
and it cannot be supposed that the advertisers seriously meant
to promise to pay money to every person who catches the
influenza at any time after the inhaling of the smoke ball. It was
urged also, that if you look at this document you will find much
vagueness as to the persons with whom the contract was
intended to be made - that, in the first place, its terms are wide
enough to include persons who may have used the smoke ball
before the advertisement was issued; at all events, that it is an
offer to the world in general, and, also, that it is unreasonable
to suppose it to be a definite offer, because nobody in their
senses would contract themselves out of the opportunity of
checking the experiment which was going to be made at their
own expense. It is also contended that the advertisement is
rather in the nature of a puff or a proclamation than a promise
or offer intended to mature into a contract when accepted. But
the main point seems to be that the vagueness of the document
shows that no contract whatever was intended. It seems to me
that in order to arrive at a right conclusion we must read this

advertisement in its plain meaning, as the public would understand it. It was intended to be issued to the public and to be read by the public. How would an ordinary person reading this document construe it? It was intended unquestionably to have some effect, and I think the effect which it was intended to have, was to make people use the smoke ball, because the suggestions and allegations which it contains are directed immediately to the use of the smoke ball as distinct from the purchase of it. It did not follow that the smoke ball was to be purchased from the defendants directly, or even from agents of theirs directly. The intention was that the circulation of the smoke ball should be promoted, and that the use of it should be increased. The advertisement begins by saying that a reward will be paid by the Carbolic Smoke Ball Company to any person who contracts the increasing epidemic after using the ball. It has been said that the words do not apply only to persons who contract the epidemic after the publication of the advertisement, but include persons who had previously contracted the influenza. I cannot so read the advertisement. It is written in colloquial and popular language, and I think that it is equivalent to this: "100*l*. will be paid to any person who shall contract the increasing epidemic after having used the carbolic smoke ball three times daily for two weeks." And it seems to me that the way in which the public would read it would be this, that if anybody, after the advertisement was published, used three times daily for two weeks the carbolic smoke ball, and then caught cold, he would be entitled to the reward. Then again it was said: "How long is this protection to endure? Is it to go on for ever, or for what limit of time?" I think that there are two constructions of this document, each of which is good sense, and each of which seems to me to satisfy the exigencies of the present action. It may mean that the protection is warranted to last during the epidemic, and it was during the epidemic that the plaintiff contracted the disease. I think, more probably, it means that the smoke ball will be a protection while it is in use. That seems to me the way in which an ordinary person would understand an advertisement about medicine, and about a specific against influenza. It could not be supposed that after you have left off using it you are still to be protected for ever, as if there was to be a stamp set upon your forehead that you were never to catch influenza because you had once used the carbolic smoke ball. I think the immunity is to last during the use of the ball. That is the way in which I should naturally read it, and it seems to be that the subsequent language of the advertisement supports that construction. It says: "During the last epidemic of influenza many thousand carbolic smoke balls were sold, and in no ascertained case was the disease contracted by those using" (not "who had used") "the carbolic smoke ball," and it concludes with saying that one smoke ball will last a family several months (which imports that it is to be efficacious while it is being used), and that the ball can be refilled at a cost of 5s. I, therefore, have myself no hesitation in saying that I think, on the construction of this advertisement, the protection was to enure during the time that the carbolic smoke ball was being used. My brother, the Lord Justice who preceded me, thinks that the contract would be sufficiently definite if you were to read it in the sense that the protection was to be warranted during a reasonable period after use. I have some difficulty myself on that point; but it is not necessary for me to consider it further, because the disease here was contracted during the use of the carbolic smoke ball.

Was it intended that the 100*l*. should, if the conditions were fulfilled, be paid? The advertisement says that 1000*l*. is lodged at the bank for the purpose. Therefore, it cannot be said that the statement that 100*l*. would be paid was intended to be a mere puff. I think it was intended to be understood by the public as an offer which was to be acted upon.

But it was said there was no check on the part of the persons who issued the advertisement, and that it would be an insensate thing to promise 100*l*. to a person who used the smoke ball unless you could check or superintend his manner of using it. The answer to that argument seems to me to be that if a person chooses to make extravagant promises of this kind he probably does so because it pays him to make them, and, if he has made them, the extravagance of the promises is no reason in law why he should not be bound by them.

It was also said that the contract is made with all the world - that is, with everybody; and that you cannot contract with everybody. It is not a contract made with all the world. There is the fallacy of the argument. It is an offer made to all the world; and why should not an offer be made to all the world which is to ripen into a contract with anybody who comes forward and performs the condition? It is an offer to become liable to any one who, before it is retracted, performs the condition, and, although the offer is made to the world, the contract is made with that limited portion of the public who come forward and perform the condition on the faith of the advertisement. It is

not like cases in which you offer to negotiate, or you issue
advertisements that you have got a stock of books to sell, or
houses to let, in which case there is no offer to be bound by any
contract. Such advertisements are offers to negotiate - offers to
receive offers - offers to chaffer as, I think, some learned
judge in one of the cases has said. If this is an offer to be bound,
then it is a contract the moment the person fulfils the
condition. That seems to me to be sense, and it is also the
ground on which all these advertisement cases have been
decided during the century; and it cannot be put better than in
Willes, J.'s, judgment in *Spencer* v. *Harding* (1870). "In the
advertisement cases," he says "there never was any doubt that
the advertisement amounted to a promise to pay the money to
the person who first gave information. The difficulty
suggested was that it was a contract with all the world. But that,
of course, was soon overruled. It was an offer to become liable
to any person who before the offer should be retracted should
happen to be the person to fulfil the contract, of which the
advertisement was an offer or tender. That is not the sort of
difficulty which presents itself here. If the circular had gone
on, 'and we undertake to sell to the highest bidder,' the reward
cases would have applied, and there would have been a good
contract in respect of the persons." As soon as the highest
bidder presented himself says, Willes, J., the person who was to
hold the vinculum juris on the other side of the contract was
ascertained, and it became settled.

Then it was said that there was no notification of the
acceptance of the contract. One cannot doubt that, as an
ordinary rule of law, an acceptance of an offer made ought to
be notified to the person who makes the offer, in order that the
two minds may come together. Unless this is done the two
minds may be apart and there is not that consensus which is
necessary according to the English law - I say nothing about the
laws of other countries - to make a contract. But there is this
clear gloss to be made upon that doctrine, that as notification of
acceptance is required for the benefit of the person who makes
the offer, the person who makes the offer may dispense with
notice to himself if he thinks it desirable to do so, and I suppose
there can be no doubt that where a person in an offer made by
him to another person, expressly or impliedly intimates a
particular mode of acceptance as sufficient to make the
bargain binding, it is only necessary for the other person to
whom such offer is made to follow the indicated method of
acceptance and if the person making the offer, expressly or

impliedly intimates in his offer that it will be sufficient to act on the proposal without communicating acceptance of it to himself, performance of the condition is a sufficient acceptance without notification.

That seems to me to be the principle which lies at the bottom of the acceptance cases, of which two instances are the well-known judgment of Mellish, L.J., in *Harris's Case* (1873), and the very instructive judgment of Lord Blackburn in *Brogden* v. *Metropolitan Ry. Co.* (1877), in which he appears to me to take exactly the line I have indicated.

Now, if that is the law, how are we to find out whether the person who makes the offer does intimate that notification of acceptance will not be necessary in order to constitute a binding bargain? In many cases you look to the offer itself. In many cases you extract from the character of the transaction that notification is not required, and in the advertisement cases it seems to me to follow as an inference to be drawn from the transaction itself that a person is not to notify his acceptance of the offer before he performs the condition, but that if he performs the condition notification is dispensed with. It seems to me that from the point of view of common sense no other idea could be entertained. If I advertise to the world that my dog is lost, and that anybody who brings the dog to a particular place will be paid some money, are all the police or other persons whose business it is to find lost dogs to be expected to sit down and write me a note saying that they have accepted my proposal? Why, of course, they at once look after the dog, and as soon as they find the dog they have performed the condition. The essence of the transaction is that the dog should be found, and it is not necessary under such circumstances, as it seems to me, that in order to make the contract binding there should be any notification of acceptance. It follows from the nature of the thing that the performance of the condition is sufficient acceptance without the notification of it, and a person who makes an offer in an advertisement of that kind makes an offer which must be read by the light of that common sense reflection. He does, therefore, in his offer impliedly indicate that he does not require notification of the acceptance of the offer.

A further argument for the defendants was that this was a nudum pactum - that there was no consideration for the promise - that taking the influenza was only a condition, and that the using the smoke ball was only a condition, and that there was no consideration at all; in fact, that there was no request, express or implied, to use the smoke ball.... The short answer, to abstain from academical discussion, is, it seems to me, that there is here a request to use involved in the offer. Then as to the alleged want of consideration. The definition of "consideration" ... which is cited and adopted by Tindal, C.J., in the case of *Laythoarp* v. *Bryant* (1836), is this: "Any act of the plaintiff from which the defendant derives a benefit or advantage, or any labour, detriment, or inconvenience sustained by the plaintiff, provided such act is performed or such inconvenience suffered by the plaintiff, with the consent, either express or implied, of the defendant." Can it be said here that if the person who reads this advertisement applies thrice daily, for such time as may seem to him tolerable, the carbolic smoke ball to his nostrils for a whole fortnight, he is doing nothing at all - that it is a mere act which is not to count towards consideration to support a promise (for the law does not require us to measure the adequacy of the consideration). Inconvenience sustained by one party at the request of the other is enough to create a consideration. I think, therefore, that it is consideration enough that the plaintiff took the trouble of using the smoke ball. But I think also that the defendants received a benefit from this user, for the use of the smoke ball was contemplated by the defendants as being indirectly a benefit to them, because the use of the smoke balls would promote their sale.

... Here, ... if you once make up your mind that there was a promise made to this lady who is the plaintiff, as one of the public - a promise made to her that if she used the smoke ball three times daily for a fortnight and got the influenza, she should have 100*l*., it seems to me that her using the smoke ball was sufficient consideration. I cannot picture to myself the view of the law on which the contrary could be held when you have once found who are the contracting parties. If I say to a person, "If you use such and such a medicine for a week I will give you 5*l*.," and he uses it, there is ample consideration for the promise.

[Lindley and A.L. Smith L.JJ. delivered concurring judgments.]

Questions

1. This leading case is quoted at length for its importance not only to the problems of offer and acceptance but also for its discussion of many other issues. What other issues do arise in the case?

2. An example of a similar range of problems arising in a modern context is *Esso Petroleum Ltd* .v. *Commissioners of Customs and Excise* (1976) see below, p. 313.

3. What sort of contract was involved in *Carlill?* If the company made an offer here, how could they have revoked it?

4. Compare the "reward" cases of *Williams* v. *Carwardine* (1833) and *R* .v. *Clarke* (1927) (Australia). What problems of revocation arise in this type of case? See, *eg Errington* v. *Errington* (1952).

5. What if the plaintiff had only seen the advertisement after she had bought the smoke ball?

2. OFFER AND INVITATION TO TREAT

Pharmaceutical Society of Great Britain v. Boots Cash Chemists (Southern) Ltd.
[*1953*] *1 Q.B. 401 (C.A.*)

[It was an offence for Boots to sell certain medicines except under the supervision of a registered pharmacist. Two customers in a "self service" shop placed such medicines selected from the open shelves in the wire baskets provided. A pharmacist was available to supervise the transaction at the cash desk. The problem at issue was, therefore, when did the contract of sale take place?]

Somervell L.J. The point taken by the plaintiffs is this: it is said that the purchase is complete if and when a customer going round the shelves takes an article and puts it in the receptacle which he or she is carrying, and that therefore, if that is right, when the customer comes to the pay desk, having completed the tour of the premises, the registered pharmacist, if so minded, has no power to say: "This drug ought not to be sold to this customer." Whether and in what circumstances he would have that power we need not inquire, but one can, of course, see that there is a difference if supervision can only be exercised at a time when the contract is completed.

I agree with the Lord Chief Justice in everything that he said, but I will put the matter shortly in my own words. Whether the view contended for by the plaintiffs is a right view depends on what are the legal implications of this layout - the invitation to the customer. Is a contract to be regarded as being completed when the article is put into the receptacle, or is this to be regarded as a more organized way of doing what is done already in many types of shops - and a bookseller is perhaps the best example - namely, enabling customers to have free access to what is in the shop, to look at the different articles, and then, ultimately, having got the ones which they wish to buy, to come up to the assistant saying "I want this"? The assistant in 999 times out of 1,000 says "That is all right," and the money passes and the transaction is completed. I agree with what the Lord Chief Justice has said, and with the reasons which he has given for his conclusion that in the case of an ordinary shop, although goods are displayed and it is intended that customers should go and choose what they want, the contract is not completed until, the customer having indicated the articles which he needs, the shop-keeper, or someone on his behalf, accepts that offer. Then the contract is completed. I can see no reason at all, that being clearly the normal position, for drawing any different implication as a result of this layout.

The Lord Chief Justice, I think, expressed one of the most formidable difficulties in the way of the plaintiffs' contention when he pointed out that, if the plaintiffs are right, once an article has been placed in the receptacle the customer himself is bound and would have no right, without paying for the first article, to substitute an article which he saw later of a similar kind and which he perhaps preferred. I can see no reason for implying from this self-service arrangement any implication other than that which the Lord Chief Justice found in it, namely, that it is a convenient method of enabling customers to see what there is and choose, and possibly put back and substitute, articles which they wish to have, and then to go up to the cashier and offer to buy what they have so far chosen. On that conclusion the case fails, because it is admitted that there was supervision in the sense required by the Act and at the appropriate moment of time. For these reasons, in my opinion, the appeal should be dismissed.

[Birkett and Romer L.JJ. concurred.]

Questions

1. What of advertisements and displays? See *Partridge* v. *Crittenden* (1968); *Fisher* v. *Bell* (1961).

2. Jane visits a motorway service area where she selects a hot meal from the counter. After waiting in the queue at the cash desk, she decides she is not hungry after all. Is she obliged to pay?

3. Who makes the offer and who accepts at an auction? See *Harris* v. *Nickerson* (1873); *Warlow* v. *Harrison* (1859); Sale of Goods Act 1979, s.57(2).

3. OFFERS AND COUNTER-OFFERS

Stevenson v. McLean
(1880) 5 Q.B.D. 346 (Q.B.D.)

[The parties were negotiating about the sale of a quantity of iron. The defendant wrote: " ... I would now sell for 40s. net cash, open till Monday." The plaintiffs telegraphed in reply, "Please wire whether you would accept forty for delivery over two months, or if not, longest limit you would give." The defendant, after

[receipt of this telegram sold the iron to a third party. The plaintiff's, not yet having received a reply to their telegram, telegraphed an acceptance of the offer to sell at 40s. cash. The plaintiff's sued the defendant for breach of contract; the defendant alleged that the plaintiffs had made a counter offer which entitled the defendant to regard the original offer as no longer open.]

Lush J. Looking at the form of the telegram, the time when it was sent, and the state of the iron market, I cannot think this is its fair meaning. The plaintiff Stevenson said he meant it only as an inquiry, expecting an answer for his guidance, and this, I think, is the sense in which the defendant ought to have regarded it.

It is apparent throughout the correspondence, that the plaintiffs did not contemplate buying the iron on speculation, but that their acceptance of the defendant's offer depended on their finding some one to take the warrants off their hands. All parties knew that the market was in an unsettled state, and that no one could predict at the early hour when the telegram was sent how the prices would range during the day. It was reasonable that, under these circumstances, they should desire to know before business began whether they were to be at liberty in case of need to make any and what concession as to the time or times of delivery, which would be the time or times of payment, or whether the defendant was determined to adhere to the terms of his letter; and it was highly unreasonable that the plaintiffs should have intended to close the negotiation while it was uncertain whether they could find a buyer or not, having the whole of the business hours of the day to look for one. Then, again, the form of the telegram is one of inquiry. It is not "I offer forty for delivery over two months," which would have likened the case to *Hyde* v. *Wrench* [see below]. . . . Here there is no counter proposal. The words are, "Please wire whether you would accept forty for delivery over two months, or, if not, the longest limit you would give." There is nothing specific by way of offer or rejection, but a mere inquiry, which should have been answered and not treated as a rejection of the offer. This ground of objection therefore fails.

Hyde v. Wrench
(1840) 3 Beav. 334 (Rolls Court)

[The defendant offered to sell his farm for £1,000. The plaintiff made an offer of £950 which was refused. The plaintiff then wrote saying that he was prepared to pay £1000 and attempted to enforce the contract of sale at that price. The court held that there was no longer an offer which he could accept.]

The Master of the Rolls [Lord Langdale]. Under the circumstances stated in this bill, I think there exists no valid binding contract between the parties for the purchase of the property. The Defendant offered to sell it for £1000, and if that had been at once unconditionally accepted, there would undoubtedly have been a perfect binding contract; instead of that, the Plaintiff made an offer of his own, to purchase the property for £950, and he thereby rejected the offer previously made by the Defendant. I think that it was not afterwards competent for him to revive the proposal of the Defendant, by tendering an acceptance of it; and that, therefore, there exists no obligation of any sort between the parties; the demurrer must be allowed.

Butler Machine Tool Co. Ltd. v. Ex-Cell-O Corporation
[1979] 1 All E.R. 965 (C.A.)

[The sellers offered to sell one of their machines to the plaintiff on their standard terms, printed on the quotation, which were stated to prevail over any terms and conditions in the buyer's order. The buyer replied by placing an order stated to be on their own terms, which inter alia contained a crucial price variation clause in conflict with the seller's terms. The sellers acknowledged receipt of the order on the buyer's form. The problem was, on whose terms had the contract been concluded?]

Lawton L.J. The modern commercial practice of making quotations and placing orders with conditions attached, usually in small print, is indeed likely, as in this case, to produce a battle of forms. The problem is how should that battle be conducted? The view taken by the judge was that the battle should extend over a wide area and the court should do its best to look into the minds of the parties and make certain assumptions. In my judgment, the battle has to be conducted in accordance with set rules. It is a battle more on classical 18th century lines when convention decided who had the right to open fire first rather than in accordance with the modern concept of attrition.

The rules relating to a battle of this kind have been known for the past 130-odd years. They were set out by the then Master of the Rolls, Lord Langdale, in *Hyde v. Wrench* (1840). . . .

When those rules are applied to this case, in my judgment, the answer is obvious. The sellers started by making an offer. That was in their quotation. The small print was headed by the following words:

"GENERAL. All orders are accepted only upon and subject to the terms set out in our quotation and the following conditions. These terms and conditions shall prevail over any terms and conditions in the Buyer's order."

That offer was not accepted. The buyers were only prepared to have one of these very expensive machines on their own terms. Their terms had very material differences in them from the terms put forward by the sellers. They could not be reconciled in any way. In the language of art 7 of the Uniform Law on the Formation of Contracts for the International Sale of Goods they did materially alter the terms set out in the offer made by the sellers.

As I understand *Hyde v. Wrench* and the cases which have followed, the consequence of placing the order in that way, if I may adopt Megaw J's words, was to kill the quotation. It follows that the court has to look at what happened after the buyers made their counter-offer. By letter dated 4th June 1969 the sellers acknowledged receipt of the counter-offer and they went on in this way: 'Details of this order have been passed to our Halifax works for attention and a formal acknowledgment of order will follow in due course.' That is clearly a reference to the printed tear-of-slip which was at the bottom of the buyers' counter-offer. By letter dated 5th June 1969 the sales office manager at the sellers' Halifax factory completed that tear-off slip and sent it back to the buyers. . . . . . .

As I pointed out in the course of argument to counsel for the sellers, if the letter of 5th June which accompanied the form acknowledging the terms which the buyers had specified had amounted to a counter-offer, then in my judgment the parties never were ad idem. It cannot be said that the buyers accepted the counter-offer by reason of the fact that ultimately they took physical delivery of the machine. By the time they took physical delivery of the machine, they had made it clear by correspondence that they were not accepting that there was any price escalation clause in any contract which they had made with the plaintiffs.

[Lord Denning M.R. and Bridge L.J. gave concurring judgments, although Lord Denning took the opportunity to criticise the traditional analysis of offer and acceptance as applied to a modern situation such as the "Battle of the Forms" cases.]

Byrne v. Van Tienhoven
(1880) 5 C.P.D. 344 (Common Pleas)

[The defendants in Cardiff posted a letter to New York offering to sell 1,000 boxes of tinplates. On October 8 they posted a letter revoking the offer. On October 11

[the plaintiffs received the first letter and telegraphed their acceptance. The second letter arrived on October 20. Had there been a revocation of the offer?]

Lindley J. There is no doubt that an offer can be withdrawn before it is accepted, and it is immaterial whether the offer is expressed to be open for acceptance for a given time or not: *Routledge* v. *Grant* (1828). For the decision of the present case, however, it is necessary to consider two other questions, viz.: 1. Whether a withdrawal of an offer has any effect until it is communicated to the person to whom the offer has been sent? 2. Whether posting a letter of withdrawal is a communication to the person to whom the letter is sent?

[The court held that a revocation to be effective must be communicated. It was not fatal to a contract that *both* parties were no longer consenting *ad idem*. This is an example of the "objective" approach of English contract law.]

I pass, therefore, to the next question, viz., whether posting the letter of revocation was a sufficient communication of it to the plaintiff. The offer was posted on the 1st October, the withdrawal was posted on the 8th, and did not reach the plaintiff until after he had posted his letter of the 11th, accepting the offer. It may be taken as now settled that where an offer is made and accepted by letters sent through the post, the contract is completed the moment the letter accepting the offer is posted . . . even although it never reaches its destination. When, however, these authorities are looked at, it will be seen that they are based upon the principle that the writer of the offer has expressly or impliedly assented to treat an answer to him by a letter duly posted as a sufficient acceptance and notification to himself, or, in other words, he has made the post office his agent to receive the acceptance and notification of it. But this principle appears to me to be inapplicable to the case of the withdrawal of an offer. In this particular case I can find no evidence of any authority in fact given by the plaintiffs to the defendants to notify a withdrawal of their offer by merely posting a letter; and there is no legal principle or decision which compels me to hold, contrary to the fact, that the letter of the 8th of October is to be treated as communicated to the plaintiff on that day or on any day before the 20th, when the letter reached them. But before that letter had reached the plaintiffs, they had accepted the offer, both by telegram and by post; and they had themselves resold the tin plates at a profit. In my opinion the withdrawal by the defendants on the 8th of October of their offer of the 1st was inoperative; and a complete contract binding on both parties was entered into on the 11th of October, when the plaintiffs accepted the offer of the 1st, which they had no reason to suppose had been withdrawn. Before leaving this part of the case it may be as well to point out the extreme injustice and inconvenience which any other conclusion would produce. If the defendants' contention were to prevail no person who had received an offer by post and had accepted it would know his position until he had waited such a time as to be quite sure that a letter withdrawing the offer had not been posted before his acceptance of it. It appears to me that both legal principles, and practical convenience require that a person who has accepted an offer not known to him to have been revoked, shall be in a position safely to act upon the footing that the offer and acceptance constitute a contract binding on both parties.

Judgment was given for the plaintiffs.

Question

What if a party only hears a rumour that the potential seller has changed his mind? See *Dickinson* v. *Dodds* (1876).

4. ACCEPTANCE

Felthouse v. Bindley
(1862) 142 E.R. 1037 (Common Pleas)

[The plaintiff, Paul Felthouse, was anxious to buy a horse forming part of the farming stock which his nephew, John Felthouse, wished to sell. A misunderstanding arose as to the price, John thinking he had sold the horse for 30 guineas, Paul thinking he had bought it for £30. Accordingly, Paul wrote to John on January 2 offering to split the difference and added, "If I hear no more about him, I consider the horse mine at £30.15s." John did not reply, but he did tell the auctioneer, Brindley, to withdraw the horse from the sale. Brindley mistakenly sold the horse to another. Paul sued Brindley, claiming that at the time of the auction on February 25, the horse already belonged to him.]

Willes, J. I am of opinion that the rule to enter a nonsuit should be made absolute. . . . It is clear that there was no complete bargain on the 2nd of January: and it is also clear that the uncle had no right to impose upon the nephew a sale of his horse for 30l. 15s, unless he chose to comply with the condition of writing to repudiate the offer. The nephew might, no doubt, have bound his uncle to the bargain by writing to him: the uncle might also have retracted his offer at any time before acceptance. It stood an open offer and so things remained until the 25th of February, when the nephew was about to sell his farming stock by auction. The horse in question being catalogued with the rest of the stock, the auctioneer (the defendant) was told that it was already sold. It is clear, therefore, that the nephew in his own mind intended his uncle to have the horse at the price which he (the uncle) had named, - 30l. 15s.: but he had not communicated such his intention to his uncle, or done anything to bind himself. Nothing, therefore, had been done to vest the property in the horse in the plaintiff down to the 25th of February, when the horse was sold by the defendant. . . .

Keating, J. I am of the same opinion. Had the question arisen as between the uncle and the nephew, there would probably have been some difficulty. But, as between the uncle and the auctioneer, the only question we have to consider is whether the horse was the property of the plaintiff at the time of the sale on the 25th of February. It seems to me that nothing had been done at that time to pass the property out of the nephew and vest it in the plaintiff.

[*Byles J.* concurred.]

Question

Suppose the auctioneer had not sold the horse, but the uncle had refused to accept delivery of the horse. Could the nephew have sued for breach of contract?

Entores Ltd. v. Miles Far East Corporation
[1955] 2 Q.B. 327 (C.A.)

[The plaintiffs in London telexed the defendant's agents in Holland making an offer. The agents sent an acceptance by telex which was received in London. An issue arose of where the contract had been made, this in turn depended upon at what point there had been acceptance of the offer.]

Lord Denning M.R. When a contract is made by post it is clear law throughout the common law countries that the acceptance is complete as soon as the letter is put into the post box, and that is the place where the contract is made. But there is no clear rule about contracts made by telephone or by Telex. Communications by these means are virtually instantaneous and stand on a different footing.

The problem can only be solved by going in stages. Let me first consider a case where two people make a contract by word of mouth in the presence of one another. Suppose, for instance, that I shout an offer to a man across a river or a courtyard but I do not hear his reply because it is drowned by an aircraft flying overhead. There is no contract at that moment. If he wishes to make a contract, he must wait till the aircraft is gone and then shout back his acceptance so that I can hear what he says. Not until I have his answer am I bound. . . .

Now take a case where two people make a contract by telephone. Suppose, for instance, that I make an offer to a man by telephone and, in the middle of his reply, the line goes "dead" so that I do not hear his words of acceptance. There is no contract at that moment. The other man may not know the precise moment when the line failed. But he will know that the telephone conversation was abruptly broken off: because people usually say something to signify the end of the conversation. If he wishes to make a contract, he must therefore get through again so as to make sure that I heard. Suppose next, that the line does not go dead, but it is nevertheless so indistinct that I do not catch what he says and I ask him to repeat it. He then repeats it and I hear his acceptance. The contract is made, not on the first time when I do not hear, but only the second time when I do hear. If he does not repeat it, there is no contract. The contract is only complete when I have his answer accepting the offer.

Lastly, take the Telex. Suppose a clerk in a London office taps out on the teleprinter an offer which is immediately recorded on a teleprinter in a Manchester office, and a clerk at that end taps out an acceptance. If the line goes dead in the middle of the sentence of acceptance, the teleprinter motor will stop. There is then obviously no contract. The clerk at Manchester must get through again and send his complete sentence. But it may happen that the line does not go dead, yet the message does not get through to London. Thus the clerk at Manchester may tap out his message of acceptance and it will not be recorded in London because the ink at the London end fails, or something of that kind. In that case, the Manchester clerk will not know of the failure but the London clerk will know of it and will immediately send back a message "not receiving." Then, when the fault is rectified, the Manchester clerk will repeat his message. Only then is there a contract. If he does not repeat it, there is no contract. It is not until his message is received that the contract is complete.

In all the instances I have taken so far, the man who sends the message of acceptance knows that it has not been received or he has reason to know it. So he must repeat it. But, suppose that he does not know that his message did not get home. He thinks it has. This may happen if the listener on the telephone does not catch the words of acceptance, but nevertheless does not trouble to ask for them to be repeated: or the ink on the teleprinter fails at the receiving end, but the clerk does not ask for the message to be repeated: so that the man who sends an acceptance reasonably believes that his message has been received. The offeror in such circumstances is clearly bound, because he will be estopped from saying that he did not receive the message of acceptance. It is his own fault that he did not get it. But if there should be a case where the offeror without any fault on his part does not receive the message of acceptance - yet the sender of it reasonably believes it has got home when it has not - then I think there is no contract.

My conclusion is, that the rule about instantaneous communications between the parties is different from the rule about the post. The contract is only complete when the acceptance is received by the offeror: and the contract is made at the place where the acceptance is received.

In a matter of this kind, however, it is very important that the countries of the world should have the same rule. I find that most of the European countries have substantially the same rule as that I have stated. Indeed, they apply it to contracts by post as well as instantaneous communications. But in the United States of America it appears as if instantaneous communications are treated in the same was as postal communications. In view of this divergence, I think that we must consider the matter on principle: and so considered, I have come to the view I have stated, and I am glad to see that Professor Winfield in this country (55 Law Quarterly Review, 514), and Professor Williston in the United States of America (Contracts, para. 82, p. 239), take the same view.

Applying the principles which I have stated, I think that the contract in this case was made in London where the acceptance was received.

Notes

The House of Lords approved this decision in *Brinkibon Ltd*. v. *Stahag Stahl* (1982).

Lord Denning has taken the view that the conventional analysis of situations into offer and acceptance is not always appropriate. See *Butler Machine Tool Co. Ltd*. v. *Ex-Cell-O Corporation* (above, p. 288); *Gibson* v. *Manchester City Council* (1979). There are certainly cases where it can become very strained. An example is the problem of cross offers (see *Tinn* v. *Hoffman* (1873)) or the peculiar facts of *Clarke* v. *Dunraven* (1897).

Questions

1. What is the legal effect of a "telemessage"?
2. Suppose the agents had replied by telephone, but it was a message dictated on to the plaintiff's answering machine. Would there have been a valid acceptance?

Chapter 2

CONSIDERATION

1. THE MEANING OF CONSIDERATION

Chappell & Co. v. Nestlé
[1960] A.C. 87 (H.L.)

[As part of a sale's promotion Nestlé's offered a record for sale at a price of 1s. 6d. plus three wrappers from their bars of chocolate. An issue arose as to whether the wrappers were part of the consideration for the contract.]

Lord Somervell of Harrow. I think they are part of the consideration. They are so described in the offer. "They," the wrappers, "will help you to get smash hit recordings." They are so described in the record itself - "all you have to do to get such new record is to send three wrappers from Nestlé's 6d. milk chocolate bars, together with postal order for 1s. 6d." This is not conclusive but, however described, they are, in my view, in law part of the consideration. It is said that when received the wrappers are of no value to Nestlé's. This I would have thought irrelevant. A contracting party can stipulate for what consideration he chooses. A peppercorn does not cease to be good consideration if it is established that the promisee does not like pepper and will throw away the corn. As the whole object of selling the record, if it was a sale, was to increase the sales of the chocolate, it seems to me wrong not to treat the stipulated evidence of such sales as part of the consideration. For these reasons I would allow the appeal.

[Lords Reid and Tucker delivered speeches allowing the appeal.]

Bainbridge v. Firmstone
(1838) 112 E.R. 1019 (Q.B.D.)

[The plaintiff, at the request of the defendant, allowed the defendant to weigh two of the plaintiff's boilers. The defendant promised to return the boilers in perfect condition, which he failed to do. The plaintiff sued, but the defendant claimed there was no consideration for his promise.]

Lord Denman C.J. It seems to me that the declaration is well enough. The defendant had some reason for wishing to weigh the boilers; and he could do so only by obtaining permission from the plaintiff, which he did obtain by promising to return them in good condition. We need not enquire what benefit he expected to derive. The plaintiff might have given or refused leave.

Patteson J. The consideration is, that the plaintiff, at the defendant's request, had consented to allow the defendant to weigh the boilers. I suppose the defendant thought he had some benefit; at any rate, there is a detriment to the plaintiff from his parting with the possession for even so short a time.

Williams and *Coleridge JJs.* concurred.

Notes

For a further discussion of consideration, see *Carlill* v. *Carbolic Smoke Ball Co.*(above, p. 283). On the requirement often stated that, "consideration must move from the promisee," see *Tweddle* v. *Atkinson* (1861) and Chapter 7.

2. CONSIDERATION AND THE TIME OF THE AGREEMENT

Lampleigh v. Braithwait
(1615) 80 E.R. 255 (Common Bench)

[Thomas Braithwait who had killed a man asked Anthony Lampleigh to obtain a pardon for him from the King. Lampleigh went to considerable trouble at his own expense, and Braithwait then promised him £100 for his troubles which he failed to pay. Lampleigh sued, Braithwait alleged that the consideration was passed and that there was therefore no contract.]

First, it was agreed, that a meer voluntary curtesie will not have a consideration to uphold an assumpsit. But if that curtesie were moved by a suit or request of the party that gives the assumpsit, it will bind, for the promise, though it follows, yet it is not naked, but couples it self with the suit before, and the merits of the party procured by that suit, which is the difference.

Judgment given for Anthony Lampleigh.

Note

A more recent illustration of the same principle is to be found in *Re Casey's Patents, Stewart* v. *Casey* (1893).

Roscorla v. Thomas
(1842) 114 E.R. 496 (Q.B.)

[The defendant sold the plaintiff a horse without, it seems, any warranty that it was sound. Subsequently the defendant claimed that it was "sound and free from vice." The plaintiff sued on the grounds that it was in fact "vicious, restive, ungovernable, and ferocious."

Lord Denman C.J. This was an action of assumpsit for breach of warranty of the soundness of a horse. The first count of the declaration, upon which alone the question arises, stated that, in consideration that the plaintiff, at the request of the defendant, had bought of the defendant a horse for the sum of 30l., the defendant promised that it was sound and free from vice. And it was objected, in arrest of judgment, that the precedent executed consideration was insufficient to support the subsequent promise. And we are of opinion that the objection must prevail.

It may be taken as a general rule, subject to exceptions not applicable to this case, that the promise must be coextensive with the consideration. In the present case, the only promise that would result from the consideration, as stated, and be coextensive with it, would be to deliver the horse upon request. The precedent sale, without a warranty, though at the request of the defendant, imposes no other duty or obligation upon him. It is clear, therefore, that the consideration stated would not raise an implied promise by the defendant that the horse was sound or free from vice.

But the promise in the present case must be taken to be, as in fact it was, express: and the question is, whether that fact will warrant the extension of the promise beyond that which would be implied by law; and whether the consideration, though insufficient to raise an implied promise, will nevertheless support an express one. And we think that it will not.

The cases in which it has been held that, under certain circumstances, a consideration insufficient to raise an implied promise will nevertheless support an express one, will be found. . . . They are cases of voidable contracts subsequently ratified, of debts barred by operation of law, subsequently revived, and of equitable and moral obligations, which, but for some rule of law, would of themselves have been sufficient to raise an implied promise. All these cases are distinguishable from, and indeed inapplicable to, the present, which appears to us to fall within the general rule, that a consideration past and executed will support no other promise than such as would be implied by law.

Judgment for the defendant.

Note

A modern illustration of the same principle is *Re McArdle* (1951).

Question

What if the defendant had made the statement about the horse *before* the plaintiff had agreed to buy it?

3. PERFORMANCE OF AN EXISTING DUTY

Ward v. Byham
[1956] 2 All E.R. 318 (C.A.)

[The defendant, who was the father of the plaintiff's illegitimate child, wrote to her saying that he would provide £1 a week maintenance "providing you can prove that she will be well looked after and happy and also that she is allowed to decide for herself whether or not she wishes to come and live with you." The father appealed against the court's judgment for the mother.]

Lord Denning. The mother now brings this action, claiming that the father should pay her £1 per week, even though she herself has married. The only point taken before us in answer to the claim is that it is said that there was no consideration for the promise by the father to pay £1 a week, because, when she looked after the child, the mother was only doing that which she was legally bound to do, and that is no consideration in law.
. . .

By statute the mother of an illegitimate child is bound to maintain it, whereas the father is under no such obligation (see s. 42 of the National Assistance Act, 1948). If she is a single woman the mother can apply to the magistrates for an affiliation order against the father, and it might be thought that consideration could be found in this case by holding that the mother must be taken to have agreed not to bring affiliation proceedings against the father. In her evidence the mother said, however, that she never at any time had any intention of bringing affiliation proceedings. It is now too late for her to bring them, because she has married and is no longer a single woman.

I approach the case, therefore, on the footing that, in looking after the child, the mother is only doing what she is legally bound to do. Even so, I think that there was sufficient consideration to support the promise. I have always thought that a promise to perform an existing duty, or the performance of it, should be regarded as good consideration, because it is a benefit to the person to whom it is given. Take this very case. It is as much a benefit for the father to have the child looked after by the mother as by a neighbour. If he gets the benefit for which he stipulated, he ought to honour his promise, and he ought not to avoid it by saying that the mother was herself under a duty to maintain the child.

I regard the father's promise in this case as what is sometimes called a unilateral contract, a promise in return for an act, a promise by the father to pay £1 a week in return for the mother's looking after the child. Once the mother embarked on the task of looking after the child, there was a binding contract. So long as she looked after the child, she would be entitled to £1 a week. . . .

[*Morris and Parker LJJ* concurred].

Notes

Forebearance to sue is also capable of amounting to consideration. Lord Denning's view of performance of an existing duty as consideration is not consistent with much of the case law on the subject. Contrast *eg Collins* v. *Godefroy* (1831) with *Glasbrook Bros.* v. *Glamorgan County Council* (1925). The performance of a contractual duty owed to a third party can amount to consideration, see *Scotson* v. *Pegg* (1861); *New Zealand Shipping Co. Ltd.* v. *Satterthwaite & Co. Ltd.* (1975). The point was authoratatively confirmed by the Privy Council in *Pau On* v. *Lau Yiu Long* (1980). What is the basis for allowing performance of a duty owed to a third party to amount to consideration? Why should cases of statutory duty be treated differently?

On performance of contractual duties, it is helpful to compare the cases of *Stilk* v. *Myrick* (1809) and *Hartley* v. *Ponsonby* (1857).

4. PART PAYMENT OF A DEBT

Foakes v. Beer
(1884) 9 App. Cas. 605 (H.L.)

[Mrs. Beer had obtained judgment against Dr. Foakes for £2090 19s. She subsequently agreed in a written memorandum that she would not "take any proceedings whatever on the judgment" if he would pay the money by instalments. By statute, a judgment debt bears interest until it is fully paid, but the agreement made no reference to interest. Dr. Foakes paid off the entire judgment and Mrs. Beer then claimed the interest as well. The House of Lords was divided on the issue of whether the agreement should properly be understood to mean that the claim to interest was waived by Mrs. Beer. They were nevertheless unanimous that, even if this were so, such an agreement would be unenforceable for lack of consideration.]

Earl of Selbourne L.C. [Having doubted whether the agreement was intended to reserve Mrs. Beer's claim to interest, continued:] But the question remains, whether the agreement is capable of being legally enforced. Not being under seal, it cannot be legally enforced against the respondent, unless she received consideration for it from the appellant, or unless, though without consideration, it operates by way of accord and satisfaction, so as to extinguish the claim for interest. What is the consideration? On the face of the agreement none is expressed, except a present payment of £500, on account and in part of the larger debt then due and payable by law under the judgment. The appellant did not contract to pay the future instalments of £150 each, at the times therein mentioned; much less did he give any new security, in the shape of negotiable paper, or in any other form. The promise de futuro was only that of the respondent, that if the half-yearly payments of £150 each were regularly paid, she would "take no proceedings whatever on the judgment." No doubt if the appellant had been under no antecedent obligation to pay the whole debt, his fulfilment of the condition might have imported some consideration on his part for that promise. But he was under that antecedent obligation; and payment at those deferred dates, by the forbearance and indulgence of the creditor, of the residue of the principal debt and costs, could not (in my opinion) be a consideration for the relinquishment of interest and discharge of the judgment, unless the payment of the £500, at the time of signing the agreement, was such a consideration. As to accord and satisfaction, in point of fact there could be no complete satisfaction, so long as any future instalment remained payable; and I do not see how any mere payments on account could operate in law as a satisfaction ad interim, conditionally upon other payments being afterwards duly made, unless there was a consideration sufficient to support the agreement while still unexecuted. Nor was anything, in fact, done by the respondent in this case, on the receipt of the last payment, which could be tantamount to an acquittance, if the agreement did not previously bind her.

The question, therefore, is nakedly raised by this appeal, whether your Lordships are now prepared, not only to overrule, as contrary to law, the doctrine stated by Sir Edward Coke to have been laid down by all the judges of the Common Pleas in *Pinnel's Case* in 1602, and repeated in his note to Littleton, sect. 344 (2), but to treat a prospective agreement, not under seal, for satisfaction of a debt, by a series of payments on account to a total amount less than the whole debt, as binding in law, provided those payments are regularly made; the case not being one of a composition with a common debtor, agreed to, inter se, by several creditors. . . . The doctrine itself, as laid down by Sir Edward Coke, may have been criticised, as questionable in principle, by some persons whose opinions are entitled to respect, but it has never been judicially overruled; on the contrary I think it has always, since the sixteenth century, been accepted as law. If so, I cannot think that your Lordships would do right, if you were now to reverse, as erroneous, a judgment of the Court of Appeal, proceeding upon a doctrine which has been accepted as part of the law of England for 280 years. . . .

The distinction between the effect of a deed under seal, and that of an agreement by parol, or by writing not under seal, may seem arbitrary, but it is established in our law; nor is it really unreasonable or practically inconvenient that the law should require particular solemnities to give to a gratuitous contract the force of a binding obligation. If the question be (as, in the actual state of the law, I think it is), whether consideration is, or is not, given in a case of this kind, by the debtor who pays down part of the debt presently due from him, for a promise by the creditor to relinquish, after certain further payments on account, the residue of the debt, I cannot say that I think consideration is given, in the sense in which I have always understood that word as used in our law. It might be (and indeed I think it would be) an improvement in our law, if a release or acquittance of the whole debt, on payment of any sum which the creditor might be content to receive by way of accord and satisfaction (though less than the whole), were held to be, generally, binding, though not under seal; nor should I be unwilling to see equal force given to a prospective agreement, like the present, in writing though not under seal; but I think it impossible, without refinements which practically alter the sense of the word, to treat such a release or acquittance as supported by any new consideration proceeding from the debtor. . . .

Lord Blackburn. [Having also considered the intention of the parties as evidenced in the memorandum, turned to the question of whether payment of a lesser sum is good satisfaction for a debt:]

This is a question, I think, of difficulty.

In Coke, Littleton 212 b, Lord Coke says: "where the condition is for payment of £20, the obligor or feoffor cannot at the time appointed pay a lesser sum in satisfaction of the whole, because *it is apparent* that a lesser sum of money *cannot* be a satisfaction of a greater. . . . If the obligor or feoffor pay a lesser sum either before the day or at another place than is limited by the condition, and the obligee or feoffor receiveth it, this is a good satisfaction." For this he cites *Pinnel's Case* (1602). That was an action on a bond for £16, conditioned for the payment of £8 10s. on the 11th of November 1600. Plea that defendant, at plaintiff's request, before the said day, to wit, on the 1st of October, paid to the plaintiff £5 2s. 2d., which the plaintiff accepted in full satisfaction of the £8 10s. The plaintiff had judgment for the insufficient pleading. But though this was so, Lord Coke reports that it was resolved by the whole Court of Common Pleas "that payment of a lesser sum on the day in satisfaction of a greater cannot be any satisfaction for the whole, because it appears to the judges that by no possibility a lesser sum can be a satisfaction to the plaintiff for a greater sum: but the gift of a horse, hawk, or robe, &c., in satisfaction is good, for it shall be intended that a horse, hawk, or robe, &c., might be more beneficial to the plaintiff than the money, in respect of some circumstance, or otherwise the plaintiff would not have accepted of it in satisfaction. But when the whole sum is due, by no intendment the acceptance of parcel can be a satisfaction to the plaintiff; but in the case at bar it was resolved that the payment and acceptance of parcel before the day in satisfaction of the whole would be a good satisfaction in regard of circumstance of time; for peradventure parcel of it before the day would be more beneficial to him than the whole at the day, and the value of the satisfaction is not material; so if I am bound in £20 to pay you £10 at Westminster, and you request me to pay you £5 at the day at York, and you will accept it in full satisfaction for the whole £10, it is a good satisfaction for the whole, for the expenses to pay it at York is sufficient satisfaction."

There are two things here resolved. First, that where a matter paid and accepted in satisfaction of a debt certain might by any possibility be more beneficial to the creditor than his debt, the Court will not inquire into the adequacy of the consideration. If the creditor, without any fraud, accepted it in satisfaction when it was not a sufficient satisfaction it was his own fault. And that payment before the day might be more beneficial, and consequently that the plea was in substance good, and this must have been decided in the case.

There is a second point stated to have been resolved, viz.: "That payment of a lesser sum on the day cannot be any satisfaction of the whole, because it appears to the judges that by no possibility a lesser sum can be a satisfaction to the plaintiff for a greater sum." This was certainly not necessary for the decision of the case; but though the resolution of the Court of Common Pleas was only a dictum, it seems to me clear that Lord Coke deliberately adopted the dictum, and the great weight of his authority makes it necessary to be cautious before saying that what he deliberately adopted as law was a mistake.

. . . .

For instance, in *Sibree* v. *Tripp* (1846) Parke, B. says, "It is clear if the claim be a liquidated and ascertained sum, payment of part cannot be satisfaction of the whole, although it may, under certain circumstances, be evidence of a gift of the remainder." And Alderson, B. in the same case says, "It is undoubtedly true that payment of a portion of a liquidated demand, in the same manner as the whole liquidated demand which ought to be paid, is payment only in part, because it is not one bargain, but two; viz. payment of part, and an agreement without consideration to give up the residue. The Courts might very well have held the contrary, and have left the matter to the agreement of the parties, but undoubtedly the law is so settled." After such strong expressions of opinion, I doubt much whether any judge sitting in a Court of the first instance would be justified in treating the question as open. But as this has very seldom, if at all, been the ground of the decision even in a Court of the first instance, and certainly never been the ground of a decision in the Court of Exchequer Chamber, still less in this House, I did think it open in your Lordships' House to reconsider this question. And, notwithstanding the very high authority of Lord Coke, I think it is not the fact that to accept prompt payment of a part only of a liquidated demand, can never be more beneficial than to insist on payment of the whole. And if it be not the fact, it cannot be apparent to the judges.

[His Lordship then considered various earlier authorities.]

What principally weighs with me in thinking that Lord Coke made a mistake of fact is my conviction that all men of business, whether merchants or tradesmen, do every day recognise and act on the ground that prompt payment of a part of their demand may be more beneficial to them than it would be to insist on their rights and enforce payment of the whole. Even where the debtor is perfectly solvent, and sure to pay at last, this often is so. Where the credit of the debtor is doubtful it must be more so. I had persuaded myself that there was no such long-continued action on this dictum as to render it improper in this House to reconsider the question. I had written my reasons for so thinking; but as they were not satisfactory to the other noble and learned Lords who heard the case, I do not now repeat them nor persist in them.

I assent to the judgment proposed, though it is not that which I had originally thought proper.

[Lords Watson and Fitsgerald also agreed that there was no consideration provided by Dr. Foakes.]

Notes

Composition agreements with creditors are an exception to the principle that payment of a lesser sum is satisfaction for a debt. See *Hirach and Punamchand* v. *Temple* (1911).

Question

Would this case be decided by a court in the same way today?

5. PROMISSORY ESTOPPEL

Central London Property Trust Ltd. v. High Trees House Ltd.
[*1947*] *K.B. 130* (*K.B.D.*)

[In September 1939 the plaintiffs had leased a block of flats to the defendants. Because of the subsequent wartime conditions many of the flats were unoccupied and the landlords agreed in 1940 to accept half-rent only. By 1945 all the flats were let and so the plaintiffs claimed the full rent for the last two quarters of 1945. The defendants pleaded in the alternative that either the agreement of 1940 operated throughout the entire remaining period of the lease or that the plaintiffs were estopped from demanding or had waived their rights to demand rent at the full rate for the period before 1945.]

Denning J. stated the facts and continued: If I were to consider this matter without regard to recent developments in the law, there is no doubt that had the plaintiffs claimed it, they would have been entitled to recover ground rent at the rate of 2,500*l.* a year from the beginning of the term, since the lease under which it was payable was a lease under seal which, according to the old common law, could not be varied by an agreement by parol (whether in writing or not), but only by deed. Equity, however stepped in, and said that if there has been a variation of a deed by a simple contract (which in the case of a lease required to be in writing would have to be evidenced by writing), the courts may give effect to it as is shown in *Berry* v. *Berry* (1929). That equitable doctrine, however, could hardly apply in the present case because the variation here might be said to have been made without consideration. With regard to estoppel, the representation made in relation to reducing the rent, was not a representation of an existing fact. It was a representation, in effect, as to the future, namely, that payment of the rent would not be enforced at the full rate but only at the reduced rate. Such a representation would not give rise to an estoppel, because, as was said in *Jorden* v. *Money* (1854), a representation as to the future must be embodied as a contract or be nothing.

But what is the position in view of developments in the law in recent years? The law has not been standing still since *Jorden* v. *Money*. There has been a series of decisions over the last fifty years which, although they are said to be cases of estoppel are not really such. They are cases in which a promise was made which was intended to create legal relations and which, to the knowledge of the person making the promise, was going to be acted on by the person to whom it was made, and which was in fact so acted on. In such cases the courts have said that the promise must be honoured. . . . As I have said they are not cases of estoppel in the strict sense. They are really promises - promises intended to be binding, intended to be acted on, and in fact acted on. *Jorden* v. *Money* can be distinguished, because there the promisor made it clear that she did not intend to be legally bound, whereas in the cases to which I refer the proper inference was that the promisor did intend to be bound. In each case the court held the promise to be binding on the party making it, even though under the old common law it might be difficult to find any consideration for it. The courts have not gone so far as to give a cause of action in damages for the breach of such a promise, but they have refused to allow the party making it to act inconsistently with it. It is in that sense, and that sense only, that such a promise gives rise to an estoppel. The decisions are a natural result of the fusion of law and equity: for the cases of *Hughes* v. *Metropolitan Ry. Co.* (1877) [His Lordship also referred to two other cases] afford a sufficient basis for saying that a party would not be allowed in equity to go back on such a promise. In my opinion, the time has now come for the validity of such a promise to be recognized. The logical consequence, no doubt is that a promise to accept a smaller sum in discharge of a larger sum, if acted upon, is binding notwithstanding the absence of consideration: and if the fusion of law and equity leads to this result, so much the better. That aspect was not considered in *Foakes* v. *Beer* (1884). At this time of day however, when law and equity have been joined together for over seventy years, principles must be reconsidered in the light of their combined effect. It is to be noticed that in the Sixth Interim Report of the Law Revision Committee, pars. 35, 40, it is recommended that such a promise as that to which I have referred, should be enforceable in law even though no consideration for it has been given by the promisee. It seems to me that, to the extent I have mentioned, that result has now been achieved by the decisions of the courts.

I am satisfied that a promise such as that to which I have referred is binding and the only question remaining for my consideration is the scope of the promise in the present case. I am satisfied on all the evidence that the promise here was that the ground rent should be reduced to 1,250*l.* a year as a temporary expedient while the block of flats was not fully, or substantially fully let, owing to the conditions prevailing. That means that the reduction in the rent applied throughout the years down to the end of 1944, but early in 1945 it is plain that the flats were fully let, and, indeed the rents received from them (many of them not being affected by the Rent Restrictions Acts), were increased beyond the figure at which it was originally contemplated that they would be let. At all events the rent from them must have been very considerable. I find that the conditions prevailing at the time when the reduction in rent was made, had completely passed away by the early months of 1945. I am satisfied that the promise was understood by all parties only to apply under the conditions prevailing at the time when it was made, namely, when the flats were only partially let, and that it did not extend any further than that. When the flats became fully let, early in 1945, the reduction ceased to apply.

In those circumstances, under the law as I hold it, it seems to me that rent is payable at the full rate for the quarters ending September 29 and December 25, 1945.

If the case had been one of estoppel, it might be said that in any event the estoppel would cease when the conditions to which the representation applied came to an end, or it also might be said that it would only come to an end on notice. In either case it is only a way of ascertaining what is the scope of the representation. I prefer to apply the principle that a promise intended to be binding, intended to be acted on and in fact acted on, is binding so far as its terms properly apply. Here it was binding as covering the period down to the early part of 1945, and as from that time full rent is payable.

I therefore give judgment for the plaintiff company for the amount claimed.

Judgment for plaintiffs.

Note

A lucid account of the background and development of the *High Trees* doctrine, as seen through the eyes of its creator, can be found in Part Five of Denning, *The Discipline of Law* (Butterworths, 1979).

Question

How, if at all, does the principle in *High Trees* differ from that laid down in *Hughes* v. *Metropolitan Railway Co*?

6. THE DEVELOPMENT OF PROMISSORY ESTOPPEL

D & C Builders Ltd. v. Rees
[1966] 2 Q.B. 617 (Q.B.D.)

Lord Denning M.R. The plaintiffs are a little company. "D" stands for Donaldson, a decorator, "C" for Casey, a plumber. They are jobbing builders. The defendant has a shop where he sells builders' materials.

In the spring of 1964 the defendant employed the plaintiffs to do work at his premises, 218, Brick Lane. The plaintiffs did the work and rendered accounts in May and June, which came to £746 13s. 1d. altogether. The defendant paid £250 on account. In addition the plaintiffs made an allowance of £14 off the bill. So in July, 1964, there was owing to the plaintiffs the sum of £482 13s. 1d. At this stage there was no dispute as to the work done. But the defendant did not pay.

On August 31, 1964, the plaintiffs wrote asking the defendant to pay the remainder of the bill. He did not reply. On October 19, 1964, they wrote again, pointing out that the "outstanding account of £480 is well overdue." Still the defendant did not reply. He did not write or telephone for more than three weeks. Then on Friday, November 13, 1964, the defendant was ill with influenza. His wife telephoned the plaintiffs. She spoke to Casey. She began to make complaints about the work: and then said: "My husband will offer you £300 in settlement. That is all you'll get. It is to be in satisfaction." Casey said he would have to discuss it with Donaldson. The two of them talked it over. Their company was in desperate financial straits. If they did not have the £300, they would be in a state of bankruptcy. So they decided to accept the £300 and see what they could do about the rest afterwards. Thereupon Donaldson telephoned to the defendant's wife. He said to her: "£300 will not even clear our commitments on the job. We will accept £300 and give you a year to find the balance." She said: "no, we will never have enough money to pay the balance. £300 is better than nothing." He said: "we have no choice but to accept." She said: "Would you like the money by cash or by cheque. If it is cash, you can have it on Monday. If by cheque, you can have it tomorrow (Saturday)."

On Saturday, November 14, 1964, Casey went to collect the money. He took with him a receipt prepared on the company's paper with the simple words: "Received the sum of £300 from

Mr. Rees." She gave him a cheque for £300 and asked for a
receipt. She insisted that the words "in completion of the
account" be added. Casey did as she asked. He added the words
to the receipt. So she had the clean receipt: "Received the sum
of £300 from Mr. Rees in completion of the account. Paid, M.
Casey." Casey gave in evidence his reason for giving it: "If I
did not have the £300 the company would have gone bankrupt.
The only reason we took it was to save the company. She knew
the position we were in.'"

The plaintiffs were so worried about their position that they
went to their solicitors. Within a few days, on November 23,
1964, the solicitors wrote complaining that the defendant had
"extricated a receipt of some sort or other" from them. They
said they were treating the £300 as a payment on account. On
November 28, 1964, the defendant replied alleging bad
workmanship. He also set up the receipt which Casey gave to
his wife, adding: "I assure you she had no gun on her." The
plaintiffs brought this action for the balance. The defendant
set up a defence of bad workmanship and also that there was a
binding settlement. The question of settlement was tried as a
preliminary issue.

The Judge made these findings:

> "I concluded that by the middle of August the sum due to
> the plaintiffs was ascertained and not then in dispute. I
> also concluded that there was no consideration to support
> the agreement of November 13 and 14. It was a case of
> agreeing to take a lesser sum when a larger sum was already
> due to the plaintiffs. It was not a case of agreeing to take a
> cheque for a smaller amount instead of receiving cash for a
> larger amount. The payment by cheque was an incidental
> arrangement."

He decided, therefore, the preliminary issue in favour of the
plaintiffs. The defendant appeals to this court. He says that
there was here an accord and satisfaction - an *accord* when the
plaintiffs agreed, however reluctantly, to accept £300 in
settlement of the account - and *satisfaction* when they
accepted the cheque for £300 and it was duly honoured. The
defendant relies on *Sibree* v. *Tripp* (1846) and *Goddard* v.
O'Brien (1882) as authorities in his favour.

This case is of some consequence: for it is a daily occurrence
that a merchant or tradesman, who is owed a sum of money, is
asked to take less. The debtor says he is in difficulties. He

offers a lesser sum in settlement, cash down. He says he cannot pay more. The creditor is considerate. He accepts the proffered sum and forgives him the rest of the debt. The question arises: Is the settlement binding on the creditor? The answer is that, in point of law, the creditor is not bound by the settlement. He can the next day sue the debtor for the balance: and get judgment. The law was so stated by Lord Coke in *Pinnel's Case* (1602) – and accepted by the House of Lords in *Foakes* v. *Beer* (1884).

Now, suppose that the debtor, instead of paying the lesser sum in cash, pays it by cheque. He makes out a cheque for the amount. The creditor accepts the cheque and cashes it. Is the position any different? I think not. No sensible distinction can be taken between payment of a lesser sum by cash and payment of it by cheque. The cheque, when given, is conditional payment. When honoured, it is actual payment. It is then just the same as cash. If a creditor is not bound when he receives payment by cash, he should not be bound when he receives payment by cheque. This view is supported by the leading case of *Cumber* v. *Wane* (1721), which has suffered many vicissitudes but was, I think, rightly decided in point of law.

Sibree v. *Tripp* (1846) is easily distinguishable. There the plaintiffs brought an action for £500. It was settled by the defendant giving three promissory notes amounting in all to £250. Those promissory notes were given upon a new contract, in substitution for the debt sued for, and not as conditional payment. The plaintiff's only remedy thenceforward was on the notes and not on the debt.

Goddard v. *O'Brien* (1882) is not so easily distinguishable. There a creditor was owed £125 for some slates. He met the debtor and agreed to accept £100 in discharge of it. The debtor gave a cheque for £100. The creditor gave a written receipt "in settlement on the said cheque being honoured." The cheque was clearly given by way of conditional payment. It was honoured. The creditor sued the debtor for the balance of £25. He lost because the £100 was paid by cheque and not by cash. The decision was criticised by Fletcher Moulton L.J. in *Hirachand Punamchand* v. *Temple* (1911), and by the editors of Smith's Leading Cases, 13th ed. (1929), Vol. 1, p. 380. It was, I think, wrongly decided. In point of law payment of a lesser sum, whether by cash or by cheque, is no discharge of a greater sum.

This doctrine of the common law has come under heavy fire. It was ridiculed by Sir George Jessel in *Couldery* v. *Bartram*

(1881). It was said to be mistaken by Lord Blackburn in *Foakes* v. *Beer*. It was condemned by the Law Revision Committee (1945 Cmd. 5449), paras. 20 and 21. But a remedy has been found. The harshness of the common law has been relieved. Equity has stretched out a merciful hand to help the debtor. The courts have invoked the broad principle stated by Lord Cairns in *Hughes* v. *Metropolitan Railway Co.* (1877).

"It is the first principle upon which all courts of equity proceed, that if parties, who have entered into definite and distinct terms involving certain legal results, afterwards by their own act or with their own consent enter upon a course of negotiation which has the effect of leading one of the parties to suppose that *the strict rights arising under the contract will not be enforced*, or will be kept in suspense, or held in abeyance, the person who otherwise might have enforced those rights *will not be allowed to enforce them when it would be inequitable having regard to the dealings which have taken place between the parties*."

It is worth noticing that the principle may be applied, not only so as to suspend strict legal rights, but also so as to preclude the enforcement of them.

This principle has been applied to cases where a creditor agrees to accept a lesser sum in discharge of a greater. So much so that we can now say that, when a creditor and a debtor enter upon a course of negotiation, which leads the debtor to suppose that, on payment of the lesser sum, the creditor will not enforce payment of the balance, and on the faith thereof the debtor pays the lesser sum and the creditor accepts it as satisfaction: then the creditor will not be allowed to enforce payment of the balance when it would be inequitable to do so. This was well illustrated during the last war. Tenants went away to escape the bombs and left their houses unoccupied. The landlords accepted a reduced rent for the time they were empty. It was held that the landlords could not afterwards turn round and sue for the balance, see *Central London Property Trust Ltd.* v. *High Trees House Ltd.* (1947). This caused at the time some eyebrows to be raised in high places. But they have been lowered since. The solution was so obviously just that no one could well gainsay it.

In applying this principle, however, we must note the qualification: The creditor is only barred from his legal rights when it would be *inequitable* for him to insist upon them.

Where there has been a *true accord*, under which the creditor voluntarily agrees to accept a lesser sum in satisfaction, and the debtor *acts upon* that accord by paying the lesser sum and the creditor accepts it, then it is inequitable for the creditor afterwards to insist on the balance. But he is not bound unless there has been truly an accord between them.

In the present case, on the facts as found by the judge, it seems to me that there was no true accord. The debtor's wife held the creditor to ransom. The creditor was in need of money to meet his own commitments, and she knew it. When the creditor asked for payment of the £480 due to him, she said to him in effect: "We cannot pay you the £480. But we will pay you £300 if you will accept it in settlement. If you do not accept it on those terms, you will get nothing. £300 is better than nothing." She had no right to say any such thing. She could properly have said: "We cannot pay you more than £300. Please accept it on account." But she had no right to insist on his taking it in settlement. When she said: "We will pay you nothing unless you accept £300 in settlement," she was putting undue pressure on the creditor. She was making a threat to break the contract (by paying nothing) and she was doing it so as to compel the creditor to do what he was unwilling to do (to accept £300 in settlement): and she succeeded. He complied with her demand. That was on recent authority a case of intimidation: see *Rookes* v. *Barnard* (1964) and *Stratford (J.T.) & Son Ltd.* v. *Lindley* (1964). In these circumstances there was no true accord so as to found a defence of accord and satisfaction: see *Day* v. *McLea* (1889). There is also no equity in the defendant to warrant any departure from the due course of law. No person can insist on a settlement procured by intimidation.

In my opinion there is no reason in law or equity why the creditor should not enforce the full amount of the debt due to him. I would, therefore, dismiss this appeal.

[Dankwerts and Winn L.JJ. gave judgments also dismissing the appeal.]

Note

In *Woodhouse Ltd.* v. *Nigerian Produce Ltd.* (1972), Lord Hailsham commented:

"I desire to add that the time may soon come when the whole sequence of cases based on promissory estoppel since the war, beginning with *Central London Property Trust Ltd.* v. *High Trees House Ltd.* (1947) may need to be reviewed and reduced to a coherent body of doctrine by the courts. I do not mean to say that any are to be regarded with suspicion. But as is common with an expanding doctrine they do raise problems of coherent exposition which have never been systematically explored."

Pending such a systematic judicial exposition, or legislative intervention, some aspects of the scope of the doctrine remain uncertain.

For example, are obligations merely suspended or extinguished by the doctrine? Must the promisee, in order to be able to rely on the doctrine, act to his detriment or is it sufficient that he simply acts in reliance upon the promise? The dicta of Lord Denning in such cases as *D & C Builders* v. *Rees* (above), *Alan* v. *El Nasr* (1972) and *Brikom Investments* v. *Carr* (1979) go further in their claims for the doctrine than some other judicial pronouncements. The House of Lords in particular seemed to take a more traditional line in *Tool Metal Manufacturing Co. Ltd.* v. *Tungsten Electric* (1955). In *Ajayi* v. *R.T. Briscoe* (1964) Lord Hodson put the matter thus:

> "Their Lordships are of opinion that the principle of law as defined by Bowen L.J. has been confirmed by the House of Lords in the case of *Tool Metal Manufacturing Co. Ltd.* v. *Tungsten Electric Co. Ltd.* (1955) where the authorities were reviewed and no encouragement was given to the view that the principle was capable of extension so as to create rights in the promisee for which he had given no consideration. The principle, which has been described as quasi estoppel and perhaps more aptly as promissory estoppel, is that when one party to a contract in the absence of fresh consideration agrees not to enforce his rights an equity will be raised in favour of the other party. This equity is, however, subject to the qualifications (1) that the other party has altered his position, (2) that the promisor can resile from his promise on giving reasonable notice, which need not be a formal notice, giving the promisee a reasonable opportunity of resuming his position, (3) the promise only becomes final and irrevocable if the promisee cannot resume his position.

If the House of Lords made a systematic explanation of the issues left open by the doctrine of promissory estoppel, how would they resolve them?

Chapter 3

INTENTION TO CREATE LEGAL RELATIONS

Esso Petroleum Ltd. v. Commissioners of Customs and Excise
[1976] 1 W.L.R. 1 (H.L.)

[As part of a sales promotion scheme Esso Petroleum displayed posters at their garages inviting customers to collect a set of coins commemorating the English squad for the World Cup. The posters stated, "One coin given with every four gallons of petrol." The Commissioners claimed that the coins were chargeable to purchase tax on the grounds that they had been sold to the customers. Esso asserted that the coins were not sold but distributed as free gifts. It therefore became relevant to consider (a) whether the coins were the subject of a legal contract, and (b) whether such a contract was a "sale."]

Viscount Dilhorne. If the coins were a free gift to every customer who purchased four gallons of petrol or multiples of that quantity, then the appeal must be dismissed. If, on the other hand, a legal contract was entered into between the customer and the dealer which, in addition to the supply of petrol, involved the dealer in a legally binding obligation to transfer a coin or coins to the customer, and if that legal contract amounted to a sale, then the appeal must be allowed.

Was there any intention on the part of the garage proprietor and also on the part of the customer who bought four gallons, or multiples of that quantity, of petrol to enter into a legally binding contract in relation to a coin or coins? In *Rose and Frank Co.* v. *J.R. Crompton and Brothers Ltd.* (1923), Scrutton L.J. said:

> "Now it is quite possible for parties to come to an agreement by accepting a proposal with the result that the agreement concluded does not give rise to legal relations. The reason of this is that the parties do not intend that their agreement shall give rise to legal relations. This intention may be implied from the subject matter of the agreement, but it may also be expressed by the parties. In social and family relations such an intention is readily implied, while in business matters the opposite result would ordinarily follow."

And Atkin L.J. said:

> "To create a contract there must be a common intention of the parties to enter into legal obligations, mutually communicated expressly or impliedly."

The facts of that case were very different from those of this. In that case there was an agreement dealing with business matters. In this case the question has to be considered whether there was any agreement as to a coin or coins between the garage proprietor and the customer and also, if there was, was it intended on both sides to be one having legal relations? If a coin was just to be given to the motorist, it would not be necessary for there to have been any agreement between him and the garage proprietor with regard to it.

In *Edwards* v. *Skyways Ltd.* (1964), where the facts were also very different from those in this case and where the plaintiff was seeking to recover the amount of an ex gratia payment, Megaw J. referred to these passages in *Rose and Frank Co.* v. *J.R. Crompton and Brothers Ltd.* and said:

> "In the present case, the subject matter of the agreement is business relations, not social or domestic matters. There was a meeting of minds – an intention to agree. There was, admittedly, consideration for the company's promise. I accept the propositions of counsel for the plaintiff that in a case of this nature the onus is on the party who asserts that no legal effect was intended, and the onus is a heavy one."

I do not wish in any way to criticise or qualify these statements, but I do not feel that they provide a sound foundation for the decision of this appeal.

True it is that the respondents are engaged in business. True it is that they hope to promote the sale of their petrol, but it does not seem to me necessarily to follow or to be inferred that there was any intention on their part that their dealers should enter into legally binding contracts with regard to the coins; or any intention on the part of the dealers to enter into any such contract or any intention on the part of the purchaser of four gallons of petrol to do so.

If in this case on the facts of this case the conclusion is reached that there was any such intention on the part of the customer, of the dealer and of the respondents, it would seem to exclude the possibility of any dealer ever making a free gift to any of his customers however negligible its value to promote his sales.

If what was described as being a gift, which would be given if something was purchased, was something of value to the purchaser, then it could readily be inferred that there was a common intention to enter into legal relations. But here, whatever the cost of production, it is clear that the coins were of little intrinsic value.

I do not consider that the offer of a gift of a free coin is properly to be regarded as a business matter in the sense in which that word was used by Scrutton L.J. in the passage cited above. Nor do I think that such an offer can be comprehended within the "business relations" which were in the *Skyways* case, as Megaw J. said "the subject-matter of the agreement." I see no reason to imply any intention to enter into contractual relations from the statements on the posters that a coin would be given if four gallons of petrol were bought.

Nor do I see any reason to impute to every motorist who went to a garage where the posters were displayed to buy four gallons of petrol any intention to enter into a legally binding contract for the supply to him of a coin. On the acceptance of his offer to purchase four gallons there was no doubt a legally binding contract for the supply to him of that quantity of petrol, but I see again no reason to conclude that because such an offer was made by him, it must be held that, as the posters were displayed, his offer included an offer to take a coin. The gift of a coin might lead to a motorist returning to the garage to obtain another one, but I think the facts in this case negative any contractual intention on his part and on the part of the dealer as to the coin and suffice to rebut any presumption there may be to the contrary.

If, however, there was any contract relating to the coin or coins, the consideration for the entry into that contract was not the payment of any money but the entry into a contract to purchase four gallons or multiples of that quantity of petrol, in which case the contract relating to the coin or coins cannot be regarded as a contract of sale.

I therefore, while of opinion that there was no legally binding contract as to the coins and so that it has not been established that they were produced for sale, am also of opinion that if there was any such contract it was not one for sale.

In my opinion this appeal should be dismissed.

Lord Simon of Glaisdale. I am, however, my Lords, not prepared to accept that the promotion material put out by Esso was not envisaged by them as creating legal relations between the garage proprietors who adopted it and the motorists who yielded to its blandishments. In the first place, Esso and the garage proprietors put the material out for their commercial advantage, and designed it to attract the custom of motorists. The whole transaction took place in a setting of business relations. In the second place, it seems to me in general undesirable to allow a commercial promoter to claim that what he has done is a mere puff, not intended to create legal relations (*cf. Carlill* v. *Carbolic Smoke Ball Co.* (1893)). The coins may have been themselves of little intrinsic value; but all the evidence suggests that Esso contemplated that they would be attractive to motorists and that there would be a large commercial advantage to themselves from the scheme, an advantage to which the garage proprietors also would share. Thirdly, I think that authority supports the view that legal relations were envisaged. In *Rose and Frank Co.* v. *J.R. Crompton and Brothers Ltd.* (1923) Scrutton L.J. said:

[His Lordship cited the same passage as above.]

In the same case Atkin L.J. said:

"To create a contract there must be a common intention of the parties to enter into legal obligations, mutually communicated expressly or impliedly. Such an intention ordinarily will be inferred when parties enter into an agreement which in other respects conforms to the rules of law as to the formation of contracts. It may be negatived impliedly by the nature of the agreed promise or promises, as in the case of offer and acceptance of hospitality, or of some agreements made in the course of family life between members of a family as in *Balfour* v. *Balfour* (1919)."

In *Edwards* v. *Skyways Ltd.* (1964) Megaw J. quoted these passages and added:

[His Lordship cited the same passage as above.]

I respectfully agree. And I venture to add that it begs the question to assert that no motorist who bought petrol in consequence of seeing the promotion material prominently displayed in the garage forecourt would be likely to bring an action in the county court if he were refused a coin. He might be a suburban Hampden who was not prepared to forgo what he conceived to be his rights or to allow a tradesman to go back on his word.

Notes

Purely domestic or social relations will not generally give rise to legal relations, as Lord Atkin observed in his citation of *Balfour* v. *Balfour* (1919). This is, however, only a starting point in the analysis of the situation not a conclusive rule. Compare, for example, *Merritt* v. *Merritt* (1970), *Jones* v. *Padavatton* (1969) and *Simpkins* v. *Pays* (1955).

Questions

1. Lord Russell of Killowen agreed with Viscount Dilhorne; Lord Wilberforce took the same view as Lord Simon on this issue.

Which view do you think is to be preferred?

2. Despite the fact that it is reached in a commercial setting, a collective agreement between an employer and a trade union will not generally give rise to legal relations (see *Ford Motor Co. Ltd.* v. *Amalgamated Union of Engineering and Foundry Workers* (1969); Trade Union and Labour Relations Act 1974, s. 18).

Why should this be so?

Chapter 4

CONTRACTUAL TERMS

1. INCORPORATION OF TERMS

Parker v. South Eastern Railway Co.
(1877) 2 C.P.D. 416

[The plaintiff deposited a bag in the defendant's cloakroom, paid the 2d. charge and received a ticket in return. The front of the ticket detailed the opening hours of the office and also the words: "See back." On the back was a clause limiting the company's liability in the case of loss to £10. A placard hung up in the cloakroom contained the same condition. The bag was lost by the defendant. The plaintiff claimed £24.10s., the value of the lost bag. The defendant claimed liability was limited to £10. The defendant appealed to the Court of Appeal against the trial judge's direction to the jury.]

Mellish L.J. In this case we have to consider whether a person who deposits in the cloak-room of a railway company, articles which are lost through the carelessness of the company's servants, is prevented from recovering, by a condition on the back of the ticket, that the company would not be liable for the loss of goods exceeding the value of 10*l.* It was argued on behalf of the railway company that the company's servants were only authorized to receive goods on behalf of the company upon the terms contained in the ticket; and a passage from Mr. Justice Blackburn's judgment in *Harris* v. *Great Western Ry. Co.* (1876) was relied on in support of their contention: "I doubt much - inasmuch as the railway company did not authorize their servants to receive goods for deposit on any other terms, and as they had done nothing to lead the plaintiff to believe that they had given such authority to their servants so as to preclude them from asserting, as against her, that the authority was so limited - whether the true rule of law is not that the plaintiff must assent to the contract intended by the defendants to be authorized, or treat the case as one in which there was no contract at all, and consequently no liability for safe custody." I am of opinion that this objection cannot prevail. It is clear that the company's servants did not exceed the authority given them by the company. They did the exact thing they were authorized to do. They were authorized to receive articles on deposit as bailees on behalf of the company, charging 2*d*. for each article, and delivering a ticket properly filled up to the person leaving the article. This is exactly what they did in the present cases, and whatever may be the legal effect of what was done, the company must, in my opinion, be bound by it. The directors may have thought, and no doubt did think, that the delivering the ticket to the person depositing the article would be sufficient to make him bound by the conditions contained in the ticket, and if they were mistaken in that, the company must bear the consequence.

The question then is, whether the plaintiff was bound by the conditions contained in the ticket. In an ordinary case, where an action is brought on a written agreement which is signed by the defendant, the agreement is proved by proving his signature, and, in the absence of fraud, it is wholly immaterial that he has not read the agreement and does not know its contents. The parties may, however, reduce their agreement into writing, so that the writing constitutes the sole evidence of the agreement, without signing it; but in that case there must be evidence independently of the agreement itself to prove that the defendant has assented to it. In that case, also, if it is proved that the defendant has assented to the writing constituting the agreement between the parties, it is, in the absence of fraud, immaterial that the defendant had not read the agreement and did not know its contents. Now if in the course of making a contract one party delivers to another a paper containing writing, and the party receiving the paper knows that the paper contains conditions which the party delivering it intends to constitute the contract, I have no doubt that the party receiving the paper does, by receiving and keeping it, assent to the conditions contained in it, although he does not read them, and does not know what they are. I hold therefore that the case of *Harris* v. *Great Western Ry. Co.* (1876) was rightly decided, because in that case the plaintiff admitted, on cross-examination, that he believed there were some conditions on the ticket. On the other hand, the case of *Henderson* v. *Stevenson* (1875) is a conclusive authority that if the person receiving the ticket does not know that there is any writing upon the back of the ticket, he is not bound by a condition printed on the back. The facts in the cases before us differ from those in both *Henderson* v. *Stevenson* and *Harris* v. *Great Western Ry. Co.* because in both the cases which have been argued before us, though the plaintiffs admitted that they knew there was writing on the back of the ticket, they swore not only that they did not read it, but that they did not know or believe that the writing contained conditions, and we are to consider whether, under those circumstances, we can lay down as a matter of law either that the plaintiff is bound or that he is not bound by the conditions contained in the ticket, or whether his being bound depends on some question of fact to be determined by the jury, and if so, whether, in the present case, the right question was left to the jury.

Now, I am of opinion that we cannot lay down, as a matter of law, either that the plaintiff was bound or that he was not bound by the conditions printed on the ticket, from the mere fact that he knew that there was writing on the ticket, but did not know that the writing contained conditions. I think there may be cases in which a paper containing writing is delivered by one party to another in the course of a business transaction, where it would be quite reasonable that the party receiving it should assume that the writing contained in it no condition, and should put it in his pocket unread. For instance, if a person driving through a turnpike-gate received a ticket upon paying the toll, he might reasonably assume that the object of the ticket was that by producing it he might be free from paying toll at some other turnpike-gate, and might put it in his pocket unread. On the other hand, if a person who ships goods to be carried on a voyage by sea receives a bill of lading signed by the master, he would plainly be bound by it, although afterwards in an action against the shipowner for the loss of the goods, he might swear that he had never read the bill of lading, and that he did not know that it contained the terms of the contract of carriage, and that the shipowner was protected by the exceptions contained in it. Now the reason why the person receiving the bill of lading would be bound seems to me to be that in the great majority of cases persons shipping goods do know that the bill of lading contains the terms of the contract of carriage; and the shipowner, or the master delivering the bill of lading, is entitled to assume that the person shipping goods has that knowledge. It is, however, quite possible to suppose that a person who is neither a man of business nor a lawyer might on some particular occasion ship goods without the least knowledge of what a bill of lading was, but in my opinion such a person must bear the consequences of his own exceptional ignorance, it being plainly impossible that business could be carried on if every person who delivers a bill of lading had to stop to explain what a bill of lading was.

Now the question we have to consider is whether the railway

company were entitled to assume that a person depositing luggage, and receiving a ticket in such a way that he could see that some writing was printed on it, would understand that the writing contained the conditions of contract, and this seems to me to depend upon whether people in general would in fact, and naturally, draw that inference. The railway company, as it seems to me, must be entitled to make some assumptions respecting the person who deposits luggage with them: I think they are entitled to assume that he can read, and that he understands the English language, and that he pays such attention to what he is about as may be reasonably expected from a person in such a transaction as that of depositing luggage in a cloak-room. The railway company must, however, take mankind as they find them, and if what they do is sufficient to inform people in general that the ticket contains conditions, I think that a particular plaintiff ought not to be in a better position than other persons on account of his exceptional ignorance or stupidity or carelessness. But if what the railway company do is not sufficient to convey to the minds of people in general that the ticket contains conditions, then they have received goods on deposit without obtaining the consent of the persons depositing them to the conditions limiting their liability. I am of opinion, therefore, that the proper direction to leave to the jury in these cases is, that if the person receiving the ticket did not see or know that there was any writing on the ticket, he is not bound by the conditions; that if he knew there was writing, and knew or believed that the writing contained conditions, then he is bound by the conditions; that if he knew there was writing on the ticket, but did not know or believe that the writing contained conditions, nevertheless he would be bound, if the delivering of the ticket to him in such a manner that he could see there was writing upon it, was, in the opinion of the jury, reasonable notice that the writing contained conditions.

I have lastly to consider whether the direction of the learned judge was correct, namely, "Was the plaintiff, under the circumstances, under any obligation, in the exercise of reasonable and proper caution, to read or to make himself aware of the condition?" I think that this direction was not strictly accurate, and was calculated to mislead the jury. The plaintiff was certainly under no obligation to read the ticket, but was entitled to leave it unread if he pleased, and the question does not appear to me to direct the attention of the jury to the real question, namely, whether the railway company did what was reasonably sufficient to give the plaintiff notice of the condition.

On the whole, I am of opinion that there ought to be a new trial.

[Baggallay L.J. concurred, but Bramwell L.J. took the view that the question was one of law and judgment ought to be entered for the defendant.]

Note

An example of failure to incorporate a term in the context of a ticket case is *Chapelton* v. *Barry UDC* (1940).

Questions

1. Mellish L.J. states that the defendant could assume the plaintiff understands English. Could as much reliance be placed on this dictum now as in 1877?

2. It is very common for a notice to incorporate by reference terms that are fully set out elsewhere in a comprehensive document. A rather extreme illustration of this to be found in *Thompson* v. *LM & S Railway* (1930). Would this case be followed today?

L'Estrange v. Graucob
[1934] 2 K.B. 394 (D.C.)

[The plaintiff signed an order form for the purchase of a cigarette vending machine which, when delivered, did not work properly. The defendants had acknowledged the order by signing a printed order confirmation agreeing to the terms in the order form. In small print, on brown paper, there was a term printed to the effect that, "any express or implied condition, statement, or warranty, statutory or otherwise not stated herein is hereby excluded." The sellers relied on this clause to exempt themselves from liability. The plaintiff asserted that she had not read the form when she signed it, knew nothing of its contents and the smallness of the print made if difficult to read.]

Maugham L.J. I regret the decision to which I have come, but I am bound by legal rules and cannot decide the case on other considerations.

The material question is whether or not there was a contract in writing between the plaintiff and the defendants in the terms contained in the brown paper document. In the case of a formal contract between seller and buyer, such as a deed, there is a presumption which puts it beyond doubt that the parties intended that the document should contain the terms of their contract. The brown paper document is not a formal instrument of that character, yet, in my opinion, having been signed it may well constitute a contract in writing. A reference to any of the text-books dealing with the law of contract will provide many cases of the verbal acceptance of a written offer, in which the Courts have held that the written offer and the acceptance, even though only verbal, together constituted a contract in writing, which could not be altered by extraneous evidence. The rule may not operate equitably in all cases, but it is unquestionably binding in law.

. . . . . .

I deal with this case on the footing that when the order confirmation was signed by the defendants confirming the order form which had been signed by the plaintiff, there was then a signed contract in writing between the parties. If that is so, then, subject to certain contingencies, there is no doubt that it was wholly immaterial whether the plaintiff read the small print or not. There can be no dispute as to the soundness in law of the statement of Mellish L.J. in *Parker* v. *South Eastern Ry. Co.*, (1877) which has been read by my learned brother, to the effect that where a party has signed a written agreement it is immaterial to the question of his liability under it that he has not read it and does not know its contents. That is true in any case in which the agreement is held to be an agreement in writing.

Scrutton L.J. . . . When a document containing contractual terms is signed, then, in the absence of fraud, or, I will add, misrepresentation, the party signing it is bound, and it is wholly immaterial whether he has read the document or not.

Judgment entered for the defendants.

Notes

With some notable exceptions, such as contracts of guarantee or for the disposition of an interest in land, it is not a formal requirement of the law that a contract be in writing. Similarly, as here, a signed document can be legally binding even if it is not emblazoned with words to the effect that, "This is a Contractual Document." For an example of the way in which the possible unfairness of the principle can be avoided, see, *eg Curtis* v. *Chemical Cleaning and Dyeing Co.* (1951).

Much legislative and judicial ingenuity has been used over the last fifty years to mitigate the possibly harsh effect of the rule in *L'Estrange* v. *Graucob*. Examples are restrictions on the exclusion of certain terms (Unfair Contract Terms Act 1977, s.6., Sched.2), or the elaborate protection given to purchasers under credit agreements provided by the Consumer Credit Act 1974. The latter Act, for example, provides for the size of type and paper to be regulated in Hire Purchase transactions.

The inclusion of "unfair" terms exempting or qualifying liability received its most thoroughgoing legislative treatment in the Unfair Contract Terms Act 1977, and see generally, below, p. 422, 428, 467.

Thornton v. Shoe Lane Parking
[1971] 2 Q.B. 163 (C.A.)

[The plaintiff drove up to the barrier of a car park and a machine automatically produced a ticket as he did so. The ticket referred to various exempting terms which could be inspected in a display panel attached to a pillar opposite the ticket machine. One of these "conditions" stated that the defendants were not liable for any injury to a customer occuring on the premises. After parking his car in the car park, the plaintiff was injured in an accident for which the defendants were partly responsible. The defendants sought to rely upon the exempting "condition."

Lord Denning M.R. We have been referred to the ticket cases of former times from *Parker* v. *South Eastern Railway Co.* (1877) to *McCutcheon* v. *David MacBrayne Ltd.* (1964). They were concerned with railways, steamships and cloakrooms where booking clerks issued tickets to customers who took them away without reading them. In those cases the issue of the ticket was regarded as an *offer* by the company. If the customer took it and retained it without objection, his act was regarded as an *acceptance* of the offer: see . . . *Thompson* v. *London, Midland and Scottish Railway Co.* (1930). These cases were based on the theory that the customer, on being handed the ticket, could refuse it and decline to enter into a contract on those terms. He could ask for his money back. That theory was, of course, a fiction. No customer in a thousand ever read the conditions. If he had stopped to do so, he would have missed the train or the boat.

None of those cases has any application to a ticket which is issued by an automatic machine. The customer pays his money and gets a ticket. He cannot refuse it. He cannot get his money back. He may protest to the machine, even swear at it. But it will remain unmoved. He is committed beyond recall. He was committed at the very moment when he put his money into the machine. The contract was concluded at that time. It can be translated into offer and acceptance in this way: the offer is made when the proprietor of the machine holds it out as being ready to receive the money. The acceptance takes place when the customer puts his money into the slot. The terms of the offer are contained in the notice placed on or near the machine stating what is offered for the money. The customer is bound by those terms as long as they are sufficiently brought to his notice before-hand, but not otherwise. He is not bound by the terms printed on the ticket if they differ from the notice, because the ticket comes too late. The contract has already been made: see *Olley* v. *Marlborough Court Ltd.* (1949). The ticket is no more than a voucher or receipt for the money that has been paid (as in the deckchair case, *Chapelton* v. *Barry Urban District Council* (1940)) on terms which have been offered and accepted before the ticket is issued.

In the present case the offer was contained in the notice at the entrance giving the charges for garaging and saying "at owner's risk," i.e., at the risk of the owner so far as damage to the car was concerned. The offer was accepted when Mr. Thornton drove up to the entrance and, by the movement of his car, turned the light from red to green, and the ticket was thrust at him. The contract was then concluded, and it could not be altered by any words printed on the ticket itself. In particular, it could not be altered so as to exempt the company from liability for personal injury due to their negligence.

Assuming, however, that an automatic machine is a booking clerk in disguise - so that the old fashioned ticket cases still apply to it. We then have to go back to the three questions put by Mellish L.J. in *Parker* v. *South Eastern Railway Co.* (1877). Telescoping the three questions, they come to this: the customer is bound by the exempting condition if he knows that the ticket is issued subject to it; or, if the company did what was reasonably sufficient to give him notice of it.

Mr. Machin admitted here that the company did not do what was reasonably sufficient to give Mr. Thornton notice of the exempting condition. That admission was properly made. I do not pause to inquire whether the exempting condition is void for unreasonableness. All I say is that it is so wide and so destructive of rights that the court should not hold any man bound by it unless it is drawn to his attention in the most explicit way. It is an instance of what I had in mind in *J. Spurling Ltd* v. *Bradshaw* (1956). In order to give sufficient notice, it would need to be printed in red ink with a red hand pointing to it - or something equally startling.

But, although reasonable notice of it was not given, Mr. Machin said that this case came within the second question propounded by Mellish L.J., namely that Mr. Thornton "knew or believed that the writing contained conditions." There was no finding to that effect. The burden was on the company to prove it, and they did not do so. Certainly there was no evidence that Mr. Thornton knew of this exempting condition. He is not, therefore, bound by it.

Mr. Machin relied on a case in this court last year - *Mendelssohn* v. *Normand Ltd*. (1970). Mr. Mendelssohn parked his car in the Cumberland Garage at Marble Arch, and was given a ticket which contained an exempting condition. There was no discussion as to whether the condition formed part of the contract. It was conceded that it did. That is shown by the report in the Law Reports at p. 180. Yet the garage company were not entitled to rely on the exempting condition for the reasons there given.

That case does not touch the present, where the whole question is whether the exempting condition formed part of the contract. I do not think it did. Mr. Thornton did not know of the condition, and the company did not do what was reasonably sufficient to give him notice of it.

I do not think the garage company can escape liability by reason of the exemption condition. I would, therefore, dismiss the appeal.

[Megaw L.J. and Sir Gordon Wilmer also gave judgments dismissing the appeal.]

Questions

1. What were the reasons which prevented the garage company relying on the exempting condition in *Mendelssohn* v. *Normand Ltd*.(1970)?

2. Would it have made any difference if Mr. Thornton had used the car park on previous occasions?

2. IMPLYING TERMS

British Crane Hire v. Ipswich Plant Hire
[*1975*] *Q.B. 303 (C.A.)*

[The defendants, who were themselves a plant hire company, hired a crane from the plaintiffs. Subsequently, the crane sank into the marshy ground where it was being used and considerable expense was incurred in retrieving it. Whether the plaintiffs or the defendants should bear this loss depended upon the incorporation of certain terms in the contract between the parties.]

Lord Denning M.R. The judge found that the printed conditions were not incorporated into the contract. The plaintiffs appeal from that finding. The facts are these: the arrangements for the hire of the crane were all on the telephone. The plaintiffs agreed to let the defendants this crane. It was to be delivered on the Sunday. The hiring charges and transport charges were agreed. Nothing was said about conditions. There was nothing in writing. But soon after the crane was delivered, the plaintiffs, in accordance with their practice, sent forward a printed form to be signed by the hirer. It set out the order, the work to be done, and the hiring fee, and that it was subject to the conditions set out on the back of the form. The defendants would ordinarily have sent the form back signed: but this time they did not do so. The accident happened before they signed it. So they never did so. But the plaintiffs say that nevertheless, from the previous course of dealing, the conditions on the form govern the relationship between the parties. They rely on . . .

[Lord Denning set out two of the terms which had the effect of making the hirer responsible for the recovery of the crane from soft ground.]

In support of the course of dealing, the plaintiffs relied on two previous transactions in which the defendants had hired cranes from the plaintiffs.

One was February 20, 1969; and the other October 6, 1969. Each was on a printed form which set out the hiring of a crane, the price, the site, and so forth; and also setting out the conditions the same as those here. There were thus only two transactions many months before and they were not known to the defendants' manager who ordered this crane. In the circumstances I doubt whether those two would be sufficient to show a course of dealing.

In *Hollier* v. *Rambler Motors* (*A.M.C.*) *Ltd.* (1972) Salmon L.J. said he knew of no case

"in which it has been decided or even argued that a term could be implied into an oral contract on the strength of a course of dealing (if it can be so called) which consisted at the most of three or four transactions over a period of five years."

That was a case of a private individual who had had his car repaired by the defendants and had signed forms with conditions on three or four occasions. The plaintiff there was not of equal bargaining power with the garage company which repaired the car. The conditions were not incorporated.

But here the parties were both in the trade and were of equal bargaining power. Each was a firm of plant hirers who hired out plant. The defendants themselves knew that firms in the plant-hiring trade always imposed conditions in regard to the hiring of plant: and that their conditions were on much the same lines. The defendants' manager, Mr. Turner (who knew the crane), was asked about it. He agreed that he had seen these conditions or similar ones in regard to the hiring of plant. He said that most of them were, to one extent or another, variations of a form which he called "the Contractors' Plant Association form." The defendants themselves (when they let out cranes) used the conditions of that form. The conditions on the plaintiffs' form were in rather different words, but nevertheless to much the same effect. . . . . . .

It is clear that both parties knew quite well that conditions were habitually imposed by the supplier of these machines: and both parties knew the substance of those conditions. In particular that if the crane sank in soft ground it was the hirer's job to recover it: and that there was an indemnity clause. In these circumstances, I think the conditions on the form should be regarded as incorporated into the contract. I would not put it so much on the course of dealing, but rather on the common understanding which is to be derived from the conduct of the parties, namely, that the hiring was to be on the terms of the plaintiff's usual conditions.

As Lord Reid said in *McCutcheon* v. *David Macbrayne Ltd.* (1964) quoting from the Scottish textbook, *Gloag on Contract,* 2nd ed. (1929),

> "The judicial task is not to discover the actual intentions of each party; it is to decide what each was reasonably entitled to conclude from the attitude of the other."

It seems to me that, in view of the relationship of the parties, when the defendants requested this crane urgently and it was supplied at once - before the usual form was received - the plaintiffs were entitled to conclude that the defendants were accepting it on the terms of the plaintiffs' own printed conditions - which would follow in a day or two. It is just as if the palintiffs had said: "We will supply it on our usual conditions," and the defendants said "Of course, that is quite understood."

Even though the judge did not find that the conditions were incorporated, he held that there was an implied term that the hirer should return the chattel to the owner at the end of the hiring. Mr. McCowan pointed out that that implied term was not distinctly pleaded or relied upon. But, nevertheless, there is much to be said for it. When a machine is let out on hire for use on marshy land, and both parties know that it may sink into a marsh, then it seems to me that, if it sinks into the marsh, it is the hirer's job to recover it, so as to restore it to the owner at the end of the hiring. Take a motor car which is let out on hire, and by reason of a gale, or an icy road, it goes off the road into a ditch. It is the hirer's job to get it back on to the road and restore it at the end of the hiring. Just as when he takes it on a long journey and falls ill a long distance away. It still is his duty to get it back and restore it to the owner at the end of the hiring. Of course, if it is lost or damaged and he can prove that it was not due to any fault on his part, he would not be liable. A bailee is not liable for loss or damage which he can prove occurred without any default on his part: but the return of the vehicle is different. It is the duty of the hirer to return the vehicle at the end of the hiring to the owner, and to pay the cost of doing so. Although he is not liable for loss or damage occurring without his fault, nevertheless he is liable to do what is reasonable to restore the property to the owner.

So, apart from the express conditions, it may well be, if it had been pleaded, that the plaintiffs could have recovered from the second mishap on an implied term.

[Megaw and Sachs L.J. concurred in dismissing the appeal.]

Question

What is the relevance, if any, of the fact that the parties were stated to be of equal bargaining power?

The Moorcock
(1889) 14 P.D. 64 (C.A.)

[The defendants contracted to allow the plaintiff to discharge his vessel at their jetty. Both parties knew that the vessel would ground at low tide. Whilst unloading, the vessel did settle on the bottom and was damaged by a ridge of hard ground under the mud. The contract did not expressly provide that it was a safe anchorage.]

Bowen L.J. The question which arises here is whether when a contract is made to let the use of this jetty to a ship which can only use it, as is known by both parties, by taking the ground, there is any implied warranty on the part of the owners of the jetty, and if so, what is the extent of the warranty. Now, an implied warranty, or, as it is called, a covenant in law, as distinguished from an express contract or express warranty, really is in all cases founded on the presumed intention of the parties, and upon reason. The implication which the law draws from what must obviously have been the intention of the parties, the law draws with the object of giving efficacy to the transaction and preventing such a failure of consideration as cannot have been within the comtemplation of either side; and I believe if one were to take all the cases, and they are many, of implied warranties or covenants in law, it will be found that in all of them the law is raising an implication from the presumed intention of the parties with the object of giving to the transaction such efficacy as both parties must have intended that at all events it should have. In business transactions such as this, what the law desires to effect by the implication is to give such business efficacy to the transaction as must have been intended at all events by both parties who are business men; not to impose on one side all the perils of the transaction, or to emancipate one side from all the chances of failure, but to make each party promise in law as much, at all events, as it must have been in the contemplation of both parties that he should be responsible for in respect of those perils or chances.

[Lord Esher M.R. and Fry L.J. concurred in affirming judgment for the plaintiff, in that the defendants had impliedly represented that reasonable care had been taken to ascertain that the river bottom was not in such condition as to cause damage to the vessel.]

Note

The reasoning of the *Moorcock* was considered and affirmed by the House of Lords in the leading case of *Liverpool Corporation* v. *Irwin* (1976). They did, however, reject Lord Denning's view that a term could be implied simply on the grounds that it was just and reasonable under the circumstances (see below).

Shell v. Lostock Garages
[1977] 1 All E.R. 481 (C.A.)

[The parties had entered into a "solus" agreement whereby Lostock Garages agreed to buy their petrol exclusively from Shell. In the course of a petrol price war, Shell reduced the price of their petrol to neighbouring garages but not to the defendant. It therefore became uneconomical for the defendant to carry on trading. When Shell sought an injunction restraining Lostock Garages from buying their petrol elsewhere, the defendant claimed as part of their defence that there was an implied term in the agreement that Shell would not abnormally discriminate against Lostock Garages in their pricing of petrol.]

Lord Denning M.R. This submission makes it necessary once again to consider the law as to implied terms. I ventured with some trepidation to suggest that terms implied by law could be brought within one comprehensive category, in which the courts could imply a term such as was just and reasonable in the circumstances: see *Greaves & Co (Contractors) Ltd v Baynham Meikle & Partners*; *Liverpool City Council v Irwin*. But, as I feared, the House of Lords have rejected it as quite unacceptable. As I read the speeches, there are two broad categories of implied terms.

(i) The first category

The first category comprehends all those relationships which are of common occurrence, such as the relationship of seller and buyer, owner and hirer, master and servant, landlord and tenant, carrier by land or by sea, contractor for building works, and so forth. In all those relationships the courts have imposed obligations on one party or the other, saying they are implied terms. These obligations are not founded on the intention of the parties, actual or presumed, but on more general considerations: see *Luxor (Eastbourne) Ltd v Cooper* (1941) per Lord Wright; *Lister v Romford Ice and Cold Storage Co. per* Viscount Simonds and Lord Tucker (both of whom give interesting illustrations); *Liverpool City Council v Irwin* per Lord Cross of Chelsea and Lord Edmund-Davies. In such relationships the problem is not solved by asking: what did the parties intend? or, would they have unhesitatingly agreed to it, if asked? It is to be solved by asking: has the law already defined the obligation or the extent of it? If so, let it be followed. If not, look to see what would be reasonable in the general run of such cases (see per Lord Cross of Chelsea) and then say what the obligation shall be. The House in *Liverpool City Council v Irwin* went through that very process. They examined the existing law of landlord and tenant, in particular that relating to easements, to see if it contained the solution to the problem; and, having found that it did not, they imposed an obligation on the landlord to use reasonable care. In these relationships the parties can exclude or modify the obligation by express words, but unless they do so, the obligation is a legal incident of the relationship which is attached by the law itself and not by reason of any implied term.

Likewise, in the general law of contract, the legal effect of frustration does not depend on an implied term. It does not depend on the presumed intention of the parties, nor on what they would have answered, if asked, but simply on what the court itself declares to amount to a frustration: see *Davis Contractors v Fareham Urban District Council* (1956) per Lord Radcliffe; *Ocean Tramp Tankers Corpn v V/O Sovfracht, The Eugenia* (1964).

(ii) The second category

The second category comprehends those case which are not within the first category. These are cases, not of common occurrence, in which from the particular circumstances a term is to be implied. In these cases the implication is based on an intention imputed to the parties from their actual circumstances: see *Luxor (Eastbourne) Ltd v Cooper* (1941) per Lord Wright. Such an imputation is only to be made when it is necessary to imply a term to give efficacy to the contract and make it a workable agreement in such manner as the parties would clearly have done if they had applied their mind to the contingency which has arisen. These are the "officious bystander" type of case: see *Lister v Romford Ice & Cold Storage Co* (1957) per Lord Tucker. In such cases a term is not to be implied on the ground that it would be reasonable, but only when it is necessary and can be formulated with a sufficient degree of precision. This was the test applied by the majority of this court in *Liverpool City Council v Irwin* (1976); and they were emphatically upheld by the House on this point; see per Lord Cross of Chelsea and Lord Edmund-Davies.

There is this point to be noted about *Liverpool City Council v Irwin*. In this court the argument was only about an implication in the second category. In the House of Lords that argument was not pursued. It was only the first category.

Into which of the two categories does the present case come? I am tempted to say that a solus agreement between supplier and buyer is of such common occurrence nowadays that it could be put into the first category; so that the law could imply a term based on general considerations. But I do not think this would be found acceptable. Nor do I think the case can be brought within the second category. If Shell had been asked at the beginnBng: "Will you agree not to discriminate abnormally against the buyer?" I think they would have declined. It might be a reasonable term, but it is not a necessary term. Nor can it be formulated with sufficient precision. On this point I agree with Kerr J. It should be noticed that in *Esso Petroleum Co Ltd v Harper's Garage (Stourport) Ltd* (1968) Mocatta J also refused to make such an implication and there was no appeal from his decision.

In the circumstances, I do not think any term can be implied.

[Ormrod **L.J.** agreed that no term could be implied.]

Bridge L.J. [dissented, stating:] It is clearly not possible to imply in this agreement a term which would inhibit Shell altogether from discriminating against Lostock. It is recognised that, in the course of normal trading, oil companies like Shell in fact negotiate marginally different rates of rebate with different dealers with whom they enter into solus agreements. In some agreements, we are told, an express term is introduced to the effect that no other buyer shall be given more favourable terms than the contracting party. But it does not follow that in the absence of any such express term Shell must be at liberty to discriminate against Lostock to any degree. An extreme example will serve to illustrate that such a freedom on the part of the plaintiffs would lead to absurdity. Suppose that an oil company concludes a five year solus agreement with A at a normal rate of rebate. If on the very next day the company were to conclude two other five year solus agreements with B and C, A's nearest competitors, giving them in each case a rebate at a rate 10p per gallon higher than the rate of rebate given to A, this would make it manifestly impossible for A to trade on the terms expressly agreed. To say that in those circumstances A must still be bound by his contract would be an absurdity. Obviously the parties as reasonable men cannot have intended such an absurdity. Accordingly it seems to me to follow that the necessary foundation for the application of the classic doctrine on which terms are implied in contracts is here present. That doctrine, as I understand it, requires that terms should be implied to prevent contractual absurdities which reasonable parties cannot have intended.

The extreme difficulty which this case presents is that of defining appropriately the degree of discrimination which any implied term is to preclude. If one were to say that Shell must not discriminate abnormally, unfairly, or unreasonably, none of those criteria indicate where the line is to be drawn with any precision. If any term is to be implied, it may be appropriate to define it by reference to the necessary effect of the discrimination on Lostock. If the effect of the discrimination is, so long as it continues, such as to render it commercially impracticable for Lostock to continue to trade on the express contractual terms, then, in my judgment, one could say with confidence that the limitation to be imposed by implication on Shell's freedom to discriminate has been exceeded.

Note

Many terms are implied by Statute, as for example ss.12 to 15 of the Sale of Goods Act 1979 (see p. 471), or the Supply of Goods and Services Act 1982 which extends analogous protection for the consumer to contracts for services.

Question

Of the two views presented, which most accurately reflects the legitimate expectations of reasonable businessmen?

3. REPRESENTATIONS AND TERMS

City and Westminster Properties (1934) Ltd. v. Mudd
[1959] Ch. 129 (Ch.)

[The defendant leased a shop from the plaintiffs annexed to which was a small room in which, as the plaintiffs knew, the defendant slept. A subsequent lease

[was negotiated which contained a clause restricting use to business purposes only. The plaintiffs had, however, made an oral undertaking to the defendant that if he signed the lease notwithstanding this clause, he could still sleep on the premises. Although the defendant thereupon signed the agreement, the plaintiffs later sued for breach of the covenant relating to use of the premises.]

Harman J. [Having rejected various other defence claims continued] There remains the so-called question of estoppel. This, in my judgment, is a misnomer and the present case does not raise the controversial issue of the *Central London Property Trust Ltd.* v. *High Trees House Ltd.* (1947) decision. This is not a case of a representation made after contractual relations existed between the parties to the effect that one party to the contract would not rely on his rights. If the defendant's evidence is to be accepted, as I hold it is, it is a case of a promise made to him before the execution of the lease that, if he would execute it in the form put before him, the landlord would not seek to enforce against him personally the covenant about using the property as a shop only. The defendant says that it was in reliance on this promise that he executed the lease and entered on the onerous obligations contained in it. He says, moreover, that but for the promise made he would not have executed the lease, but would have moved to other premises available to him at the time. If these be the facts, there was a clear contract acted upon by the defendant to his detriment and from which the plaintiffs cannot be allowed to resile.

    . . . The plea that this was a mere licence retractable at the plaintiffs' will does not bear examination. The promise was that so long as the defendant personally was tenant, so long would the landlords forbear to exercise the rights which they would have if he signed the lease. He did sign the lease on this promise and is therefore entitled to rely on it so long as he is personally in occupation of the shop.

                                           Judgment for the defendant.

Notes

This case provides a striking example of how the device of a "collateral" contract can override even the terms of a formal signed document (*cf. L'Estrange* v. *Graucob*, above).

For further examples of a collateral contract, see *De Lassalle* v. *Guildford* (1901); *Shanklin Pier Ltd.* v. *Detel Products Ltd.* (1951).

If no collateral contract can be discovered by the court, it may sometimes be difficult to ascertain whether a statement is a term of the contract or merely a representation. Contrast, for example, *Oscar Chess* v. *Williams* (1957) with *Dick Bentley Productions Ltd.* v. *Harold Smith* (*Motors*) *Ltd.* (1965). The importance of the distinction lies in the remedy available, which may be either for breach of contract or misrepresentation (see Chap. 5).

Question

If the promise made by the plaintiffs had contractual force, what was the consideration which the defendant gave for it?

4. THE RELATIVE IMPORTANCE OF CONTRACTUAL TERMS

A/S Awilco v. Fulvia Sp A di Navigazione of Cagliari; The Chikuma
[1981] 1 All E.R. 652 (H.L.)

[A charterparty, in a form commonly used, provided that unless "punctual and regular payment" of the hire charge was made, the owners were entitled to withdraw the vessel from the charterers. On one occasion the charterers paid in a way that effectively gave the owners an overdraft facility for the amount of the monthly hire as opposed to an equivalent to an unconditional cash payment. If the owners had wished to draw on the money immediately, it would probably have cost them no more than $100 in interest charges in the context of a monthly payment from the charterers of nearly $69,000 and a charterparty of several years duration. The owners claimed, nevertheless, that because of the technical failure to make an unconditional payment, they had not been punctually paid and were entitled to withdraw the ship.]

Lord Bridge. It has often been pointed out that shipowners and charterers bargain at arm's length. Neither class has such a preponderance of bargaining power as to be in a position to oppress the other. They should be in a position to look after themselves by contracting only on terms which are acceptable to them. Where, as here, they embody in their contracts common form clauses, it is, to my mind, of overriding importance that their meaning and legal effect should be certain and well understood. The ideal at which the courts should aim, in construing such clauses, is to produce a result such that in any given situation both parties seeking legal advice as to their rights and obligations can expect the same clear and confident answer from their advisers and neither will be tempted to embark on long and expensive litigation in the belief that victory depends on winning the sympathy of the court. This ideal may never be fully attainable, but we shall certainly never even approximate to it unless we strive to follow clear and consistent principles and steadfastly refuse to be blown off course by the supposed merits of individual cases.

[Lords Diplock, Simon, Edmund-Davies and Scarman concurred in giving judgment in favour of the owners.]

Notes

Although their Lordships did not actually use the terminology of "conditions" and "warranties," the effect of the decision is that the "punctual and regular payment" clause in such a charterparty is a "condition," which is strictly construed.

Even, however, in commercial matters the courts have sometimes taken a more flexible approach to the importance of terms as illustrated by the next case.

Hong Kong Fir Shipping Co. Ltd. v. Kawasaki Kisen Kaisha Ltd.
[1962] 2 Q.B. 26 (H.L.)

[The plaintiffs chartered a ship to the defendants for two years, by an agreement which stated that the ship was "in every way fitted for ordinary cargo service." In fact the engines were elderly and the crew required to maintain them incompetent. The result was that several months of the charter were wasted in delays. The defendants accordingly claimed that the agreement was at an end and repudiated the charter. The plaintiffs, whose ship it was, sued for damages for wrongful repudiation. The precise status of this "seaworthiness clause" therefore had to be considered.]

Lord Diplock. [Having stated that contractual undertakings cannot all be categorised as either "conditions" or "warranties" continued] Lawyers tend to speak of this classification as if it were comprehensive, partly for the historical reasons which I have already mentioned and partly because Parliament itself adopted it in the Sale of Goods Act, 1893, as respects a number of implied terms in contracts for the sale of goods and has in that Act used the expressions "condition" and "warranty" in that meaning. But it is by no means true of contractual undertakings in general at common law.

No doubt there are many simple contractual undertakings, sometimes express but more often because of their very simplicity ("It goes without saying") to be implied, of which it can be predicated that every breach of such an undertaking must give rise to an event which will deprive the party not in default of substantially the whole benefit which it was intended that he should obtain from the contract. And such a stipulation, unless the parties have agreed that breach of it shall not entitle the non-defaulting party to treat the contract as repudiated, is a "condition." So too there may be other simple contractual undertakings of which it can be predicated that *no* breach can give rise to an event which will deprive the party not in default of substantially the whole benefit which it was intended that he should obtain from the contract; and such a stipulation, unless the parties have agreed that breach of it shall entitle the non-defaulting party to treat the contract as repudiated, is a "warranty."

There are, however, many contractual undertakings of a more complex character which cannot be categorised as being "conditions" or "warranties," if the late nineteenth-century meaning adopted in the Sale of Goods Act, 1893, and used by Bowen L.J. in *Bentsen* v. *Taylor, Sons & Co.* (1893) be given to those terms. Of such undertakings all that can be predicated is that some breaches will and others will not give rise to an event which will deprive the party not in default of substantially the whole benefit which it was intended that he should obtain from the contract; and the legal consequences of a breach of such an undertaking, unless provided for expressly in the contract, depend upon the nature of the event to which the breach gives rise and do not follow automatically from a prior classification of the undertaking as a "condition" or a "warranty." For instance, to take Bramwell B.'s example in *Jackson* v. *Union Marine Insurance Co. Ltd.* (1874) itself, breach of an undertaking by a shipowner to sail with all possible dispatch to a named port does not necessarily relieve the charterer of further performance of his obligation under the charterparty, but if the breach is so prolonged that the contemplated voyage is frustrated it does have this effect.

. . . . . .

As my brethren have already pointed out, the shipowners' undertaking to tender a seaworthy ship has, as a result of numerous decisions as to what can amount to "un-seaworthiness," become one of the most complex of contractual undertakings. It embraces obligations with respect to every part of the hull and machinery, stores and equipment and the crew itself. It can be broken by the presence of trivial defects easily and rapidly remediable as well as by defects which must inevitably result in a total loss of the vessel.

Consequently the problem in this case is, in my view, neither solved nor soluble by debating whether the shipowner's express or implied undertaking to tender a seaworthy ship is a "condition" or a "warranty." It is like so many other contractual terms an undertaking one breach of which may give rise to an event which relieves the charterer of further performance of his undertakings if he so elects and another breach of which may not give rise to such an event but entitle him only to monetary compensation in the form of damages. It is, with all deference to Mr. Ashton Roskill's skilful argument, by no means surprising that among the many hundreds of previous cases about the shipowner's undertaking to deliver a seaworthy ship there is none where it was found profitable to discuss in the judgments the question whether that undertaking is a "condition" or a "warranty"; for the true answer, as I have already indicated, is that it is neither, but one of that large class of contractual undertakings one breach of which may have the same effect as that ascribed to a breach of "condition" under the Sale of Goods Act, 1893, and a different breach of which may have only the same effect as that ascribed to a breach of "warranty" under that Act.

. . . . . .

What the judge had to do in the present case, as in any other case where one party to a contract relies upon a breach by the other party as giving him a right to elect to rescind the contract, and the contract itself makes no express provision as to this, was to look at the events which had occurred as a result of the breach at the time at which the charterers purported to rescind the charterparty and to decide whether the occurrence of those events deprived the charterers of substantially the whole benefit which it was the intention of the parties as expressed in the charterparty that the charterers should obtain from the further performance of their own contractual undertakings.

One turns therefore to the contract, the Baltime 1939 charter, of which Sellers L.J. has already cited the relevant terms. Clause 13, the "due diligence" clause, which exempts the shipowners from responsibility for delay or loss or damage to goods on board due to unseaworthiness, unless such delay or loss or damage has been caused by want of due diligence of the owners in making the vessel seaworthy and fitted for the voyage, is in itself sufficient to show that the mere occurrence of the events that the vessel was in some respect unseaworthy when tendered or that such unseaworthiness had caused some delay in performance of the charterparty would not deprive the charterer of the whole benefit which it was the intention of the parties he should obtain from the performance of his obligations under the contract - for he undertakes to continue to perform his obligations notwithstanding the occurrence of such events if they fall short of frustration of the contract and even deprives himself of any remedy in damages unless such events are the consequence of want of due diligence on the part of the shipowner.

The question which the judge had to ask himself was, as he rightly decided, whether or not at the date when the charterers purported to rescind the contract, namely, June 6, 1957, or when the shipowners purported to accept such rescission, namely, August 8, 1957, the delay which had already occurred as a result of the incompetence of the engine-room staff, and the delay which was likely to occur in repairing the engines of the vessel and the conduct of the shipowners by that date in taking steps to remedy these two matters, were, when taken together, such as to deprive the charterers of substantially the whole benefit which it was the intention of the parties they should obtain from further use of the vessel under the charterparty.

In my view, in his judgment - on which I would not seek to improve - the judge took into account and gave due weight to all the relevant considerations and arrived at the right answer for the right reasons.

Judgment for the plaintiffs.

Note

In substance, the "innominate term" predates the *Hong Kong Fir* case even though that case was the first to discuss it. An earlier example is *Aerial Advertising Co.v. Batchelor's Peas Ltd* .(1938). The advantages of flexibility in regarding a term as "innominate" have to be set against the uncertainty which is thereby produced. Cases which seem to follow the *Hong Kong Fir* approach such as *Cehave N.V. v. Bremer Handelsgesselschaft mbH* (*The Hansa Nord*) (1976) and *Reardon Smith Line* v. *Hansen Tangen* (1976) can be contrasted with *The Michalis Angelos* (1971) where the House of Lords affirmed the value of the distinction between "conditions" and "warranties."

Chapter 5

MISREPRESENTATION

1. THE MEANING OF MISREPRESENTATION

Bisset v. Wilkinson
[1927] A.C. 177 (P.C.)

[Bisset was selling two plots of land in New Zealand to Wilkinson for the purpose of sheep farming. In the course of negotiations, Bisset expressed the view that if the land were worked properly it could carry 2,000 sheep. Both parties knew that the land concerned had never been used for sheep-farming. The issue arose of whether or not this was an actionable misrepresentation.]

Lord Merrivale. In an action for rescission, as in an action for specific performance of an executory contract, when misrepresentation is the alleged ground of relief of the party who repudiates the contract, it is, of course, essential to ascertain whether that which is relied upon is a representation of a specific fact, or a statement of opinion, since an erroneous opinion stated by the party affirming the contract, though it may have been relied upon and have induced the contract on the part of the party who seeks rescission, gives no title to relief unless fraud is established. The application of this rule, however, is not always easy, as is illustrated in a good many reported cases, as well as in this. A representation of fact may be inherent in a statement of opinion and, at any rate, the existence of the opinion in the person stating it is a question of fact. In *Karberg's Case* Lindley L.J., in course of testing a representation which might have been, as it was said to be by interested parties, one of opinion or belief, used this inquiry: "Was the statement of expectation a statement of things not really expected?" The Court of Appeal applied this test and rescinded the contract which was in question. In *Smith* v. *Land and House Property Corporation* (1884) there came in question a vendor's description of the tenant of the property sold as "a most desirable tenant" - a statement of his opinion, as was argued on his behalf in an action to enforce the contract of sale. This description was held by the Court of Appeal to be a misrepresentation of fact, which, without proof of fraud, disentitled the vendor to specific performance of the contract of purchase. "It is often fallaciously assumed," said Bowen L.J., "that a statement of opinion cannot involve the statement of fact. In a case where the facts are equally well known to both parties, what one of them says to the other is frequently nothing but an expression of opinion. The statement of such opinion is in a sense a statement of fact, about the condition of the man's own mind, but only of an irrelevant fact, for it is of no consequence what the opinion is. But if the facts are not equally well known to both sides, then a statement of opinion by one who knows the facts best involves very often a statement of a material fact, for he impliedly states that he knows facts which justify his opinion.

[His Lordship considered the particular facts of this case.]

As was said by *Sim J.*: "In ordinary circumstances, any statement made by an owner who has been occupying his own farm as to its carrying capacity would be regarded as a statement of fact. . . . This, however, is not such a case. . . . In these circumstances . . . the defendants were not justified in regarding anything said by the plaintiff as to the carrying capacity as being anything more than an expression of his opinion on the subject." In this view of the matter their Lordships concur.

Judgment for the appellant, Bisset.

Note

The statement in *Bisset* v. *Wilkinson* was regarded under the circumstances merely as an expression of opinion. In *Smith* v. *Land and House Property Corporation* (1884) the statement was in reality one of fact because the vendors were well aware that the tenant paid only "by driblets under pressure." There was therefore an implied statement of fact in the vendors assertion which was quite untrue, namely that they knew facts which justified their opinion.

2. SILENCE AS MISREPRESENTATION

Wales v. Wadham
[1977] 2 All E.R. 125

[Mr. Wales and his wife, who were in the process of obtaining a divorce, entered into a compromise agreement whereby in return for a capital payment of £13,000 she agreed not to make a claim for maintenance. She had previously stated her intention not to remarry, and did not inform her husband that she had, by the time of the agreement, changed her mind on this issue. The husband would have had no obligation to maintain his wife after her remarriage. Mr. Wales subsequently brought an action for rescission of the agreement.]

Tudor Evans J. I must now consider the husband's submission that the wife's statement to him that she would not remarry amounts to a misrepresentation which induced him to enter the contract. It is the husband's case that had he been aware of the true fact he would never have made the offer to pay £13,000. This was intended to commute his liability for periodical payments, a liability which, in the event, he would never have had. In order to prove a fraudulent misrepresentation, the husband must show that the wife made a statement of fact which was false to her knowledge or that she was reckless as to its truth, and that such misrepresentation was intended to, and did, cause the husband to enter the contract. It is submitted that even if the wife's statement that she would never remarry was honestly held, she was under a duty to tell the husband of her changed circumstances, but that she failed to do so. Counsel has referred me to *With v. O'Flanagan* (1936) in the Court of Appeal. In that case, during course of negotiations for the sale of a medical practice, the vendor made representations to the purchaser about the existing nature of the practice which, by the time when the contract was signed, were untrue. The value of the practice had declined in the meantime because of the vendor's inability to attend to it through illness. Lord Wright MR quoted, with approval, observations of Fry J in *Davies v London and Provincial Marine Insurance Co* (1878) where he said:

> "So, again, if a statement has been made which is true at the time, but which during the course of negotiations becomes untrue, then the person who knows that it has become untrue is under an obligation to disclose to the other the change of circumstances."

The representations in both of these cases related to existing fact and not to a statement of intention in relation to future conduct. A statement of intention is not a representation of existing fact, unless the person making it does not honestly hold the intention he is expressing, in which case there is a misrepresentation of fact in relation to the state of that person's mind. That does not arise on the facts as I have found them. On the facts of this case, the wife made an honest statement of her intention which was not a representation of fact, and I can find no basis for holding that she was under a duty in the law of contract to tell the husband of her change of mind. Counsel for the wife submits that, apart from any other consideration, the wife's objection to remarriage after divorce and her specific statements to the husband that she would not remarry, do not have the quality of representations in the sense that at her age she could not seriously be taken as representing that she would never change her mind. I accept that submission. It seems to me that when after a marriage which had lasted for some 26 years the wife told the husband she would never marry again she was not representing to the husband that, she then being barely 50, she would never change her mind. The wife's objections to remarriage on religious grounds could not, in themselves, amount to a representation. They were simply general opinions expressed during the existence of the marriage, and not in any way made in contemplation by either party of a contract. With respect to the specific statements, as I have said, I am satisfied that the wife made them in an attempt to save her marriage and I am satisfied she was not representing that she would never change her mind . . . .

I must now consider the submission of the husband that the contract in this case was one requiring uberrima fides. Such contracts are an exception to the common law rule that a party may remain silent about material facts when negotiating a contract, and that such silence does not amount to a misrepresentation. I have been referred to *Bell v Lever Bros Ltd* (1932), where Lord Thankerton said:

> "The most familiar of these exceptions is found in the case of policies of insurance, as to which Blackburn J says, in *Fletcher v Krell*, "mercantile custom has established the rule with regard to concealment of material facts in policies of assurance, but in other cases there must be an allegation of moral guilt or fraud." Other exceptions are found in case of trustee and cestui que trust and of a company issuing a prospectus and an applicant for shares, but the number of exceptions is limited, and no authority has been cited which extends the exceptions to cover a case such as the present."

Further examples are contracts of partnership and suretyship but there is no case in which the principle has been extended to contracts between a husband and wife, although counsel for the husband has referred to a number of authorities in the 19th century concerned with deeds of separation, in which he submits the duty to disclose has been recognised. I shall refer to these cases at a later stage. The first submission is that the contract in the present case is similar to a contract of insurance.

It is pointed out that contracts of insurance are speculative in nature in the sense that an insurer can only compute his risk on the basis of what he is told by the proposed assured. I have been referred to an early case, *Carter v Boehm* (1766), where Lord Mansfield CJ said:

> "Insurance is a contract upon speculation. The special facts, upon which the contingent chance is to be computed, lie most commonly in the knowledge of the *insured* only: the under-writer trusts to his representation, and proceeds upon confidence that he does not keep back any circumstance in his knowledge, to mislead the under-writer into a belief that the circumstance does not exist ..."

It is said that the husband in the present case was computing or compromising in a single sum a future and uncertain liability to maintain the wife and that the likelihood of the wife's remarriage was a material fact in the computation which should have been disclosed. I cannot accept that there is any analogy between a contract of insurance and the contract in the present case. In contracts of insurance, the material facts on which the insurer decides whether to assume the risk and, if so, on what terms, lie exclusively within the knowledge of the insured. Contracts requiring uberrima fides are based on the fact that, from the very necessity of the case, only one party possesses knowledge of all the material facts. In the case of life assurance, for example, only the proposed assured can know the state of his health, past or present. The contract in the present case was one in which material facts on both sides were withheld. Neither side made full disclosure. The husband admitted in cross-examination that he did not disclose his income. ... On the wife's side, she did not disclose that between the end of October 1972, when the husband made the offer, and February 1973, when counsel agreed the terms in settlement of all the wife's claims for ancillary relief for maintenance, that she had an arrangement to marry Mr Wadham. No questions were asked of the wife's financial position nor whether she intended to marry at any time in the future. It seems to me that the negotiations and the agreement reached was a compromise without full disclosure on either side. I can find no similarity at all to a contract of insurance.

Judgment for the wife.

3. *TERMS AND NEGLIGENT MISREPRESENTATION*

Esso Petroleum Co. Ltd. v. Mardon
[1976] 2 All E.R. 5 (C.A.)

[Esso had bought a site for development as a petrol station. Their very experienced sales representative assured the defendant that the garage would have a throughput of petrol of some 200,000 gallons per year. The defendant doubted this but ultimately, in reliance upon the representative's estimate, signed the tenancy agreement. In fact, the petrol sales were less than half the estimate. In the resulting litigation the defendant counterclaimed against Esso on the basis of the negligent statement made by their representative.]

Lord Denning M.R. . . .

Collateral warranty

Ever since *Heilbut Symons & Co. v Buckleton* (1913) we have had to contend with the law as laid down by the House of Lords that an innocent misrepresentation gives no right to damages. In order to escape from that rule, the pleader used to allege - I often did it myself - that the misrepresentation was fraudulent, or alternatively a collateral warranty. At the trial we nearly always succeeded on collateral warranty. We had to reckon, of course, with the dictum of Lord Moulton that "such collateral contracts must from their very nature be rare." But more often than not the court elevated the innocent misrepresentation into a collateral warranty; and thereby did justice - in advance of the Misrepresentation Act 1967. I remember scores of cases of that kind, especially on the sale of a business. A representation as to the profits that had been made in the past was invariably held to be a warranty. Besides that experience, there have been many cases since I have sat in this court where we have readily held a representation - which induces a person to enter into a contract - to be a warranty sounding in damages. I summarised them in *Dick Bentley Productions Ltd. v Harold Smith (Motors) Ltd.* (1965) when I said:

"Looking at the cases once more, as we have done so often, it seems to me that if a representation is made in the course of dealings for a contract for the very purpose of inducing the other party to act on it, and it actually induces him to act on it by entering into the contract, that is prima facie ground for inferring that the representation was intended as a warranty. It is not necessary to speak of it as being collateral. Suffice it that the representation was intended to be acted on and was in fact acted on."

Counsel for Esso retaliated, however, by citing *Bisset v Wilkinson* where the Privy Council said that a statement by a New Zealand farmer that an area of land "would carry 2,000 sheep" was only an expression of opinion. He submitted that the forecast here of 200,000 gallons was an expression of opinion and not a statement of fact; and that it could not be interpreted as a warranty or promise.

Now, I would quite agree with counsel for Esso that it was not a warranty - in this sense - that it did not *guarantee* that the throughput *would be* 200,000 gallons. But, nevertheless, it was a forecast made by a party, Esso, who had special knowledge and skill. It was the yardstick . . . by which they measured the worth of a filling station. They knew the facts. They knew the traffic in the town. They knew the throughput of comparable stations. They had much experience and expertise at their disposal. They were in a much better position than Mr Mardon to make a forecast. It seems to me that if such a person makes a forecast - intending that the other should act on it and he does act on it - it can well be interpreted as a warranty that the forecast is sound and reliable in this sense that they made it with reasonable care and skill. It is just as if Esso said to Mr Mardon: "Our forecast of throughput is 200,000 gallons. You can rely on it as being a sound forecast of what the service station should do. The rent is calculated on that footing." If the forecast turned out to be an unsound forecast, such as no person of skill or experience should have made, there is a breach of warranty. Just as there is a breach of warranty when a forecast is made "expected to load" by a certain date if the maker has no reasonable grounds for it: see *Samuel Sanday v Keighley Maxted & Co.* (1922), or bunkers "expected 600/700 tons": see *The Pantanassa* (1958) by Diplock J. It is very different from the New Zealand case where the land had never been used as a sheep farm and both parties were equally able to form an opinion as to its carrying capacity.

In the present case it seems to me that there was a warranty that the forecast was sound, that is that Esso had made it with reasonable care and skill. That warranty was broken. Most negligently Esso made a "fatal error" in the forecast they stated to Mr Mardon, and on which he took the tenancy. For this they are liable in damages. The judge, however, declined to find a warranty. So I must go further.

Negligent misrepresentation

Assuming that there was no warranty, the question arises whether Esso are liable for negligent mis-statement under the doctrine of *Hedley Byrne & Co Ltd v Heller & Partners Ltd* (1964). It has been suggested that *Hedley Byrne* cannot be used so as to impose liability for negligent pre-contractual statements; and that, in a pre-contract situation, the remedy (at any rate before the 1967 Act) was only in warranty or nothing. Thus in *Hedley Byrne* itself Lord Reid said: "Where there is a contract there is no difficulty as regards the contracting parties: the question is whether there is a warranty." And in *Oleificio Zucchi SPA v Northern Sales Ltd.* (1965) McNair J said: " . . . as at present advised, I consider the submission advanced by the buyers - that the ruling in [*Hedley Byrne*] applies as between contracting parties, is without foundation." As against these, I took a different view in *McInerny v Lloyds Bank Ltd.* (1974), when I said: " . . . if one person, by a negligent mis-statement, induces another to enter into a contract - with himself or a third person - he may be liable in damages."

It follows that I cannot accept counsel for Esso's proposition. It seems to me that *Hedley Byrne,* properly understood, covers this particular proposition: if a man, who has or professes to have special knowledge or skill, makes a representation by virtue thereof to another - be it advice, information or opinion - with the intention of inducing him to enter into a contract with him, he is under a duty to use reasonable care to see that the representation is correct, and that the advice, information or opinion is reliable. If he negligently gives unsound advice or misleading information or expresses an erroneous opinion, and thereby induces the other side into a contract with him, he is liable in damages. This proposition is in line with what I said in *Candler v Crane Christmas & Co* (1951), which was approved by the majority of the Privy Council in *Mutual Life & Citizens' Assurance Ltd v Evatt,* (1971). And the judges of the Commonwealth have shown themselves quite ready to apply *Hedley Byrne* between contracting parties: see, in Canada, *Sealand of the Pacific Ltd v Ocean Cement Ltd* (1973) and, in New Zealand, *Capital Motors Ltd v Beecham* (1975).

Applying this principle, it is plain that Esso professed to have - and did in fact have - special knowledge or skill in estimating the throughput of a filling station. They made the representation - they forecast a throughput of 200,000 gallons

- intending to induce Mr Mardon to enter into a tenancy on the faith of it. They made it negligently. It was a "fatal error." And thereby induced Mr Mardon to enter into a contract of tenancy that was disastrous to him. For this misrepresentation they are liable in damages.

[Ormrod and Shaw L.JJ. concurred in giving judgment for the defendant on the counterclaim.]

Question

Even though there may be a cause of action in both contract and tort in these circumstances, why might a litigant prefer to bring his action under the Misrepresentation Act 1967?

4. MISREPRESENTATION AND THE MISREPRESENTATION ACT 1967

Howard Marine & Dredging Co. Ltd. v. A. Ogden and Son (Excavations) Ltd.
[*1978*] *Q.B. 574 (C.A.)*

[Ogdens wished to hire some barges for removing large quantities of clay. The carrying capacity of the barges to be used was crucial as this would affect, for example, how quickly the job could be done. They approached Howards, who hired out barges, and on enquiring as to their capacity received an oral reply from their representative Mr. O'Loughlin which proved to be incorrect in that it was too high. The mistake arose from the maker's reliance on the entry in Lloyds Register (which was usually accurate) instead of checking the ship's documents which were in their possession. When the error became apparent, Ogdens refused to make further hire payments. Howards, the plaintiffs, withdrew the barges and claimed for hire payments. Ogdens counterclaimed on the grounds of misrepresentation.]

Lord Denning M.R. (dissenting):

The collateral oral warranties

Ogdens submitted that, in the two telephone conversations in April 1974, Howards gave oral warranties as to the carrying capacity of the barges: and that, on the faith of these warranties, they tendered for the main excavation contract and entered into it: that the warranties are therefore binding on Howards on the authority of such cases as *Shanklin Pier Ltd.* v. *Detel Products Ltd.* (1951) and *Wells (Merstham) Ltd.* v. *Buckland Sand and Silica Ltd.* (1965). Further, that at the interview of July 11, 1974, Howards gave a further oral warranty as to the carrying capacity of the barges: and that, on the faith of it, they did order the barges and took them on hire under the charterparties.

On this point we were, as usual, referred to *Heilbut, Symons & Co.* v. *Buckleton* (1913). That case has come under considerable criticism lately, particularly in view of the contemporaneous decision of the House of Lords in *Schawel* v. *Reade* (1912). ... Much of what was said in *Heilbut, Symons & Co.* v. *Buckleton* is now out of date, as I mentioned in *J. Evans & Sons (Portsmouth) Ltd.* v. *Andrea Merzario Ltd.* (1976) and *Esso Petroleum Co. Ltd.* v. *Mardon* (1976). No doubt it is still true to say, as Holt C.J. said: "an affirmation at the time of the sale is a warranty, provided it appears as evidence to be so intended" – which I take to mean intended to be binding.

Applying this test, I cannot regard any of the oral representations made in April 1974 as contractual warranties. Ogdens invited offers from five different owners of barges. These five made separate offers. Howards made their written offer "subject to availability and contract": which shows that they were not binding themselves to anything at that stage. It cannot be supposed that in the telephone conversations they were binding themselves contractually to anything. Nor would I regard the statement at the interview of July 11, 1974, as a contractual warranty. It was made three months before the barges were delivered. And meanwhile there was the "on-hire condition survey": and the exchange of the draft charterparties – in which you would expect any contractual terms to be included.

I agree with the judge that there were no collateral warranties here.

Negligent misrepresentations

Ogdens contended next that the representations by Howards, as to the carrying capacity of the barges, were made negligently: and that Howards are liable in damages for negligent misrepresentation on the principles laid down in *Hedley Byrne & Co. Ltd.* v. *Heller & Partners Ltd.* (1964).

This raises the vexed question of the scope of the doctrine of *Hedley Byrne*. It was much discussed in the Privy Council in *Mutual Life and Citizens' Assurance Co. Ltd.* v. *Evatt* (1971) and in this court in *Esso Petroleum Co. Ltd.* v. *Mardon* (1976). To my mind one of the most helpful passages is to be found in the speech of Lord Pearce in *Hedley Byrne & Co. Ltd.* v. *Heller & Partners Ltd.* (1964):

" . . . To import such a duty (of care) the representation must normally, I think, concern a business or professional transaction whose nature makes clear the gravity of the inquiry and the importance and influence attached to the answer . . . A most important circumstance is the form of the inquiry and of the answer."

To this I would add the principle stated by Lord Reid and Lord Morris of Borth-y-Gest in the Privy Council case, *Mutual Life and Citizens' Assurance Co. Ltd.* v. *Evatt* (1971), which I would adopt in preference to that stated by the majority:

" . . . when an inquirer consults a business man in the course of his business and makes it plain to him that he is seeking considered advice and intends to act on it in a particular way . . . his action in giving such advice . . . (gives rise to) . . . a legal obligation to take such care as is reasonable in the whole circumstances."

Those principles speak of the "gravity of the inquiry" and the seeking of "considered advice." Those words are used so as to exclude representations made during a casual conversation in the street; or in a railway carriage; or an impromptu opinion given offhand; or "off the cuff" on the telephone. To put it more generally, the duty is one of honesty and no more whenever the opinion, information or advice is given in circumstances in which it appears that it is unconsidered and it would not be reasonable for the recipient to act on it without taking further steps to check it. . . .

Applying this test, it seems to me that at these various conversations Mr. O'Loughlin was under a duty to be honest, but no more. Take the first two conversations. They were on the telephone. The callers from the north wanted to know what was the capacity of the barges. Mr. O'Loughlin answered it offhand as best he could, without looking up the file. If they had wanted considered advice, they should have written a letter and got it in writing. Take the last conversation. It was on an occasion when Mr. O'Loughlin went up to the north to discuss all sorts of things. In the course of it, he was asked again the capacity of the barges. He had not got the file with him, so he answered as best he could from memory. To my mind in those circumstances it was not reasonable for Ogdens to act on his answers without checking them. They ought either to have got him to put in writing - that would have stressed the gravity and importance of it - or they ought to have got expert advice on their own behalf - especially in a matter of such importance to them. So I agree with the judge that there was not such a situation here as to give rise to a duty of care: or to make Howards liable for negligent misrepresentation at common law.

The Misrepresentation Act 1967

Alternatively Ogdens claim damages for innocent misrepresentation under the Misrepresentation Act 1967. It says in section 2: . . . [see p. 464]

This enactment imposes a new and serious liability on anyone who makes a representation of fact in the course of negotiations for a contract. If that representation turns out to be mistaken - then however innocent he may be - he is just as liable as if he made it fraudulently. But how different from times past! For years he was not liable in damages at all for innocent misrepresentation: see *Heilbut, Symons & Co.* v. *Buckleton* (1913). Quite recently he was made liable if he was proved to have made it negligently: see *Esso Petroleum Co. Ltd.* v. *Mardon* (1976). But now with this Act he is made liable - unless he proves - and the burden is on him to prove - that he had reasonable ground to believe and did in fact believe that it was true.

Section 2(1) certainly applies to the representation made by Mr. O'Loughlin on July 11, 1974, when he told Ogdens that each barge could carry 1,600 tonnes. The judge found that it was a misrepresentation: that he said it with the object of getting the hire contract for Howards. They got it: and, as a result, Ogdens suffered loss. But the judge found that Mr. O'Loughlin was not negligent: and so Howards were not liable for it.

The judge's finding was criticised before us: because he asked himself the question: was Mr. O'Loughlin negligent? Whereas he should have asked himself: did Mr. O'Loughlin have reasonable ground to believe that the representation was true? I think that criticism is not fair to the judge. By the word "negligent" he was only using shorthand for the longer phrase contained in section 2(1) which he had before him. And the judge, I am sure, had the burden of proof in mind: for he had come to the conclusion that Mr. O'Loughlin was not negligent. The judge said in effect: "I am satisfied that Mr. O'Loughlin was not negligent": and being so satisfied, the burden need not be further considered . . . .

. . . . . .

It seems to me that when one examines the details, the judge's view was entirely justified. He found that Mr. O'Loughlin's state of mind was this: Mr. O'Loughlin had examined Lloyd's Register and had seen there that the deadweight capacity of each barge was 1,800 tonnes. That figure stuck in his mind. The judge found that "the 1,600 tonnes was arrived at by knocking off what he considered a reasonable margin for fuel, and so on, from the 1,800 tonnes summer deadweight figure in Lloyd's Register, which was in the back of his mind." The judge said that Mr. O'Loughlin had seen at some time the German shipping documents and had seen the deadweight figure of 1,055.135 tonnes: but it did not register. All that was in his mind was the 1,800 tonnes in Lloyd's Register which was regarded in shipping circles as the Bible. That afforded reasonable ground for him to believe that the barges could each carry 1,600 tonnes pay load: and that is what Mr. O'Loughlin believed.

So on this point, too, I do not think we should fault the judge. It is not right to pick his judgment to pieces - by subjecting it - or the shorthand note - to literal analysis. Viewing it fairly, the judge (who had section 2(1) in front of him) must have been of opinion that the burden of proof was discharged.

The exception clause

If I be wrong so far, however, there remains the exception clause in the charterparty. It was, as I have said, included throughout all the negotiations: and no objection was ever taken to it. The important words are:

"... charterers' acceptance of handing over the vessel shall be conclusive that [she is] . . . in all respects fit for the intended and contemplated use by the charterers and in every other way satisfactory to them."

In the old days we used to construe such an exception clause strictly against the party relying on it: but there is no need - and I suggest no warrant - any longer for construing it so strictly. The reason is that now by section 3 of the Misrepresentation Act 1967 the provision is of no effect except to the extent that the court may allow reliance on it as being fair and reasonable in the circumstances of the case. Under this section the question is not whether the provision itself is reasonable: but only whether "reliance on it [is] fair and reasonable in the circumstances of the case."

If the clause itself is reasonable, that goes a long way towards showing that the reliance on it is fair and reasonable. It seems to me that the clause was itself fair and reasonable. The parties here were commercial concerns and were of equal bargaining power. The clause was not foisted by one on the other in a standard printed form. It was contained in all the drafts which passed between them, and it was no doubt given close consideration by both sides, like all the other clauses, some of which were amended and others not. It was a clause common in charterparties of this kind: and is familiar in other commercial contracts, such as construction and engineering contracts . . . . It is specially applicable in cases where the contractor has the opportunity of checking the position for himself. It tells him that he should do so: and that he should not rely on any information given beforehand, for it may be inaccurate. Thus it provides a valuable safeguard against the consequences of innocent misrepresentation.

. . . I would do nothing to impair its efficacy. I would allow Howards to rely on it.

Bridge L.J. [Having also rejected the collateral warranty argument, and after citing section 2(1) of the Act continued:]

The first question then is whether Howards would be liable in damages in respect of Mr. O'Loughlin's misrepresentation if it had been made fraudulently, that is to say, if he had known that it was untrue. An affirmative answer to that question is inescapable. The judge found in terms that what Mr. O'Loughlin said about the capacity of the barges was said with the object of getting the hire contract for Howards, in other words, with the intention that it should be acted on. This was clearly right. Equally clearly the misrepresentation was in fact acted on by Ogdens. It follows, therefore, on the plain language of the statute that, although there was no allegation of fraud, Howards must be liable unless they proved that Mr. O'Loughlin had reasonable ground to believe what he said about the barges' capacity.

It is unfortunate that the judge never directed his mind to the question whether Mr. O'Loughlin had any reasonable ground for his belief. The question he asked himself, in considering liability under the Misrepresentation Act 1967, was whether the innocent misrepresentation was negligent. He concluded that if Mr. O'Loughlin had given the inaccurate information in the course of the April telephone conversations he would have been negligent to do so but that in the circumstances obtaining at the Otley interview in July there was no negligence. I take it that he meant by this that on the earlier occasions the circumstances were such that he would have been under a duty to check the accuracy of his information, but on the later occasions he was exempt from any such duty. I appreciate the basis of this distinction, but it seems to me, with respect, quite irrelevant to any question of liability under the statute. If the representee proves a misrepresentation which, if fraudulent, would have sounded in damages, the onus passes immediately to the representor to prove that he had reasonable ground to believe the facts represented. In other words the liability of the representor does not depend upon his being under a duty of care the extent of which may vary according to the circumstances in which the representation is made. In the course of negotiations leading to a contract the statute imposes an absolute obligation not to state facts which the representor cannot prove he had reasonable ground to believe.

Although not specifically posing the question of whether he had reasonable ground for his belief, the judge made certain findings about Mr. O'Loughlin's state of mind. He said:

> "Mr. O'Loughlin looked at the documents of the ships he was in charge of including HB2 and HB3's German documents. He is not a master of maritime German. He saw, but did not register, the deadweight figure of 1,055.135 tonnes. Being in the London office he went to the City and looked up Lloyd's Register. There he noted that the summer loading deadweight figure for B41 and B45, described as TM sand carriers, was 1,800 tonnes. This figure stayed in his mind. But it was one of Lloyd's Register's rare mistakes."

[Having considered the evidence in the case]

I am fully alive to the dangers of trial by transcript and it is to be assumed that Mr. O'Loughlin was perfectly honest throughout. But the question remains whether his evidence, however benevolently viewed, is sufficient to show that he had an objectively reasonable ground to disregard the figure in the ship's documents and to prefer the Lloyd's Register figure. I think it is not. . . . Accordingly I conclude that Howards failed to prove that Mr. O'Loughlin had reasonable ground to believe the truth of his misrepresentation to Mr. Redpath.

Having reached a conclusion favourable to Ogdens on the issue of liability under the Misrepresentation Act 1967, I do not find it necessary to express a concluded view on the issue of negligence at common law. As at present advised I doubt if the circumstances surrounding the misrepresentation at the Otley interview were such as to impose on Howards a common law duty of care for the accuracy of the statement. If there was such a duty, I doubt if the evidence established a breach of it.

[His Lordship then considered the exception clause:]

A clause of this kind is to be narrowly construed. It can only be relied on as conclusive evidence of the charterers' satisfaction in relation to such attributes of the vessel as would be apparent on an ordinary examination of the vessel. I do not think deadweight capacity is such an attribute. It can only be ascertained by an elaborate calculation or by an inspection of the ship's documents. But even if, contrary to this view, the clause can be read as apt to exclude liability for the earlier misrepresentation, Howards still have to surmount the restriction imposed by section 3 of the Misrepresentation Act 1967, which provides: . . . [See p. 465]

What the judge said in this matter was: "If the wording of the clause is apt to exempt from responsibility for negligent misrepresentation as to carrying capacity, I hold that such exemption is not fair and reasonable." The judge having asked himself the right question and answered it as he did in the exercise of the discretion vested in him by the Act, I can see no ground on which we could say that he was wrong.

I would accordingly allow the appeal to the extent of holding that Ogdens establish liability against Howards under section 2(1) of the Misrepresentation Act 1967 for any damages they suffered as a result of Mr. O'Loughlin's misrepresentation at the Otley interview in the terms as found by the judge.

[*Shaw LJ* expressed the view that there was a cause of action in negligence at common law, but otherwise concurred with Bridge L.J.]

Judgment for the defendants.

Question

There were three main claims in the defendant's counterclaim. What were they? On which one did they ultimately succeed?

Note

For an example of a clause in a common form contract purporting to restrict liability for misrepresentation which was considered not to be fair and reasonable, see *Walker* v. *Boyle* (1982).

Chapter 6

MISTAKE

1. MISTAKE AS TO THE EXISTENCE OF THE SUBJECT-MATTER

Lever Brothers Ltd. v. Bell
[1931] 1 K.B. 557

[The facts are set out later at p. 358.]

Wright J. The mistake here invoked is of that type which has often been discussed, and has been described by various terms – for instance, as being mistake of subject matter, or substance, or essence, or fundamental basis. However described, what is meant is some mistake or misapprehension as to some facts (which term here includes particular private rights, as held in *Cooper* v. *Phibbs* (1867)), which, by the common intention of the parties, whether expressed or more generally implied, constitute the underlying assumption without which the parties would not have made the contract they did. The simplest and oldest illustration of such mistake is where the parties contracted to sell and buy a specific chattel which at the date of the contract, though both parties thought it existing, had ceased to exist: in that event, however absolute the terms of the contract, there is in law no binding contract, and this principle is now embodied in the Sale of Goods Act, 1893, s.6. The principle was applied in a sense to the sale of a cargo sold c.i.f. which had, before the date of the contract, owing to sea damage, been properly sold by the shipmaster at a port of refuge, and hence became, without the knowledge of either party, incapable of delivery, though it may be that it still existed: *Couturier* v. *Hastie* (1852). The contract in such cases is void. . . . In . . . *Scott* v. *Coulson* (1903), there was a contract for the sale of a life policy, but before that the assured had died, both parties to the contract being in ignorance of that fact. This transaction was set aside, and Vaughan Williams L.J. thus stated his conclusion: "If we are to take it that it was common ground that, at the date of the contract for the sale of this policy, both the parties to the contract supposed the assured to be alive, it is true that both parties entered into this contract upon the basis of a common affirmative belief that the assured was alive; but as it turned out that this was a common mistake, the contract was one which cannot be enforced. This is so at law; and the plaintiffs do not require to have recourse to equity to rescind the contract, if the basis which both parties recognized as the basis is not true."

Note

The case was subsequently appealed to the House of Lords, see below.

2. MISTAKE AS TO QUALITY

Bell v. Lever Brothers
[*1932*] *A.C. 161 (H.L.)*

[Lever Brothers appointed Bell as managing director of a company in which they had a controlling interest at an annual salary of £8,000 for a period of five years. Because of a merger Bell's services were no longer required and Lever Brothers paid him £30,000 compensation for his loss of employment. They subsequently discovered that during his employment he had committed various acts which would have entitled them to terminate his employment without any compensation at all, although it was also found that Bell had not been fraudulent in failing to reveal these actions. Lever Brothers sued for rescission of the agreement and for the recovery of the £30,000. One of the bases for this claim was that there was a common mistake rendering the contract void.]

Lord Atkin. Two points present themselves for decision. Was the agreement of March 19, 1929, void by reason of a mutual mistake of Mr. D'Arcy Cooper and Mr. Bell?

Could the agreement of March 19, 1929, be avoided by reason of the failure of Mr. Bell to disclose his misconduct in regard to the cocoa dealings?

My Lords, the rules of law dealing with the effect of mistake on contract appear to be established with reasonable clearness. If mistake operates at all it operates so as to negative or in some cases to nullify consent. The parties may be mistaken in the identity of the contracting parties, or in the existence of the subject-matter of the contract at the date of the contract, or in the quality of the subject-matter of the contract. These mistakes may be by one party, or by both, and the legal effect may depend upon the class of mistake above mentioned. Thus a mistaken belief by A. that he is contracting with B., whereas in fact he is contracting with C., will negative consent where it is clear that the intention of A. was to contract only with B. So the agreement of A. and B. to purchase a specific article is void if in fact the article had perished before the date of sale. In this case, though the parties in fact were agreed about the subject-matter, yet a consent to transfer or take delivery of something not existent is deemed useless, the consent is nullified. As codified in the Sale of Goods Act the contract is expressed to be void if the seller was in ignorance of the destruction of the specific chattel. I apprehend that if the seller with knowledge that a chattel was destroyed purported to sell it to a purchaser, the latter might sue for damages for non-delivery though the former could not sue for non-acceptance, but I know of no case where a seller has so committed himself. This is a case where mutual mistake certainly and unilateral mistake by the seller of goods will prevent a contract from arising. Corresponding to mistake as to the existence of the subject-matter is mistake as to title in cases where, unknown to the parties, the buyer is already the owner of that which the seller purports to sell to him. The parties intended to effectuate a transfer of ownership: such a transfer is impossible: the stipulation is naturali ratione inutilis. This is the case of *Cooper* v. *Phibbs* (1867) where A. agreed to take a lease of a fishery from B., though contrary to the belief of both parties at the time A. was tenant for life of the fishery and B. appears to have had no title at all. To such a case Lord Westbury applied the principle that if parties contract under a mutual mistake and misapprehension as to their relative and respective rights the result is that the agreement is liable to be set aside as having proceeded upon a common mistake. Applied to the context the statement is only subject to the criticism that the agreement would appear to be void rather than voidable. Applied to mistake as to rights generally it would appear to be too wide. Even where the vendor has no title, though both parties think he has, the correct view would appear to be that there is a contract: but that the vendor has either committed a breach of a stipulation as to title, or is not able to perform his contract. The contract is unenforceable by him but is not void.

Mistake as to quality of the thing contracted for raises more difficult questions. In such a case a mistake will not affect assent unless it is the mistake of both parties, and is as to the existence of some quality which makes the thing without the quality essentially different from the thing as it was believed to be. Of course it may appear that the parties contracted that the article should possess the quality which one or other or both mistakenly believed it to possess. But in such a case there is a contract and the inquiry is a different one, being whether the contract as to quality amounts to a condition or a warranty, a different branch of the law. The principles to be applied are to be found in two cases which, as far as my knowledge goes, have always been treated as authoritative expositions of the law. The first is *Kennedy* v. *Panama Royal Mail Co.* (1867).

In that case the plaintiff had applied for shares in the defendant company on the faith of a prospectus which stated falsely but innocently that the company had a binding contract with the Government of New Zealand for the carriage of mails. On discovering the true facts the plaintiff brought an action for the recovery of the sums he had paid on calls. The defendants brought a cross action for further calls. Blackburn J., in delivering the judgment of the Court (Cockburn C.J., Blackburn, Mellor and Shee JJ.), said: "The only remaining question is one of much greater difficulty. It was contended by Mr. Mellish, on behalf of Lord Gilbert Kennedy, that the effect of the prospectus was to warrant to the intended shareholders that there really was such a contract as is there represented, and not merely to represent that the company *bona fide* believed it; and that the difference in substance between shares in a company with such a contract and shares in a company whose supposed contract was not binding, was a difference in substance in the nature of the thing; and that the shareholder was entitled to return the shares as soon as he discovered this, quite independently of fraud, on the ground that he had applied for one thing and got another. And, if the invalidity of the contract really made the shares he obtained different things in substance from those which he applied for, this would, we think, be good law. The case would then resemble *Gompertz* v. *Bartlett* (1853) and *Gurney* v. *Womersley* (1854), where the person who had honestly sold what he thought a bill without recourse to him, was nevertheless held bound to return the price on its turning out that the supposed bill was a forgery in the one case, and void under the stamp laws in the other; in both cases the ground of this decision being that the thing handed over was not the thing paid for. A similar principle was acted on in *Ship's Case* (1865). There is, however, a very important difference between cases where a contract may be rescinded on account of fraud, and those in which it may be rescinded on the ground that there is a difference in substance between the thing bargained for and that obtained. It is enough to show that there was a fraudulent representation as to any part of that which induced the party to enter into the contract which he seeks to rescind; but where there has been an innocent misrepresentation or misapprehension, it does not authorize a rescission unless it is such as to show that there is a complete difference in substance between what was supposed to be and what was taken, so as to constitute a failure of consideration. For example, where a horse is bought under a belief that it is sound, if the purchaser was induced to buy by a fraudulent representation as to the horse's soundness, the contract may be rescinded. If it was induced by an honest misrepresentation as to its soundness, though it may be clear that both vendor and purchaser thought that they were dealing about a sound horse and were in error, yet the purchaser must pay the whole price unless there was a warranty; and even if there was a warranty, he cannot return the horse and claim back the whole price, unless there was a condition to that effect in the contract: *Street* v. *Blay* (1831)."

The Court came to the conclusion in that case that, though there was a misapprehension as to that which was a material part of the motive inducing the applicant to ask for the shares, it did not prevent the shares from being in substance those he applied for.

The next case is *Smith* v. *Hughes* (1871), the well known case as to new and old oats. . . .

[See p. 371. Lord Atkin gave the facts and quoted from the judgments in that case.]

The Court ordered a new trial. It is not quite clear whether they considered that if the defendant's contention was correct, the parties were not ad idem or there was a contractual condition that the oats sold were old oats. In either case the defendant would succeed in defeating the claim.

In these cases I am inclined to think that the true analysis is that there is a contract, but that the one party is not able to supply the very thing whether goods or services that the other party contracted to take; and therefore the contract is unenforceable by the one if executory, while if executed the other can recover back money paid on the ground of failure of the consideration.

We are now in a position to apply to the facts of this case the law as to mistake so far as it has been stated. It is essential on this part of the discussion to keep in mind the finding of the jury acquitting the defendants of fraudulent misrepresentation or concealment in procuring the agreements in question. Grave injustice may be done to the defendants and confusion introduced into the legal conclusion, unless it is quite clear that in considering mistake in this case no suggestion of fraud is admissible and cannot strictly be regarded by the judge who has to determine the legal issues raised. The agreement which is said to be void is the agreement contained in the letter of March 19, 1929, that Bell would retire from the Board of the Niger Company and its subsidiaries, and that in consideration of his doing so Levers would pay him as compensation for the termination of his agreements and consequent loss of office the sum of 30,000*l*. in full satisfaction and discharge of all claims and demands of any kind against Lever Brothers, the Niger Company or its subsidiaries. The agreement, which as part of the contract was terminated, had been broken so that it could be repudiated. Is an agreement to terminate a broken contract different in kind from an agreement to terminate an unbroken contract, assuming that the breach has given the one party the right to declare the contract at an end? I feel the weight of the plaintiffs' contention that a contract immediately deter-minable is a different thing from a contract for an unexpired term, and that the difference in kind can be illustrated by the immense price of release from the longer contract as compared with the shorter. And I agree that an agreement to take an assignment of a lease for five years is not the same thing as to take an assignment of a lease for three years, still less a term for a few months. But, on the whole, I have come to the conclusion that it would be wrong to decide that an agreement to terminate a definite specified contract is void if it turns out that the agreement had already been broken and could have been terminated otherwise. The contract released is the identical contract in both cases, and the party paying for release gets exactly what he bargains for. It seems immaterial that he could have got the same result in another way, or that if he had known the true facts he would not have entered into the bargain. A. buys B.'s horse; he thinks the horse is sound and he pays the price of a sound horse; he would certainly not have bought the horse if he had known as the fact is that the horse is unsound. If B. has made no representation as to soundness and has not contracted that the horse is sound, A. is bound and cannot recover back the price. A. buys a picture from B.; both A. and B. believe it to be the work of an old master, and a high price is paid. It turns out to be a modern copy. A. has no remedy in the absence of representation or warranty. A. agrees to take on lease or to buy from B. an unfurnished dwelling-house. The house is in fact uninhabitable. A. would never have entered into the bargain if he had known the fact. A. has no remedy, and the position is the same whether B. knew the facts or not, so long as he made no representation or gave no warranty. A. buys a roadside garage business from B. abutting on a public thoroughfare: unknown to A., but known to B., it has already been decided to construct a byepass road which will divert substantially the whole of the traffic from passing A.'s garage. Again A. has no remedy. All these cases involve hardship on A. and benefit B., as most people would say, unjustly. They can be supported on the ground that it is of paramount importance that contracts should be observed, and that if parties honestly comply with the essentials of the formation of contracts - i.e., agree in the same terms on the same subject-matter - they are bound, and must rely on the stipulations of the contract for protection from the effect of facts unknown to them.

This brings the discussion to the alternative mode of expressing the result of a mutual mistake. It is said that in such a case as the present there is to be implied a stipulation in the contract that a condition of its efficacy is that the facts should be as understood by both parties - namely, that the contract could not be terminated till the end of the current term. The question of the existence of conditions, express or implied, is obviously one that affects not the formation of contract, but the investigation of the terms of the contract when made. A condition derives its efficacy from the consent of the parties, express or implied. They have agreed, but on what terms. One term may be that unless the facts are or are not of a particular nature, or unless an event has or has not happened, the contract is not the take effect. With regard to future facts such a condition is obviously contractual. Till the event occurs the parties are bound. Thus the condition (the exact terms of which need not here be investigated) that is generally accepted as underlying the principle of the frustration cases is contractual, an implied condition. Sir John Simon formulated for the assistance of your Lordships a proposition which should be recorded: "Whenever it is to be inferred from the terms of a contract or its surrounding circumstances that the consensus has been reached upon the basis of a particular contractual assumption, and that assumption is not true, the contract is avoided: i.e., it is void ab initio if the assumption is of present fact and it ceases to bind if the assumption is of future fact."

I think few would demur to this statement, but its value depends upon the meaning of "a contractual assumption," and also upon the true meaning to be attached to "basis," a metaphor which may mislead. When used expressly in contracts, for instance, in policies of insurance, which state that the truth of the statements in the proposal is to be the basis of the contract of insurance, the meaning is clear. The truth of the statements is made a condition of the contact, which failing, the contract is void unless the condition is waived. The proposition does not amount to more than this that, if the contract expressly or impliedly contains a term that a particular assumption is a condition of the contract, the contract is avoided if the assumption is not true. But we have not advanced far on the inquiry how to ascertain whether the contract does contain such a condition. Various words are to be found to define the state of things which made a condition. "In the contemplation of both parties fundamental to the continued validity of the contract," "a foundation essential to its existence," "a fundamental reason for making it," are phrases found in the important judgment of Scrutton L.J. in the present case. The first two phrases appear to me to be unexceptionable. They cover the case of a contract to serve in a particular place, the existence of which is fundamental to the service, or to procure the services of a professional vocalist, whose continued health is essential to performance. But "a fundamental reason for making a contract" may, with respect, be misleading. The reason of one party only is presumably not intended, but in the cases I have suggested above, of the sale of a horse or of a picture, it might be said that the fundamental reason for making the contract was the belief of both parties that the horse was sound or the picture an old master, yet in neither case would the condition as I think exist. Nothing is more dangerous than to allow oneself liberty to construct for the parties contracts which they have not in terms made by importing implications which would appear to make the contract more businesslike or more just. The implications to be made are to be no more than are "necessary" for giving business efficacy to the transaction, and it appears to me that, both as to existing facts and future facts, a condition would not be implied unless the new state of facts makes the contract something different in kind from the contract in the original state of facts. Thus, in *Krell* v. *Henry* (1903), Vaughan Williams L.J. finds that the subject of the contract was "rooms to view the procession": the postponement, therefore, made the rooms not rooms to view the procession. This also is the test finally chosen by Lord Sumner in *Bank Line* v. *Arthur Capel & Co.* (1919), agreeing with Lord Dunedin in *Metropolitan Water*

Board v. *Dick Kerr* (1918), where, dealing with the criterion for determining the effect of interruption in "frustrating" a contract, he says: "An interruption may be so long as to destroy the identity of the work or service, when resumed, with the work or service when interrupted." We there get a common standard for mutual mistake, and implied conditions whether as to existing or as to future facts. Does the state of the new facts destroy the identity of the subject-matter as it was in the original state of facts? To apply the principle to the infinite combinations of facts that arise in actual experience will continue to be difficult, but if this case results in establishing order into what has been a somewhat confused and difficult branch of the law it will have served a useful purpose.

I have already stated my reasons for deciding that in the present case the identity of the subject-matter was not destroyed by the mutual mistake, if any, and need not repeat them.

[Lord Atkin then went on to hold that there was no duty on Bell to disclose the improper transactions. The relationship of employer and employee is not of the kind mentioned at p. 343 as being of *uberrimae fidei* (of the utmost good faith).]

The result is that in the present case servants unfaithful in some of their work retain large compensation which some will think they do not deserve. Nevertheless it is of greater importance that well established principles of contract should be maintained than that a particular hardship should be redressed; and I see no way of giving relief to the plaintiffs in the present circumstances except by confiding to the Courts loose powers of introducing terms into contracts which would only serve to introduce doubt and confusion where certainty is essential.

[Lord Blanesburgh and Lord Thankerton agreed with Lord Atkin in giving judgment for the defendant Bell.

Viscount Hailsham and Lord Warrington dissented on the grounds that the erroneous assumption of the parties was indeed fundamental, "as fundamental to the bargain as any error one can imagine."]

Note

Of the nine judges who were at different times involved in the case, six disagreed with the majority in the House of Lords.

Questions

1. Was the conclusion which Lord Atkin came to in the final paragraph of his judgment really so inevitable? Were the principles enunciated in his judgment correctly applied to the facts?
2. Would *Bell's* case be decided in the same way today?

3. *MISTAKE AND EQUITY*

Solle v. Butcher
[1950] 1 K.B. 671 (C.A.)

[A agreed to let a flat to B for seven years at a rent of £250 a year. Both parties assumed that the Rent Acts did not apply to the property. In fact, it was so subject and the maximum rent permitted was only £140. The plaintiff sued to recover the amount of rent paid out over and above the rate of £140 per year; the defendant counterclaimed for rescission of the agreement on the grounds of mistake. One of the results of the application of the Rent Acts was that notice to increase the rent from the permitted amount of £140 could not be given during the currency of the contractual tenancy. The landlord therefore stood to lose after both parties had entered an agreement under a serious misapprehension as to the nature of the property.]

Denning L.J. In this plight the landlord seeks to set aside the lease. He says, with truth, that it is unfair that the tenant should have the benefit of the lease for the outstanding five years of the term at 140*l.* a year, when the proper rent is 250*l.* a year. If he cannot give a notice of increase now, can he not avoid the lease? The only ground on which he can avoid it is on the ground of mistake. It is quite plain that the parties were under a mistake. They thought that the flat was not tied down to a controlled rent, whereas in fact it was. In order to see whether the lease can be avoided for this mistake it is necessary to remember that mistake is of two kinds: the first, mistake which renders the contract void, that is, a nullity from the beginning, which is the kind of mistake which was dealt with by the courts of common law; and, secondly, mistake which renders the contract not void, but voidable, that is, liable to be set aside on such terms as the court thinks fit, which is the kind of mistake which was dealt with by the courts of equity. Much of the difficulty which has attended this subject has arisen because, before the fusion of law and equity, the courts of common law, in order to do justice in the case in hand, extended this doctrine of mistake beyond its proper limits and held contracts to be void which were really only voidable, a process which was capable of being attended with much injustice to third persons who had bought goods or otherwise committed themselves on the faith that there was a contract. In the well-known case of *Cundy* v. *Lindsay* (1878), Cundy suffered such an injustice. He bought the handkerchiefs from the rogue, Blenkarn, before the Judicature Acts came into operation. Since the fusion of law and equity, there is no reason to continue this process, and it will be found that only those contracts are now held void in which the mistake was such as to prevent the formation of any contract at all.

Let me first consider mistakes which render a contract a nullity. All previous decisions on this subject must now be read in the light of *Bell* v. *Lever Bros. Ld.* (1932). The correct interpretation of that case, to my mind, is that, once a contract has been made, that is to say, once the parties, whatever their inmost states of mind, have to all outward appearances agreed with sufficient certainty in the same terms on the same subject matter, then the contract is good unless and until it is set aside for failure of some condition on which the existence of the contract depends, or for fraud, or on some equitable ground. Neither party can rely on his own mistake to say it was a nullity from the beginning, no matter that it was a mistake which to his mind was fundamental, and no matter that the other party knew that he was under a mistake. A fortiori, if the other party did not know of the mistake, but shared it. The cases where goods have perished at the time of sale, or belong to the buyer, are really contracts which are not void for mistake but are void by reason of an implied condition precedent, because the contract proceeded on the basic assumption that it was possible of performance. So far as cases later than *Bell* v. *Lever Bros., Ld.* (1932) are concerned, I do not think that *Sowler* v. *Potter* (1940) can stand with *King's Norton Metal Co. Ld.* v. *Edridge* (1897), which shows that the doctrine of French law as enunciated by Pothier is no part of English law. Nor do I think that the contract in *Nicholson and Venn* v. *Smith-Marriott* (1947) was void from the beginning.

Applying these principles, it is clear that here there was a contract. The parties agreed in the same terms on the same subject-matter. It is true that the landlord was under a mistake which was to him fundamental: he would not for one moment have considered letting the flat for seven years if it meant that he could only charge 140*l.* a year for it. He made the fundamental mistake of believing that the rent he could charge was not tied down to a controlled rent; but, whether it was his own mistake or a mistake common to both him and the tenant, it is not a ground for saying that the lease was from the beginning a nullity. Any other view would lead to remarkable results, for it would mean that, in the many cases where the parties mistakenly think a house is outside the Rent Restriction Acts when it is really within them, the tenancy would be a nullity, and the tenant would have to go; with the result that the tenants would not dare to seek to have their rents reduced to the permitted amounts lest they should be turned out.

Let me next consider mistakes which render a contract voidable, that is, liable to be set aside on some equitable ground. Whilst presupposing that a contract was good at law, or at any rate not void, the court of equity would often relieve a party from the consequences of his own mistake, so long as it could do so without injustice to third parties. The court, it was said, had power to set aside the contract whenever it was of opinion that it was unconscientious for the other party to avail himself of the legal advantage which he had obtained: *Torrance* v. *Bolton* (1872) per James L.J.

The court had, of course, to define what it considered to be unconscientious, but in this respect equity has shown a progressive development. It is now clear that a contract will be set aside if the mistake of the one party has been induced by a material misrepresentation of the other, even though it was not fraudulent or fundamental; or if one party, knowing that the other is mistaken about the terms of an offer, or the identity of the person by whom it is made, lets him remain under his delusion and concludes a contract on the mistaken terms instead of pointing out the mistake. That is, I venture to think, the ground on which the defendant in *Smith* v. *Hughes* (1871) would be exempted nowadays, and on which, according to the view by Blackburn J. of the facts, the contract in *Lindsay* v. *Cundy* (1878), was voidable and not void; and on which the lease in *Sowler* v. *Potter* (1940), was, in my opinion, voidable and not void.

A contract is also liable in equity to be set aside if the parties were under a common misapprehension either as to facts or as to their relative and respective rights, provided that the misapprehension was fundamental and that the party seeking to set it aside was not himself at fault. That principle was first applied to private rights as long ago as 1730 in *Lansdown* v. *Lansdown* (1730). There were four brothers, and the second and third of them died. The eldest brother entered on the lands of the deceased brothers, but the youngest brother claimed them. So the two rival brothers consulted a friend who was a local schoolmaster. The friend looked up a book which he then had with him called the Clerk's Remembrancer and gave it as his opinion that the lands belonged to the youngest brother. He recommended the two of them to take further advice, which at first they intended to do, but they did not do so; and, acting on the friend's opinion, the elder brother agreed to divide the estate with the younger brother, and executed deeds and bonds giving effect to the agreement. Lord Chancellor King declared that the documents were obtained by a mistake and by a misrepresentation of the law by the friend, and ordered them to be given up to be cancelled. He pointed out that the maxim ignorantia juris non excusat only means that ignorance cannot be pleaded in excuse of crimes. Eighteen years later, in the time of Lord Hardwicke, the same principle was applied in *Bingham* v. *Bingham* (1748).

If and in so far as those cases were compromises of disputed rights, they have been subjected to justifiable criticism, but, in cases where there is no element of compromise, but only of mistaken rights, the House of Lords in 1867 in the great case of *Cooper* v. *Phibbs* (1867), affirmed the doctrine there acted on as correct. In that case an uncle had told his nephew, not intending to misrepresent anything, but being in fact in error, that he (the uncle) was entitled to a fishery; and the nephew after the uncle's death, acting in the belief of the truth of what the uncle had told him, entered into an agreement to rent the fishery from the uncle's daughters, whereas it actually belonged to the nephew himself. The mistake there as to the title to the fishery did not render the tenancy agreement a nullity. If it had done, the contract would have been void at law from the beginning and equity would have had to follow the law. There would have been no contract to set aside and no terms to impose. The House of Lords, however, held that the mistake was only such as to make it voidable, or, in Lord Westbury's words, "liable to be set aside" on such terms as the court thought fit to impose; and it was so set aside.

The principle so established by *Cooper* v. *Phibbs* (1867), has been repeatedly acted on: see, for instance, *Earl Beauchamp* v. *Winn* (1873), and *Huddersfield Banking Co. Ltd.* v. *Lister* (1895). It is in no way impaired by *Bell* v. *Lever Bros. Ld.* (1932), which was treated in the House of Lords as a case at law depending on whether the contract was a nullity or not. If it had been considered on equitable grounds, the result might have been different. In any case, the principle of *Cooper* v. *Phibbs* has been fully restored by *Norwich Union Fire Insurance Society Ltd.* v. *William H. Price, Ld.* (1934).

Applying that principle to this case, the facts are that the plaintiff, the tenant, was a surveyor who was employed by the defendant, the landlord, not only to arrange finance for the purchase of the building and to negotiate with the rating authorities as to the new rateable values, but also to let the flats. He was the agent for letting, and he clearly formed the view that the building was not controlled. He told the valuation officer so. He advised the defendant what were the rents which could be charged. He read to the defendant an opinion of counsel relating to the matter, and told him that in his opinion he could charge 250*l.* and that there was no previous control. He said that the flats came outside the Act and that the defendant was "clear." The defendant relied on what the plaintiff told him, and authorized the plaintiff to let at the rentals which he had suggested. The plaintiff not only let the four other flats to other people for a long period of years at the new rentals, but also took one himself for seven years at 250*l.* Now he turns round and says, quite unashamedly, that he wants to take advantage of the mistake to get the flat at 140*l.* a year for seven years instead of the 250*l.* a year, which is not only the rent he agreed to pay but also the fair and economic rent; and it is also the rent permitted by the Acts on compliance with the necessary formalities. If the rules of equity have become so rigid that they cannot remedy such an injustice, it is time we had a new equity, to make good the omissions of the old. But, in my view, the established rules are amply sufficient for this case.

On the defendant's evidence, which the judge preferred, I should have thought there was a good deal to be said for the view that the lease was induced by an innocent material misrepresentation by the plaintiff. It seems to me that the plaintiff was not merely expressing an opinion on the law: he was making an unambiguous statement as to private rights; and a misrepresentation as to private rights is equivalent to a misrepresentation of fact for this purpose: *MacKenzie* v. *Royal Bank of Canada* (1934). But it is unnecessary to come to a firm conclusion on this point, because, as Bucknill L.J. has said, there was clearly a common mistake, or, as I would prefer to describe it, a common misapprehension, which was fundamental and in no way due to any fault of the defendant; and *Cooper* v. *Phibbs* (1867), affords ample authority for saying that, by reason of the common misapprehension, this lease can be set aside on such terms a the court thinks fit.

. . . . . .

The terms will be complicated by reason of the Rent Restriction Acts, but it is not beyond the wit of man to devise them. Subject to any observations which the parties may desire to make, the terms which I suggest are these: the lease should only be set aside if the defendant is prepared to give an undertaking that he will permit the plaintiff to be a licensee of the premises pending the grant of a new lease. Then, whilst the plaintiff is a licensee, the defendant will in law be in possession of the premises, and will be able to serve on the plaintiff, as prospective tenant, a notice under s.7, sub-s.4, of the Act of 1938 increasing the rent to the full permitted amount. The defendant must further be prepared to give an undertaking that he will serve such a notice within three weeks from the drawing up of the order, and that he will, if written request is made by the plaintiff, within one month of the service of the notice, grant him a new lease at the full permitted amount of rent, not, however, exceeding 250*l.* a year, for a term expiring on September 29, 1954, subject in all other respects to the same covenants and conditions as in the rescinded lease. If there is any difference of opinion about the figures stated in the notice, that can, of course, be adjusted during the currency of the lease. If the plaintiff does not choose to accept the licence or the new lease, he must go out. He will not be entitled to the protection of the Rent Restriction Acts because, the lease being set aside, there will be no initial contractual tenancy from which a statutory tenancy can spring.

[Bucknill L.J. concurred in giving judgment in the terms indicated by Denning L.J. Jenkins L.J. dissented.]

Notes

For a similar approach to problems of mistake, see *Grist* v. *Bailey* (1967) and *Magee* v. *Pennine Insurance Co. Ltd.* (1969). Would the well-known case of *Leaf* v. *International Galleries* (1950) now be disposed of using the court's equitable jurisdiction?

4. MISTAKE AS TO THE AGREEMENT BETWEEN THE PARTIES

Smith v. Hughes
(1871) L.R. 6 Q.B. 507 (Q.B.)

[The defendant was shown a sample of oats by the plaintiff. He wanted old oats as the plaintiff apparently knew. The defendant agreed to buy them, labouring under the misapprehension that they were old oats, which was the only kind he had any use for. There was no evidence of fraud, but there was a conflict of evidence over whether or not the parties had specifically referred to "old oats" or just "oats." When he realised the mistake, the defendant refused to accept the oats and the plaintiff sued for the price. The judge directed the jury to consider two questions. First, had the parties used the word "old" of the oats? If so, judgment for the defendant. If not, then secondly, did they believe that the plaintiff believed the defendant to believe, or to be under the impression, that he was contracting for old oats? If so, again there would be judgment for the defendant. The jury found for the defendant, and the plaintiff appealed on the grounds that the judge had misdirected the jury.]

Cockburn C.J. It is to be regretted that the jury were not required to give specific answers to the questions so left to them. For, it is quite possible that their verdict may have been given for the defendant on the first ground; in which case there could, I think, be no doubt as to the propriety of the judge's direction; whereas now, as it is possible that the verdict of the jury - or at all events of some of them - may have proceeded on the second ground, we are called upon to consider and decide whether the ruling of the learned judge with reference to the second question was right.

For this purpose we must assume that nothing was said on the subject of the defendant's manager desiring to buy *old* oats, nor of the oats having been said to be old; while, on the other hand, we must assume that the defendant's manager believed the oats to be old oats, and that the plaintiff was conscious of the existence of such belief, but did nothing, directly or indirectly, to bring it about, simply offering his oats and exhibiting his sample, remaining perfectly passive as to what was passing in the mind of the other party. The question is whether, under such circumstances, the passive acquiescence of the seller in the self-deception of the buyer will entitle the latter to avoid the contract. I am of opinion that it will not.

The oats offered to the defendant's manager were a specific parcel, of which the sample submitted to him formed a part. He kept the sample for twenty-four hours, and had, therefore, full opportunity of inspecting it and forming his judgment upon it. Acting on his own judgment, he wrote to the plaintiff, offering him a price. Having this opportunity of inspecting and judging of the sample, he is practically in the same position as if he had inspected the oats in bulk. It cannot be said that, if he had gone and personally inspected the oats in bulk, and then, believing - but without anything being said or done by the seller to bring about such a belief - that the oats were old, had offered a price for them, he would have been justified in repudiating the contract, because the seller, from the known habits of the buyer, or other circumstances, had reason to infer that the buyer was ascribing to the oats a quality they did not possess, and did not undeceive him.

I take the true rule to be, that where a specific article is offered for sale, without express warranty, or without circumstances from which the law will imply a warranty - as where, for instance, an article is ordered for a specific purpose - and the buyer has full opportunity of inspecting and forming his own judgment, if he chooses to act on his own judgment, the rule caveat emptor applies. If he gets the article he contracted to buy, and that article corresponds with what it was sold as, he gets all he is entitled to, and is bound by the contract. Here the defendant agreed to buy a specific parcel of oats. The oats were what they were sold as, namely, good oats according to the sample. The buyer persuaded himself they were old oats, when they were not so; but the seller neither said nor did anything to contribute to his deception. He has himself to blame. The question is not what a man of scrupulous morality or nice honour would do under such circumstances.

The case put of the purchase of an estate, in which there is a mine under the surface, but the fact is unknown to the seller, is one in which a man of tender conscience or high honour would be unwilling to take advantage of the ignorance of the seller; but there can be no doubt that the contract for the sale of the estate would be binding. . . . . . .

Now, in this case, there was plainly no legal obligation in the plaintiff in the first instance to state whether the oats were new or old. He offered them for sale according to the sample, as he had a perfect right to do, and gave the buyer the fullest opportunity of inspecting the sample, which, practically, was equivalent to an inspection of the oats themselves. What, then, was there to create any trust or confidence between the parties, so as to make it incumbent on the plaintiff to communicate the fact that the oats were not, as the defendant assumed them to be, old oats? If, indeed, the buyer, instead of acting on his own opinion, had asked the question whether the oats were old or new, or had said anything which intimated his understanding that the seller was selling the oats as old oats, the case would have been wholly different; or even if he had said anything which shewed that he was not acting on his own inspection and judgment, but assumed as the foundation of the contract that the oats were old, the silence of the seller, as a means of misleading him, might have amounted to a fraudulent concealment, such as would have entitled the buyer to avoid the contract. Here, however, nothing of the sort occurs. The buyer in no way refers to the seller, but acts entirely on his own judgment. . . . . . .

It only remains to deal with an argument which was pressed upon us, that the defendant in the present case intended to buy old oats, and the plaintiff to sell new, so the two minds were not ad idem; and that consequently there was no contract. This argument proceeds on the fallacy of confounding what was merely a motive operating on the buyer to induce him to buy with one of the essential conditions of the contract. Both parties were agreed as to the sale and purchase of this particular parcel of oats. The defendant believed the oats to be old, and was thus induced to agree to buy them, but he omitted to make their age a condition of the contract. All that can be said is, that the two minds were not ad idem as to the age of the oats; they certainly were ad idem as to the sale and purchase of them. Suppose a person to buy a horse without a warranty, believing him to be sound, and the horse turns out unsound, could it be contended that it would be open to him to say that, as he had intended to buy a sound horse, and the seller to sell an unsound one, the contract was void, because the seller must have known from the price the buyer was willing to give, or from his general habits as a buyer of horses, that he thought the horse was sound? The cases are exactly parallel.

The result is that, in my opinion, the learned judge of the county court was wrong in leaving the second question to the jury, and that consequently, the case must go down to a new trial.

Blackburn J. The jury were directed that, if they believed the word "old" was used , they should find for the defendant - and this was right; for if that was the case, it is obvious that neither did the defendant intend to enter into a contract on the plaintiff's terms, that is, to buy this parcel of oats without any stipulation as to their quality; nor could the plaintiff have been led to believe he was intending to do so.

But the second direction raises the difficulty. I think that, if from that direction the jury would understand that they were first to consider whether they were satisfied that the defendant intended to buy this parcel of oats on the terms that it was part of his contract with the plaintiff that were old oats, so as to have the warranty of the plaintiff to that effect, they were properly told that, if that was so, the defendant could not be bound to a contract without any such warranty unless the plaintiff was misled. But I doubt whether the direction would bring to the minds of the jury the distinction between agreeing to take the oats under the belief that they were old, and agreeing to take the oats under the belief that the plaintiff contracted that they were old.

The difference is the same as that between buying a horse believed to be sound, and buying one believed to be warranted sound; but I doubt if it was made obvious to the jury, and I doubt this the more because I do not see much evidence to justify a finding for the defendant on this latter ground if the word "old" was not used. There may have been more evidence than is stated in the case; and the demeanour of the witnesses may have strengthened the impression produced by the evidence there was; but it does not seem a very satisfactory verdict if it proceeded on this latter ground. I agree, therefore, in the result that there should be a new trial.

New Trial ordered.

Notes

Whilst an agreement mistake as to the quality of the subject-matter will not normally be sufficient, it may be otherwise if the mistake of quality was so great that it really amounted to a mistake of identity, see *Nicholson & Venn* v. *Smith-Marriott* (1947).

Although it may not always be very apparent, there is a distinction drawn between mistake as to a quality and mistake as to the subject-matter. The latter provides a basis for operative mistake. Examples are the decisions in *Scriven Bros & Co.* v. *Hindley & Co.* (1913) and *Raffles* v. *Wichelhaus* (1864).

Question

What is the *ratio decidendi* of *Smith* v. *Hughes*? What of Denning L.J.'s approach to the case in *Solle* v. *Butcher* (above, p. 368)?

5. MISTAKE AS TO IDENTITY

Cundy v. Lindsay
(1878) 3 App. Cas. 459 (H.L.)

[A respectable firm of merchants called "Blenkiron & Co." carried on business at 123 Wood Street, London. A rogue called Blenkarn hired a room, also in Wood Street and placed an order for handkerchiefs with Lindsay & Co. The order came in a letter which gave the Wood Street address and was signed in such a way that it could have been read as "Bleniron & Co." The plaintiffs delivered the handkerchiefs, the rogue failed to pay. Before the fraud was discovered Cundy had bought the goods in good faith from Blenkarn. Lindsay sued Cundy for conversion. The question therefore arose as to the status of the agreement between Lindsay and the rogue. If it was only voidable, title has passed to Cundy. If it was void, Lindsay had never lost title to the goods.]

Lord Cairns L.C. Now, my Lords, there are two observations bearing upon the solution of that question which I desire to make. In the first place, if the property in the goods in question passed, it could only pass by way of contract; there is nothing else which could have passed the property. The second observation is that, your Lordships are not here embarrassed by any conflict of evidence, or any evidence whatever as to conversations or as to acts done, the whole history of the whole transaction lies upon paper. The principal parties concerned, the Respondents and *Blenkarn,* never came in contact personally - everything that was done was done by writing. What has to be judged of, and what the jury in the present case had to judge of, was merely the conclusion to be derived from that writing, as applied to the admitted facts of the case.

Now, my Lords, discharging that duty and answering that inquiry, what the jurors have found is in substance this: it is not necessary to spell out the words, because the substance of it is beyond all doubt. They have found that by the form of the signatures to the letters which were written by *Blenkarn,* by the mode in which his letters and his applications to the Respondents were made out, and by the way in which he left uncorrected the mode and form in which, in turn, he was addressed by the Respondents that by all those means he led, and intended to lead, the Respondents, to believe, and they did believe, that the person with whom they were communicating was not *Blenkarn,* the dishonest and irresponsible man, but was a well known and solvent house of *Blenkiron & Co.,* doing business in the same street. My Lords, those things are found as matters of fact, and they are placed beyond the range of dispute and controversy in the case.

If that is so, what is the consequence? It is that *Blenkarn* - the dishonest man, as I call him - was acting here just in the same way as if he had forged the signature of *Blenkiron & Co.,* the respectable firm, to the applications for goods, and as if, when, in return, the goods were forwarded and letters were sent, accompanying them, he had intercepted the goods and intercepted the letters, and had taken possession of the goods, and of the letters which were addressed to, and intended for, not himself but, the firm of *Blenkiron & Co.* Now, my Lords, stating the matter shortly in that way, I ask the question, how is it possible to imagine that in that state of things any contract could have arisen between the Respondents and *Blenkarn,* the dishonest man? Of him they knew nothing, and of him they never thought. With him they never intended to deal. Their minds never, even for an instant of time rested upon him, and as between him and them there was no *consensus* of mind which could lead to any agreement or any contract whatever. As between him and them there was merely the one side to a contract, where, in order to produce a contract, two sides would be required. With the firm of *Blenkiron & Co.* of course there was no contract, for as to them the matter was entirely unknown, and therefore the pretence of a contract was a failure.

The result, therefore, my Lords, is this, that your Lordships have not here to deal with one of those cases in which there is *de facto* a contract made which may afterwards be impeached and set aside, on the ground of fraud; but you have to deal with a case which ranges itself under a completely different chapter of law, the case namely in which the contract never comes into existence. My Lords, that being so, it is idle to talk of the property passing. The property remained, as it originally had been, the property of the Respondents, and the title which was attempted to be given to the Appellants was a title which could not be given to them.

My Lords, I therefore move your Lordships that this appeal be dismissed with costs, and the judgment of the Court of Appeal affirmed.

[Lords Hatherley, Penzance and Gordon concurred.]

Question

Compare the view of Lord Denning at p. 366. Which view is to be preferred?

Lewis v. Averay
[1972] 1 Q.B. 198 (C.A.)

[A rogue offered to buy the plaintiff's car, falsely claiming to be Richard Green, an actor who portrayed the part of Robin Hood. In support of his claim he produced a pass to Pinewood Studios with his name and photograph on it. After paying with a worthless cheque, he sold the car to an innocent purchaser, Averay. When Lewis discovered what had happened, he sued Averay for conversion. The central issue which faced the court was therefore identical to that which arose in *Cundy* v. *Lindsay*.]

Lord Denning M.R. The real question in the case is whether on May 8, 1969, there was a contract of sale under which the property in the car passed from Mr. Lewis to the rogue. If there was such a contract, then, even though it was voidable for fraud, nevertheless Mr. Averay would get a good title to the car. But if there was no contract of sale by Mr. Lewis to the rogue - either because there was, on the face of it, no agreement between the parties, or because any apparent agreement was a nullity and void ab initio for mistake, then no property would pass from Mr. Lewis to the rogue. Mr. Averay would not get a good title because the rogue had no property to pass to him.

There is no doubt that Mr. Lewis was mistaken as to the identity of the person who handed him the cheque. He thought that he was Richard Greene, a film actor of standing and worth: whereas in fact he was a rogue whose identity is quite unknown. It was under the influence of that mistake that Mr. Lewis let the rogue have the car. He would not have dreamed of letting him have it otherwise.

What is the effect of this mistake? There are two cases in our books which cannot, to my mind, be reconciled the one with the other. One of them is *Phillips* v. *Brooks Ltd.* (1919) where a jeweller had a ring for sale. The other is *Ingram* v. *Little* (1961) where two ladies had a car for sale. In each case the story is very similar to the present. A plausible rogue comes along. The rogue says he likes the ring, or the car, as the case may be. He asks the price. The seller names it. The rogue says he is prepared to buy it at that price. He pulls out a cheque book. He writes, or prepares to write, a cheque for the price. The seller hesitates. He has never met this man before. He does not want to hand over the ring or the car not knowing whether the cheque will be met. The rogue notices the seller's hesitation. He is quick with his next move. He says to the jeweller in *Phillips* v. *Brooks*: "I am Sir George Bullough of 11 St. James's Square"; or to the ladies in *Ingram* v. *Little* "I am P.G.M. Hutchinson of Stanstead House, Stanstead Road, Caterham"; or to the post-graduate student in the present case: "I am Richard Greene, the film actor of the Robin Hood series." Each seller checks up the information. The jeweller looks up the directory and finds there is a Sir George Bullough at 11 St. James's Square.

The ladies check up too. They look at the telephone directory and find there is a "P.G.M. Hutchinson of Stanstead House, Stanstead Road, Caterham." The post-graduate student checks up too. He examines the official pass of the Pinewood Studios and finds that it is a pass for "Richard A. Green" to the Pinewood Studios with this man's photograph on it. In each case the seller feels that this is sufficient confirmation of the man's identity. So he accepts the cheque signed by the rogue and lets him have the ring, in the one case, and the car and logbook in the other two cases. The rogue goes off and sells the goods to a third person who buys them in entire good faith and pays the price to the rogue. The rogue disappears. The original seller presents the cheque. It is dishonoured. Who is entitled to the goods? The original seller? Or the ultimate buyer? The courts have given different answers. In *Phillips* v. *Brooks*, the ultimate buyer was held to be entitled to the ring. In *Ingram* v. *Little* the original seller was held to be entitled to the car. In the present case the deputy county court judge has held the original seller entitled.

It seems to me that the material facts in each case are quite indistinguishable the one from the other. In each case there was, to all outward appearance, a contract: but there was a mistake by the seller as to the identity of the buyer. This mistake was fundamental. In each case it led to the handing over of the goods. Without it the seller would not have parted with them.

This case therefore raises the question: What is the effect of a mistake by one party as to the identity of the other? It has sometimes been said that if a party makes a mistake as to the identity of the person with whom he is contracting there is no contract, or, if there is a contract, it is a nullity and void, so that no property can pass under it. This has been supported by a reference to the French jurist Pothier; but I have said before, and I repeat now, his statement is no part of English law. . . .

For instance, in *Ingram* v. *Little* (1961) the majority of the court suggested that the difference between *Phillips* v. *Brooks* (1919) and *Ingram* v. *Little* was that in *Phillips* v. *Brooks* the contract of sale was concluded (so as to pass the property to the rogue) before the rogue made the fraudulent misrepresentation . . . : whereas in *Ingram* v. *Little* the rogue made the fraudulent misrepresentation before the contract was concluded. My own view is that in each case the property in the goods did not pass until the seller let the rogue have the goods.

Again it has been suggested that a mistake as to the identity of a person is one thing: and a mistake as to his attributes is another. A mistake as to identity, it is said, avoids a contract: whereas a mistake as to attributes does not. But this is a distinction without a difference. A man's very name is one of his attributes. It is also a key to his identity. If then, he gives a false name, is it a mistake as to his identity? or a mistake as to his attributes? These fine distinctions do no good to the law.

As I listened to the argument in this case, I felt it wrong that an innocent purchaser (who knew nothing of what passed between the seller and the rogue) should have his title depend on such refinements. After all, he has acted with complete circumspection and in entire good faith: whereas it was the seller who let the rogue have the goods and thus enabled him to commit the fraud. I do not, therefore, accept the theory that a mistake as to identity renders a contract void. I think the true principle is that which underlies the decision of this court in *King's Norton Metal Co. Ltd.* v. *Edridge Merrett & Co. Ltd.* (1897) and of Horridge J. in *Phillps* v. *Brooks* (1919), which has stood for these last 50 years. It is this: When two parties have come to a contract – or rather what appears, on the face of it, to be a contract - the fact that one party is mistaken as to the identity of the other does not mean that there is no contract, or that the contract is a nullity and void from the beginning. It only means that the contract is voidable, that is, liable to be set aside at the instance of the mistaken person, so long as he does so before third parties have in good faith acquired rights under it.

Applied to the cases such as the present, this principle is in full accord with the presumption stated by Pearce L.J. and also Devlin L.J. in *Ingram* v. *Little* (1961). When a dealing is had between a seller like Mr. Lewis and a person who is actually there present before him, then the presumption in law is that there is a contract, even though there is a fraudulent impersonation by the buyer representing himself as a different man than he is. There is a contract made with the very person there, who is present in person. It is liable no doubt to be avoided for fraud, but it is still a good contract under which title will pass unless and until it is avoided. In support of that presumption, Devlin L.J. quoted, at p. 66, not only the English case of *Phillips* v. *Brooks*, but other cases in the United States where "the courts hold that if A appeared in person before B, impersonating C, an innocent purchaser from A gets the property in the goods against B." That seems to me to be right in principle in this country also.

In this case Mr. Lewis made a contract of sale with the very man the rogue, who came to the flat. I say that he "made a contract" because in this regard we do not look into his intentions, or into his mind to know what he was thinking or into the mind of the rogue. We look to the outward appearances. On the face of the dealing, Mr. Lewis made a contract under which he sold the car to the rogue, delivered the car and the logbook to him, and took a cheque in return. The contract is evidenced by the receipts which were signed. It was, of course, induced by fraud. The rogue made false representations as to his identity. But it was still a contract, though voidable for fraud. It was a contract under which this property passed to the rogue, and in due course passed from the rogue to Mr. Averay, before the contract was avoided.

Though I very much regret that either of these good and reliable gentlemen should suffer, in my judgment it is Mr. Lewis who should do so. I think the appeal should be allowed and judgment entered for the defendant.

[Phillimore L.J. concurred stating that he thought the case was on all fours with

Phillips v. *Brooks.* Megaw L.J. concurred stating that the plaintiff had merely made a mistake as to an attribute of the rogue, his credit worthiness.]

Questions

How can *Cundy* v. *Lindsay* and *Lewis* v. *Averay* be distinguished? Are Lord Denning's dicta compatible with the decision in the earlier case?

6. NON EST FACTUM

Saunders v. Anglia Building Society
[1971] A.C. 1004 (H.L.)

[Mrs. Gallie, a 78 year old widow, was deceived by her nephew, Wally Parkin, into assigning the leasehold interest in her house to a dishonest acquaintance of the nephew, one Lee. She had thought she was merely making a gift of the house to Parkin to enable him to raise money, something she was content to do. The dishonest Lee then mortgaged the house to a building society but defaulted on the mortgage payments. When the building society, who of course were unaware of the way Mr. Lee had obtained title to the property, sought possession of the house they were met by the defence of *non est factum*.]

Lord Pearson. I must, however, deal specifically with the broad principle stated by the Master of the Rolls as his conclusion from his investigation of the law, at pp. 36-37:

" . . . whenever a man of full age and understanding, who can read and write, signs a legal document which is put before him for signature - by which I mean a document which, it is apparent on the face of it, is intended to have legal consequences - then, if he does not take the trouble to read it, but signs it as it is, relying on the word of another as to its character or contents or effect, he cannot be heard to say that it is not his document. By his conduct in signing it he has represented, to all those into whose hands it may come, that it is his document: and once they act upon it as being his document, he cannot go back on it, and say it was a nullity from the beginning."

In applying the principle to the present case, the Master of the Rolls said, at p. 37:

" . . . Mrs. Gallie cannot in this case say that the deed of assignment was not her deed. She signed it without reading it, relying on the assurance of Lee that it was a deed of gift to Wally. It turned out to be a deed of assignment to Lee. But it was obviously a legal document. She signed it: and the building society advanced money on the faith of it being her document. She cannot now be allowed to disavow her signature."

There can be no doubt that this statement of principle by the Master of the Rolls is not only a clear and concise formulation but also a valuable guide to the right decision to be given by a court in any ordinary case. The danger of giving an undue extension to the plea of non est factum has been pointed out in a number of cases. For instance in *Muskham Finance Ltd.* v. *Howard* (1963) Donovan L.J. delivering the judgment of the court said:

> "The plea of non est factum is a plea which must necessarily be kept within narrow limits. Much confusion and uncertainty would result in the field of contract and elsewhere if a man were permitted to try to disown his signature simply by asserting that he did not understand that which he had signed."

. . . . . .

The principle stated by the Master of the Rolls can and should be applied so as to confine the scope of the plea of non est factum within narrow limits. It rightly prevents the plea from being successful in the normal case of a man who, however much he may have been misinformed about the nature of a deed or document, could easily have ascertained its true nature by reading it and has taken upon himself the risk of not reading it.

I think, however, that unless the doctrine of non est factum, as it has been understood for at least a hundred years, is to be radically transformed, the statement of principle by the Master of the Rolls, taken just as it stands, is too absolute and rigid and needs some amplification and qualification. Doubts can be raised as to the meaning of the phrase "a man of full age and understanding, who can read and write." There are degrees of understanding and a person who is a great expert in some subjects may be like a child in relation to other subjects. Does the phrase refer to understanding of things in general, or does it refer to capacity for understanding (not necessarily in more than a general and elementary way) legal documents and property transactions and business transactions?

In my opinion, the plea of non est factum ought to be available in a proper case for the relief of a person who for permanent or temporary reasons (not limited to blindness or illiteracy) is not capable of both reading and sufficiently understanding the deed or other document to be signed. By "sufficiently understanding" I mean understanding at least to the point of detecting a fundamental difference between the actual document and the document as the signer had believed it to be. There must be a proper case for such relief. There would not be a proper case if (a) the signature of the document was brought about by negligence of the signer in failing to take precautions which he ought to have taken, or (b) the actual document was not fundamentally different from the document as the signer believed it to be. I will say something later about negligence and about fundamental difference.

In the present case the plaintiff was not at the material time a person who could read, because on the facts found she had broken her spectacles and could not effectively read without them. In any case her evidence (unless it was deliberately false, which has not been argued) shows that she had very little capacity for understanding legal documents and property transactions, and I do not think a reasonable jury would have found that she was negligent. In my opinion, it would not be right to dismiss the plaintiff's appeal on the ground that the principle stated by the Master of the Rolls is applicable to her case. I do not think it is.

The principle as stated is limited to a case in which it is apparent on the fact of the document that it is intended to have legal consequences. That allows for possible success of the plea in a case such as *Lewis* v. *Clay* (1897) where Clay had been induced to sign promissory notes by the cunning deception of a false friend, who caused him to believe that he was merely witnessing the friend's signature on several private and highly confidential documents, the material parts of which had been covered up.

I wish to reserve the question whether the plea of non est factum would ever be rightly successful in a case where (1) it is apparent on the face of the document that it is intended to have legal consequences; (2) the signer of the document is able to read and sufficiently understand the document; (3) the document is fundamentally different from what he supposes it to be; (4) he is induced to sign it without reading it. It seems unlikely that the plea ought ever to succeed in such a case, but it is inadvisable to rule out the wholly exceptional and unpredictable case.

I have said above that the statement of principle by the Master of the Rolls needs to be amplified and qualified unless the doctrine of non est factum, as it has been understood for at least a hundred years, is to be radically transformed. What is the doctrine, and should it be radically transformed?

As to the early history, the authorities referred to in the judgment of Byles J. in *Foster* v. *Mackinnon* (1869) (and also referred to in *Holdsworth's History of English Law*, Vol. 8, pp. 50-51) were cited in the argument of this appeal. Having considered them I think they show that the law relating to the plea of non est factum remained in an undeveloped state until the judgment in *Foster* v. *Mackinnon*, and the modern development began with that judgment. It was the judgment of the court (Bovill C.J., Byles, Keating and Montague Smith JJ.) delivered by Byles J. He said, at p. 711:

> "It seems plain, on principle and on authority, that, if a blind man, or a man who cannot read, or who for some reason (not implying negligence) forbears to read, has a written contract falsely read over to him, the reader misreading to such a degree that the written contract is of a nature altogether different from the contract pretended to be read from the paper which the blind or illiterate man afterwards signs; then, at least if there be no negligence, the signature so obtained is of no force. And it is invalid not merely on the ground of fraud, where fraud exists, but on the ground that the mind of the signer did not accompany the signature; in other words, that he never intended to sign, and therefore in contemplation of law never did sign, the contract to which his name is appended."

In my opinion, the essential features of the doctrine are contained in that passage and the doctrine does not need any radical transformation. A minor comment is that the phrase "who for some reason (not implying negligence) forbears to read" is (to use a currently fashionable word) too "permissive" in its tone. If a person forbears to read the document, he nearly always should be reckoned as negligent or otherwise debarred from succeeding on the plea of non est factum.

The passage which I have set out from Byles J.'s judgment, though I think it contains the essential features, was only a brief summary in a leading judgment, and there are further developments which need to be considered.

Ascertainment of the intention: I think the doctrine of non est factum inevitably involves applying the subjective rather than the objective test to ascertain the intention. It takes the intention which a man has in his own mind rather than the intention which he manifests to others (the intention which as reasonable men they would infer from his words and conduct).

There are, however, some cases in which the subjective test of intention can be applied so as to produce the same result as would be produced by the objective test. Suppose a man signs a deed without knowing or inquiring or having any positive belief or formed opinion, as to its nature or effect: he signs it because his solicitor or other trusted adviser advises him to do so. Then his intention is to sign the deed that is placed before him, whatever it may be or do. That is the intention in his own mind as well as the intention which by signing he manifests to others. Examples of this will be found in *Hunter* v. *Walters* (1871); *National Provincial Bank of England* v. *Jackson* (1886); *King* v. *Smith* (1900). In *King* v. *Smith*, Farwell J., at p. 430, cited and relied upon a passage in the judgment of Mellish L.J. in *Hunter* v. *Walters* (1871) where he said:

> "When a man knows that he is conveying or doing something with his estate, but does not ask what is the precise effect of the deed, because he is told it is a mere form, and has such confidence in his solicitor as to execute the deed in ignorance, then, in my opinion, a deed so executed, although it may be voidable upon the ground of fraud, is not a void deed."

Farwell J. said that Mr. King "had absolute confidence in his solicitor, and executed any deed relating to his property that Eldred put before him."

I think this principle affords a solution to a problem that was raised in the course of the argument. Suppose that the very busy managing director of a large company has a pile of documents to be signed in a few minutes before his next meeting, and his secretary has arranged them for maximum speed with only the spaces for signature exposed, and he "signs them blind," as the saying is, not reading them or even looking at them. He may be exercising a wise economy of his time and energy. There is the possibility of some extraneous document, involving him in unexpected personal liability, having been fraudulently inserted in the pile, but this possibility is so improbable that a reasonable man would disregard it: *Bolton* v. *Stone* (1951). Such conduct is not negligence in any ordinary sense of the word. But the person who signs documents in this way ought to be held bound by them, and ought not to be entitled to avoid liability so as to shift the burden of loss on to

an innocent third party. The whole object of having documents
signed by him is that he makes them his documents and takes
responsibility for them. He takes the chance of a fraudulent
substitution. I think the right view of such a case is that the
person who signs intends to sign the documents placed before
him, whatever they may be, and so there is no basis on which he
could successfully plead non est factum.

Negligence: It is clear that by the law as it was laid down in
Foster v. *Mackinnon* (1869) a person who had signed a
document differing fundamentally from what he believed it to
be would be disentitled from successfully pleading non est
factum if his signing of the document was due to his own
negligence. The word "negligence" in this connection had no
special technical meaning. It meant carelessness and in each
case it was a question of fact for the jury to decide whether the
person relying on the plea had been negligent or not. In *Foster*
v. *Mackinnon* the Lord Chief Justice had told the jury that, if
the indorsement was not the defendant's signature, or if, being
his signature, it was obtained upon a fraudulent representation
that it was a guarantee, and the defendant signed it without
knowing that it was a bill, and under the belief that it was a
guarantee and if the defendant was not guilty of any negligence
in so signing the paper, the defendant was entitled to the
verdict. On appeal this direction was held to be correct. In
Vorley v. *Cooke* (1857) Stuart V.-C. said:

> "It cannot be said that Cooke's conduct was careless or rash.
> He was deceived, as anyone with the ordinary amount of
> intelligence and caution would have been deceived, and he
> is therefore entitled to be relieved."

Whatever may be thought of the merits of the decision in that
case, this passage illustrates the simple approach to the
question whether the signer of the deed had been negligent or
not. Similarly, in *Lewis* v. *Clay* (1898), Lord Russell of
Killowen C.J. left to the jury the question: "Was the defendant,
in signing his name as he did, recklessly careless, and did he
thereby enable Lord William Nevill to perpetrate the fraud?"
. . . . . .

The degree of difference required: The judgments in the
older cases used a variety of expressions to signify the degree or
kind of difference that, for the purposes of the plea of non est
factum, must be shown to exist between the document as it was
and the document as it was believed to be. More recently there

has been a tendency to draw a firm distinction between (a) a difference in character or class, which is sufficient for the purposes of the plea, and (b) a difference only in contents, which is not sufficient. This distinction has been helpful in some cases, but, as the judgments of the Court of Appeal have shown, it would produce wrong results if it were applied as a rigid rule for all cases. In my opinion, one has to use a more general phrase, such as "fundamentally different" or "radically different" or "totally different."

I would dismiss the appeal.

[Lords Reid, Hodson, Wilberforce and Viscount Dilhorne concurred in the view that Mrs. Gallie had not established her plea of *non est factum*.]

Note

Even though a plea of *non est factum* may fail, a defendant may still Auccessfully plead that the transaction be set aside on the basis of undue influence. See, *eg A von Finance Co. Ltd.* v. *Bridger* (1985) and below, p. 403.

Chapter 7

PRIVITY

Tweddle v. Atkinson
(*1861*) *1 B. & S. 393 (Q.B.)*

[As part of a marriage settlement William Guy and John Tweddle agreed with each other that they would provide a sum of money for William Tweddle. Guy died without having paid the money so William Tweddle sued his executors for the £200 which he considered had been promised to him.]

Crompton J. It is admitted that the plaintiff cannot succeed unless this case is an exception to the modern and well established doctrine of the action of assumpsit. At the time when the cases which have been cited were decided the action of assumpsit was treated as an action of trespass upon the case, and therefore in the nature of a tort; and the law was not settled, as it now is, that natural love and affection is not a sufficient consideration for a promise upon which an action may be maintained; nor was it settled that the promisee cannot bring an action unless the consideration for the promise moved from him. The modern cases have, in effect, overruled the old decisions; they shew that the consideration must move from the party entitled to sue upon the contract. It would be a monstrous proposition to say that a person was a party to the contract for the purpose of suing upon it for his own advantage, and not a party to it for the purpose of being sued. It is said that the father in the present case was agent for the son in making the contract, but that argument ought also to make the son liable upon it. I am prepared to overrule the old decisions, and to hold that, by reason of the principles which now govern the action of assumpsit, the present action is not maintainable.

[Wightman and Blackburn JJ. concurred in giving judgment for the defendant.]

Dunlop v. Selfridge
[*1915*] *A.C. 847 (H.L.)*

[Dunlop, the plaintiffs who were the appellants in the House of Lords, sold tyres to Dew & Co. under a contract which stated that the buyers would not sell the tyres below a certain price and that a similar term would be part of any agreement between Dew & Co. and subsequent purchasers. Dew & Co. sold tyres

[to Selfridge, the respondents, who also agreed not to sell below the fixed price and to pay Dunlop £5 for every tyre sold in breach of this agreement. Selfridge did later supply tyres to customers below the fixed price, and Dunlop sued for damages and an injunction in an attempt to restrain them from doing so.]

Viscount Haldane L.C. My Lords, in the law of England certain principles are fundamental. One is that only a person who is a party to a contract can sue on it. Our law knows nothing of a jus quaesitum tertio arising by way of contract. Such a right may be conferred by way of property, as, for example, under a trust, but it cannot be conferred on a stranger to a contract as a right to enforce the contract in personam. A second principle is that if a person with whom a contract not under seal has been made is to be able to enforce it consideration must have been given by him to the promisor or to some other person at the promisor's request. These two principles are not recognized in the same fashion by the jurisprudence of certain Continental countries or of Scotland, but here they are well established. A third proposition is that a principal not named in the contract may sue upon it if the promisee really contracted as his agent. But again, in order to entitle him so to sue, he must have given consideration either personally or through the promisee, acting as his agent in giving it.

My Lords, in the case before us, I am of opinion that the consideration, the allowance of what was in reality part of the discount to which Messrs. Dew, the promisees, were entitled as between themselves and the appellants, was to be given by Messrs. Dew on their own account, and was not in substance, any more than in form, an allowance made by the appellants. The case for the appellants is that they permitted and enabled Messrs. Dew, with the knowledge and by the desire of the respondents, to sell to the latter on the terms of the contract of January 2, 1912. But it appears to me that even if this is so the answer is conclusive. Messrs. Dew sold to the respondents goods which they had a title to obtain from the appellants independently of this contract. The consideration by way of discount under the contract of January 2 was to come wholly out of Messrs. Dew's pocket, and neither directly nor indirectly out of that of the appellants. If the appellants enabled them to sell to the respondents on the terms they did, this was not done as any part of the terms of the contract sued on.

No doubt it was provided as part of these terms that the appellants should acquire certain rights, but these rights appear on the face of the contract as jura quaesita tertio, which the appellants could not enforce. Moreover, even if this difficulty can be got over by regarding the appellants as the principals of Messrs. Dew in stipulating for the rights in question, the only consideration disclosed by the contract is one given by Messrs. Dew, not as their agents, but as principals acting on their own account.

. . . . . .

Lord Dunedin. My Lords, I confess that this case is to my mind apt to nip any budding affection which one might have had for the doctrine of consideration. For the effect of that doctrine in the present case is to make it possible for a person to snap his fingers at a bargain deliberately made, a bargain not in itself unfair, and which the person seeking to enforce it has a legitimate interest to enforce. Notwithstanding these considerations I cannot say that I have ever had any doubt that the judgment of the Court of Appeal was right.

My Lords, I am content to adopt from a work of Sir Frederick Pollock, to which I have often been under obligation, the following words as to consideration: "An act or forbearance of one party, or the promise thereof, is the price for which the promise of the other is bought, and the promise thus given for value is enforceable." (Pollock on Contracts, 8th ed., p. 175.)

Now the agreement sued on is an agreement which on the face of it is an agreement between Dew and Selfridge. But speaking for myself, I should have no difficulty in the circumstances of this case in holding it proved that the agreement was truly made by Dew as agent for Dunlop, or in other words that Dunlop was the undisclosed principal, and as such can sue on the agreement. None the less, in order to enforce it he must show consideration, as above defined, moving from Dunlop to Selfridge.

In the circumstances, how can he do so? The agreement in question is not an agreement for sale. It is only collateral to an agreement for sale; but that agreement for sale is an agreement entirely between Dew and Selfridge. The tyres, the property in which upon the bargain is transferred to Selfridge, were the property of Dew, not of Dunlop, for Dew under his agreement with Dunlop held these tyres as proprietor, and not as agent. What then did Dunlop do, or forbear to do, in a question with Selfridge? The answer must be, nothing. He did not do anything, for Dew, having the right of property in the tyres, could give a good title to any one he liked, subject, it might be, to an action of damages at the instance of Dunlop for breach of contract, which action, however, could never create a vitium reale in the property of the tyres. He did not forbear in anything, for he had no action against Dew which he gave up, because Dew had fulfilled his contract with Dunlop in obtaining, on the occasion of the sale, a contract from Selfridge in the terms prescribed.

To my mind, this ends the case. That there are methods of framing a contract which will cause persons in the position of Selfridge to become bound, I do not doubt. But that has not been done in this instance; and as Dunlop's advisers must have known of the law of consideration, it is their affair that they have not so drawn the contract.

I think the appeal should be dismissed.

Lord Parker of Waddington. My Lords, even assuming that the undertaking upon which this action is funded was given by the respondents to Messrs. A. J. Dew & Co. as agents for the appellants, and was intended to enure for their benefit, the appeal cannot succeed unless the undertaking was founded on a consideration moving from the appellants, and in my opinion there was no such consideration. The appellants did not give or give up anything on the strength of the undertaking. They had sold tyres to Messrs. A. J. Dew & Co. on the terms that the latter should not resell them at prices less than those specified in the appellants' price list, except that Messrs. A. J. Dew & Co. were to be at liberty to allow to persons legitimately engaged in the motor trade a certain discount off such price list, if they, as agents for the appellants, obtained from such persons a written undertaking such as that upon which this action is founded. In reselling these tyres to the respondents, and obtaining from the respondents the undertaking in question, Messrs. A. J. Dew & Co. admittedly committed no breach of contract. The sale was, of course, a good consideration for the undertaking moving from Messrs. A. J. Dew & Co., but the appellants, in whose favour the undertaking was given, being in the position of volunteers not parties to the contract of sale, cannot sue on it. The case was argued on behalf of the appellants as though what was done by Messrs. A. J. Dew & Co. would have been unlawful but for the leave and licence of the appellants, and that such leave and licence, though general in form, must be taken as given on the occasion of each sale, in consideration of the undertaking. I cannot accept this contention. In the first place, it is wrong to speak of an exception from a restrictive contract as importing any leave or licence at all. But for any contract to the contrary, Messrs. A. J. Dew & Co. were entitled to resell the goods supplied to them by the appellants upon any terms they might think fit, and in reselling as they did there was no breach of any restrictive contract. Even, however, if the sale can be considered as lawful only by licence of the appellants, the licence was given once for all in their contract to Messrs. A. J. Dew & Co., and was not given as part of the terms upon which any particular sale was allowed.

The appeal fails on this ground and should be dismissed with costs.

[Lords Atkinson, Sumner and Parmoor all gave speeches dismissing Dunlop's appeal.]

Note

The area of resale price maintenance is now governed by the Resale Prices Act 1976, which places severe restrictions on such agreements (see H.S.B., p. 403).

Question

Lord Dunedin comments that the contract could have been framed in such a way as to bind Selfridge. How could this have been done?

Beswick v. Beswick
[*1968*] *A.C. 58 (H.L.)*

[Peter Beswick, who was elderly and in poor health, sold his business to his nephew, John, on terms that Peter would receive a weekly payment for the rest of his life, and in the event of his death, his widow was to receive £5 per week. Peter died soon afterwards but John only made one payment to the widow. She thereupon sued the nephew (i) as administratix of her husband's estate, and (ii) in her personal capacity. In the Court of Appeal, Lord Denning M.R. and Dankwerts L.J. considered that section 56 of the Law of Property Act 1925 had abrogated the rule in *Tweddle* v. *Atkinson*, so enabling the widow to bring a claim under (ii). Section 56(1) of the Act states, "A person may take an immediate or other interest in land or other property, or the benefit of any condition, . . . covenant or agreement . . . respecting land or other property, although he may not be named as a party to the conveyance or other instrument . . ." Section 205 of the Act contains a definition of "property" as including "any thing in action, and any interest in real or personal property" "unless the context otherwise requires."]

Lord Pearce. My Lords, if the annuity had been payable to a third party in the lifetime of Beswick senior and there had been default, he could have sued in respect of the breach. His administratrix is now entitled to stand in his shoes and to sue in respect of the breach which has occurred since his death.

It is argued that the estate can only recover nominal damages and that no other remedy is open, either to the estate or to the personal plaintiff. Such a result would be wholly repugnant to justice and commonsense. And if the argument were right it would show a very serious defect in the law.

In the first place, I do not accept the view that damages must be nominal. Lush L.J. in *Lloyds's* v. *Harper* said:

> "Then the next question which, no doubt, is a very important and substantial one, is, that Lloyd's having sustained no damage themselves, could not recover for the losses sustained by third parties by reason of the default of Robert Henry Harper as an underwriter. That, to my mind, is a startling and alarming doctrine, and a novelty, because I consider it to be an established rule of law that where a contract is made with A for the benefit of B, A can sue on the contract for the benefit of B, and recover all that B could have recovered if the contract had been made with B himself."

. . . I agree with the comment of Windeyer J. in the case of *Coulls* v.*Bagot's Executor and Trustee Co. Ltd.* in the High Court of Australia that the words of Lush L.J. cannot be accepted without qualification and regardless of context and also with his statement:

> "I can see no reason why in such cases the damages which A would suffer upon B's breach of his contract to pay C $500 would be merely nominal: I think that in accordance with the ordinary rules for the assessment of damages for breach of contract they could be substantial. They would not necessarily be $500; they could I think be less or more."

In the present case I think that the damages, if assessed, must be substantial. It is not necessary, however, to consider the amount of damages more closely since this is a case in which, as the Court of Appeal rightly decided, the more appropriate remedy is that of specific performance.

The administratrix is entitled, if she so prefers, to enforce the agreement rather than accept its repudiation, and specific performance is more convenient than an action for arrears of payment followed by separate actions as each sum falls due. Moreover, damages for breach would be a less appropriate remedy since the parties to the agreement were intending an annuity for a widow; and a lump sum of damages does not accord with this. And if (contrary to my view) the argument that a derisory sum of damages is all that can be obtained be right, the remedy of damages in this case is manifestly useless.

The present case presents all the features which led the equity courts to apply their remedy of specific performance. The contract was for the sale of a business. The defendant could on his part clearly have obtained specific performance of it if Beswick senior or his administratrix had defaulted. Mutuality is a ground in favour of specific performance.

Moreover, the defendant on his side has received the whole benefit of the contract and it is a matter of conscience for the court to see that he now performs his part of it. Kay J. said in *Hart* v. *Hart*:

> " . . . when an agreement for valuable consideration . . . has been partially performed, the court ought to do its utmost to carry out that agreement by a decree for specific performance."

What, then, is the obstacle to granting specific performance?

It is argued that since the widow personally had no rights which she personally could enforce the court will not make an order which will have the effect of enforcing those rights. I can find no principle to this effect. The condition as to payment of an annuity to the widow personally was valid. The estate (though not the widow personally) can enforce it. Why should the estate be barred from exercising its full contractual rights merely because in doing so it secures justice for the widow who, by a mechanical defect of our law, is unable to assert her own rights? Such a principle would be repugnant to justice and fulfil no other object than that of aiding the wrongdoer. I can find no ground on which such a principle should exist.

. . . . . .

In my opinion, the plaintiff as administratrix is entitled to a decree of specific performance.

It is not, therefore, strictly necessary to deal with the respondent's argument that the plaintiff is entitled at common law or, by reason of section 56 of the Law of Property Act, 1925, to sue in her personal capacity. The learned Master of the Rolls expressed the view that at common law the widow was entitled to sue personally; but this view was not argued before your Lordships. He distinguished *Tweddle* v. *Atkinson* (1861). In *Smith and Snipes Hall Farm Ltd.* v. *River Douglas Catchment Board* (1949) and *White* v. *John Warwick & Co. Ltd.* (1953) the same learned judge had given his reasons for thinking that *Tweddle* v. *Atkinson* was wrongly decided and was out of line with the law as it had been settled in previous centuries. On the other hand, in *Coulls* v. *Bagot's Executor and Trustee Co. Ltd.* (1967) a survey of the cases from Tudor times led Windeyer J. to a different conclusion, namely that:

> "The law was not in fact 'settled' either way during the two hundred years before 1861. But it was, on the whole, moving towards the doctrine that was to be then and thereafter taken as settled."

But the greatest difficulty in the way of the widow's right to sue personally is that two cases in this House, *Dunlop Pneumatic Tyre Co. Ltd.* v. *Selfridge & Co. Ltd.* (1915) and *Midland Silicones Ltd.* v. *Scruttons Ltd.,* (1962) clearly accepted the principle that a third party cannot sue on a contract to which he was not a party.

The majority of the Court of Appeal expressed the view that this principle had been abolished by section 56 of the Law of Property Act. If, however, a far reaching and substantial alteration had been intended by Parliament, one would expect it to be expressed in clear terms. Yet the terms of section 56(1) are far from clear and appear to be simply an enlargement of a section passed 80 years before. Further, section 56 is to be found in a part of the Act devoted to the technicalities of conveyancing rather than the creation of rights. The cross heading of that part of the Act is "Conveyances and other Instruments." And the second part of the section deals with a small question of formality. The important innovations in the law of property were contained in the two Acts of 1922 and 1924, but this alleged innovation was not among them. It first appears in the 1925 Law of Property Act. That was a consolidation Act and therefore, one should not find a substantial innovation in it. . . .

[Lords Reid, Hodson, Guest and Upjohn delivered judgments also dismissing the defendant's appeal and granting a decree of specific performance.]

Jackson v. Horizon Holidays
[1975] 1 W.L.R. 1468 (C.A.)

[The plaintiff contracted with the defendants for a holiday in Ceylon for himself, his wife and children. When they arrived they discovered that the plumbing was inadequate, the room had mould growing up the walls and the food was distasteful. Clearly there was a breach of contract. The difficulty was that the "damage" extended not only to the plaintiff but also to his family who were not parties to the contract. The issue arose as to how such damage was to be treated.]

Lord Denning M.R. On this question a point of law arises. The judge said that he could only consider the mental distress to his wife and children. He said:

> "The damages are the plaintiff's . . . I can consider the effect upon his mind of the wife's discomfort, vexation, and the like, although I cannot award a sum which represents her own vexation."

Mr. Davies, for Mr. Jackson, disputes that proposition. He submits that damages can be given not only for the leader of the party - in this case, Mr. Jackson's own distress, discomfort and vexation - but also for that of the rest of the party.

We have had an interesting discussion as to the legal position when one person makes a contract for the benefit of a party. In this case it was a husband making a contract for the benefit of himself, his wife and children. Other cases readily come to mind. A host makes a contract with a restaurant for a dinner for himself and his friends. The vicar makes a contract for a coach trip for the choir. In all these cases there is only one person who makes the contract. It is the husband, the host or the vicar, as the case may be. Sometimes he pays the whole price himself. Occasionally he may get a contribution from the others. But in any case it is he who makes the contract. It would be a fiction to say that the contract was made by all the family, or all the guests, or all the choir, and that he was only an agent for them. Take this very case. It would be absurd to say that the twins of three years old were parties to the contract or that the father was making the contract on their behalf as if they were principals. It would equally be a mistake to say that in any of these instances there was a trust. The transaction bears no resemblance to a trust. There was no trust fund and no trust property. No, the real truth is that in each instance, the father, the host or the vicar, was making a contract himself for the benefit of the whole party. In short, a contract by one for the benefit of third persons.

What is the position when such a contract is broken? At present the law says that the only one who can sue is the one who made the contract. None of the rest of the party can sue, even though the contract was made for their benefit. But when that one does sue, what damages can he recover? Is he limited to his own loss? Or can he recover for the others? Suppose the holiday firm puts the family into a hotel which is only half built and the visitors have to sleep on the floor? Or suppose the restaurant is fully booked and the guests have to go away, hungry and angry, having spent so much on fares to get there? Or suppose the coach leaves the choir stranded halfway and they have to hire cars to get home? None of them individually can sue. Only the father, the host or the vicar can sue. He can, of course, recover his own damages. But can he not recover for the others? I think he can. The case comes within the principle stated by Lush L.J. in *Lloyds's* v. *Harper* (1880):

> "I consider it to be an established rule of law that where a contract is made with *A*. for the benefit of *B*., *A*. can sue on the contract for the benefit of *B*., and recover all that *B*. could have recovered if the contract had been made with *B*. himself."

It has been suggested that Lush L.J. was thinking of a contract in which A was trustee for B. But I do not think so. He was a common lawyer speaking of common law. His words were quoted with considerable approval by Lord Pearce in *Beswick* v. *Beswick* (1968). I have myself often quoted them. I think they should be accepted as correct, at any rate so long as the law forbids the third persons themselves from suing for damages. It is the only way in which a just result can be achieved. Take the instance I have put. The guests ought to recover from the restaurant their wasted fares. The choir ought to recover the cost of hiring the taxis home. Then is no one to recover from them except the one who made the contract for their benefit? He should be able to recover the expense to which he has been put, and pay it over to them. Once recovered, it will be money had and received to their use. (They might even if desired, be joined as plaintiffs). If he can recover for the expense, he should also be able to recover for the discomfort, vexation and upset which the whole party have suffered by reason of the breach of contract, recompensing them accordingly out of what he recovers.

Applying the principles to this case, I think that the figure of £1,100 was about right. It would, I think, have been excessive if it had been awarded only for the damage suffered by Mr. Jackson himself. But when extended to his wife and children, I do not think it is excessive. People look forward to a holiday. They expect the promises to be fulfilled. When it fails, they are greatly disappointed and upset. It is difficult to assess in terms of money; but it is the task of the judges to do the best they can. I see no reason to interfere with the total award of £1,100. I would therefore dismiss the appeal.

[Orr and James L.JJ. agreed in giving judgment for the plaintiff.]

Note

In *Woodar Investment Development Ltd.* v. *Wimpey Construction UK Ltd.* (1980) the case of *Jackson* was criticised by the House of Lords. Lord Wilberforce commented:

"I am not prepared to dissent from the actual decision in that case. It may be supported either as a broad decision on the measure of damages (per James L.J.) or possibly as an example of a type of contract - examples of which are persons contracting for family holidays, ordering meals in restaurants for a party, hiring a taxi for a group - calling for special treatment. As I suggested in *New Zealand Shipping Co. Ltd.* v. *A M. Satterthwaite & Co. Ltd.* (1975) there are many situations of daily life which do not fit neatly into conceptual analysis, but which require some flexibility in the law of contract. *Jackson's* case may well be one."

He then went on to criticise reliance upon the passage from Lush L.J. in *Lloyd's* v. *Harper* (1880).

Lord Russel of Killowen stated:

"I do not criticize the outcome of that case: the plaintiff had bought and paid for a high class family holiday: he did not get it, and therefore he was entitled to substantial damages for the failure to supply *him* with one. It is to be observed that the order of the Court of Appeal as drawn up did not suggest that any part of the damages awarded to him were "for the use and benefit of" any member of his family. It was a special case quite different from the instant case on the Transworld point. I would not, my Lords, wish to leave the *Jackson* case without adverting with respectful disapproval to the reliance there placed by Lord Denning M.R. - not for the first time - on an extract taken from the judgment of Lush L.J. in *Lloyd's* v. *Harper* (1880). That case was plainly a case in which a trustee or agent was enforcing the rights of a beneficiary or principal, there being therefore a fiduciary relationship. Lord Denning in *Jackson's* case said . . . :

"The case comes within the principle stated by Lush L.J. in *Lloyd's* v. *Harper* (1880): 'I consider it to be an established rule of law that where a contract is made with *A.* for the benefit of *B., A*. can sue on the contract for the benefit of *B.* and recover all that *B.* could have recovered if the contract had been made with *B*. himself'."

Lord Denning continued: "It has been suggested that Lush L.J. was thinking of a contract in which A was trustee for B. But I do not think so. He was a common lawyer speaking of common law." I have already indicated that in all the other judgments the matter proceeded upon a fiduciary relationship between A and B: and Lush L.J. in the same passage makes it plain that he does also; for he says:

"It is true that the person [B] who employed him [the broker A] has a right, if he pleases, to take action himself and sue upon the contract made by the broker for him, for he [B] *is a principal party to the contract*."

To ignore that passage is to divorce the passage quoted by Lord Denning from the fiduciary context in which it was uttered, the context of principal and agent, a field with which it may be assumed Lush L.J. was familiar. I venture to suggest that the brief quotation should not be used again as support for a proposition which Lush L.J. cannot have intended to advance.

Chapter 8

DURESS, UNDUE INFLUENCE AND ILLEGALITY

1. DURESS

A. Threats

Barton v. Armstrong
[1975] 2 W.L.R. 1050 (P.C.)

[Armstrong threatened Barton, the appellant, with death if the latter would not agree to buy out Armstrong's interest in a business. Barton executed the deed but subsequently brought an action against Armstrong on the grounds that the transaction should be set aside because of the threats. There was evidence that Barton in fact executed the deed because he thought it was a satisfactory business arrangement. On this basis the trial judge dismissed the claim because he found that the threats were not the predominant reason why the appellant had entered the agreement. The Court of Appeal of New South Wales also dismissed the appeal and held that the appellant was not entitled to succeed unless he established that, but for the threats, he would not have signed the agreement. In this he had failed. The appellant appealed to the Privy Council.]

Lord Cross. Their Lordships turn now to consider the question of law which provoked a difference of opinion in the Court of Appeal Division. It is hardly surprising that there is no direct authority on the point, for if A threatens B with death if he does not execute some document and B, who takes A's threats seriously, executes the document it can be only in the most unusual circumstances that there can be any doubt whether the threats operated to induce him to execute the document. But this is a most unusual case and the findings of fact made below do undoubtedly raise the question whether it was necessary for Barton in order to obtain relief to establish that he would not have executed the deed in question but for the threats. In answering this question in favour of Barton, Jacobs J.A. relied both on a number of old common law authorities on the subject of "duress" and also - by way of analogy - on later decisions in equity with regard to the avoidance of deeds on the ground of fraud. Their Lordships do not think that the common law authorities are of any real assistance for it seems most unlikely that the authors of the statements relied on had the sort of problem which has arisen here in mind at all. On the other hand they think that the conclusion to which Jacobs J.A. came was right and that it is supported by the equity decisions. The scope of common law duress was very limited and at a comparatively early date equity began to grant relief in cases where the disposition in question had been procured by the exercise of pressure which the Chancellor considered to be illegitimate - although it did not amount to common law duress. There was a parallel development in the field of dispositions induced by fraud. At common law the only remedy available to the man defrauded was an action for deceit but equity in the same period in which it was building up the doctrine of "undue influence" came to entertain proceedings to set aside dispositions which had been obtained by fraud: see *Holdsworth, A History of English Law,* vol. V (1924), pp. 328-329. There is an obvious analogy between setting aside a disposition for duress or undue influence and setting it aside for fraud. In each case - to quote the words of Holmes J. in *Fairbanks* v. *Snow* (1887) - "the party has been subjected to an improper motive for action." Again the similarity of the effect in law of metus and dolus in connection with dispositions of property is noted by Stair in his *Institutions of the Law of Scotland,* New ed. (1832), Book IV, title 40.25. Had Armstrong made a fraudulent misrepresentation to Barton for the purpose of inducing him to execute the deed of January 17, 1967, the answer to the problem which has arisen would have been clear. If it were established that Barton did not allow the representation to affect his judgment then he could not make it a ground for relief even though the representation was designed and known by Barton to be designed to affect his judgment. If on the other hand Barton relied on the misrepresentation Armstrong could not have defeated his claim to relief by showing that there were other more weighty causes which contributed to his decision to execute the deed, for in this field the court does not allow an examination into the relative importance of contributory causes.

"Once make out that there has been anything like deception, and no contract resting in any degree on that foundation can stand": *per* Lord Cranworth L.J. in *Reynell* v. *Sprye* (1852) - see also the other cases referred to in *Cheshire and Fifoot's Law of Contract,* 8th ed. (1972), pp. 250-251. Their Lordship think that the same rule should apply in cases of duress and that if Armstrong's threats were "a" reason for Barton's executing the deed he is entitled to relief even though he might well have entered into the contract if Armstrong had uttered no threats to induce him to do so.

[Their Lordships went on to decide that the onus was on the respondent, Armstrong, to prove that the threats did not contribute to the appellant's decision to sign the deed. The proper inference from the facts was that, although the appellant might have executed the deed anyway, the threats contributed to the decision. The deeds were accordingly executed under duress.]

Judgment for the appellant.

[Lord Kilbrandon and Sir Garfield Barwick agreed. Lords Wilberforce and Simon dissented on the basis that there was no justification for interfering with the lower courts findings of fact.]

B. Economic Duress

Pau On v. Lau Yiu Long
[1980] A.C. 614 (P.C.)

Lord Scarman. Duress, whatever form it takes, is a coercion of the will so as to vitiate consent. Their Lordships agree with the observation of Kerr J. in *Occidental Worldwide Investment Corporation* v. *Skibs A/S Avanti* (1976) that in a contractual situation commercial pressure is not enough. There must be present some factor "which could in law be regarded as a coercion of his will so as to vitiate his consent." This conception is in line with what was said in this Board's decision in *Barton* v. *Armstrong* (1976) by Lord Wilberforce and Lord Simon of Glaisdale - observations with which the majority judgment appears to be in agreement. In determining whether there was a coercion of will such that there was no true consent, it is material to inquire whether the person alleged to have been coerced did or did not protest; whether, at the time he was allegedly coerced into making the contract, he did or did not have an alternative course open to him such as an adequate legal remedy; whether he was independently advised; and whether after entering the contract he took steps to avoid it. All these matters are, as was recognised in *Maskell* v. *Horner* (1915), relevant in determining whether he acted voluntarily or not.

[Their Lordships noted that the facts in this case disclosed commercial pressure, not coercion.]

It is therefore, unnecessary for the Board to embark upon an inquiry into the question whether English law recognises a category of duress known as "economic duress." But, since the question has been fully argued in this appeal, their Lordships will indicate very briefly the view which they have formed. At common law money paid under economic compulsion could be recovered in an action for money had and received *Astley* v. *Reynolds* (1731). The compulsion had to be such that the party was deprived of "his freedom of exercising his will" (see p. 916). It is doubtful, however, whether at common law any duress other than duress to the person sufficed to render a contract voidable: see *Blackstone's Commentaries,* Book 1, 12th ed. pp. 130-131 and *Skeate* v. *Beale* (1841). American law (*Williston on Contracts*, 3rd ed.) now recognises that a contract may be avoided on the ground of economic duress. The commercial pressure alleged to constitute such duress must, however, be such that the victim must have entered the contract against his will, must have had no alternative course open to him, and must have been confronted with coercive acts by the party exerting the pressure: *Williston on Contracts*, 3rd ed., vol. 13 (1970), section 1603. American judges pay great attention to such evidential matters as the effectiveness of the alternative remedy available, the fact or absence of protest, the availability of independent advice, the benefit received, and the speed with which the victim has sought to avoid the contract. Recently two English judges have recognised that commercial pressure may constitute duress the pressure of which can render a contract voidable: Kerr J. in *Occidental Worldwide Investment Corporation* v. *Skibs A/S Avanti* (1976) and Mocatta J. in *North Ocean Shipping Co. Ltd.* v. *Hyundai Construction Co. Ltd.* (1979). Both stressed that the pressure must be such that the victim's consent to the contract was not a voluntary act on his part. In their Lordships' view, there is nothing contrary to principle in recognising economic duress as a factor which may render a contract voidable, provided always that the basis of such recognition is that it must amount to a coercion of will, which vitiates consent. It must be shown that the payment made or the contract entered into was not a voluntary act.

Notes

The growth of the doctrine of economic duress is a good example of the courts developing a traditional common law concept and applying it to modern conditions. The House of Lords explicity recognised the doctrine in *Universe Tankships of Monrovia* v. *International Transport Workers Federation* (1983), note in particular the judgments of Lords Diplock and Scarman.

The ambit of the doctrine will no doubt be developed further in subsequent cases. Two examples of, on the facts, unsuccessful claims of economic duress are, *North Ocean Shipping Co.Ltd.v. Hyundai Construction Co. Ltd., The Atlantic Baron* (1978) and *Alec Lobb Ltd.v. Total Oil G B. Ltd.*(1983).

2. UNDUE INFLUENCE

National Westminster Bank v. Morgan
[1985] 2 W.L.R. 588 (H.L.)

[Mrs. Morgan and her husband entered into an agreement with the bank to charge their house in order to secure a bridging loan. The object was to prevent the family house being repossessed by a mortgagee, which was imminent. The bank subsequently sought to enforce the charge. The wife claimed that the bank manager had exercised undue influence upon her. The trial judge found that the transaction had not been manifestly disadvantageous to the wife, the manager had not put pressure on her, and there was not such a relationship between the parties (examples include parent and child, solicitor and client, doctor and patient) as to give rise to the presumption of undue influence. The judge accordingly gave judgment for the bank. The Court of Appeal allowed an appeal by the wife. They found that the facts did give rise to a presumption of undue influence, and that as a matter of law, there was no need to show that the influenced party had necessarily been put at a disadvantage. The bank appealed. A further motivation of the appeal was a clarification of the law laid down in what had previously been a leading case on the matter, *Lloyds Bank Ltd.v. Bundy* (1975).]

Lord Scarman. My Lords, I believe that the Lord Justices were led into a misinterpretation of the facts by their use, as is all too frequent in this branch of the law, of words and phrases such as "confidence," "confidentiality," "fiduciary duty." There are plenty of confidential relationships which do not give rise to the presumption of undue influence (a notable example is that of husband and wife, *Bank of Montreal* v. *Stuart* (1911)); and there are plenty of non-confidential relationships in which one person relies upon the advice of another, e.g. many contracts for the sale of goods.

. . . . . .

But, further, the view of the law expressed by the Court of Appeal was, as I shall endeavour to show, mistaken. Dunn L.J., while accepting that in all the reported cases to which the court was referred the transactions were disadvantageous to the person influenced, took the view that in cases where public policy requires the court to apply the presumption of undue influence there is no need to prove a disadvantageous transaction.

[His Lordship considered an authority relied upon by the Court of Appeal involving gifts and rejected it as support for such a proposition.]

... I know of no reported authority where the transaction set aside was not to the manifest disadvantage of the person influenced. It would not always be a gift: it can be a "hard and inequitable" agreement (*Ormes* v. *Beadel* (1860)); or a transaction "immoderate and irrational" (*Bank of Montreal* v. *Stuart* (1911)) or "unconscionable" in that it was a sale at an undervalue (*Poosathurai* v. *Kannappa Chettiar* (1919)). Whatever the legal character of the transaction, the authorities show that it must constitute a disadvantage sufficiently serious to require evidence to rebut the presumption that in the circumstances of the relationship between the parties it was procured by the exercise of undue influence. In my judgment, therefore, the Court of Appeal erred in law in holding that the presumption of undue influence can arise from the evidence of the relationship of the parties without also evidence that the transaction itself was wrongful in that it constituted an advantage taken of the person subjected to the influence which, failing proof to the contrary, was explicable only on the basis that undue influence had been exercised to procure it.

The principle justifying the court in setting aside a transaction for undue influence can now be seen to have been established by Lindley L.J. in *Allcard* v. *Skinner* (1887). It is not a vague "public policy" but specifically the victimisation of one party by the other. It was stated by Lindley L.J. in a famous passage:

> "The principle must be examined. What then is the principle? Is it that it is right and expedient to save persons from the consequences of their own folly? or is it that it is right and expedient to save them from being victimised by other people? In my opinion the doctrine of undue influence is founded upon the second of these two principles. Courts of equity have never set aside gifts on the ground of the folly, imprudence, or want of foresight on the part of donors. The courts have always repudiated any such jurisdiction. *Huguenin* v. *Baseley* (1807) is itself a clear authority to this effect. It would obviously be to encourage folly, recklessness, extravagance and vice if persons could get back property which they foolishly made away with, whether by giving it to charitable institutions or by bestowing it on less worthy objects. On the other hand, to protect people from being forced, tricked or misled in any way by others into parting with their property is one of the most legitimate objects of all laws; and the equitable

doctrine of undue influence has grown out of and been developed by the necessity of grappling with insidious forms of spiritual tyranny and with the infinite varieties of fraud."

. . . . . .

The wrongfulness of the transaction must, therefore, be shown: it must be one in which an unfair advantage has been taken of another.

The doctrine is not limited to transactions of gift. A commercial relationship can become a relationship in which one party assumes a role of dominating influence over the other. In *Poosathurai's* case (1919), the Board recognised that a sale at an undervalue could be a transaction which a court could set aside as unconscionable if it was shown or could be presumed to have been procured by the exercise of undue influence. Similarly a relationship of banker and customer may become one in which the banker acquires a dominating influence. If he does and a manifestly disadvantageous transaction is proved, there would then be room for the court to presume that it resulted from the exercise of undue influence.

This brings me to *Lloyds Bank Ltd.* v. *Bundy* (1975). It was, as one would expect, conceded by counsel for the respondent that the relationship between banker and customer is not one which ordinarily gives rise to a presumption of undue influence: and that in the ordinary course of banking business a banker can explain the nature of the proposed transaction without laying himself open to a charge of undue influence. This proposition has never been in doubt, though some, it would appear, have thought that the Court of Appeal held otherwise in *Lloyds Bank Ltd.* v. *Bundy.* If any such view has gained currency, let it be destroyed now once and for all time .. .. Your Lordships are, of course, not concerned with the interpretation put upon the facts in that case by the Court of Appeal: the present case is not a rehearing of that case. The question which the House does have to answer is: did the court in *Lloyds Bank Ltd.* v. *Bundy* accurately state the law?

Lord Denning M.R. believed that the doctrine of undue influence could be subsumed under a general principle that English courts will grant relief where there has been "inequality of bargaining power". He deliberately avoided reference to the will of one party being dominated or overcome by another. The majority of the court did not follow him; they based their decision on the orthodox view of the doctrine as

expounded in *Allcard* v. *Skinner*. The opinion of the Master of
the Rolls, therefore, was not the ground of the court's decision,
which was to be found in the view of the majority, for whom
Sir Eric Sachs delivered the leading judgment.

Nor has counsel for the respondent sought to rely on Lord
Denning M.R.'s general principle: and, in my view, he was
right not to do so. The doctrine of undue influence has been
sufficiently developed not to need the support of a principle
which by its formulation in the language of the law of contract
is not appropriate to cover transactions of gift where there is no
bargain. The fact of an unequal bargain will, of course, be a
relevant feature in some cases of undue influence. But it can
never become an appropriate basis of principle of an equitable
doctrine which is concerned with transactions "not to be
reasonably accounted for on the ground of friendship,
relationship, charity, or other ordinary motives on which
ordinary men act" (Lindley L.J. in *Allcard* v. *Skinner*, at p.
185). And even in the field of contract I question whether there
is any need in the modern law to erect a general principle of
relief against inequality of bargaining power. Parliament has
undertaken the task - and it is essentially a legislative task - of
enacting such restrictions upon freedom of contract as are in its
judgment necessary to relieve against the mischief: for
example, the hire-purchase and consumer protection
legislation, of which the Supply of Goods (Implied Terms) Act
1973, Consumer Credit Act 1974, Consumer Safety Act 1978,
Supply of Goods and Services Act 1982 and Insurance
Companies Act 1982 are examples. I doubt whether the courts
should assume the burden of formulating further restrictions.

...... A meticulous examination of the facts of the present
case reveals that Mr. Barrow never "crossed the line" Nor was
the transaction unfair to Mrs. Morgan. The bank was,
therefore, under no duty to ensure that she had independent
advice. It was an ordinary banking transaction whereby Mrs.
Morgan sought to save her home; and she obtained an honest
and truthful explanation of the bank's intention which,
notwithstanding the terms of the mortgage deed which in the
circumstances the trial judge was right to dismiss as
"essentially theoretical," was correct: for no one has suggested
that Mr. Barrow or the bank sought to make Mrs. Morgan
liable, or to make her home the security, for any debt of her
husband other than the loan and interest necessary to save the
house from being taken away from them in discharge of their
indebtedness to the building society.

For these reasons, I would allow the appeal. In doing so, I would wish to give a warning. There is no precisely defined law setting limits to the equitable jurisdiction of a court to relieve against undue influence. This is the world of doctrine, not of neat and tidy rules. The courts of equity have developed a body of learning enabling relief to be granted where the law has to treat the transaction as unimpeachable unless it can be held to have been procured by undue influence. It is the unimpeachability at law of a disadvantageous transaction which is the starting-point from which the court advances to consider whether the transaction is the product merely of one's folly or of the undue influence exercised by another. A court in the exercise of this equitable jurisdiction is a court of conscience. Definition is a poor instrument when used to determine whether a transaction is or is not unconscionable: this is a question which depends upon the particular facts of the case.

[Lords Keith, Roskill, Bridge and Brandon all concurred in giving judgment for the bank.]

Note

An example of a successful plea of undue influence is the case of *Avon Finance Co.Ltd v. Bridger*(1985), although the judgment of Lord Denning M.R. must now be read in the light of Lord Scarman's strictures in the case of *Morgan* above. A further recent discussion of this area is to be found in *Coldunell Ltd. v. Gallon and another* (1986).

3. ILLEGALITY

Pearce v. Brooks
(1866) L.R. 1 Ex. 213 (Exchequer Chamber)

[The plantiff sued the defendant on what was an early example of a hire purchase agreement. The defendant alleged that the plantiff could not recover on the basis, in effect, that the contract was tainted with illegality. One of the issues that arose was whether it must be proved in such a case that the plantiff expected to be paid out of the proceeds of the immoral act, or whether it was enough simply that it was known that the defendant would apply the article for an immoral purposes.]

Bramwell B. There is no doubt that the woman was a prostitute; no doubt to my mind that the plaintiffs knew it; there was cogent evidence of the fact, and the jury have so found. The only fact really in dispute is for what purpose was the brougham hired, and if for an immoral purposes, did the plaintiffs know it? At the trial I doubted whether there was evidence of this, but, for the reasons I have already stated, I think the jury were entitled to infer, as they did, that it was hired for the purposes of display, that is, for the purpose of enabling the defendant to pursue her calling, and that the plaintiffs knew it.

That being made out, my difficulty was, whether, though the defendant hired the brougham for that purpose, it could be said that the plaintiffs let it for the same purpose. In one sense, it was not for the same purpose. It a man were to ask for duelling pistols, and to say: "I think I shall fight a duel to-morrow," might not the seller answer: "I do not want to know your purpose; I have nothing to do with it; that is your business: mine is to sell the pistols, and I look only to the profit of trade." No doubt the act would be immoral, but I have felt a doubt whether it would be illegal; and I should still feel it, but that the authority of *Cannan* v. *Bryce* (1819) *M'Kinnell* v. *Robinson* (1838) concludes the matter. In the latter case the plea does not say that the money was lent on the terms that the borrower should game with it; but only that it was borrowed by the defendant, and lent by the plaintiff "for the purpose of the defendant's illegally playing and gaming therewith." The case was argued by Mr. Justice Crompton against the plea, and by Mr. Justice Wightman in support of it; and the considered judgment of the Court was delivered by Lord Abinger, who says . . . : "As the plea states that the money for which the action is brought was lent for the purpose of illegally playing and gaming therewith, at the illegal game of 'Hazard,' this money cannot be recovered back, on the principle, not for the first time laid down, but fully settled in the case of *Cannan* v. *Bryce.* This principle is that the repayment of money, lent for the express purpose of accomplishing an illegal object, cannot be enforced." This Court, then, following *Cannan* v. *Bryce,* decided that it need not be part of the bargain that the subject of the contract should be used unlawfully, but that it is enough if it is handed over for the purpose that the borrower shall so apply it. We are, then, concluded by authority on the point; and, as I have no doubt that the finding of the jury was right, the rule must be discharged.

[Pollock C.B., Martin and Pigott BB. concurred in giving judgment for the defendant.]

Note

The intricacies of the law relating to illegality, and its effects on the rights of the contracting parties, are somewhat complex (see for example, H.S.B., pp. 416-

424). Even if the agreement does contain an "illegal" element, a plaintiff is not necessarily without remedy. For example, it may be possible to "sever" the offending element or find a collateral contract as in *Strongman* (1945) v. *Simcock* (1955). A further example is set out below.

Shelley v. Paddock
[1979] 1 Q.B. 120 (Q.B.)

[Miss Shelley, the plaintiff, wished to buy a house in Spain. She entered into an agreement with the defendants, who in fact did not have authority to sell and were acting fraudulently, for the purchase of a house and duly paid over the purchase price. In fact, such a payment was illegal, being in breach of the then existing exchange control legislation which required Treasury consent for such a transaction. The plaintiff was completely unaware of this requirement and had acted quite innocently. The defendants were unable to convey a title to the house, and Miss Shelley brought an action in the tort of deceit for the return of the purchase price of £9,400. The defendants claimed, *inter alia*, that the plaintiff was unable to recover the payment because the agreement by which she had paid the money was an illegal transaction.]

Bristow J. [having outlined the facts continued] At any rate, what she did clearly was a breach of section 5 of the Exchange Control Act 1947. What is the effect of this?

The first expression of the principle of law with which we have to deal to which reference is made when this sort of problem arises was enunciated by Lord Mansfield as long ago as the 1770s. The case in which he enunciated it was *Holman* v. *Johnson* (1775):

"The objection, that a contract is immoral or illegal as between plaintiff and defendant, sounds at all times very ill in the mouth of the defendant. It is not for his sake, however, that the objection is ever allowed; but it is founded in general principles of policy, which the defendant has the advantage of, contrary to the real justice, as between him and the plaintiff, by accident, if I may say so. The principle of public policy is this; ex dolo malo non oritur actio. No court will lend its aid to a man who founds his cause of action upon an immoral or illegal act. If, from the plaintiff's own stating or otherwise, the cause of action appears to arise ex turpi causa, or the transgression of a positive law of this country, there the court says he has no right to be assisted. It is upon that ground the court goes; not for the sake of the defendant, but because they will not lend their aid to such plaintiff. So if the plaintiff and defendant were to change sides, and the defendant was to bring his action against the plaintiff, the latter would then have the advantage of it; for where both are equally in fault, potior est conditio defendentis."

The Latin is perhaps not unimportant in appreciating the principle and the reason for it. "Dolo malo" can be translated accurately as "a dirty trick." "Turpis" means shameful, wicked, disgraceful. Both the Latin words involve the stigma of blameworthy conduct.

The application of the principle between 1775 and 1977 has been the subject of a vast wealth of judicial authority, which is examined in all the textbooks. I do not propose to try to make any elaborate review of the authorities. Among other cases, there are cases in which a plaintiff who, in order to maintain his action, has disclosed that he has been involved in a breach of the Exchange Control Act 1947, and has been told that he cannot recover because of this principle. But in nearly all the cases, and certainly in the exchange control cases, the breach of the Exchange Control Act 1947 has been deliberate. If, as I find in this case, the plaintiff genuinely had not any idea that there was such a thing, does her innocence in this respect make any difference? Clearly, where somebody deliberately breaks the law, it would be absurd for the courts to lend their assistance to that person to establish rights which result from a deliberate breach of the law. Nearly all the cases involve perfectly deliberate breaches of the law at the time the transaction was entered into from which the rights sought to be established depend. I asked Mr. Barker whether there were any cases in which somebody who genuinely did not know that they were breaking the law had been held unable to succeed because of this principle. There is such a case, decided in the Court of Appeal in 1963. It is *J.M. Allan (Merchandising) Ltd.* v. *Cloke* (1963). It is the only case where a plaintiff did not know when the transaction was entered into that it was being entered into in breach of the law. It is a case which is of course binding upon me. But in that case the contract in breach of the law which was entered into was the hiring of a roulette outfit, wheel plus cloth plus croupier's rake, for the express purpose of what was in fact an illegal way of playing roulette. So that you had a continuing contract under which the hirer was seeking to recover the rent of the outfit, and although the court expressly held that both parties did not realise that the particular game for which the outfit was hired was illegal, for the court to enforce that contract once it was known it was illegal would clearly have been against public policy, just as in any other of the cases where a deal is entered into with knowledge that it is illegal.

The facts in this case are very different. The plaintiff does not sue on the contract. She says: "I have been defrauded. I sue in tort. It is true that I paid money in breach of the Exchange Control Act 1947" - she does not say that, but I do - "and I am asking for damages from the people who defrauded me, not for my money back."

In my judgment, there is nothing in the wealth of authority which has arisen on this principle, and nothing in the decision of the Court of Appeal in *J.M. Allan (Merchandising) Ltd.* v. *Cloke* - by which I am bound and which I respectfully regard as entirely correct and in accordance with principle - which prevents me from asking myself: given that the plaintiff did not know, how does the principle encapsulated in the Latin "dolus malus" or "turpis causa" apply to her? In my judgment, public policy does not require, and the law as I understand it and the principle enunciated by Lord Mansfield does not require, that the court shall not lend its assistance to the plaintiff in order to give her compensation for the wrong committed to her by the fraud of the defendants. In my judgment, she is entitled to succeed in this action. She is entitled to recover as damages for fraud the equivalent of what she paid the defendants, that is to say £9,400.

[The Court also awarded the plaintiff her expenses in making two abortive trips to Spain and £500 for her mental and physical suffering caused by the defendants' fraudulent conduct.]

Note

Bristow J.'s decision was subsequently upheld by the Court of Appeal (1980).

Chapter 9

DISCHARGE

1. PERFORMANCE

A. Exact and Substantial Performance

Cutter v. Powell
(1795) 101 E.R. 573 (K.B.)

[Cutter agreed to serve as second mate on a ship bound from Kingston, Jamaica, to Liverpool. The agreement between the parties stated "Ten days after the ship 'Governor Parry', myself master, arrives at Liverpool, I promise to pay to Mr. T. Cutter the sum of thirty guineas, provided he proceeds, continues and does his duty as second mate in the said ship from hence to the port of Liverpool, Kingston July 31, 1793." Unfortunately Cutter died on the voyage before reaching Liverpool. His widow sued for the wages he had earned up to the date of his death; the defendant claimed that the agreement was one entire contract which had not been performed.]

Lord Kenyon Ch.J. I should be extremely sorry that in the decision of this case we should determine against what had been the received opinion in the mercantile world on contracts of this kind, because it is of great importance that the laws by which the contracts of so numerous and so useful a body of men as the sailors are supposed to be guided should not be overturned. Whether these kind of notes are much in use among the seamen, we are not sufficiently informed; and the instances now stated to us from Liverpool are too recent to form any thing like usage. But it seems to me at present that the decision of this case may proceed on the particular words of this contract and the precise facts here stated, without touching marine contracts in general. That where the parties have come to an express contract none can be implied has prevailed so long as to be reduced to an axiom in the law. Here the defendant expressly promised to pay the intestate thirty guineas, provided he proceeded, continued and did his duty as second mate in the ship from Jamaica to Liverpool; and the accompanying circumstances disclosed in the case are that the common rate of wages is four pounds per month, when the party is paid in proportion to the time he serves: and that this voyage is generally performed in two months. Therefore if there had been no contract between these parties, all that the intestate could have recovered on a quantum meruit for the voyage would have been eight pounds, whereas here the defendant contracted to pay thirty guineas provided the mate continued to do his duty as mate during the whole voyage, in which case the latter would have received nearly four times as much as if he were paid for the number of months he served. He stipulated to receive the larger sum if the whole duty were performed, and nothing unless the whole of that duty were performed: it was a kind of insurance. On this particular contract my opinion is formed at present; at the same time I must say that if we were assured that these notes are in universal use, and that the commercial world have received and acted upon them in a different sense, I should give up my own opinion.

[Ashurst, Grose and Lawrence JJ. concurred.]

Question

If the facts of *Cutter* v. *Powell* were to recur today, how would the court approach the problem?

Hoenig v. Isaacs
[1952] 2 All E.R. 176 (C.A.)

[An interior decorator agreed to decorate and furnish a flat for £750. The defendant paid £400 on account but refused to pay the remaining £350 on the grounds that the design and workmanship was faulty. It was found by the official referee that there were defects but that the cost of remedying these came to some £56. The plaintiff claimed the £350; the official referee held there had been substantial compliance, and awarded him £294, being the balance claimed less the cost of rectifying the defects. The defendant appealed.]

Somervell L.J., stated the facts and continued. Counsel for the defendant submits that the decision of the official referee is wrong in law. He submits that this is an entire contract which, on the findings of fact, has not been performed. On the well-known principle applied to the facts of that case in *Cutter* v. *Powell* he submitted that the plaintiff cannot, therefore, recover on his contract. He was not concerned to dispute that on this basis the plaintiff might on the facts of this case be entitled to recover on a quantum meruit. Such a claim has never been put forward. If it were, he submits that the amount recoverable would be the fair value of what was done and delivered. The learned official referee found that there had been a substantial compliance with the contract. Counsel submits that, if his first point is right, this does not enable the plaintiff to succeed. If necessary, he submits that on his findings of fact the learned official referee was wrong as a matter of law in holding that there had been substantial compliance. [His Lordship referred to the official referee's findings as to the wardrobe door, the bookshelf, and the bookcase, and continued:] If any issue arises whether the breaches were substantial, I think it must be based on the items to which I have referred, bearing in mind, of course, that there were some additional minor defects.

The official referee regarded the principle laid down in *H. Dakin & Co., Ltd.* v. *Lee* (1916) as applicable. The contract in that case was for repairs to a house. The official referee before whom the case came in the first instance found that the work as completed did not accord with the contract in certain respects. He proceeded to hold that the plaintiff could not recover any part of the contract price or any sum in respect of the contract work. This decision was reversed in the Divisional Court and their decision was affirmed by this court. In support of the official referee's decision it was argued that the plaintiff could not recover either on the contract or on a quantum meruit. No new contract on the latter basis could be implied from the fact that the defendant by continuing to live in her house had enjoyed the benefit of what had been done.

In *Eshelby* v. *Federated European Bank, Ltd.* (1932) *Greer, L.J.* clearly felt some difficulty about *H. Dakin & Co., Ltd.* v. *Lee* (1916) as possibly inconsistent with *Cutter* v. *Powell* (1795), and the cases following that decision and deciding that where work is to be done for a sum named neither that sum nor any part of it can be recovered while the work remains undone. We were referred to a number of these cases and I have considered those authorities and others. Each case turns on the construction of the contract. In *Cutter* v. *Powell* the condition for the promissory note sued on was that the sailor should proceed to continue and do his duty as second mate in the ship from Jamaica to the port of Liverpool. The sailor died before the ship reached Liverpool and it was held his estate could not recover either on the contract or on a quantum meruit. It clearly decided that his continuing as mate during the whole voyage was a condition precedent to payment. It did not decide that if he had completed the main purpose of the contract, namely, serving as mate for the whole voyage, the defendant could have repudiated his liability by establishing that in the course of the voyage the sailor had, possibly through inadvertence, failed on some occasion in his duty as mate whereby some damage had been caused. In these circumstances, the court might have applied the principle applied to ordinary contracts for freight. The shipowner can normally recover nothing unless the goods are carried to their agreed destination. On the other hand, if this is done, his claim is not defeated by the fact that some damage has been done to the goods in transit which has resulted from a breach of the contract. The owner of the goods has his remedy by cross-action: *Dakin* v. *Oxley* (1864). The damage might, of course, be so great as to raise the question whether what was agreed to be carried had substantially arrived (*ibid*). *Sinclair* v. *Bowles* (1829) is often cited as an illustration of the *Cutter* v. *Powell* principle. The plaintiff had undertaken to repair chandeliers and make them "complete" or "perfect". This he, quite plainly on the evidence and findings of the jury, failed to do. It may, perhaps, be regarded as a case where, on the construction of the contract, having regard to the subject-matter, there was no scope for terms collateral to the main purpose.

The principle that fulfilment of every term is not necessarily a condition precedent in a contract for a lump sum is usually traced back to a short judgment of Lord Mansfield, C.J., in *Boone* v. *Eyre* (1779) - the sale of the plantation with its slaves. Lord Mansfield said . . . :

" . . . where mutual covenants go to the whole of the consideration on both sides, they are mutual conditions, the one precedent to the other. But where they go only to a part, where a breach may be paid for in damages, there the defendant has a remedy on his covenant, and shall not plead it as a condition precedent".

One is very familiar with the application of this principle in the law relating to the sale of goods. Quoad stipulations which are conditions, the *Cutter* v. *Powell* principle is applicable. If they are not all performed the other party can repudiate, but there will not have been, as there was in *Cutter* v. *Powell*, a partial performance. But there may be other terms, collateral to the main purpose, the breach of which in English law gives rise to a claim for damages, but not to a right to reject the goods and treat the contract as repudiated: see definition of warranty, Sale of Goods Act, 1893, s. 62.

In a contract to erect buildings on the defendant's land for a lump sum, the builder can recover nothing on the contract if he stops before the work is completed in the ordinary sense - in other words, abandons the contract. He is also usually in a difficulty in recovering on a quantum meruit because no new contract can be inferred from the mere fact that the defendant remains in possession of his land: *Sumpter* v. *Hedges* (1898). In *Appelby* v. *Myers* (1867) while the work was in progress the premises and the work so far done on them were destroyed by fire and the court held both parties excused. At the end of his judgment Blackburn, J., after referring to *Cutter* v. *Powell*, *Sinclair* v. *Bowles* (1829), and that line of cases, said . . . :

" . . . the plaintiffs, having contracted to do an entire work for a specific sum, can recover nothing unless the work be done . . . "

in *H. Dakin & Co. Ltd.* v. *Lee* Lord Cozens-Hardy, M.R., I think, had this principle in mind when he said . . .

"The work was finished - and when I say this I do not wish to prejduce matters, but I cannot think of a better word to use at the moment."

The question here is whether in a contract for work and labour for a lump sum payable on completion the defendant can repudiate liability under the contract on the ground that the work though "finished" or "done" is in some respects not in accordance with the contract. *H. Dakin & Co., Ltd.* v. *Lee* (1916) is, of course, binding on us, but counsel for the defendant submitted that it was an exception to a general rule applying to contracts such as that in issue here and should be confined within as narrow limits as possible. I agree with the learned editor of the notes to *Cutter* v. *Powell* in *Smith's Leading Cases*, . . . that *H. Dakin & Co., Ltd.* v. *Lee*, so far from being an exception, re-affirmed the true position on the construction of this class of contract on which doubts had been thrown by taking certain observations out of their context.

. . . . .

The learned official referee regarded *H. Dakin & Co., Ltd.* v. *Lee* as laying down that the price must be paid subject to set-off or counterclaim if there was a substantial compliance with the contract. I think on the facts of this case where the work was finished in the ordinary sense, though in part defective this is right. It expresses in a convenient epithet what is put from another angle in the Sale of Goods Act, 1893. The buyer cannot reject if he proves only the breach of a term collateral to the main purpose. I have, therefore, come to the conclusion that the first point of counsel for the defendant fails.

The learned official referee found that there was substantial compliance. Bearing in mind that there is no appeal on fact, was there evidence on which he could so find? The learned official referee having, as I hold, properly directed himself, this becomes, I think, a question of fact. The case on this point was, I think, near the border line, and if the finding had been the other way I do not think we could have interfered. Even if I had felt we could interfere, the defendant would be in a further difficulty. The contract included a number of chattels. If the defendant wished to repudiate his liability under the contract he should not, I think, have used those articles, which he could have avoided using. On this view, though it is not necessary to decide it, I think he put himself in the same position as a buyer of goods who by accepting them elects to treat a breach of condition as a breach of warranty.

I now come to the final question, the measure of damages. It seems from the argument that the defendant regards the price of £750 as excessive irrespective of any relief by way of reduction of price or on his counterclaim. He was anxious to put the plaintiff in the position of having to sue on a quantum meruit for the value of the work done and he was anxious to tender evidence designed, no doubt, to show that the work done was worth much less than £750. The learned official referee excluded this evidence. The measure he applied was the cost of putting the work in accordance with the contract and on this basis such evidence was rightly excluded. The defendant is bound, he held, to pay for the furniture supplied less the cost of putting right the defects. This I think is, as the learned official referee thought, in accordance with *H. Dakin & Co., Ltd.* v. *Lee.* Lord Cozens-Hardy, M.R., there said . . . :

"the builders are entitled to recover the contract price, less so much as it is found ought to be allowed in respect of the items which the official referee has found to be defective".

This seems to follow what was said by Parke B., in *Mondel* v. *Steel* (1841). In dealing with the procedural point he said . . . that the defendant need not bring a cross-action but can diminish the price.

" . . . by showing how much less the subject-matter of the contract was worth, by reason of the breach of contract."

I therefore think the appeal must be dismissed.

[Denning and Romer L.JJ. concurred in dismissing the appeal.]

Note

A case to contrast with the above is *Bolton* v. *Mahadeva* (1972). The cost of remedying defects was there £174 in the context of a price of £560 to install central heating. The Court of Appeal refused to allow the plaintiff's claim for payment of the agreed lump sum since they did not regard the performance as substantial.

B. *Acceptance of Part Performance*

Sumpter v. Hedges
[1898] 1 Q.B. 673 (C.A.)

[The plaintiff, a builder, agreed to erect certain buildings on the defendant's land for £565. After completing £333 worth of work he abandoned the contract, and the defendant had to complete the work himself. The builder sued the defendant on a *quantum meruit*.]

Collins L.J. I agree. I think the case is really concluded by the finding of the learned judge to the effect that the plaintiff had abandoned the contract. If the plaintiff had merely broken his contract in some way so as not to give the defendant the right to treat him as having abandoned the contract, and the defendant had then proceeded to finish the work himself, the plaintiff might perhaps have been entitled to sue on a quantum meruit on the ground that the defendant had taken the benefit of the work done. But that is not the present case. There are cases in which, though the plaintiff has abandoned the performance of a contract, it is possible for him to raise the inference of a new contract to pay for the work done on a quantum meruit from the defendant's having taken the benefit of that work, but, in order that that may be done, the circumstances must be such as to give an option to the defendant to take or not to take the benefit of the work done. It is only where the circumstances are such as to give that option that there is any evidence on which to ground the inference of a new contract. Where, as in the case of work done on land, the circumstances are such as to give the defendant no option whether he will take the benefit of the work or not, then one must look to other facts than the mere taking the benefit of the work in order to ground the inference of a new contract. In this case I see no other facts on which such an inference can be founded. The mere fact that a defendant is in possession of what he cannot help keeping, or even has done work upon it, affords no ground for such an inference. He is not bound to keep unfinished a building which in an incomplete state would be a nuisance on his land. I am therefore of opinion that the plaintiff was not entitled to recover for the work which he had done.

[Smith and Chitty L.JJ. concurred in dismissing the appeal.]

C. Vicarious Performance

British Waggon Co. v. Lea
(1880) 5 Q.B.D. 149 (Q.B.)

[The plaintiffs let a number of railway wagons to the defendants under a contract which required the latter to keep them in good repair. Consequent upon the liquidation of the plaintiffs' company, the task of maintaining the wagons was assigned to another company. The defendants resisted an action for the rent on the trucks on the grounds that the plaintiffs were, in effect, in breach of contract in not themselves maintaining the trucks.]

Cockburn C.J. The main contention on the part of the defendants, however, was that, as the Parkgate Company had, by assigning the contracts, and by making over their repairing stations to the British Company, incapacitated themselves to fulfil their obligation to keep the waggons in repair, that company had no right, as between themselves and the defendants, to substitute a third party to do the work they had engaged to perform, nor were the defendants bound to accept the party so substituted as the one to whom they were to look for performance of the contract; the contract was therefore at an end.

[His Lordship considered an authority involving the repair of a carriage.]

In like manner, where goods are ordered of a particular manufacturer, another, who has succeeded to his business, cannot execute the order, so as to bind the customer, who has not been made aware of the transfer of the business, to accept the goods. The latter is entitled to refuse to deal with any other than the manufacturer whose goods he intended to buy. For this *Boulton* v. *Jones* (1857) is a sufficient authority. The case of *Robson* v. *Drummond* (1831) comes nearer to the present case, but is, we think, distinguishable from it. We entirely concur in the principle on which the decision in *Robson* v. *Drummond* rests, namely, that where a person contracts with another to do work or perform service, and it can be inferred that the person employed has been selected with reference to his individual skill, competency, or other personal qualification, the inability or unwillingness of the party so employed to execute the work or perform the service is a sufficient answer to any demand by a stranger to the original contract of the performance of it by the other party, and entitles the latter to treat the contract as at an end, notwithstanding that the person tendered to take the place of the contracting party may be equally well qualified to do the service. Personal performance is in such a case of the essence of the contract, which, consequently, cannot in its absence be enforced against an unwilling party. But this principle appears to us inapplicable in the present instance, inasmuch as we cannot suppose that in stipulating for the repair of these waggons by the company - a rough description of work which ordinary workmen conversant with the business would be perfectly able to execute - the defendants attached any importance to whether the repairs were done by the company, or by any one with whom the company might enter into a subsidiary contract to do the work. All that the hirers, the defendants, cared for in this stipulation was that the waggons should be kept in repair; it was indifferent to them by whom the repairs should be done. Thus if, without going into liquidation, or assigning these contracts, the company had entered into a contract with any competent party to do the repairs, and so had procured them to be done, we cannot think that this would have been a departure from the Berms of the contract to keep the waggons in repair. . . . . . .

Much work is contracted for, which it is known can only be executed by means of subcontracts; much is contracted for as to which it is indifferent to the party for whom it is to be done, whether it is done by the immediate party to the contract, or by someone in his behalf. In all these cases the maxim Qui facit per alium facit per se applies.

Judgment for the plaintiff.

2. AGREEMENT

In Chapter 2 we have seen how the doctrine of consideration and promissory estoppel affect the formation and operation of a contract. The law will not generally enforce a gratuitous promise, or permit reliance upon an equally gratuitous waiver of the other party's obligations. Similar principles apply, albeit at a different stage, to the discharge of a contract by agreement. They are not, therefore, dealt with at length again here (see H.S.B., pp. 429-432).

An illuminating example is provided by *Charles Rickards Ltd*. v. *Oppenhaim* (1950). The defendant ordered a body to be built on a car chassis, the work to be completed within "six or seven months." At the end of this time the work was not finished, but he agreed to wait another three months. On this aspect of the case see below:

Charles Rickards Ltd. v. Oppenhaim
[*1950*] *1 K.B. 616*

Denning L.J. If this had been originally a contract without any stipulation as to time and, therefore, with only the implication of reasonable time, it may be that the plaintiffs could have said that they had fulfilled the contract; but in my opinion the case is very different when there was an initial contract, making time of the essence of the contract: "within six or at the most, seven "months." I agree that that initial time was waived by reason of the requests that the defendant made after March, 1948, for delivery; and that, if delivery had been tendered in compliance with those requests, the defendant could not have refused to accept the coach-body. Suppose, for instance, that delivery had been tendered in April, May, or June, 1948: the defendant would have had no answer. It would be true that the plaintiffs could not aver and prove they were ready and willing to deliver in accordance with the original contract. They would have had, in effect, to rely on the waiver almost as a cause of action. At one time there would have been theoretical difficulties about their doing that. It would have been said that there was no consideration; or, if the contract was for the sale of goods, that there was nothing in writing to support the variation. There is the well-known case of *Plevins* v. *Downing* (1876), coupled with what was said in *Besseler, Waechter, Glover & Co.* v. *South Derwent Coal Co. Ld.* (1938), which gave rise to a good deal of difficulty on that score; but all those difficulties are swept away now. If the defendant, as he did, led the plaintiffs to believe that he would not insist on the stipulation as to time, and that, if they carried out the work, he would accept it, and they did it, he could not afterwards set up the stipulation as to the time against them. Whether it be called waiver or forbearance on his part, or an agreed variation or substituted performance, does not matter. It is a kind of estoppel. By his conduct he evinced an intention to affect their legal relations. He made, in effect, a promise not to insist on his strict legal rights. That promise was intended to be acted on, and was in fact acted on. He cannot afterwards go back on it. I think not only that that follows from *Panoutsos* v. *Raymond Hadley Corporation of New York* (1917), a decision of this

court, but that it was also anticipated in *Bruner* v. *Moore* (1904).
It is a particular application of the principle which I
endeavoured to state in *Central London Property Trust Ld.* v.
High Trees House Ltd. (1947).

[In fact, the car was not delivered within even the extended time and the
defendant thereupon gave reasonable notice that unless it was ready by a certain
date, he would not accept it. It was not ready, and by his actions the defendant
had once again made time of the essence in the contract. The plaintiffs were
therefore in clear breach of contract and their action failed.]

Note

See also, for an example of discharge by "accord and satisfaction," *British
Russian Gazette Ltd.* v. *Associated Newspapers Ltd.* (1933).

3. BREACH

Photo Production Ltd. v. Securicor
[1980] A.C. 827 (H.L.)

[Securicor had been employed to provide a night patrol service to their client's
factory. In the course of such a visit one of Securicor's employees decided to light
a small fire. It become a big one. The result was £615,000 worth of damage to the
factory, although it was found that the employee did not intend to burn down the
premises and that Securicor had not been negligent in employing or supervising
him. The fee for the provision of the service was only £8.15s. a week. When sued,
Securicor relied upon an exemption clause which stated:]

"Under no circumstances shall the company [Securicor] be responsible for any
injurious act or default by any employee of the company unless such act or
default could have been foreseen and avoided by the exercise of due diligence
on the part of the company as his employer, nor, in any event, shall the
company be held responsible for (a) any loss suffered by the customer through
burglary, theft, fire or any other cause, except insofar as such loss is solely
attributable to the negligence of the company's employees acting within the
course of their employment. . . . "

The Court of Appeal, following the *Harbutt's Plasticine* case gave
judgment for the plaintiffs on the grounds that there had been a fundamental
breach of the contract which brought it to an end, so preventing reliance upon
the exemption clause. In the alternative, the clause could not be construed to
apply to the events which had actually occurred. The defendants appealed.]

Lord Wilberforce [After stating that the *ratio decidendi* of the
Suisse Atlantique case (1967) was accurately summarised in the
headnote, which stated, "the question whether an exceptions
clause was applicable where there was a fundamental breach of
contract was one of the true construction of the contract,"
continued:]

1. The doctrine of "fundamental breach" in spite of its
imperfections and doubtful parentage has served a useful
purpose. There was a large number of problems, productive of
injustice, in which it was worse than unsatisfactory to leave

exception clauses to operate. Lord Reid referred to these in the *Suisse Atlantique* case (1967), pointing out at the same time that the doctrine of fundamental breach was a dubious specific. But since then Parliament has taken a hand: it has passed the Unfair Contract Terms Act 1977. This Act applies to consumer contracts and those based on standard terms and enables exception clauses to be applied with regard to what is just and reasonable. It is significant that Parliament refrained from legislating over the whole field of contract. After this Act, in commercial matters generally, when the parties are not of unequal bargaining power, and when risks are normally borne by insurance, not only is the case for judicial intervention undemonstrated, but there is everything to be said, and this seems to have been Parliament's intention, for leaving the parties free to apportion the risks as they think fit and for respecting their decisions.

At the stage of negotiation as to the consequences of a breach, there is everything to be said for allowing the parties to estimate their respective claims according to the contractual provisions they have themselves made, rather than for facing them with a legal complex so uncertain as the doctrine of fundamental breach must be. What, for example, would have been the position of the respondents' factory if instead of being destroyed it had been damaged, slightly or moderately or severely? At what point does the doctrine (with what logical justification I have not understood) decide, ex post facto, that the breach was (factually) fundamental before going on to ask whether legally it is to be regarded as fundamental? How is the date of "termination" to be fixed? Is it the date of the incident causing the damage, or the date of the innocent party's election, or some other date? All these difficulties arise from the doctrine and are left unsolved by it.

At the judicial stage there is still more to be said for leaving cases to be decided straightforwardly on what the parties have bargained for rather than upon analysis, which becomes progressively more refined, of decisions in other cases leading to inevitable appeals. The learned judge was able to decide this case on normal principles of contractual law with minimal citation of authority. I am sure that most commercial judges have wished to be able to do the same: see *Trade and Transport Inc.* v. *Ilno Kaiun Kaisha Ltd.* (1973), *per* Kerr J. In my opinion they can and should.

2. The case of *Harbutt* (1970) must clearly be overruled. It would be enough to put that upon its radical inconsistency with

the *Suisse Atlantique* case (1967). But even if the matter were res integra I would find the decision to be based upon unsatisfactory reasoning as to the "termination" of the contract and the effect of "termination" on the plaintiffs' claim for damage. I have, indeed been unable to understand how the doctrine can be reconciled with the well accepted principle of law, stated by the highest modern authority, that when in the context of a breach of contract one speaks of "termination," what is meant is no more than that the innocent party or, in some cases, both parties, are excused from further performance. Damages, in such cases, are then claimed under the contract, so what reason in principle can there be for disregarding what the contract itself says about damages - whether it "liquidates" them, or limits them, or excludes them? These difficulties arise in part from uncertain or inconsistent terminology. A vast number of expressions are used to describe situations where a breach has been committed by one party of such a character as to entitle the other party to refuse further performance: discharge, rescission, termination, the contract is at an end, or dead, or displaced clauses cannot survive, or simply go. I have come to think that some of these difficulties can be avoided; in particular the use of "rescission," even if distinguished from rescission ab initio, as an equivalent for discharge, though justifiable in some contexts (see *Johnson* v. *Agnew* (1980)) may lead to confusion in others. To plead for complete uniformity may be to cry for the moon. But what can and ought to be avoided is to make use of these confusions in order to produce a concealed and unreasoned legal innovation: to pass, for example, from saying that a party, victim of a breach of contract, is entitled to refuse further performance, to saying that he may treat the contract as at an end, or as rescinded, and to draw from this the proposition, which is not analytical but one of policy, that all or (arbitrarily) some of the clauses of the contract lose, automatically, their force, regardless of intention.

If this process is discontinued the way is free to use such words as "discharge" or "termination" consistently with principles as stated by modern authority which *Harbutt's* case (1970) disregards. I venture with apology to relate the classic passages. In *Heyman* v. *Darwins Ltd.* (1942) Lord Porter said:

> "To say that the contract is rescinded or has come to an end or has ceased to exist may in individual cases convey the truth with sufficient accuracy, but the fuller expression

that the injured party is thereby absolved from future performance of his obligations under the contract is a more exact description of the position. Strictly speaking, to say that on acceptance of the renunciation of a contract the contract is rescinded is incorrect. In such a case the injured party may accept the renunciation as a breach going to the root of the whole of the consideration. By that acceptance he is discharged from further performance and may bring an action for damages, but the contract itself is not rescinded."

And similarly Lord Macmillan . . . : see also *Boston Deep Sea Fishing and Ice Co.* v. *Ansell* (1888), *per* Bowen L.J. In *Lep Air Services Ltd.* v. *Rolloswin Investments Ltd.* (1973), my noble and learned friend, Lord Diplock, drew a distinction (relevant for that case) between primary obligations under a contract, which on "rescission" generally come to an end, and secondary obligations which may then arise. Among the latter he includes an obligation to pay compensation, i.e., damages. And he states in terms that this latter obligation "is just as much an obligation arising from the contract as are the primary obligations that it replaces." My noble and learned friend has developed this line of thought in an enlightening manner in his opinion which I have now had the benefit of reading.

These passages I believe to state correctly the modern law of contract in the relevant respects: they demonstrate that the whole foundation of *Harbutt's* case (1970) is unsound.

. . . . . .

3. I must add to this, by way of exception to the decision not to "gloss" the *Suisse Atlantique* (1967) a brief observation on the deviation cases, since some reliance has been placed upon them, particularly upon the decision of this House in *Hain Steamship Co. Ltd.* v. *Tate and Lyle Ltd.* (1936) (so earlier than the *Suisse Atlantique*) in the support of the *Harbutt* doctrine. I suggested in the *Suisse Atlantique* that these cases can be regarded as proceeding upon normal principles applicable to the law of contract generally viz., that it is a matter of the parties' intentions whether and to what extent clauses in shipping contracts can be applied after a deviation, i.e., a departure from the contractually agreed voyage or adventure. It may be preferable that they should be considered as a body of authority sui generis with special rules derived from historical and commercial reasons. What on either view they cannot do is to lay down different rules as to contracts generally from those

later stated by this House in *Heyman* v. *Darwins Ltd*. (1942)....

4. It is not necessary to review fully the numerous cases in which the doctrine of fundamental breach has been applied or discussed. Many of these have now been superseded by the Unfair Contract Terms Act 1977. Others, as decisions, may be justified as depending upon the construction of the contract (see *Levison* v. *Patent Steam Carpet Cleaning Co. Ltd*. (1978)) in the light of well known principles such as that stated in *Alderslade* v. *Hendon Laundry Ltd*. (1945).

In this situation the present case has to be decided. As a preliminary the nature of the contract has to be understood. Securicor undertook to provide a service of periodical visits for a very modest charge which works out at 26p. per visit. It did not agree to provide equipment, it would have no knowledge of the value of the plaintiffs' factory: that and the efficacy of their fire precautions, would be known to the respondents. In these circumstances nobody could consider it unreasonable that as between these two equal parties the risk assumed by Securicor should be a modest one, and that the respondents should carry the substantial risk of damage or destruction.

The duty of Securicor was, as stated, to provide a service. There must be implied an obligation to use due care in selecting their patrolmen, to take care of the keys and, I would think, to operate the service with due and proper regard to the safety and security of the premises. The breach of duty committed by Securicor lay in a failure to discharge this latter obligation. Alternatively it could be put upon a vicarious responsibility for the wrongful act of Musgrove - viz., starting a fire on the premises: Securicor would be responsible for this upon the principle stated in *Morris* v. *C. W. Martin & Sons Ltd*. (1966). This being the breach, does condition 1 apply? It is drafted in strong terms, "Under no circumstances" ... "any injurious act or default by any employee." These words have to be approached with the aid of the cardinal rules of construction that they must be read contra proferentem and that in order to escape from the consequences of one's own wrongdoing, or that of one's servant, clear words are necessary. I think that these words are clear. The respondents in fact relied upon them for an argument that since they exempted from negligence they must be taken as not exempting from the consequence of deliberate acts. But this is a perversion of the rule that if a clause can cover something other than negligence, it will not be applied to negligence. Whether, in addition to negligence, it covers other, e.g., deliberate, acts, remains a matter of construction requiring, of course, clear words. I am of opinion that it does, and being free to construe and apply the clause, I must hold that liability is excluded. On this part of the case I agree with the judge and adopt his reasons for judgment. I would allow the appeal.

[Lords Keith and Scarman agreed with Lord Wilberforce.
Lords Diplock and Salmon gave judgments also allowing the appeal.]

Ailsa Craig Fishing Co. Ltd. v. Malvern Fishing Co. Ltd.
[1983] 1 All E.R. 101 (H.L.)

[Here Securicor agreed to provide security services for certain vessels moored in Aberdeen harbour. As a result of their failure to perform the contract two ships sank. They sought to rely on a limitation clause which greatly restricted their liability to pay damages in such an event. The Scottish Court of Session held that Securicor's liability was limited by the clause even though there had been a total failure by them to perform the contract. There was an appeal to the House of Lords.]

Lord Wilberforce. My Lords, the only questions for decision in these appeals are (i) whether the liability of the respondents, Securicor (Scotland) Ltd, under a short-term contract made on 31 December 1971, has been effectively limited by a special condition in that contract, and if so (ii) [what were the damages].

Whether a condition limiting liability is effective or not is a question of construction of that condition in the context of the contract as a whole. If it is to exclude liability for negligence, it must be most clearly and unambiguously expressed, and, in such a contract as this, must be construed contra proferentem. I do not think that there is any doubt so far. But I venture to add one further qualification, or at least clarification: one must not strive to create ambiguities by strained construction, as I think the appellants have striven to do. The relevant words must be given, if possible, their natural, plain meaning. Clauses of limitation are not regarded by the courts with the same hostility as clauses of exclusion; this is because they must be related to other contractual terms, in particular to the risks to which the defending party may be exposed, the remuneration which he receives and possibly also the opportunity of the other party to insure.

It is clear, on the findings of Lord Ordinary (Wylie), that the respondents were negligent as well as in material breach of their contractual obligations. The negligence consisted in a total or partial failure to provide the service contract for, viz "continuous security cover for your [the appellants'] vessels from 1900 hours on 31/12/71 until 0700 hours on 5/1/72" over the increased area specified in the contract. It is arguable, in my opinion, that the failure was not total, in that some security against some risks was provided, though not that which was necessary to prevent the actual damage which occurred. But I do not think that it makes a difference as regards the applicability of the clause of limitation whether this is right or not, and since their Lordships in the Inner House were of opinion that the failure was total, I will proceed on the assumption that this was so.

The clause of limitation was as follows (condition 2(f) of the special conditions of the contract):

> "If, pursuant to the provisions set out herein, any liability on the part of the Company shall arise (whether under the express or implied terms of this Contract, or at Common law, or in any other way) to the customer for any loss or damage of whatever nature arising out of or connected with the provision of, or purported provision of, or failure in provision of, the services covered by this Contract, such liability shall be limited to the payment by the Company by way of damages of a sum [alternatives are then stated to which I shall refer later]."

This clause is on the face of it clear. It refers to failure in provision of the services covered by the contract. There is no warrant as a matter of construction for reading "failure" as meaning "partial failure," i.e. as excluding "total failure" and there is no warrant in authority for so reading the word as a matter of law.

[Lords Elynn-Jones, Salmon, Fraser and Lowry all concurred in dismissing the appeal.]

George Mitchell (Chesterhall) Ltd. v. Finney Lock Seeds
[1983] 1 All E.R. 108 (C.A.)

Lord Denning M.R. Some farmers, called George Mitchell (Chesterhall) Ltd, ordered 30 lb of cabbage seed. It was supplied. It looked just like cabbage seed. No one could say it was not. The farmers planted it over 63 acres. Six months later there appeared out of the ground a lot of loose green leaves. They looked like cabbage leaves but they never turned in. They had no hearts. They were not "cabbages" in our common parlance because they had no hearts. The crop was useless for human consumption. Sheep or cattle might eat it if hungry enough. It was commercially useless. The price of the seed was £192. The loss to the farmers was over £61,000. They claimed damages from the seed merchants, Finney Lock Seeds Ltd. The judge awarded them that sum with interest. The total comes to nearly £100,000.

The seed merchants appeal to this court. They say that they supplied the seed on a printed clause by which their liability was limited to the cost of the seed, that is £192. They rely much on two recent cases in the House of Lords: *Photo Production Ltd* v *Securicor Transport Ltd* (1980) and *Ailsa Craig Fishing Co Ltd* v *Malvern Fishing Co Ltd* (1983) (the two *Securicor* cases).

For the last 25 years these farmers, and other farmers in the maritime belt, have got their seed from Finneys who get it from Holland. Finneys had a representative, Mr Wing. He called on the farmers each year. At Christmas 1973 he came. They gave him an order by word of mouth for 30 lb of Finneys Late Dutch Special Cabbage Seed. There was no order in writing. In February 1974 the seeds arrived. The invoice gave the date of despatch as 14 February 1974:

> "30 lbs Cabbage Finneys Late Dutch Special £192.00 . . . IMPORTANT. – For Seeds Act statutory declarations, Conditions of Sale etc., see reverse."

Then on the back there were in small printed [*sic*] many conditions of sale. Included in them was the clause relied on by Finneys. They say that their liability was limited to the return of the price, £192, and that they are not liable for the £61,000 claimed.

Are the conditions part of the contract?

The farmers were aware that the sale was subject to some conditions of sale. All seed merchants have conditions of sale. They were on the back of the catalogue. They were also on the back of the invoice each year. So it would seem that the farmers were bound at common law by the terms of them. The inference from the course of dealing would be that the farmers had accepted the conditions as printed, even though they had never read them and did not realise that they contained a limitation on liability.

But, in view of modern developments, it is to be noticed that the conditions were not negotiated at all between any representative bodies. They were not negotiated by the National Farmers' Union. They were introduced by the seed merchants by putting them in their catalogue and invoice, and never objected to by the farmers.

It is also to be noticed that the farmers never thought of insuring against any breach of contract by the seedsmen. It would be difficult to get any quotation. It might be possible for the seed merchants to insure themselves, something in the nature of a product liability insurance. Some seed merchants do so.

The printed condition here

The limitation clause here is of long standing in the seed trade. It has been in use for many years. The material part of it is as follows:

> "All Seeds, Bulbs, Corms, Tubers, Roots, Shrubs, Trees and Plants (hereinafter referred to as 'Seeds or Plants') offered for sale or sold by us to which the Seeds Act 1920 or the Plant Varieties and Seeds Act 1964 as the case may be and the Regulations thereunder apply have been tested in accordance with the provisions of the same. In the event of any seeds or plants sold or agreed to be sold by us not complying with the express terms of the contract of sale or with any representation made by us or by any duly authorised agent or representative on our behalf prior to, at the time of, or in any such contract, or any seeds or plants proving defective in varietal purity *we will, at our option, replace the defective seeds or plants, free of charge to the buyer or will refund all payments made to us by the buyer in respect of the defective seeds or plants and this shall be the limit of our obligation. We hereby exclude all liability for any loss or damage arising from the use of any seeds or plants supplied by us and for any consequential loss or damage arising out of such use* or any failure in the performance of or any defect in any seeds or plants supplied by us *or for any other loss or damage whatsoever save for, at our option, liability for any such replacement or refund as aforesaid.* In accordance with the established custom of the Seed Trade any express or implied condition, statement or warranty, statutory or otherwise, not stated in

these Conditions is hereby excluded. *The price of any seeds or plants sold or offered for sale by us is based upon the foregoing limitations upon our liability. The price of such seeds or plants would be much greater if a more extensive liability were required to be undertaken by us.*" (My emphasis.)

The natural meaning

There was much discussion before us as to the construction of that condition. I am much impressed by the words I have emphasised. Taking the clause in its natural plain meaning, I think it is effective to limit the liability of the seed merchants to a return of the money or replacement of the seeds. The explanation they give seems fair enough. They say that it is so as to keep the price low, and that if they were to undertake any greater liability the price would be much greater.

After all, the seed merchants did supply seeds. True, they were the wrong kind altogether. But they were seeds. On the natural interpretation, I think the condition is sufficient to limit the seed merchants to a refund of the price paid or replacement of the seeds.

The hostile meaning

Before the decisions of the House of Lords in the two *Securicor* cases, I would have been inclined to decide the case as the judge did. I would have been "hostile" to the clause. I would have said that the goods supplied here were different *in kind* from those that were ordered, and that the seed merchants could not avail themselves of the limitation clause. But in the light of the House of Lords cases, I think that that approach is not available.

I am particularly impressed by the words of Lord Wilberforce in the *Ailsa Craig* case (1983) where he said:

" . . . one must not strive to create ambiguities by strained construction, as I think the appellants have striven to do. The relevant words must be given, if possible, their natural, plain meaning. Clauses of limitation are not regarded by the courts with the same hostility as clauses of exclusion; this is because they must be related to other contractual terms, in particular to the risks to which the defending party may be exposed, the remuneration which he receives and possibly also the opportunity of the other party to insure."

To my mind these two cases have revolutionised our approach to exemption clauses. In order to explain their importance, I propose to take you through the story.

The heyday of freedom of contract

None of you nowadays will remember the trouble we had, when I was called to the Bar, with exemption clauses. They were printed in small print on the back of tickets and order forms and invoices. They were contained in catalogues or timetables. They were held to be binding on any person who took them without objection. No one ever did object. He never read them or knew what was in them. No matter how unreasonable they were, he was bound. All this was done in the name of "freedom of contract." But the freedom was all on the side of the big concern which had the use of the printing press. No freedom for the little man who took the ticket or order form or invoice. The big concern said, "Take it or leave it." The little man had no option but to take it. The big concern could and did exempt itself from liability in its own interest without regard to the little man. It got away with it time after time. When the courts said to the big concern, "You must put it in clear words," the big concern had no hesitation in doing so. It knew well that the little man would never read the exemption clauses or understand them.

It was a bleak winter for our law of contract. It is illustrated by two cases, *Thompson* v *London Midland and Scottish Rly Co* (1930) (in which there was exemption from liability, not on the ticket, but only in small print at the back of the timetable, and the company were held not liable) and *L'Estrange* v *F Graucob Ltd* (1934) (in which there was complete exemption in small print at the bottom of the order form, and the company were held not liable). [See p. 322.]

The secret weapon

Faced with this abuse of power, by the strong against the weak, by the use of the small print of the conditions, the judges did what they could to put a curb on it. They still had before them the idol, "freedom of contract." They still knelt down and worshipped it, but they concealed under their cloaks a secret weapon. They used it to stab the idol in the back. This weapon was called "the true construction of the contract." They used it with great skill and ingenuity. They used it so as to depart from the natural meaning of the words of the exemption clause and to put on them a strained and unnatural construction. In case after case, they said that the words were not strong enough to give the big concern exemption from liability, or that in the circumstances the big concern was not entitled to rely on the exemption clause. If a ship deviated from the contractual voyage, the owner could not rely on the exemption clause. If a warehouseman stored the goods in the wrong warehouse, he could not pray in aid the limitation clause. If the seller supplied goods different in kind from those contracted for, he could not rely on any exemption from liability. If a shipowner delivered goods to a person without production of the bill of lading, he could not escape responsibility by reference to an exemption clause. In short, whenever the wide words, in their natural meaning, would give rise to an unreasonable result, the judges either rejected them as repugnant to the main purpose of the contract or else cut them down to size in order to produce a reasonable result. This is illustrated by these cases in the House of Lords: *Glynn* v *Margetson & Co* (1893), *London and North Western Rly Co* v *Neilson* (1922), *Cunard Steamship Co Ltd* v *Buerger* (1927); and by these in the Privy Council: *Canada Steamship Lines Ltd* v *R* (1952), *Sze Hai Tong Bank Ltd* v *Rambler Cycle Co Ltd* (1959); and innumerable cases in the Court of Appeal, culminating in *Levison* v *Patent Steam Carpet Cleaning Co Ltd* (1978). But when the clause was itself reasonable and gave rise to a reasonable result, the judges upheld it, at any rate when the clause did not exclude liability entirely but only limited it to a reasonable amount. So, where goods were deposited in a cloakroom or sent to a laundry for cleaning, it was quite reasonable for the company to limit their liability to a reasonable amount, having regard to the small charge made for the service. These are illustrated by *Gibaud* v *Great Eastern Rly Co* (1921), *Alderslade* v *Hendon Laundry Ltd* (1945) and *Gillespie Bros & Co Ltd* v *Roy Bowles Transport Ltd* (1973).

Fundamental breach

No doubt had ever been cast thus far by anyone. But doubts arose when in this court, in a case called *Karsales (Harrow) Ltd* v. *Wallis* (1956), we ventured to suggest that if the big concern was guilty of a breach which went to the "very root" of the contract, sometimes called a "fundamental breach", or at other times a "total failure" of its obligations, then it could not rely on the printed clause to exempt itself from liability. This way of putting it had been used by some of the most distinguished names in the law, such as Lord Dunedin in *W & S Pollock & Co v Macrae* (1922) Lord Atkin and Lord Wright in *Hain Steamship Co Ltd* v *Tate & Lyle Ltd* (1936) and Devlin J in *Smeaton Hanscomb & Co Ltd* v *Sassoon I Setty Son & Co (No 1)* (1953). But we did make a mistake, in the eyes of some, in elevating it, by inference, into a "rule of law". That was too rude an interference with the idol of "freedom of contract". We ought to have used the secret weapon. We ought to have said that in each case, on the "true construction of the contract" in that case, the exemption clause did not avail the party where he was guilty of a fundamental breach or a breach going to the root. That is the lesson to be learnt from the "indigestible" speeches in *Suisse Atlantique Societe d'Armement Maritime SA* v *NV Rotterdamsche Kolen Centrale* (1967). They were all obiter dicta. The House were dealing with an agreed damages clause and not an exemption clause and the point had never been argued in the courts below at all. It is noteworthy that the House did not overrule a single decision of the Court of Appeal. Lord Wilberforce appears to have approved them . . . At any rate, he cast no doubt on the actual decision in any case.

The change in climate

In 1969 there was a change in climate. Out of winter into spring. It came with the first report of the Law Commission on Exemption Clauses in Contracts (Law Com No 24) which was implemented in the Supply of Goods (Implied Terms) Act 1973. In 1975 there was a further change. Out of spring into summer. It came with their second report on Exemption Clauses (Law Com No 69) which was implemented by the Unfair Contract Terms Act 1977. No longer was the big concern able to impose whatever terms and conditions it liked in a printed form, no matter how unreasonable they might be. These reports showed most convincingly that the courts could and should only enforce them if they were fair and reasonable in themselves and it was fair and reasonable to allow the big concern to rely on them. So the idol of "freedom of contract" was shattered. In cases of personal injury or death, it was not permissible to exclude or restrict liability at all. In consumer contracts any exemption clause was subject to the test of reasonableness.

These reports and statutes have influenced much the

thinking of the judges. At any rate, they influenced me as you will see if you read *Gillespie Bros & Co Ltd* v. *Roy Bowles Transport Ltd* (1973) and *Photo Production Ltd* v. *Securicor Transport Ltd* (1978):

> "Thus we reach, after long years, the principle which lies behind all our striving: the court will not allow a party to rely on an exemption or limitation clause in circumstances in which it would not be fair or reasonable to allow reliance on it; and, in considering whether it is fair and reasonable, the court will consider whether it was in a standard form, whether there was equality of bargaining power, the nature of the breach, and so forth."

The effect of the changes

What is the result of all this? To my mind it heralds a revolution in our approach to exemption clauses; not only where they exclude liability altogether and also where they limit liability; not only in the specific categories in the Unfair Contract Terms Act 1977, but in other contracts too. Just as in other fields of law we have done away with the multitude of cases on "common employment," "last opportunity", "invitees" and "licensees" and so forth, so also in this field we should do away with the multitude of cases on exemption clauses. We should no longer have to go through all kinds of gymnastic contortions to get round them. We should no longer have to harass our students with the study of them. We should set about meeting a new challenge. It is presented by the test of reasonableness.

The two Securicor cases

The revolution is exemplified by the recent two *Securicor* cases in the House of Lords (*Photo Production Ltd* v *Securicor Transport Ltd* (1980) and *Ailsa Craig Fishing Co Ltd* v *Malvern Fishing Co Ltd* (1983)). In each of them the Securicor company provided a patrolman to keep watch on premises so as to see that they were safe from intruders. They charged very little for the service. In the *Photo Production* case it was a factory with a lot of paper in it. The patrolman set light to it and burnt down the factory. In the *Ailsa Craig* case it was a quay at Aberdeen where ships were berthed. The patrolman went off for the celebrations on New Year's Eve. He left the ships unattended. The tide rose. A ship rose with it. Its bow got "snubbed" under the deck of the quay. It sank. In each case the owners were covered by insurance. The factory owners had their fire insurance. The shipowners had their hull insurance. In each case the Securicor company relied on a limitation clause. Under it they were protected from liability beyond a limit which was quite reasonable and their insurance cover was limited accordingly. The issue in practical terms was: which of the insurers should bear the loss? The question in legal terms in each case was whether Securicor could avail themselves of the limitation clause. In each case the House held that they could.

In the first case the House made it clear that the doctrine of "fundamental breach" was no longer applicable. They replaced it by the test of reasonableness. That was the test applied by the trial judge MacKenna J. which I myself quoted with approval. He said:

> "Condition 1, as I construe it, is, I think, a reasonable provision . . . Either the owner of the premises, or the person providing the service, must bear the risk. Why should the parties not agree to its being borne by the [owner of the premises]? He is certain to be insured against fire and theft, and is better able to judge the cover needed than the party providing the service . . . That is only another way of shifting the risk from the party who provides the service to the party who receives it. There is, as I have said, nothing unreasonable, nothing impolitic, in such a contract."

His judgment was approved by the House of Lords, who themselves held that the limitation clause was valid because it was a reasonable way of opportioning the risks, as between the insurers on either side. I would set out two passages to prove it. Lord Wilberforce said . . . :

> "Securicor undertook to provide a service of periodical visits for a very modest charge which works out at 26p per visit. It did not agree to provide equipment. It would have no knowledge of the value of Photo Productions' factory; that, and the efficacy of their fire precautions, would be known to Photo Productions. In these circumstances nobody could consider it unreasonable that as between these two equal parties the risk assumed by Securicor should be a modest one, and that Photo Productions should carry the substantial risk of damage or destruction."

And Lord Diplock said:

> "For the reasons given by Lord Wilberforce it seems to me
> that this apportionment of the risk of the factory being
> damaged or destroyed by the injurious act of an employee
> of Securicor while carrying out a visit to the factory is one
> which reasonable businessmen in the position of Securicor
> and Photo Productions might well think was the most
> economical. An analogous apportionment of risk is
> provided for by the Hague Rules in the case of goods
> carried by sea under bills of lading."

I do hope, however, that we shall not often have to consider
the new-found analysis of contractual obligations into
"primary obligations", "secondary obligations", "general
secondary obligations" and "anticipatory secondary obligations". No doubt it is logical enough, but it is too esoteric
altogether. It is fit only for the rarified atmosphere of the
House of Lords. Not at all for the chambers of the practitioner.
Let alone for the student at the university.

In the second case the House made a distinction between
clauses which excluded liability altogether, and those which
only limited liability to a certain sum. Exclusion clauses were
to be construed strictly contra proferentem, whereas limitation
clauses were to be construed naturally. This must be because a
limitation clause is more likely to be reasonable than an
exclusion clause. If you go by the plain, natural meaning of the
words (as you should do) there is nothing to choose between
them. As Lord Sumner said fifty years ago in *Atlantic Shipping
and Trading Co* v *Louis Dreyfus & Co* (1922):

> "There is no difference in principle between words
> which save them from having to pay at all and words which
> save them from paying as much as they would otherwise
> have had to pay."

If you read the speeches in the *Ailsa Craig* case, it does look
as if the House of Lords were relying on the reasonableness of
the limitation clause. They held it was applicable even though
the failure of the Securicor company was a "total failure" to
provide the service contracted for. They also said, obiter, that
they would construe an exclusion clause much more strictly,
just as was done in the old cases decided in the winter time. But
I would suggest that the better reason is because it would not be

fair or reasonable to allow the propounder of them to rely on them in the circumstances of the case.

The Supply of Goods (*Implied Terms*) *Act 1973*

In any case the contract for these cabbage seeds was governed by s 4 of the Supply of Goods (Implied Terms) Act 1973: see now s 55(4) as set out in para 11 of Sch 1 to the Sale of Goods Act 1979. That section says that in the case of a contract of sale of goods any term "is . . . not enforceable to the extent that it is shown that it would not be fair or reasonable to allow reliance on the term". That provision is exactly in accord with the principle which I have advocated above. So the ultimate question, to my mind, in this case is just this: to what extent would it be fair or reasonable to allow the seed merchants to rely on the limitation clause?

Fair and reasonable

There is only one case in the books so far on this point. It is *R W Green Ltd* v *Cade Bros Farm* (1978). There Griffiths J held that it was fair and reasonable for seed potato merchants to rely on a limitation clause which limited their liability to the contract price of the potatoes. That case was very different from the present. The terms had been evolved over twenty years. The judge said . . . : "They are therefore not conditions imposed by the strong upon the weak; but are rather a set of trading terms upon which both sides are apparently content to do business." The judge added . . . : "No moral blame attaches to either party; neither of them knew, nor could be expected to know, that the potatoes were infected." In that case the judge held that the clause was fair and reasonable and that the seed merchants were entitled to rely on it.

Our present case is very much on the borderline. There is this to be said in favour of the seed merchants. The price of this cabbage seed was small: £192. The damages claimed are high: £61,000. But there is this to be said on the other side. The clause was not negotiated between persons of equal bargaining power. It was inserted by the seed merchants in their invoices without any negotiation with the farmers.

To this I would add that the seed merchants rarely, if ever, invoked the clause. Their very frank director said: "The trade does not stand on the strict letter of the clause . . . Almost invariably when a customer justifiably complains, the trade pays something more than a refund." The papers contain many illustrations where the clause was not invoked and a settlement was reached.

Next, I would point out that the buyers had no opportunity at all of knowing or discovering that the seed was not cabbage seed, whereas the sellers could and should have known that it was the wrong seed altogether. The buyers were not covered by insurance against the risk. Nor could they insure. But, as to the seed merchants, the judge said:

> "I am entirely satisfied that it is possible for seedsmen to insure against this risk. I am entirely satisfied that the cost of so doing would not materially raise the price of seeds on the market. I am entirely satisfied that the protection of this clause for the purposes of protecting against the very rare case indeed, such as the present, is not reasonably required. If and in so far as it may be necessary to consider the matter, I am also satisfied that it is possible for seedsmen to test seeds before putting them on to the market."

To that I would add this further point. Such a mistake as this could not have happened without serious negligence on the part of the seed merchants themselves or their Dutch suppliers. So serious that it would not be fair to enable them to escape responsibility for it.

In all the circumstances I am of opinion that it would not be fair or reasonable to allow the seed merchants to rely on the clause to limit their liability.

I would dismiss the appeal accordingly.

[Oliver and Kerr L.JJ. also gave judgments dismissing the appeal.]

Note

As regards exemption clauses, reference should also be made to the discussion of incorporation at p. 318 and the terms of the Unfair Contract Terms Act 1977 at p. 467.

4. FRUSTRATION

Krell v. Henry
[1903] 2 K.B. 740 (C.A.)

[The defendant made a written agreement for the hire of a suite of rooms overlooking the coronation procession of Edward VII. The agreement did not expressly mention the procession, but both parties understood that this was the reason for the hire. The procession was cancelled, but the plaintiff nevertheless sued for the balance of the hire fee. The plaintiff appealed to the Court of Appeal against the trial judge's judgment for the defendant.]

Vaughan Williams L.J. The real question in this case is the extent of the application in English law of the principle of the Roman law which has been adopted and acted on in many English decisions, and notably in the case of *Taylor* v. *Caldwell* (1863). That case at least makes it clear that "where, from the nature of the contract, it appears that the parties must from the beginning have known that it could not be fulfilled unless, when the time for the fulfilment of the contract arrived, some particular specified thing continued to exist, so that when entering into the contract they must have contemplated such continued existence as the foundation of what was to be done; there, in the absence of any express or implied warranty that the thing shall exist, the contract is not to be considered a positive contract, but as subject to an implied condition that the parties shall be excused in case, before breach, performance becomes impossible from the perishing of the thing without default of the contractor." Thus far it is clear that the principle of the Roman law has been introduced into the English law. The doubt in the present case arises as to how far this principle extends. The Roman law dealt with obligationes de certo corpore. Whatever may have been the limits of the Roman law, the case of *Nickoll* v. *Ashton* (1901) makes it plain that the English law applies the principle not only to cases where the performance of the contract becomes impossible by the cessation of existence of the thing which is the subject-matter of the contract, but also to cases where the event which renders the contract incapable of performance is the cessation or non-existence of an express condition or state of things, going to the root of the contract, and essential to its performance. It is said, on the one side, that the specified thing, state of things, or condition the continued existence of which is necessary for the fulfilment of the contract, so that the parties entering into the contract must have contemplated the continued existence of that thing, condition, or state of things as the foundation of what was to be done under the contract, is limited to things which are either the subject-matter of the contract or a condition or state of things, present or anticipated, which is expressly mentioned in the contract. But, on the other side, it is said that the condition or state of things need not be expressly specified, but that it is sufficient if that condition or state of things clearly appears by extrinsic evidence to have been assumed by the parties to be the foundation or basis of the contract, and the event which causes the impossibility is of such a character that it cannot reasonably be supposed to have been in the contemplation of the contracting parties when the contract was made. In such a case the contracting parties will not be held bound by the general words which, though large enough to include, were not used with reference to a possibility of a particular event rendering performance of the contract impossible. I do not think that the principle of the civil law as introduced into the English law is limited to cases in which the event causing the impossibility of performance is the destruction or non-existence of some thing which is the subject-matter of the contract or of some condition or state of things expressly specified as a condition of it. I think that you first have to ascertain, not necessarily from the terms of the contract, but, if required, from necessary inferences, drawn from surrounding circumstances recognised by both contracting parties, what is the substance of the contract, and then to ask the question whether that substantial contract needs for its foundation the assumption of the existence of a particular state of things. If it does, this will limit the operation of the general words, and in such case, if the contract becomes impossible of performance by reason of the non-existence of the state of things assumed by both contracting parties as the foundation of the contract, there will be no breach of the contract thus limited. Now what are the facts of the present case?

[His Lordship stated them.]

In my judgment the use of the rooms was let and taken for the purpose of seeing the Royal procession. It was not a demise of the rooms, or even an agreement to let and take the rooms. It is a licence to use rooms for a particular purpose and none other. And in my judgment the taking place of those processions on the days proclaimed along the proclaimed route, which passed 56A, Pall Mall, was regarded by both contracting parties as the foundation of the contract; and I think that it cannot reasonably be supposed to have been in the contemplation of the contracting parties, when the contract was made, that the coronation would not be held on the proclaimed days, or the processions not take place on those days along the proclaimed route; and I think that the words imposing on the defendant the obligation to accept and pay for the use of the rooms for the named days, although general and unconditional, were not used with reference to the possibility of the particular contingency which afterwards occurred. It was suggested in the course of the argument that if the occurrence, on the proclaimed days, of the coronation and the procession in this case were the foundation of the contract, and if the general words are thereby limited or qualified, so that in the event of the non-occurrence of the coronation and procession along the proclaimed route they would discharge both parties from further performance of the contract, it would follow that if a cabman was engaged to take some one to Epsom on Derby Day at a suitable enhanced price for such a journey, say 10*l*., both parties to the contract would be discharged in the contingency of the race at Epsom for some reason becoming impossible; but I do not think this follows, for I do not think that in the cab case the happening of the race would be the foundation of the contract. No doubt the purpose of the engager would be to go to see the Derby, and the price would be proportionately high; but the cab had no special qualifications for the purpose which led to the selection of the cab for this particular occasion. Any other cab would have done as well. Moreover, I think that, under the cab contract, the hirer, even if the race went off, could have said, "Drive me to Epsom; I will pay you the agreed sum; you have nothing to do with the purpose for which I hired the cab," and that if the cabman refused he would have been guilty of a breach of contract, there being nothing to qualify his promise to drive the hirer to Epsom on a particular day. Whereas in the case of the coronation, there is not merely the purpose of the hirer to see the coronation procession, but it is the coronation procession and the relative position of the rooms which is the basis of the contract as much for the lessor as the hirer; and I think that if the King, before the coronation day and after the contract, had died, the hirer could not have insisted on having the rooms on the days named. It could not in the cab case be reasonably said that seeing the Derby race was the foundation of the contract, as it was of the licence in this case. Whereas in the present case, where the rooms were offered and taken; by reason of their peculiar suitability from the position of the rooms for a view of the coronation procession, surely the view of the coronation procession was the foundation of the contract, which is a very different thing from the purpose of the man who engaged the cab - namely, to see the race - being held to be the foundation of the contract. Each case must be judged by its own circumstances. In each case one must ask oneself, first, what, having regard to all the circumstances, was the foundation of the contract? Secondly, was the performance of the contract prevented? Thirdly, was the event which prevented the performance of the contract of such a character that it cannot reasonably be said to have been in the contemplation of the parties at the date of the contract? If all these questions are answered in the affirmative (as I think they should be in this case), I think both parties are discharged from further performance of the contract. I think that the coronation procession was the foundation of this contract, and that the non-happening of it prevented the performance of the contract; and, secondly, I think that the non-happening of the procession, to use the words of Sir James Hannen in *Baily* v. *De Crespigny* (1869) was an event "of such a character that it cannot reasonably be supposed to have been in the contemplation of the contracting parties when the contract was made, and that they are not to be held bound by general words which, though large enough to include, were not used with reference to the possibility of the particular contingency which afterwards happened." The test seems to be whether the event which causes the impossibility was or might have been anticipated and guarded against. It seems difficult to say, in a case where both parties anticipate the happening of an event, which anticipation is the foundation of the contract, that either party must be taken to have anticipated, and ought to have guarded against, the event which prevented the performance of the contract. In both *Jackson* v. *Union Marine Insurance Co.* (1874) and *Nickoll* v. *Ashton* (1901) the parties might have anticipated as a possibility that perils of the sea might delay the ship and frustrate the commercial venture: in the former case the carriage of the goods to effect which the charterparty was entered into; in the latter case the sale of the goods which were to be shipped on the steamship which was delayed. But the Court held in the former case that the basis of the contract was that the ship would arrive in time to carry out the contemplated commercial venture, and in the latter that the steamship would arrive in time for the loading of the goods the subject of the sale. I wish to observe that cases of this sort are very different from cases where a contract or warranty or representation is implied, such as was implied in *The Moorcock* (1889), and refused to be implied in *Hamlyn* v. *Wood* (1891). But *The Moorcock* is of importance in the present case as shewing that whatever is the suggested implication - be it condition, as in this case, or warranty or representation - one must, in judging whether the implication ought to be made, look not only at the words of the contract, but also at the surrounding Dacts and the knowledge of the parties of those facts. There seems to me to be ample authority for this proposition.

[His Lordship cited the relevant authorities.]

I see no difficulty whatever in the case. It is not essential to the application of the principle of *Taylor* v. *Caldwell* that the direct subject of the contract should perish or fail to be in existence at the date of performance of the contract. It is sufficient if a state of things or condition expressed in the contract and essential to its performance perishes or fails to be in existence at that time. In the present case the condition which fails and prevents the achievement of that which was, in the contemplation of both parties, the foundation of the contract, is not expressly mentioned either as a condition of the contract or the purpose of it; but I think for the reasons which I have given that the principle of *Taylor* v. *Caldwell* (1863) ought to be applied. This disposes of the plaintiff's claim for 50*l.* unpaid balance of the price agreed to be paid for the use of the rooms.

Judgment for the defendant.

Note

For an example of a "coronation case" in which it was held that the contract had not been frustrated, contrast *Herne Bay Steam Boat Company* v. *Hutton* (1903).

Fibrosa Spolka Akcyjna v. Fairbairn Lawson Combe Barbour Ltd.
[1943] A.C. 32 (H.L.)

[Fairbairn agreed to make some machinery for Fibrosa (a Polish company) in July 1939 for a price of £4,800. Of this amount £1,600 was payable in advance although only £1,000 was in fact paid over by Fibrosa. By September 1940 the place of delivery in Poland was under German occupation and the contract was therefore frustrated. Fibrosa claimed the return of their £1,000. The Court of Appeal rejected the claim relying on the authority of *Chandler* v. *Webster* (1904). This, another "coronation case", had stated that where money was payable before the frustrating event, it could not be recovered on the grounds that frustration only operated from the time of the frustrating event. It did not therefore affect rights which had accrued before this. Fibrosa appealed to the House of Lords.]

Viscount Simon L.C.

[Having considered the implications of *Chandler* v. *Webster* continued:]

If we are to approach this problem anew, it must be premised that the first matter to be considered is always the terms of the particular contract. If, for example, the contract is "divisible" in the sense that a sum is to be paid over in respect of completion of a defined portion of the work, it may well be that the sum is not returnable if completion of the whole work is frustrated. If the contract itself on its true construction stipulates for a particular result which is to follow in regard to money already paid, should frustration afterwards occur, this governs the matter. The ancient and firmly established rule that freight paid in advance is not returned if the completion of the voyage is frustrated: *Byrne* v. *Schiller* (1871) should, I think, be regarded as a stipulation introduced into such contracts by custom, and not as the result of applying some abstract principle. And so, a fortiori, if there is a stipulation that the prepayment is "out and out." To take an example, not from commerce, but from sport, the cricket spectator who pays for admission to see a match cannot recover the entrance money on the ground that rain has prevented play if, expressly or by proper implication, the bargain with him is that no money will be returned. Inasmuch as the effect of frustration may be explained as arising from an implied term: see *Joseph Constantine Steamship Line, Ld.* v. *Imperial Smelting Corporation Ld.* (1942); it is tempting to speculate whether a further term could be implied as to what was to happen, in the event of frustration, to money already paid, but, if the parties were assumed to have discussed the point when entering into the contract, they could not be supposed to have agreed on a simple formula which would be fair in all circumstances, and all that could be said is that, in the absence of such agreement, the law must decide. The question now to be determined is whether, in the absence of a term in the contract dealing with the matter, the rule which is commonly called the rule in *Chandler* v. *Webster* (1904) should be affirmed.

[His Lordship considered the case noting that it had been criticised.]

The locus classicus for the view which has hitherto prevailed is to be found in the judgment of Collins M.R. in *Chandler* v. *Webster*. It was not a considered judgment, but it is hardly necessary to say that I approach this pronouncement of the then Master of the Rolls with all the respect due to so distinguished a common lawyer. When his judgment is studied, however, one cannot but be impressed by the circumstance that he regarded the proposition that money in such cases could not be recovered back as flowing from the decision in *Taylor* v. *Caldwell* (1863). *Taylor* v. *Caldwell,* however, was not a case in which any question arose whether money could be recovered back, for there had been no payment in advance, and there is nothing in the judgment of Blackburn J., which, at any rate in terms, affirms the general proposition that "the loss lies where it falls." The application by Collins M.R. of *Taylor* v. *Caldwell* to the actual problem with which he had to deal in *Chandler* v. *Webster* deserves close examination. He said: "The plaintiff contends that he is entitled to recover the money which he had paid on the ground that there has been a total failure of consideration. He says that the condition on which he paid the money was that the procession should take place, and that, as it did not take place, there has been a total failure of consideration. That contention does no doubt raise a question of some difficulty, and one which has perplexed the courts to a considerable extent in several cases. The principle on which it has been dealt with is that which was applied in *Taylor* v. *Caldwell* – namely, that where, from causes outside the volition of the parties, something which was the basis of, or essential to the fulfilment of, the contract has become impossible, so that, from the time when the fact of that impossibility has been ascertained, the contract can no further be performed by either party, it remains a perfectly good contract up to that point, and everything previously done in pursuance of it must be treated as rightly done, but the parties are both discharged from further performance of it. If the effect were that the contract were wiped out altogether, no doubt the result would be that money paid under it would have to be repaid as on a failure of consideration. But that is not the effect of the doctrine; it only releases the parties from further performance of the contract. Therefore the doctrine of failure of consideration does not apply."

It appears to me that the reasoning in this crucial passage is open to two criticisms: (*a*) The claim of a party, who has paid money under a contract, to get the money back, on the ground that the consideration for which he paid it has totally failed, is not based on any provision contained in the contract, but arises because, in the circumstances that have happened, the law gives a remedy in quasi-contract to the party who has not got that for which he bargained. It is a claim to recover money to which the defendant has no further right because in the circumstances that have happened the money must be regarded as received to the plaintiff's use. It is true that the effect of frustration is that, while the contract can no further be performed, "it remains a perfectly good contract up to that point, and everything previously done in pursuance of it must be treated as rightly done," but it by no means follows that the situation existing at the moment of frustration is one which leaves the party that has paid money and has not received the stipulated consideration without any remedy. To claim the return of money paid on the ground of total failure of consideration is not to vary the terms of the contract in any way. The claim arises not because the right to be repaid is one of the stipulated conditions of the contract, but because, in the circumstances that have happened, the law gives the remedy. It is the failure to distinguish between the action of assumpsit for money had and received in a case where the consideration has wholly failed, and an action on the contract itself, which explains the mistake which I think has been made in applying English law to this subject-matter. Thus, in *Blakeley* v. *Muller & Co.* (1903), Lord Alverstone C.J. said, "I agree that *Taylor* v. *Caldwell* applies, but the consequence of that decision is that neither party here could have sued on the contract in respect of anything which was to be done under it after the procession had been abandoned." That is true enough, but it does not follow that because the plaintiff cannot sue "on the contract" he cannot sue dehors the contract for the recovery of a payment in respect of which consideration has failed. In the same case, Wills J. relied on *Appleby* v. *Myers* (1867) where a contract was made for the erection by A. of machinery on the premises of B., to be paid for on completion. There was no prepayment and in the course of the work the premises were destroyed by fire. It was held that both parties were excused from further performance, and that no liability accrued on either side, but the liability referred to was liability under the contract, and the learned judge seems to have thought that no action to recover money in such circumstances as the present could be conceived of unless there was a term of the contract, express or implied, which so provided. Once it is realized that the action to recover money for a consideration that has wholly failed rests, not on a contractual bargain between the parties, but, as Lord Sumner said in *Sinclair* v. *Brougham* (1914), "upon a notional or imputed promise to repay," or (if it is preferred to omit reference to a fictitious promise) upon an obligation to repay arising from the circumstances, the difficulty in the way of holding that a prepayment made under a contract which has been frustrated can be recovered back appears to me to disappear. (*b*) There is, no doubt, a distinction between cases in which a contract is "wiped out altogether," e.g., because it is void as being illegal from the start or as being due to fraud which the innocent party has elected to treat as avoiding the contract, and cases in which intervening impossibility "only releases the parties from further performance of the contract." But does the distinction between these two classes of case justify the deduction of Collins M.R. that "the doctrine of failure of consideration does not apply" where the contract remains a perfectly good contract up to the date of frustration? This conclusion seems to be derived from the view that, if the contract remains good and valid up to the moment of frustration, money which has already been paid under it cannot be regarded as having been paid for a consideration which has wholly failed. The party that has paid the money has had the advantage, whatever it may be worth, of the promise of the other party. That is true, but it is necessary to draw a distinction. In English law, an enforceable contract may be formed by an exchange of a promise for a promise, or by the exchange of a promise for an act - I am excluding contracts under seal - and thus, in the law relating to the formation of contract, the promise to do a thing may often be the consideration, but when one is considering the law of failure of consideration and of the quasi-contractual right to recover money on that ground, it is, generally speaking, not the promise which is referred to as the consideration, but the performance of the promise. The money was paid to secure performance and, if performance fails the inducement which brought about the payment is not fulfilled.

If this were not so, there could never be any recovery of money, for failure of consideration, by the payer of the money in return for a promise of future performance, yet there are endless examples which show that money can be recovered, as for a complete failure of consideration, in cases where the promise was given but could not be fulfilled. . . . A simple illustration of the same result is an agreement to buy a horse, the price to be paid down, but the horse not to be delivered and the property not to pass until the horse had been shod. If the horse dies before the shoeing, the price can unquestionably be recovered as for a total failure of consideration, notwithstanding that the promise to deliver was given. This is the case of a contract de certo corpore where the certum corpus perishes after the contract is made, but, as Vaughan Williams L.J.'s judgment in *Krell* v. *Henry* (1903) explained, the same doctrine applies "to cases where the event which renders the contract incapable of performance is the cessation or non-existence of an express condition or state of things, going to the root of the contract, and essential to its performance." I can see no valid reason why the right to recover prepaid money should not equally arise on frustration arising from supervening circumstances as it arises on frustration from destruction of a particular subject-matter. The conclusion is that the rule in *Chandler* v. *Webster* (1904) is wrong, and that the appellants can recover their 1000*l*.

While this result obviates the harshness with which the previous view in some instances treated the party who had made a prepayment, it cannot be regarded as dealing fairly between the parties in all cases, and must sometimes have the result of leaving the recipient who has to return the money at a grave disadvantage. He may have incurred expenses in connexion with the partial carrying out of the contract which are equivalent, or more than equivalent, to the money which he prudently stipulated should be prepaid, but which he now has to return for reasons which are no fault of his. He may have to repay the money, though he has executed almost the whole of the contractual work, which will be left on his hands. These results follow from the fact that the English common law does not undertake to apportion a prepaid sum in such circumstances . . . . It must be for the legislature to decide whether provision should be made for an equitable apportionment of prepaid moneys which have to be returned by the recipient in view of the frustration of the contract in respect of which they were paid. I move that the appeal be allowed, and that judgment be entered for the appellants.

[Lords Atkin, Russel, MacMillan, Wright, Roche and Porter concurred.]

Notes

The legislature's response to Viscount Simon's criticisms was the Law Reform (Frustrated Contracts) Act 1943, for which see p. 461. Since, however, this Act does not apply to every contract and may be excluded by the parties themselves, the common law remains important.

The somewhat complex provisions of this Act are subjected to a detailed and helpful commentary in the judgment of Robert Goff J. in *BP Exploration* v. *Hunt (No. 2)* (1979).

Question

How would the cases of *Cutter* v. *Powell* (see p. 412), and *Fibrosa* be decided under the terms of the 1943 Act?

Chapter 10

REMEDIES

1. REMOTENESS OF DAMAGE

**Victoria Laundry (Windsor) Ltd. v. Newman
Industries Ltd.**
[1949] 2 K.B. 528 (C.A.)

[The plaintiffs, who were launderers and dyers, required a larger boiler to expand
their business. The defendants agreed to install a boiler on June 5, 1946 but in
breach of contract it was not delivered until November 8, 1946. The plaintiffs
claimed under two heads: (i) £16 a week damages for loss of profits for the extra
custom they could have taken on, and (ii) £262 a week which they could have
obtained under certain lucrative contracts with the Ministry of Supply.]

Asquith L.J. [delivering the judgment of the court (Tucker,
Asquith and Singleton L.JJ.)] The authorities on recovery of
loss of profits as a head of damage are not easy to reconcile. At
one end of the scale stand cases where there has been non-
delivery or delayed delivery of what is on the face of it
obviously a profit-earning chattel; for instance, a merchant or
passenger ship: see *Fletcher* v. *Tayleur* (1855); *In re Trent and
Humber Company, ex parte Cambrian Steam Packet Company*
(1868); or some essential part of such a ship; for instance, a
propeller, in *Wilson* v. *General Ironscrew Company* (1887), or
engines, *Saint Line* v. *Richardson* (1940). In such cases loss of
profit has rarely been refused. A second and intermediate class
of case in which loss of profit has often been awarded is where
ordinary mercantile goods have been sold to a merchant with
knowledge by the vendor that the purchaser wanted them for
resale; at all events, where there was no market in which the
purchaser could buy similar goods against the contract on the
seller's default, see, for instance, *Borries* v. *Hutchinson* (1865).
At the other end of the scale are cases where the defendant is
not a vendor of the goods, but a carrier, see, for instance,
Hadley v. *Baxendale* (1854) and *Gee* v. *Lancashire and
Yorkshire Railway* (1860). In such cases the courts have been
slow to allow loss of profit as an item of damage. This was not,
it would seem, because a different principle applies in such
cases, but because the application of the same principle leads to

different results. A carrier commonly knows less than a seller
about the purposes for which the buyer or consignee needs the
goods, or about other "special circumstances" which may cause
exceptional loss if due delivery is withheld.

Three of the authorities call for more detailed examination.
First comes *Hadley* v. *Baxendale* (1854) itself. Familiar though
it is, we should first recall the memorable sentence in which the
main principles laid down in the case are enshrined: "Where
two parties have made a contract which one of them has
broken, the damages which the other party ought to receive in
respect of such breach of contract should be such as may fairly
and reasonably be considered as either arising naturally, *i.e.*
according to the usual course of things, from such breach of
contract itself, or such as may reasonably be supposed to have
been in the contemplation of both parties, at the time they
made the contract, as the probable "result of the breach of it."
The limb of this sentence prefaced by "either" embodies the
so-called "first" rule that prefaced by "or" the "second." In
considering the meaning and application of these rules, it is
essential to bear clearly in mind the facts on which *Hadley* v.
Baxendale (1854) proceeded. The head-note is definitely
misleading in so far as it says that the defendant's clerk, who
attended at the office, was told that the mill was stopped and
that the shaft must be delivered immediately. The same
allegation figures in the statement of facts which are said ... to
have "appeared" at the trial before Crompton J. If the Court of
Exchequer had accepted these facts as established, the court
must, one would suppose, have decided the case the other way
round; must, that is, have held the damage claimed was
recoverable under the second rule. But it is reasonably plain
from Alderson B's judgment that the court rejected this
evidence, for ... he says: "We find that the only circumstances
here communicated by the plaintiffs to the defendants at the
time when the contract was made were that the article to be
carried was the broken shaft of a mill and that the plaintiffs
were the millers of that mill," and it is on this basis of fact that
he proceeds to ask, "How do these circumstances show
reasonably that the profits of the mill must be stopped by an
unreasonable delay in the delivery "of the broken shaft by the
carrier to the third person?"

British Columbia Sawmills v. *Nettleship* (1868) annexes to
the principle laid down in *Hadley* v. *Baxendale* (1854) a rider
to the effect that where knowledge of special circumstances is
relied on as enhancing the damage recoverable that knowledge

must have been brought home to the defendant at the time of the contract and in such circumstances that the defendant impliedly undertook to bear any special loss referable to a breach in those special circumstances. The knowledge which was lacking in that case on the part of the defendant was knowledge that the particular box of machinery negligently lost by the defendants was one without which the rest of the machinery could not be put together and would therefore be useless.

Cory v. *Thames Ironworks Company* (1868) - a case strongly relied on by the plaintiffs - presented the peculiarity that the parties contemplated respectively different profit-making uses of the chattel sold by the defendant to the plaintiff. It was the hull of a boom derrick, and was delivered late. The plaintiffs were coal merchants, and the obvious use, and that to which the defendants believed it was to be put, was that of a coal store. The plaintiffs, on the other hand, the buyers, in fact intended to use it for transhipping coals from colliers to barges, a quite unprecedented use for a chattel of this kind, one quite unsuspected by the sellers and one calculated to yield much higher profits. The case accordingly decides, inter alia, what is the measure of damage recoverable when the parties are not ad idem in their contemplation of the use for which the article is needed. It was decided that in such a case no loss was recoverable beyond what would have resulted if the intended use had been that reasonably within the contemplation of the defendants, which in that case was the "obvious" use. This special complicating factor, the divergence between the knowledge and contemplation of the parties respectively, has somewhat obscured the general importance of the decision, which is in effect that the facts of the case brought it within the first rule of *Hadley* v. *Baxendale* (1854) and enabled the plaintiff to recover loss of such profits as would have arisen from the normal and obvious use of the article. The "natural consequence," said Blackburn J., of not delivering the derrick was that 420*l*. representing those normal profits was lost. Cockburn C.J., interposing during the argument, made the significant observation: "No doubt in order to recover damage arising from a special purpose the buyer must have communicated the special purpose to the seller; but there is one thing which must always be in the knowledge of both parties, which is that the thing is bought for the purpose of being in some way or other profitably applied." This observation is apposite to the present case. These three cases have on many occasions been approved by the House of Lords without any material qualification.

What propositions applicable to the present case emerge from the authorities as a whole, including those analysed above? We think they include the following: -

(1.) It is well settled that the governing purpose of damages is to put the party whose rights have been violated in the same position so far as money can do so, as if his rights had been observed: (*Sally Wertheim* v. *Chicoutimi Pulp Company* (1911)). This purpose, if relentlessly pursued, would provide him with a complete indemnity for all loss de facto resulting from a particular breach, however improbable, however unpredictable. This, in contract at least, is recognized as too harsh a rule. Hence,

(2.) In cases of breach of contract the aggrieved party is only entitled to recover such part of the loss actually resulting as was at the time of the contract reasonably forseeable as liable to result from the breach.

(3.) What was at that time reasonably so foreseeable depends on the knowledge then possessed by the parties or, at all events, by the party who later commits the breach.

(4.) For this purpose, knowledge "possessed" is of two kinds; one imputed, the other actual. Everyone, as a reasonable person, is taken to know the "ordinary course of things" and consequently what loss is liable to result from a breach of contract in that ordinary course. This is the subject matter of the "first rule" in *Hadley* v. *Baxendale*. But to this knowledge, which a contract-breaker is assumed to possess whether he actually possesses it or not, there may have to be added in a particular case knowledge which he actually possesses, of special circumstances outside the "ordinary course of things," of such a kind that a breach in those special circumstances would be liable to cause more loss. Such a case attracts the operation of the "second rule" so as to make additional loss also recoverable.

(5.) In order to make the contract-breaker liable under either rule it is not necessary that he should actually have asked himself what loss is liable to result from a breach. As has often been pointed out, parties at the time of contracting contemplate not the breach of the contract, but its performance. It suffices that, if he had considered the question, he would as a reasonable man have concluded that the loss in question was liable to result (see certain observations of Lord du Parcq in the recent case of *A/B Karlshamns*

Oljefabriker v. *Monarch Steamship Company Limited* (1949)).

(6.) Nor, finally, to make a particular loss recoverable, need it be proved that upon a given state of knowledge the defendant could, as a reasonable man, foresee that a breach must necessarily result in that loss. It is enough if he could foresee it was likely so to result. It is indeed enough, to borrow from the language of Lord du Parcq in the same case, . . . if the loss (or some factor without which it would not have occurred) is a "serious possibility" or a "real danger." For short, we have used the word "liable" to result. Possibly the colloquialism "on the cards" indicates the shade of meaning with some approach to accuracy.

If these, indeed, are the principles applicable, what is the effect of their application to the facts of this case?

[The court held that the defendants, as an engineering company who were not therefore mere "laymen" in the matter, could reasonably foresee that loss of business profit would result from the delay in delivery. They were not, however, aware of the especially lucrative supply contract and so were not liable for the loss of profits on those contracts.]

Note

The principles of the rule in *Hadley* v. *Baxendale* were subsequently considered by the House of Lords in *Koufos* v. *C. Czarnikow Ltd. (The Heron II)* (1969). The judgments, although refining it somewhat, appear to leave the principles of the rule essentially intact.

2. QUANTIFICATION

Chaplin v. Hicks
[1911] 2 K.B. 786 (C.A.)

[The defendant agreed with the plaintiff that if she attended an audition along with 49 other actresses she would have the chance of being one of the 12 chosen for employment as an actress. The plaintiff, in breach of contract, failed to give her a reasonable opportunity to attend but claimed that only nominal damages could be recovered for a loss of such a speculative kind.]

Vaughan Williams L.J. It was said that the plaintiff's chance of winning a prize turned on such a number of contingencies that it was impossible for any one, even after arriving at the conclusion that the plaintiff had lost her opportunity by the breach, to say that there was any assessable value of that loss. It is said that in a case which involves so many contingencies it is impossible to say what was the plaintiff's pecuniary loss. I am unable to agree with that contention. I agree that the presence of all the contingencies upon which the gaining of the prize might depend makes the calculation not only difficult but incapable of being carried out with certainty or precision. The proposition is that, whenever the contingencies on which the result depends are numerous and difficult to deal with, it is impossible to recover any damages for the loss of the chance or opportunity of winning the prize. In the present case I understand that there were fifty selected competitors, of whom the plaintiff was one, and twelve prizes, so that the average chance of each competitor was about one in four. Then it is said that the questions which might arise in the minds of the judges are so numerous that it is impossible to say that the case is one in which it is possible to apply the doctrine of averages at all. I do not agree with the contention that, if certainty is impossible of attainment, the damages for a breach of contract are unassessable. I agree, however, that damages might be so unassessable that the doctrine of averages would be inapplicable because the necessary figures for working upon would not be forthcoming; there are several decisions, which I need not deal with, to that effect. I only wish to deny with emphasis that, because precision cannot be arrived at, the jury has no function in the assessment of damages.

In early days when it was necessary to assess damages, no rules were laid down by the Courts to guide juries in the assessment of damages for breach of contract; it was left to the jury absolutely. But in course of time judges began to give advice to juries; as the stress of commerce increased, let us say between the reigns of Queen Elizabeth and Queen Victoria, rule after rule was suggested by way of advice to juries by the judges when damages for breach of contract had to be assessed. But from first to last there were, as there are now, many cases in which it was difficult to apply definite rules. In the case of a breach of a contract for the delivery of goods the damages are usually supplied by the fact of there being a market in which similar goods can be immediately bought, and the difference between the contract price and the price given for the substituted goods in the open market is the measure of damages; that rule has been always recognized. Sometimes, however, there is no market for the particular class of goods; but no one has ever suggested that, because there is no market, there are no damages. In such a case the jury must do the best they can, and it may be that the amount of their verdict will really be a matter of guesswork. But the fact that damages cannot be assessed with certainty does not relieve the wrong-doer of the necessity of paying damages for his breach of contract. I do not wish to lay down any such rule as that a judge can in every case leave it to the jury to assess damages for a breach of contract. There are cases, no doubt, where the loss is so dependent on the mere unrestricted volition of another that it is impossible to say that there is any assessable loss resulting from the breach. In the present case there is no such difficulty. It is true that no market can be said to exist. None of the fifty competitors could have gone into the market and sold her right; her right was a personal right and incapable of transfer. But a jury might well take the view that such a right, if it could have been transferred, would have been of such a value that every one could recognize that a good price could be obtained for it. My view is that under such circumstances as those in this case the assessment of damages was unquestionably for the jury. The jury came to the conclusion that the taking away from the plaintiff of the opportunity of competition, as one of a body of fifty, when twelve prizes were to be distributed, deprived the plaintiff of something which had a monetary value. I think that they were right and that this appeal fails.

Note

For another example of the courts' willingness to award damages in cases where exact quantification is difficult or impossible, see *Jackson* v. *Horizon Holidays* above, p. 397.

3. *AGREED DAMAGES AND PENALTIES*

Dunlop Pneumatic Tyre Co. Ltd. v. New Garage and Motor Co. Ltd.
[1915] A.C. 79 (H.L.)

Lord Dunedin. I do not think it is advisable to attempt any detailed review of the various cases, but I shall content myself with stating succinctly the various propositions which I think are deducible from the decisions which rank as authoritative: -

1. Though the parties to a contract who use the words "penalty" or "liquidated damages" may prima facie be supposed to mean what they say, yet the expression used is not conclusive. The Court must find out whether the payment stipulated is in truth a penalty or liquidated damages. This doctrine may be said to be found passim in nearly every case.
2. The essence of a penalty is a payment of money stipulated as in terrorem of the offending party; the essence of liquidated damages is a genuine covenanted pre-estimate of damage

(*Clydebank Engineering and Shipbuilding Co.* v. *Don Jose Ramos Yzquierdo y Castaneda* (1905)).

3. The question whether a sum stipulated is penalty or liquidated damages is a question of construction to be decided upon the terms and inherent circumstances of each particular contract, judged of as at the time of the making of the contract, not as at the time of the breach (*Public Works Commissioner* v. *Hills* (1906) and *Webster* v. *Bosanquet* (1912)).

4. To assist this task of construction various tests have been suggested, which if applicable to the case under consideration may prove helpful, or even conclusive. Such are:

(*a*) It will be held to be penalty if the sum stipulated for is extravagant and unconscionable in amount in comparison with the greatest loss that could conceivably be proved to have followed from the breach. (Illustration given by Lord Halsbury in *Clydebank Case*).

(*b*) It will be held to be a penalty if the breach consists only in not paying a sum of money, and the sum stipulated is a sum greater than the sum which ought to have been paid (*Kemble* v. *Farren* (1829)). This though one of the most ancient instances is truly a corollary to the last test. Whether it had its historical origin in the doctrine of the common law that when A. promised to pay B. a sum of money on a certain day and did not do so, B. could only recover the sum with, in certain cases, interest, but could never recover further damages for non-timeous payment, or whether it was a survival of the time when equity reformed unconscionable bargains merely because they were unconscionable, - a subject which much exercised Jessel M.R. in *Wallis* v. *Smith* (1882) - is probably more interesting than material.

(*c*) There is a presumption (but no more) that it is penalty when "a single lump sum is made payable by way of compensation, on the occurrence of one or more or all of several events, some of which may occasion serious and others but trifling damage" (Lord Watson in *Lord Elphinstone* v. *Monkland Iron and Coal Co.* (1886)).

On the other hand:

(*d*) It is no obstacle to the sum stipulated being a genuine pre-estimate of damage, that the consequences of the breach are such as to make precise pre-estimation almost an impossibility. On the contrary, that is just the situation when it is probable that pre-estimated damage was the true bargain between the parties (*Clydebank Case*, Lord Halsbury; *Webster* v. *Bosanquet*, Lord Mersey (1912)).

4. MITIGATION

Pilkington v. Wood
[*1953*] *Ch. 770 (Ch.)*

[The plaintiff's solicitor, the defendant, who had acted for him in the purchase of a house, had negligently and in breach of contract failed to notice that there was a defect in the title to the property. The only issue was as to the measure of damages.]

Harman J. It would appear then at first sight that the measure of the defendant's liability is the diminution in value of the property; that is to say, the difference between the value in 1950, the date of the plaintiff's purchase of the property with a good title and with the title which it in fact had.

The defendant, however, argues that it is the duty of the plaintiff before suing him in damages to seek to recover damages against his vendor Colonel Wilks under the covenant for title implied by reason of the conveyance as beneficial owner. It is said that this duty arises because of the obligation which rests on a person injured by a breach of contract to mitigate the damages. This suggestion seems to me to carry the doctrine of mitigation a stage further than it has been carried in any case to which I have been referred. The classic statement of the doctrine is that of Lord Haldane in *British Westinghouse Electric and Manufacturing Co. Ld.* v. *Underground Electric Railways Company of London Ld.* (1912) The Lord Chancellor expressed it thus:

"The quantum of damage is a question of fact, and the only guidance the law can give is to lay down general principles which afford at times but scanty assistance in dealing with particular cases. The judges who give guidance to juries in these cases have necessarily to look at their special character, and to mould, for the purposes of different kinds of claim, the expression of the general principles which apply to them, and this is apt to give rise to an appearance of ambiguity. Subject to these observations I think that there are certain broad principles which are quite well settled. The first is that, as far as possible, he who has proved a breach of a bargain to supply what he contracted to get is to be placed, as far as money can do it, in as good a situation as if the contract had been performed. The fundamental basis is thus compensation for pecuniary loss naturally flowing from the breach; but this first principle is qualified by a second, which imposes on a plaintiff the duty of taking all reasonable steps to mitigate the loss consequent on the breach, and debars him from claiming any part of the damage which is due to his neglect to take such steps. In the words of James L.J. in *Dunkirk Colliery Co.* v. *Lever (1878)*, 'the person who has broken the contract is not to be exposed to additional cost by reason of the plaintiffs not doing what they ought to have done as reasonable men, and the plaintiffs not being under any obligation to do anything otherwise than in the ordinary course of business.' "

For the present purpose it seems to me that it is apposite to state the plaintiff's rights in the words of Scrutton L.J. in *Payzu Ld.* v. *Saunders* (1919) thus: "he can recover no more than he would have suffered if he had acted reasonably, because any further damages do not reasonably follow from the defendant's breach. . . . "

Ought then the plaintiff as a reasonable man to enter on the litigation suggested? It was agreed that the defendant must offer him an indemnity against the costs, and it was suggested on the defendant's behalf that if an adequate indemnity were offered, if, secondly, the proposed defendant appeared to be solvent, and if, thirdly, there were a good prima facie right of action against that person, it was the duty of the injured party to embark on litigation in order to mitigate the damage suffered. This is a proposition which, in such general terms, I am not prepared to accept, nor do I think I ought to entertain it here, because I am by no means certain that the foundations for it exist.

It may be conceded that the indemnity offered would be adequate and that Colonel Wilks is a man of substance. It was clear, however, that he would resist any claim and would in his turn claim over against his solicitors, for that was his attitude in the witness-box.

About the third condition much more doubt exists.

[His Lordship discussed the point.]

I do not propose to attempt to decide whether an action against Colonel Wilks would lie or be fruitful. I can see it would be one attended with no little difficulty. I am of opinion that the so-called duty to mitigate does not go so far as to oblige the injured party, even under an indemnity, to embark on a complicated and difficult piece of litigation against a third party. The damage to the plaintiff was done once and for all *directly* the voidable conveyance to him was executed. This was the direct result of the negligent advice tendered by his solicitor, the defendant, that a good title had been shown; and, in my judgment, it is no part of the plaintiff's duty to embark on the proposed litigation in order to protect his solicitor from the consequences of his own carelessness.

Chapter 11

SELECTED STATUTES

Law of Property Act 1925

40. - (1) No action may be brought upon any contract for the sale or other disposition of land or any interest in land, unless the agreement upon which such action is brought, or some memorandum or note thereof, is in writing, and signed by the party to be charged or by some other person thereunto by him lawfully authorised.

Law Reform (Frustrated Contracts) Act 1943

Adjustment of rights and liabilities of parties to frustrated contracts

1. - (1) Where a contract governed by English law has become impossible of performance or been otherwise frustrated, and the parties thereto have for that reason been discharged from the further performance of the contract, the following provisions of this section shall, subject to the provisions of section two of this Act, have effect in relation thereto.

(2) All sums paid or payable to any party in pursuance of the contract before the time when the parties were so discharged (in this Act referred to as "the time of discharge") shall, in the case of sums so paid, be recoverable from him as money received by him for the use of the party by whom the sums were paid, and, in the case of sums so payable, cease to be so payable:

Provided that, if the party to whom the sums were so paid or payable incurred expenses before the time of discharge in, or for the purpose of, the performance of the contract, the court may, if it considers it just to do so having regard to all the circumstances of the case, allow him to retain or, as the case may be, recover the whole or any part of the sums so paid or payable, not being an amount in excess of the expenses so incurred.

(3) Where any party to the contract has, by reason of anything done by any other party thereto in, or for the purpose of, the

performance of the contract, obtained a valuable benefit (other than a payment of money to which the last foregoing subsection applies) before the time of discharge, there shall be recoverable from him by the said party such sum (if any), not exceeding the value of the said benefit to the party obtaining it, as the court considers just, having regard to all the circumstances of the case and, in particular, -

(*a*)   the amount of any expenses incurred before the time of discharge by the benefited party in, or for the purpose of, the performance of the contract, including any sums paid or payable by him to any other party in pursuance of the contract and retained or recoverable by that party under the last foregoing subsection, and

(*b*)   the effect, in relation to the said benefit, of the circumstances giving rise to the frustration of the contract.

(4) In estimating, for the purposes of the foregoing provisions of this section, the amount of any expenses incurred by any party to the contract, the court may, without prejudice to the generality of the said provisions, include such sums as appears to be reasonable in respect of overhead expenses and in respect of any work or services performed personally by the said party.

(5) In considering whether any sum ought to be recovered or retained under the foregoing provisions of this section by any party to the contract, the court shall not take into account any sums which have, by reason of the circumstances giving rise to the frustration of the contract, become payable to that party under any contract of insurance unless there was an obligation to insure imposed by an express term of the frustrated contract or by or under any enactment.

(6) Where any person has assumed obligations under the contract in consideration of the conferring of a benefit by any other party to the contract upon any other person, whether a party to the contract or not, the court may, if in all the circumstances of the case it considers it just to do so, treat for the purposes of subsection (3) of this section any benefit so conferred as a benefit obtained by the person who has assumed the obligations as aforesaid.

Provision as to application of this Act

2. - (1) This Act shall apply to contracts, whether made before or after the commencement of this Act, as respects which the time of discharge is on or after the first day of July, nineteen hundred and forty-three, but not to contracts as respects which the time of discharge is before the said date.

(2) This Act shall apply to contracts to which the Crown is a party in like manner as to contracts between subjects.

(3) Where any contract to which this Act applies contains any provision which, upon the true construction of the contract, is intended to have effect in the event of circumstances arising which operate, or would but for the said provision operate, to frustrate the contract, or is intended to have effect whether such circumstances arise or not, the court shall give effect to the said provision and shall only give effect to the foregoing section of this Act to such extent, if any, as appears to the court to be consistent with the said provision.

(4) Where it appears to the court that a part of any contract to which this Act applies can properly be severed from the remainder of the contract, being a part wholly performed before the time of discharge, or so performed except for the payment in respect of that part of the contract of sums which are or can be ascertained under the contract, the court shall treat that part of the contract as if it were a separate contract and had not been frustrated and shall treat the foregoing section of this Act as only applicable to the remainder of that contract.

(5) This Act shall not apply -

(*a*)   to any charterparty, except a time charterparty or a charterparty by way of demise, or to any contract (other than a charterparty) for the carriage of goods by sea; or

(*b*)   to any contract of insurance, save as is provided by subsection (5) of the foregoing section; or

(*c*)   to any contract to which section seven of the Sale of Goods Act, 1893 (which avoids contracts for the sale of specific goods which perish before the risk has passed to the buyer) applies, or to any other contract for the sale, or for the sale and delivery, of specific goods, where the contract is frustrated by reason of the fact that the goods have perished.

Misrepresentation Act 1967

Removal of certain bars to rescission for innocent misrepresentation

1. - Where a person has entered into a contract after a misrepresentation has been made to him, and -

(*a*)   the misrepresentation has become a term of the contract; or

(*b*)   the contract has been performed;

or both, then, if otherwise he would be entitled to rescind the contract without alleging fraud, he shall be so entitled, subject to the provisions of this Act, notwithstanding the matters mentioned in paragraphs (*a*) and (*b*) of this section.

Damages for misrepresentation

2. - (1) Where a person has entered into a contract after a misrepresentation has been made to him by another party thereto and as a result thereof he has suffered loss, then, if the person making the misrepresentation would be liable to damages in respect thereof had the misrepresentation been made fraudulently, that person shall be so liable notwithstanding that the misrepresentation was not made fraudulently, unless he proves that he had reasonable ground to believe and did believe up to the time the contract was made that the facts represented were true.

(2) Where a person has entered into a contract after a misrepresentation has been made to him otherwise than fraudulently, and he would be entitled, by reason of the misrepresentation, to rescind the contract, then, if it is claimed, in any proceedings arising out of the contract, that the contract ought to be or has been rescinded the court or arbitrator may declare the contract subsisting and award damages in lieu of rescission, if of opinion that it would be equitable to do so, having regard to the nature of the misrepresentation and the loss that would be caused by it if the contract were upheld, as well as to the loss that rescission would cause to the other party.

(3) Damages may be awarded against a person under subsection (2) of this section whether or not he is liable to damages under subsection (1) thereof, but where he is so liable any award under the said subsection (2) shall be taken into account in assessing his liability under the said subsection (1).

Avoidance of certain provisions excluding liability for misrepresentation

3. - If a contract contains a term which would exclude or restrict -

(a) any liability to which a party to a contract may be subject by reason of any misrepresentation made by him before the contract was made; or

(b) any remedy available to another party to the contract by reason of such a misrepresentation,

that term shall be of no effect except in so far as it satisfies the requirement of reasonableness as stated in section 11(1) of the Unfair Contract Terms Act 1977; and it is for those claiming that the term satisfies that requirement to show that it does.

Unsolicited Goods and Services Act 1971

Rights of recipient of unsolicited goods

1. - (1) In the circumstances specified in the following subsection, a person who after the commencement of this Act receives unsolicited goods, may as between himself and the sender, use, deal with or dispose of them as if they were an unconditional gift to him, and any right of the sender to the goods shall be extinguished.

(2) The circumstances referred to in the preceding subsection are that the goods were sent to the recipient with a view to his acquiring them, that the recipient has no reasonable cause to believe that they were sent with a view to their being acquired for the purposes of a trade or business and has neither agreed to acquire nor agreed to return them, and either -

(a) that during the period of six months beginning with the day on which the recipient received the goods the sender did not take possession of them and the recipient did not unreasonably refuse to permit the sender to do so; or

(b) that not less than thirty days before the expiration of the period aforesaid the recipient gave notice to the sender in accordance with the following subsection, and that during the period of thirty days beginning with the day on which the notice was given the sender did not take possession of the goods and the recipient did not unreasonably refuse to permit the sender to do so.

(3) A notice in pursuance of the preceding subsection shall be in writing and shall –

(*a*)   state the recipient's name and address and, if possession of the goods in question may not be taken by the sender at that address, the address at which it may be so taken;

(*b*)   contain a statement, however expressed, that the goods are unsolicited,

and may be sent by post.

(4) In this section "sender," in relation to any goods, includes any person on whose behalf or with whose consent the goods are sent, and any other person claiming through or under the sender or any such person.

Demands and threats regarding payment

2. – (1) A person who, not having reasonable cause to believe there is a right to payment, in the course of any trade or business makes a demand for payment, or asserts a present or prospective right to payment, for what he knows are unsolicited goods sent (after the commencement of this Act) to another person with a view to his acquiring them, shall be guilty of an offence and on summary conviction shall be liable to a fine not exceeding [level 4 on the standard scale].

(2) A person who, not having reasonable cause to believe there is a right to payment, in the course of any trade or business and with a view to obtaining any payment for what he knows are unsolicited goods sent as aforesaid –

(*a*)   threatens to bring any legal proceedings; or

(*b*)   places or causes to be placed the name of any person on a list of defaulters or debtors or threatens to do so; or

(*c*)   invokes or causes to be invoked any other collection procedure or threatens to do so,

shall be guilty of an offence and shall be liable on summary conviction to a fine not exceeding [level 5 on the standard scale].

Unfair Contract Terms Act 1977

Negligence liability

2. - (1) A person cannot by reference to any contract term or to a notice given to persons generally or to particular persons exclude or restrict his liability for death or personal injury resulting from negligence.

(2) In the case of other loss or damage, a person cannot so exclude or restrict his liability for negligence except in so far as the term or notice satisfies the requirement of reasonableness.

(3) Where a contract term or notice purports to exclude or restrict liability for negligence a person's agreement to or awareness of it is not of itself to be taken as indicating his voluntary acceptance of any risk.

Liability arising in contract

3. - (1) This section applies as between contracting parties where one of them deals as consumer or on the other's written standard terms of business.

(2) As against that party, the other cannot by reference to any contract term -

(*a*)   when himself in breach of contract, exclude or restrict any liability of his in respect of the breach; or

(*b*)   claim to be entitled -

  (i)   to render a contractual performance substantially different from that which was reasonably expected of him, or

  (ii)   in respect of the whole or any part of his contractual obligation, to render no performance at all,

except in so far (in any of the cases mentioned above in this subsection) the contract term satisfies the requirement of reasonableness.

. . . . .

Sale and hire-purchase

6. - (1) Liability for breach of the obligations arising from -

(*a*)   section 12 of the Sale of Goods Act 1979 (seller's implied undertakings as to title, etc.);

(*b*)   section 8 of the Supply of Goods (Implied Terms) Act 1973 (the corresponding thing in relation to hire-purchase),

cannot be excluded or restricted by reference to any contract term.

(2) As against a person dealing as consumer, liability for breach of the obligations arising from –

(*a*)   section 13, 14 or 15 of the 1979 Act (seller's implied undertakings as to conformity of goods with description or sample, or as to their quality or fitness for a particular purpose);

(*b*)   section 9, 10 or 11 of the 1973 Act (the corresponding things in relation to hire-purchase),

cannot be excluded or restricted by reference to any contract term.

(3) As against a person dealing otherwise than as consumer, the liability specified in subsection (2) above can be excluded or restricted by reference to a contract term, but only in so far as the term satisfies the requirement of reasonableness.

(4) The liabilities referred to in this section are not only the business liabilities defined by section 1(3), but include those arising under any contract of sale of goods or hire-purchase agreement.

. . . . .

The "reasonableness" test

11. – (1) In relation to a contract term, the requirement of reasonableness for the purposes of this Part of this Act, section 3 of the Misrepresentation Act 1967 and section 3 of the Misrepresentation Act (Northern Ireland) 1967 is that the term shall have been a fair and reasonable one to be included having regard to the circumstances which were, or ought reasonably to have been, known to or in the contemplation of the parties when the contract was made.

(2) In determining for the purposes of section 6 or 7 above whether a contract term satisfies the requirement of reasonableness, regard shall be had in particular to the matters specified in Schedule 2 to this Act; but this subsection does not prevent the court or arbitrator from holding, in accordance with any rule of law, that a term which purports to exclude or restrict any relevant liability is not a term of the contract.

(3) In relation to a notice (not being a notice having contractual effect), the requirement of reasonableness under this Act is that it should be fair and reasonable to allow reliance on it, having regard to all the circumstances obtaining when the liability arose or (but for the notice) would have arisen.

(4) Where by reference to a contract term or notice a person seeks to restrict liability to a specified sum of money, and the question arises (under this or any other Act) whether the term or notice satisfies the requirement of reasonableness, regard shall be had in particular (but without prejudice to subsection (2) above in the case of contract terms) to -

(*a*) the resources which he could expect to be available to him for the purpose of meeting the liability should it arise; and

(*b*) how far it was open to him to cover himself by insurance.

(5) It is for those claiming that a contract term or notice satisfies the requirement of reasonableness to show that it does.

"Dealing as consumer"

12. - (1) A party to a contract "deals as consumer" in relation to another party if -

(*a*) he neither makes the contract in the course of a business nor holds himself out as doing so; and

(*b*) the other party does make the contract in the course of a business; and

(*c*) in the case of a contract governed by the law of sale of goods or hire-purchase, or by section 7 of this Act, the goods passing under or in pursuance of the contract are of a type ordinarily supplied for private use or consumption.

(2) But on a sale by auction or by competitive tender the buyer is not in any circumstances to be regarded as dealing as consumer.

(3) Subject to this, it is for those claiming that a party does not deal as consumer to show that he does not.

Varieties of exemption clause

13. - (1) To the extent that this Part of this Act prevents the exclusion or restriction of any liability it also prevents -

(*a*)   making the liability or its enforcement subject to restrictive or onerous conditions;

(*b*)   excluding or restricting any right or remedy in respect of the liability, or subjecting a person to any prejudice in consequence of his pursuing any such right or remedy;

(*c*)   excluding or restricting rules of evidence or procedure;

and (to that extent) sections 2 and 5 to 7 also prevent excluding or restricting liability by reference to terms and notices which exclude or restrict the relevant obligation or duty.

(2) But an agreement in writing to submit present or future differences to arbitration is not to be treated under this Part of this Act as excluding or restricting any liability.

. . . . .

SCHEDULE 2

"GUIDELINES" FOR APPLICATION OF REASONABLENESS TEST

The matters to which regard is to be had in particular for the purposes of sections 6(3), 7(3) and (4), 20 and 21 are any of the following which appear to be relevant –

(*a*)   the strength of the bargaining positions of the parties relative to each other, taking into account (among other things) alternative means by which the customer's requirements could have been met;

(*b*)   whether the customer received an inducement to agree to the term, or in accepting it had an opportunity of entering into a similar contract with other persons, but without having to accept a similar term;

(*c*)   whether the customer knew or ought reasonably to have known of the existence and extent of the term (having regard, among other things, to any custom of the trade and any previous course of dealing between the parties);

(*d*)   where the term excludes or restricts any relevant liability if some condition is not complied with, whether it was reasonable at the time of the contract to expect that compliance with that condition would be practicable;

(*e*)   whether the goods were manufactured, processed or adapted to the special order of the customer.

Sale of Goods Act 1979

Goods which have perished
6. Where there is a contract for the sale of specific goods, and the goods without the knowledge of the seller have perished at the time when the contract is made, the contract is void.

Implied terms about title, etc.
12. - (1) In a contract of sale, other than one to which subsection (3) below applies, there is an implied condition on the part of the seller that in the case of a sale he has a right to sell the goods, and in the case of an agreement to sell he will have such a right at the time when the property is to pass.

(2) In a contract of sale, other than one to which subsection (3) below applies, there is also an implied warranty that -

(*a*)   the goods are free, and will remain free until the time when the property is to pass, from any charge or encumbrance not disclosed or known to the buyer before the contract is made, and

(*b*)   the buyer will enjoy quiet possession of the goods except so far as it may be disturbed by the owner or other person entitled to the benefit of any charge or encumbrance so disclosed or known.

(3) This subsection applies to a contract of sale in the case of which there appears from the contract or is to be inferred from its circumstances an intention that the seller should transfer only such title as he or a third person may have.

(4) In a contract to which subsection (3) above applies there is an implied warranty that all charges or encumbrances known to the seller and not known to the buyer have been disclosed to the buyer before the contract is made.

(5) In a contract to which subsection (3) above applies there is also an implied warranty that none of the following will disturb the buyer's quiet possession of the goods, namely-

(*a*)   the seller;

(*b*)   in a case where the parties to the contract intend that the seller should transfer only such title as a third person may have, that person;

(*c*)   anyone claiming through or under the seller or that third person otherwise than under a charge or encumbrance disclosed or known to the buyer before the contract is made.

(6) . . .

Sale by description

13. - (1) Where there is a contract for the sale of goods by description, there is an implied condition that the goods will correspond with the description.

(2) If the sale is by sample as well as by description it is not sufficient that the bulk of the goods corresponds with the sample if the goods do not also correspond with the description.

(3) A sale of goods is not prevented from being a sale by description by reason only that, being exposed for sale or hire, they are selected by the buyer.

(4) . . .

Implied terms about quality or fitness

14. - (1) Except as provided by this section and section 15 below and subject to any other enactment, there is no implied condition or warranty about the quality or fitness for any particular purpose of goods supplied under a contract of sale.

(2) Where the seller sells goods in the course of a business, there is an implied condition that the goods supplied under the contract are of merchantable quality, except that there is no such condition-

(*a*)   as regards defects specifically drawn to the buyer's attention before the contract is made; or

(*b*)   if the buyer examines the goods before the contract is made, as regards defects which that examination ought to reveal.

(3) Where the seller sells goods in the course of a business and the buyer, expressly or by implication, makes known-

(*a*)   to the seller, or

(*b*)   where the purchase price or part of it is payable by instalments and the goods were previously sold by a credit-broker to the seller, to that credit-broker, any particular purpose for which the goods are being bought, there is an implied condition that the goods supplied under the contract are reasonably fit for that purpose, whether or not that is a purpose for which such goods are commonly supplied, except where the circumstances show that the buyer does not rely, or that it is unreasonable for him to rely, on the skill or judgment of the seller or credit-broker.

(4) An implied condition or warranty about quality or fitness for a particular purpose may be annexed to a contract of sale by usage.

(5) The preceding provisions of this section apply to a sale by a person who in the course of a business is acting as agent for another as they apply to a sale by a principal in the course of a business, except where that other is not selling in the course of a business and either the buyer knows that fact or reasonable steps are taken to bring it to the notice of the buyer before the contract is made.

(6) Goods of any kind are of merchantable quality within the meaning of subsection (2) above if they are as fit for the purpose or purposes for which goods of that kind are commonly bought as it is reasonable to expect having regard to any description applied to them, the price (if relevant) and all the other relevant circumstances.

(7) . . .

(8) . . .

Sale by sample

15. - (1) A contract of sale is a contract for sale by sample where there is an express or implied term to that effect in the contract.

(2) In the case of a contract for sale by sample there is an implied condition -

(*a*)　　　that the bulk will correspond with the sample in quality;

(*b*)　　　that the buyer will have a reasonable opportunity of comparing the bulk with the sample;

(*c*)　　　that the goods will be free from any defect, rendering them unmerchantable, which would not be apparent on reasonable examination of the sample.

(3) In subsection (2)(*c*) above "unmerchantable" is to be construed in accordance with section 14(6) above.

(4) . . .

. . . . .

Auction sales

57. - (1) Where the goods are put up for sale by auction in lots, each lot is prima facie deemed to be the subject of a separate contract of sale.

(2) A sale by auction is complete when the auctioneer announces its completion by the fall of the hammer, or in other customary manner; and until the announcement is made any bidder may retract his bid.

(3) A sale by auction may be notified to be subject to a reserve or upset price, and a right to bid may also be reserved expressly by or on behalf of the seller.

(4) Where a sale by auction is not notified to be subject to a right to bid by or on behalf of the seller, it is not lawful for the seller to bid himself or to employ any person to bid at the sale, or for the auctioneer knowingly to take any bid from the seller or any such person.

(5) A sale contravening subsection (4) above may be treated as fraudulent by the buyer.

(6) Where, in respect of a sale by auction, a right to bid is expressly reserved (but not otherwise) the seller or any one person on his behalf may bid at the auction.

APPENDIX

Since the publication of *"A" Level Law* in 1983 Parliament has enacted the Police and Criminal Evidence Act 1984 and the Prosecution of Offences Act 1985, both of which are largely based on the recommendations of the Royal Commission on Criminal Procedure, Cmnd. 8092 (1981). The substantive provisions of the former have not yet been brought into force since the police need time to prepare themselves for the substantial changes introduced by the Act, and while the latter has been brought into force the Crown Prosecution Service is not yet fully operational. But since it appears inevitable that the Police and Criminal Evidence Act will be brought into force in the near future, and that the Crown Prosecution Service will soon be fully operational, what follows may now be substituted for what appears in the text of H.S.B. at pp. 80-95.

Criminal Proceedings

Under the existing law a prosecution may be instituted by anyone subject to certain exceptions where the consent of the Attorney-General or Director of Public Prosecutions is required. In practice most prosecutions are brought by the police but the role of other official agencies is significant. The police have limited resources and hence offences against the revenue, or customs and excise legislation, or under the legislation relating to factories or weights and measures, will be left to the bodies charged with the enforcement of the relevant legislation. Private (*i.e.* non-official) prosecution is dwarfed by public prosecution but it cannot be dismissed as unimportant. More than the occasional cause célèbre results from a private prosecution.

Essentially all prosecutions are governed by the same rules. The prosecutor, be he a Crown Prosecutor or a factory inspector or just John Citizen, directs the prosecution and a "private" prosecution does not differ from a "public" prosecution in its incidents. The decision making power, subject to cases where a consent is required, rests with the prosecutor and not with the lawyers he may instruct. The lawyer may advise against a prosecution but it is the prosecutor who decides.

Prosecutions instituted other than by the police are unaffected by the Prosecution of Offences Act 1985. The D.P.P., however, continues to be able to exercise control over such prosecutions for his duty to take over certain proceedings (*e.g.* offences against the state), and his power to take over the conduct of any criminal proceedings at any stage are confirmed by section 6 of the Act.

But the powers of the police in this regard are profoundly affected by the Act. While it will still be for the police to initiate prosecutions it is, by section 3(1), "the duty of the Director to take over the conduct of all criminal proceedings . . . instituted on behalf of a police force." The substantial change effected is that it is not for the police to determine the course and conduct of criminal proceedings; the decision making power is transferred to an independent prosecuting service. This, the principal aim of the Act, was supported by all parties during its passage through Parliament.

To this end the Act sets up a national prosecuting service (the Crown Prosecution Service) headed by the D.P.P. It is for the D.P.P. to divide England and Wales into areas and to designate a Chief Crown Prosecutor, who will in turn be assisted by Crown Prosecutors, for each area and who will have, subject to the directions of the D.P.P., all the powers of the D.P.P. in his area.

What it is hoped the Crown Prosecution Service will achieve is consistent prosecution policies and standards throughout the country; freedom from undue local influence; accountability to Parliament; and an attractive career structure for those involved in the service. Only through a national structure, it was thought, could all these desiderata be met.

(1) Police powers: general

The substantial responsibility for the prevention and investigation of crime remains, of course, with the police. For this purpose the constable (all police officers are constables regardless of their rank within the force) is accorded more extensive powers than those accorded the ordinary citizen, and in the exercise of those powers he is answerable to the law. In the conduct of his office the constable may be subject to the orders of his superiors. A senior officer may, for example, direct his subordinates as to where and when they are to patrol but he cannot lawfully order them not to enforce particular laws or not to enforce the law against particular individuals. A constable cannot defend unlawful conduct by a plea of superior orders.

Unlike the citizen, a constable has a legal duty to enforce the law and if, without lawful authority or reasonable excuse, he fails to do so he is guilty of an offence. This does not mean that a constable must necessarily prosecute for every infraction that comes to his notice. Life would become intolerable for both the citizen and the constable if the latter did not occasionally turn a blind eye or issue a friendly caution. But in 1978 a constable was fined on a charge of misconduct as a police officer where he deliberately refrained from intervening in a brawl outside a club when from the cries and screams it was clear that someone was being done a serious injury (*Dytham* (1979)). The court said that his failure to act in this situation, where life itself was at risk, was such as to injure the public interest and to call for condemnation and punishment.

When a crime has been committed, indeed when any event has occurred, any person is at liberty to ask questions of participants or witnesses, and any participant or witness is equally at liberty to refuse to answer any such questions. In practice the police usually secure the co-operation of witnesses and, contrary to the image fostered in detective fiction, most crime is uncovered by information volunteered by members of the public. The informant thus plays a central role in the detection and prosecution of crime. Most of us are informants at one time or another, perhaps reporting a theft or burglary or volunteering evidence concerning a road traffic accident.

Socially we draw a distinction between the *informant* who volunteers his information disinterestedly except for an interest in the proper enforcement of the law, and the *informer* who trades his information for some advantage to himself which may be financial or otherwise. To take the matter a stage further, the informer may affect to join the participants in their criminal enterprise only to inform on them, or may even (and at this stage he is referred to as an *agent provacateur*) incite or instigate crime by others.

These are muddy waters. In dealing with terrorist organisations bent on the wholesale destruction of life, few would question the propriety of undercover police infiltration for the purpose of securing the conviction and punishment of the terrorists. But what of the inspector who orders a drink after hours with a view to entrapping the friendly publican? Or the woman police officer who affects to be pregnant to secure evidence against an alleged back-street abortionist? Or the agent who has "laid-on" a robbery so that his principals may be caught red-handed?

The courts have ruled unequivocally that "entrapment" is not a defence to the perpetrators. On the other hand the courts have recognised that law enforcement should not overstep the mark. This mark is ill-defined and it may be that the mark for offences of terrorism is not the same as it is for offences of shoplifting, but the courts are strongly inclined to reduce an otherwise appropriate sentence where it appears that the participants might or would not have committed the offence but for instigation by an agent. The Law Commission considered this matter (Law Comm. No. 83) and proposed that it should be made an offence positively to instigate, incite or persuade another to commit an offence but no action has been taken on this recommendation.

Another general problem concerns the interception of communications. Clearly eavesdropping is lawful; if X on a bus relates to Y in a loud voice his part in a murder, he has only himself to blame if a police officer sitting behind him hears all. In one case (*Maqsud Ali* (1916)) the police placed two men suspected of murder in a room which contained a concealed microphone and the court allowed the taped recording, tantamount to a confession, to be given in evidence.

This leads to a consideration of telephone tapping and the interception of mail. Traditionally it has been assumed that the Crown (the power came to be exercised by the Secretary of State under a warrant issued by him) may lawfully intercept letters and this power was extended to telegrams and then to telephone communications. By convention warrants to intercept communications were issued only exceptionally in cases of serious crime where other methods of obtaining evidence had been tried and failed.

The legality of this practice was challenged in *Malone* v. *Commissioner of Metropolitan Police* (1979) where Malone's telephone had been tapped pursuant to a warrant and in connection with offences of handling stolen property. Megarry V.-C. held that Malone's action failed because there was no positive law against tapping, no property right of Malone's had been invaded, and English law did not recognise any right of privacy. Malone, however, pursued the matter to the European Court alleging a breach of Article 8 of the European Convention on Human Rights which provides that everyone has "the right to respect for his private and family life, his home and his correspondence." Article 8, goes on to provide that there shall be no interference with this right "except such as in accordance with law and is necessary in a democratic society . . . for the prevention of disorder or crime. . . . " The court declared Malone's application admissible on the grounds that English procedures relating to interception failed to satisfy Article 8.

The outcome was that Parliament placed the law on a statutory footing in the Interception of Communications Act 1985. The Act makes it an offence for any person, other than as authorised by the Act, to intercept a communication in course of transmission by post or by means of a public telecommunication system. The Secretary of State, however, is authorised to issue a warrant for interception in specified cases (where he considers it necessary in the interests of national security, preventing or detecting serious crime, or of safeguarding economic well-being) subject to requirements as to form, extent and duration. The Act further sets up a Tribunal to which any person who believes his communications have been intercepted may complain and if the Tribunal finds that there has been a contravention of the Act it shall, *inter alia,* make a report to the Prime Minister, and may order the destruction of the intercepted material or may make an order for compensation.

Finally, the Act provides for the appointment of a person who has held high judicial office as a Commissioner whose function it is to keep under review the carrying out by the Secretary of State of his functions under the Act and to report thereon to the Prime Minister and to Parliament.

(2) Police powers: interrogation

It has been pointed out that everyone is at liberty to refuse to answer questions whoever poses the questions. If a man has nothing to hide, however, he is normally more than willing to answer questions whether put by the police, the press or his next-door neighbour.

But if a man is, *or is thought to be,* a participant in events that might show him in a discreditable light (most obviously a crime) then he would be best advised to stay silent at least until he receives professional legal advice. Our law has long recognised this right of silence *and* has additionally taken the view that usually no adverse inferences may be drawn from an accused's refusal to answer questions. Hence no deduction of guilt may be drawn from an accused's silence in response to police questions or from his refusal to give evidence in court.

The law may thus be said to be favourable to the suspect or accused. And it goes further than this. A confession is not admissible against a defendant unless it is proved that it was not obtained by oppression or as a consequence of anything done or said which might render any confession unreliable. Not only is the rack proscribed but also a confession obtained by a promise of bail or other favourable treatment may be equally inadmissible.

But if this is the law, the reality is somewhat different. Few can resist the urge to communicate with a fellow human being even if he happens to be a police officer whose interest lies in securing evidence, most especially a confession, about a crime which the suspect is thought to have committed. The contest of wits may not be an equal one. The suspect (unless he is an old hand) is in foreign territory, his movements are controlled and he is dependent on his captors for his means of existence. He may have been stripped, for reasons of evidence or security, of possessions which are important to his dignity. The police officer, on the other hand, is entirely familiar with the environment and has all the trappings of control and authority.

It is probably the case that no interrogation is entirely "fair" as any errant schoolboy brought before his headmaster will testify. The headmaster brings the pupil to *his* office, unfamiliar territory to the pupil, and will subtly use the trappings of his office to erode the boy's confidence. The headmaster who needs to resort to beatings or threats or inducements to obtain damaging admissions cannot have read any worthwhile books on his trade in the last half century.

It is at this point that the Police and Criminal Evidence Act 1984 contains a comprehensive restatement of the law which aims to regularise the conduct of interrogation and in some respects to revise it. What is presently obscure or opaque is governed by comprehensive provisions in the Act and further supplemented by Codes of Practice which will replace the Judges' Rules (see H.S.B., pp. 84 and 91) with much more detailed provisions.

It will remain the law, of course, that other than by authority of law (almost invariably following arrest) no one can be compelled to go to a police station and, still less, can he be compelled to give evidence against himself. It is still not uncommon to hear or read following a report of crime that a man is at a certain police station "helping the police with their inquiries." It is of course open to suspects voluntarily to attend a police station and to submit to questioning but such public-spiritedness in suspects is very much the exception. A suspect can be lawfully detained only following a lawful arrest; there is no obligation on him to help and the police have no power to detain him for questioning. If a person is held against his will, that is, it is made clear to him that he is not a free agent, he is unlawfully detained unless he has been given a valid ground for his detention. It is true that the Act refers in Part IV to "detention" while in Part III it refers to "arrest" but "detention" here is simply a convenient way of referring to that period which the suspect is constrained to be in police custody; the assumption always is that it has been preceded by a valid arrest and that the detention is in right of the arrest.

While the provisions in the Act are extensive it may be that they can be fairly summarised under three heads: (a) the timescale; (b) administrative supervision; and (c) detainee's rights.

(a) *The timescale* (see Figure 1)

For convenience Figure 1 assumes the suspect arrives at a police station on the dot of midnight but at whatever time he arrives the timescale for subsequent action remains the same.

Little needs to be said of the suspect who is (i) promptly released without being charged (though he may be bailed to return to the station at some specified later stage in which case his further detention is governed by the timescale); or who is (ii) promptly charged and promptly released with or without bail; or (iii) promptly charged and kept in custody except to note that in this case the custody officer must review the situation and may yet release the suspect with or without bail.

The real problem concerns the suspect who is neither released nor charged but is kept in detention so that further inquiries (including questioning of the suspect) may be made. In his case the really critical stages are Stage 5 at which he can be further detained only on the authorisation of a superintendent; Stage 6 after which he can be detained only if, after a hearing at which the suspect is entitled to be legally represented, a magistrates' court issues a warrant (or successive warrants) of further detention; and Stage 7 at which he must be charged or released.

Figure 1

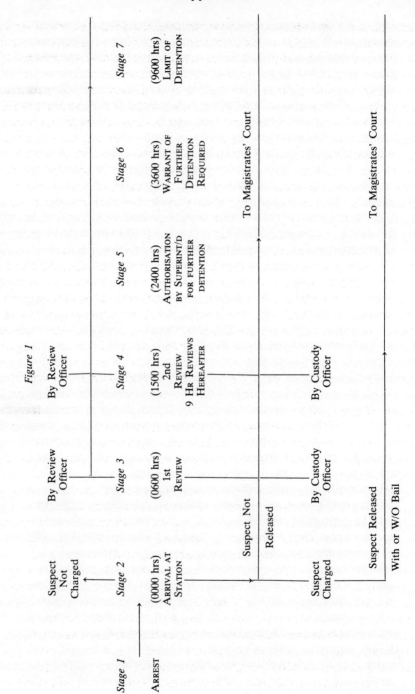

(b) *Administrative supervision*

A general feature of the Act is the provision for what might be called administrative supervision which will necessitate what may prove to be an enormous increase in paperwork as the police are required to log their actions and to record their reasons therefore. Some might regard this as, at best, a useless imposition, or, at worst, a brake on efficiency, but the idea seems to be - certainly a good one in principle - that the police will be obliged to think carefully about what they are doing and to closely consider the justification for doing it. Allied to that the review officer or the custody officer as the case may be provides an element of impartial supervision of the suspect's case. He may be entirely impartial since he himself will be a police officer but he must be an officer who is not himself involved in investigating the case against the suspect. Detention, or continued detention thus has to be justified by the officers conducting the inquiry to their superiors.

(c) *Detainee's rights*

The detainee has two rights. One concerns his right to have someone informed of his arrest and the place where he is held. This was first introduced by section 62 of the Criminal Law Act 1977 and it will be enlarged and improved upon by section 56 of the Police and Criminal Evidence Act. Delay in according this right is now permissible *only* where (i) a serious arrestable offence has been committed ("serious arrestable offence" has an extensive definition in s.116 but may broadly be said to extend to an arrestable offence, as to which see below p. 485, the commission of which has led, or is likely to lead, to serious harm to the state, the person, or to cause substantial financial gain or loss); and (ii) a superintendent is satisfied that one of the conditions in section 56(5) is met (broadly these refer to cases where disclosure would impede the course of justice as by alerting associates or preventing the recovery of property); and (iii) in any event the right of notification cannot be delayed for more than 36 hours. Moreover the suspect must be told the reason for any denial of his right and this must be recorded.

The other concerns access to a solicitor. At present this is governed by administrative directions appended to the Judges' Rules but now appears for the first time in statutory form in section 58 of the Act. This provision closely follows section 56 in that it may be delayed only for the same reasons and for the same time.

Under both section 56 and section 58 it appears that the initiative - "if he so requests" - must come from the suspect but the Codes of Practice make it clear that the suspect must be informed of these rights as soon as practicable (even if the police are minded to deny him their immediate exercise) and in the case of legal advice the suspect who does not wish to avail himself of it must sign a waiver clause to that effect. One further point in this connection concerns the practicality of access. All very well if the suspect is Mr. Big who has prompt access to a solicitor at all hours, not so good for Widow Twanky who has never fallen foul of the law before. During ordinary office hours she can be put into contact with a duty solicitor but real problems may arise at night and at weekends.

Quite what effect the Act and the Codes of Practice will have on the actual conduct of interrogations remains to be seen. The Codes of Practice are certainly more detailed and precise than the Judges Rules. The suspect will normally have had the opportunity of exercising his rights of notification and access since it can only be exceptionally that these rights will be denied. Thereafter there are detailed provisions concerning the proper treatment of the suspect during his confinement. As to questioning this is normally (unless the urgency of inquiries makes this impracticable) to be carried out during the working day and no one session should exceed two hours without a break, though a break may be delayed if there are reasonable grounds for believing that it would involve a risk of harm to persons or serious loss of property, unnecessary delay to the suspect's release from custody, or would otherwise prejudice the investigation.

The Codes of Practice continue the requirement of the Judges' Rules for cautioning the subject that he is not obliged to say anything whenever a police officer has grounds to believe that the suspect has committed an offence, and in any event on arrest. The suspect must be cautioned before questioning and must be reminded at the beginning of any subsequent session that he is still under caution.

But perhaps the most striking innovation is the commitment to the tape-recording of interviews contained in section 60 of the Act. This places a duty on the Home Secretary to issue a Code of Practice for the tape-recording of interviews. But this cannot be done overnight and it is envisaged that tape-recording will be introduced experimentally and selectively in the first instance. There are difficulties to be overcome (including a marked lack of enthusiasm for tape-recording on the part of the police) but the present expectation is that it will eventually form part of the routine.

(3) Police Powers: arrest

While the Police and Criminal Evidence Act restates and revises much of the law relating to arrest, it does not provide a code in the sense of providing a comprehensive and exclusive statement of the law. For example, the common law power to arrest for breach of the peace remains unaffected by the Act. Though the Act constitutes the most extensive review of arrest it will still be necessary in some particulars to resort to the common law.

The Royal Commission identified two principal defects in the existing system. One was its complexity, particularly in relation to statutory powers of arrest (see H.S.B. p. 86). The other was the issue of underreach and overreach in that sometimes powers of arrest were not available where they were obviously required and sometimes accorded where they were not required. The Commission proposed, broadly, that the power of arrest should be available only where it was necessary for the proper enforcement of the law. Thus, for example, it would be available to deal with bank robbers but not to deal with an elderly shoplifter who fully co-operates with the authorities. The Commission's proposals in this regard were not fully accepted and powers of arrest may be summarised as follows.

(a) *Arrest for arrestable offences*

The general powers of arrest presently found in section 2 of the Criminal Law Act 1967 are re-enacted by section 24 of the Police and Criminal Evidence Act 1984. The section authorises any person, whether a constable or not, to arrest without warrant: (i) anyone who is, or who is reasonably believed to be, in the act of committing an arrestable offence; and (ii) where an arrestable offence has been committed, anyone who has, or is reasonably believed to have been, guilty of the offence.

The section then confers further powers on constables who may additionally arrest a person; (iii) where there are reasonable grounds for believing that he has committed an arrestable offence; and (iv) where a person is, or is reasonably believed to be, about to commit an arrestable offence. Moreover, a constable, but not a private citizen, is authorised to enter (if needs be by force) any place where the suspect is or is reasonably believed to be for the purpose of effecting an arrest.

So the powers of a constable are somewhat more extensive than those of a private citizen. Under (iv) a constable has a prophylactic power; he may arrest a man whom he reasonably believes to be about to throw a brick through a shop window while the citizen must wait until the window is broken. The additional power conferred on a constable under (iii) may be simply illustrated. Suppose a bookshop manager sees a shopper behaving in a way that reasonably leads the manager to believe that the shopper has taken a copy of Hogan, Seago and Bennett's "*A*" *Level Law* from the shelves and secreted it in his coat. In fact the shopper had been bent on stealing this priceless work but, guessing that he was being observed, had changed his mind. The manager follows the shopper into the street where the arrests him. In these circumstances the manager is not protected by the section because *no arrestable offence has in fact been committed* and is thus liable to pay damages for the unlawful arrest (false imprisonment). Had the manager communicated his reasonable suspicions to a passing constable and had the constable effected the arrest then neither would be liable; the manager because he has not made the arrest, and the constable because he is protected by (iii), (see *Walters* v. *W. H. Smith* (1914)).

Had the manager arrested the shopper at the very shelf where the manager reasonably believed he was stealing then the manager would have been protected by (i) which protects the manager even if the theft has not been committed so long as he reasonably believes the shopper to be in the *act of committing*. But once the shopper has left the premises he can no longer be said to be in the act of committing the theft.

It may seen odd that a citizen may be liable for an unlawful arrest even though he has acted reasonably on the available evidence. Not surprisingly the so-called "citizen's arrest" is very much the exception; it is usually possible, and certainly safer, to leave these matters to the police.

An arrestable offence is also similarly defined in both Acts (namely, as any offence for which the sentence is fixed by law or any offence for which a person over 21 may be sentenced to five years' imprisonment) but the Police and Criminal Evidence Act then goes on to include within the definition of arrestable offence certain offences not carrying five years' imprisonment. Some of the offences so added (for example, going equipped for stealing contrary to the Theft Act 1968, s.25, and taking vehicles contrary to Theft Act 1968, s.12) already carry a power of arrest, but others (for example, indecent assault on a female contrary to the Sexual Offences Act 1956, s.14) become arrestable offences for the first time. The significance of including any offence in the category of arrestable offences is that the power of arrest exists even though the "necessity" principles which are required by the next category are not met. Hence, for example, the elderly shoplifter may be arrested even though he co-operates fully with the police and an arrest is not "necessary" to secure compliance with the law.

(b) *General arrest powers under section 25*

Somewhat paradoxically section 25 is concerned with powers of arrest for non-arrestable offences. The idea is simple enough. If certain conduct is made a crime (be it failing to sign a driving licence, or dropping litter, or taking the eggs of a protected bird) then the police must be given the necessary powers to enforce that law effectively and that means that every offence must have the ultimate long-stop of arrest if only for the purpose of identifying the suspect.

At a stroke section 25 effects a considerable simplification. The constable is no longer burdened with having to memorise over one hundred statutory powers of arrest, and the citizen is not threatened with the risk of arrest provided he is co-operative and gives his name and address, and presents no further danger to himself or others.

(i) *The identification requirements.* The ordinary run of case will present no difficulty since people ordinarily carry adequate evidence of identity (driving licence, credit cards). But it must not be supposed that people are required to carry and furnish means of identity; the constable must have reasonable grounds for suspecting that the name furnished is not the real name of the suspect and a mere failure on the suspect's part to provide confirmatory evidence would not constitute reasonable grounds. It will often prove possible for the police to confirm a name and address by contacting headquarters on their radios.

(ii) *The preventive requirements.* Under Section 25 the police are also accorded powers of arrest where there are reasonable grounds for suspecting that an offence has been, or is being, committed and there are also reasonable grounds for believing that arrest is necessary to prevent the suspect causing physical harm to himself or another, suffering physical injury to himself, causing loss of or damage to property, committing an offence against public decency, or causing an unlawful obstruction of the highway.

Typically these powers might be used where the suspect has committed an offence involving drunkenness (drunk in a public place, for example) and his arrest is necessary because he cannot safely convey himself, or a child accompanying him, across the road; or of a "flasher" who has been causing alarm and annoyance to passing women by exposing himself.

(c) *Other statutory powers of arrest*

It might be thought in view of the foregoing powers that there was no need for any additional statutory powers of arrest but section 26 preserves some statutory powers of arrest which are set out in Schedule 2. The rationale of these offences appears to be that there are some cases where, though the offence is not an arrestable offence and there is no difficulty in indentifying the suspect an arrest must be made if the law is to be properly enforced. Thus, for example, a deserter from the armed forces may be arrested and returned to the relevant authority even though his identity is not in question.

(d) *Arrest for breach of the peace*

The power of a constable at common law to arrest for a breach of the peace committed in his presence remains unaffected by the Act. To a suggestion during debate in Parliament that this power should be put on a statutory basis, the Government replied that this would be unacceptable because the common law basis of the power provides the police with a degree of flexibility, particularly when responding to situations requiring urgent intervention, which is not readily susceptible to precise statutory formulation. A breach of the peace is conduct which involves, or threatens, violence to the person or significant harm to property. Fighting in the street provides a common occasion for the exercise of the power and here the constable does not have to pass on the merits; he may properly arrest all the combattants though it turns out that one or more of them was acting in lawful self-defence.

(e) *Arrest for fingerprinting*

By section 27 of the Act the police are empowered to require a person convicted of a recordable (this will probably be defined to mean an offence punishable by imprisonment) offence who has not at any time been in police detention to present himself for fingerprinting and if he does not he may be arrested.

(f) *Arrest under warrant*

Apart from powers of arrest without warrant, an arrest may also be effected under warrant. Warrants of arrest are usually issued by a magistrate after hearing evidence on oath and may be issued for both arrestable and non-arrestable offences. A warrant may be executed anywhere within the jurisdiction and reciprocal arrangements exist with Scotland, Northern Ireland and the Irish Republic. A constable who in good faith executes a warrant according to its terms incurs no liability to the suspect even though the warrant proves to be unlawful. The officer need not have the warrant in his possession but the suspect must be shown it as soon as practicable.

(g) *General requirements of a valid arrest*

(i) *Reasonable grounds.* All powers of arrest are conditioned by the requirement that reasonable grounds must exist for the suspicion on which the arrest is based. Reasonable cause cannot be defined in the abstract and has to be related to the circumstances of the case. Clearly a constable is not required to have an open-and-shut case against the suspect because it is his *suspicion* that he must justify, not prove that the suspect committed the offence. But deprivation of liberty is a serious matter and can be justified only where good grounds exist for the suspicion. This requires, at the least, that the officer be open-minded and that he makes such inquiries as are practicable in the circumstances. The officer may act on information provided by third parties if it has every appearance of being reliable and leads to a reasonable inference of the suspect's guilt. It would, for example, be reasonable for the officer to rely on a report given him by a store-detective whom the officer knows to be experienced and reliable, but not on an anonymous tip-off given hurriedly over the telephone. One exception, of little practical importance, to the requirement for reasonable cause is where the officer's suspicions, though unfounded on any evidence available, turn out to be right. If, for example, an officer following a report of burglary arrests X just on a hunch, he will be liable in damages if his intuition is wrong but will not be liable if it turns out that X did in fact commit the crime.

(ii) *Notification of grounds of arrest.* An arrest is lawful only if the suspect is given a *valid* reason for it. The suspect is entitled to know why he is being deprived of his liberty so that he can meet the case against him. In *Christie* v. *Leachinsky* (1947) police found Leachinsky in possession of stolen cloth and arrested him under the Liverpool Corporation Act 1921 (it might be noted in passing that powers of arrest may be conferred by local as well as general statutes) on a charge of unlawful possession. This Act did confer a power of arrest for unlawful possession but only when the identity of the suspect was unknown and Leachinsky was well known to the officers concerned. It was held by the House of Lords that a suspect is entitled to know the valid ground for his arrest and since Leachinsky was given no such valid ground he was entitled to damages. It appears in this case that the police might have had reasonable grounds for suspecting that Leachinsky had received the cloth knowing it to be stolen and might have validly arrested him under the then Larceny Act 1916 which conferred an arrest power whether the suspect's identity was or was not known. But an arrest cannot be justified by showing that a power did exist if only the police had remembered it; and still less by showing that the suspect had committed some other arrestable offence.

In *Christie* v. *Leachinsky* it was said that the party arresting need not use technical language so long as the suspect knows for what he is arrested. The police are well advised to use unmistakable language, *e.g.* "I arrest you for stealing this watch/murdering your mother-in-law." But, and so long as the import is clear to the suspect, it would do to say "You're nicked laddie for lifting this watch/doing away with your dear old mother-in-law."

Section 28 of the Police and Criminal Evidence Act continues the requirement that the suspect be informed of the ground of his arrest unless it is not reasonably practicable by reason of the suspect having escaped from arrest before the information could be given. This marks another departure from the existing law which does not require the suspect to be informed of the ground of the arrest where it is patently obvious why he is being arrested.

(iii) *Use of force.* Section 3 of the Criminal Law Act 1967 which permits the use of such force as is reasonable in the prevention of crime and in the arrest of offenders (see H.S.B., p. 208) continues in force. In addition section 117 of the Police and Criminal Evidence Act states that where any provision of the Act confers a power on a constable not being a power which may be exercised only with the consent of some person other than a constable, the constable may use reasonable force, if necessary, in the exercise of the power. What is reasonable, of course, depends on the circumstances. While necessity must always exist for the use of the force, force is not justified simply because it is necessary if it is not also reasonable. If the only way to bring a fleeing shoplifter to justice is to gun him down this might be necessary but would not be reasonable and he will have to be allowed to go free.

(4) Police powers: search and seizure

Just as the Police and Criminal Evidence Act seeks to rationalise and simplify the law relating to the melange of powers of arrest, so too the Act seeks to bring order to what can fairly be described as the ragbag of powers of search and seizure (see H.S.B., p. 89). The new powers may be summarised as follows.

(a) *Search for stolen or prohibited articles*
Where a constable has reasonable grounds for suspecting that when in a public place a person has, or a vehicle contains, stolen goods or prohibited articles (articles are prohibited if they are made or adapted, or intended by the possessor, for causing injury or for use in connection with burglary, theft, deception or taking motor vehicles) he may detain that person or vehicle for the purpose of a search.

It has often been maintained that constables exercising powers of search do so on flimsy grounds, following no more than a hunch. To counter this possibility the Act by section 3 introduces the safeguard of requiring the constable to record, at the time, or as soon as practicable, the object of the search and his grounds for making it, and the suspect is entitled to have a copy of this record. As has been indicated, the requirement for records and reasons is general to the scheme of the Act and may turn out to constitute a brake on precipitate and unthinking police action.

(b) *Road checks*
It has apparently long been the practice of the police to conduct checks on vehicles leaving a particular area where it is known that a crime has been committed and when there is

reason to think that a suspect may be apprehended. Obviously this involved stopping and searching the vehicles of many innocent persons and the Royal Commission, considering that the practice was of doubtful validity, proposed that it should be put on a statutory basis. Accordingly section 3 provides that an officer not below the rank of superintendent may authorise a road check where there are reasonable grounds for believing that a serious arrestable offence has been, or will be, committed, that the suspect is still in, or is about to enter, the area in order that vehicles may be checked with a view to ascertaining whether the suspect or a witness is in any such vehicle. Once again records must be kept and reasons recorded.

(c) *Entry and search of premises under warrant*

Under the existing law justices have certain specific powers to issue search warrants but no general powers to issue warrants to search for evidence of crime. The Act provides, by section 8, that justices may issue a search warrant where there are reasonable grounds for suspecting that a serious arrestable offence has been committed and that there is likely to be on the premises material of substantial evidential value. The Act, however, makes provision for "excluded material" (for example, personal records and journalistic material) which can be seized only after application to a circuit judge.

(d) *Entry for purpose of arrest and search consequent upon arrest*

In order to effect a lawful arrest the police are empowered by section 17 to enter any place where the suspect is or is reasonably suspected of being. Attendant upon this the police may search the premises but the search may be conducted only by a constable in uniform and only to the extent that it is exercised to discover evidence relating to the offence for which the arrest is made or for a related offence. Thus if the entry is to arrest a suspect for theft, the police may, if it is reasonable to suspect that evidence of the theft (or a related offence such as handling) may be uncovered, conduct a search for that purpose but not for evidence of other crimes.

(e) *Entry and search after arrest*

It may happen that the police arrest a suspect for, say, theft, not at his own premises but in some other place. Nevertheless, they may have reasonable grounds for suspecting that a search of his premises will reveal evidence relating to that offence or to a similar offence, for example handling. A search in such circumstances must ordinarily be authorised, under section 18 of the Act, by an officer not below the rank of inspector but can be authorised by a constable of lower rank provided it is necessary for the effective investigation of the offence and is notified as soon as practicable to an officer not below the rank of inspector.

(f) *Search upon arrest*

Where a person is arrested he may by section 32 of the Act be searched where there are reasonable grounds for believing that the suspect may be a danger to himself or others, that he has anything that might assist him to escape, or anything that might be evidence relating to an offence. The constable may "frisk" the suspect but he cannot require him to remove any of his clothing in public other than an outer coat, jacket and gloves.

(g) *Search upon detention*

If the suspect is to be detained at a police station the custody officer must record everything which the suspect has with him when arrested and may seize anything which he believes may be used to cause physical injury or damage property, or to interfere with evidence or to effect an escape; and anything which he reasonably believes may constitute evidence: section 54. The custody officer may seize anything falling within these categories but must tell the suspect the reason for the seizure; otherwise clothing and personal effects may not be seized. A suspect may co-operate in this procedure but if he does not he may be searched against his will though this must be done by an officer of the same sex as the suspect.

(h) *Intimate searches*

An officer of at least the rank of superintendent may by section 55 authorise an intimate search (*i.e.* a search of the body orifices) where he has reasonable grounds for believing that the suspect has concealed on him anything with which he may do injury or a Class A drug. This form of search is governed by stringent conditions as to place, manner of search and documentation but may be conducted against the will of the suspect.

An officer of at least the rank of superintendent may also authorise, again subject to strict conditions as to manner and documentation, the taking of an intimate sample (*i.e.* a sample of blood, semen or any other tissue fluid, urine, saliva or pubic hair, or a swab taken from a body orifice) but only where the suspect consents in writing. Without the suspect's consent no intimate sample may be taken but if the suspect refuses without good cause then a court or a jury may draw such inferences from that refusal as appear proper.

Non-intimate samples (*e.g.* a sample of hair other than pubic hair, a sample taken from under the fingernails) may also be taken with the written consent of the suspect but in this case they may be taken without his consent if the taking is authorised by an officer of at least the rank of superintendent who has reasonable cause to believe that the sample will tend to confirm or disprove the suspect's involvement in a serious arrestable offence. Once again, of course, there are strict conditions as to manner and documentation.

(i) *Search in general*

Even this brief survey will indicate that the Police and Criminal Evidence Act accords extensive powers of search of persons, premises and vehicles. They are certainly more extensive than existing common law powers (*e.g.* in permitting the issue of search warrants to search premises where there are reasonable grounds for suspecting that evidence relating to a serious arrestable offence may be discovered) but in some instances (*e.g.* intimate searches) it is difficult to say how far the new powers may differ from the old in the absence of rulings by the courts. If the Act has extended powers of search it has also clarified them so that the police and the citizen know more precisely what is permitted and what is not. While the provisions of the Act, especially in relation to documentation may appear to be prolix, the particular powers of search are exhaustively (save for the power to enter premises to prevent a breach of the peace when the common law is preserved) defined and, of course, the provisions as to documentation are intended as a check on arbitrary action since at every relevant stage reasons have to be given and recorded for action taken.

(5) Police powers: illegally obtained evidence

Except as authorised by law any arrest, search, seizure or interrogation is unlawful. Frequently the illegality will give rise to civil remedy or even a criminal prosecution. Thus if the suspect is not informed of the grounds of his arrest he may sue for false imprisonment; if an intimate search is made without the appropriate assents he may sue for assault; if there is an unauthorised search of his premises he may sue for trespass, and so on. But the risk of civil proceedings, which will only be pursued where the plaintiff has access to the necessary resources and is sufficiently determined, is at best a fitful safeguard.

Moreover breaches of the Act or of the Codes of Practice do not necessarily afford rights of redress on the suspect. If, for example, the suspect is improperly denied his rights to have someone informed of the arrest or to consult with a solicitor, it does not appear that he has any civil redress. So far as the Codes of Practice are concerned, it is specifically provided (s.67(10)) that a breach of the Codes shall not of itself render a police officer liable to criminal or civil proceedings. It is, however, provided (s.67(8)) that a police officer shall be liable to disciplinary proceedings for failure to comply with any provision of a Code. Though the effectiveness of this sanction must be largely in the hands of the police themselves, it may be assumed that it carries some potency.

A final sanction is the possibility that evidence obtained in breach of the Act or of the Codes may be rendered inadmissible with the attendant risk that the prosecution will fail. Two provisions of the Act are relevant. The first is section 76 which continues the former law and requires the exclusion of any confession which has been obtained by oppression of the person who made it, or where it was made in consequence of anything said or done which is likely to render it unreliable and it is for the prosecution to prove beyond reasonable doubt that it was not so obtained.

The second is section 78 which provides that a court may refuse to allow evidence to be given if it appears that having regard to all the circumstances "the admission of the evidence would have such an adverse effect on the fairness of the proceedings that the court ought not to admit it." Quite how this provision will be interpreted is as yet unclear. In the past the courts have been reluctant to exclude illegally obtained evidence provided they have been satisfied that it was not obtained by oppression or inducement and that it is relevant to the issues in the case. But the assumption underlying section 78 seems to be that there would be at least some cases where though the evidence was not obtained by oppression or inducement (*i.e.* not excluded by virtue by section 76) it would nevertheless be excluded under section 78 because of its adverse effect on the fairness of the proceedings. Suppose that the facts of *Prager* (H.S.B., p. 84) were to recur and fall to be considered under the Act. There would seem to be clear breaches of the Codes of Practice in the failure to inform Prager of his right to remain silent and in the protracted nature of the questioning. No doubt such breaches would now be relied upon as some evidence of oppression but if the court is satisfied that the confession was not obtained by oppression within section 76, what grounds are there for excluding it under section 78? This section does not allow the court to exclude evidence because the court disapproves of the police tactics in obtaining it, but only where its admission would adversely affect the fairness of the subsequent proceedings. It may be, therefore, that section 78 will prove to add little or nothing to section 76.

(6) Complaints against the police and police accountability

Inevitably policing attracts complaints and it is essential to both the police and the public that a fair system should exist for airing and investigating these complaints. The police themselves are well aware that in a democratic society their effectiveness depends in large measure in securing the confidence, and therefore the co-operation, of the public.

A complaint at the one extreme may involve little more than an allegation of incivility and, at the other, may involve an allegation of a serious criminal offence. A complaint may be made about the conduct of a particular officer or it may be made about policing in general. Examples of the latter may be an allegation that blacks are being subject to harassment by the police, or a complaint that an area is insufficiently policed resulting in soliciting by prostitutes becoming an intolerable nuisance. The procedures which govern complaints against the police and complaints about policing have overlapping elements but call for separate discussion.

(a) *Complaints against the police*

The Police and Criminal Evidence Act revises the procedure for dealing with complaints against the police.

Where a complaint is received by a chief officer of police it is his duty to refer it to the appropriate authority. In the case of complaints relating to any senior officer (an officer above the rank of chief superintendent) the appropriate authority is the Commissioner of Police for the Metropolis in the case of the metropolitan police, and the police authority in the case of provincial forces. If the complaint relates to an officer below this rank the appropriate authority is the chief officer himself.

Where the chief officer is the appropriate authority he must record the complaint and then consider whether it is suitable for informal resolution. The idea here is to provide for the resolution of minor complaints, which do not involve a criminal or disciplinary charge, without recourse to the formal procedure of an investigation. If, however, the matter is not suitable for informal resolution, or informal resolution proves impossible, the chief constable must appoint an officer (in practice usually the deputy Chief Constable) to investigate the complaint.

If the complaint relates to a senior officer the procedure is the same in that if it is a minor matter not involving a criminal charge or disciplinary offence the authority will in the first place seek informal resolution, and only if that fails will an officer be appointed to investigate the complaint.

Following the investigation a report is sent to the appropriate authority. If this reveals the commission of a criminal offence then when the officer concerned is a senior officer the D.P.P. must be informed, and where he is not a senior officer the D.P.P. must be informed if the report discloses the commission of a criminal offence and recommends that the officer be prosecuted in respect of it. If the investigation discloses no criminal offence the officer in charge of the investigation must consider whether disciplinary proceedings should be brought. The discipline regulations are made by the Home Secretary and cover all aspects of policing; as has been indicated breach of the Codes of Practice is made a disciplinary offence by the Act and provision is additionally made for racially discriminatory behaviour to be made a disciplinary offence.

The consequence of an adverse finding in disciplinary proceedings can be serious, involving loss of pay, reduction in rank, or even dismissal. Provision is accordingly made for the opportunity to be legally represented at a hearing before a disciplinary tribunal and for an appeal to the Secretary of State.

The Act also sets up a new Police Complaints Authority which will replace the Police Complaints Board and will have additional powers. The P.C.A. provides the independent element in relation to complaints against the police and none of its members may be a person who is or has been a constable. The appropriate authority must refer to the P.C.A. any complaint alleging that the conduct complained of resulted in death or serious injury, any complaint specified in regulations to be made by the Secretary of State; and may refer any other complaint though it is not required to do so. But the P.C.A.'s role is not confined to passively receiving references from the appropriate authority and they may supervise the investigation of any complaint, though it is not one the P.C.A. is required to supervise, if they consider that it is desirable in the public interest that they should do so. It appears to be intended that the P.C.A. should have an active, independent and genuinely supervisory role in order to dispel fears held in some parts of the community that the police in dealing with complaints against their own members might be less than impartial.

(b) *Complaints about policing*

The last section dealt with complaints against the police in the narrow sense under procedures set out inb the Police and Criminal Evidence Act. But these by no means exhaust the procedures, both formal and informal for dealing with complaints about the police which may range from a criticism in a letter written to a local newspaper to a high level tribunal of inquiry.

By way of introduction it is necessary to know something of the constitutional position of the police. As we have seen (H.S.B., p. 81) a constable's primary duty is to keep the peace and in the exercise of his functions he is answerable to the law. So it is essentially with a chief constable, except that his responsibilities are general as well as particular. The office is one of enormous power for it is the chief constable who decides upon the disposition of his force, the allocation of resources, the determination of priorities as between the various police functions, the methods of policing to be used and so on. With these immense powers come immense responsibilities. He has to balance the requirements of law enforcement against a wider, if ill-defined, public interest which includes the maintenance of strict impartiality in his force and the retention of public confidence in it. He must decide upon the strategies for dealing with pickets at the factory gate, demonstrations outside an embassy, or rioters on the streets; it will be for him to indicate when and what force may be used.

In this he is subject to the law as *R.* v. *Metropolitan Police Commissioner, ex p. Blackburn (No. 1)* (1968) shows. The Commissioner had issued a directive to his force which, in effect, said that the Gaming Act was not to be enforced since its provisions were virtually unworkable. In the result the Commissioner withdrew this instruction but the Court of

Appeal was clear that, had he not, mandamus would have issued to compel him to do so. It was not open to a chief constable to refuse altogether to enforce particular legislation because he thought it unworkable and a waste of valuable police time.

But too much must not be read into this decision for its prctical effect is limited. The indefatigable Mr. Blackburn (one of life's natural litigants) brought a further action (*R. v. Metropolitan Police Commissioner, ex p. Blackburn (No. 3)* (1973)) to compel the Commissioner to enforce the laws against obscenity more vigorously in central London. The court refused to interfere; there was no suggestion that the Commissioner had abdicated his responsibility for enforcing the obscenity laws and it was for him to decide, along with all other competing demands on the police resources, what priority to accord the enforcement of these laws.

Of more importance as a practical matter is "political" control. At the national level the Home Secretary has considerable potential for control in that he has power to withhold the grants payable from central funds to police forces and there are fewer more potent controls than the financial one. The Home Secretary may also call upon a chief (or a deputy or assistant) constable to retire in the interests of efficiency (a power that has been used only once) though an inquiry must be held if the officer concerned wishes to dispute the matter. Finally, the Home Secretary may cause a local inquiry to be held "into any matter connected with the policing of any area." Such inquiries in the past have been concerned with particular allegations of misconduct, such as fabricating evidence or using violence against suspects in custody, but could be used to investigate matters of policing policy.

At the local level there is the police authority which is comprised (except for London where the Home Secretary is the police authority) as to two-thirds from the elected councillors for that area and as to one third from magistrates for that area. It is the duty of the police authority "to secure the maintenance of an adequate and efficient police force" for the area, to appoint the chief constable, and to determine the number of persons in each rank which is to constitute the establishment of the force.

But on the critical question of the relationship between the chief constable and the police authority, the legislation says next to nothing. The chief constable is required to make an annual report to his authority "on the policing during that year" and the authority may from time to time require reports on matters connected with policing; but information which it is not in the public interest to divulge or which is not needed for the authority to discharge its functions may be withheld by the chief constable on the authority of the Home Secretary. The result is that the divisions of functions and authority as between the police authority and the chief constable is highly uncertain. On more than one occasion this had led to confrontations which have not been satisfactorily nor authoritatively resolved.

The Police and Criminal Evidence Act introduces a new dimension by providing that arrangements shall be made in each police area for obtaining the views of people in that area about matters concerning the policing in that area and for obtaining their co-operation in the prevention of crime. This continues the development begun by the Home Office for the establishment of local liaison committees following Lord Scarman's report on the Brixton riots of 1980. It is difficult to resist the sense of arrangements which make the responsibility for the enforcement of the law a community responsibility. The police will inevitably be in the front line but to operate effectively they must enjoy the confidence, the respect and the goodwill of the disparate communities they serve. The police officer is not the unthinking arm of the law and the skills required of him extend far beyond a mechanistic knowledge of his powers.

INDEX